Basic Skills in English

11

Contents of the Teacher's Edition

Components of *Basic Skills in English*

Student Texts

Red Level / **Grade 7**

Green Level / **Grade 8**

Orange Level / **Grade 9**

Blue Level
Blue Level / **Grade 10**

Yellow Level / **Grade 11**

Purple Level / **Grade 12**

Teacher's Editions

Practice Books/Duplicating Masters

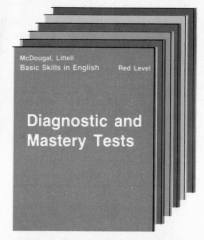

Diagnostic and Mastery Tests

The only English series for students reading *below* grade level . . . with content that is *on* grade level!

Ever since its introduction, *Basic Skills in English* has been the only series of its kind—a composition/grammar series for students reading below grade level. It's a program designed to teach all essential skills while helping students learn with confidence and achieve success.

The 1985 edition maintains the tone, format, and clear instruction that teachers praised in the earlier edition. It then builds on this success with more practice exercises, greatly expanded instruction in the process of writing, and new material on study and research skills, speaking and listening, critical thinking, and more. *Basic Skills in English* provides:

Clear, readable presentation for below-level readers

The series offers a controlled reading level, a one-step-at-a-time approach, and success-directed lessons. As a result, students read with ease and master skills gradually, gaining confidence as they progress (see pages T4–T5).

Comprehensive coverage of on-level skills

Students reading below grade level need the same skills and preparation that average students do. That's why *Basic Skills in English* provides thorough instruction in all the language basics: composition, grammar, and related language skills (see pages T6–T7).

So complete, you can be sure your students will learn all essential English skills.

All students need the same skills, regardless of their reading abilities. That's why *Basic Skills in English* teaches all of the essential concepts and skills that students are expected to master at their grade level. It's a comprehensive program that provides instruction in *all* the language basics: composition; grammar, usage, and mechanics; and related language skills.

Composition

In-depth writing instruction teaches students the skills and techniques they'll need to write effectively:

Process of Writing
Students learn the three stages of the process of writing . . . pre-writing, writing, and revising . . . then use the process consistently throughout the program.

Types of writing
The series teaches students the various elements and techniques that characterize narrative, descriptive, and explanatory writing.

Forms of writing
Students learn and practice the different forms of writing that they will use in school and in everyday life. Lessons on sentences, paragraphs, compositions, reports, and research papers give students the essential skills they need.

Part 5 **Return to the Scene**

Revising Your Descriptive Paragraph

Part 4 **Put It There!**

Writing the First Draft

Part 3 **A Certain Feeling**

Pre-Writing: Creating Mood

Here's the Idea Have you ever read a really scary mystery novel or ghost story? What scared you? Was it just the story, or was it also the way the writer described what was happening? Most writers, especially when they are describing someone or something, try to suggest a certain feeling to the reader. This feeling is called **mood**.

Writers suggest mood through the language they use. Suppose a writer is describing the park in winter. The writer wants the reader to feel that the park is a pleasant place, alive with happy people. The writer might fill his description with words like these:

Nouns	Adjectives	Verbs	Adverbs
couples	crisp	skate	merrily
flurries	smiling	stroll	gently
snowballs	sunny	frolic	excitedly

Now suppose that the writer wants to suggest a different mood to the reader. The writer wants the reader to feel that the park is a cold, dead place. In that case, he or she might use words like these:

Nouns	Adjectives	Verbs	Adverbs
slush	biting	howled	harshly
clouds	frozen	stung	terribly
storm	bare	whipped	miserably

Think about the kind of mood you want to suggest in your description. Make lists of nouns, adjectives, verbs, and adverbs that will help you to suggest that feeling.

122

Grammar, usage, and mechanics

Basic Skills in English offers exceptionally clear, to-the-point instruction in grammar, usage, and mechanics. A flexible handbook format allows for developmental teaching, skills review, and student reference. And each section includes a wealth of varied exercises that are both fun and instructive. The series pays special attention to problems of usage and speech that often present difficulties for less able students.

Related language skills

Separate chapters teach the related skills students need for effective communication and for successful learning in every subject area:

Critical thinking
Topics include distinguishing fact and opinion, avoiding errors in reasoning, and drawing conclusions.

Vocabulary
The series develops skills such as discovering word meaning from context and recognizing word parts.

Levels of language
Students learn about standard and nonstandard English, slang, jargon, regional language, and more.

Life skills
Letters, forms, applications, résumés, and interviews are a few of the topics taught throughout the program.

Study and research
Students learn skills such as following directions, completing research, and preparing for tests.

Speaking and listening
Skills include presenting formal and informal speeches, evaluating speeches, and participating in group discussions.

Possessive Pronouns and Contractions

Some contractions are formed by joining a pronoun and a verb, omitting one or more letters. The apostrophe shows where letters are left out.

it's = it + is   they're = they + are
you're = you + are   who's = who + is

The possessive forms of the pronouns *its, your, their,* and *whose* sound the same as these contractions: *it's, you're, they're,* and *who's.* Because they sound alike, the contractions and possessives are sometimes confused.

Wrong: The groundhog saw it's shadow.
Right: The groundhog saw its shadow.

Right: You're (You are) late for your appointment.
Right: They're (They are) planning to show their slides.
Right: Who's (Who is) favored to win?

Exercise A Write the correct word from the two in parentheses.

1. (They're, Their) going to pick up the uniforms.
2. Have you made up (you're, your) mind?
3. (You're, Your) idea might work.
4. Are you sure that (they're, their) coming?
5. (Who's, Whose) going to the Eagles concert?
6. (They're, Their) glad (its, it's) Friday.
7. (Who's, Whose) going to remove the spider?
8. The amusement park gave free passes to (it's, its) first 500 entrants.
9. (Who's, Whose) bike is chained to the tree?
10. (Who's, Whose) got a dime that I can borrow?

Exercise B Write the words for which the contractions in these sentences stand.

1. It's twenty miles from this tow
2. The book is called *Who's Who*

444

Part 4
Wanted!

Reading Help-Wanted Ads

Here's the Idea An important step in looking for a job is finding out what jobs are available. You can do this by checking the help-wanted ads in your local newspaper. These ads are organized alphabetically by job title. Ads for full-time jobs are usually listed separately from ads for part-time jobs. A help-wanted ad may contain any or all of the following information:

1. Job title
2. Job description
3. Skills or experience required
4. Days or shifts to be worked
5. Number of hours per week
6. Salary or wages to be paid
7. How to contact the employer

Read the help-wanted ads carefully. Note details such as those listed above. Decide whether your skills and experience match those required for the job. Also decide whether you are available at the times given in the ad.

Check It Out Read the following help-wanted ads.

OFFICE—Filing Clerk. Full-time days, M-F. Filing for busy medical office. Some scheduling of appts. Exper. preferred. Start at $5.20 hr. Call Dr. Plessas, 555-1263.

RETAIL SALES, bakery. Christmas holiday only. Full-time, evenings. Weekends included. Mature, experienced person pref. Call Sandi, 555-2800.

STOCK & CLEAN UP work. 15 hrs./wk., after school and wknds. Apply in person. Melinke Auto Supply, 253 Warrington Rd.

333

As students progress, they build on the success they've already achieved.

Success-directed lessons, a controlled reading level, and a one-step-at-a-time approach combine to make concepts more accessible to students. As a result, they read with ease and master skills gradually, gaining confidence as they progress.

Success-directed lessons

The short, highly-structured lessons are fail-proof . . . every student can achieve success.

Here's the Idea
The main idea of the lesson is presented in a clear, concise manner. Explanations are especially easy to understand.

Check It Out
High-interest examples and models illustrate the main idea of the lesson. Questions help students focus on key points.

Try Your Skill
These highly-structured, success-directed exercises allow students to apply the skill they have learned.

Keep This in Mind
For further reinforcement, a boxed summary highlights the main idea of the lesson.

Now Write
The second exercise is a writing application that gives students independent practice in using the skill.

Part 9 **Top It Off**

The First Draft: Ending a Paragraph

Here's the Idea   Have you ever watched a television show and waited for a thrilling ending, only to find that the episode would be continued the next week? It is not a very satisfying experience. That is why you must include a good ending when you write a paragraph.

A good ending sentence is important to a paragraph. It sums up, or ties together, the ideas of the paragraph. It may also explain the importance of the ideas presented.

An ending sentence should not introduce any new information. A good ending makes a clear, final statement that works well with the other sentences in the paragraph. In fact, an ending sentence often restates the idea of the topic sentence in a slightly different way.

A good ending sentence should also be interesting. Whenever you write a paragraph, try to express your idea in an ending sentence that is memorable as well as clear.

Check It Out   Read the following paragraph.

New highway lights, not flying saucers, are responsible for a recent wave of UFO sightings. At about the same time that new highway lights were installed on Route 31 in our town, people began reporting UFO sightings. The highway lights are bright orange disks that light up the night sky in an eerie way. However, when a group of residents studied several photographs taken of these lights, they agreed that the lights resembled the UFO's they had reported. Our town's close encounter turned out to be much closer than we thought.

- Does the ending sentence tie together the ideas of the paragraph?

92

Try Your Skill   Read these three paragraphs with poorly written ending sentences. Then rewrite the endings. Make your endings clear and interesting.

1   We trudged through the swamp, jars held ready. Each time one of us saw a frog or tadpole, a cry went up. Then all of us would come sloshing to where the sighting had been made, ready to lunge with our jars. Usually, we turned around and around without success. *This was the second field trip for our biology class.*

2   Television news coverage is different from newspaper reporting. The best stories for TV news are those having strong visual elements. Such visible events often deal with violence, death, or disaster. Newspapers, on the other hand, rely more on words than on pictures to tell stories. Therefore, newspapers usually have a better balance of stories than television stations do. *It is better to read a newspaper.*

3   Pike, the superintendent in our building, lets me use the tools in his basement workshop. I go down to the basement whenever I have free time. I gather my tools from the pegboard panel on the prickly cement wall behind the workbench. As I cut, sand, and hammer, time passes quickly. I enjoy the whine of the saw and the smell of freshly cut wood. *I can even taste the sawdust in the air.*

Keep This in Mind

- A good ending sentence should sum up the main idea of a paragraph. It should also be interesting.

Now Write   Now you are ready to write a strong ending for your own paragraph. Review what you have written. It is a good idea to read your work aloud, at least to yourself. Then write an ending that sums up your idea in an interesting way. Save your paragraph in your folder.

93

Controlled reading level

While the content of each text is on grade level, the readability has been carefully controlled so that it does not interfere with the concepts.

The language and tone of the instruction is encouraging and conveys confidence in the student's ability. To further motivate students, the text uses lively, high-interest models and exercises.

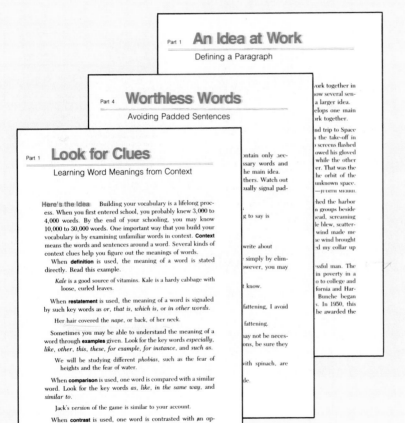

Part 1 **An Idea at Work**

Defining a Paragraph

Part 4 **Worthless Words**

Avoiding Padded Sentences

Part 1 **Look for Clues**

Learning Word Meanings from Context

Here's the Idea   Building your vocabulary is a lifelong process. When you first entered school, you probably knew 3,000 to 4,000 words. By the end of your schooling, you may know 10,000 to 30,000 words. One important way that you build your vocabulary is by examining unfamiliar words in context. **Context** means the words and sentences around a word. Several kinds of context clues help you figure out the meanings of words.

When **definition** is used, the meaning of a word is stated directly. Read this example.

Kale is a good source of vitamins. Kale is a hardy cabbage with loose, curled leaves.

When **restatement** is used, the meaning of a word is signaled by such key words as *or*, *that is*, *which is*, or *in other words*.

Her hair covered the *nape*, or back, of her neck.

Sometimes you may be able to understand the meaning of a word through **examples** given. Look for the key words *especially*, *like*, *other*, *this*, *these*, *for example*, *for instance*, and *such as*.

We will be studying different *phobias*, such as the fear of heights and the fear of water.

When **comparison** is used, one word is compared with a similar word. Look for the key words *as*, *like*, *in the same way*, and *similar to*.

Jack's *version* of the game is similar to your account.

When **contrast** is used, one word is contrasted with an opposite word. Look for the key words *although*, *but*, *unlike*, *while*, *on the contrary*, and *on the other hand*.

2

One-step-at-a-time approach

Each lesson follows a consistent, manageable format that focuses on one . . . and only one . . . topic at a time.

Single-concept lessons

So that students master skills gradually, lessons focus on a single skill and develop it. Later lessons review and build on the concept, helping students retain what they've learned.

Developmental sequence

Instruction moves logically from the word, to the sentence, to the paragraph, and on to longer types of writing.

Using the Teacher's Edition

The Teacher's Edition for each level provides step-by-step teaching strategies for presenting, developing, reinforcing, and reviewing each lesson.

Full-size student pages
Student pages are reproduced full size for ease in reading.

Objectives
Knowing what the objectives are can make your teaching more directed and purposeful.

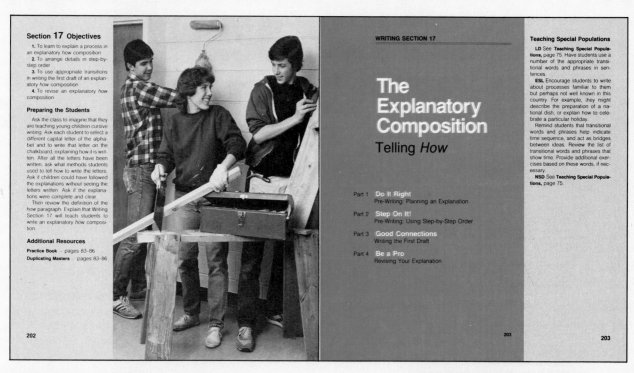

Preparing the students
The Teacher's Edition suggests ideas for motivating and preparing students prior to every new section.

Additional resources
A detailed list directs you to extra practice, review, and tests.

Teaching special populations
At the beginning of each writing section and at the end of each handbook, the Teacher's Edition explains difficulties faced by the special student. Strategies are presented for helping students for whom English is a second language, students with learning disabilities, and students who speak nonstandard dialects.

Lesson objectives
Objectives are clearly stated in terms of student performance.

Presenting the lesson
Teaching suggestions stress points to emphasize, possible areas of difficulty, and ways to use the exercises effectively.

Answers
For your convenience, exercise answers are printed on or beside the student page.

Optional practice
Additional ideas are provided for drill, review, or reinforcement.

Part 7

Objective
To revise a report

Presenting the Lesson
1. Have students read **Here's the idea.** Outline the revision questions on the chalkboard as you discuss them.
2. Have students examine the revised paragraph in **Check It Out.** Help the class recognize that the paragraph's overall organization has been revised to more effectively introduce the topic.
3. Assign **Try Your Skill.**
4. Read **Keep This in Mind.**
5. Assign **Now Write.** Point out that first drafts tend to be messy when they are revised, as in the sample in **Check It Out.** Students should not worry about neatness at this point as long as their revisions are legible.

Individualizing the Lesson

Less-Advanced Students
After students have made major revisions in their reports, devote one class period to proofreading for errors in grammar and mechanics. Note on the chalkboard any points of punctuation, grammar, capitalization, and spelling that the class has found troublesome. Urge students to keep an eye out for errors that they have made in the past. Instruct them to look up questionable items in the dictionary or Handbook. Finally, have students exchange papers near the end of the period and help their classmates proofread.

250

Part 7 — Check Up
Revising a Report

Here's the Idea Now that you have a first draft, you're almost finished. However, you have a few more steps to complete. Revising your report is the first of these steps.

As you revise your work, remember that a report depends on an accurate presentation of facts. Check the accuracy of dates and figures. Make sure that special words and names are spelled correctly. You may have to go back and check your sources.

Try reading your report aloud to yourself. Sometimes your ears will catch mistakes that your eyes have missed. As you read your report, ask yourself these questions.

1. Does my introduction tell the reader what my report will be about? Is the introduction interesting and informative?
2. Does the report follow my outline?
3. Are all of the facts and dates accurate? Do they develop my topic thoroughly?
4. Have I used quotation marks when copying a writer's work word for word?
5. Is each paragraph about one main idea? Does each fact in a paragraph develop that main idea?
6. Have I used effective transitions between sentences and paragraphs?
7. Does my conclusion summarize the main ideas?

Proofreading is the last step in revising. Read your paper carefully. Look for and correct any errors in grammar, capitalization, punctuation, and spelling. Once again, check dates, figures, and the spelling of special words and names.

Check It Out Read this revised introductory paragraph.

250

A hero is a person who is known for special achievements. The names of such heroes are honored. However, there are also lesser known people who have performed acts of bravery. The Carnegie Hero Fund honors these heroes. Americans have respected men and women who have excelled in government, the arts, sports, and the sciences

· What has the writer done to improve the paragraph?

Try Your Skill This concluding paragraph has been revised, but it has not been proofread. The paragraph has five errors in grammar and mechanics. Find and correct these errors.

Today, the carnegie Hero Fund is more than seventy-five years old. During its existance, it has considered more than 50,000 heroic acts. It has awarded more than thirteen million dollars, to more than 6,300 winners. It is visable evidence that there is a deep admiration of people who help others. In this Democratic spirit, brave human beings—Whatever their sex, race, age, or background—become honored heroes.

· ... for organization, and for word choice.
· Proofread your report to correct errors in grammar, capitalization, punctuation, and spelling.

Now Write Using the guidelines in this lesson, revise your report. Then proofread it. Save your revised work.

251

Advanced Students
After students have revised their reports, duplicate one paragraph from each of several revised drafts, each illustrating a different item that has been revised. Point out the improvements that have been made and have the class suggest further improvements. Then give students a chance to further revise their reports.

Optional Practice
Have the class revise the following paragraph from the body of a report, which does not stick to one main idea.

A great variety of dinosaurs existed. Some were vegetarians and some were meat-eaters. There were horned dinosaurs such as triceratops and duck-billed dinosaurs like corythosaurus. The name "dinosauria" means "terrible lizard." There were even bird-sized dinosaurs.

Extending the Lesson
Invite students who wrote especially good reports to read them to the class. Just as the class learned about the Carnegie Hero Fund from the textbook, they can also learn about their classmates' topics. A similar exercise is to read a few good reports yourself. After a report is read, ask what the class especially liked about the report.

251

On-page teaching suggestions
The text provides ideas for motivating the student, presenting the lesson, and providing enrichment.

Individualizing
Each section provides approaches for adjusting the basic lesson to different levels of ability or skill development.

Extending the lesson
An enrichment lesson or exercise suggests way students can apply the concepts outside of the English classroom.

Guidelines for evaluating composition
Special pages offer guidelines for teaching and evaluating student writing, including an evaluation form.

T9

Other McDougal, Littell Programs

Building English Skills

Building English Skills is the only complete, developmental grammar and composition program for grades 1–12. Skills are developed sequentially from one grade to the next, with each level reinforcing and extending the skills learned earlier.

The McDougal, Littell Literature Series

The *McDougal, Littell Literature* Series for grades 7–12 provides an in-depth presentation of literary types at every level to give students a strong grasp of the possibilities of each genre.

Reading Literature Series

Reading Literature is a new literature program for grades 7–12 that combines high-quality literature selections with developmental instruction in reading skills. The program builds skills in comprehension, reading literature, vocabulary, and writing. In addition, related skills such as study and research, speaking and listening, and critical thinking are reinforced throughout.

Teaching Special Populations

Many classrooms in our society include students with special language needs. Some of these students may have learning disabilities (LD). Others may be learning English as their second language (ESL). Still others may speak a nonstandard dialect of English (NSD). These students are likely to encounter special difficulties in mastering some of the concepts and acquiring some of the skills presented in *Basic Skills in English*.

The purpose of this section is to make the classroom teacher aware of these students and the learning difficulties they may face. A teacher who understands the special needs of these students can make certain that they are not penalized for learning deficiencies beyond their control. At the same time, the teacher will be better equipped to help these students fulfill their potential.

The text for *Basic Skills in English* has been reviewed by consultants whose areas of expertise include the problems faced by LD, ESL and NSD students in the English classroom. Our consultants' general suggestions for adapting *Basic Skills in English* to the special needs of these students are provided on the following pages. Additionally, specific suggestions for teaching special populations are presented at the beginning of each writing section and at the back of this book.

Special Consultants

Rebecca Benjamin, Educational Consultant, Albuquerque, New Mexico

Grace Massey Holt, Instructor of English as a Second Language, California State University, Sacramento, California

Dr. Eleanor Wall Thonis, District Psychologist, Wheatland School District, Wheatland, California

Karen Bustelo Wehle, S.L.D. Teacher, Leon County School District, Tallahassee, Florida

Virginia Woods, Secondary Resource Teacher, Dripping Springs Independent School District, Dripping Springs, Texas

Following are some general strategies for modifying lessons and assignments to help LD, ESL, and NSD students overcome some of their difficulties.

Learning Disabled Students

LD students typically have average or above average potential. However, specific areas of deficiency, which vary from student to student, can make the processing of information and the acquisition of skills difficult. There are many learning problems that can be included under the general heading "learning disabilities."

Specific areas of dysfunction include auditory memory, auditory discrimination, visual memory, visual discrimination, fine motor coordination, gross motor coordination, written expression, and oral expression.

It is important for the teacher to realize that these learning difficulties are beyond the students' control. Learning disabilities may be the result of brain damage, central nervous system dysfunction, mild cerebral palsy, or other physical impairment. Therefore, what may appear to be inattentiveness or an uncooperative attitude on the part of a student may actually be a sign of his or her inability to learn through conventional methods. Nevertheless, learning disabled students can compensate for their handicaps and overcome their problems. This is most likely to occur when teachers understand their students' strengths and limitations and are willing to adjust assignments and the presentation of material to maximize the chances for success.

Whenever possible, the teacher should work with counselors and special education teachers to determine the specific nature of a student's disability. This will allow the teacher to devise strategies for circumventing the disability. Some general strategies that apply to many kinds of learning disabilities are presented here. However, the teacher is encouraged to improvise new methods and to modify material as necessary for individual students.

General Areas of Difficulty

Whatever the nature of a student's disability, there are certain predictable problems that will impede his or her efforts to learn:

1. short attention span
2. poor memory
3. difficulty in generalizing
4. hyperactivity
5. distractability
6. low motivation
7. poor motor coordination

These problems of concentration and memory are usually compounded by low levels of acquired skills:

1. low reading level
2. inability to organize work and ideas
3. laborious and illegible handwriting

General Strategies

There are several strategies the teacher can use to counter learning disabilities.

1. Seat the students in the front of the classroom where there are no obstructions to sight or hearing.
2. Present essential information both orally and in writing. Reinforce written material in the text with oral explanation or with tape recordings made by the teacher, the student, or the student's parents. Write oral instructions and assignments on the board, and provide a written study guide that highlights the key points of oral presentations.
3. Supply visual aids whenever possible, to reinforce

material from the text. Simple charts, diagrams, photographs, and other illustrations may help to clarify the relationships among ideas.

4. Repeat important ideas frequently and begin each lesson with a summary of the material covered the previous day. This will help students to compensate for poor short- and long-term memory. Repeat assignments more than once, and give them both orally and in writing.

5. Demonstrate the correct way to complete an assignment. Work one or more problems on the board, showing the students how to go about answering them. Break down the assignment into steps, and be sure that the order of the steps is clear.

6. Give two grades for written work, one for content and another for mechanics. This two-grade system rewards students for good ideas despite mechanical shortcomings. Do not penalize students with visual disabilities for misspellings.

7. Allow students to answer test questions orally, either directly to the teacher or into a tape recorder. This can help to eliminate the anxiety caused by the prospect of writing under the pressure of time.

8. Help the students find shortcuts so that they can avoid writing long or difficult words repeatedly. When complete words or sentences are unnecessary, devise abbreviatons. For example, use *D., Int., Imp.,* and *E* instead of *Declarative, Interrogative, Imperative,* and *Exclamatory* for completing exercises on the types of sentences. Allow LD students to print rather than write if printing is easier and more legible. You might also suggest that students with writing difficulties learn to type.

Modification of Material

The teacher may find that some modification of the course material in *Basic Skills in English* will be necessary so that learning disabled students can keep pace with the rest of the class.

1. Break long-term assignments into shorter, individual tasks that can be assigned on a step-by-step, short-term basis.

2. Shorten and simplify all regularly assigned work; these students must put extra time and effort into completing their work. When possible, allow the students to select one, or a few, of several questions, topics, or exercises.

3. Simplify the assignments for written paragraphs and compositions, and allow students to work with partners or to put first drafts on tape.

4. If the reading level of a Section is too advanced, explain important vocabulary words and concepts before asking the students to read it.

5. Either supplement or replace difficult terms from the text with simpler ones. For example, when teaching the types of sentences, supplement or replace the terms *Declarative, Interrogative, Imperative,* and *Exclamatory* with words like *Statement, Question, Command,* and *Strong Feeling.*

6. Review "Study and Research Skills" with LD students several times during the year. This chapter will help them to overcome their difficulties in organizing work and ideas.

English as a Second Language

Students whose first language is not English face a number of challenges. These vary in difficulty depending on their native language and culture and their familiarity with American language and culture. In general, speakers of Indo-European languages, such as German and Spanish, will probably have fewer problems learning English grammar and adapting to American culture than will, for example, speakers of Oriental languages. However, most ESL students share one distinct disadvantage: they lack their classmates' years of experience with the English language, experience which is necessary to the thorough understanding of most standard textbooks. For these students, the problems of using textbooks fall into two categories: difficulty with the complexity of language and unfamiliarity with cultural references.

The Sections of *Basic Skills in English* are written at a level that may be difficult for many ESL students. Moreover, the exercises and assignments require students to analyze and manipulate a language that many ESL students will not yet have acquired fully. Once a teacher is aware of these problems, he or she can implement certain techniques for reducing the difficulties ESL students face.

General Strategies for Countering Language Barriers

To help students overcome these difficulties posed by an unfamiliar language, the following strategies may be employed:

1. Introduce new topics at a slower pace, and provide guided practice with increased feedback and monitoring.
2. Read aloud the essential parts of each Section, allowing time for explanation, examples, and the answering of questions.
3. In explaining any abstract concept such as "unity," it is better to go to the specific example first, pointing out the elements that show unity before giving the definition. Beginning from the concrete and particular enables ESL students to follow to the general or abstract.
4. Shorten assignments for these students and allow extra time for the acquisition of concepts.
5. Simplify all activities and exercises linguistically

whenever possible. Exercises from intermediate ESL books would be helpful.
6. Build into the activities as many visuals, manipulatives, and concrete experiences as possible. The teacher may have to illustrate and demonstrate meanings as if with small children. However, these aids should not be presented in a condescending manner—the age and intelligence of the students must be respected.
7. Suggest that students work as a group whenever possible. Allowing each student to go through activities with the group before having to do it individually gives him or her enough concrete practice and confidence to try it alone.
8. Correct written exercises and compositions carefully so that students will not continue to practice mistakes.
9. Precede *every* writing activity for ESL students with a similar oral activity; these students must have opportunities to speak and express themselves *before* writing. This procedure provides students with an opportunity to separate the tasks of clarifying ideas and translating them into correct written form.
10. Encourage ESL students to keep journals in English, recording thoughts and impressions without concern for grammar, spelling, and pronunciation. It will help them to develop fluency and build confidence and enjoyment in their writing, and it will free them from anxieties about absolute correctness.
11. To reduce the demands on the teacher's time, recruit advanced students to help the ESL students understand written materials and to monitor their practice.

General Strategies for Countering Culture Differences

The other major problem area for ESL students will be

the many cultural references that appear in the text. Some ESL students will have trouble determining gender from proper names alone. They may also have difficulty understanding references to national holidays, sports, individual teams, famous people, geography, foods, and popular culture. Slang, jargon, and idiomatic expressions are tied directly to a specific culture and are often impossible to translate. The following approaches could alleviate these problems:

1. Encourage class discussion to clarify cultural references and provide general information to the whole class. This and other oral work will greatly facilitate the ESL student's acquisition of English.
2. Encourage discussion of differences and similarities between ESL student's language and English. In covering verb tenses, for example, ask the ESL student to explain how his or her language expresses ideas of time. Such comparisons would benefit the American students by exposing them to aspects of language that are not part of their own linguistic experience.
3. Encourage ESL students to write about their native customs, holidays, geography, celebrities, and foods.
4. Encourage ESL students to read material, at an appropriate level, about specifically American people, places, and events. You might even provide these students with newspapers and popular magazines to read and discuss. This will help them acquire the common stock of information familiar to most Americans.

Speakers of Nonstandard Dialects

Everyone speaks some sort of dialect. The speech of Americans in one section of the country differs in at least some aspects of pronunciation, vocabulary, and grammar from the speech of people in other sections.

In addition, certain social, ethnic, and racial groups share a distinct way of speaking. Sometimes, however, the dialect common to a particular group departs so much for the most widely used and accepted dialects that it is termed "nonstandard." It is with students who speak such a dialect that this section is concerned.

Teachers must be aware that nonstandard dialects are legitimate language variations. These dialects follow regular phonological and semantic rules and serve the needs of the speech communities that use them. Speakers of "nonstandard" dialects are not necessarily careless speakers of English, nor should the variant features of these dialects be considered "errors." On the other hand, speakers of these dialects should be led to recognize that they cannot participate fully in mainstream American culture and society without understanding and effectively employing its language, standard English.

General Strategies

The teacher of NSD students should bear in mind that one need not, and indeed should not, eradicate one dialect in order to teach another. Instead, the teacher should implement the following strategies:

1. Encourage students to learn the patterns and usages of standard English for use in contexts where it is considered more appropriate: for academic writing and speech; in job applications and interviews; at work, if co-workers or superiors use standard English.
2. Encourage students to use the dialect that sounds natural both to speaker and listener in informal, casual, and family settings.
3. Tape-record samples of speech from various settings: playing fields, family gatherings, classrooms, committee meetings. Guide students in analyzing the vocabulary, sentence patterns, and grammar

used in these different contexts. This practice will make them see that various forms exist within a single language, each form being appropriate in a certain setting. It has proven to be a non-threatening way to increase all students' awareness of linguistic variation and to demonstrate that shifting from one form of speech to another does not involve a loss of identity.

4. When covering the Writing Sections have the NSD students keep journals, in whatever dialect is natural and comfortable, of thoughts, feelings, impressions, and experiences. Read the journals periodically and comment in writing about potential uses for the material in later compositions. Do not "correct" variations from standard usage or point out misspellings. Such nonjudgmental reading, discussion, and subsequent use of the journal entries will reinforce the lesson that writing in standard English is not abandoning one's identity but communicating it to a wider audience.

5. Establish small-group "workshops" consisting of four or five students, and have them collaborate in making suggestions for revision of written work. This strategy educates all of the students about the various dialects spoken in class.

6. Take note of the areas of grammatical variations that appear in the NSD students' written work, and be prepared to help the students with any problems that arise from these differences. Speakers of so-called Black English, for example, may have trouble with verb usage, for some of the principles of standard grammar and usage do not match their speech patterns. For similar reasons speakers of Hawaiian dialect may encounter difficulties with articles and pronouns. Other groups may have trouble with word order in sentences. Provide extra coaching, more details explanations, and additional practice, until the students have mastered the unfamiliar parts of standard dialect.

Specific suggestions for teaching composition to special populations appear at the beginning of each Composition Section of this book.

Specific suggestions for teaching grammar, usage, and mechanics to special populations appear at the end of this book.

Basic Skills in English

Purple Level

Yellow Level

Blue Level

Orange Level

Green Level

Red Level

Basic Skills in English

Yellow Level

Joy Littell, EDITORIAL DIRECTOR

McDougal, Littell & Company
Evanston, Illinois
New York   Dallas   Sacramento

AUTHORS

Joy Littell, Editorial Director, McDougal, Littell & Company

The Editorial Staff of McDougal, Littell & Company

Kraft and Kraft, Developers of Educational Materials, Stow, Massachusetts

CONSULTANTS

Carole B. Bencich, Coordinator of Secondary Language Arts, Brevard County School Board, Rockledge, Florida

Dr. Sheila F. S. Ford, Coordinator for Secondary Language Arts, Spring Branch Independent School District, Houston, Texas

Marietta H. Hickman, English Department Chairman, Wake Forest-Rolesville High School, Wake Forest, North Carolina

Mary Evans Roberts, Supervisor of English and Language Arts, Savannah-Chatham Public Schools, Savannah, Georgia

ISBN: 0-86609-502-0   TE ISBN: 0-86609-503-9

Acknowledgments

Simon & Schuster: for entries on pages 17, 27, 29, 30, 32, 33, 40, and 440 from *Webster's New World Dictionary*, Students Edition; copyright © 1981 by Simon & Schuster, Inc. Bryna Untermeyer: For "The Fox and the Grapes" by Joseph Lauren, from *Story Poems*, edited by Louis Untermeyer; copyright © 1957 by Simon & Shuster, Inc.

85 86 87 88 / 12 11 10 9 8 7 6 5 4 3 2

Composition

Handbook

Section 1 Objectives

1. To learn word meanings by using context clues
2. To infer word meanings from context clues
3. To recognize base words
4. To recognize and know the meanings of common prefixes
5. To recognize and know the meanings of common suffixes
6. To recognize and understand common Latin roots in words
7. To recognize and understand combinations from Greek
8. To use antonyms and synonyms effectively
9. To use vivid sensory details in writing
10. To recognize new language in the fields of science and technology

Preparing the Student

Have students listen to Prokofiev's *Peter and the Wolf* played once without words and once with the words. Explain that while communication is generally thought to be a verbal activity, much communication is nonverbal. After listening to the version without words, ask students to give their version of the story. Play it again, this time with words, and see how different the intended version is from their interpretation. Point out that the more precise the message, the easier it is to understand.

Additional Resources

Mastery Test — pages 11–12 in the test booklet

Practice Book — pages 1–10

Duplicating Masters — pages 1–10

Developing Your Vocabulary

Teaching Special Populations

LD Provide additional oral exercises to reinforce the vocabulary concepts presented in this Section. Additionally, alter the text and ancillary exercises to meet the needs of your students.

Help students understand context clues by providing additional fill-in-the-blank exercises.

Most LD students will have difficulty memorizing the definitions for prefixes, suffixes, and roots. Allow them extra time with these exercises, and provide materials such as flashcards, lists, and worksheets.

Provide opportunities for students to list synonyms and antonyms of simple words, so that they grasp the difference between the two concepts.

ESL This Section is important for ESL students as they build their knowledge of the structure of English. Allow extra time for students to grasp the concept of *inference*. Be sure they understand the meaning of each base, prefix, and suffix. Stress especially the importance of using precise words. Also note that it is to their advantage to use newer dictionaries, so that they can understand the language of contemporary technology.

NSD Help students understand the function of the various suffixes.

Have students list standard words that they misuse, and drill them on the pronunciation of these words.

Part 1

Discoveries

Learning Word Meanings from Context

Objective

To learn word meanings by using context clues

Presenting the Lesson

1. Read aloud and discuss **Here's the Idea.** On the chalkboard list the five types of context clues and discuss their differences.

definition
restatement
examples
comparison
contrast

2. Read and discuss **Check It Out.** Ask students to identify which context clue is used in each sentence.

3. Assign and discuss **Try Your Skill.** You may want students having difficulty to work in small groups.

4. Read aloud **Keep This in Mind** and then assign **Now Write.**

Individualizing the Lesson

Less-Advanced Students

Have students bring in articles from periodicals such as *Time, National Geographic,* or *Science Digest.* Working in small groups, have them identify one example of each type of context clue.

Advanced Students

Have each student find one example of each type of context clue in periodicals. Then have them use each word that has been defined in an original sentence that displays their understanding of the word.

Here's the Idea   English has a larger, more varied vocabulary than most other languages. It includes a total of about 600,000 different words. In everyday situations, you usually recognize from 30,000 to 40,000 words. In speaking and writing, you may use 10,000.

One way to develop your vocabulary continually is to examine words in context. **Context** is the words and sentences within which a given word appears. Clues in the context can help you to figure out the meanings of unfamiliar words.

When **definition** is used in context, the meaning of an unfamiliar word is stated directly. Here is an example.

Jean is taking a *yoga* class at the YWCA. *Yoga* is a system of controlled breathing and exercises.

When **restatement** is used, the meaning of a new word is explained. Look for the key words *or, that is,* or *which is.*

The City Council approved a three percent tax *rebate.* That is, taxpayers will receive a return equal to three percent of their taxes.

You may be able to understand the meaning of a word through **examples** given. Look for the key words *especially, like, other, this, such as, for example,* and *for instance.*

Pasta, such as spaghetti and macaroni, makes a filling and inexpensive meal.

When **comparison** is used, one word is compared with a similar word. Look for the key words *as, like, in the same way,* and *similar to.*

Ralph's *astute* answer was as clever as the teacher's question.

When **contrast** is used, a word is compared with an opposite word. Look for the key words *although, but, unlike, while, on the contrary,* and *on the other hand.*

That perfume is *subtle,* but this one has quite a sharp scent.

Check It Out Read the following sentences.

1. I didn't understand the speaker's *dialect.* A dialect is a form of a language with its own vocabulary and pronunciation.
2. Dan's latest *objective,* or goal, is to run two miles every day.
3. Radioactive elements, such as *uranium* and *radium,* must be stored safely.
4. This *minestrone* is similar to Grandma's vegetable soup.
5. Although I was *punctual,* Donna was late for our meeting.

• What is the meaning of each italicized word? What context clue is used in each sentence?

Try Your Skill Choose four of these words: *artist, cashier, electrician, reporter, salesperson, secretary.* Write sentences that explain each word. Use key words as context clues.

Keep This in Mind

• Develop your vocabulary by examining unfamiliar words in context. Helpful context clues are definition, restatement, examples, comparison, and contrast.

Now Write Copy five unfamiliar words used in a textbook. Use context clues to write a definition of each word. Check your meanings in a dictionary. Label your paper **Discoveries,** the title of this lesson. Keep your work in your folder.

Have students select five key words—three concrete and two abstract—to use in sentences. The meanings of the key words should be revealed through context clues. Have students exchange papers and write definitions of the key words.

Extending the Lesson

Lead a class discussion on the benefits of understanding and using context clues. Be sure students understand that context clues can help them not only to understand more completely what they read but also to make their own writing clearer and more interesting.

Part 2

Objective

To infer word meanings from context clues

Presenting the Lesson

1. Read aloud and discuss **Here's the Idea.** Give particular attention to the example paragraph and how it defines *serene.* Stress that the entire paragraph should be read before attempting to define the unknown word.

2. Read and discuss **Check It Out.** Ask students to give the meaning of *apprentice.*

3. Assign and discuss **Try Your Skill.** You may want to do this exercise orally. Look up words in the dictionary for exact definitions.

4. Read aloud **Keep This in Mind** and then assign **Now Write.**

Individualizing the Lesson

Less-Advanced Students

Have students write four or five sentences that infer the meaning of *frugal.*

Advanced Students

Ask students to find two unfamiliar words in the dictionary. Have them write several sentences for each which infer rather than directly state the meaning of the word. Have students read their sentences aloud and ask for volunteers to try and define the key words.

Optional Practice

Read the following paragraphs aloud. Ask students to try to infer the

Drawing Conclusions

Inferring Meaning from Context

Here's the Idea The meaning of an unfamiliar word is not always made clear through direct context clues. However, the surrounding sentences may help you make a good guess at the meaning of an unfamiliar word. You may be able to read between the lines and draw a conclusion about the meaning of the word. This process is called **inference.**

The main idea of a passage or an entire paragraph may be related to the meaning of an unfamiliar word. In the following paragraph, for example, try to *infer* the meaning of the word *serene.*

> Jill had managed to stay *serene* in spite of a trying day. In the morning she didn't panic when she discovered that her bicycle had a flat tire. At lunch, she was patient with the freshman who tipped over her soup. She even remained unruffled during our surprise quiz in math this afternoon.

From the clues supplied in this paragraph, you can infer that *serene* means "quiet, calm, undisturbed."

Check It Out Read the following paragraph.

> When I finish high school, I am going to become an *apprentice* in the printing industry. For three years I will work with a master typesetter to learn all the phases of typesetting and printing. I will become familiar with various kinds of presses and with other printing machinery. I will also receive a salary while I learn the business.

- What can you infer about the meaning of *apprentice?*

Try Your Skill As you read these passages, try to infer the meanings of the italicized words. Write definitions for them.

1. My cousin's *dilapidated* car is as unsafe as it looks. The fenders are one color, the roof another, and the trunk a third. The tires are bald. Only one of the brake lights is working. Each visible part of the car is rusty, dented, or worn. It is impossible for me to imagine that this car was ever new.

2. Critics point out that one bad side effect of watching too much violent television is increased *irascibility* in young children. Preschoolers who watch more than three hours a day are more quick-tempered and irritable than those whose viewing is more limited.

3. The most *prodigious* tides in the world occur in the Bay of Fundy, between Maine and Nova Scotia. In most other places, the difference between high and low tide is only a few feet. However, near the narrow mouth of the Bay of Fundy, the tides rise more than fifty feet! Because of these awesome tides, these waters are considered quite dangerous.

4. Shoveling snow became a *lucrative* activity for me last winter. The heavy snowfalls set records. People in my neighborhood paid me extra money to shovel the large drifts that buried driveways, cars, and sidewalks. In fact, I made more money in one month than I had during the last three winters put together.

Keep This in Mind

- Inference is the process of using clues to draw a conclusion. Inferences about unfamiliar words can be drawn from the main ideas of paragraphs.

Now Write Suppose that you want to write a description of a friend who is especially *thoughtful*. Write four or five sentences that suggest this quality without defining it directly. Label your paper **Drawing Conclusions** and put it into your folder.

meaning of the italicized words. Have them check their meanings in the dictionary.

Many politicians are masters at the art of *circumlocution*. This fact is often best illustrated in press conferences. In response to a controversial question posed by a reporter, some politicians can talk for several minutes without ever really answering the question.

Most Americans would find it difficult to adapt to the *ascetic* lifestyle of a monk. Garage door openers, dishwashers, garbage disposals, stereos, and color televisions—the luxuries that many pampered Americans consider necessities—are missing from the life of a Franciscan monk.

The sudden collapse of the Brennan Dam sent a *torrent* of devastation into the St. Thomas Valley. Within a matter of hours, however, numerous organizations and individuals met the *exigency* of the situation with food, clothing, shelter, and medical help.

Extending the Lesson

Ask students to complete this sentence with a specific personality trait: "I wish I could be more _____." Have them add three sentences which suggest this trait, beginning with: "Then I would . . ." Collect the finished papers and read them aloud without identifying the personality trait. Let the class try to infer the trait from the passage.

The Heart of the Matter

Base Words

To recognize base words

Presenting the Lesson

1. Read aloud and discuss **Here's the Idea.** Write the list of words formed from *use* on the chalkboard. Although prefixes and suffixes change the word, focus attention on the base word.

2. On the chalkboard, write the list of words in **Check It Out** that are formed from *trust*. Have students come to the board and circle the base word, the prefix, and the suffix.

3. Assign **Try Your Skill.** Point out that base words are complete words themselves.

4. Read aloud **Keep This in Mind** and then assign **Now Write.**

Individualizing the Lesson

Less-Advanced Students

Have students reread **Here's the Idea.** Ask each student to write the base word for *preheat, undress, reclaim,* and *movable.* Then have students use each word (with the prefix) in a sentence.

Advanced Students

Duplicate the following paragraph. It contains five italicized words which have been changed by the addition of either a prefix or a suffix. Have students write the prefix, suffix, and base word for each word in italics.

No one could duplicate his skill. He would be *imprisoned* in a room at night with the lock clamped on the outside of the door, and the next morn-

Here's the Idea　Many of the longer words in English are made of more than one part. Some of these words may seem complicated and impossible to understand at first. If you know how to recognize the parts, however, you can take long words apart. You can separate one part from another. If you know the meanings of a number of word parts, you can often piece together a meaning for the whole word.

The three key word parts are base words, prefixes, and suffixes. A **base word** is a shorter English word around which a longer word is built. A **prefix** is a word part added at the beginning of a base word. A **suffix** is a word part added at the end of a base word.

Study this list of words that have been built from the base word *use.* How is the meaning of *use* included in the meaning of each longer word?

disuse	"lack of use"
misuse	"use improperly"
reuse	"use again"
us**able**	"that can be used; ready for use"
use**less**	"having no use"
use**ful**	"having many uses; helpful"
reus**able**	"that can be used again"

Notice that the spelling of the base word may change when an ending is added.

Check It Out　Examine these words and their definitions.

dis**trust**	"lack of trust; suspicion"
mis**trust**	"lack of trust; suspicion"

trustful   "full of trust or confidence"
mistrustful   "full of suspicion"
trusty   "that can be trusted or relied upon"

- What is the base word in each longer word?
- What parts have been added in each word? Is each part a prefix or a suffix?
- How does the meaning of the longer word include the meaning of the base word?

Try Your Skill   The words in each of the following groups have the same base word. For each group, write the <u>base word</u>.

1. discredit   noncredit   creditable
2. action   inaction   react   reaction
3. remove   movable   immovable   removable
4. conceivable   inconceivable   preconceived
5. construction   misconstruct   reconstruct
6. replace   displace   misplace   replaceable
7. incorrect   correctable   correction
8. disassemble   preassembled   reassemble   assembly
9. flexible   flexion   inflexible
10. dishonor   honorable   dishonorable

Keep This in Mind

- A base word is a word from which other words can be made by adding new parts.
- The new parts may be added at the beginning of the base word, at the end, or in both places.

Now Write   Choose one word from each of the ten groups in **Try Your Skill.** Write the meaning of each word you choose. Then use each word in a sentence. Label your paper **The Heart of the Matter** and keep it in your folder.

ing he would be seen *nonchalantly* strolling through the marketplace, while on the outside of the door the lock remained *unopened.* He could manage this even with his hands and feet chained. Some maintained that he practiced black magic and owned a cap which made him *invisible,* capable of squeezing through cracks in the wall; others said that he was *merely* a master of illusion.

—I. B. Singer

Optional Practice

Ask students to form as many words as possible by using the following base words: *know, nature, credit,* and *comfort.*

Extending the Lesson

Ask students to bring in the front page of the daily newspaper. Working in groups (less-advanced students with advanced students), have them find as many words as they can which have a prefix, suffix or both. Then have students write the base word and its definition.

Part 4

A Word Divided

Objective

To recognize and know the meanings of common prefixes

Presenting the Lesson

1. Ask students to define *prefix*. Then read aloud **Here's the Idea**. Point out that the words *soil* and *compact* are base words, while the prefix *sub-* gives these words a new meaning. Review the prefixes on page 8. Ask students to think of more words with these prefixes.

2. Read aloud and discuss **Check It Out**. Ask students to identify the meaning of each prefix.

3. Discuss and assign **Try Your Skill**. Point out that base words are complete words by themselves. Discuss students' answers when they have finished.

4. Read aloud **Keep This in Mind** and then assign **Now Write**.

Individualizing the Lesson

Less-Advanced Students

Have students reread **Here's the Idea**. From the examples, have them select two words with prefixes. Ask them to use each word in three original sentences.

Advanced Students

Have students add two different prefixes to *count*, *pay*, and *place*. Then have them use each word in an original sentence.

Optional Practice

Distribute a list of thirty definitions of words containing prefixes. Have

Recognizing Prefixes

Here's the Idea   Another good way to develop your vocabulary is to examine the parts of an unfamiliar word. In English, many words are made up of parts that work together. If you learn some of the most common word parts, you will be able to learn many new words.

A **prefix** is a word part with its own meaning that is added to the beginning of a base word. For instance, the prefix *sub-* means "under" or "less than." Once you know the meaning of this prefix, you will know that *subsoil* is "a layer of soil beneath the surface soil." You will also see that a *subcompact* is "a car that is smaller than a compact." Notice how the addition of the prefix affects the meanings of the base words *soil* and *compact*.

Study this list of common prefixes, their meanings, and examples of their use. Some prefixes have more than one meaning.

Prefix	Meaning	Example
dis-	"opposite of" or "away"	dishonest, displace
in- (also il-, im-, and ir-)	"not"	inability, illogical, immature, irreplaceable
mis-	"wrong, bad"	misbehavior
non-	"not"	nonfiction
pre-	"before"	prepay
re-	"again" or "back"	remarry, regain

Do not expect to find prefixes in all words. Check a word and its history in a dictionary to determine if the word has a prefix.

Check It Out   Examine these words and their definitions.

discomfort—"lack of comfort; distress"

disarm—"to take away weapons; to reduce forces"

inattentive—"not attentive; careless"

illimitable—"not limited; without bounds"

immobile—"not movable; motionless"

irrational—"not reasonable; absurd"

misfortune—"bad luck; trouble"

nonessential—"not essential; unnecessary"

precaution—"care taken beforehand"

rearrange—"to arrange again or differently"

repay—"to pay back"

- What is the prefix in each? What is the base word?

Try Your Skill   Twelve of the following words have prefixes. For each word that has a prefix, write the prefix and its meaning, plus the base word. For example, for the word *preview* you would write: pre (before) + view.

1. miscount
   mis (wrong) + count
2. distrust
   dis (not) + trust
3. pressure
4. redecorate
   re (again) + decorate
5. incapable
   in (not) + capable
6. nonskid
   non (not) + skid
7. miserable
8. reenlist
   re (again) + enlist
9. mispronounce
   mis (wrong) + pronounce
10. preelection
    pre (before) + election
11. disinterested
    dis (not) + interested
12. prepackage
    pre (before) + package
13. irresistible
    ir (not) + resistible
14. nonrestricted
    non (not) + restricted
15. distant

Keep This in Mind

- A prefix is a word part added at the beginning of a base word. A prefix has its own meaning. Learn the meanings of common prefixes.

Now Write   Use a dictionary to find six unfamiliar words containing each of the six prefixes that you have learned. List these words and define them. Finally, study them. Label your paper **A Word Divided** and keep it in your folder.

students identify the words that have been defined. If they have difficulty, suggest using a dictionary. Have students choose ten words to use in sentences.

Extending the Lesson

Write the following words on the chalkboard: *place, take, locate, pay, stop, activate, correct,* and *judge.* Have students form as many words as possible by using these base words in combination with the prefixes from this Section. Write the new words on the chalkboard and have students give definitions for these words, checking a dictionary when necessary.

Objective

To recognize and know the meanings of common suffixes

Preparing the Lesson

1. Read aloud **Here's the Idea.** Review the seven common suffixes and have students think of additional words containing these suffixes.

2. Read and discuss **Check It Out.** Point out that certain base words change their spelling when a suffix is added. Review the meaning of each suffix.

3. Assign and discuss **Try Your Skill.** Students may refer to the list of suffixes on page 10. Have students exchange papers to check answers.

4. Read aloud **Keep This in Mind,** and assign **Now Write.** Tell students that words with suffixes are listed at the end of the dictionary entry for the base word.

Individualizing the Lesson

Less-Advanced Students

Have students reread **Here's the Idea.** Choose three words with suffixes from the examples and have students use each in a sentence. Then have students write sentences using only the base word.

Advanced Students

Have students add two different suffixes to *civil, faith,* and *operate.* Then have them write a sentence using each new word.

On End

Recognizing Suffixes

Here's the Idea   A word part added at the end of a base word is called a **suffix.** Like a prefix, a suffix has a meaning of its own that changes the meaning of the base word. Also like a prefix, a suffix may have more than one meaning or more than one form. For instance, the suffix *-er* or *-or* means "a person or thing that does something." Thus, a *counselor* is "a person who counsels or advises."

Unlike prefixes, however, suffixes usually affect the spelling of the base words. Sometimes the final consonant is doubled. For example, *shop* becomes *shopper.* Sometimes the final letter is dropped. For example, *move* becomes *movable.* Sometimes the final letter of the base word is changed. For example, *penny* becomes *penniless.*

Study this list of common suffixes, their meanings, and examples of their use.

Suffix	Meaning	Example
-able or **-ible**	"can be, having this quality"	lovable, sensible
-less	"without"	thoughtless
-ful	"full of, having"	doubtful
-ous	"full of, having"	courageous
-ist	"a person who does something"	biologist
-ion	"act of, result of, condition of"	correction
-y	"tending to be, characterized by"	foggy

Check It Out   Examine these words and their definitions.

social   sociable—"enjoying the company of others; friendly"
permit   permissible—"that can be permitted; allowable"
artless—"lacking skill or art; simple; natural"
pity   pitiful—"deserving pity because it is sad or pathetic"
space   spacious—"having more than enough space; large"
naturalist—"a person who studies animals and plants"
formation—"something formed, arranged, or positioned"
faulty—"having faults; imperfect"

- What is the suffix in each? What is the base word?

Try Your Skill   Number your paper from 1 to 15. Find the suffix in each of the following words. Write the base word and the meaning of the suffix for each word. Check the spelling of the base word if necessary. For instance, for the word *typist* you would write: type + a person who does.

fame + having
1. famous
home + without
2. homeless
violin + one skilled in
3. violinist
tax + able to
4. taxable
reflect + the act of
5. reflection

delight + full of
6. delightful
convert + able to
7. convertible
noise + full of
8. noisy
mystery + full of
9. mysterious
wave + full of
10. wavy

guitar + one skilled in
11. guitarist
price + without
12. priceless
cup + full of
13. cupful
reason + able to
14. reasonable
translate + the result of
15. translation

Keep This in Mind

- A suffix is a word part added at the end of a base word. A suffix has its own meaning. Learn the meanings of some of the most common suffixes. Use a dictionary to check the spelling of a word when you add a suffix.

Now Write   Use a dictionary to help you find seven words, each containing a different one of the seven suffixes you have learned. List the new words. Define them and study them. Label your paper **On End** and put it into your folder.

11

Optional Practice

Divide the class into two groups. Using a list of words containing all seven suffixes, alternate between the two groups and ask for definitions of each word. Ask a volunteer to write the definitions on the chalkboard. Have one student be a dictionary judge.

Extending the Lesson

Ask students to bring in the front page of a daily newspaper. Have them circle all the words containing the suffixes presented in this lesson. Then ask them to use each word in a sentence. Suggest using a dictionary if they have trouble.

The Root of the Matter

Objective

To recognize and understand common Latin roots in words

Presenting the Lesson

1. Review the use and meaning of prefixes and suffixes. Read aloud and discuss **Here's the Idea**. Have students identify the base words, prefixes, and suffixes in *prearrange*, *weightless*, and *inapplicable*. Ask students how a base word differs from a root. Have students study the chart on page 12.

2. Read aloud the words in **Check It Out**. Have students identify the Latin root.

3. Assign **Try Your Skill**. Discuss how the roots relate to the meaning of each word. Show students how to find the history of a word in the dictionary. After students have completed the exercise, discuss the history of each word.

4. Read aloud **Keep This in Mind** and assign **Now Write**.

Individualizing the Lesson

Less-Advanced Students

Have students carefully read **Here's the Idea** and study the chart on page 12. Selecting one Latin root from the chart, have students find another word in the dictionary with the same root. Have them use the word in a sentence.

Advanced Students

Ask students to look up the meanings of *mental/demented*, and

Using Roots from Latin

Here's the Idea   You have learned that a prefix, such as *dis-*, meaning "opposite," can be added to a base word, such as *loyal*. The word formed, *disloyal*, means "without loyalty, faithless." You have also learned that a suffix, such as *-y*, meaning "characterized by," can be added to a base word, such as *sleep*. The word formed, *sleepy*, means "likely to fall asleep, drowsy." In these examples, it is clear that base words are separate words with their own meanings.

Some words are formed from a different kind of word part, called a **root**. Usually, a root is not an English word by itself. Nevertheless, a root has a meaning of its own. Because so many of the words in English come from Latin, the most common roots also come from Latin.

Study these four common Latin roots, their meanings, and examples of words in which they appear.

Latin Root	Meaning	Example
cred	"believe"	*credit*, meaning "belief or trust; approval; confidence"
duc, duct, duce	"lead"	*introduction*, meaning "something that leads into or prepares the way for"
fac, fact	"make"	*factory*, meaning "a building in which things are made"
pos, pon	"place or set"	*position*, meaning "the place where a person or thing is, especially in relation to others"

Check It Out   Examine these words and their definitions.

cred creed—"a brief statement of beliefs"
incredible—"unbelievable"
produce—"to lead or bring forth; to create"
deduce—"to figure out by logical reasoning"
factor—"any condition that makes something happen"
manufacture—"to make goods, especially by machinery"
positive—"definitely set; sure"
impose—"to place something on, such as a burden, tax, or regulation"

- What is the Latin root in each example? How is the meaning of the root related to the meaning of the whole word?

Try Your Skill   Copy the following words, circling the Latin root in each. Use the meaning of the root to help you figure out the meaning of the word. Then check the history and the meaning of each word in a dictionary.

creditable   abduct   fact   posture
accredit   aqueduct   facility   compose

Keep This in Mind
- A root is a part of a word and has a meaning of its own. Many common roots come from Latin. Learn some of the Latin roots, and you will have a clue to the meaning of many unfamiliar words.

Now Write   Using a dictionary, find four new words containing each of the four Latin roots you have learned. List and define the new words. Finally, study the roots. Label your paper **The Root of the Matter.** Put it into your folder.

statue/stature in a dictionary. Have them identify the Latin roots and use each word in a sentence.

Optional Practice
Give each student two words with different Latin roots. Have them define each word and explain its history.

Extending the Lesson
Divide the class into four groups and assign one Latin root to each group. Have students look through magazine articles or newspaper stories to find at least four words containing the Latin root they were given. Then have students define each word they find.

Part 7

Objective

To recognize and understand combinations from Greek

Presenting the Lesson

1. Read aloud and discuss **Here's the Idea.** Have students think of as many words containing *micro-* and *-ology* as possible. Have the students study the chart on page 14.

2. Read aloud the words in **Check It Out.** Have students identify the Greek roots in each word.

3. Assign **Try Your Skill.** Discuss how Greek roots relate to the meaning of the word.

4. Read aloud **Keep This in Mind** and then assign **Now Write.**

Individualizing the Lesson

Less-Advanced Students

Have students reread **Here's the Idea** and study the chart on page 14. Selecting two Greek roots from the chart, have students find two new words in the dictionary containing the same roots. Then have them use each new word in a sentence.

Advanced Students

Using the dictionary, have students find three words containing the Greek root *graph* or *chrono.* Have them write the definitions for each word they find and then use each one in a sentence.

Through the Centuries

Combinations from Greek

Here's the Idea   Like Latin, Greek has contributed many word parts to English. There are, for instance, several words made from the Greek root *micro,* meaning "very small."

You are probably familiar with a *micro*wave oven. You have used a *micro*scope in science class. You may have read *micro*film in your school library. You may listen to a pocket stereo made possible through *micro*miniaturization of electronic parts. The meaning "very small" is important in each of these words.

Study these six common Greek roots, their meanings, and examples of words in which they appear. Notice that the forms of some roots may change slightly.

Greek Root	Meaning	Example
micro	"small"	*microfiche,* a card with print too small to read without magnification
bio	"life"	*biosphere,* the part of the earth and its atmosphere where living things are found
chrono	"time"	*chronic,* lasting for a long time
ology	"science"	*biology,* the science that studies life
graph	"writing"	*graphite,* the material used to make pencils
metron	"measure"	*chronometer,* an extremely accurate timepiece

Check It Out   Examine these words and their definitions.

bio graph
        biography—"writing about a person's life"
chrono ology
      chronology—"the study of time; a sequence of events"
chrono graph
    chronograph—"a machine that keeps a written record of time"
micro bio ology
     microbiology—"the branch of biology that studies the smallest
                living things"
micro metron
    micrometer—"a tool for measuring very small distances"

- What Greek root or roots are in each example? How is the meaning of each Greek root related to the meaning of the whole word?

Try Your Skill   Copy the following words, circling the Greek root or roots in each. Use the meanings of the roots to help you figure out the meaning of each word. Write what you think each word means. Then check the history and the meaning of each word in a dictionary.

micro	micro	bio
microcircuit	micronutrient	biochemistry
bio metron	bio	chrono
biometrics	biosatellite	synchronize
chrono	graph	metron
anachronism	epigraph	symmetry

Keep This in Mind

- Many English words are made from Greek roots. If you learn some of the Greek roots, you will have a clue to the meanings of many unfamiliar words.

Now Write   Using a dictionary, find six new words containing each of the six new Greek roots you have learned. List and define the new words. Finally, study the words. Label your paper **Through the Centuries.** Put it into your folder.

Optional Practice

Give each student three words with different Greek roots. Have students define the words, give the history, and use each one in a sentence.

Extending the Lesson

Divide the class into five groups and assign each group one Greek root. Have students read newspaper stories or magazine articles and circle all the words which contain their Greek root. Have them define each word they find and use it in a sentence.

Part 8

Objective

To use synonyms and antonyms effectively

Presenting the Lesson

1. Read aloud **Here's the Idea.** Write *synonym, synonymy, antonym,* and *thesaurus* on the chalkboard. Ask students to define these words. Show the class a copy of *Roget's Thesaurus* and explain how to use it.

2. Read and discuss **Check It Out.** Discuss the meanings of the synonyms.

3. Read aloud the instruction for **Try Your Skill,** and assign the exercise. After students have finished, compare their answers.

4. Read aloud **Keep This in Mind** and then assign **Now Write.**

Individualizing the Lesson

Less-Advanced Students

Have students reread **Here's the Idea.** Ask them to look up *anger* and *intelligent* in the dictionary. Then have them write down the synonyms and antonyms listed for these words.

Advanced Students

Ask students to use a thesaurus to find two synonyms for the following words: *divide, eager,* and *walk.* Then have them write one sentence for each synonym.

Optional Practice

Have students identify the follow-

In the Right

Using Words Precisely

Here's the Idea   If you use language carelessly, you run two risks. First, your writing may be dull or boring. Second, and more important, your ideas may be misunderstood. Thus, it is important to choose specific words that express the precise meaning you have in mind.

To use words precisely, you need to learn to choose among synonyms. **Synonyms** are words with nearly the same meaning. For example, the words *easy, effortless, smooth,* and *simple* are synonyms. The meanings of synonyms may be quite similar, but the differences are usually important. These important shades of meaning are often explained in a dictionary. A *synonymy* (si nän′ ə mē) is the list of synonyms and their shades of meaning that is given at the end of some entries in a dictionary.

Synonyms are also given in another helpful reference book called a *thesaurus* (thi sôr′ əs). A thesaurus gives many synonyms for each word or idea listed.

To use words precisely, you also need to learn to use antonyms. **Antonyms** are words with opposite meanings. For example, *find—lose, arrive—depart,* and *ancient—modern* are pairs of antonyms. Antonyms will help you to show contrasts. For example, you might write, "In Rome the remains of *ancient* buildings are an important part of the *modern* city." You will find antonyms given in some dictionaries and in a thesaurus.

Check It Out   Look at the synonymy given at the end of a dictionary entry for *sad,* and then answer these questions.

- Which synonym for *sad* suggests discouragement?
- What are antonyms for *sad?*

SYN.—**sad** is the simple, general term, implying anything from a mild unhappiness that is over quickly to a feeling of great, deep grief; **sorrowful** implies a sadness caused by some specific loss, disappointment, etc. *[her death left him sorrowful]*; **melancholy** suggests a more or less continuing mournfulness or gloominess, or, often, merely a deep thoughtfulness *[a melancholy view of life and its misfortunes]*; **dejected** implies discouragement or a sinking of spirits, as because of frustration; **depressed** suggests a mood of worry and hopelessness, as because of feeling tired or useless *[the unhappy ending left him feeling depressed]*; **doleful** implies a mournful, often exaggerated, sadness *[the doleful look on a lost child's face]* —**ANT.** **happy, cheerful**

Try Your Skill   Choose the synonym that best fits each sentence. Use a dictionary or thesaurus to help you.

1. I couldn't risk driving far on these (<u>bad</u>, wicked, severe, defective) tires.

2. Dr. McKenna hoped that her patient would (reply, answer, <u>respond</u>, retort) to the bright light.

3. You can turn to your elders for (<u>intelligent</u>, clever, alert, smart) advice on many practical matters.

4. The youngest children (chuckled, <u>laughed</u>, snickered, guffawed) at the clown's wonderful, silly tricks.

> **Keep This in Mind**
>
> • Use a dictionary or thesaurus to check the meanings of words. Learn to use words precisely.

Now Write   Choose two of the synonyms and one antonym for *sad* shown in **Check It Out.** Use each correctly in a sentence that shows its precise meaning. Label your paper **In the Right** and put it into your folder.

ing pairs of words as synonyms or antonyms. Have them define the words.

S civil-polite   A antique-modern
S attain-achieve   A fail-succeed
S grand-major   A chief-subordinate

Extending the Lesson

Have students look up synonyms for *heavy* and *mystery.* As a class, compose sentences for each synonym listed, and write these on the chalkboard. Make sure students' sentences illustrate the proper use of each synonym.

Part 9

Objective

To use vivid sensory details in writing

Presenting the Lesson

1. Read aloud **Here's the Idea.** On the chalkboard write the five senses: *sight, hearing, touch, taste,* and *smell.* Ask students which senses are used in the example paragraph. Then open the classroom door and ask students to write down the sounds they hear in the building. Have volunteers read aloud their sensory details. Encourage students to become more aware of the surroundings through their senses.

2. Read and discuss **Check It Out.** Ask students to look up unfamiliar words.

3. Go over the lists of sensory words on pages 20–21. Then assign **Try Your Skill.**

4. Read aloud **Keep This in Mind** and assign **Now Write.**

Individualizing the Lesson

Less-Advanced Students

Ask students to reread **Here's the Idea.** Have them list as many sensory details about their experience during a thunderstorm as possible. Have them share their sensory details with their classmates.

Advanced Students

Have students review the list of sensory hearing words on page 18. Then have each student select a machine or mechanical device, such as a blender, a power saw, or

---

Special Effects

Building a Vocabulary of the Senses

Here's the Idea   Your five senses are constantly giving you specific information. Much of the time, you do not pay particular attention to sensory details. However, if you stop and focus on each of your senses, you will realize the variety of impressions that you are receiving. When you write, you can use these sensory details to describe an experience and bring it to life.

Through the use of sensory details you can make any experience vivid. For example, suppose that you were home alone during a power failure. Can you imagine that experience as you read the following paragraph?

I felt the sudden silence. The radio stopped. The furnace ceased its steady rumbling. The refrigerator stopped its droning hum. The only sounds were those of the wind whistling and the creaking of the old house. As I sat in the silence, I felt a chilly draft. I shivered and moved toward the window. I watched the sky darken as the storm thundered into the valley.

To learn how to use sensory details effectively, you need to do three things. First, train yourself to be more aware of your senses. Notice the details of your surroundings. Second, build a vocabulary of the senses. Become familiar with the sensory words such as those listed on pages 20 and 21 at the end of this lesson. Finally, use your sensory vocabulary effectively. Select sensory words that describe your experience precisely.

Check It Out   Look at these examples of sensory words.

Sight:	silver, curved, sparkling, massive
Hearing:	thud, whine, hiss, rustle, sigh
Touch:	lukewarm, spongy, wooly, waxy

Taste: bittersweet, mellow, medicinal, savory
Smell: earthy, pungent, briny, musty

- Which of these sensory words are new to you? What do they mean? Think of an object or place that might be described by each of these words.

Try Your Skill   Think of two specific places that fit any of the general categories below. Name the two places and then list as many sensory words as you can think of that describe each one. Be specific. Try to use all of your senses.

a museum	a gymnasium
a department store	a classroom
an amusement park	a room
a restaurant	a garage

Keep This in Mind

- Use your senses to learn about your surroundings. Build a vocabulary of the senses. When you write, use vivid sensory details that bring an experience to life.

Now Write   Think of a place where you go to rest or relax. List as many sensory details about the place as you can. Try to use all of your senses. Choose specific, precise words. You may want to refer to the sample lists on the following pages. Label your paper **Special Effects.** Keep it in your folder.

an automobile engine and write a list of sensory words to describe the different noises it would make if it were in use. Ask students to think about all the sounds: starting, running, and shutting-off.

Optional Practice

Fill a paper bag with different objects of various sizes and textures, such as a nail file, a rock, a teabag, wet spaghetti, a sponge, or a flower. Have students close their eyes, choose an object from the bag and describe how it feels. Pass the bag around the classroom asking students to use good sensory words to describe the objects.

Extending the Lesson

Ask students to imagine what it would be like to live underwater. Have them list as many sensory details as possible to describe their underwater existence. Be sure they attempt to use all five senses. When they have finished, list on the chalkboard the words and phrases which are most vivid, precise, or imaginative.

A List of Sight Words

colorless	round	dotted	tidy
white	flat	freckled	handsome
ivory	curved	wrinkled	tall
yellow	wavy	striped	lean
gold	ruffled	bright	muscular
orange	oval	clear	sturdy
lime	angular	shiny	healthy
green	triangular	sparkling	fragile
turquoise	rectangular	jeweled	pale
blue	square	fiery	sickly
pink	hollow	sheer	small
maroon	narrow	drab	large
lavender	crooked	dark	massive
purple	lumpy	old	immense
gray	swollen	worn	attractive
silver	long	messy	perky
hazel	wiry	cluttered	showy
black	shapeless	clean	shadowy

A List of Hearing Words

crash	squawk	crackle	chime
thud	whine	buzz	laugh
bump	bark	clink	gurgle
boom	bleat	hiss	giggle
thunder	bray	snort	guffaw
bang	blare	bellow	sing
roar	rumble	growl	hum
scream	grate	whimper	mutter
screech	slam	stammer	murmur
shout	clap	snap	whisper
yell	stomp	rustle	sigh
whistle	jangle	whir	hush

A List of Taste Words

oily	rich	bland	ripe
buttery	hearty	tasteless	medicinal
salty	mellow	sour	fishy
bitter	sugary	vinegary	spicy
bittersweet	crisp	fruity	hot
sweet	savory	tangy	burnt

A List of Smell Words

sweet	piney	acrid	sickly
scented	pungent	burnt	stagnant
fragrant	spicy	gaseous	musty
aromatic	gamy	putrid	moldy
perfumed	fishy	spoiled	dry
fresh	briny	sour	damp
earthy	sharp	rancid	dank

A List of Touch Words

cool	wet	silky	sandy
cold	slippery	velvety	gritty
icy	spongy	smooth	rough
lukewarm	mushy	soft	sharp
tepid	oily	wooly	thick
warm	waxy	furry	dry
hot	fleshy	feathery	dull
steamy	rubbery	fuzzy	thin
sticky	bumpy	hairy	fragile
damp	crisp	leathery	tender

Part 10

Objective

To recognize new language in the fields of science and technology

Presenting the Lesson

1. Read aloud **Here's the Idea.** Ask students to try and define the new meanings of *loop, menu, bit, scroll, crash,* and *bug.* Have students offer additional words they know which now have new meanings.

2. Read aloud **Check It Out.** Ask students to define these words and write sentences using each one. This can be done on the chalkboard.

3. Read aloud and assign **Try Your Skill.** Suggest special dictionaries or glossaries which would give the specialized use of these words.

4. Read aloud **Keep This in Mind** and assign **Now Write.**

Individualizing the Lesson

Less-Advanced Students

Have students look up the meanings for *hardware* and *touchdown* in the dictionary. Have them write down one familiar and one new meaning for each word. Then ask students to use each word in two sentences.

Advanced Students

Have students look up these words in the dictionary: *quark, petrodollars,* and *SALT.* Ask them to write down their meanings and the fields from which they originate. Then have them use each word in a sentence.

Satellites and Silicon

Language for Special Fields

Here's the Idea   Our world changes at a rapid pace. People the world over influence our lives. They invent new machines, new processes, new ways of working and living. The English language changes to keep up with the times.

As the world changes, English grows and changes to enable us to communicate with each other. New words are created. Old words are given new meanings. New terms may be created by combining words that already exist, either with other existing words or with new ones.

The computer industry, for example, has added a new vocabulary to English. Some computer words are just old words with new meanings. Do you know what these computer terms mean?

loop   menu   bit   scroll   crash   bug

Other computer terms are entirely new. Some are acronyms. Others are compounds. Still others started out as slang terms among computer designers and hobbyists (or "hackers"). How many of these terms can you define?

RAM   printout   software   byte   user-friendly

Other areas of science, technology, and medicine also add words to your language. Which of these words do you know?

interferon   fly-by   genetic engineering

As time passes, the world changes. To understand the changing world, you must keep up with changes in the language. Since many dictionaries do not include definitions of the newest terms, you must turn elsewhere. Ask teachers for explanations of terms in their fields. Look for a glossary of terms at the end of a recent book on the subject.

Check It Out   The following terms are all recent additions to English. They have specialized meanings in science, technology, or medicine. Some of them have older, more familiar meanings. Others are made up of two familiar words. Study them carefully. Find out what their meanings are.

Answers will vary. See current dictionaries/encyclopedias.

cursor   gene splicing   chip   floppy disk

bubble memory   spacewalk   industrial robot

- Do you see how English words can take on brand new meanings to describe new ideas and inventions?

Try Your Skill   Look up each of the following words in a dictionary. Write one familiar meaning for each word. Then write each word's new meaning in the field of computers, space exploration, medicine, or technology.

mouse   scan   core   boot

Keep This in Mind

- As the world changes, the vocabulary of English changes. New words are added. New meanings are added to old words.
- Dictionaries may not include definitions of the newest terms. Ask teachers for explanations of terms in their fields. Look for glossaries in recent books.

Now Write   Label your paper **Satellites and Silicon.** During the next two days, make a list of new technological terms that appear in a local newspaper. By asking experts, determine the meaning of each term. Next to each term, write its meaning. Share your words with your classmates. Save your work in your folder.

Section 2 Objectives

1. To become familiar with the organization of a dictionary

2. To understand and use the information contained in a dictionary entry

3. To gain skill in understanding the meaning of a word in a particular context

Preparing the Students

Ask students where they think they could find the answers to these questions.

When was William Penn born?
What is a pilot light?
When is Memorial Day?
What is the abbreviation for *millimeter*?
Where is Cape Cod?
How is silkscreening done?

The class may be surprised to find out that a good dictionary can answer all of these questions

Ask students when and how they use dictionaries. Explain that this Section will help them to use dictionaries more effectively.

Additional Resources

Mastery Test — pages 13–14 in the test booklet
Practice Book — pages 11–13
Duplicating Masters — pages 11–13

24

Using a Dictionary

Teaching Special Populations

LD Provide additional exercises in alphabetizing, and allow students to use simplified dictionaries.

Duplicate additional entries for students to read and discuss as a group. Allow students to complete the more difficult exercises in pairs.

ESL Be sure ESL students understand pronunciation symbols and accent marks. Have students look up various words and pronounce them in class.

ESL students may be confused by words that have multiple meanings and functions in English. Review with students the parts of speech, and give additional examples of words that are used in more than one way.

NSD Emphasize the exercises on pronunciation with NSD students. List on the chalkboard words that are frequently mispronounced, and conduct oral drills based on those words.

Objective

To become familiar with the organization of a dictionary

Presenting the Lesson

1. Read aloud **Here's the Idea.** Examine several types of dictionaries, and show students the kinds of information contained in each. Discuss the differences between an unabridged and an abridged dictionary. Point out the guide words in a dictionary and explain their purpose.

2. Have students study and discuss **Check It Out.** Show them the key to symbols and abbreviations in a dictionary.

3. Give each student a dictionary and assign **Try Your Skill.**

4. Read aloud **Keep This in Mind** and then assign **Now Write.**

Individualizing the Lesson

Less-Advanced Students

Have students reread **Here's the Idea.** Working in pairs, have one student look through his or her dictionary and give five words to the other student. Then have the second student find and write the guide words for each entry given.

Advanced Students

Have students answer the following questions.   Answers will vary.

1. Would the entry *ace* be found on the page with the guide words *accolade* and *accouterment*? Why or why not?
2. What word precedes *mascara* in the dictionary?

Words To Guide You

Using a Dictionary

Here's the Idea   A dictionary is a useful reference book containing lists of words and information about the words. Whenever you use words, you will want to use a dictionary. When you read, you will see unfamiliar words or words used in unfamiliar ways. A dictionary will help you to understand the meanings of the words you see. When you write, you will be searching continually for the right words. A dictionary will help you to choose the right words and to use them correctly.

There are several kinds of dictionaries you might find helpful. Usually you will be able to find what you need in an abridged, or shortened, dictionary. Sometimes, however, you may need an unabridged dictionary. This contains nearly all of the words in a language, including those that are rare. There are also specialized dictionaries that include only words used with a single subject, such as music.

Become familiar with the dictionaries you use. You will find that every dictionary organizes information in its own way and uses its own symbols and abbreviations. Read the introduction to a dictionary for an explanation of its format.

All dictionaries list words in alphabetical order. In addition, all dictionaries have two guide words in large, bold print at the top of each page to help you locate words listed on the page. The left guide word is the same as the first word on the page. The right guide word is the same as the last word on the page. When you are looking for a word, flip through the dictionary until you find the page where your word comes alphabetically between the guide words.

Check It Out   Look at the top portion of a dictionary page, on the following page.

Gan·y·mede (gan′ə mēd) *Gr. Myth.* a beautiful youth who was cupbearer to the gods

gaol (jāl) *n. Brit. sp. of* JAIL —**gaol′er** *n.*

gap (gap) *n.* [ON. < *gapa*, to yawn, GAPE] **1.** a hole or opening made by breaking, tearing, etc.; breach **2.** a mountain pass or ravine **3.** an empty space or time; blank **4.** a difference in ideas, natures, etc. **5.** *same as* SPARK GAP —*vi.* **gapped, gap′ping** to come apart; open

gape (gāp) *vi.* **gaped, gap′ing** [< ON. *gapa*, to yawn < IE. base *ghe-*] **1.** to open the mouth wide, as in yawning **2.** to stare with the mouth open, as in wonder **3.** to open wide, as a chasm —*n.* **1.** an open-mouthed stare **2.** a yawn **3.** a wide opening **4.** *Zool.* the measure of the widest possible opening of a mouth or beak —**the gapes 1.** a disease of poultry and birds, causing them to gape **2.** a fit of yawning —**gap′er** *n.* —**gap′ing·ly** *adv.*

☆ **gar** (gär) *n., pl.* **gar, gars:** see PLURAL, II, D, 2 [contr. < GARFISH] any of a group of freshwater ganoid fishes with long, narrow bodies, long, beaklike snouts, and many sharp teeth

G.A.R. Grand Army of the Republic

ga·rage (gə räzh′, -räj′; *Brit.* gar′äzh) *n.* [Fr. < *garer*, to GUARD] **1.** a closed shelter for automobiles **2.** a business establishment where automobiles are repaired, stored, etc. —*vt.*

GAR
(to 10 ft. long)

gar·goyle (gär′goil) *n.* [< OFr. *gargouille:* see GARGLE] **1.** a waterspout, usually in the form of a carved fantastic creature, sticking out from the gutter of a building **2.** a person with very strange or grotesque features

GARGOYLE

Gar·i·bal·di (gar′ə bôl′dē; *It.* gä rē bäl′dē), **Giu·sep·pe** (joō zep′pe) 1807-82; It. patriot & general: leader in movement to unify Italy

gar·ish (ger′ish) *adj.* [prob. < ME. *gauren*, to stare] too bright or gaudy; showy —see SYN. at GAUDY —**gar′ish·ly** *adv.* —**gar′ish·ness** *n.*

gar·land (gär′lənd) *n.* [< OFr. *garlande*] a wreath of flowers, leaves, etc. —*vt.* to form into or decorate with a garland or garlands

Gar·land (gär′lənd) [after A. *Garland*, U.S. attorney general (1885-89)] city in NE Tex.: suburb of Dallas: pop. 81,000

gar·lic (gär′lik) *n.* [< OE. < *gar*, a spear (see GORE³) + *leac*, a leek] **1.** a bulbous plant of the lily family **2.** its strong-smelling bulb, made up of small sections called cloves, used as a seasoning —**gar′lick·y** *adj.*

gar·ment (gär′mənt) *n.* [< OFr. *garnement* < *garnir:* see GARNISH] **1.** any article of clothing **2.** a covering —*vt.* to clothe

gar·ner (gär′nər) *n.* [< OFr. < L. *granarium* < *granum*, GRAIN] **1.** a place for storing grain; granary **2.** a store of something —*vt.* **1.** to gather up and store in or as in a granary **2.** to get or earn [to *garner* praise] **3.** to collect or gather [to *garner* data]

- In what order are the words in each column listed? What special symbols are used? What are the guide words? Would you find the word *garden* on this page?

Try Your Skill
Look up each word in a dictionary and write the guide words for that page.

fireworks	synonym	phase	elegant
jackpot	atmosphere	century	limelight
kettle	typical	bouquet	carburetor

Keep This in Mind

- A dictionary is a reference book that lists words alphabetically and explains each word.

Now Write
In learning about governments you may see the following words: *aristocracy, communism, constitution, democracy, fascism, monarchy, nation,* and *republic.* Find each word in a dictionary and list the guide words on the page. Use four of the words in sentences. Label your paper **Words To Guide You** and put it into your folder.

---

3. What words appear between *torque* and *tortilla*?

Optional Practice

Photocopy one page from the dictionary. Give students one copy each plus five nonsense words. Ask them to insert the nonsense words in the proper alphabetical position.

Extending the Lesson

Ask students to put the following words in alphabetical order following the style used in the dictionary.

3 newlywed
2 New Deal
1 newborn
4 new math
6 New World
5 newsletter

Then ask students to give the guide words that appear on the page containing each word in this list.

Part 2

Objective

To understand and use the information contained in a dictionary entry

Presenting the Lesson

1. Make sure that each student has his or her own dictionary for this entire lesson. If necessary, divide the class into groups to share dictionaries. Read aloud **Here's the Idea** paying special attention to the boldfaced words. Point out that each dictionary has its own symbols to indicate the primary and secondary accents on words.

Explain the abbreviations for the parts of speech. Review *word origin* and *synonyms*. Be sure students read the information about how the dictionary is organized and understand the purpose of the various sections in the dictionary.

2. Have students study and discuss the entry given in **Check It Out.** Ask the class to explain the key symbols that the dictionary entry uses. Have students identify the information included in the entry as well as answering the questions from **Check It Out.**

3. Assign and discuss **Try Your Skill.**

4. Read aloud **Keep This in Mind** and then assign **Now Write.**

Individualizing the Lesson

Less-Advanced Students

Have students carefully reread **Here's the Idea.** Ask them to use the

---

In Search

Reading a Dictionary Entry

Here's the Idea Each dictionary entry contains much more than the meaning of a word. It also has information to help you understand a word and use it correctly.

The **entry word** itself appears in bold print and is divided into syllables. The word *memorable*, for example, is entered as **mem·o·ra·ble.** Refer to the entry word whenever you need to divide a word at the end of a line of writing.

The **pronunciation** of a word is given in parentheses. Use the symbols and accent marks to help you sound out an unfamiliar word. The word *commercial*, for example, appears as (kə mur′ shəl). Refer to the explanation of symbols often shown at the bottom of a page. You will usually find the complete explanation at the front of the dictionary.

The **part of speech** of a word is indicated by an abbreviation in bold print. *Noun*, for example, is abbreviated *n.* and *adjective* is *adj.* Refer to the complete list of abbreviations usually presented in the front of the dictionary. Some words can be used as more than one part of speech. If so, the other parts of speech will be indicated later in an entry.

If a word has **special forms** or **endings,** they will be included next in the entry. The entry for the irregular verb *see*, for example, includes the forms **saw, seen, seeing.** Plural endings of some nouns are also shown. For the noun *hero*, for example, the plural ending **-oes** is shown.

The **origin,** or **history,** of a word is given next, usually in brackets. The symbol < means "came from." Abbreviations, such as *Gr.* and *L.*, stand for the languages from which words came, such as Greek and Latin. Refer to the complete list of abbreviations used in your dictionary. This list is usually given at the front of the dictionary.

Definitions are given next. The most common definition of a word is often given first. When a word has a special meaning within a field, that meaning will be noted. One definition of *return*, for instance, says "*Sports* to hit, run, or throw back a ball."

Sometimes a word may have a special meaning in casual conversation and informal writing. This is called a *colloquial* meaning and is usually indicated in a dictionary. For instance, one definition of *character* is "[Colloq.] an odd or peculiar person." Slang—very informal, popular language—is also indicated in the dictionary. For instance, one definition of *charge*, as a noun, is "[Slang] a thrill."

Some dictionaries also list **synonyms** and **antonyms** at the ends of certain entries. A *synonymy* may explain a group of synonyms and their shades of meaning. For example, at the end of the entry for *sharp*, its synonyms *keen* and *acute* are also explained. *Dull*, an antonym for *sharp*, is also listed.

From all of these examples, you can see how much useful information is presented in an entry in a good dictionary.

Check It Out   Examine the dictionary entry below and then answer the questions at the top of page 30.

> **tune** (tōōn, tyōōn) *n.* [ME., var. of *tone*, TONE] **1.** a series of musical tones with a regular rhythm; melody; air **2.** the condition of having correct musical pitch, or of being in key; also, harmony; concord: now chiefly in phrases **in tune, out of tune** [a violin that is *in tune;* a person *out of tune* with the times] —*vt.* **tuned, tun′ing 1.** to adjust (a musical instrument) to some standard of pitch [to *tune* a piano] **2.** to adapt (music, the voice, etc.) to some pitch, tone, etc. **3.** to adjust (an electronics circuit, a motor, etc.) to the proper or desired performance —*vi.* to be in tune; harmonize —see **SYN.** at MELODY —**call the tune** to be in control —**change one's tune** to change one's attitude or manner: also **sing a different tune** —**to the tune of** [Colloq.] to the amount of —**tune in 1.** to adjust a radio or television receiver to a given frequency or channel so as to receive (a specified station, program, etc.) ☆**2.** [Slang] to become or make aware, knowing, etc. —**tune out 1.** to adjust a radio or television receiver so as to get rid of (interference, etc.) **2.** [Slang] to stop paying attention to, showing interest in, etc. — **tune up 1.** to adjust (musical instruments) to the same pitch **2.** to put (an engine) into good working condition

pronunciation guide in their dictionaries to identify the following phonetically spelled words.

lurk
lerk

shadow
shad′ō

tattoo,
ta tū′

gobble
gob′ əl

vague
vāg

orb
ôrb

Advanced Students

Have students visit the library and examine and report on the specialized dictionaries they find there. Have them explain the different ways each dictionary organizes its information.

Optional Practice

Have each student use one page of a dictionary to develop the following list.

1. all words that are nouns
2. all three-syllable words
3. all words with an accented second syllable
4. all words of Latin origin
5. all words having synonyms

Extending the Lesson

Divide the class into four groups and have them prepare twenty questions about interesting information that can be found in dictionaries. Collect the questions and give them to different groups. See if the students in each group can find the answers to the questions they are given.

- How many syllables are there in *tune?* From what language did *tune* come? What parts of speech can *tune* be? Which definition is most familiar to you? Where would you find synonyms for *tune?* What informal expressions include *tune?*

Try Your Skill   Read this entry and answer the questions.

ice (īs) *n.* [OE. *is*]   **1.** water frozen solid by cold   **2.** a piece, layer, or sheet of this   **3.** anything like frozen water in appearance, etc.   **4.** coldness in manner or attitude   **5.** *a)* a frozen dessert, usually of water, fruit juice, and sugar   *b)* [Brit.] ice cream   ☆**6.** [Slang] diamonds —*vt.* **iced, ic′ing**   **1.** to change into ice; freeze   **2.** to cover with ice   **3.** to cool by putting ice on, in, or around *[to ice a drink]*   **4.** to cover with icing *[to ice a cake]*   **5.** *Ice Hockey* to shoot (the puck) from defensive to offensive territory —*vi.* to freeze (often with *up* or *over*) —**break the ice**   **1.** to make a start by getting over the first problems   **2.** to make a start toward getting better acquainted —☆**cut no ice** [Colloq.] to have no effect —☆**on ice** [Slang]   **1.** in readiness or reserve   **2.** sure to result in victory or success *[this game is on ice]* —**on thin ice** [Colloq.] in a risky situation

1. As what parts of speech can *ice* be used?
2. What endings does the verb *ice* have?
3. From what language does *ice* come?
4. State a specialized meaning of *ice*.
5. What informal expressions use the word *ice?*

Keep This in Mind

- A dictionary entry contains the meanings of a word and other useful information.

Now Write   Use a dictionary to find words with these characteristics. Each word should have one characteristic. Label your paper **In Search of** and put it into your folder.

1. two pronunciations
2. two parts of speech
3. has come from French
4. meaning in a special field
5. an informal meaning
6. an antonym

A Fitting Choice

Finding the Meaning of a Word

Here's the Idea   As you look through a dictionary, you will soon notice that many words have more than one meaning. Whenever you check a word in the dictionary, read all of its meanings. Find the meaning that fits the context in which you found the word or intend to use it.

For instance, the simple word *turn* has a surprising number of meanings. *Webster's New World Dictionary, Students Edition,* gives forty-three meanings for *turn* as a verb. The same entry gives sixteen meanings for *turn* as a noun, and sixteen phrases that include the word. In the following examples, notice how the context helps you determine the correct meaning.

1. It was my *turn* to pitch the ball.
(In this context, *turn* means "the right or chance to do something, especially in regular order.")
2. Marcia *turned* several plans over in her mind.
(Here, *turn* means "to think about, to ponder.")
3. *Turn* your chair away from the window.
(Here, *turn* means "to change the position or direction of.")
4. Hot weather will *turn* milk.
(Here, *turn* means "to make sour.")
5. My sister Barbara just *turned* sixteen.
(Here, *turn* means "to reach or pass.")
6. Grandpa was born at the *turn* of the century.
(Here, *turn* means "the time of change.")
7. Her fall off the ladder gave us quite a *turn*.
(Here, *turn* means "a sudden, brief shock.")

From these few examples, it is clear how many meanings can be contained in a single entry.

Some words seem to be repeated in more than one entry. For

Objective

To gain skill in understanding the meaning of a word in a particular context

Presenting the Lesson

1. Read aloud **Here's the Idea.** Explain how there can be several different meanings for the same word. Write *homograph* on the chalkboard. Ask students to explain the difference between a homograph and a word that has more than one meaning. Ask students to look through the dictionary to find an example of a homograph.

2. Read and discuss **Check It Out.** Point out that the raised numbers after entry words denote homographs. Have students think up sentences using the different definitions of *match*.

3. Assign **Try Your Skill** to groups of four. Ask each group to select which meaning of *pound* best fits the five sentences. Have groups compare answers.

4. Read aloud **Keep This in Mind** and then assign **Now Write.**

Individualizing the Lesson

Less-Advanced Students

Ask students to look up the word *brief* in the dictionary, and to examine its definitions. Ask them to use *brief* in three different sentences, first as an adjective, then as a noun, and finally as a verb.

Advanced Students

Have students write sentences for the words below. Remind students that their sentences should illustrate the word as defined and as the part of speech given.

maxim—"a short rule of conduct; proverb" n.

saddle—"to burden" v.

subject—"cause to undergo or experience something" v.

novel—"of a new kind or nature; unfamiliar" adj.

beam—"to look or smile brightly" v.

Optional Practice

Divide the class into four groups. Have them look through the dictionary and find three homographs. Have each group write the two different meanings of a homograph on the chalkboard and ask the rest of the class to come up with the word. For example, "single" and "bottom of the foot" both come from *sole*.

Extending the Lesson

Have students use their dictionaries to find the meanings of the following homographs—*net, deck, box, spell*. Have them use these homographs in sentences.

instance, you will find the word *lean* entered twice: *lean*[1], a verb, means "to bend from an upright position" or "to depend on for help"; *lean*[2], an adjective, means "thin, containing little or no fat." In each entry, *lean* has a different origin and different meanings. Such words are called *homographs*. Homographs have the same spelling, although they may have different pronunciations. Notice that each entry is not a shade of meaning of one word. It is actually a different word. When you notice a word with more than one entry, be sure to read all of the entries to find the meaning you want.

Check It Out   Read these dictionary entries.

> **match**[1] (mach) *n.* [< OFr. *mesche*, prob. < L. *myxa*, lamp wick < Gr.] **1.** orig., a wick or cord prepared to burn at a uniform rate, used for firing guns or explosives **2.** a slender piece of wood, cardboard, etc. tipped with a composition that catches fire by friction, sometimes only on a specially prepared surface
> **match**[2] (mach) *n.* [OE. (ge)*mæcca*, a mate < base of *macian*, MAKE] **1.** any person or thing equal or similar to another in some way; specif., *a)* a person, group, or thing able to cope with another as an equal [he met his *match* in chess when he played her] *b)* a counterpart or facsimile **2.** two or more persons or things that go together in appearance, size, etc. [a purse and shoes that are a good *match*] **3.** a contest or game; competition [a tennis *match*] **4.** a marriage or mating **5.** a person regarded as a suitable mate —*vt.* **1.** to join in marriage; mate **2.** to compete with successfully [he was able to *match* his opponent] **3.** to put in opposition (*with*); pit (*against*) [to match one's strength against an enemy] **4.** to be equal, similar, or suitable to [he could never *match* her in an argument] **5.** to make, show, or get a competitor, counterpart, or equivalent to [*match* this cloth] **6.** to suit or fit (one thing) to another **7.** to fit (things) together **8.** to compare ☆**9.** *a)* to flip or reveal (coins) to decide something contested, the winner being determined by the combination of faces thus exposed *b)* to match coins with (another person) —*vi.* to be equal, similar, suitable, etc. in some way —**match′a·ble** *adj.* —**match′er** *n.*

- Which definition of *match* fits the context of the sentence: My family came to my wrestling *match*?
- From what language is *match*[1]? *match*[2]? Which of the meanings of *match*[2] are most familiar to you?

Try Your Skill   Read the following dictionary entries and sentences. Determine which meaning of *pound* fits the context of each sentence and write your answer.

pound¹ (pound) *n., pl.* **pounds**, sometimes **pound** [OE. *pund* < L. *pondo*, abl. of *pondus*, weight, akin to *pendere*: see PENDANT] **1.** a unit of weight, equal to 16 oz. (7,000 grains) avoirdupois or 12 oz. (5,760 grains) troy: abbrev. **lb.** **2.** *a)* the monetary unit of the United Kingdom (in full, **pound sterling**) equal to 100 (new) pennies or, in the earlier system, to 20 shillings: symbol £ *b)* the monetary unit of various other countries, as of Ireland, Israel, etc. See MONETARY UNITS, table

pound² (pound) *vt.* [OE. *punian*] **1.** to beat to a pulp, powder, etc. [to *pound* corn into meal] **2.** to strike or drive with repeated heavy blows [to *pound* nails into a board] **3.** to make by pounding [he *pounded* a cabinet together] —*vi.* **1.** to deliver repeated, heavy blows (*at* or *on* a door, etc.) **2.** to move with heavy steps, thumps, etc. [he *pounded* down the hall] **3.** to beat heavily; throb [her heart *pounded* from the exercise] —*n.* a pounding, or the sound of it —see SYN. at BEAT —☆**pound one's ear** [Slang] to sleep —**pound out** **1.** to flatten, smooth, etc. by pounding **2.** to produce (musical notes, typed copy, etc.) with a very heavy touch —☆**pound the pavement** [Slang] to walk the streets, as in looking for work —**pound'er** *n.*

pound³ (pound) *n.* [< OE. *pund-*] **1.** an enclosed place for keeping animals, esp. stray animals [the city dog *pound*] **2.** a place of confinement, as for arrested persons **3.** an enclosed area for catching or keeping fish

1. The almonds must be *pounded* into paste for the cake.
2. They found the lost dog at the city *pound*.
3. The bear *pounded* through the woods.
4. Have you ever seen a British *pound* note?
5. The mysterious noise caused my heart to *pound*.

Keep This in Mind

- When you look up a word in the dictionary, determine which meaning fits the context.
- Sometimes a word has more than one entry, with a different meaning and origin for each.

Now Write   Use a dictionary to find one example of a word with many different meanings and one example of a homograph. For each example, copy three definitions. Then write a sentence using each of the meanings you have written. Label your paper **A Fitting Choice** and put it into your folder.

Section 3 Objectives

1. To recognize standard and nonstandard English

2. To recognize formal and informal English

3. To recognize and avoid slang in formal writing and speech

4. To understand the use and misuse of jargon

5. To recognize regional language and understand its uses

Preparing the Students

On the chalkboard write *standard*, *nonstandard*, *formal*, *informal*, *slang*, *jargon*, and *regional dialects*. Point out to students that there are at least 2,798 separate languages currently being spoken around the world. Like most other languages, English has sub-languages contained within it. Each of these sub-languages contributes to making our language a personal means of expression. Explain to students that Section 3 will introduce them to different types of English.

Additional Resources

Mastery Test — page 15 in the test booklet

Practice Book — pages 14–18

Duplicating Masters — pages 14–18

The Right Language at the Right Time

Teaching Special Populations

LD Discuss with students situations in which slang is appropriate and inappropriate. Simplify instructions for the exercises provided in the text.

ESL Use native English speakers to present examples of standard and nonstandard and formal and informal language.

Explain that in English, double negatives are not considered correct. Refer students to appropriate Sections in the Handbook for subject-verb agreement and pronoun usage.

Stress that "television language" is not formal English. Review with students the words they know that are slang. Ask them under what circumstances they use slang in their cultures.

NSD Help students understand why standard usage is important. Emphasize that all languages have speakers of different dialects, but that in order to communicate well in a society, speakers must use language understood by most of the population.

Provide students with additional practice in identifying nonstandard and informal usages.

Objective

To recognize standard and non-standard English

Presenting the Lesson

1. Read aloud **Here's the Idea** and have students carefully examine the chart on page 36. Discuss the meaning of *standard*. Ask students if the sentences written in non-standard English have a different meaning from those written in standard English. Explain that while non-standard English can be understood by some people, its use will not allow students to communicate effectively with the greatest number of people.

2. Read **Check It Out.** Ask students to explain what is nonstandard about each second sentence.

3. Assign **Try Your Skill.** Have students write their choices on the chalkboard.

4. Read aloud **Keep This in Mind** and assign **Now Write.**

Individualizing the Lesson

Less-Advanced Students

Have students reread **Here's the Idea.** Ask them to find the meaning of *standard* in the dictionary. Discuss with students some situations when the use of nonstandard English is not only inappropriate but also clearly limiting (for example, a job interview, a letter of request or complaint, and so on).

Advanced Students

Ask students what is nonstandard about the following quotation. Then

Special Occasions

Standard and Nonstandard English

Here's the Idea Singers, dancers, and actors often wear special costumes when they perform. These costumes are appropriate for entertaining others. However, they are not appropriate for going to an interview or sitting in a classroom.

Similarly, some types of language are right only in certain situations. In this chapter you will learn about several types of language and when they are appropriate. Two common types of language are standard English and non-standard English. The following chart describes these two types of language.

Using Standard and Nonstandard English	
Definition and Use	**Examples**
Standard English is language that follows the rules of good grammar and usage. Standard English is acceptable in all situations.	1. I don't want anything. 2. Call Jim and me tonight. 3. I'm not going.
Nonstandard English is language that does not follow the rules of good grammar and usage. Nonstandard English should not be used in most situations, especially in discussions, in speeches, or in most kinds of writing.	1. I don't want nothing. 2. Call Jim and I tonight. 3. I ain't going.

Use standard English for speeches, class discussions, compositions, and reports. Use it on the job. Also use standard English when you meet new people. Always proofread your writing to avoid using nonstandard English.

Check It Out   Read the following sentences.

Standard English	Nonstandard English
1. The President himself signed the letter.	1. The President hisself signed the letter.
2. I told you about those others.	2. I told you about them others.
3. Susan doesn't work here.	3. Susan don't work here.
4. She and I are friends.	4. Her and me are friends.

- What is nonstandard about each second sentence?

Try Your Skill   From each pair, choose the sentence that is written in standard English.

1. Leave the dog run free.
   Let the dog run free. s
2. Yolanda dances beautifully. s
   Yolanda dances beautiful.
3. Them answers were right; I'm real sure.
   Those answers were right; I'm really sure. s
4. It don't make no difference to Andy and me.
   It doesn't make any difference to Andy and me. s

Keep This in Mind

- Standard English follows the rules of good grammar and usage.

Now Write   Write a paragraph telling what you hope to do after high school. Exchange papers with a classmate. Correct any examples of nonstandard English in your friend's paper.

37

lead a discussion about why nonstandard English may be used in literature.

It worried me till I couldn't get no sleep. Here I go preachin' and I'd say "By God, this time I ain't gonna do it." And right while I said it, I knowed I was.   —John Steinbeck

Optional Practice

Ask students to rewrite the following sentences changing nonstandard English into standard English.

1. Susan and me are the only persons who done the assignment correct.
2. Mario throwed the paper away yesterday.
3. The letter from the senator was sent to Julio and I.
4. Don't worry about nothing, we'll be just fine on the camping trip.

Extending the Lesson

Have students find works of fiction in which the author has deliberately used nonstandard English to help portray a character. Remind students that this is the only legitimate use for nonstandard English in their writing.

One Way or Another

Formal and Informal English

Presenting the Lesson

1. Read aloud **Here's the Idea.** Discuss the differences between formal and informal English. Ask students when it would be best to use formal English, and when informal English would be appropriate.

2. Read **Check It Out.** Ask students which words should be used in formal situations and which should be used in informal ones.

3. Have students read the paragraph in **Try Your Skill** and rewrite it using formal English. Write some of the revised paragraphs on the chalkboard.

4. Read aloud **Keep This in Mind** and then assign **Now Write.**

Individualizing the Lesson

Less-Advanced Students

Have students reread **Here's the Idea,** paying close attention to the differences in the two paragraphs. Ask them to consider three occasions when formal English should be used, and three occasions when informal English would be appropriate.

Advanced Students

Have students choose a specific topic either from art, history, or science. Ask them to write a paragraph on their topic using the formal language of a report. Then have them

Here's the Idea   Standard English is spoken and written in many different situations. Some of these situations are more formal than others. In order to suit your language to the occasion, you must understand how to use two different kinds of standard English. These kinds are called formal and informal English.

Formal English is language that is right for serious or important occasions. It is the language that is used in sermons and lectures. It is also used in reports, serious essays, and official documents. If you were asking the president of a company for a job interview, you would use formal English.

> Formal English: Mr. MacIntire, may I call your secretary for an appointment to talk to you about a job with your company? I will be graduating from high school next spring and have some ideas that may benefit both your company and me.

Informal English is the comfortable but correct language used in everyday situations. It is the language of conversations, letters, and informal talks. It is also the language of most newspapers and magazines. If you were talking to a friend about an upcoming interview, you would use informal English.

> Informal English: Hi, Jim! I got the interview. How about that! I'm going in tomorrow. I'll call you later and tell you all about it. Wish me luck—I'll need it.

Whenever you are speaking or writing, choose language that is right for the situation. If the situation is formal, use formal language. If the situation is informal, use informal language.

Check It Out   Read the following pairs of words.

F	I
children	kids
appropriate	okay
Wonderful!	Wow!
unfortunate	too bad
cannot	can't

- Which word in each pair would you use in a formal situation? Which would you use in an informal situation?

Try Your Skill   The following paragraph contains a mixture of formal and informal English. Revise the paragraph. Replace all informal language with language that is right for a report.

Revisions will vary.

Some animals are highly social. Prairie dogs, for example, live in burrows placed a little way apart. These collections of burrows are really neat. They're like a little neighborhood or something. Furthermore, prairie dogs act much like human neighbors. They all do their share to keep their communities in good condition. They also warn one another if an enemy, such as a coyote, comes messing around looking for trouble. Prairie dogs are really something else!

Keep This in Mind

- Formal English is appropriate for serious or important occasions.
- Informal English is appropriate for conversations, letters, and informal talks.

Now Write   Imagine that you are the captain or manager of a sports team. You wish to congratulate a player on the team for his or her performance. Write a paragraph telling what you might say. Use informal English. Then, rewrite the paragraph for use in a formal speech at a sports banquet.

rewrite the paragraph in informal English as if they were including it in a letter to a friend.

Optional Practice

Ask students to rewrite the following paragraph using formal English.

Answers will vary.

The chronometer is a mechanical piece for keeping real good time. The chronometer was made better by the English clockmaker John Harrison in 1759. This thing helped sailors figure out longitude correctly for the first time.

Extending the Lesson

Have students look through newspapers, magazines, or books to find two paragraphs which are examples of formal English and two which are examples of informal English. Have students share their paragraphs with the class.

Part 3 · **Far Out!**

Using and Misusing Slang

<table>
<tr><td>

Objective

To recognize and avoid slang in formal writing and speech

Presenting the Lesson

1. Read aloud **Here's the Idea.** Point out that slang is not considered standard English. Slang is a specialized vocabulary of fad words and expressions. It is usually devised with the intent of restricting understanding to members of a certain group, such as teenagers.

2. Read **Check It Out.** Write the six expressions on the chalkboard and ask students to give the meanings of these slang expressions. Ask if they can provide additional expressions with the same or similar meanings.

3. Read and assign **Try Your Skill.** Have the class do this exercise orally.

4. Read aloud **Keep This in Mind** and assign **Now Write.**

Individualizing the Lesson

Less-Advanced Students

Have students write five slang words or expressions and use each one in a sentence. Have them rewrite the sentences replacing the slang with a standard English word or phrase.

Advanced Students

Ask students to match the slang word with its standard English meaning. Then have them use each slang word in a sentence.

</td><td>

Here's the Idea   When using the dictionary, you may have noticed that some words are labeled "slang." Here is an example:

> **spiff·y** (spif′ē) *adj.* **spiff′i·er, spiff′i·est** [< dial. *spiff*, well-dressed person] [Old Slang] neat and trim; smart or dapper

Slang is language made of fad words and phrases that are not accepted as standard English. Most slang is popular only for a short time. The word *spiffy*, for example, was extremely popular in the 1950's. Today, it is rarely used. Other slang terms that have now become outdated are the words *keen, marvy,* and *far out.* At different times, each of these slang terms has been used to mean "wonderful or interesting."

Slang is not considered standard English. It is also not always understood by everyone. Therefore, slang should never be used in compositions, reports, formal speeches, or business situations. It may be used in casual conversations, for informal talks, or in the dialogue of a short story.

Be especially careful not to use slang in formal writing. When you revise the work you do for school, always look for examples of slang. Replace any that you find. If you are unsure whether a given word is slang, look it up in a dictionary.

Check It Out   The following slang terms all have the same or similar meanings. Read this list of terms.

shake a leg	get down	go to town
lean on it	hit it	pour it on

- What slang meaning is shared by these terms?
- How many of these terms have you heard before? How many are unfamiliar to you?

</td></tr>
</table>

Try Your Skill   Identify the slang terms in the following sentences. Then, rewrite each sentence. Replace each slang term with a standard word or phrase.

1. Mark needs to mellow out a little; perhaps he should go on vacation.

2. His first film made big bucks, but his second was a real bust.

3. I saw a group of people protesting nukes.

4. If you forget your lines, you'll have to wing it.

5. My klutzy cat knocked a picture from the bookcase.

Keep This in Mind

- Slang, a type of nonstandard English, is made of fad words and phrases.
- Do not use slang in formal writing or speech.
- Use slang only in casual conversation or in the dialogue of a short story.

Now Write   The following paragraph from an old detective story contains many outdated slang words and phrases. Rewrite the paragraph. Replace the outdated slang with standard English.

What do I like about Rosie? Well, let me give you a for instance. Several years ago, she was all set to marry this palooka named Tommy Bayles. But old Tommy blew it when he said Rosie would have to quit this high-class, muckety-muck job she had downtown. When Rosie stopped laughing, she gave him the gate. Since then, lots of guys have thought Rosie was just the bee's knees, but old Rosie just ignores them. She's staying on the shelf and making her own way. I tell you, that Rosie has a mind of her own. I mean, she's got a real head on her shoulders. That's why she and I are pals.

a dogs   e a dullard; a bore
b jive   c jail
c pokey a feet
d bread b nonsense talk
e nerd   d money

Optional Practice

Ask students to look through a slang dictionary and find five slang words or expressions which relate to one topic, such as money, music, cars, etc. Have students use each word in a sentence and share these with the class.

Extending the Lesson

Ask students to keep a notebook of slang words or expressions they read in books, newspapers, and magazines, or that they hear from friends or family. Have them give a definition and the standard English word or expression for each slang word they find. After one or two weeks have students share their notebook entries with one another.

Part 4

Objective

To understand the use and misuse of jargon

Presenting the Lesson

1. Read aloud **Here's the Idea.** Point out that jargon, like slang, is also used by a particular group of people. However, jargon differs from slang in that jargon is usually reserved for occupational or professional activities. Jargon grows out of the need to find an expedient way of communicating ideas among people who share a common professional or occupational vocabulary.

2. Write the six words from **Check It Out** on the chalkboard. Ask students if any of these words are familiar to them. Have students provide additional words associated with the railroad industry.

3. Assign **Try Your Skill.** Have students check the appropriate meanings in the dictionary.

4. Read aloud **Keep This in Mind** and then assign **Now Write.**

Individualizing the Lesson

Less-Advanced Students

Point out that many fields have contributed jargon words to the English language. Ask students to find the specific meaning to each jargon word from the following lists.

Sports	Print Media
slider	byline
dugout	filler
shutout	slug
receiver	lead

Part 4

Shop Talk

Using and Misusing Jargon

Here's the Idea As you have already learned in this chapter, different occasions call for different types of language. For example, workers in many fields have special words and phrases that they use to describe their jobs. The words and phrases used to describe such specialized activities are called jargon. A farmer, for example, may use the following jargon to describe farm machinery:

baler	grub hook
binder	middlebreaker
combine	rotary plow
cultivator	snap machine
disk harrow	thresher

Farmers can use terms like these when talking to one another. This is because most farmers know the jargon of farming. However, most non-farmers do not understand such jargon. Therefore, a farmer who is talking to a non-farmer must either avoid these terms or define them as they come up in the conversation.

By using jargon, workers are able to communicate with one another quickly and easily. However, jargon must be used only with certain audiences. Whenever you write or speak about a specialized activity, first decide whether your audience is familiar with the jargon of that activity. If your audience is not familiar with the activity, use as little jargon as possible. When you do use a jargon word, define the word to avoid confusing your listeners or readers.

Check It Out Read the following words from the jargon of railway workers.

gondola car	flat car	piggyback
roomette	cannonball	brakie

- Are you familiar with any of these words?
- Would you understand these words if a railway worker used them when speaking to you?
- Look up each word. Do any of these words have other meanings that are not related to railroads?

Try Your Skill   The following words are from the jargon of sports. Look up each word in a dictionary. Tell what the word means. Also tell what sport the word is used in. Then, use each word in a sentence.   Answers below. Sentences will vary.

1. icing	6. birdie
2. dribble	7. iron cross
3. bunt	8. knockout
4. slalom	9. snorkel
5. love	10. wicket

Keep This in Mind

- Words and phrases used to describe specialized activities are called jargon.
- Use jargon only when it is appropriate to your audience.

Now Write   Choose an activity with which you are very familiar. Make a list of the jargon words used by others who are familiar with this activity. Define each word.

1. hockey—violation of rules   2. basketball—bounce the ball by tapping it with one hand
3. baseball—to bat the ball lightly without swinging   4. skiing—downhill race over a zigzag course
5. tennis—a score of zero   6. golf—a score of one stroke under par for a hole
7. gymnastics—a movement on the rings with the body upright and arms extended sideways
8. boxing—victory won when the opponent is knocked down and cannot rise before the count of ten
9. swimming—device to breath underwater, or the act of doing such
10. cricket—sets on vertical sticks with two small pieces resting on top of it
    croquet—small wire arches through which the balls must be hit

Ask students to find the meaning of the following jargon words. To increase the level of difficulty in this exercise, do not inform the students what fields these words come from.

Music	Film
axe	shot
gig	fade
number	pan
riff	dupe
ivories	gaffer
pit	auteur

Optional Practice

Ask students to look through newspaper or magazine ads and find ten jargon words. Students will find it helpful to use trade journals such as *Sports Illustrated*, *Omni*, *Wall Street Journal*, *Forbes*, *Car & Driver*, etc.

Extending the Lesson

Ask students to select a particular subject or business which interests them. Have them visit or telephone a professional from the field they have chosen, and request a brief interview. During their interview, have each student find out at least ten jargon words that are unique to the specific field or business. Then have students bring their lists to class and compare the jargon words they have found. For students having difficulty with this exercise, suggest possible places they could visit, such as the post office, the phone company, a restaurant, a print shop, a fish hatchery, a farm, or an airport.

Part 5

Objective

To recognize regional language and understand its uses

Presenting the Lesson

1. Read aloud **Here's the Idea.** Point out that people from different regions have different ways of saying the same thing, or pronouncing the same words. Ask for volunteers to pronounce the words *orange* and *roof*; or to tell what they call a *doughnut*, a *living room* or a *soft drink*.

2. Write the twelve words on the chalkboard. Find out which words students use, and which ones they have never heard of.

3. Read aloud the passage from **Try Your Skill.** As a class, find the examples of dialect.

4. Read aloud **Keep This in Mind** and assign **Now Write.**

Individualizing the Lesson

Less-Advanced Students

The following groups of words are used in different regions of the country. Have students indicate the ones they use.

flapjacks	bags	sofa
pancakes	sacks	couch
griddlecakes	pokes	davenport
fried cakes	totes	divan

Advanced Students

Ask students to provide three different words for each of the following. Have them use a dictionary for additional help.

On Location

Regional Language

Here's the Idea   The way you speak or write is the result of many influences. For example, people in different areas of the country speak and write differently. The types of language used in various parts of the country are called **regional dialects.**

Regional dialects differ in three ways. First, they differ in vocabulary. In the North and Midwest, for example, most people speak of *breakfast, lunch,* and *dinner.* In many areas of the South, these meals are called *breakfast, dinner,* and *supper.*

Second, regional dialects differ in pronunciation. In some areas of New England, for example, speakers often drop the *r* sound from some words and add it to other words.

Pahk the *cah.*   What's the *idear?*

Third, regional dialects sometimes differ in grammar. For example, a speaker in the South or Midwest would say "Mr. Wilkes stood *in* line for three hours." Some speakers in the North would say "Mr. Wilkes stood *on* line for three hours."

Dialects add variety and interest to our language. Much outstanding writing uses various American regional dialects. However, dialects can also be a source of confusion. When writing or talking to one another, speakers of different dialects should try to use language that everyone will understand.

American dialects have become increasingly similar because of television, education, and travel. However, for years to come, you can expect that a person from Boston will not talk like a person from Charleston or Chicago.

Check It Out   The following are some words used in different areas of the country. The words in each group all have the same meaning. Read these words.

corn on the cob	veranda	stream
sweet corn	terrace	brook
table corn	stoop	branch
roasting ears	porch	creek

- Which of these words are used in your region?

Try Your Skill   The following passage is about a family that has returned home after a flood. Find examples of dialect.

"The henhouse is gone," sighed the woman.

"N the pigpen," sighed the man.

They spoke without bitterness.

"Ah reckon them chickens is all done drowned."

"Yeah."

"Miz Flora's house is gone, too," said the little girl.

They looked at the clump of trees where their neighbor's house had stood.

"Lawd!"

"Yuh reckon anybody knows where they is?"

"Hard t tell."

The man walked down the slope and stood uncertainly.

"There wuz a road erlong here somewheres," he said.

But there was no road now. Just a wide sweep of yellow, scalloped silt.

—RICHARD WRIGHT

Keep This in Mind

- The types of language used in various parts of the country are called regional dialects.
- Regional dialects differ in vocabulary, pronunciation, and grammar.

Now Write   Watch two or three television programs that are set in different parts of the country. Make notes on any examples of regional dialect that you hear. Bring these notes to class.

garden patch
cloudburst
mantle

Optional Practice

Write the following phrases on the chalkboard.

a paved road
to do housework
a cover for a bed
the sound a horse makes
a long sandwich with meats and cheeses

Ask students to provide the word or words they commonly call these things.

Extending the Lesson

Ask students to interview a relative or friend who has lived in another region of the country. Have students make a list of five words or expressions with which they are unfamiliar (for example, freeway/expressway/turnpike; cookout/bar-be-que; or vest/waistcoat).

Section 4 Objectives

1. To write clear and effective sentences
2. To include only related details in a sentence
3. To avoid writing repetitive sentences and unsupported statements
4. To avoid padding a sentence with useless words or phrases
5. To avoid overloading a sentence with too many ideas

Preparing the Students

Tell students to imagine that they have received the following telegram:

"Two enormous sacks of gold, small shiny disks, click, quick, the dark place is in the north; finders, keepers."

Point out that this message uses specific vocabulary, but still makes no sense. Explain that a sentence must be clear and direct to effectively convey an idea to the reader.

Now read the following telegram to the students:

"Hidden in a dark cave, north of town, are two enormous sacks of shiny gold coins. Whoever finds them may keep them."

Emphasize that by expressing complete thoughts in clear and direct sentences, this telegram communicates effectively. Point out that this Section will help students to write effective sentences.

Additional Resources

Mastery Test — pages 16–17 in the test booklet
Practice Book — pages 19–23
Duplicating Masters — pages 19–23

Controlling Your Sentences

Teaching Special Populations

LD The exercises in this Section will be difficult for most LD students. Break down the instructions into simple steps, and state how the students should prepare their work before handing it in.

Provide students with additional practice in locating unrelated details in sentences. Write examples on the chalkboard, and have students as a group identify what belongs in each sentence and what doesn't.

ESL Many ESL students will be uncomfortable paring down their sentences. Stress to these students that more words in a sentence does not necessarily improve the sentence. Show many padded examples that clearly need pruning.

Allow students sufficient time to complete the exercises in this Section. Many students will have to look up words in a dictionary in order to complete the exercises. If possible, pair ESL students with native English speakers and have them complete the exercises together.

NSD Have students complete the more difficult exercises as a group. Require students to write examples of empty and padded sentences of their own, and to revise those sentences.

Part 1

Objective

To write clear and effective sentences

Presenting the Lesson

1. Read aloud **Here's the Idea.** Emphasize the definition of *sentence.* Discuss the meaning of each of the quotations, and ask the class what makes each sentence interesting and memorable. As an experiment, have students paraphrase the sentences to compare with the originals.

2. Read and discuss **Check It Out.** Ask students what these sentences have in common. Point out how each one expresses an idea directly and with precise language.

3. Assign and discuss **Try Your Skill.** Have students share their sentences. Discuss clarity and directness.

4. Read **Keep This in Mind.**

5. Assign **Now Write.** Encourage students to revise their sentences until they are clear and precise.

Individualizing the Lesson

Less-Advanced Students

Refer students to Handbook Section 1. Have them review the elements of a complete sentence. Students should understand basic sentence mechanics, such as noun and verb agreement.

Advanced Students

Ask students to bring to class a quotation they are especially fond of. It may be a sentence they have read in a book or periodical, or it

In the Clear

Using Sentences

Here's the Idea   Individual words usually express parts of thoughts. A **sentence** is a group of words that expresses a complete thought.

Good sentences express complete thoughts clearly and directly. A good sentence has something to say. The idea that it expresses may be either humorous or serious, but it is always clear. A good sentence also expresses an idea in a direct and imaginative way.

Read these examples of effective, interesting sentences.

> A light heart lives long. —WILLIAM SHAKESPEARE
> A wise man will make more opportunities than he finds.
>   —FRANCIS BACON
> Remember, no one can make you feel inferior without your consent. —ELEANOR ROOSEVELT
> The language of friendship is not words but meanings.
>   —HENRY DAVID THOREAU
> Please all and you please none. —AESOP

Each of these sentences has expressed one idea in a clear, direct, and original way. You can see how powerful a single sentence can be. When you write a sentence, use your senses and your imagination to express an idea in an effective way.

Check It Out   Read the following sentences.

1. As Nancy raced to the exit, she searched the crowd for a police officer.
2. The patient's room was dark and smelled of antiseptic.
3. Homemade soup makes a light, tasty, and economical meal.

4. All citizens should participate in government by voting in elections.

5. Refugees are people who flee their homes or countries to seek safety during times of war and trouble.

- Does each sentence express a single, complete thought? Is each sentence clear and interesting?

Try Your Skill   Write one sentence in response to each of the following directions. Use real or imaginary details to make your sentences clear and effective.

1. Tell one thing that you usually do after school.
2. Describe something that you own.
3. Explain how to save money.
4. Explain why passengers should wear seat belts in cars.
5. Explain what a basketball is.
6. Describe your favorite meal.
7. Tell one event that happened to your family.
8. Explain what a doctor is.

Keep This in Mind

- A sentence is a group of words that expresses a complete thought. A good sentence is clear and interesting.

Now Write   Write five original sentences. One should tell part of a story. One should describe something. One should explain one step of a process. One should explain why something is useful. One should explain what something is.

Before you write, think about each sentence. Decide what point you are trying to make and how you can best make it. Be specific. Label your paper **In the Clear** and put it into your folder.

may be an aphorism, such as "It's always darkest before the dawn." Have the students explain why their quotation is meaningful and memorable to them.

Optional Practice

Ask students to use their imagination as they complete the following sentences. After finishing the exercise, call on students to read their completed sentences aloud. Sentences will vary.

1. Being sixteen years old means _____

2. The home of the future will _____
3. Everyone should _____
4. No one knows why _____
5. When I woke up this morning _____

Extending the Lesson

1. Show students a few pictures, using photographs from magazines or photography books. Have students write clear, interesting sentences as captions for the photographs.

2. Bring to class a few record albums by popular singers or bands. As you play the albums, ask students to write sentences from the songs that they find especially interesting and memorable. After listening to several songs, have students read their sentences aloud and explain their choices.

Objective

To include only related details in a sentence

Presenting the Lesson

1. Read aloud **Here's the Idea.** Emphasize that details are important to make sentences interesting. However, details must be related to the main idea of the sentence. Ask students to suggest other details that could logically be added to the two sentences about volleyball and poetry.

2. Have students work in pairs to discuss **Check It Out.** Ask each pair to rewrite the sentences, deleting unnecessary details and adding related details. Have students compare their sentences.

3. Assign and discuss **Try Your Skill.** Discuss which details are unnecessary and why. Have volunteers read their revised sentences.

4. Read aloud **Keep This in Mind** and then assign **Now Write.**

Individualizing the Lesson

Less-Advanced Students

1. Some students may have difficulty recognizing unrelated details. Work with students as a group on the first two sentences of **Try Your Skill.** Point out how unrelated details cause confusion, while related details add to the meaning of a sentence.

2. If students have difficulty choosing a topic for **Now Write,** suggest the general topics of *music,* *sports,* and *holidays.*

Part 2

Beware of Detours

Keeping to the Point

Here's the Idea   A well-written sentence expresses one idea as clearly and directly as possible.

> The volleyball sailed over our heads.
> First prize in the poetry competition was awarded to Sandra.

Sometimes you may want to add details to a sentence to make it more interesting. Related details are those that support the main idea. By adding related details, you can add meaning to a sentence.

> The volleyball hit by Ms. Powers sailed over our heads.

Here, the added detail is related to the volleyball shot.

> First prize in the poetry competition was awarded to Sandra for her poem "Spring."

In this sentence, the added detail is related to the poem.

Whenever you include details in a sentence, be sure they are related to the main idea. Unrelated details will confuse the meaning of the sentence.

> The volleyball, which we also use for soccer, sailed over our heads.

The added detail is not related to the volleyball shot.

> First prize in the poetry competition was awarded to Sandra Morrison, who is six feet tall.

The added detail is about Sandra. However, the main idea of the sentence is the poetry prize.

Avoid using unrelated details in sentences that you write. Use only interesting and specific details that are related to the main idea. Be sure to keep to the point.

Check It Out   Read the following sentences.

1. My locker, which I share with Dan, is on the third floor.
2. Maria's father, who was born in Mexico, works at city hall.
3. Barrel racing, a sport I've never tried, is popular in many Western states.
4. Open the green door, which used to be brown, at the end of this hallway and you'll see the office.

- In each sentence, what unrelated detail should be omitted? Are there any related details that you might add?

Try Your Skill   Rewrite the following sentences, which contain unrelated details. Use related details.

1. Firefighters, who work long shifts, save many lives.
2. Mrs. Collins, who has two children, gives weekly quizzes.
3. You can park in the lot near the library, one of my favorite places to study.
4. An aunt of mine wrote a book, with her picture on the cover, about how to start a small business.
5. Hundreds of volunteers, mostly local college students, helped rescue birds hurt by the oil spill.

Keep This in Mind

- Use related details that add interest and meaning to the main idea of a sentence. Omit unrelated details that interrupt and confuse the meaning.

Now Write   Write four sentences about subjects that interest you. Use related details that support the main idea of each sentence. Be sure that each sentence keeps to the point. Label your paper **Beware of Detours.** Keep it in your folder.

Advanced Students

Divide students into two groups. Have each group write several sentences which contain unrelated details. Then, have two groups trade papers. Each group should identify the unrelated details from the other group's sentences. Have students correct the sentences by adding related details.

Optional Practice

Ask students to take out the sentences they wrote for **Now Write** in Part 1 of this Section. Have students rewrite their original sentences, adding a related detail to each sentence.

Extending the Lesson

Have each student write a brief sentence on a blank piece of paper and then pass the paper to the person behind them. Tell students to add a related detail to the sentence they receive. Rotate the papers once more and have the students again add a related detail. Finally, return the papers to the original owners so they can check that all details are related. Have students read the sentences aloud.

Objective

To avoid writing repetitive sentences and unsupported statements

Presenting the Lesson

1. Read aloud **Here's the Idea.** Ask the class to define the term *empty sentence* and identify the two types of empty sentences. Call on individual students to give more examples of empty sentences.

2. Read and discuss **Check It Out.** Have students discuss different ways of improving each sentence.

3. Assign **Try Your Skill.** Have groups of three discuss what makes each sentence empty. Have the groups rewrite the sentences and then read aloud their new sentences.

4. Read **Keep This in Mind** and then assign **Now Write.** Have students exchange papers to check that empty sentences have been corrected.

Individualizing the Lesson

Less-Advanced Students

Have students form two or three small groups. Pass out letters to the editor or advertisements from the local paper. Have each group look for empty sentences and discuss ways of improving the sentences.

Advanced Students

Have students complete the same exercise as the less-advanced students, but individually. When students have discovered

Empty-Handed

Avoiding Empty Sentences

Here's the Idea   Some sentences do not make a point either clearly or completely. They are called **empty sentences.**

One kind of empty sentence repeats an idea.

The experiment failed because we were unsuccessful with it.

To fail at something means "to be unsuccessful," so the second part of the sentence is a useless repetition. You can see that this kind of sentence goes nowhere.

To improve this kind of empty sentence, you must avoid the repetition. Sometimes you may choose to make the sentence simpler. It is more likely, though, that you will choose to add related information.

The experiment failed.
The experiment failed because we tried to rush it.

There is also another kind of empty sentence. This second kind of empty sentence states a strong opinion. However, the opinion is not supported by facts, reasons, or examples.

Radio talk shows are boring.

You can see that such a strong statement is empty of meaning to a reader unless it is explained. You can improve this kind of empty sentence by adding the supporting evidence necessary to complete the idea. Supporting evidence may be given in the same sentence or in another sentence.

Radio talk shows are boring when their hosts are not well informed about the topics discussed.
Radio talk shows are boring. Often their hosts are not well informed about the topics discussed.

Supporting evidence for such ideas might also be provided in paragraphs or compositions.

Check It Out   Read the following empty sentences.

1. Everyone should learn to drive.
2. Roller skating is popular now, and many people enjoy it.
3. Hockey is the most exciting sport.
4. I can't do this problem because it's too hard.
5. The team was exhausted, and the players needed rest.
6. The crumbling pavement on Maple Avenue needs repair.

- Which sentences repeat an idea? Which sentences state an unsupported opinion? How would you improve each of these empty sentences?

Try Your Skill   Rewrite each of these empty sentences.

1. Keeping wild animals as pets is cruel.
2. The team played so well that they were excellent.
3. People who won't change their opinions are annoying.
4. I find it hard to remember names because I'm forgetful.
5. Outdoor jobs are the most satisfying.

Keep This in Mind

- Sentences that repeat an idea or state an unsupported opinion are empty sentences. Improve a sentence that repeats an idea by simplifying it or by adding related information. Improve a sentence with an unsupported opinion by adding supporting evidence that explains the opinion.

Now Write   Label your paper *Empty Sentences*. Write, or find, three examples of each kind of empty sentences. Improve the sentences by avoiding repetition or by supplying facts or reasons. Write the improved sentences.

and corrected empty sentences, have them exchange papers and check one another's revisions.

Optional Practice

Ask students to identify which of the following sentences are empty. Have students correct empty sentences by avoiding repetition or by supporting an opinion.

1. Theo tripped over his untied shoelaces.
2. Maria led the group down the dark stairway and they followed her.
3. Basketball is the best sport.
4. We couldn't find Tim's house because we didn't know how to get there.
5. I went for a swim because I was hot and sweaty.
6. Our streets have too much traffic because there are too many cars using them.
7. To ease congestion on city streets, people should take up bicycle riding.

Extending the Lesson

Ask the class to suggest the names of five TV shows or current movies. Write these names on the chalkboard. Have students choose a show and write their opinion of it, including supporting evidence in the statement. Then have all students who wrote about the same TV show or movie form a panel to read their opinions. Allow each panel to debate these opinions for a few minutes.

Objective

To avoid padding a sentence with useless words or phrases

Presenting the Lesson

1. Announce to the class: "This lesson, you know, because of the fact that so many students pad sentences, teaches that the point is to avoid unnecessary words and also phrases, you see." Ask the students how your statement could be worded more simply and concisely. Read aloud **Here's the Idea.** Write *padded sentence* on the chalkboard and ask students to define it.

2. Read and discuss **Check It Out.** Have students suggest two or three different ways to make each sentence more concise. Write revised sentences on the chalkboard.

3. Have students work in pairs to complete **Try Your Skill.** Ask students to check each other's sentences to see that all padding is eliminated.

4. Read aloud **Keep This in Mind** and then assign **Now Write.**

Individualizing the Lesson

Less-Advanced Students

Remind students that how we *write* and how we *speak* are often two different things. Point out that many phrases used in a casual conversation, such as "you know," or "you see," are quite unnecessary and clumsy when written.

Advanced Students

Play a brief tape-recording of people conversing. Ask students to

Stay Trim

Avoiding Padded Sentences

Here's the Idea   A **padded sentence** contains unnecessary words. The main idea of a padded sentence is smothered by extra words.

Several unnecessary phrases usually signal padded sentences and should be avoided.

in my opinion, I think	well
what I mean is that	you see
what I'm saying is	you know
the point is	due to the fact that
the thing is	because of the fact that
the reason is	on account of the fact that

You can usually improve a padded sentence simply by eliminating the useless expressions. Sometimes, however, you may need to revise the sentence totally.

Padded: What I mean is that winter is my favorite season.
Improved: Winter is my favorite season.

Padded: It is becoming easier all the time to take good pictures indoors owing to the fact that color film now available is very sensitive to light.
Improved: Since color film is now more sensitive to light, taking good pictures indoors is easier.

Many groups of words using *who is, which is,* or *that is* also pad sentences unnecessarily. Be sure to use such expressions only when they add to the meaning of a sentence.

Padded: The auto show, which is being held at the Civic Center, continues through next week.
Improved: The auto show at the Civic Center continues through next week.

Check It Out   Read the following padded sentences.

1. Have you ever tried halvah, which is a kind of candy made with sesame seeds, nuts, and honey?

2. Well, Bonnie said that what she wanted was only a fair chance to audition for the part.

3. Hang gliding attracts people who like risk on account of the fact that it requires skill and luck.

4. The construction crew had to stop working until spring because of the fact that the ground became frozen.

5. I am going to write about careers in the field of communications, which includes jobs in TV production, you know.

• How would you improve each of these sentences?

Try Your Skill   Rewrite the following padded sentences. Improve them by eliminating useless words or by revising a sentence completely.

1. On account of the fact that Saturn has rings, it is one of the most beautiful planets to observe.

2. Brian called Ramon, who is his best friend.

3. What I'm trying to say is what an exciting story you wrote.

4. The reason Dad becomes tired so easily is due to the fact that he has just recovered from the flu.

5. Kate tried on her new sweater, which is red.

Keep This in Mind

• Sentences that include unnecessary words are padded sentences. Improve a padded sentence by eliminating the useless expressions or by revising the sentence totally.

Now Write   Label your paper *Padded Sentences*. Write, or find, five examples of padded sentences. Then improve the sentences. Eliminate an unnecessary expression or revise the sentence totally. Keep your paper in your folder.

write each unnecessary phrase they hear. Have students compare lists. Play the tape again.

Optional Practice

Tell students to pretend they are writing telegrams, in which they are charged for each word. Ask them to rewrite these padded sentences without eliminating any ideas.

Answers will vary.

1. Now you can pick up your order due to the fact that it is ready and waiting.

2. What I mean to say is I hope you'll see why I want to say I'm sorry.

3. The train that came from Los Angeles didn't leave on time, so that's the reason we'll be later than we thought.

4. Friends who are true friends, in my opinion, ought to keep secrets on account of the fact that they should be loyal.

Extending the Lesson

Discuss with students the use of padded language in business communications. Point out that common business expressions such as "regarding yours of the 22nd" are examples of padded language that should be avoided.

Part 5 · Heavyweights

Avoiding Overloaded Sentences

Objective

To avoid overloading a sentence with too many ideas

Presenting the Lesson

1. Read aloud **Here's the Idea.** Point out the differences in the two passages about the local radio station. Discuss the passages with students. Have them point out why the second passage is better. Write an overloaded sentence on the chalkboard and ask for a definition, making sure that students can tell the difference between a padded sentence and an overloaded sentence. Ask students where they usually see or hear overloaded sentences. Ask how they should be revised.

2. Read and discuss **Check It Out.** Ask students if the overloaded sentence has been broken up logically.

3. Assign **Try Your Skill.** When students have completed the exercise, have them share their revisions with the class. See if students agree on the number of sentences needed to revise each overloaded sentence in the exercise.

4. Assign **Now Write.** You might suggest that students listen to conversations in the halls or cafeteria to gather examples of overloaded sentences.

Individualizing the Lesson

Less-Advanced Students

Students may have difficulty recognizing overloaded sentences as distinct from complex or padded sentences. Work with students on

Here's the Idea   There will be times when you need to express a complex idea in writing. However, you should not try to include too many ideas in a single sentence. Sentences having too many ideas are called **overloaded sentences.**

Overloaded sentences usually contain several thoughts loosely joined by *and*. The word *and* is used incorrectly when it is used to connect ideas that are not closely related.

> Our local radio station has a preference for fire stories, and every nightly newscast seems to include a story about a fire, and I have also noticed that other stations have their own favorite kinds of stories that are repeated often.

From this example, you can see how confusing an overloaded sentence is. Which is the main idea? It is impossible for a reader to know.

You can avoid such confusion. Separate an overloaded sentence into several shorter sentences.

> Our local radio station has a preference for fire stories. Every nightly newscast seems to include a story about a fire. I have also noticed that other stations seem to have their own favorite kinds of stories.

Whenever you write, make sure that each sentence contains only one main idea or related ideas.

Check It Out   Read this overloaded sentence.

Overloaded: Every year when safety inspections are required, I promise to take our car to be inspected early, and every year I promise, and yet I always find that I leave this task until the last possible day, and I have to rush around anxiously trying to have the inspection completed by the deadline.

Improved: Every year when safety inspections are required, I promise to take our car to be inspected early. Although I promise, I always find that I leave this task until the last possible day. Then I have to rush around anxiously trying to have the inspection completed by the deadline.

• How has this overloaded sentence been improved?

Try Your Skill   Improve these overloaded sentences.

1. It used to be that if you went to the movies you could choose from among many different films, and now there seem to be fewer movies playing, and they play for longer periods of time, and theaters in the same area will be showing the same films.

2. In my opinion, this country's lawmakers should resolve the question of whether an eighteen-year-old is a child or an adult, and the laws should be consistent, so that they are the same from state to state, and they will not be confusing as they are now.

3. As recently as 1979, the town of Kelso in California had no television at all because the mountains around this remote town interfered with TV reception, and it surprises me that no one has studied children who grew up there to see if they are different in any way from children who have watched TV.

Keep This in Mind

• Sentences containing too many ideas are overloaded sentences. Improve an overloaded sentence by separating it into shorter sentences.

Now Write   Label your paper *Overloaded Sentences*. Write, or find, four examples of overloaded sentences. Improve the sentences by separating the main ideas into several shorter sentences. Keep your work in your folder.

an individual basis through **Try Your Skill.** Have students discuss their sentences in **Now Write.**

Advanced Students

For **Now Write,** have students work individually. When they have completed the exercise, pair the students and have them exchange their original overloaded sentence. Each student should rewrite one or two of his or her partner's sentences. Have students discuss their revisions.

Optional Practice

Organize students into two or three groups. Have each group invent a news story and write several overloaded sentences about it. In discussion, have students suggest changes and necessary revisions to the sentences.

Extending the Lesson

Find a paragraph from a short story that the class would enjoy. Combine the sentences in the paragraph, using a series of conjunctions. Distribute copies of this overloaded sentence, and ask students to revise it.

Section 5 Objectives

1. To combine closely related sentences with a comma and *and*, *but*, or *or*

2. To join closely related sentence parts with *and*, *but*, or *or*

3. To combine closely related sentences by adding single words from one sentence to the other

4. To combine sentences by adding groups of words from one sentence to the other

5. To improve writing by combining sentences

Preparing the Students

Read the following paragraph.

The sun was bright. The mid-March air was still very cold. Danielle sat on the front porch. Robert sat there, too. They were thinking about summer. Danielle wished she could go swimming. Robert wished he could play baseball.

Point out that although each sentence is clear and makes sense, the paragraph seems choppy and dull.

Tell the class that in this Section they will learn how to improve their sentences by combining them. Then read this revised paragraph to the class.

The sun was bright, but the mid-March air was still very cold. Danielle and Robert sat on the front porch, thinking about summer. Danielle wished she could go swimming, and Robert wished he could play baseball.

Additional Resources

Mastery Test — page 18 in the test booklet

Practice Book — pages 24–28

Duplicating Masters — pages 24–28

Sentence Combining

Teaching Special Populations

LD Provide students with additional sets of short, related sentences and have students combine those sentences. Be sure to provide instructions after each sentence, (for example, *join with "but"*). You might want to delete or simplify some of the more difficult exercises.

ESL Students may not understand at first that combining sentences does not weaken the meaning of the sentences. Explain that the sentences or parts of sentences being combined are logically related. Give students examples of sentences that should not be combined as well as sentences that should be combined.

Remind students that some words can be used in more than one way. Be sure students understand what each sentence means in each exercise.

NSD Give students additional practice in using coordinating conjunctions. Explain that the words *but, and,* and *or* have very specific meanings, and are not interchangeable. Give students examples of sentences where these conjunctions are used properly, and examples of sentences where they are misused.

Objective

To combine closely related sentences with a comma and *and, but,* or *or*

Presenting the Lesson

1. Read aloud **Here's the Idea.** Point out the differences between each of the three types of sentence combinations: stating similar ideas, stating contrasting ideas, or offering a choice between ideas. Discuss how the sentences have been improved and made more interesting.

2. Read and discuss **Check It Out.** Be sure students understand the different ways and reasons for combining sentences.

3. Assign **Try Your Skill.** Have students complete the exercise in pairs. Discuss how each sentence has been improved.

4. Read aloud **Keep This in Mind** and assign **Now Write.** Remind students that each conjunction, *and, but,* and *or,* has its own specific purpose. Have students decide why each sentence should be combined.

Individualizing the Lesson

Less-Advanced Students

Refer students to the Handbook, Section 11, especially Parts 1 and 2. Have students work in pairs to complete **Now Write.**

Advanced Students

For each sentence in **Now Write,** have students explain their choice of *and, but,* or *or* to combine the sentences.

60

Join Forces

Combining Sentences

Here's the Idea   Whenever you write, you should try to show how your ideas are related to each other. Often you can do this by combining sentences that state similar ideas. Two sentences that state similar ideas of equal importance can usually be joined with a comma and the word *and*.

> Linda drew a picture of the school mascot. Geraldo printed the picture on the T-shirts.

> Linda drew a picture of the school mascot, **and** Geraldo printed the picture on the T-shirts.

Sometimes two sentences state contrasting ideas of equal importance. You can usually join these sentences with a comma and the word *but*.

> The hockey team won the regionals. It lost the state tournament.

> The hockey team won the regionals, **but** it lost the state tournament.

Finally, two sentences may offer a choice between ideas of equal importance. You can join these sentences with a comma and the word *or*.

> Were you able to buy tickets? Was the concert sold out?

> Were you able to buy tickets, **or** was the concert sold out?

Check It Out   Read the following sentences.

1. The sun was hot, and the hikers were thirsty.
2. Is Lake Mead a natural lake, or is it a reservoir?
3. The two cars collided, but no one was injured.

- Which sentence combines similar ideas of equal importance?
- Which sentence combines contrasting ideas of equal importance?
- Which sentence combines ideas of equal importance and offers a choice between them?

Try Your Skill   Combine each pair of sentences.

1. The mayor held a news conference. She did not announce plans to seek another term. (Join with **, but**.)

2. A surprise snowstorm hit Atlanta. Traffic slowed to a crawl. (Join with **, and**.)

3. Are you going to the speech club banquet? Do you have to work that evening? (Join with **, or**.)

4. People began lining up at dawn. By noon the line was two blocks long. (Join with **, and**.)

Keep This in Mind

- Use a comma and *and* to combine sentences that state similar ideas of equal importance.
- Use a comma and *but* to combine sentences that state contrasting ideas of equal importance.
- Use a comma and *or* to combine sentences that offer a choice between ideas of equal importance.

Now Write   Combine each pair of sentences using **, and** or **, but** or **, or**. Label your paper **Join Forces.** Save it in your folder.

1. Everyone grew silent. The President began to speak.
2. We followed the instructions. The experiment failed.
3. Is the amusement park open in the winter? Is it only open during the summer?
4. The airplane had engine trouble. It arrived safely.
5. Did you purchase this sweater? Was it given to you?

61

Optional Practice

Pass out a short editorial from the local paper or a newsmagazine. Ask students to locate all of the combined sentences in the editorial. Discuss the reasons for each combined sentence, and how the editorial is made effective by sentence combining.

Extending the Lesson

Have students combine a sentence in part 1 with a sentence in part 2 below. Students should be prepared to state why they chose to combine two sentences, and why they used *and, but,* or *or.*

1. The ocean was very rough.
   It was a cold afternoon.
   Did you buy that cabinet at the store?
   The storm blew in from the north.

2. The sun was brilliant.
   The little boat was tossed about.
   It was still sunny to the south.
   Did you make that cabinet yourself?

Objective

To join closely related sentence parts with *and*, *but*, or *or*

Presenting the Lesson

1. Read aloud **Here's the Idea.** Tell students that sentence parts are combined for the same reasons that entire sentences are combined. Point out that repeated words are dropped. Discuss how much better the sentences read when repeated words are dropped.

2. Read and discuss **Check It Out.** Make sure students understand which words to drop, and how sentences should be combined.

3. Assign **Try Your Skill.** Have students share their sentences. Point out how each sentence is more effective after combining.

4. Read aloud **Keep This in Mind** and assign **Now Write.** For sentence 3, remind students that the pronoun *he* stands for the noun, *reporter*.

Individualizing the Lesson

Less-Advanced Students

1. Complete **Try Your Skill** orally in class.

2. Have students complete **Now Write** in pairs. Have them explain why they used a particular conjunction with each sentence.

Advanced Students

1. Have students complete **Try Your Skill** individually.

2. For **Now Write,** have each student make up one extra pair of sen-

The Parts Department

Combining Sentence Parts

Here's the Idea   You have seen that you can join entire sentences. You can also join related sentence parts. If sentence parts state similar ideas of equal importance, you can join them with *and*.

> The gardener cleared the weeds. *The gardener* planted some tulips.
>
> The gardener cleared the weeds and planted some tulips.

Notice that when you combine sentence parts, you drop any repeated words. In the example above, these repeated words are shown in italics.

Sometimes two sentence parts state contrasting ideas of equal importance. You can usually join these sentence parts with *but*.

> Ants are attracted to sugar. *Ants are* repelled by cinnamon.
>
> Ants are attracted to sugar but repelled by cinnamon.

Sentence parts may also offer a choice between ideas of equal importance. Such parts can usually be joined with *or*.

> The director may choose the location. The producer *may choose the location.*
>
> The director or the producer may choose the location.

Check It Out   Read the following sentences.

1. Martha loves television. Martha hates the commercials. Martha loves television but hates the commercials.

2. Henry wrapped the glasses in paper. Henry packed them into cartons. Henry wrapped the glasses in paper and packed them into cartons.

3. Is the pool private? Is the pool open to the public? Is the pool private or open to the public?

- Which sentence combines similar parts of equal importance?
- Which sentence combines contrasting parts of equal importance?
- Which sentence combines parts that offer a choice between ideas of equal importance?

Try Your Skill Combine each pair of sentences by following the directions in parentheses. Leave out the italicized words.

1. The horses paraded around the circus ring. The bears *paraded around the circus ring.* (Join with *and.*)
2. The film was praised by the critics. *The film* didn't do well at the box office. (Join with *but.*)
3. The assembly hall is used for concerts. *The assembly hall is used for* basketball games. (Join with *and.*)
4. The squirrels ate the peanut butter. *The squirrels* wouldn't touch the crackers. (Join with *but.*)

Keep This in Mind

- Join sentence parts that state similar ideas of equal importance with *and.*
- Join sentence parts that state contrasting ideas of equal importance with *but.*
- Join sentence parts that offer a choice between ideas of equal importance with *or.*

Now Write Combine each pair of sentences. Use *and, but,* or *or* to join sentence parts. Label your paper **The Parts Department.** Save it in your folder.

1. The directing in the movie was wonderful. The acting in the movie was wonderful.
2. My sister wants to be a dancer. My sister hates to practice.
3. Will the reporter submit the story? Will he file it away?
4. This shop sells makeup. This shop sells costume jewelry.

tences that can be combined. Have students trade papers and combine the extra sentence pair.

Optional Practice

Pass out copies of the following paragraph to the class. Have students form pairs to revise the paragraph by combining sentences and sentence parts. You may want less-advanced students to pair with advanced students in this exercise.

Answers will vary.

Adolfo walked straight up to the stage. He was very nervous inside. He felt butterflies in his stomach. The auditorium lights dimmed. The stage lights came on. Adolfo knew it was now or never. He picked up the microphone. He started to sing. As the music rang out, he gained confidence. A career in music was something he had always dreamed of.

Extending the Lesson

Have students read the letters-to-the-editor from the local paper. Ask students to pick out sentences which could be combined to create a better piece of writing.

Objective

To combine closely related sentences by adding single words from one sentence into the other

Presenting the Lesson

1. Read aloud **Here's the Idea.** Emphasize that for each sentence pair, only one sentence states the main idea. The second sentence adds an important detail to the main idea. Be sure students note that they must sometimes change the ending of a word when inserting it into a sentence.

2. Read and discuss **Check It Out.** Have students note that words added to a sentence can come from these parts of speech: verbs, adverbs, nouns, or adjectives. All of these words become modifiers.

3. Assign **Try Your Skill.** Have students share their sentences and discuss how the sentences have been changed.

4. Read **Keep This in Mind** and then assign **Now Write.** Check to see that students have added the correct word with the proper ending.

Individualizing the Lesson

Less-Advanced Students

Assist students with **Now Write** on an individual basis. Ask students to be especially careful when changing endings on the added words.

Advanced Students

Have students write out each word they added to a sentence in **Now Write.** Have students write what that part of speech was before they

64

One at a Time

Combining by Adding Single Words

Here's the Idea   Sometimes two sentences are very closely related. One sentence in the pair states a main idea. The second sentence adds only one important word to the idea. You may be able to combine such sentences by adding the one important word to the sentence that states the main idea.

> The street musicians wore costumes. *The costumes were* colorful.
>
> The street musicians wore colorful costumes.

Notice that the word *colorful* was added to the first sentence. The words in italics were dropped.

Occasionally you will have to change the form of a word when you add it to a sentence. You may have to change the ending of the word by adding *-ing, -ed,* or *-ly.*

> The ship rolled in the waves. *The waves* pounded *the ship.*
> The ship rolled in the pounding waves.
>
> Phil has been making pottery. *He* glazes *the pottery.*
> Phil has been making glazed pottery.
>
> Clara offered pointers to the other swimmers. *Clara was* patient.
> Patiently, Clara offered pointers to the other swimmers.

Check It Out   Study the following examples.

1. The desk top is made of mahogany.
   The desk top has varnish *on it.*
   The desk top is made of varnished mahogany.
2. A storm beat against the windows of our cabin.
   The storm raged.
   A raging storm beat against the windows of our cabin.

64

3. The first baseman threw the ball to the shortstop.
The first baseman was quick.
  The first baseman quickly threw the ball to the shortstop.
4. Nancy bandaged her brother's knee.
   Nancy worked carefully.
   Nancy carefully bandaged her brother's knee.

• What words have been added to each sentence?

Try Your Skill   Combine each pair of sentences.

1. Put that plate on the bottom of the stack. *The plate has a crack.* (End the important word with **-ed.**)
2. The governor's aide arrived. *This happened* later.
3. In Yellowstone Park there are ten thousand hot springs. *They* bubble. (End the important word with **-ing.**)
4. We must act. *Our actions must be* immediate. (End the important word with **-ly.**)

Keep This in Mind

• Sometimes one sentence states a main idea and a second sentence adds one important word. Combine these sentences by adding the important word to the first sentence.
• When you add a word to a sentence, you may have to change the ending of the word to *-ing,* *-ed,* or *-ly.*

Now Write   Choose the important word from the second sentence in each pair. Add it to the first sentence. Remember that you may have to change the ending of the added word. Label your paper **One at a Time.** Save it in your folder.

1. Across the canal was a green light. The light flickered.
2. Today, shoppers fill the square. The shoppers are busy.
3. We ship the fresh fish in ice. We crush the ice.
4. A hawk circled overhead. The hawk circled lazily.

added it to the sentence. Then, have them write what part of speech the word became after they added it.

Optional Practice

Have students complete the following exercise by adding one important word to the first sentence from the second sentence in each pair.

1. The wind blew across the mountain.   *[fierce]*
   The wind was fierce.
2. Martin slipped off the log.   *[wet]*
   The log was wet.
3. Anna ran over to her cousin's house.   *[quickly]*
   She ran quickly.
4. Louis has a new dictionary.   *[Spanish]*
   It is a Spanish dictionary.

Extending the Lesson

Refer students to Writing Section 4, Part 5. Lead a class discussion on the differences between overloaded sentences, and sentences which can be effectively combined.

Objective

To combine sentences by adding groups of words from one sentence to the other

Presenting the Lesson

1. Read aloud **Here's the Idea.** Tell students that adding one word to a sentence is not enough at times. Adding a group of words may be necessary to create a clear and complete sentence. Point out that it is important *where* in a sentence groups of words are added.

2. Read and discuss **Check It Out.** Ask students to comment on where the groups of words were added to each sentence.

3. Assign **Try Your Skill.** Have students work in pairs to complete the exercise. Discuss why certain words were dropped from each sentence.

4. Read **Keep This in Mind** and then assign **Now Write.** Ask students to think about *where* their words should be added to the sentences.

Individualizing the Lesson

Less-Advanced Students

For **Now Write,** ask students to first consider how their added words affect each sentence. Do the words tell more about a person or thing? Do the words tell more about an action? Do the words add to the entire meaning of the sentence? Assist students individually to be sure they understand where to add their words.

Group Effort

Adding Groups of Words

Here's the Idea   You learned that sometimes you can add a single word to a sentence. At other times you can combine sentences by adding a group of words.

Edna was holding a kitten. *The kitten was* in her arms.

Edna was holding a kitten in her arms.

The group of words may tell more about a person or thing. If so, add it near the words that name the person or thing.

The students arrive today. *The students are* from Sweden.

The students from Sweden arrive today.

The group of words may describe an action. If so, add it near the words that name the action.

The students arrived last week. *The students arrived* from St. Louis.

The students arrived from St. Louis last week.

The group of words may add information to the entire main idea of the other sentence. If so, you may add it at the beginning or at the end.

The lute was a popular instrument. *The lute was popular* in the fifteenth century.

The lute was a popular instrument in the fifteenth century.

In the fifteenth century, the lute was a popular instrument.

Check It Out   Study the following examples.

1. I found an old letter. The letter was from my great-grandmother.

I found an old letter from my great-grandmother.

2. A candidates' debate will be held. The debate will be at the National Guard Armory.

A candidates' debate will be held at the National Guard Armory.

- What words were added to each sentence?
- What words were dropped?

Try Your Skill

Combine each group of sentences. Leave out the italicized words.

1. The Lakers took the lead. *The Lakers did this* with seconds left in the game.
2. The white house is ours. *The white house is* on the corner.
3. The jewelry was beautiful. *It was* at the crafts show.
4. The race car developed engine trouble. *The car developed trouble* on the last lap.
5. Many people are concerned. *Their concern is* about low-cost housing.

Keep This in Mind

- A sentence may contain a group of words that adds information to another sentence. Often you can combine the sentences by adding the group of words.

Now Write

Combine each group of sentences by adding a group of words to the first sentence. Leave out any unnecessary words.

1. Rarotonga is an island. It is in the South Pacific.
2. The pain began to go away. The pain was in my side.
3. The van delivered the ice. The van is from Gardner's Market.
4. We were ready to leave. We were ready before daylight.
5. Karen and Larry waited. Karen and Larry were at the subway entrance.

For **Now Write,** have students explain orally where their words should be added to each sentence, and why.

Optional Practice

Have students work in small groups to rearrange the following combined sentences. Ask them what is wrong with each combined sentence.   Answers will vary.

1. Baton Rouge is a town. It is on the Mississippi River.
   On the Mississippi River, Baton Rouge is a town.
2. Miners drilled into the earth. Miners drilled for gold.
   For gold, miners drilled into the earth.
3. Josey slapped the volleyball. She slapped it over the net.
   Over the net, Josey slapped the volleyball.

Extending the Lesson

Ask a volunteer to write a simple sentence on the chalkboard. Ask another volunteer to write a different sentence about the same subject, next to the first sentence. In class discussion, have students suggest ways of combining the two sentences. Have them apply their knowledge of sentence-combining to several different sentences.

Part 5

Objective

To improve writing by combining sentences

Presenting the Lesson

1. Read aloud **Here's the Idea.** Have students pay special attention to the chart "Combining Ideas in Sentences." Encourage students to use their sentence-combining skills when they revise their writing.

2. Read and discuss **Check It Out.** Discuss which of the two paragraphs is more interesting to read and why.

3. Assign **Try Your Skill.** Ask students to exchange papers and check each other's sentences. Have volunteers read revised sentences aloud.

4. Read **Keep This in Mind** and then assign **Now Write.** Encourage students to review difficult lessons in this Section before revising the paragraph.

Individualizing the Lesson

Less-Advanced Students

Have students copy the chart on page 68 into their notebooks or folders. Tell them to refer to it whenever they write.

Advanced Students

Have students complete **Now Write** individually. Have them discuss which rules they used to combine sentences.

Winning Combinations

Using Combining Skills in Writing

Here's the Idea   By combining sentences, you can show how your ideas are related. You can also add variety to your writing. The following chart describes the many ways that you have learned to combine sentences.

Combining Ideas in Sentences

1. Use a comma and the words *and*, *but*, and *or* to combine related sentences.

2. Use *and*, *but*, and *or* to combine related sentence parts.

3. Add single words from one sentence to another. If necessary, change the forms of the words by adding *-ing*, *-ed*, or *-ly*.

4. Add groups of words from one sentence to another. Place the added words near the words that they describe.

Use your sentence-combining skills whenever you revise your writing. The new sentences make your writing clearer and more interesting to read.

Check It Out   Read the following paragraphs.

1. At ten o'clock, Nan was still waiting. The other hikers hadn't arrived. She sat on a log. She sat for a while. Sunlight fell through the leaves above. The sunlight flickered. Birds chirped in their nests. The birds were cheerful.

2. At ten o'clock, Nan was still waiting, but the other hikers hadn't arrived. She sat for a while on a log. Flickering sunlight fell through the leaves above. Cheerful birds chirped in their nests.

- In which paragraph are related ideas combined?
- How was each pair of sentences combined?

Try Your Skill   Improve the following sentences by combining each pair. Leave out the italicized words.

1. Mardi Gras is a festival that is held each year in New Orleans. *The festival is* exciting. (Add the important word.)
2. During Mardi Gras, people wear masks. *People also wear* fancy costumes. (Join the sentence parts.)
3. Organizations called *krewes* hold parties. Their members dance through the streets. (Join the two sentences.)
4. The festival climaxes with a parade. *The parade is* grand. (Add the important word.)
5. Formal dances are held. *These take place* after the parade. (Add the group of words.)

Keep This in Mind

- Use your combining skills whenever you revise your writing.
- Combine sentences or sentence parts.
- Add single words or groups of words.

Now Write   Revise the following paragraph by combining the sentences. Label your paper **Winning Combinations.** Save it in your folder.

The drama club will begin its next production. This will happen soon. Ms. Sanchez will direct Kaufman and Hart's play *You Can't Take It with You.* The play is delightful. We need performers. We also need people for the technical crew. Auditions will be held on April 8. The auditions will be in the auditorium. If you want to try out, get a copy of the play. Get the copy from Ms. Sanchez. She will explain the audition procedures. She will also take the names of students who want to work backstage.

Optional Practice

Use an old grade-school primer to find examples of simple sentences which could be effectively combined. Pass out copies to the class. Have students combine sentences using the methods they have learned in this Section.

Extending the Lesson

Find a paragraph from a short story your class might enjoy. Break up complex sentences into short, simple sentences and distribute copies to the class. Ask students to suggest sentence-combining revisions to the paragraph.

Section 6 Objectives

1. To know that a paragraph is a group of sentences developing one main idea

2. To recognize and write unified paragraphs

3. To recognize and write effective topic sentences

4. To identify and skillfully use the four ways of developing a paragraph: sensory details, specific examples, facts and statistics, or incidents or anecdotes

5. To recognize the three types of paragraphs: narrative, descriptive, and explanatory

Preparing the Students

Pair students and have them interview each other. Questions might be about family, hobbies, employment, and future plans. When interviews are completed, have students report on them.

When students have finished, ask how the information could have been written in sentence form. Ask if all the information could be included in one paragraph. Point out that a paragraph is made of a group of sentences which develop one main idea. Explain that information gathered through their interviews deals with many ideas, and would have to be developed in separate paragraphs. Explain that this Section will teach students what makes a successful paragraph.

Additional Resources

Mastery Test — pages 19–20 in the test booklet

Practice Book — pages 29–33

Duplicating Masters — pages 29–33

Examining the Paragraph

Teaching Special Populations

LD Stress that a paragraph is much more than a series of sentences. Explain that a paragraph always has a structure. Show students how a paragraph is unified by writing one on the chalkboard, and explaining the function of each sentence in that paragraph. Or, ask students what each sentence adds to the main idea of the paragraph.

Provide students with additional examples of each type of paragraph. Ask them to identify the characteristics of narrative, descriptive, and explanatory paragraphs.

ESL Allow students enough time to read each of these lessons before discussing them in class. Provide additional paragraph samples for student discussion. Be sure students understand the vocabulary necessary for an understanding of this Section: *paragraph, unity, topic sentence, sensory details, specific examples, facts, statistics, anecdotes, narrative, descriptive,* and *explanatory*.

Give extra practice and close guidance for exercises involving topic sentences. Suggest to students that they write about topics they know well.

Read aloud the examples of each type of paragraph. Point out that inflections and tonal changes reflect the type of paragraph being read.

NSD Point out that paragraphs aren't simply a collection of sentences. Duplicate for student discussion examples of paragraphs that are unified, and examples or paragraphs that need much revision.

Objective

To know that a paragraph is a group of sentences developing one main idea

Presenting the Lesson

1. Read aloud **Here's the Idea.** Discuss the definition of a paragraph. Have students read each paragraph and decide what idea each group of sentences develops. Ask them how each group develops an idea in a different way.

2. Read aloud the instructions for **Try Your Skill.** Have students work in groups of three and have each group discuss all three paragraphs. Discuss students' answers.

3. Read aloud **Keep This in Mind** and then assign **Now Write.**

Individualizing the Lesson

Less-Advanced Students

Have students reread **Here's the Idea.** Then write the following topic sentence on the board:

Some of my friends have outrageous nicknames.

Ask students to suggest sentences that help to develop this topic.

Advanced Students

Have each student write a paragraph using the topic sentence from **Less-Advanced Students.** Ask volunteers to share their paragraphs with the class. Have students save their paragraphs for specific revisions when they study Section 7.

A Good Group

Defining a Paragraph

Here's the Idea   You have examined words and sentences. Now you will examine paragraphs. A **paragraph** is a group of sentences dealing with one main idea. Notice how the sentences in each of these groups work together.

1   Nothing could have kept me there in the house that night. My mind held nothing but the driving desire to follow Shane. I waited, hardly daring to breathe, while Mother watched him go. I waited until she turned to Father, bending over him; then I slipped around the doorpost out to the porch. I thought for a moment she had noticed me, but I could not be sure and she did not call to me. I went softly down the steps and into the freedom of the night.   —JACK SCHAEFER

2   There were no shops on the wide street that Billy Weaver was walking along, only a line of tall houses on each side, all of them identical. They had porches and pillars and four or five steps going up to their front doors. It was obvious that once upon a time they had been very elegant residences. Now, however, even in the darkness, Billy could see that the paint was peeling from the woodwork on their doors and windows. All of these handsome white houses were cracked and blotchy from neglect.   —ROALD DAHL

3   Years ago, illiteracy was not as serious a handicap to employment as it is today. Society needed many unskilled workers. Today, however, it is very difficult for people who cannot read to find jobs. There are very few jobs that do not require at least some reading ability. For this reason alone, reading must be viewed as a valuable, practical skill.

Check It Out   Examine the three groups of sentences above.

- Are these groups of sentences paragraphs? Does each group of sentences deal with one idea?

Try Your Skill   One of the groups below is a paragraph. Two are not. For the paragraph, write the main idea. For the groups that are not paragraphs, explain why they are not.

1   In Lexington, Virginia, there is an odd Civil War relic— Stonewall Jackson's horse, which has been stuffed. The horse is displayed on the campus of the Virginia Military Institute. More women are now enrolling in military academies. Little Sorrel, Jackson's horse, still wears a saddle and bridle. Does not have one main idea.

2   Day after day, Luis followed the same routine after school. He took a crosstown bus home, where he worked for two hours on his homework. He cooked dinner, so that it would be ready when his mother returned from work. Later, while she washed the dishes, Luis spread out his paints and materials on the kitchen table. He painted until he was too tired to work any more. Finally he went to bed. He dreamed of the day when his work would hang in a downtown art gallery.

3   Old buildings that once would have been torn down are now being restored. This nationwide trend is partly due to rising interest in the architecture of the past century or so. It is also due to rising building costs and the money saved in renovation. It is becoming more difficult for a person to purchase a home. People must come up with a big down payment and take a loan at high interest rates. Does not have one main idea.

Keep This in Mind

- A paragraph is a group of sentences dealing with one main idea.

Now Write   Rewrite those groups of sentences in **Try Your Skill** that are not paragraphs by changing or omitting sentences that do not belong. Label your paper **A Good Group.**

73

Part 2

Objective

To recognize and write unified paragraphs

Presenting the Lesson

1. Read aloud and discuss **Here's the Idea.** Ask for a volunteer to read aloud the paragraph about sand castles.

2. Read aloud and discuss the paragraph from **Check It Out.** Ask students to identify the main idea in this paragraph, and to decide if the paragraph has unity.

3. Read aloud the instructions from **Try Your Skill.** Have students work in pairs to discuss the unity of the three paragraphs. Have them indicate the sentences which do not belong.

4. Read aloud **Keep This in Mind** and then assign **Now Write.**

Individualizing the Lesson

Less-Advanced Students

Have students reread **Here's the Idea.** Ask them to keep a list of important concepts and definitions that pertain to paragraphs. Their first entries should include a *main idea* and *unity*.

Advanced Students

Have students bring in paragraphs from magazines or newspapers. Ask them to decide if the paragraphs have unity and to explain why.

Optional Practice

Ask students to rewrite the paragraphs from **Try Your Skill** which

---

Of One Mind

Recognizing Unity in a Paragraph

Here's the Idea   Paragraphs are organized units of ideas. Each paragraph deals with one main idea. Every sentence in a paragraph should be related to that main idea. When all of the sentences work together, a paragraph has **unity.**

A unified paragraph follows a plan. Suppose that a paragraph deals with storms on the surface of the sun. Every sentence in that paragraph should include related information. Sentences about solar energy or sunny days would not belong in such a paragraph. They might be good sentences, but they would belong in other paragraphs.

Notice how these sentences relate to the idea of sand castle contests.

> Sand castle contests are attracting crowds on both the East and West coasts. Contestants use wet sand to build elaborate structures with high walls, towers, and moats. Some contestants use knives or sticks to carve the sand. Others use only their hands. The castles are soon demolished by the wind and waves. These unusual creations can usually be studied only in photographs.

Check It Out   Read the following paragraph.

> When you use yeast in baking, its temperature is very important. Yeast is alive, and cold temperatures stop its growth. Too much heat, on the other hand, kills it completely. Ideally, the liquid ingredients in which yeast is dissolved should be about 110 degrees. At this temperature, the liquid should feel warm but not hot to your touch. If the temperature is correct, you can be reasonably sure that the yeast will do its work.

- Do all of the sentences relate to one main idea? Does the paragraph have unity?

Try Your Skill   Read the following paragraphs. Decide if each has unity. If a paragraph does not have unity, write the sentence or sentences that do not belong.

1   ESP is not confined to human beings. There are documented instances in which dogs and cats have shown remarkable psychic powers. Some animals have traveled to find their owners after the owners have moved hundreds of miles away. People should not leave pets without first making careful arrangements for them. Other animals have warned humans about earthquakes. Does not have unity.

2   There are advantages to driving an older car. For one thing, you will probably worry less about the car being damaged or stolen. You will also find that many older models are easier for you to repair yourself. Finally, keeping an older car for several years will save you money. Has unity.

3   It was a terrible sight. The force of the tornado had completely destroyed several buildings in the downtown area. Uprooted trees blocked the streets. Pieces of glass were scattered everywhere. The results of the damaging storm could be seen for miles. Tornadoes don't last very long. They are short-lived, though powerful. Does not have unity.

Keep This in Mind

- All the sentences in a paragraph should relate to one main idea. Then a paragraph has unity.

Now Write   Write the name of someone you admire. Write one sentence that sums up your thoughts about the person. Below that sentence, list five more sentences related to the main idea. Label your paper **Of One Mind.**

they have decided do not exhibit unity. Have them take out the sentences which don't belong, and replace them with sentences which are consistent with the main idea of the paragraph.

Extending the Lesson

Have students read the following paragraph about rocks. Ask them if the entire paragraph is unified. If they feel that it lacks unity, ask them to indicate the sentences which do not belong. Answers will vary.

A rock may be thought of as an aggregate of minerals. Some rocks, such as limestone, consist entirely of a single mineral. In most cases, however, a rock consists of a few major minerals together with a number of minor minerals. Gems are minerals that have ornamental value. Most gemstones have three qualities that set them apart from common minerals. By understanding the differences between rocks of many types, and how they were formed, geologists have been able to better understand the earth's history.

I Declare!

Using a Topic Sentence

To recognize and write effective topic sentences

Presenting the Lesson

1. Read aloud and discuss **Here's the Idea.** Ask students what other ideas could be developed from the topic *February.* Refer to the paragraphs from Parts 1 and 2 and ask students to identify the topic sentences in each paragraph.

2. Read and discuss **Check It Out.**

3. Assign **Try Your Skill.** Discuss students' answers. Try to agree on the best topic sentence for each paragraph.

4. Read aloud **Keep This in Mind** and then assign **Now Write.**

Individualizing the Lesson

Less-Advanced Students

Have students reread **Here's the Idea.** Have them add *topic sentence* to their list of important definitions. Ask students which of the following sentences would be good topic sentences and why.

1. A hippopotamus has a large mouth with two long tusks.
2. Many animals live peacefully in Yellowstone National Park.
3. The old abandoned McEnnis house has a mysterious history.
4. Many people consider the abacus the first calculator.

Advanced Students

Ask students to write three topic sentences which could be developed into three different paragraphs about musical instruments.

Here's the Idea   A **topic sentence** states the main idea of a paragraph in a clear, direct way. A topic sentence is helpful to both readers and writers. It helps readers group related ideas together in their minds. It helps writers keep their ideas organized.

A topic sentence should also state an idea that can be developed by the other sentences in the paragraph. Suppose you were writing a paragraph about February. The sentence "February is the second month of the year" is too narrow to be a good topic sentence. It makes a statement of fact that cannot be developed. A better topic sentence might be "February contains two of my favorite holidays." This topic sentence offers an idea that promises more. It can be supported and developed by other sentences in the paragraph.

The topic sentence is often the first sentence in a paragraph. Used in this position, it prepares a reader for the statements that follow. However, the topic sentence may be used anywhere in a paragraph where it states the main idea most clearly.

Check It Out   Read the following paragraph.

My sister Mary is hard of hearing and needs to wear a hearing aid. Sometimes Mary uses her hearing problem to her own advantage. If we are having a disagreement and she wants to infuriate me, she can. She simply turns off her hearing aid. I find myself arguing emotionally, but Mary does not hear a word I say.

• Which is the topic sentence? Is it too narrow to be developed? State the main idea of this paragraph.

Try Your Skill   Read each paragraph below. Write the <u>topic</u> <u>sentence</u>. If the topic sentence is too narrow, label it *Narrow*. Then rewrite it so that it is a better topic sentence.

1   <u>Ice fishing is not as rugged as it may appear to be.</u> First of all, there are ways to fight the cold. This can be accomplished with warm clothing, portable shelters, and heaters. Second, portable radios and TV's help fishers pass the time on the ice. Third, a grateful family is likely to show its appreciation to the person who brings home fresh fish during the winter.

        Narrow
2   <u>My birthday is July 12.</u> To celebrate this year, I invited five friends to a cookout. Last year my family planned a special day's trip to Jones Beach. When I was younger, my favorite celebration was an afternoon of rides at a carnival.

        Narrow
3   <u>Our dog Duke is a watchdog.</u> Duke is always alert and on guard. Whenever a stranger approaches our house, Duke rises to meet him. The stranger cannot pass until Duke is assured by a family member that the person is a friend. We all feel safer knowing that Duke is around to protect us.

Keep This in Mind

- A topic sentence states the main idea of a paragraph. The sentence should deal with an idea that can be developed in a paragraph in a meaningful way.

Now Write   Think of three topics that you might develop into paragraphs. For each paragraph, write a topic sentence that states the main idea. Label your paper **I Declare!** and put it into your folder.

Part 4

Objective

To identify and skillfully use the four ways of developing a paragraph: sensory details, specific examples, facts and statistics, or incidents or anecdotes

Presenting the Lesson

1. Read aloud **Here's the Idea.** Ask students to identify the topic sentence in each of the four paragraphs. Write the four ways of developing paragraphs on the chalkboard. Under the heading *sensory details* ask students to list the details from the first paragraph. Under *specific examples,* ask students to list the examples given in the second paragraph. Continue this for *facts and statistics* and *incidents or anecdotes.*

2. Read and discuss **Check It Out.** Ask students to point out the sensory details in this paragraph. Also, ask students to indicate the topic sentence.

3. Assign and discuss **Try Your Skill.**

4. Read aloud **Keep This in Mind** and then assign **Now Write.**

Individualizing the Lesson

Less-Advanced Students

Have students reread **Here's the Idea.** Ask them to add the four ways of developing a paragraph to their list. Ask students to identify how the following paragraph is developed.

facts and statistics

An earthquake is a trembling or shaking movement of the earth's surface. Great earthquakes usually begin with slight tremors, rapidly increase to

From the Ground Up

Ways of Developing a Paragraph

Here's the Idea The main idea of a paragraph is stated in the topic sentence. The other sentences in the paragraph should develop and support that idea. You can develop a paragraph with sensory details, specific examples, facts and statistics, and incidents or anecdotes.

Sensory details tell how something looks, smells, tastes, feels, and sounds.

> The forest was engulfed in flames. Everywhere Jeff looked he saw sheets of orange-yellow fire. All he could taste was smoke. Around him, trees exploded in the intense heat. The suffocating smell of burning pine was everywhere.

Use **specific examples** to develop a general statement.

> The Indian tribes in North America used deer for almost everything. The flesh was used for food, the hide for moccasins and clothes, and the antlers for tool handles. The cords and sinews that connected the muscles of the deer to the bones were used for thread with which to sew clothing. The hooves were made into glue.—ROSEBUD YELLOW ROBE

Use **facts and statistics** to make an idea clear or to support an opinion.

> Amelia Earhart was the first woman to fly the Atlantic. In May, 1932, she made the solo flight in a single-engine Lockheed Vega. She was beset by bad weather. The wings of her plane coated with ice, forcing her to fly as close as seventy-five feet above the waves part of the time. Fifteen hours after her departure from Long Island, she landed in a farmer's pasture in Ireland.
> —*The Women's Book of World Records and Achievements*

Incidents or anecdotes can help you to illustrate a point.

My grandmother is a very patient woman. I remember a morning when she and I went fishing. For two hours we cast our lines with no success. I suggested leaving, but grandmother wouldn't hear of it. "The fish are here," she said. "They're just not ready to bite." Minutes later, I felt a tug on my line. Soon we had both caught our limit. "Patience," my grandmother reminded me later, "is a virtue."

Check It Out   Read the following paragraph.

Second Street was peaceful. There was no traffic at that hour. Steve stood in the deserted street looking up at the rows of apartment windows with their shades still drawn. The sky was still dark, but the air was fresh. Steve began bouncing the basketball he had been carrying. A little later, he heard a shout from an eighth-floor window. "Be right down," Chris hollered.

• How is the topic sentence developed?

Try Your Skill   Copy the topic sentence in this paragraph. How is the main idea developed?

Ben struggled to climb the muddy trail. His woolen shirt was not heavy enough to protect him from the sharp thorns. His compass and canteen hung from his belt and clanged against each other. His shoes were caked with mud. sensory details

Keep This in Mind

• The main idea of a paragraph can be developed with sensory details, specific examples, facts and statistics, or incidents or anecdotes.

Now Write   Take out the paper labeled **I Declare!** Choose one topic sentence. List three sensory details, three specific examples, three facts and statistics, or one incident or anecdote that would develop the main idea. Save your work.

one or more violent shocks, and diminish gradually. The immediate cause of most earthquakes is the sudden release of stress along a *fault,* or fracture in the earth's crust, resulting in the movement of opposing blocks of rock past one another.

Advanced Students

Ask students to pretend they are tour agents. Have them describe a trip they are offering. Ask them which of the four different ways of developing a paragraph would best suit their descriptions. Have them list five sensory details, specific examples, or facts and statistics as preparation for their guide. Students may want to use more than one type of detail in their descriptions.

Optional Practice

Discuss techniques used in advertisements to sell products. Ask students to describe the ads that they like best. Ask them if the ads use details, examples, or facts and figures. On the chalkboard, list memorable ads and the way their message is developed. Then ask students to choose a product, write a sentence stating why the consumer should buy it, and add three details, examples, or facts and figures to support the main idea. Have students share their "ads" with the class.

Part 5   What's Your Line?

Objective

To recognize the three types of paragraphs: narrative, descriptive, and explanatory

Presenting the Lesson

1. Read aloud **Here's the Idea.** Point out that different ideas require different methods of presentation. For example, the story of a rafting trip down the Colorado River would be written as a narrative while a paragraph telling about a solar eclipse might work well using a descriptive or explanatory form.

2. Have students read the paragraphs from **Check It Out** and answer the questions. Also, have them identify the topic sentence in each paragraph.

3. Assign and discuss **Try Your Skill.** Have students explain what makes each of these sentences fit the category they have chosen.

4. Read aloud **Keep This in Mind** and then assign **Now Write.**

Individualizing the Lesson

Less-Advanced Students

Have students reread **Here's the Idea,** and add the terms *narrative, descriptive,* and *explanatory* to their list of definitions. Ask students to bring to class one example of each type of paragraph.

Advanced Students

Have students reread **Here's the Idea.** Ask them to think of two topics for each type of paragraph.

Recognizing Three Kinds of Paragraphs

Here's the Idea   Any paragraph you may write fits into one of three main categories. It might be a story, a description, or an explanation. Each kind of paragraph presents a topic in a different way.

A **narrative** paragraph tells a story or relates events. All events, real or imaginary, are usually told in the order in which they happened.

A **descriptive** paragraph is a word picture of an object, a scene, or a person. Its vivid sensory details usually create a certain mood.

An **explanatory** paragraph explains something. It may explain a process, state an opinion, or present a definition.

Check It Out   Read the following paragraphs.

1   Willard Farquar felt his weight change the steps under his feet into an escalator. He cursed under his breath, but let them carry him. He was carried up to the tall, blue entrance doors, which silently parted when he was five meters away. The escalator changed to a slideway that carried him into a softly gleaming, high-domed room. "Martian peace to you, Willard Farquar," an invisible voice chanted.   —FRITZ LEIBER

2   One summer morning I lay on the sand after swimming in the small lake in the park. The sun beat down—it was almost noon. The water shone like steel. It was motionless except for the feathery curl behind a distant swimmer. From my position I was looking at a rectangle with sun, sand, water, a few solitary people, and around it all a border of dark, rounded oak trees. Ever since I had begun taking painting lessons, I had made small frames with my fingers, to look out at everything.

—EUDORA WELTY

3   The term *checkmate* comes from the game of chess. It describes the situation in which a player attacks the opponent's king so that no defense or escape is possible. This is then the end of the game. The word *checkmate* comes originally from a Persian word *shāhmāt*, meaning "the king is dead." The word *checkmate* is now also used to mean "to defeat completely."

- Which paragraph is narrative? Which is descriptive? Which is explanatory?

Try Your Skill   As you read the following topic sentences decide what kind of paragraph they would most likely be part of. Write *Narrative*, *Descriptive*, or *Explanatory*. Answers may vary.

1. The Golden Gate Bridge glowed in the brilliant orange light of the sunset. D
2. One glance told me I had made a terrible mistake. N
3. The Jerusalem artichoke is a vegetable that few people recognize. E
4. Some old radio shows are still popular. E
5. Gilbert seemed to be having a run of bad luck. E or N

Keep This in Mind

- A narrative paragraph tells a story or relates events.
- A descriptive paragraph creates a word picture.
- An explanatory paragraph explains a process, states an opinion, or states a definition.

Now Write   Review your work labeled **From the Ground Up.** Write which of the three kinds of paragraphs you would use for this topic. Explain why this choice seems best. Label your paper **What's Your Line?** Keep your work in your folder.

Section **7** Objectives

1. To understand the steps in the process of writing a paragraph

2. To know how and where to search for topics for a paragraph

3. To know how to narrow a topic for a paragraph

4. To be aware of purpose and audience in writing

5. To write a topic sentence that is informative, interesting, and direct

6. To select the method of paragraph development that best suits the main idea

7. To choose a method of organization that suits the purpose of a paragraph

8. To put pre-writing notes in sentence form in a first draft

9. To end a paragraph with an interesting sentence that sums up the main idea

10. To revise the content, presentation, and style of a paragraph

Preparing the Students

Explain to students that the next logical step after learning about words and sentences is to learn about paragraphs. Tell students that in this Section they will learn what makes a well-written paragraph.

Additional Resources

Mastery Test — pages 21–22 in the test booklet

Practice Book — pages 34–43

Duplicating Masters — pages 34–43

Teaching Special Populations

LD Provide LD students with individual guidance and reinforcement as they complete the assignments

Writing a Paragraph

in Writing Sections 7–20. Check each student's work as he or she completes each step in the composing process.

Revision skills are difficult for LD students. Allow extensive practice in simple revision skills. Provide incentives for revised papers, and allow students to exchange and improve each other's work.

Some students may be more successful if allowed to record their first drafts on a tape recorder, or if they can work with a more skilled student.

For each assignment, discuss possible topics with students, or provide them with a list from which to choose. Discuss each topic in class before assigning the writing exercises.

ESL If students have trouble locating and using reference material, work through the library skills presented in Section 22. Some students might gain confidence in their writing skills if you assign a native English speaker to help them write down their ideas. Offer additional help as needed.

Give students individual attention during the pre-writing stages, especially as they narrow topics. Pair students and have them review each other's spelling, capitalization, grammar, and punctuation.

NSD Tell students that many writers use nonstandard dialects, informal language, abbreviations, and so on in their first drafts. Explain that this sometimes helps writers get their thoughts down on paper. Tell students that they can do the same, but stress that they must standardize their language when they revise.

Objective

To understand the steps in the process of writing a paragraph

Presenting the Lesson

1. Read aloud and discuss **Here's the Idea.** Write the steps in the process of writing on the chalkboard. Lead students in a discussion of why they think these steps are necessary for writing a good paragraph.

2. Read and discuss **Check It Out.** Ask students to point out how the pre-writing notes are incorporated into the first draft.

3. Assign **Try Your Skill.** Go over the students' answers, pointing out the logic that should govern their choices.

4. Read **Keep This in Mind** aloud and then assign **Now Write.** Bring in examples of journals written by famous writers. Make sure students understand that their journals are not to be graded, that they are just personal writing books.

Individualizing the Lesson

Less-Advanced Students

Have students continue their list of important terms and definitions. Be sure they include *paragraph*, *specific*, and *general*.

Advanced Students

Give students some specific topics to write about in their journals: a description of an unusual person they might have seen in a public

Get in Step

Writing as a Process

Here's the Idea   To write a good paragraph, follow a step-by-step plan. This plan is called the process of writing. There are three stages: pre-writing, writing the first draft, and revising.

Pre-writing includes all the planning you do before you actually begin to write. Choosing a topic, narrowing it, gathering information, and organizing ideas are all parts of pre-writing.

Writing the first draft involves turning your pre-writing ideas into sentences and paragraphs. First, you write a topic sentence that states your main idea. Then you use your pre-writing notes to develop your subject. Don't be afraid to experiment.

Revising is the stage when you correct and improve your first draft. You organize your ideas and proofread your writing.

Check It Out   Read the following note and paragraph.

General topic: Georgia

Narrowed topic: Savannah in the spring

Pre-Writing Notes: horse-drawn carriages, restored old buildings—tours, historical district, beautiful parks, flowers

First Draft and Revision:

Savannah Georgia is ~~nice~~ *magical* in the spring. Horses *clip-clop* go through the historical district. They pull old carriages with tourists ~~in them.~~ *ing antique loaded* The historical district ~~is where they have~~ *In beautiful old* houses *have been restored* ~~that are fixed up~~ to look like they *did before the Civil War.* used to. These houses are ~~around~~ *surround* squares *filled* with lots of flowers. *azaleas and jasmine.* ~~Its no wonder it is~~ *Savannah is* called *rightly* the bell of the south.

84

- Explain how the writer followed each stage in the process of writing.

Try Your Skill Make three columns on your paper. Title one column *Pre-Writing*, the second column *Writing the First Draft*, and the third column *Revising*. Put each of the following writing activities in the appropriate column.

Rev changing general verbs to specific ones

First writing a rough version of a paragraph

Pre choosing a general subject

First writing an ending

proofreading Rev

gathering details Pre

organizing ideas Pre

narrowing a subject Pre

Keep This in Mind

- The process of writing includes three main stages: pre-writing, writing the first draft, and revising.
- Pre-writing includes all of the planning you do before you write.
- Use the first draft to turn your ideas into sentences.
- When you revise your work, you can improve and correct your writing.

Now Write Most experienced writers agree that one way to become a good writer is through practice. You can practice writing by keeping a journal. A journal is a notebook where you can record your thoughts, experiences, and reactions to the world around you. Keeping a journal allows you to practice your writing and at the same time build a rich storehouse of writing ideas.

Begin your journal today. On a piece of paper, write about an interesting event you experienced this week. You might also write about a conversation you had, or one you overheard. When you get a notebook for your journal, add this paper to it.

place, their reaction to a certain school rule, a conversation they overheard, etc.

Optional Practice

Have students write in their journals for the first five or ten minutes of each class. Encourage them to copy favorite passages from their reading into their journals. Emphasize that the journals are not only for practicing writing, but also a source book of ideas for future writing assignments.

Extending the Lesson

Have students begin a collection of paragraphs that appeal strongly to them as readers. Set a goal of five paragraphs to be collected by each student during his or her study of this Section. Above each paragraph, the students should write one sentence explaining what he or she liked about it. Under the paragraph the student should record the author and source of the paragraph.

Your Choice

Pre-Writing: Choosing a Topic

To know how and where to search for topics for a paragraph

Presenting the Lesson

1. Read and discuss **Here's the Idea.** Have students discuss their own writing experiences. Ask them how they usually go about choosing a topic to write about. Take time to go over each technique; for example, for *Reading* give students fifteen minutes to look through a variety of magazines and books. Then have them discuss and record ideas that come to them.

2. Read and discuss **Check It Out.** List the ideas on the chalkboard.

3. Assign **Try Your Skill.** Encourage each group to come up with as many ideas as possible.

4. Read **Keep This in Mind** and then assign **Now Write.** Have students indicate which method of choosing a topic they used.

Individualizing the Lesson

Less-Advanced Students

Allow enough class time to lead students through a practice run of all the ways to find subjects.

Advanced Students

To provide students with practice in interviewing, invite an interesting person to class (a writer, if possible). Have the students prepare for the interview by developing appropriate questions.

Here's the Idea   The first step in writing a paragraph is to choose a topic. One way to do this is to examine your own interests, ideas, and opinions. What interests you? What things do you consider important? Answering these questions will help you find a topic that you will enjoy developing. Here are four other ways to find writing ideas for paragraphs:

Journal Writing   Keep a daily journal in which you record your experiences, thoughts, and feelings. Write in this journal as often as you can. Soon you will have collected many ideas that you can use for writing assignments.

Brainstorming   Another way to search for ideas is by brainstorming. Start with a general idea, such as *camping* or *football*. Then, in five or ten minutes, write down as many thoughts as you can about the subject. At the end of this time, you will have many possible ideas for writing.

Clustering   Clustering is a form of brainstorming. Write your general idea on a piece of paper and circle it. Then write a related idea, circle it, and connect it to the general idea. Continue in this fashion, writing down ideas connected to the general idea and to other related ideas.

Interviews and Discussions   Another source of writing ideas is other people. If you know someone who has an interesting hobby, you can interview him or her about it. Listen carefully and ask questions, and you will soon gather enough details for a paragraph. Class discussions or conversations with friends can also yield writing ideas. Again, listen carefully and ask questions.

Reading   Reading can be more than a source of knowledge and enjoyment. It can also be a source of new ideas. If a particular book, magazine article, or newspaper story interests you, make some general notes about it in your journal. You might also clip out interesting articles and save them.

Check It Out   Read these two entries from a journal:

April 10   My sixteenth birthday! Finally, I get to drive—*if* I pass the test. Mom has invited some of my friends for dinner tonight. It's supposed to be a surprise, but Willy let the cat out of the bag.

May 14   I found out today I got a summer job. I'll start work next month as a day camp leader. I'll be responsible for eight children with cerebral palsy. I hope I'll do okay. I'm kind of nervous.

• What writing ideas can you find in these journal entries?

Try Your Skill   Read the following list of general topics. With your classmates, pick out one general topic and discuss it for four or five minutes. See how many good topics you can find for paragraphs.

sports   music   school life
jobs   animals   summer

Keep This in Mind

• When choosing a topic to write about, consider what interests you and what is important to you.
• Five good ways to find subjects are journal writing, brainstorming, clustering, interviewing and discussing, and reading.

Now Write   Make a list of four or five topics that you would be interested in writing a paragraph about. Use one or more of the methods suggested in this lesson. Save your writing ideas in your folder.

Have students bring copies of a newspaper to class. Have them go through the paper for ideas for paragraph topics. You might specifically refer them to advice columns, front-page news, sports columns, and editorial cartoons.

Extending the Lesson

Set aside a section of a bulletin board for an idea corner. Have the students bring in and post interesting news articles, quotations, and photographs.

Part 3

Pre-Writing: Narrowing a Topic

To know how to narrow a topic for a paragraph

Presenting the Lesson

1. Read and discuss **Here's the Idea.** Ask students why they think it's important to narrow a topic. Point out that these six questions are the same ones a newspaper reporter asks when writing a story.

2. Read and discuss **Check It Out.** Write the questions and their answers on the chalkboard.

3. Assign **Try Your Skill.** It is suggested you do this exercise as an in-class activity.

4. Read **Keep This in Mind.** Write the questions on the board for reinforcement.

5. Assign **Now Write.** Have volunteers read their narrowed topics to the class.

Individualizing the Lesson

Less-Advanced Students

Do only one topic for **Try Your Skill.** Do this topic as an oral class exercise. Write student responses on the board.

Advanced Students

Remind students that a topic can be narrowed too far, that they might find themselves "stretching" information or padding sentences. Lead a class discussion on how to know when a topic has been narrowed enough.

Here's the Idea   Many topics, such as *music* or *school*, are too broad to be developed in a single paragraph. Such topics must be narrowed to make them more specific.

One good way to narrow a topic is to ask questions beginning with *who, what, when, where, why,* and *how.* For example, to narrow the broad topic *music,* you could begin with several *who* questions:

> Who is my favorite singer? instrumentalist?
> Who won this year's Grammy Award for best rock album?

You might also ask several *what* questions:

> What was the first concert I went to?
> What do I remember about my first guitar lesson?

Suppose you decided to write about the first concert you went to. You could continue to narrow this topic by asking questions like these:

> **Who?**   Michael Jackson
> **Where?**   Madison Square Garden, New York
> **Why?**   my favorite performer

Asking such questions will help you to find a topic that is narrow enough to be covered well in a paragraph. These questions will also help you to find specific details to include in your paragraph. The more specific you make your paragraph, the more interesting it will be to your readers.

Check It Out   Read the paragraph on the next page, and then answer the questions that follow.

I never would have discovered the flute if it hadn't been for my older sister, Lisa. Two years ago, she asked me to a concert by John Galway at Orchestra Hall. I wasn't very interested in the idea, but that soon changed. When I heard the first silvery notes from Galway's flute, I was in awe. From that moment, I knew I wanted to play the flute. Thanks to Lisa, I discovered the beauty of this musical instrument.

- What questions do you think this student might have asked to narrow her topic? How did she answer them?

Try Your Skill   Choose two of these general topics and write them on your paper. Narrow each topic by asking *Who? What? When? Where? Why?* or *How?*

animals   television   dreams   friends   games   future

Keep This in Mind

- Narrow a general topic by answering *who, what, when, where, why,* and *how* questions. Make sure that you have a specific topic that you can write about in an interesting and informative paragraph.

Now Write   Choose one of the general topics you listed in the **Try Your Skill** from the last lesson. Narrow the topic so that you can write an interesting and informative paragraph about it. Ask *who, what, when, where, why,* and *how* questions to help you. Write your narrowed topic on a piece of paper. Save it in your folder.

Part 4 Improve Your Aim

Pre-Writing: Audience and Purpose

Part 4

Objective

To be aware of purpose and audience in writing

Presenting the Lesson

1. Read and discuss **Here's the Idea.** Ask students what the difference between writing for their parents and writing for their friends would be: would they use different language, different details and examples, etc.? Then ask them why their purpose for writing is important. Go over the example on page 91 and ask how the different audiences would affect the way the paragraph is written.

2. Read and discuss **Check It Out.** Ask students who the intended audience probably is.

3. Assign **Try Your Skill.** Have volunteers read their lists of details.

4. Read **Keep This in Mind** and then assign **Now Write.** Explain to students that in longer pieces of writing, they will actually write out their statement of purpose (*thesis statement*).

Individualizing the Lesson

Less-Advanced Students

Do **Try Your Skill** orally in class. If possible, lead the class through different audience reactions.

Advanced Students

Have students bring into class three newspaper or magazine articles clearly intended for three different audiences, but all about the same subject.

Here's the Idea Suppose that a speaker from the auto industry were to give a talk at your school. What would you think if the speaker used many technical terms that only an expert would understand? How would you feel if the speaker just explained that cars come in different sizes, shapes, and colors? In both cases, you would probably be bored. The first talk would be too complicated. The second would be too simple. Neither talk would be right for its audience.

Before writing a paragraph, always ask these questions:

What is my purpose?
Who are the people in my audience?

The answers to these questions will help you to focus your ideas. They will also help you to suit your writing to your readers.

Your **purpose** is what you want to accomplish with your writing. To determine your purpose, think about why you have chosen your topic. Do you want to tell a story? Do you want to define your subject? to describe it? to compare or contrast it to something else? to analyze it? Also think about whether your aim is to inform, to persuade, or to entertain your readers.

The **audience** is all the people who will read your writing. You should consider the ages and interests of these people. You should also consider how much your readers already know about your subject. Suppose, for example, that you are writing a paragraph about how to throw a curve ball. You would write in one way for the members of your baseball team. You would write in another way for readers who know little about baseball.

Here is an example of how a writer's purpose and audience can help determine how a paragraph will be developed:

Topic: mountain climbing

Purposes: *to describe* my first experience as a climber
to convince people that climbing is dangerous
to explain the types of equipment needed

Audiences: experienced climbers
beginning climbers
people interested in outdoor sports

Check It Out   Read this paragraph.

From the first day Sluggo arrived at our house, he was boss. Our five-year-old cat Nancy took one look at the three-month-old kitten and ran for cover. The chase was on. Sluggo is always the chaser and Nancy the chased. In contrast to Sluggo's mad dashing from room to room, Nancy tiptoes silently. Sluggo wriggles away if I try to hold him. Nancy, on the other hand, loves to curl up in my lap, purring contentedly. Whoever thinks all cats are alike hasn't met my two furry friends!

• What is the purpose of this paragraph?

Try Your Skill   If the above writer had wanted to convince a cat hater that cats are loving, gentle pets, the details would have been different. List three or four details that might be included if that were the purpose of the paragraph.

Keep This in Mind

• Your purpose is what you want to accomplish with your writing. The audience is all of the people who will read your writing.
• Identifying purpose and audience will help you to select details and suit your writing to your audience.

Now Write   On a sheet of paper, write the purpose of the paragraph you plan to write. Then write a brief description of the people who will read your paragraph. Save these notes.

Have students decide whether the following paragraph is written for adults, children, or a specialist in a certain field. Ask them to explain their decision.

Baby tigers usually don't get their first teeth until they are two weeks old. The cubs spend their first few months playing and chasing their tails. They start to learn to hunt when they are about six months old. At two years old they can take care of themselves.
—*National Geographic World*

Extending the Lesson

To emphasize the importance of audience to the writer, have students find out how the same topic (for example, a biography or scientific phenomena) is dealt with in a children's book, an encyclopedia, and a technical publication.

Part 5

Objective

To write a topic sentence that is informative, interesting, and direct

Presenting the Lesson

1. Write the words *topic sentence* on the chalkboard and list under them the goals for writing good topic sentences. Then read and discuss **Here's the Idea,** referring back to the list as you discuss each point.

2. Read and discuss **Check It Out.** Ask students why they feel these sentences are effective or not effective.

3. Assign and discuss **Try Your Skill.** Have volunteers read their revised sentences.

4. Read **Keep This in Mind** and then assign **Now Write.** Ask students to explain the final choice of their topic sentence.

Individualizing the Lesson

Less-Advanced Students

As students work on **Now Write,** check their topic sentences and offer advice while they are still composing. It will probably be best to emphasize the idea of *specific information* since the terms *direct* and *interesting* are more abstract qualities.

Advanced Students

Have students find well-written topic sentences that follow the guidelines in Part 5. Ask students to explain why they consider the sentences direct, interesting, and informative. Make a display of their sentences.

Attention Please

Pre-Writing: Creating a Topic Sentence

Here's the Idea   A good topic sentence will do several things. First, it should state the main idea of the paragraph clearly. That is, it should tell the reader what the paragraph will be about. Second, it should capture the reader's attention. If the topic sentence is not interesting, the reader may not want to finish reading the paragraph. The following rules will help you to accomplish these goals when writing topic sentences.

1. Make it informative. Stick to a single idea. Do not wander from your topic. Do not introduce unnecessary information. Avoid rambling, overloaded topic sentences such as the following:

> Paul Revere was a naval captain and patriot who was born in Boston, and he warned the colonists that the British were coming, and he was also an accomplished silversmith.

Instead, make a statement that introduces just one idea.

> Paul Revere, the Revolutionary War hero, was an accomplished silversmith.

2. Make it interesting. Try to find an unusual aspect of your subject to write about in your sentence. You can also add interest to your subject by approaching it in an unusual way:

> Paul Revere rode into the pages of American history.

3. Make it direct. Introduce the topic, not yourself. Do not begin with such phrases as *I think*, *I feel*, or *I believe*. Avoid wordy sentences such as the following:

> I want to write about the fact that Paul Revere actually made two famous rides, not one.

Instead, state your topic directly:

Paul Revere actually made two famous rides, not one.

Check It Out   Read the following topic sentences.

1. Friday the thirteenth was a lucky day for me.
2. If you ever see a mop wearing a blue bow, that's my dog Fluffy.
3. Amphibians are animals that are at home both on land and in water.
4. You can grow vegetables even if you live in an apartment.

• Is each of these sentences informative, direct, and interesting? Explain your answer.

Try Your Skill   Rewrite these sentences. Find a more informative, direct, and interesting way to state the same main ideas.

1. There are fifty states in the United States, but Alaska is the one I'm most interested in.
2. I guess if I put my mind to it I could tell you a thing or two about modern music.
3. Molly, who likes the spring season best, said that she was prepared for a long winter.
4. In biology, the day that students dissect an animal, which is usually a frog, is a memorable day.

Keep This in Mind

• Write a topic sentence that is informative, interesting, and direct.

Now Write   From your folder, take out the topic you chose and narrowed for your paragraph. Write several topic sentences that state the main idea of your paragraph. Experiment with your topic sentences. Try to express your main idea in several different ways. Make your sentences informative, interesting, and direct. Save your topic sentences in your folder.

93

Objective

To select the method of paragraph development that best suits the main idea

Presenting the Lesson

1. Read and discuss **Here's the Idea.** List the different kinds of details on the board. Ask students for examples of topics that might use each type of detail. Then discuss the methods students might use for gathering these details.

2. Read and discuss **Check It Out.** Ask students what type of details are included in these notes.

3. Assign **Try Your Skill.** Have volunteers read their answers. Point out that some topics might be developed with more than one kind of detail, and that those details might be gathered in more than one way.

4. Read **Keep This in Mind** and then assign **Now Write.**

Individualizing the Lesson

Less-Advanced Students

1. Do **Try Your Skill** as an oral exercise.

2. Begin **Now Write** in class and check to see that the students are choosing workable methods of gathering details.

Advanced Students

Display a photograph of an interesting individual or scene. Have each student list details about the subject of the picture; tell them that they should first list details for a descriptive paragraph and then list details for an explanatory paragraph.

Collecting Data

Pre-Writing: Developing a Paragraph

Here's the Idea   In Part 5 you learned how to write a topic sentence to express the main idea of a paragraph. Once you have written a topic sentence, you can then look for specific details to support and develop your main idea. The following types of details are helpful in developing different kinds of paragraphs.

sensory details   facts and statistics
specific examples   incidents or anecdotes

Always look for details that suit your purpose. If you want to write a descriptive paragraph, look for sensory details. These are details that tell how a subject looks, sounds, tastes, feels, and smells. If you want to express an opinion, look for facts and statistics to use as support. If you want to prove a point, you may consider telling an anecdote. If you want to explain or define a general idea, you may decide to give specific examples to make the idea clearer.

To gather the details you need, use any of the following methods: personal observation, brainstorming, interviewing, discussion, research, and general reading. Again, choose a method that suits your purpose. If you want to describe a scene in nature, go to the scene and make some personal observations. If you want to find facts to back up an opinion, do some research in such reference works as encyclopedias and almanacs. Choose the sources of information that are most likely to provide reliable information about your topic. For more information on choosing sources, see Critical Thinking, pages 273–291.

Check It Out   Read the following list of pre-writing notes.

Topic: The Grand Canyon

227 miles long, one mile deep, 18 miles wide in places
Carved out by erosion—Colorado River, weather
In deepest part, the stone is two billion years old
Cliffs, hills, and slopes of many colors

- How do you think the writer gathered these details?

Try Your Skill   What kinds of details might you use to develop each of the following topic sentences? How might you gather these details?

1. A rainy Saturday needn't be a washout. spec. ex.
2. Niagara Falls is an important source of energy. facts and stat.
3. I feel damp whenever I remember my ride on the "Maid of the Mist" at Niagara Falls. sens. det. incid. or anec.
4. Sixteen is not too young to drive. spec. ex. incid or anec.
5. Lion tamers go through intense training. spec. ex.

Keep This in Mind

- You can develop your paragraph with sensory details, facts and statistics, specific examples, or incidents or anecdotes.
- Gather details and ideas for your paragraph through personal observation, brainstorming, discussions, interviews, research, and general reading.
- Gather details and ideas that will support your purpose and appeal to your audience.

Now Write   Read the topic sentence you wrote in the last lesson. Look over your notes on purpose and audience. Then decide what kinds of information you need to develop your paragraph. Use whichever method of gathering details will give you the kinds of details you need. Save your pre-writing notes.

95

Ask students which of the methods they would be most likely to use in gathering material for the following topic sentences. Answers may vary.

1. The father penguin "baby-sits" with his children. specific examples
2. The peddler's truck was piled high with fruit. sensory details
3. I have never believed in ghosts. facts and statistics
4. Some animals make better pets than others. specific examples
5. I shall never forget our midnight guest. incidents or anecdotes

Extending the Lesson

Have students find four different paragraphs in a magazine or literature text; one should use sensory details, one should use specific details, one should use facts and statistics, and one should use incidents or anecdotes to develop the main idea.

Part 7

Objective

To choose a method of organization that suits the purpose of a paragraph

Presenting the Lesson

1. Review the types of details that students have been learning: sensory details, specific examples, facts and statistics, and incidents or anecdotes.

2. Read and discuss **Here's the Idea.** Explain that these are all orders with which to organize their details. Students will probably grasp *chronological, most familiar to least familiar,* and *spatial order* easily, but will need more help with *order of importance* and *general to specific order,* as well as *comparison and contrast.* Be prepared with several example paragraphs of each kind of order.

3. Read and discuss **Check It Out.** Ask students to identify the type of details used in this paragraph.

4. Assign **Try Your Skill.** Point out that sometimes more than one type of organization is appropriate for a topic.

5. Read **Keep This in Mind** and then assign **Now Write.**

Individualizing the Lesson

Less-Advanced Students

1. Do **Try Your Skill** as a group exercise.

2. Have students who are having trouble with organization work with a partner on **Now Write.**

3. Have students add these terms and their definitions to their vocab-

96

One After Another

Pre-Writing: Organizing a Paragraph

Here's the Idea   Suppose that every time you took notes in class you simply jotted the notes onto pieces of scrap paper. You then shoved the papers into your book bag. What would happen when it came time to study for a test? Of course, your notes would be a mess. Only when information is organized logically can it be understood readily. The same is true when you are writing a paragraph. If your ideas are not organized logically, your readers may not understand what you are trying to say. Here are some methods you can use.

Chronological Order   Use chronological order when you are telling a story or explaining how something is done. Present the events in the order in which they occurred or should occur.

Spatial Order   Spatial order helps you to present the sensory details of a description. It allows your readers to see how the things you are describing are related in space to other things.

Order of Importance   Use this order when giving reasons, facts, or examples to support an opinion. Present each detail, in order, from least important idea to the most important.

General to Specific   Use this order to define an object or idea. Begin with a general statement. Then add specific details.

Most Familiar to Least Familiar   Use this order when defining or describing. Begin with details that are familiar to your readers. Then introduce less familiar ideas and details.

Comparison and Contrast   Comparison and contrast can help you to show the similarities and differences between two subjects. Begin by describing how the subjects are alike. Then, show how they are different. You can also do the reverse.

Check It Out   Read the following paragraph.

We walked down the quaint village street with a row of elms on each side of it. Just beyond were two ancient stone pillars, weather-stained and lichen-blotched, bearing upon their summits a shapeless something which had once been the rampant lion of Birlstone Manor. A short walk along the winding drive with such sward and oaks around it as one only sees in rural England, then a sudden turn, and the long, low house of dingy, liver-colored brick lay before us, with an old-fashioned garden of cut yews on each side of it. As we approached it, there was the wooden drawbridge and the beautiful, broad moat as still and luminous as quicksilver in the cold, winter sunshine.

—SIR ARTHUR CONAN DOYLE

- What is the purpose of this paragraph?
- What kind of organization has the writer used?

Try Your Skill   Below is a list of topics for a paragraph. For each topic, choose a good method of organization.

1. Waxing a car is a simple process.
2. The emu and the penguin are both flightless birds, yet they lead very different lives.
3. Perseverance is a special quality that is often defined in the motto, "If at first you don't succeed, try, try, again."
4. Toxic waste is a problem that deserves our attention.
5. Aunt Sarah's home is a beautiful, old Victorian house, filled with treasured antiques.

Keep This in Mind

- Organize the details of your paragraph in a clear, logical order.
- Choose an order that best suits the purpose of your paragraph.

Now Write   Take out your pre-writing notes and organize them. Choose a method of organization that suits the purpose of your paragraph. Save your organized notes in your folder.

ulary lists: *chronological, spatial, comparison,* and *contrast.*

Advanced Students

For extra practice of *most familiar to least familiar* organization of material, have each student think of a topic on which he or she has specialized knowledge (such as a hobby, ethnic custom, academic subject, etc.). Have them write and then organize their notes in this order.

Optional Practice

Have students choose a good method of organization for each of the following topics. Have them explain their choices. Answers will vary.

1. reasons to travel by plane
2. a bird's-eye view
3. radio versus television
4. looking down a hallway
5. how to make a wood carving

Extending the Lesson

Have students find six paragraphs that illustrate each of the types of organization presented in this Part. Have students present their paragraphs to the class.

Objective

To put pre-writing notes in sentence form in a first draft

Presenting the Lesson

1. Read and discuss **Here's the Idea.** Emphasize the experimental nature of the first draft. Point out that although transitions can be used in the first draft, sometimes they are added during the revision stage. Ask students which transitions go with which form of organization.

2. Read and discuss **Check It Out.** Ask students to identify the method of organization used in this paragraph (spatial).

3. Read **Try Your Skill** with the class and determine the kind of organization used before assigning the exercise.

4. Review **Try Your Skill.**

5. Assign **Now Write.** Have students put their notes into an order before they begin their first draft. If necessary, review the different orders presented on page 96.

Individualizing the Lesson

Less-Advanced Students

Do **Try Your Skill** as an in-class exercise. As suggestions for transitions are given, discuss the appropriateness of these choices.

Advanced Students

Encourage students to add several new ideas to their first draft that are not in their notes.

Trial Run

Writing the First Draft

Here's the Idea When you have finished the pre-writing steps described in Parts 1–7, you should have a topic sentence and an organized list of details. The next step in the writing process is to turn your pre-writing notes into sentences. This step is called writing the first draft.

The main point of writing a first draft is to get all your ideas down in sentence form. Do not worry about the details of grammar, capitalization, punctuation, and spelling at this point. You will have time later to correct any mistakes you might make. Instead, concentrate on what you want to say. Feel free to change, take out, or add ideas as you write.

As you turn your ideas into sentences, try to make one sentence flow smoothly into the next. Use transitional words and phrases to help your readers understand the relationships between your ideas more easily.

In a paragraph that is organized in chronological order, use transitional words and phrases that express time. Examples include the words *first, next, then,* and *finally.*

In a paragraph that is organized in spatial order, use transitional words and phrases that relate to place or position. Some words and phrases that are useful in descriptive paragraphs are *next to, above, under, over, beside,* and *behind.*

A paragraph that is organized in some other way may use any of a great number of transitional words and phrases. Some words that are often used include *therefore, as a result, on the other hand, similarly,* and *in contrast.*

Check It Out Read this descriptive paragraph.

The fortune-teller sat in the shadows. In front of her was a deck of tarot cards and beside the deck was a crystal ball. On every finger of the gypsy's hands were large, flashy rings. A bright, flowered scarf was wrapped around her head. From her ears dangled huge hoop earrings that jingled like bells whenever she nodded her head.

- What transitional words and phrases did the writer use?

Try Your Skill Add transitional words and phrases to the following paragraph. Use transitions that help show the kind of order being used in the paragraph.

Carlos steadied himself in the starting blocks. He looked up at the track ahead of him. The gun went off. He jumped out of the blocks. He was running at an all-out sprint. He passed several runners. Two runners were still ahead of him. He passed one. He passed the other. His legs ached and his heart was pounding. He rounded the last turn in first place. He crossed the finish line. Carlos found out he had set a new school record.

Keep This in Mind

- The first draft is your first chance to put your ideas into sentence form.
- When writing a first draft, let your thoughts and ideas flow freely. Use transitional words and phrases to help make your ideas and organization clear.

Now Write Take out your topic sentences and your organized pre-writing notes. Choose the topic sentence that you like the best. Then, write the body of your paragraph. Use your organized notes to guide you. In the next lesson, you will write an ending for your paragraph. Save your first draft in your folder.

Have students reread the paragraphs in **Check It Out** and **Try Your Skill.** Discuss how the writers' audiences and purposes affected the content and language of the paragraphs.

Extending the Lesson

Invite a professional writer (newspaper, advertising agency, etc.) to your class. Ask the writer to explain and perhaps to demonstrate the process he or she follows when writing.

Objective

To end a paragraph with an interesting sentence that sums up the main idea

Presenting the Lesson

1. Read and discuss **Here's the Idea.** Emphasize the point that a good ending sentence should be interesting, as well as sum up the idea of the paragraph.

2. Read and discuss **Check It Out.** Ask students to identify the order of the details in this paragraph (chronological).

3. Read and assign **Try Your Skill.** It is suggested that students do this exercise with a partner.

4. Read **Keep This in Mind** and then assign **Now Write.**

Individualizing the Lesson

Less-Advanced Students

Do **Try Your Skill** as an oral in-class exercise. You may wish to supply additional practice paragraphs if necessary.

Advanced Students

Have students bring three paragraphs to class with interesting ending sentences. Have students discuss what makes these sentences interesting.

Optional Practice

Ask the class to write an ending sentence for the following brief paragraph.

> The Vikings were a warlike people who lived in northern Europe from about 800 to 1050 A.D. They built and

---

Top It Off

The First Draft: Ending a Paragraph

Here's the Idea   Have you ever seen a great television show that was spoiled by a bad ending? If so, you know how important a good ending is. This is why you must pay particular attention to the last sentence in every paragraph you write.

A good ending sentence sums up, or ties together, the ideas presented in the rest of the paragraph. An ending sentence may also explain the importance of these ideas. In either case, a good ending helps readers to make sense of what they have just read.

An ending sentence should not introduce any new information. It should make a clear, final statement that follows logically from the other sentences in the paragraph. In fact, an ending sentence may simply restate the idea of the topic sentence using different words.

A good ending sentence is also interesting. Whenever you write a paragraph, try to express your central idea in an ending sentence that your readers will want to remember.

Check It Out   Read this real-life account.

My adjustment to my new world was a very difficult one. I ran into problems with my classmates almost immediately after returning to school. Everything proceeded smoothly enough until the entire class was out on the playground during recess. A large group of children gathered around me the moment I finally reached the playground. "Hey, Harold," asked one of the boys, "what is it really like to be completely blind?"   —HAROLD KRENTS

- Does the ending sentence sum up the main idea of this paragraph? Does the ending capture your interest?

Try Your Skill Read these paragraphs and rewrite the poorly written endings. Try to make your concluding sentences interesting.

1   Levin Hutchins was a clockmaker who lived in Concord, New Hampshire. He was also a creature of habit. It was Hutchins's rule to get up at four o'clock sharp every day. He was upset with himself whenever he overslept. In 1787, when he was only twenty-six, Hutchins decided to attach a bell to the timing mechanism of one of his clocks. *Although he hadn't invented the first clock, which had been invented many years before, Hutchins invented the first alarm clock.*

2   Hercules was one of the most powerful heroes of Greek legends. He performed twelve impossible tasks. He killed two giant snakes when he was a baby. When he became a man, his weapon was a bow so big that no other person on earth could shoot an arrow with it. Hercules killed a huge, ferocious lion with his bare hands. He also won a battle against a nine-headed snake monster. *I like to read about heroes.*

3   You can create an inexpensive art object by using colored sand. First, buy several packages of sand in different colors. Next, find a clear glass container such as a vase, drinking glass, or jar. Then, carefully spoon one layer of sand at a time into your container. As the artist, you will choose the order of colors used and the thickness of the layers. *You can make many sand objects.*

Keep This in Mind

- A good ending sentence should sum up the main idea of a paragraph. It should also be interesting.

Now Write It is your turn to write a strong ending to your own paragraph. Read your first draft. Think about what you have written. Then write an ending that sums up the main idea in an interesting way. Save your completed first draft in your folder.

101

sailed faster ships than anyone before them had ever done. They were also traders and explorers.

Extending the Lesson

Bring in examples of good paragraphs to class and have students discuss how the ending sentence ties together the whole paragraph and how it relates to the topic sentence. Have students identify the key idea that is repeated in the final sentence.

Part 10

Objective

To revise the content, presentation, and style of a paragraph

Presenting the Lesson

1. Ask students to suggest what a writer might look for when revising a paragraph. Then read and discuss **Here's the Idea.** Make sure students understand the words *content, presentation,* and *style.* Ask students to explain the difference between *revising* and *proofreading.*

2. Read and discuss **Check It Out.**

3. Assign **Try Your Skill.** It is suggested that this exercise be done in class.

4. Read **Keep This in Mind** and then assign **Now Write.** Remind students to read their paragraphs one last time after they have done their revising and proofreading.

Individualizing the Lesson

Less-Advanced Students

Before students revise their first drafts, discuss with them those changes that they intend to make.

Advanced Students

Have students make up a mechanics checklist to use when revising their writing (Sections 13–16 of the Handbook will help). Duplicate the list for the use of all the students.

Optional Practice

Display some first drafts of paragraphs from your files on an overhead projector. Have students revise these paragraphs with you in

Just So

Revising a Paragraph

Here's the Idea   Revising is the final step in the process of writing. To revise a paragraph, you must read it carefully several times. As you read, look for ways to improve what you have written.

Begin by looking for ways to improve your **content.** The content includes all the ideas and details you have presented. First, make sure that your topic sentence is direct, interesting, and informative. Second, make sure that your paragraph has unity. A paragraph has unity if all its details are related to the single idea given in the topic sentence. Third, make sure that you have developed your main idea fully. If you need more details to support your main idea, add them.

Next, check the **presentation** of your ideas. Presentation refers to the way in which your ideas are organized. Make sure that your paragraph has coherence. A paragraph has coherence if its ideas are arranged in a clear, logical order. The ideas in the paragraph should flow smoothly from one to the other. The method of organization used should suit your purpose.

Then read your paragraph aloud to check its **style.** Style refers to the kind of language that you have used. Make sure that your words are right for your audience and your topic. Replace any dull or uninteresting language you find. Use strong, specific verbs, adverbs, and adjectives to make your writing come to life.

Now you must proofread your paragraph. Again, read your paragraph carefully. Look for and correct any errors in grammar, capitalization, punctuation, and spelling. When you have revised and proofread your paragraph, make a final copy of your work. Proofread this copy one last time, and correct any errors you find.

Check It Out   Read this partially revised paragraph.

You may have heard the expression "Time is money."

Food can be money. Edible money has been used from
~~Did you know that~~ *Did you know that*

Ancient Times up to the present Century. In ancient egypt
merchants paid their helpers with
people used grain ~~for money.~~ Roman solders was paid~~in~~ *with* salt.
valuable
Pepper was so ~~good~~ during the middle Ages that it was used
Near the end of
more often ~~to pay for things~~ *as currency* than as a spice. ~~In~~ World War II

the germans, when there official currency became worthless,
We should all be thankful
~~used coffee and sugar as money.~~ Today we use credit cards for *that*
paper, coins, and
money. *It could get pretty sticky*
carrying jelly doughnuts in your wallet.

- What changes have been made to improve the content, presentation, and style of this paragraph?
- What revising step has not yet been done?

Try Your Skill   The paragraph in **Check It Out** has been revised for content, presentation, and style. However, it still has errors in grammar and mechanics. Try your skill at finding and correcting these errors.

> ### Keep This in Mind
> - Revise the first draft of your paragraph for content, presentation, and style. Then proofread it for errors in grammar and mechanics.

Now Write   Revise your paragraph, following the guidelines in this lesson. When you are satisfied that your paragraph is the best it can be, make a neat, clean final copy. Save your finished paragraph in your folder.

103

class. Point out that there is always more than one "correct" way to revise a paragraph.

Extending the Lesson

Put together a publication of students' paragraphs. Have a student committee work on the organization and layout. Duplicate and distribute the booklet throughout the school.

Section 8 Objective

To understand the three main stages of the writing process: pre-writing, writing the first draft, and revising

Presenting the Lesson

To introduce the idea of the process of writing, ask students to imagine that they are reporters assigned to write a story about an important event. Ask them what they would have to do in order to write such a story: gather facts and details, decide on the ost important part of the story (main point), organize the information, etc. Point out that everyone who writes goes through these stages, that no one just sits down and writes well unless he or she thinks about and plans the writing first. Tell students that good writers constantly rethink and rearrange what they have written in an effort to express themselves more clearly.

Remind students that they used the process of writing to produce a paragraph in Section 7. Explain that this Section will give them a chance to see how to use the process of writing in a step-by-step order.

Review with students all the activities that are part of the process of writing that they learned in the previous Section. Stress the importance of each stage.

Use the pre-writing example on page 107 to illustrate each activity listed under *Pre-Writing* on pages 106–107. Discuss ways to find ideas for topics and then the importance of limiting a subject adequately. Point out that by narrowing a topic, a writer can then focus on a

The Process of Writing

more unusual or interesting aspect of the topic. Explain that the time spent on pre-writing saves time later, because it helps make writing the first draft and revising much easier.

Read and discuss *Writing the First Draft*. Compare the illustration on page 108 with the pre-writing illustration on page 107. Have students find any ideas in the first draft that were not in the pre-writing notes.

Read the *Revising* section, taking time with each paragraph. Make sure students understand why these three aspects of writing are important. Go over the proofreading symbols. Use these marks when you grade students' papers, so students become familiar with them and use them themselves. Discuss the difference between proofreading and revision; make sure students understand why both are important. You may want to introduce your students to the following evaluating techniques:

Peer evaluation—Pairs or small groups evaluate each other's work.

Conference—Oral evaluations by the teacher concentrate on both strengths and problems.

Editorial groups—Students work as authors, editors, and proofreaders.

Clinics—Students with similar writing problems receive concentrated instruction from the teacher.

Tutoring—A student weak in one area is paired with a student who is strong in the same area.

Discuss *The Final Copy*. Compare the first draft on page 108 with the final copy on page 111. Ask students why revisions were made. Point out how neat the final copy of the paragraph is and ask students why the final copy should look like this and not like the revised paragraph on page 110.

Additional Resources

Practice Book — pages 44–45
Duplicating Masters — pages 44–45

Teaching Special Populations

LD See **Teaching Special Populations,** pages 82–83.

ESL discuss this Section slowly and thoroughly with ESL students. Introduce and review with them the important vocabulary: *pre-writing, subject, purpose, audience, details, first draft, revision, content, presentation, style,* and *proofreading.*

Review spelling, capitalization, grammar, and punctuation skills as necessary.

NSD See **Teaching Special Populations,** pages 82–83.

The Process of Writing

Throughout the rest of this book, you will be learning about and practicing many different kinds of writing. You will write narratives, descriptions, explanations, and a research paper. Although the kind of writing you do will change, one aspect of your writing will remain the same. You will always use the three stages of the process of writing—pre-writing, writing the first draft, and revising—to plan, write, and improve your paragraphs and compositions.

Pre-Writing A football coach wouldn't send his team onto the field without a game plan. A builder wouldn't start digging the foundation for a skyscraper without an architect's plans. Careful planning is important to nearly all activities. It increases the odds that the outcome of the activity will be successful.

As a writer, you need to plan, too. The planning stage of the process of writing is called pre-writing. During pre-writing, you will complete the following activities.

1. Choose and narrow a subject. Look for a subject that interests you and that you know something about or want to learn about. You can find interesting writing ideas through brainstorming, clustering, reading, research, interviewing, discussing, and looking in your journal. Then narrow your subject so that it is specific enough to be covered well in a paragraph, a composition, or a research paper.

2. Define your purpose. Why are you writing? Do you want to tell a story, describe something or someone, explain a process, express an opinion, or define something? Knowing your purpose will help you to focus your writing.

3. Identify your audience. Who are your readers? What are their interests and opinions? How old are they? How much do they know about your subject? If you know your audience, you can suit your writing to your readers.

4. Gather details. Look for details, ideas, and other information to support and develop your topic. You can use sensory details, specific examples, facts and statistics, or incidents or anecdotes. You can use the same techniques to gather information that you used to choose a topic.

5. Organize your information. You must arrange the details you have gathered into a logical order. Some methods of organization you can use are chronological order, spatial order, the order of importance, general to specific order, most familiar to least familiar order, and comparison and contrast. Whichever method you choose, be sure that it suits the type of writing you are doing.

Pre-Writing

You list possible topics and select one.

You identify your purpose and audience.

the hail storm
my new nephew
the Olympics

our cactus garden
my hospital experience
Mexico City

Purpose: to describe waking up in the hospital
Audience: my classmates

① waking up, groggy
   sound of buzzer
② white plaster cast
④ dry throat
③ tube on arm
⑥ moped accident

⑧ fine in a few days
   no clock
   Memorial Hospital
⑤ doctor enters
⑦ broken arm / concussion

You list details, choose those that develop your topic, and organize them.

Writing the First Draft   When you have finished all of your planning, you are ready to write your first draft. A first draft is like the sketches an artist draws before he or she begins a painting. Like the artist, you want to see how well things fit, whether anything needs to be added, taken out, or moved.

When you write a first draft, concentrate on turning your details into sentences and paragraphs. Follow your organized pre-writing notes as you write, but don't be afraid to experiment with the order of your ideas. Let your ideas flow naturally as you write. Don't interrupt this flow by questioning your grammar, capitalization, punctuation, or spelling. You will have time later to correct any mistakes you make.

Writing the First Draft

You write a paragraph about your topic.

> I woke up feeling funny. I heard voices. Slowly I opened my eyes. My left arm was in a cast. I was in a strange room. My right arm had a tube taped to it. My throat was sore. I was confused. Suddenly a door opened up. A doctor with her assistants said my name. She said that while riding my moped I had slipped on some oil. I broke my arm and got a concusion. She said I was okay. I could leave in a few days. I smiled and thanked her and fell asleep.

Revising   A first draft is just a rough version of your written work. During the third stage of the process of writing, called revising, you smooth out the rough edges. You work to improve what you have written, to make your writing the best it can be.

When you revise, you should pay attention to three important aspects of your writing: content, presentation, and style.

Content refers to the ideas and details you have presented. To check the content of your writing, ask yourself these questions.

1. Does each topic sentence express the main idea of a paragraph?
2. Do all of my details relate directly to my main idea?
3. Have I included enough details to develop my main idea fully?
4. Does my conclusion sum up my ideas?
5. Have I fulfilled my purpose?

Presentation refers to the way your writing is organized. The following questions will help you to check your presentation.

1. Does my writing have a clear beginning, middle, and ending?
2. Have I arranged my details in a logical order?
3. Does my method of organization suit the kind of writing I am doing?
4. Do my ideas flow smoothly from one to another?

Style refers to the way you have expressed yourself in your writing. Most writers have different styles. Still, there are some examples of good style that are common to all writers.

1. Is each topic sentence interesting enough to capture a reader's attention? Is each topic sentence direct, not wordy?
2. Have I used lively, vivid language?
3. Is my language well suited to my audience?
4. Have I included transitional words and phrases to help the reader see how my ideas are connected?

Proofreading When you are satisfied with the content, presentation, and style of your writing, proofread your work. Look for and correct any errors in grammar, capitalization, punctuation, and spelling. When you proofread, use a dictionary and the Handbook sections of this book to check your work.

As you revise your first draft, use the following proofreading marks to show your corrections and changes.

Proofreading Symbols

Symbol	Meaning	Example
∧	add	would ∧gone (*have* added above)
≡	capitalize	United states
/	make lower case	our club President
∿	reverse	t h i e r
ℒ	take out	finished the the race
¶	make new paragraph	....be over. ¶New ideas
⊙	period	....and stop⊙Before we
⋀	add comma	Red, blue ⋀and green are

Revising

You rewrite. You express your idea in a different way.

I woke up feeling funny. I heard voices. *dazed and groggy. In the distance,* (funny → dazed and groggy)

Slowly I opened my eyes. My left arm *forced* *open* *stretched out beside me,*

was in a cast. I was in a strange room. *wrapped* *white plaster* *found myself*

My right arm had a tube taped to it.

My throat was sore. I was confused. *felt parched and scratchy.* *clear*

Suddenly a door opened up. A doctor *My mind*

with her assistants said my name. *accompanied by* *spoke*

She said that while riding my moped, *told me*

I had slipped on some oil. I broke my *skidded* *a patch of* *had* *n*

arm and got a concussion. She said I *suffered mild* *s* *The doctor assured me that*

was okay. I could leave in a few days. *I was not in any danger and that the hospital*

I smiled and thanked her and fell asleep. *Smiling weakly, I* *drifted off into a deep sleep.*

Notice how the paragraph has been improved.

The Final Copy   When you have finished revising and proof-reading your writing, copy it in its final form. Write carefully. Make your work as neat as possible. Proofread your final copy. Neatly correct any errors you find.

Final Copy

I woke up feeling dazed and groggy. In the distance, I heard voices. Slowly, I forced my eyes open. I found myself in a strange room. My left arm, stretched out beside me, was wrapped in a white plaster cast. My right arm had a clear tube taped to it. My throat felt parched and scratchy. My mind was confused. Suddenly, a door opened. A doctor, accompanied by her assistants, spoke my name. She told me that while riding my moped, I had skidded on a patch of oil. I had broken my arm and suffered a mild concussion. The doctor assured me that I was not in any danger and that I could leave the hospital in a few days. Smiling weakly, I thanked her and drifted off into a deep sleep.

Now you are ready to begin learning and practicing different kinds of writing. Whenever and whatever you write, follow all the stages of the process of writing. Each time you write, you will be learning something about writing and about yourself.

Section **9** Objectives

1. To develop a narrative paragraph with specific and sensory details

2. To use chronological order to organize the incidents in a narrative paragraph

3. To distinguish between first- and third-person point of view

4. To use transitional words and phrases to show chronological order

5. To revise a narrative paragraph so that it is clear, lively, and interesting

Preparing the Students

Review the paragraphs in Section 6, pages 80–81. Ask students which of these paragraphs tells a story. Explain that a paragraph that tells a story is called a *narrative.* Tell students that in this Section they will learn special techniques for writing a good narrative paragraph.

Additonal Resources

Mastery Test — page 23 in the test booklet

Practice Book — pages 46–50

Duplicating Masters — pages 46–50

The Narrative Paragraph

Teaching Special Populations

LD See **Teaching Special Populations,** pages 82–83.

ESL Present additional exercises for using transitions that show chronological order.

Be sure students understand what is meant by *point-of-view*. Have them tell brief stories based on folk tales in first-person point of view, and ask another student to re-tell that story from third-person point of view. Point out the change of verb tense.

Help students choose topics for their narrative paragraphs.

NSD See **Teaching Special Populations,** pages 82–83. Tell students to check their paragraphs for pronoun agreement.

Part 1

What's the Story?

Objective

To develop a narrative paragraph with specific and sensory details

Presenting the Lesson

1. Read and discuss the first two paragraphs of **Here's the Idea.**

2. Tell students that the next two paragraphs will help them narrow their topic and find specific and sensory details. Make sure they understand what the word *sensory* means.

3. Read and discuss **Check It Out.**

4. Assign **Try Your Skill.** Ask for volunteers to read their details. Ask students how they found their sensory details: did they use their memories, imagination, etc.?

5. Review **Keep This in Mind.**

6. Assign **Now Write.** If students can not think of a story to write about, refer them to their journals for ideas.

Individualizing the Lesson

Less-Advanced Students

Have students work with a partner to do **Try Your Skill.**

Advanced Students

Have each student find, in a short story or a novel, one paragraph developed with specific sensory details. Have students share their paragraphs with the class.

Optional Practice

Once students have decided on a story to narrate, you can help them select specific and sensory details

Pre-Writing: Developing a Narrative

Here's the Idea A narrative paragraph is one that tells a story. You can write a narrative to describe an experience, provide an example, or entertain. A narrative paragraph may stand alone or it may be used as part of a speech, a composition, or a report.

To write a narrative paragraph, first choose a story that you want to tell. The story may be about a real experience such as something that happened to you while on vacation. The story may also be totally imaginary. In either case, the story must be a brief one. Otherwise, you will not be able to develop it fully in a single paragraph.

When you have chosen a general idea for a story, make your topic more specific. Do this by asking questions that begin with *who*, *what*, *when*, *where*, *why*, and *how*. The answers to these questions will help you to focus your ideas. The answers will also provide you with some details to tell your story.

When you have a more specific topic, make a list of every event that you want to include. Even a very short story may contain many separate events. Consider how the things in your story look, sound, feel, taste, and smell. Then, list the details that will appeal to the senses of your readers. Together these two types of details will help you to write a vivid narrative.

Check It Out Look at this list of details.

who:	Jeff and me
what:	grudge match in tennis
where:	school tennis court
when:	after school
why:	to prove girls are as good in athletics as boys
how:	won with self confidence

Now read the narrative.

Jeff was always bragging that boys were better athletes than girls. So I challenged him to a tennis match after school to prove that he was wrong. We each won one game and then I lost a game. Jeff was so pleased with his apparent victory that he started making mistakes. But, it hardly mattered. I was rushing every shot. I didn't feel I had control of the ball. I needed to relax. I decided to change racquets between sets for luck. I got my confidence back. I moved in after my serves and put his returns away. It worked—my game—and match!

- What separate events help to tell the story?
- What sensory details does the story include?

Try Your Skill Recall a particular situation in which you were frightened or taken by surprise. On your paper, list *Who? What? When? Where? Why?* and *How?* Recall and list sensory details about the situation.

> ### Keep This in Mind
> - A narrative paragraph tells a brief story. The story may be true or imaginary.
> - Gather specific details for a narrative paragraph by asking *who, what, when, where, how,* and *why* questions.
> - Develop a narrative paragraph with specific and sensory details.

Now Write Think about a brief story you would like to tell. The story may be true or imaginary. Make a list of the events that will tell your story. Save your pre-writing notes in your folder.

by guiding them through a visualization of the experience. Have them close their eyes and picture the setting. Then have them think about the main event and those events that lead up to it. Ask them to remember how they felt. Encourage students to search for specific words that precisely describe the scene and their feelings.

Extending the Lesson

Have students bring in comic strips that tell a story. Have students list any specific or sensory details that they would need to write a narrative paragraph based on the cartoon.

Part 2

Objective

To use chronological order to organize the incidents in a narrative paragraph

Presenting the Lesson

1. Read and discuss **Here's the Idea.** Be sure the students understand the term *chronological order.* Have them list the incidents in the sample paragraph.

2. Read and discuss **Check It Out.** Ask students to find words in the paragraph that tell "time" order.

3. Assign **Try Your Skill.** Ask volunteers to share their lists with the class.

4. Read **Keep This in Mind** and then assign **Now Write.** Encourage students to add more information to their notes as they organize.

Individualizing the Lesson

Less-Advanced Students

1. Ask volunteers to share their organized notes from **Now Write** with the class. Show the writers how to add necessary details to their notes.

2. Ask students to write down "time" words that they can use to make chronological order clearer in their paragraphs.

Advanced Students

Explain that chronological order does not always start at the beginning of an event and move progressively toward the end. Ask students to find examples of movies or books that start in the middle or the end of the action and move

---

Moment to Moment

Pre-Writing: Using Chronological Order

Here's the Idea   Most stories are told in **chronological order.** In other words, the events are presented in the order in which they occurred. Notice the use of chronological order in the following example.

> When I was free for a few hours, I explored the foothills. I would leave the town and head toward the point of the foothills nearest my home. There I would test my legs and lungs against the hillside. It was hard work. At first, I ran two miles at the fast pace of perhaps five or six miles an hour. Then, I climbed a hillside of five hundred feet or more in elevation. At last, I returned to home and bed, dead tired, every muscle of my legs aching. Time and again I followed this routine.
>
> —WILLIAM O. DOUGLAS

Before writing a narrative paragraph, always organize the list of events you want to include. Arrange these events in the order that they occurred. By using chronological order, you will make it easier for your reader to follow what is happening in your story.

Check It Out   Now read this imaginary narrative.

> He was an old man who fished alone in a small boat in the Gulf Stream and he had gone eighty-four days now without taking a fish. In the first forty days, a boy had been with him. However, after forty days without a fish the boy's parents had told him that the old man was now definitely and finally unlucky. At their orders, the boy had gone in another boat that caught three good fish the first week. It made the boy sad to see the old man come in each day with his boat empty, and he always went down to help him.   —ERNEST HEMINGWAY

- Are the events of this narrative in chronological order? Explain your answer.

Try Your Skill   Assume you are going to write a narrative paragraph about getting ready for school in the morning. Make a list of everything you do. Then arrange that list in chronological order.

Keep This in Mind

- The events of a narrative paragraph are organized in chronological order.

Now Write   Examine the pre-writing notes you made in the last lesson. Arrange the events and details in chronological order. You can add or take out details as you see fit. Save your organized notes in your folder.

backwards in time to previous events (*flashback*).

Optional Practice

Show students a picture of an action scene. Have students decide what is happening *now*, what might have happened *before*, and what will happen *next*. Explain that they are dealing with chronological order.

Extending the Lesson

Have students bring in brief newspaper articles and trace the chronology of the incidents covered in the stories.

Part 3

Part 3

Who Sees What?

Objective

To distinguish between first- and third-person point of view

Presenting the Lesson

1. Read and discuss **Here's the Idea.** Go over the difference between third-person limited and third-person omniscient. Have extra examples on hand, in case students have trouble with these concepts.

2. Read and discuss **Check It Out.** Point out how the paragraph using the first-person makes the reader feel more a part of the action, while the third-person narrative has a more objective feeling.

3. Assign **Try Your Skill.** Have volunteers read their sentences to the class.

4. Read **Keep This in Mind.**

5. Assign **Now Write.** Ask students to write down which pronouns they will be using for their point of view.

Individualizing the Lesson

Less-Advanced Students

Do **Try Your Skill** as an in-class exercise. Discuss the different effect each point of view has on the reader.

Advanced Students

Have students choose details and a point of view for a narrative paragraph about a nonhuman: a pet, a computer, a video game, a hockey stick, a radio, etc.

Pre-Writing: Choosing a Point of View

Here's the Idea   Every narrative has an author. He or she is the person who *writes* the story. Every narrative also has a narrator. He or she is the person who *tells* the story. Sometimes the narrator is a character in the story. At other times, the narrator may be an outsider, someone who is not in the story at all. When you choose a narrator to tell your story, you are choosing a **point of view.** Point of view means the eyes and mind through which something is written.

Point of view is an important choice when you are writing a narrative paragraph. As a pre-writing step, you must decide which of the three different points of view you will use.

One point of view you may choose is the **first-person point of view.** When you use this point of view, you use the first-person pronoun *I.* The character *I* is the narrator. Your reader will know only what the narrator knows.

With **third-person point of view,** the third-person pronouns *he, she,* and *they* are used. Your story is told by an outsider. who cannot tell what any character is thinking or feeling. Thus, this point of view is called **third-person limited.**

A second type of third-person point of view is called **third-person omniscient.** *Omniscient* means "knowing all things." The pronouns *he, she,* and *they* are used. This narrator knows what each character is thinking and feeling.

Check It Out   Read the following two narrative paragraphs.

1   Once, while I was baby-sitting for Jim and Jenny Lee, I decided to take them shopping. As we entered Filene's, I saw my friend Maria and stopped to say hello. One minute the

twins were right next to me, but the next minute they had disappeared. At first, I was frantic. I ran up and down nearby aisles, calling their names. Finally, I had an inspiration—try the toy department! first-person

2   Steve and Maria were delighted to run into each other in Filene's. Steve remembered how much fun they'd had last summer as lifeguards at Harbor Beach Park. As they chatted, Steve failed to notice that Jim and Jenny had drifted off. When the twins found the toy department, they broke into a run. Jim had never seen so many model trains before. Jenny couldn't wait to find out what was inside a huge box of building materials. By then, Steve was searching for the missing twins. third-person

- What is the point of view of each paragraph?

Try Your Skill   Suppose that you arrive home to find that no one is there and you have forgotten your key. While you are trying to find a way in, a stranger appears on the scene. First, write several sentences that relate these events from the first-person point of view. Relate the same events from the third-person limited and the third-person omniscient points of view.

> ### Keep This in Mind
>
> - With the first-person point of view, the narrator, *I*, tells what the characters say and do.
> - With the third-person limited point of view, the narrator is an observer.
> - With the third-person omniscient point-of-view, the narrator is "all knowing." He or she tells everything—actions, thoughts, and feelings.

Now Write   Take out the pre-writing notes you organized in the previous lesson. Choose a point of view that seems suited to the story you have chosen to tell. Write down your choice in your pre-writing notes. Save your notes in your folder.

Have students look through their literature anthology and identify stories written from the first-person point of view and from the third-person point of view.

Extending the Lesson

Have students write a statement about themselves and something they like or dislike (*I am the only person in my family who doesn't like chocolate*). Then have them exchange papers and write the same statement in third-person limited and then omniscient point of view.

Objective

To use transitional words and phrases to show chronological order

Presenting the Lesson

1. Read and discuss **Here's the Idea.** Remind students that a first draft is to be a flowing of ideas, not a finished copy. Ask students why a narrative may not need a topic sentence. Go over the list of transitional words and phrases and challenge students to think of a sentence for each one.

2. Read **Check It Out.** Take time to point out the use of vivid verbs and adjectives in this paragraph.

3. Assign **Try Your Skill.**

4. Read **Keep This in Mind** and then assign **Now Write.** Encourage students to search for specific verbs and adjectives that would make their writing more interesting.

Individualizing the Lesson

Less-Advanced Students

Give students individual help with their first drafts. Allow class time for them to do their writing.

Advanced Students

Read a short story aloud in class. Ask students to write a one-paragraph summary of the plot. Remind them to use transitions.

Optional Practice

Ask students to find a narrative paragraph that contains at least three transitions. Have volunteers

120

As Time Goes By

Writing the First Draft

Here's the Idea During the pre-writing stage of writing a narrative paragraph, you chose a group of events to tell about. You arranged these events in chronological order. You also chose a point of view from which to tell your story. Having done these things, you are now ready to write your first draft.

As you begin writing the first draft, remember that you are telling a story. Therefore, you do not have to begin with a topic sentence that states the main idea. Instead, you may write a sentence that sets the scene or that tells about the first event. The other events of the narrative should then follow in order.

There are many special words and phrases that you can use to make the order of events clear. These are called transitional words and phrases. They allow you to show how much time has passed between events in a narrative. Here is a list of useful transitional words and phrases:

first	now	when	at the same time
then	before	soon	by the time
next	earlier	suddenly	at the beginning
while	after	immediately	in the middle
last	later	finally	at the end

Notice that these words and phrases all deal with time. They tell the reader *when* each event in the story takes place. In addition to the transitional words and phrases above, you may want to use time words and phrases that are more specific. For example, you may need to write *after ten minutes, at noon,* or *in September.* Use a variety of transitional words or phrases to tell your reader exactly when each event takes place.

120

Check It Out   Read this narrative paragraph.

We reached the beach late in the afternoon. The tide was high and the surf was heavy. I dived in and rode a couple of waves, but they had reached that stage of power in which you could feel the whole strength of the ocean in them. The second wave, as it tore toward the beach with me, spewed me a little ahead of it, encroaching rapidly; suddenly it was immeasurably bigger than I was, it rushed me from the control of gravity and took control of me itself; the wave threw me down in a primitive plunge without a bottom, then there was a bottom, grinding sand, and I skidded onto the shore. The wave hesitated, balanced there, and then hissed back toward the deep water, its tentacles not quite interested in me enough to drag me with it.
                                                      —JOHN KNOWLES

- What transitional words and phrases has the author used in this paragraph?
- Do the transitional words and phrases help to show time and order?

Try Your Skill   Look again at the narrative paragraph by William O. Douglas on page 116. Find and list the transitional words and phrases he used.

Keep This in Mind

- Transitional words and phrases that tell *when* help to show chronological order in a narrative paragraph.

Now Write   Begin writing the first draft of your narrative paragraph. For now, just write to get your ideas into paragraph form. Let your thoughts and ideas flow freely. Don't hesitate to make changes as you write. Remember to include transitional words and phrases that tell *when*. Save your first draft in your folder.

write their paragraphs on the chalkboard, leaving a blank space for the transitions. Have the class suggest words or phrases that would fit into the blanks.

Extending the Lesson

Point out to the students that the word *narrator* comes from the same base word as *narrative*. Ask someone who often tells stories (librarian, speech teacher, etc.) to narrate a story to the class. Afterward, discuss how the specific details, chronological order, point of view, and transitions all worked together to make the story-telling interesting.

Part 5

Objective

To learn to revise a narrative paragraph so that it is clear, lively, and interesting

Presenting the Lesson

1. Read and discuss **Here's the Idea.** Go over the four questions to ask when revising. Discuss the idea of strong verbs. Review the paragraph on page 121 with the students, asking them to point out the strong verbs that are used. If necessary, review linking verbs with the class.

2. Read and discuss **Check It Out.** Point out the strong adjectives as well as the verbs in this paragraph.

3. Assign **Try Your Skill.** Have students read their revised paragraphs aloud. Explain that there is often more than one synonym for a word.

4. Read **Keep This in Mind** and then assign **Now Write.**

Individualizing the Lesson

Less-Advanced Students

Do **Try Your Skill** as a class exercise. Make sure that students realize that there is no one right answer to this exercise.

Advanced Students

Discuss different ways to make a paragraph more effective: ask students what feeling present tense gives to a narrative, and what feeling past tense would give (immediacy vs. thinking over a situation). Ask students what verbs they might choose if they were trying to convey

Achieving Excellence

Revising Your Narrative Paragraph

Here's the Idea   Revising is the last stage in the process of writing a narrative paragraph. When you revise, you change parts of your story to make it clearer and more interesting.

Here are some questions to ask yourself as you revise your narrative:

1. Have I included specific and sensory details in my narrative?
2. Have I arranged the events in chronological order?
3. Have I made the order of the events clear by using transitional words and phrases?
4. Have I used only one point of view?

When writing a narrative, always try to use language that is specific. This will make your story more vivid to your readers. Avoid such general verbs as *walk*. Replace any such verbs with ones that are more specific. For example, the verb *walk* could be replaced by *amble*, *tiptoe*, or *march*. Choose the verb that fits the particular action you are describing.

The lazy boy *ambled* down the hall.
Cautiously, Sarah *tiptoed* up the steps to the attic.
Luis *marched* into the room with a scowl on his face.

Also avoid weak linking verbs. These include all forms of the verb *be*, such as *is*, *were*, or *had been*. Instead, use strong verbs that show action, such as *leap*, *dunked*, or *flew*.

Once you have checked the ideas, organization, and word choice in your paragraph, proofread it carefully. Find and correct any errors in grammar, capitalization, punctuation, and spelling.

Check It Out   Notice how the author has used strong and specific verbs in this paragraph.

> Kino deftly slipped his knife into the edge of the shell. Through the knife he could feel the muscle tighten hard. He worked the blade lever-wise and the closing muscle parted and the shell fell apart. The lip-like flesh writhed up and then subsided. Kino lifted the flesh, and there it lay, the great pearl, perfect as the moon. It captured the light and refined it and gave it back in silver incandescence. It was as large as a seagull's egg. It was the greatest pearl in the world.
>
> —JOHN STEINBECK

- Which verbs in particular make this paragraph come alive?

Try Your Skill   Replace the verbs in italics below with stronger, more specific verbs.

> Jerome *ran* up the alley, terrified and nearly out of breath. He *ran* into a garbage can, which *made noise* as it *moved* along the pavement. Behind him, the huge dog was closing in. It *went* past the intersection and *came* into the alley at incredible speed. With one last, desperate effort, Jerome *put* himself through an open window in the house at the end of the alley. He *turned* and *shut* the window just as the snarling dog reached the house.

Keep This in Mind

- When revising a narrative paragraph, add strong and specific verbs to make the story come alive.

Now Write   Revise your first draft. Follow the guidelines in this lesson, adding strong, specific verbs where necessary. Proofread your paper for errors in grammar and mechanics. Then make a final copy of your narrative. Save it in your folder.

a feeling of anger and what they might choose if trying to present a feeling of happiness.

Optional Practice

Have students find the strong verbs in the following paragraph.

> Cinnamon has <u>spiced</u> the lives of a lot of people. Ancient Romans <u>prized</u> it for use in perfumes and scented oils. The Greeks and Romans also <u>flavored</u> their foods with cinnamon. Some people <u>treasured</u> it for medicinal uses, and others thought it valuable enough to use for money.
>
> —*National Geographic World*

Extending the Lesson

Ask the class to find well-written examples of narrative paragraphs in fiction and nonfiction. Encourage them to look in magazines as well as in books. Have them read the passages aloud and explain why they find the writing effective.

Section **10** Objectives

1. To use sensory details gathered from observation or memory to develop a descriptive paragraph

2. To use spatial order to organize a description

3. To use appropriate pronouns, verbs, adjectives, and adverbs to create mood in a descriptive paragraph

4. To use transitional words and phrases to show spatial order

5. To revise the first draft of a descriptive paragraph

Preparing the Students

Tell the class that descriptive paragraphs tell what a place, person, or thing is like. Have students close their eyes as you read this paragraph.

As far as he could see the trees were standing up against the sky. Not one tree, not two, not a dozen, but the thousands he had planted in seed and sprout. And not little trees, no, not saplings, not little tender shoots, but great trees, huge trees, trees as tall as ten men, green and green and huge and round and full, trees shimmering their metallic leaves, trees whispering, trees in a line over hills, lemon trees, lime trees, redwoods and mimosas and oaks and elms and aspens, cherry, maple, ash, apple, orange, eucalyptus, stung by a tumultuous rain, nourished by alien and magical soil and, even as he watched, throwing out new branches, popping open new buds.

—Ray Bradbury

Ask students what makes this paragraph vivid. Ask which words make the scene come to life. Explain that good descriptive paragraphs like this one are vivid and

The Descriptive Paragraph

appeal to the senses. Tell students that this Section will help them to write good descriptive paragraphs. Tell them to think about descriptive paragraphs as pictures painted with words.

Additional Resources

Mastery Test — page 24 in the test booklet

Practice Book — pages 51–55

Duplicating Masters — pages 51–55

Teaching Special Populations

LD See **Teaching Special Populations,** pages 82–83. Remind students to refer to the lists of sensory words on pages 20–21.

ESL Review with students the sensory words listed on pages 20–21. Have the class as a group suggest sensory details for various things brought to class (a piece of marble, broccoli, a scented sticker, a stone etc.).

Be sure students understand the meanings of transitional words that show spatial order. Provide them with additional oral or written exercises.

As an additional assignment, have students describe a place in their native country.

NSD See **Teaching Special Populations,** pages 82–83.

Objective

To use sensory details gathered from observation or memory to develop a descriptive paragraph

Presenting the Lesson

1. Read aloud **Here's the Idea.** Have students read Shirley Jackson's paragraph. Ask them what sensory details are used to make the description come to life. Stress the importance of gathering vivid sensory details through observation.

2. Divide students into small groups and assign **Check It Out.** Have them pick out sensory details in the paragraph. Have students identify which senses the description appeals to.

3. Assign **Try Your Skill.** Stress that students narrow their chosen topic so they can list specific sensory details.

4. Assign **Now Write.** Remind students that this is the first step in writing a descriptive paragraph.

Individualizing the Lesson

Less-Advanced Students

1. Students may have difficulty in choosing and narrowing a topic. They may want to use the topic they chose in **Try Your Skill.**

2. To assist students in recognizing sensory details, give each student a photograph of a scene. Have students imagine that they are in the picture, and to think of the sights, smells, sounds, tastes, and textures they would experience. Have students list these details.

126

Making Sense

Pre-Writing: Gathering Sensory Details

Here's the Idea   A **descriptive paragraph** is like a painting. It presents a picture of a real or imaginary person, place, or thing. To make this picture live in the reader's mind, the writer of a descriptive paragraph uses sensory details. **Sensory details** describe things that can be *seen, heard, felt, smelled,* or *tasted.* Notice the use of sensory details in the following paragraph.

From halfway down the block, Miss Strangeworth could catch the heavy scent of her roses, and she moved a little more quickly. The perfume of roses meant home, and home meant the Strangeworth House on Pleasant Street. Miss Strangeworth stopped at her own front gate, as she always did, and looked with deep pleasure at her house, with the red and pink and white roses massed along the narrow lawn, and the rambler going up along the porch; and the neat, the unbelievably trim lines of the house itself, with its slimness and its washed white look. Every window sparkled, every curtain hung stiff and straight, and even the stones of the front walk were swept and clear.

—SHIRLEY JACKSON

To write a descriptive paragraph, you must first choose a subject. Once this is done, you must gather sensory details to create a vivid picture for your reader. One way to gather sensory details is through observation. Suppose, for example, that you want to describe a crowd of fans at a football game. To do this, you could go to a game and take notes. Your notes would include the things that you could see, hear, touch, taste, and smell. Another source of sensory details is your memory. If, for example, you wanted to describe a scene from your childhood, you could simply picture the scene in your mind. However, your memory of the scene would have to be clear enough to provide all the details you need. Whenever you write a description, try

126

to choose details that are specific enough to give your reader a clear picture of your subject.

Check It Out   Read the following description.

> The lamplight in the Store gave a soft make-believe feeling to our world that made me want to whisper and walk about on tiptoe. The odors of onions and oranges and kerosene had been mixing all night and wouldn't be disturbed until the wooden slat was removed from the door and the early morning air forced its way in with the bodies of people who had walked miles to reach the pickup place.   —MAYA ANGELOU

- What sensory details does this description use?

Try Your Skill   Read the following general topics. Choose one and narrow it so that it is more specific. For example, if you choose "a friend," narrow this topic to a specific friend. Then list as many sensory details as you can about your topic.

a kitchen	a friend	a traffic jam
a garden	a relative	a holiday celebration

Keep This in Mind

- Use sensory details to create a vivid description.
- Gather sensory details through observation or from your memory.

Now Write   Make a list of persons (an unusual neighbor, a bus driver), places (an abandoned house, a shopping mall), and objects (a painting, an exotic sports car) that you might want to describe.

Choose one of these subjects as a topic for your descriptive paragraph. Be sure your subject is narrow enough to be described well in just one paragraph. Make a list of sensory details that will help you to describe your subject. Save these notes.

Advanced Students

Give students the following list and ask them to use their imaginations as they make each item in the first column more vivid and specific by adding sensory details to it. Have them write their details in the second column.

Example:

horse   silky black mare
apple
trophy
crowd
snow
ambulance

Optional Practice

Ask students to look around the classroom and note what it looks, smells, and sounds like. Have them write a list of sensory details that describe the classroom. Ask students to read their lists and compare them with others.

Extending the Lesson

Ask students to picture in their minds the school cafeteria. Tell them to write a list of descriptive details about the cafeteria. Have students compare their lists. Stress that it is necessary to use as many of the five senses as possible to give the audience a clear idea of the topic.

Part 2

Objective

To use spatial order to organize a description

Presenting the Lesson

1. Read aloud **Here's the Idea.** Write *spatial order* on the chalkboard and ask students to define it.

2. Read and discuss **Check It Out.** Ask students whether the description has been organized from top-to-bottom, side-to-side, or around in a circle. Have a volunteer make a diagram of the workroom on the chalkboard.

3. Assign **Try Your Skill.** Have students work in pairs to complete the exercise. Remind them to use specific sensory details.

4. Read aloud **Keep This in Mind** and then assign **Now Write.**

Individualizing the Lesson

Less-Advanced Students

Have students reread **Here's the Idea.** Tell them to visualize their topic, starting at one point and working their way to a finish.

Advanced Students

Have students bring to class a descriptive real estate ad from a local paper. Discuss how the details have been organized in these ads. Then ask students to write a real estate ad for a home of their choice. Remind them to use spatial order to organize their copy.

Directional Signals

Pre-Writing: Using Spatial Order

Here's the Idea   As you learned in Part 1, a descriptive paragraph uses sensory details to create a vivid picture. These details are most effective when they are organized in a logical way.

The details in a description are often arranged according to spatial order. **Spatial order** shows how one detail in a description is related in space to other details. Using spatial order, you might describe a subject from top to bottom or from bottom to top. You might also describe it from left to right, from right to left, from near to far, or from far to near. Be sure to choose a pattern of spatial order that suits your subject. For example, you would be more likely to describe a tree from top to bottom than from near to far. Notice the use of spatial order in this description:

> Bonsai—the Oriental art of growing miniature trees—is my new hobby. My bonsai tree is prickly juniper, only eighteen inches high. I have carefully shaped my dwarf tree so that it resembles an umbrella. At the top, the spice-scented needles are tightly bunched. Below this cluster of needles, the tiny trunk is twisted and wrinkled. Below that, the roots of the juniper are covered with moss. The base of the bonsai tree is a shallow dish in which the tiny juniper is growing.

Sometimes it's difficult to arrange the details in a description according to spatial order. Suppose you were trying to describe the atmosphere at a rock concert or your feeling of exhilaration after winning a first place in a track meet. These descriptions are not well suited to spatial arrangement. Instead, you might arrange the details in whatever order you want the reader to notice them. Always arrange your details in an order that suits the kind of paragraph you are writing.

Check It Out   Read this description.

   Last weekend I helped my mother turn our once cluttered basement into a well-organized workroom for her new upholstery business. At the foot of the stairs we set up a display of fabric selections. Above the fabrics we stapled pictures of finished products. Along the wall to the left of the stairs we arranged samples of a variety of wood stains and varnishes. Beside this display, we set her sewing machine. On the adjoining wall we placed her workbench. Above the workbench, we hung her tools. Finally, we moved two newly reupholstered chairs against the fourth wall to show customers the end products of my mother's skills.

- How does this description use spatial order?

Try Your Skill   Imagine that you have been asked to write a description of a street in your town. You might choose the street on which you live. You might also choose a street in the business district. Choose a street, and make a list of sensory details that you could use to describe it. Arrange your details according to spatial order.

Keep This in Mind

- Use spatial order or some other logical order to organize the details in your description.

Now Write   Read your pre-writing notes from the last lesson. Arrange your details in a logical order. Save your organized notes in your folder.

Optional Practice

   Pass out copies of this description of a castle. Have students rearrange the details in a logical spatial order; from top to bottom, side to side, etc. Answers will vary.

5 A wooden walkway led around the top of the walls.

8 A deep moat surrounded the castle.

3 At the very top of the highest turret, a red and white flag fluttered.

1 The castle had four turrets on top.

9 A drawbridge hung over the moat, suspended with strong iron chains.

2 The southeast turret was the highest.

6 The walls were built with blocks of dark gray stone.

4 The sound of a trumpet could be heard, blaring from another turret.

7 Slender, leaded glass windows were set in the castle walls.

Extending the Lesson

   Refer students to the photograph on page 112. Ask them to describe the picture, starting from the front and working towards the background. Have students note other sensory details they might notice if they were in the scene such as sounds, smells, etc.

Part 3

Objective

To use appropriate pronouns, verbs, adjectives, and adverbs to create mood in a descriptive paragraph

Presenting the Lesson

1. Read aloud **Here's the Idea.** Write the following sentence on the chalkboard: "Thunder was in the mountains." Ask the class if they get a sense of mood from the statement. Ask students to suggest possible verbs and adverbs that are stronger and more specific to develop the mood. Discuss how the sentence is changed by use of strong, specific language.

2. Read **Check It Out.** Ask students what specific words help to create the mood of the paragraph. Ask whether these words are verbs, adverbs, nouns, or adjectives.

3. Assign **Try Your Skill.** Have students work in pairs or small groups to complete the exercise. Have them share their ideas.

4. Read **Keep This in Mind** and then assign **Now Write.** Tell the class that every description can create a mood. Even boredom is a mood. Ask students to choose verbs, adverbs, nouns, and adjectives carefully, and to be sure their words develop the mood they wish to create.

Individualizing the Lesson

Less-Advanced Students

1. Refer students to Handbook Section 6, Part 1.

Words Have Feelings

Pre-Writing: Creating Mood

Here's the Idea   Have you ever wondered why people enjoy listening to music? The answer, of course, is that music stirs powerful feelings in people. Music can make you feel happy, sad, tender, peaceful, or excited. These feelings are called **mood.**

Mood is extremely important in a description. Before you begin writing, you must decide what mood you want your writing to suggest. Mood is suggested by the language a writer uses. Nouns, verbs, adjectives, and adverbs can all suggest mood. For example, suppose you were going to describe a beach scene. To create one kind of mood, one that suggested a positive feeling, you might choose words like these:

Nouns	Adjectives	Verbs	Adverbs
sea gulls	sunny	lapping	brightly
sand castle	sparkling	splash	contentedly
popsicles	breezy	laughing	softly

To suggest a very different mood about the beach, you might use words like these:

Nouns	Adjectives	Verbs	Adverbs
sand fly	crowded	crash	hotly
sunburn	blinding	scream	fiercely
litter	sticky	shatter	harshly

When you are planning your description, think about the feeling you want to suggest. Write lists of nouns, adjectives, verbs, and adverbs that will help you to create a specific mood.

Check It Out   Read the following paragraph.

When I think of the home town of my youth, all that I seem to remember is dust—the brown, crumbly dust of late summer— arid, sterile dust that gets into the eyes and makes them water, gets into the throat and between the toes of bare brown feet. I don't know why I should remember only the dust. Surely there must have been lush green lawns and paved streets under leafy shade trees somewhere in town; but memory is an abstract painting—it does not present things as they are, but rather as they *feel*. And so, when I think of that time and that place, I remember only the dry September of the dirt roads and grass- less yards of the shanty-town where I lived.

—EUGENIA COLLIER

· What words help to create the mood of this paragraph?

Try Your Skill   Assume you have been asked to write a de- scription of a large sporting goods store on the first day of their annual "Half-Price Madness Sale." Write a brief statement indi- cating the mood you want to create. Then make a list of nouns, adjectives, verbs, and adverbs that will help you to suggest that feeling.

Keep This in Mind

· Mood is the feeling suggested by a piece of writing.
· Writers express mood through the language they use.

Now Write   Review the pre-writing notes you have made for your descriptive paragraph. What mood do you want to create in your description? Make a list of nouns, adjectives, verbs, and adverbs that will help you create that mood. Save your list in your folder. Use these words when you write your first draft.

131

2. Students may need assistance in discovering particularly strong verbs and modifiers. Have students form small groups and pass out the- sauruses from the school library. Give each group a few modifiers such as *sad, peaceful, angry,* or *happy*. Ask each group to find five verbs or adjectives that reflect each of these moods. Ask them to find strong, specific words.

Advanced Students

Tell students to imagine they are going on a boat ride. Ask them to make two lists; one with all the words they can think of to describe a terrible ride, and one with vocabu- lary to describe a wonderful ride. Encourage students to seek vivid, strong, and specific words.

Optional Practice

Copy and distribute the following paragraph. Have students replace weak, general language with strong, specific language to create a mood. Ahswers will vary.

Kyle moved down the street. He was in a hurry. Up ahead, he could see smoke coming out of his family's apartment building. Fire trucks and police cars went by very fast as he went on his way. People ran around and he could hear loud voices. The scene was one of complete chaos.

Extending the Lesson

Bring a variety of record albums to class: classical, folk, rock, jazz, etc. For each selection you play, ask the class to suggest words to de- scribe how the music made them feel. Ask the class about the mood of each piece of music. Discuss what images come to mind when listening to the music.

Objective

To use transitional words and phrases to show spatial order

Presenting the Lesson

1. Read aloud **Here's the Idea.** Remind students that they are trying to create a clear word picture for their readers. Transitional words and phrases are necessary for clarity. Have a volunteer read aloud the description of a bonsai tree on page 128. Ask the class to identify the transitions which help show spatial order.

2. Read and discuss **Check It Out.** Have students compare the transitions in this paragraph with those in the bonsai description on page 128. Ask a volunteer to draw a map of the Pompeii area on the chalkboard.

3. Assign **Try Your Skill.** Have students share their personal descriptions with each other.

4. Read **Keep This in Mind** and then assign **Now Write.** Remind students to begin their paragraphs with a strong topic sentence that introduces their subject.

Individualizing the Lesson

Less-Advanced Students

Students may need help writing their topic sentences. Have students think of three or four different topic sentences and help them to choose the one that best suits their description. Refer students to Section 8 to review all of the important stages of the process of writing.

Can You Place It?

Writing the First Draft

Here's the Idea When you write narrative paragraphs, you use transitional words and phrases to show *when* things occur. When you write descriptive paragraphs, you should use other transitions to show *where* things are. Here are some transitional words and phrases that help to show spatial order in descriptive paragraphs:

above	beside	in the center	over
against	between	near	side by side
ahead of	by	next to	south
alongside	down	north	throughout
at the end of	east	on	to the left
at the top	facing	on the bottom	to the right
around	in	on the corner	under
below	in back of	on the edge	up
beneath	in front of	outside	west

As you write the first draft of a descriptive paragraph, use transitions such as these. They will help your readers to understand where each item in the description is in relation to other items. You may place a transitional word or phrase at the beginning, in the middle, or at the end of a sentence, as follows:

Beside the curb sat a wet, shaggy dog.
Only the chimney could be seen *above* the flood waters.
The monkeys scurried in the trees *overhead*.

Check It Out Read this paragraph.

Until that year, Pompeii was a prosperous city of 25,000 people. Nearby was the Bay of Naples, an arm of the blue Mediterranean. Rich men came down from wealthy Rome, 125 miles to the north, to build luxurious seaside villas. Fertile farmlands occupied the fields surrounding Pompeii. Rising sharply behind the city was the 4,000-foot bulk of Mount Vesuvius, a grass-covered slope where the shepherds of Pompeii took their goats to graze. Pompeii was a busy city and a happy one. —ROBERT SILVERBERG

- What words and phrases in this paragraph tell *where?*

Try Your Skill The following paragraph contains blanks where transitional words and phrases should be inserted. Add transitional words and phrases to this paragraph. Use words from the list in this lesson or any others that tell *where.* Be aware that there are no right or wrong answers. Use any words or phrases you want to create a personal description. Compare your description with those of your classmates.

_____, a path wound its way through the forest. We decided to explore the path. _____, silver spruce trees pointed skyward. A narrow stream gurgled along _____. Red-winged blackbirds chattered _____ in the trees. _____, we spied a fawn. Its mother followed _____. _____, the forest was alive.

Keep This in Mind

- In a description, transitional words and phrases that tell *where* can be used to show spatial order.

Now Write Write the first draft of your descriptive paragraph. Follow your organized pre-writing notes as you write. Introduce the subject of your description in your topic sentence. Develop your description with sensory details in the body of your paragraph. Use transitional words and phrases to show the order of your details. Sum up your description in a strong ending sentence. Save your first draft in your folder.

Part 5

Objective

To revise the first draft of a descriptive paragraph

Presenting the Lesson

1. Read aloud **Here's the Idea.** Discuss each question. Tell students to refer to these questions as they revise their paragraphs, and to make sure each question can be answered affirmatively.

2. Read and discuss **Check It Out.** Ask students whether the details in this paragraph have been organized effectively.

3. Assign **Try Your Skill.** Ask students to take their time, and examine the paragraph closely for errors.

4. Read aloud **Keep This in Mind** and then assign **Now Write.** Encourage students to rewrite entire sentences, if necessary, to make their descriptions the best they can be.

Individualizing the Lesson

Less-Advanced Students

1. Discuss the importance of using as many of the five senses as possible in a description. Not every description will use all five, but students should try to give their readers a variety of sensory details.

2. Have students work in pairs as they complete **Now Write.** Point out that one person may catch an error that another person overlooked.

Advanced Students

Ask these students to concentrate on refining the words they want

Revising Your Descriptive Paragraph

Here's the Idea   The first draft of your descriptive paragraph is just a rough version of what you want to say. It must be revised before it can be considered finished.

When you revise your paragraph, ask yourself these questions.

1. Is my topic sentence interesting? Is it informative?

2. Are the details in my description vivid? Can the reader see, hear, taste, smell, or feel what I am describing?

3. Did I include enough details to develop the description?

4. Are my details arranged in a logical order?

5. Have I used transitional words and phrases to show order? Do these words and phrases lead from one detail to the next?

6. Have I used specific language to suggest a particular mood?

When you have finished revising, check for errors in grammar, capitalization, punctuation, and spelling. Correct any errors that you find.

Check It Out   Read the following descriptive paragraph.

The professor had succeeded in making a French garden in Hamilton. There was not a blade of grass; it was a tidy half-acre of glistening gravel and glistening shrubs and bright flowers. There were trees, of course; a spreading horse-chestnut, a row of slender Lombardy poplars at the back, along the white wall, and in the middle two symmetrical round-topped linden trees. Masses of green-brier grew in the corners, the prickly stems interwoven and clipped until they were like great bushes. There was a bed for salad herbs. Salmon pink geraniums dripped over the wall. The French marigolds and dahlias were just now at their best—such dahlias as no one else in Hamilton could grow.

—WILLA CATHER

- Does the topic sentence introduce the subject of the description?
- What sensory details does this description include? Are there enough details to develop the description?
- What mood does the description suggest? What words help to create that feeling?

Try Your Skill Proofread the following paragraph. You should be able to find and correct nine errors in grammar, usage, and mechanics.

The sleeck Indy race car was fastened securely to the trailer. The nose of the car was fited with a wide, ground-effects spoiler. Gawdy product decals decorated the front end. Further back, a narrow plastic windscreen wrapped around the cockpit. Nestled in the rear of the car, was a awesome, chrome Turbocharged engine. A row of exhaust pipes were protruding from it. Above the engine, another spoiler was positioned to catch the wind and keep the car from flying off the track. Four fat black tires set at the corners of the car. With it's metallic silver paint and aerodynamic body, the car could have been mistaken for a starship from another galaxy.

Keep This in Mind

- When revising your descriptive paragraph:
- Be sure to use specific sensory details.
- Arrange your details in a logical order.
- Use transitional words and phrases that tell *where*.
- Use specific nouns, adjectives, verbs, and adverbs that will suggest a particular mood.

Now Write Revise your descriptive paragraph, using the guidelines in this lesson. Then proofread your description for errors in grammar and mechanics. Correct any errors you find. Make a neat final copy and save it in your folder.

to use in their descriptions. Guide them in their choice of specific language.

Optional Practice

Have students choose partners. Distribute the following paragraph and ask students to revise it, paying careful attention to the guidelines for revising a description. Answers will vary.

Inside the abandoned mining shaft it was real dark. There was a few old rusted coal cars around. Water dripped from the dark roof. An axe rested against a stack of old timber railroad tyes. The air was damp and chilly. Strange, gurgling sounds of running water could be heard deep in the shaft. Outside, the sun was shining and it was a beautiful spring day. But not inside the mine shaft.

Extending the Lesson

Ask the class to think about why people see certain things differently. For example, one person might feel exhilarated and cheerful when standing atop a tall building or mountain. Another person might feel terror in the same circumstance. Lead a discussion with the students on how they feel about a rainy day, fog, a crowded beach, etc. Ask students to reflect on the different moods each scene brings to mind.

Section **11** Objectives

1. To know that an explanatory paragraph explains how to do something or how something works or happens

2. To know that an explanatory paragraph must contain all the necessary steps of the process

3. To know that each step in the process must be arranged in step-by-step order

4. To know how to use transitional words and phrases to show step-by-step order

5. To know and use the guidelines for revising an explanatory paragraph

Preparing the Students

Ask students to define the word *process*. Point out to them that they observe or take part in processes every day: starting the car, watching a football game, even writing a paragraph. Explain to the students that this Section will teach them how to explain processes clearly and completely.

Additional Resources

Mastery Test — page 25 in the test booklet

Practice Book — pages 56–59

Duplicating Masters — pages 56–59

The Explanatory Paragraph

Explaining a Process

Teaching Special Populations

LD See **Teaching Special Populations,** pages 82–83. Be sure students understand the concept of step-by-step order.

ESL Discuss with students how the concepts and vocabulary of time vary from culture to culture. Provide students with additional exercises on transitional words that show time.

NSD See **Teaching Special Populations,** pages 82–83. Have students read their revised paragraphs aloud to a partner, and have the partner note where further revision in language is necessary.

Let Me Tell You

Pre-Writing: Explaining a Process

Objectives

1. To know that an explanatory paragraph explains how to do something or how something works or happens

2. To know that an explanatory paragraph must contain all the necessary steps of the process

Presenting the Lesson

1. Read aloud **Here's the Idea.** Stress that an explanatory paragraph can explain how to do something or how something works or happens.

2. Ask for a volunteer to read the paragraph from **Check It Out.** Have students answer the questions following the paragraph.

3. Read aloud and assign **Try Your Skill.**

4. Read aloud **Keep This in Mind** and then assign **Now Write.**

Individualizing the Lesson

Less-Advanced Students

Have students think of examples for each type of explanatory paragraph.

Advanced Students

Have students bring to class one example of each type of explanatory paragraph. For example, a recipe would be a good example of an explanatory paragraph telling how to do something. Display these paragraphs in class.

Here's the Idea   Hardly a day goes by that you don't explain something to someone. You might explain how you made that delicious carrot cake, how your science experiment went, or how to get to the concert without fighting traffic. All of these are explanations of how to do something or how something happens or works.

You can develop a written explanation of a process by writing an explanatory paragraph. You could write an explanatory paragraph to explain how to paint a car, how to string a violin, or how earthquakes happen. When you choose your topic, be sure to choose one that interests you. Also, choose a topic that is narrow enough to be developed in just one paragraph.

After you have chosen your topic, you will have to list all the important steps of the process. For example, if you had chosen the topic "How to Make the Hottest Chili in Town," your notes would include everything from the purchasing of all the ingredients to the final seasoning just before serving.

When you write your pre-writing notes, be sure to include all the necessary steps of the process. If you leave any steps out, your readers may become confused. Write each step clearly and simply so that your explanation will be easy to understand.

Check It Out   Read the following explanatory paragraph that explains a process.

There is an art to taking a good photograph. The first step is to decide exactly what you want in the picture. This step is called "composing" the picture. When you have composed the picture the way you want it, your next step is to focus the subject. This requires turning the focusing ring on the lens until the image you see through the camera is crisp and sharply defined. The next step is to set the f-stop by turning the f-stop ring on the lens. This adjusts the amount of light entering the camera so that the picture will be properly exposed. Now you are ready to press the shutter release and take a beautiful photograph.

- What process is explained in this paragraph?
- Are all the steps included?
- Is each step explained simply and clearly?

Try Your Skill The first step in writing your explanatory paragraph about a process is choosing your topic. Take some time to think about processes that interest you and that you are familiar with. You can choose to explain how to do something, how something works, or how something happens. Make a list of six different processes that you could write an explanatory paragraph about. Be sure each topic is narrow enough to be covered well in a paragraph. Save your list in your folder.

Keep This in Mind

- An explanatory paragraph explains how to do something or how something works or happens.
- Include all the necessary steps of the process.
- Explain each step clearly and simply.

Now Write Look over the list of six topics you developed in **Try Your Skill.** Choose one topic for the explanatory paragraph you will write. Then make a list of all of the important steps involved in the process you have chosen to explain. Don't leave out any important steps. Save your pre-writing notes in your folder.

Part 2

First Things First

Objective

To know that each step in the process must be arranged in step-by-step order

Pre-Writing: Using Step-by-Step Order

Presenting the Lesson

1. Read aloud **Here's the Idea.** On the chalkboard write *step-by-step order.* Point out that once all the necessary steps of a process have been determined, they must be arranged in the proper order. This order is called *step-by-step order.*

2. Have a student read aloud the paragraph from **Check It Out.** Ask students to answer the questions from this exercise.

3. Assign **Try Your Skill.**

4. Read aloud **Keep This in Mind** and then assign **Now Write.**

Individualizing the Lesson

Less-Advanced Students

Have students reread **Here's the Idea.** Then have them work on **Try Your Skill** in pairs.

Advanced Students

After students have completed **Now Write,** ask them to mix up the step-by-step order of their pre-writing notes. Have students exchange these mixed up notes and put them back into the correct step-by-step order.

Optional Practice

Have students put the following pre-writing notes for polishing silver into correct step-by-step order.

Here's the Idea   When a mechanic replaces the parts of a car, he or she must place the parts in the right order. Otherwise, the car will not run properly. When you write a paragraph, you must also place the parts in the right order. Otherwise, your readers will become confused.

In an explanatory paragraph that explains a process, information should be presented in **step-by-step order.** This is the order in which something happens or is done. To organize your explanation, begin with your pre-writing notes. These list every step in the process that you are writing about. Decide which is the first step in the process. Place this step first. Then, decide which is the second step. Place this step second. Continue in this way until you reach the last step. By placing each step in the proper order, you can make certain that your reader will understand the process from beginning to end.

Check It Out   Read the following paragraph.

There's really nothing to painting a room. Of course, the first thing to do is buy paint. After buying the paint, open the paint and put the brush in. Start painting. Of course, you need to cover all the furniture when you get home. You must mask around areas you don't want painted, such as windows, trim, and light switch plates. Before you go and buy the paint, be sure you know exactly what color you want. It is helpful if you bring a piece of material from a couch or draperies so that the color of the paint will match. I mentioned earlier that it is important to cover the furniture. This should be one of the first things you do. Also, before you cover the furniture, it helps to move it all to the center of the room so it is not in the way when you paint. When you are all finished remember to put the brushes away. All brushes should be washed thoroughly before putting them away.

- What process is explained in this paragraph?
- Is this paragraph organized in step-by-step order? Explain your answer.

Try Your Skill   Rewrite the paragraph in **Check It Out.** Place all of the steps in proper step-by-step order. If you feel any steps are missing, add them. Compare your rewritten paragraph with those of your classmates.

Keep This in Mind

- Step-by-step order is the order in which the steps of a process happen or are to be done.
- Use step-by-step order to organize the details in an explanatory paragraph explaining a process.

Now Write   Organize your pre-writing notes from **Now Write** in the last lesson into step-by-step order. Be certain that all the necessary steps are included and are arranged in the order in which they happen or should be done. Save your organized notes in your folder.

6 buff to shine
5 wipe off polish
4 let dry to haze
1 shake polish
3 spread polish over silver
2 apply polish to cloth

Extending the Lesson

Have students find out the proper way to raise and lower the American flag. Suggest they call their local police or fire department for information. Be sure they include the steps involved for folding the flag. Have them arrange the steps in correct step-by-step order.

Part 3

Objective

To know how to use transitional words and phrases to show step-by-step order

Presenting the Lesson

1. Read aloud **Here's the Idea.** On the chalkboard write *topic sentence* and *transitional words and phrases.* Review with students the function of a good topic sentence. Explain that transitional words and phrases guide the reader from one step of the process to the next.

2. Ask for a volunteer to read the paragraph from **Check It Out.** Have students discuss the questions from this exercise.

3. Assign **Try Your Skill.**

4. Read aloud **Keep This in Mind** and then assign **Now Write.**

Individualizing the Lesson

Less-Advanced Students

Have students make a numerical list including each important step from the paragraph in **Check It Out.**

Advanced Students

Have students concentrate specifically on transitional words and phrases. Have them review **Here's the Idea** to familiarize themselves with some useful words and phrases. Ask them to think about appropriate transitional words and phrases that will help them when writing their explanatory compositions.

Trial Run

Writing the First Draft

Here's the Idea   The best way to begin the first draft of your explanatory paragraph is with a good topic sentence. This sentence should tell your readers exactly what process you intend to explain. It should also capture your reader's attention. Avoid dull topic sentences such as the following:

> In this paragraph I will explain how to throw a football properly.

This sentence lets the reader know what to expect. However, it is not very interesting. This topic sentence is much better:

> To throw a football properly, you have to know all the right moves.

After you have written your topic sentence explain, in order, all the steps in your process. Present each step in a separate sentence. Use transitional words and phrases to guide your readers from step to step. The following words and phrases are particularly useful in paragraphs that explain processes.

first	when	the next step	finally
second	afterwards	at the same time	then
third	later	while	next
as	after that	following that	at last
	at least	the last step	

Of course, you are not limited to these particular words and phrases. You may also use any other transitions.

Check It Out   Read the following paragraph.

> An omelet is a quick and tasty breakfast. First, whisk together three eggs and a tablespoon of cream or milk until all is

well blended. Then prepare a filling. Chopped vegetables, shredded cheeses, and crumbled bacon or sausage are all delicious possibilities. As soon as the eggs and filling are ready, melt a tablespoon of butter in an omelet pan over medium heat. When the butter has melted, slowly pour in the eggs. Once the eggs on the bottom have set, lift the edge of the omelet with a spatula and tilt the pan so that the uncooked eggs on top will run under and cook. Now that the omelet is almost cooked through, sprinkle the filling over the top. Next, use your spatula to carefully fold the omelet in half. Cook the folded omelet for several minutes so that the filling heats through. Finally, slide the omelet onto a warm plate, garnish with a sprinkling of chopped parsley or some other herbs, and dig in!

- What process is explained in this paragraph?
- Are the steps arranged in proper step-by-step order?

Try Your Skill   Reread the paragraph in **Check It Out**. Make a list of all of the transitional words and phrases that have been used to lead the reader from one step in the process to the next step.

Keep This in Mind

- Begin an explanatory paragraph with an informative and interesting topic sentence.
- Use correct step-by-step order.
- Use transitional words and phrases to show step-by-step order and to help your readers move easily from one idea to the next.

Now Write   Write the first draft of your explanatory paragraph that explains a process. Follow your organized pre-writing notes which should include all of the necessary steps of the process you are explaining. Start with a good topic sentence and use step-by-step order. Save your first draft in your folder.

Optional Practice

Have students write several possible topic sentences for their paragraphs. Volunteers should read their sentences, and the class should decide which of the sentences from each list is the most interesting, direct, and informative.

Extending the Lesson

Have students make lists of the specific transitional words and phrases they used in their paragraphs. Duplicate each list and distribute them for future reference.

Part 4

The Final Touch

Revising Your Explanatory Paragraph

Objective

To know and use the guidelines for revising an explanatory paragraph

Presenting the Lesson

1. Read aloud **Here's the Idea** and discuss each question.

2. Read and discuss the revised paragraph in **Check It Out.**

3. Assign and discuss **Try Your Skill.** Point out that transitional words and phrases help the reader move easily from one idea to the next.

4. Read aloud **Keep This in Mind** and then assign **Now Write.**

Individualizing the Lesson

Less-Advanced Students

Work with students on revising their paragraphs. First point out the strengths of each student's work. Then guide them to discover their weaknesses and errors.

Advanced Students

Have students work in pairs to revise their paragraphs. Point out that this system will give them more objectivity in their revisions.

Optional Practice

Project volunteers' revised paragraphs on an opaque projector. Have the class suggest further constructive revisions.

Here's the Idea   Every step in an explanatory paragraph should be explained clearly and completely. Nothing in the paragraph should keep the reader from understanding the process being explained. Therefore, you must revise your paragraph carefully. When you revise, read your rough draft several times. As you read, ask these questions.

1. Is the topic sentence interesting? Does it tell what process I am explaining?
2. Have I included all the important steps in the process?
3. Are the steps organized in the order in which they happen?
4. Is each step explained clearly and completely?
5. Do my transitions guide my reader from step to step?

Once you have revised your content, organization, and word choice, proofread the paragraph. Find and correct any errors.

Check It Out   Read the following revised paragraph.

Teaching your dog to perform simple tricks can be a rewarding experience.
~~Most dogs enjoy performing tricks.~~ You may want to teach your dog to shake hands. *First,* Decide what simple command you will use. *Second,* Call your dog by *its* name and make it sit in front of you. Keep *your dog's* ~~its~~ attention through constant eye contact. *Next,* Say the dog's name followed by the command. *At the same time,* Gently nudge the dog's paw. Repeat these steps until the first time your dog correctly responds to your command. *Then,* Immediately reward the dog with a dog biscuit and a great deal of praise.

- How has the writer improved the topic sentence?
- What transitional words have been added? How do they improve the paragraph?

Try Your Skill Examine the following explanatory paragraph. Revise it, paying particular attention to transitions and to providing a clear and interesting topic sentence.

You take a pail and add a mild soap and fill it with water. Bring it out to your car. Hose down the car with water. Using a soft sponge or towel, wet it with the soapy solution and begin washing your car. Start with the top. Don't wash the windows with soap or they will become smeary in the rain. Don't wash the entire car without rinsing it as you go along. Be sure to wash the hubcaps and the tires with a stiff brush. Dry the car. Move the car into the shade and apply a good paste wax. Let it dry to a haze before rubbing it off. Rub it off. Clean the windows inside and out. Vacuum the interior of the car. Your car is the cleanest on the block now!

Keep This in Mind

- Revise your explanatory paragraph so that it begins with an informative and interesting topic sentence.
- Include all the necessary steps of the process and order them in step-by-step order.
- Use transitional words and phrases to show the order of each step and to help your readers move easily from one idea to the next.
- Proofread your paragraph for errors in grammar and mechanics.

Now Write Using the questions in this lesson, revise your explanatory paragraph. Remember to proofread for errors in grammar and mechanics. When you have finished revising your paragraph, make a final copy. Save your work.

145

Have a class discussion in which students offer information about how they get their writing ideas and what they consider when they revise their work.

Section 12 Objectives

1. To write an explanatory paragraph that expresses an opinion

2. To know that opinions are supported with accurate facts and logical reasons

3. To organize facts and reasons in order of importance

4. To use transitional words and phrases to introduce ideas and show the order of their importance

5. To write the first draft of an explanatory paragraph that presents an opinion

6. To revise an explanatory paragraph that presents an opinion

Preparing the Students

On the chalkboard write *opinion* and *fact.* Ask students to give their own definitions of these words. List their definitions. Then have them look up these two words in the dictionary.

Ask students to decide whether the following statements are opinions or facts.

F 1. The 1984 Summer Olympics were held in Los Angeles, California.

O 2. Jesse Owens was the greatest American track and field athlete.

F 3. Uri Gagarin was the first person to orbit the earth.

O 4. The 55 mph speed limit is too low.

O 5. Capital punishment should be banned.

F 6. The continent with the greatest number of countries is Africa.

Additional Resources

Mastery Test — page 26 in the test booklet

Practice Book — pages 60–63

Duplicating Masters — pages 60–63

The Explanatory Paragraph

Presenting an Opinion

Teaching Special Populations

LD See **Teaching Special Populations,** pages 82–83.

ESL Students may be shy of stating opinions in class. Some may feel it impolite to overtly disagree with a teacher or with classmates. To help students become comfortable stating opinions, discuss several topics in class that will elicit opposing opinions.

Be sure students understand how to indicate sequence and order of importance of their ideas.

Students may not realize that modals are expressed in the inflection of the verb. Explain the function of words that indicate mood, such as *may, can, should* or *must*.

NSD See **Teaching Special Populations,** pages 82–83.

Mind and Matter

Pre-Writing: Developing an Opinion

Presenting the Lesson

1. Read aloud **Here's the Idea.** On the chalkboard write *judgment, prediction,* and *statement of obligation.* Ask students to provide examples of these kinds of opinions.

Point out that explanatory paragraphs that present an opinion, like all other explanatory paragraphs, need a strong topic sentence. The topic sentence will be a statement of opinion, and therefore must be clear and concise. Explain that the topic sentence will be followed by facts and logical reasons that support it.

2. Read the pre-writing notes from **Check It Out.** Have students discuss the questions orally.

3. Assign **Try Your Skill.** For less-advanced students, have them work in pairs.

4. Read aloud **Keep This in Mind** and then assign **Now Write.**

Individualizing the Lesson

Less-Advanced Students

Have students carefully reread **Here's the Idea.** Have them work in small groups to choose topics and write topic sentences. Help them to choose appropriate facts and supporting reasons.

Here's the Idea   In the last chapter, you learned how to write an explanatory paragraph that tells how. Such paragraphs are used to explain processes. In this chapter, you will learn how to write an explanatory paragraph that tells why. Such paragraphs are used to express and support opinions.

Everyone has opinions. An opinion is a belief you hold. Your opinion might be a judgment, a prediction, or a statement of obligation. A judgment tells how you feel about something.

> Aerobic exercise is the best exercise of all.

A prediction tells what you think will happen in the future.

> During the next twenty years, computers will play an increasingly important role in everyday life.

A statement of obligation tells what you believe ought to be done about something.

> Governments should fund public transportation to reduce air pollution from cars.

Always begin your pre-writing notes for this explanatory paragraph by stating an opinion. This opinion can be the topic sentence of your paragraph. Try to write the opinion as simply and directly as possible.

The next step in developing your paragraph is to list reasons and facts that support your opinion. The reasons should be logical. The facts should be accurate and provable. Try to list enough supporting facts and opinions to convince your readers that your opinion is sound.

Check It Out   Read the following statement of an opinion and the reasons and facts supporting it.

Opinion: All automobile drivers and passengers should be required to wear seat belts.
　　　　　—lowers insurance costs due to decreased injuries
　　　　　—lessens chance of injury in crash
　　　　　—saves lives

- Is the opinion a judgment, a prediction, or a statement of obligation?
- Is the opinion supported with logical reasons and accurate facts?

Try Your Skill　From the following list of opinions choose one you agree with. Support that opinion with four or five accurate facts or logical reasons. Save your work in your folder.

1. Women should receive equal pay for equal work.
2. Holidays have become too commercial.
3. Employers should not be allowed to pay teenagers less than the minimum wage.
4. Those people who are eligible to vote should use that right.
5. America should explore the use of solar power more extensively.

Keep This in Mind

- When you want to present your opinion about something, write an explanatory paragraph.
- Always support your opinion with accurate facts and logical reasons.

Now Write　What do you feel strongly about? Spend time thinking about an issue or subject that interests you. Write a clear and direct sentence that states your opinion. Then, list accurate facts and logical reasons that support your belief. Save your pre-writing notes in your folder.

Advanced Students

Ask students to bring in three editorials which focus on issues of interest to students. Ask students to determine if the editorials are judgments, predictions, or statements of obligation.

Optional Practice

Divide the class into two groups—A and B. Give each group the same opinion (do not give it in sentence form). Have group A list as many facts and reasons as they can in support of the opinion, and have group B list as many facts and reasons as they can against the opinion. Ask each group to save their lists.

Extending the Lesson

Have groups A and B each write a clear and direct topic sentence stating the group's position. Then ask each group to neatly indicate the most important of the supporting reasons they listed. Be sure students save their work.

Objective

To organize facts and reasons in order of importance

Presenting the Lesson

1. Read aloud **Here's the Idea.** On the chalkboard write *order of importance.* Be sure that students fully understand this method of organization.

On the chalkboard write the three reasons students should participate in local elections. Have students discuss if the reasons are listed in order of importance from least important to most important.

2. Read aloud the pre-writing notes. Ask students for a volunteer to read the paragraph from **Check It Out.**

3. Assign **Try Your Skill.**

4. Read aloud **Keep This in Mind** and then assign **Now Write.**

Individualizing the Lesson

Less-Advanced Students

Have students reread **Here's the Idea** and **Check It Out.** Have them work in pairs as they do **Now Write,** checking one another's work.

Advanced Students

Ask students to share their organized pre-writing notes with the class. Have the class determine whether or not the organization makes sense.

The Order of Things

Pre-Writing: Organizing an Opinion

Here's the Idea As you already know, the ideas in a paragraph should be organized logically. By following a logical order, you help your reader to understand how your ideas are related. When you write an explanatory paragraph in order to present an opinion, organize your ideas according to the **order of importance.** In other words, order your ideas from the least important to the most important.

Begin by stating your opinion. This will be your topic sentence. Then, organize the supporting ideas from your pre-writing notes. These will make up the body of your paragraph. Start with the least important of your supporting ideas. Place this idea first. Then, find the next most important supporting idea. Place this second. Continue in this way until you reach the most important supporting idea of all.

Suppose, for example, that you are writing about why students should become involved in local elections. You might organize your supporting ideas from most important to least important, as follows:

1. gives students something to do after school
2. helps students to learn about important local issues
3. teaches students how their political system works

Check It Out Examine the following pre-writing notes.

Opinion: more jobs should be available for teenagers

Reasons: want something to do
need to earn money
teenagers are good workers
need to learn responsibility

Now read the following paragraph.

More jobs should be made available for teenagers. First of all, teenagers want something to do other than just "hanging out." Like everybody else, teens want to feel as if they are contributing to society. Second, teenagers are good workers. They are energetic, and they are often willing to take jobs that older people don't want. More important, teenagers need to earn money. By the time a person is sixteen or seventeen years old, it's not right to expect Mom and Dad to pay for everything. Teens want to be able to pay their own share and to be able to buy for themselves the things that they want. Finally, working teaches reponsibility. Working teens learn to deal with money and with people. They also learn some important things about themselves. Providing more jobs for teens is a way for society to encourage self-sufficiency and responsibility among young people.

- Does the topic sentence state an opinion clearly?
- Are the supporting reasons in this paragraph arranged in the order of their importance? Explain your answer.

Try Your Skill   Look over the pre-writing notes you made in **Try Your Skill** in the last lesson. Organize them in the order of importance, from the least important to the most important.

Keep This in Mind

- Organize your facts and reasons in order of their importance, from the least important idea to the most important.

Now Write   Look at the pre-writing notes you made in the last lesson for your explanatory paragraph. Which of the reasons or facts you listed to support your opinion is the most important? Which is the next in importance? Examine your notes carefully. Arrange your reasons or facts from the least important idea to the most important. Save your organized pre-writing notes in your folder.

Optional Practice

Have students form groups A and B again. Have them arrange, in order of importance from least important to most important, the pre-writing notes from **Optional Practice** in the last lesson.

Extending the Lesson

Find editorials or statements of opinion from magazines or newspapers that would be of interest to the class. Have students read and discuss the opinions giving close attention to the topic sentences and the order in which the supporting facts and reasons have been organized.

Objectives

1. To use transitional words and phrases to introduce ideas and show the order of their importance

2. To write the first draft of an explanatory paragraph that presents an opinion

Presenting the Lesson

1. Read aloud **Here's the Idea.** On the chalkboard write the words *topic sentence, transitional words and phrases,* and *concluding sentence.* Point out that the guidelines from **Here's the Idea** will help students present their opinions clearly and convincingly.

2. Have a student read the paragraph from **Check It Out.** Have the class discuss the questions pertaining to the paragraph.

3. Assign **Try Your Skill.**

4. Read aloud **Keep This in Mind** and then assign **Now Write.**

Individualizing the Lesson

Less-Advanced Students

Have students reread **Here's the Idea.** Before assigning **Try Your Skill,** divide the students into small groups to do the exercise.

Advanced Students

Have students pay special attention to their topic sentences. Remind them that this is when they should get their reader's attention. Have them study editorials from newspapers or magazines to understand how professionals create attention-grabbing topic sentences.

152

Here's Why

Writing the First Draft

Here's the Idea   When you write the first draft of an explanatory paragraph that presents an opinion, always keep your purpose in mind. Your purpose is to explain your opinion as convincingly as possible. The following guidelines will help you to present your opinions forcefully.

1.   Make sure your topic sentence states your opinion directly. Avoid beginning your topic sentence with *I feel, I think, I believe,* or *In my opinion.* Such sentence openers will make your opinion sound weak. Compare the following topic sentences. Which sounds stronger?

> I feel that, perhaps, our school should start a summer theater program.
> Our school should start a summer theater program.

2.   Use transitional words and phrases to connect your ideas. There are two kinds of transitions you can use. One kind introduces reasons or facts. *Because, so, since, if, therefore,* and *as a result* are transitions of this kind. Another useful type of transition shows order of importance. *First, second, more important, most important,* and *finally* are transitions of this kind.

3.   End your paragraph with a strong concluding sentence. This sentence may restate your opinion in different words. It may also summarize the ideas you have given to support your opinion.

Check It Out   Read the following paragraph.

152

Every high school student should work for a candidate in a local election campaign. First of all, it is a public service to help candidates by stuffing envelopes and answering phones. More important, by becoming involved, the student will learn first-hand what issues are important to the community and how local government works. As a result, the student will be better prepared to participate as an informed citizen.

- Does the topic sentence state an opinion directly?
- Is the supporting evidence organized in order of importance? Which transitions are used?
- Does the concluding sentence sum up the argument?

Try Your Skill Reread the paragraph in **Check It Out.** Write two different ending sentences for this paragraph. Be sure each sentence sums up the opinion or the reasons that support it.

Keep This in Mind

- State your opinion clearly and directly in the topic sentence.
- Use transitional words and phrases to introduce your reasons and show the order of their importance.
- Write a strong concluding sentence to sum up your ideas.

Now Write Present your opinion by writing the first draft of your explanatory paragraph. Be sure to include a clear topic sentence, transitional words and phrases, and a strong ending sentence to conclude your paragraph and sum up your opinion and reasons. Save your first draft in your folder.

Optional Practice

Again, divide students into groups A and B. Have each group write a first draft of an explanatory paragraph from the notes they organized in **Optional Practice** from the previous lesson.

Extending the Lesson

Have students bring to class letters-to-the-editor from newspapers or magazines. Explain that these opinion paragraphs are written by people just like themselves. Have students apply what they have learned about this kind of explanatory paragraph to *evaluate* the letters. Instruct students to look for good topic sentences, and to see if the reasons offered in the letters have been organized in order of their importance.

Part 4

Objective

To revise an explanatory paragraph that presents an opinion

Presenting the Lesson

1. Read aloud **Here's the Idea.** Discuss with students each of the guidelines for revising their explanatory paragraphs.

2. Read and discuss how the paragraph from **Check It Out** has been revised.

3. Assign **Try Your Skill.**

4. Read aloud **Keep This in Mind.** Ask if students have any questions.

5. Assign **Now Write.**

Individualizing the Lesson

Less-Advanced Students

Have students carefully study the guidelines for revision. Ask them to give special attention to ordering their reasons from the least important to the most important and to using transitions that indicate this order.

Advanced Students

Have students reread **Here's the Idea.** When revising their paragraphs, instruct students to give special attention to their closing sentence. Point out that since this is the last impression their readers will have of their opinion, students will want to make their concluding sentence as strong and conclusive as they can.

Optional Practice

Divide students into groups A and B. Have each group evaluate the

154

Last, But Not Least

Revising Your Explanatory Paragraph

Here's the Idea   When you have completed the first draft, you are ready to revise your paragraph. As when revising other types of paragraphs, read your paragraph over several times. Check your content and organization as you read. Ask yourself the following questions to identify possible areas of improvement.

1. Does your topic sentence state your opinion clearly and directly?

2. Is your paragraph unified? Have you supported your opinion with enough evidence? Are your facts accurate? Are your reasons logical?

3. Have you presented your supporting ideas in order from least important to most important?

4. Is your paragraph coherent? Have you used transitional words and phrases to show how your supporting ideas are related?

5. Does your paragraph end with a strong concluding sentence? Does this sentence restate your opinion or summarize your supporting ideas?

After you have made any necessary revisions, proofread your paragraph. Correct any errors in grammar, punctuation, capitalization, and spelling.

Check It Out   Notice how the following explanatory paragraph has been revised.

- How has this paragraph been improved through revision?

154

Everyone who wants to join a team should. ~~Because~~ every-
one needs ~~exersize~~ *exercise* and being on a team ~~helps.~~ A player ~~could~~
~~still not make a teem if everyone else were better. And a player~~
~~could enjoy a sport and be very good at it.~~ ~~Tryouts should not~~
~~be part of school team sports.~~ Also school teams should not ~~just~~
~~be there~~ to win games. You ~~should learn~~ about a sport and how
to play it ~~in school.~~

Handwritten annotations: be allowed to. First of all, / is an enjoyable way to work out. / and / team someone / Moreover, / Finally, / formed just / ing / well is the most important part of school athletics.

Try Your Skill   Revise this paragraph.

In my opinion, I think that automobile drivers and pasengers
should be recquired to wear seat belts. Wearing a seat belt
would lower the cost of insurance. If you have a seat belt on,
you have a better chance of not being hurt in a crash. Seat belts
save lives, too. That's my opinion.

Keep This in Mind

- State an opinion clearly and directly in an explanatory paragraph that presents an opinion.
- Use accurate facts and logical reasons to support
  the opinion.
- Make sure the supporting evidence is arranged in
  order of importance from the least important idea
  to the most important.
- Use transitional words and phrases to present reasons and facts and to show their order.
- End the paragraph with a strong concluding sentence that sums up your opinion.

Now Write   Revise the first draft of your explanatory para-
graph presenting an opinion. Use the questions in this lesson to
guide your revision. Make a final copy and save it.

first draft they completed in the previous lesson and revise it according
to the guidelines presented on page
154.

Extending the Lesson

When students have finished revising their group paragraph, have
each group select a speaker. Ask
each speaker to read the group's
paragraph. Ask students to decide
which group's opinion has been
presented with the most interesting
topic sentence, the best supporting
reasons and facts, and the most effective concluding sentence.

Section **13** Objectives

1. To know that an explanatory paragraph can state a definition

2. To know that a successful definition includes both the general and specific characteristics of the subject being defined

3. To learn that an explanatory paragraph stating a definition begins with a general statement followed by specific details

4. To write a first draft of a paragraph which states and develops a definition

5. To revise a paragraph that states a definition

Preparing the Students

On a table, display a small telescope, a microscope, a pair of eyeglasses, and some binoculars. Have students examine each instrument.

Point out that each instrument belongs to a general class of optical instruments used to enhance vision. However, each of these optical aids has specific qualities which distinguishes it from the others. Ask students to name several specific characteristics of each instrument.

Then explain to students that a definition first places a subject in a general class and then offers specific characteristics that make the subject different from other members of that class.

Additional Resources

Mastery Test — page 27 in the test booklet

Practice Book — pages 64–67

Duplicating Masters — pages 64–67

The Explanatory Paragraph

Stating a Definition

Teaching Special Populations

LD See **Teaching Special Populations,** pages 82–83.

ESL Present students with several clear definitions, and ask them whether the definitions seem complete. Have students choose simple, concrete terms for their own definitions, or prepare a list of words from which they can choose. Review dictionary skills as necessary.

NSD See **Teaching Special Populations,** pages 82–83. Have students look up the words they are defining in a dictionary first.

Part 1

Objectives

1. To know that an explanatory paragraph can state a definition

2. To know that a successful definition includes both the general and specific characteristics of the subject being defined

Presenting the Lesson

1. Read aloud **Here's the Idea.** Stress the three things that a good definition does. Point out that this type of explanatory paragraph often requires students to do research to find facts and statistics.

2. Have the class carefully examine the pre-writing notes for the *hang glider* paragraph in **Check It Out.** Have students answer the questions.

3. Assign **Try Your Skill.**

4. Read aloud **Keep This in Mind** and then assign **Now Write.**

Individualizing the Lesson

Less-Advanced Students

Have students reread **Here's the Idea.** Suggest that students work in pairs to do the exercise from **Try Your Skill.** Have students compare their one-sentence definitions.

Advanced Students

Ask students to reread **Here's the Idea.** Have them write a one-sentence definition for two of the following topics:

ice fishing
rhubarb
osmosis
squash racket

158

On Your Terms

Pre-Writing: Learning About Definitions

Here's the Idea   In the last two sections, you have learned to write paragraphs that explain processes and present opinions. Now you're going to write a third kind of explanatory paragraph—an explanatory paragraph that states a definition. What is defined may be a real object like a *bobsled* or *ozone*. What is defined may also be a term or an idea, like *food chain* or *leadership*.

A good definition does three things. First, it gives the subject to be defined. Next, it puts that subject in its general class. Then, by giving specific characteristics, it shows how the subject is different from all the other members of its class.

Imagine that you want to define a *zucchini*. First, you would write that a zucchini is a vegetable. That puts it in its general class. How is a zucchini different from other vegetables? A zucchini is a squash. However, because there are several other kinds of squash besides zucchini, you might add that a zucchini is a summer squash. Because there are many types of summer squash, you could add that a zucchini is shaped like a cucumber. Because there are other cucumber-shaped summer squashes, you can add that the zucchini has a smooth, dark green skin. Now you have a complete definition.

Your complete definition might be stated like this: A zucchini is a smooth-skinned, dark green, cucumber-shaped vegetable that belongs to the summer squash family.

When you have a one-sentence definition of your subject, you must gather details to expand and develop the definition. Choose facts and figures and specific examples as you gather your pre-writing notes. Gather facts and figures through research. Specific examples will come from your own experience.

158

When you are ready to write your paragraph, the one-sentence definition you have composed will become your topic sentence. The details you have gathered will make up the body of your definition.

Check It Out   Read these pre-writing notes.

Topic: Hang glider

Notes: an aircraft
triangular sail; often bright, vivid colors
frame measures about 18 feet
no engine; powered by air currents
pilot hangs underneath
steers with a control bar
first became popular in U.S. in 1970's

- To what general class does the hang glider belong?
- What features distinguish the hang glider from other members of its class?

Try Your Skill   Use the notes in **Check It Out** to write a one-sentence definition of a hang glider. The definition should give the word to be defined, its general class, and one or two distinguishing characteristics.

Keep This in Mind

- An explanatory paragraph can state a definition.
- A good definition puts a subject into its general class, then shows its particular characteristics.

Now Write   Think of a real object, a term, or an idea that you want to define. Write a one-sentence definition of the word. You may want to use a dictionary or an encyclopedia to help you. Then make a list of details that will help you to develop the definition of your subject. Save your notes in your folder.

159

Part 2

Objective

To learn that an explanatory paragraph stating a definition begins with a general statement followed by specific details

Presenting the Lesson

1. Read aloud **Here's the Idea.** Point out that an explanatory paragraph stating a definition starts with a general statement which names the subject, the general class to which it belongs, and a few of its particular characteristics. This is followed by additional information which helps the reader gain a clear understanding of what is being defined.

2. Ask for a volunteer to read the paragraph from **Check It Out.**

3. Assign **Try Your Skill.**

4. Read aloud **Keep This in Mind** and then assign **Now Write.**

Individualizing the Lesson

Less-Advanced Students

Have students reread **Here's the Idea.** Pair students to do the exercise from **Try Your Skill.**

Advanced Students

Have students reread the paragraph from **Check It Out.** Ask them to think of other ways this paragraph on the guitar could be organized.

Optional Practice

Explain that explanatory paragraphs can be developed by using facts or statistics, examples, or comparisons and contrasts. Using the four terms from **Try Your Skill,**

160

Pre-Writing: Organizing a Definition

Here's the Idea   At this stage in the process of writing your explanatory paragraph, you should have all of the information you need to develop your definition. Before you can start writing, however, you have to organize your information.

A definition can be organized in a number of ways. Usually, a definition begins with a general statement. This general statement names the subject, its general class, and a few particular characteristics. The general statement is then followed by specific details that add to the reader's understanding of the subject. These details should be organized logically. If the subject is unfamiliar to your readers, or is a technical or scientific term, you may want to begin with the most familiar details. Then, as your reader's understanding grows, you can introduce less familiar details that further define your subject.

However you decide to organize your definition, be sure to choose a method that is well suited to your subject.

Check It Out   Read this explanatory paragraph.

The guitar is a stringed musical instrument. Historians believe that the guitar was first developed in Egypt about 5,000 years ago. The modern guitar was created in the late 1800's in Spain. Made of a light wood, it has curved sides and is shaped somewhat like an hourglass. It is played by plucking the strings with the fingers or with a small, flat object called a *pick*. Guitars usually have six strings, although some have as many as twelve, and some have as few as four.

- How was this explanatory paragraph organized? Explain your answer.

160

Try Your Skill   Write a one-sentence three-part general definition of each of these terms.

dictator   woodpecker
sailboat   tollway

Keep This in Mind

- An explanatory paragraph that states a definition should begin with a general statement. That statement should be followed by specific details.

Now Write   Organize the pre-writing notes you have gathered for your explanatory paragraph. Choose a method that best suits the subject. Save your organized notes in your folder.

have students think about which method of development would best suit each term. Discuss their answers.

Extending the Lesson

Ask students to bring in three examples of explanatory paragraphs which state a definition. For additional practice, have them try to find paragraphs which use different methods of development.

Objective

To write a first draft of a paragraph which states and develops a definition

Presenting the Lesson

1. Read aloud **Here's the Idea.** Point out that a successful explanatory paragraph needs an interesting and informative topic sentence, supporting information to develop the definition, and a strong concluding sentence.

2. Ask for a volunteer to read the paragraph from **Check It Out.**

3. Assign **Try Your Skill.**

4. Read aloud **Keep This in Mind** and then assign **Now Write.**

Individualizing the Lesson

Less-Advanced Students

Have students reread **Here's the Idea.** Suggest they work in pairs to complete the exercise from **Try Your Skill.**

Advanced Students

Have students concentrate on the best method for organizing their paragraph. Suggest they reread the paragraphs on the *guitar* and on the *rival* to help them organize their own definition.

Optional Practice

Reproduce three explanatory paragraphs which state a definition. Omit the topic sentence. Give one copy of any paragraph to each student and have them provide an interesting and informative topic sentence.

Writing the First Draft

Here's the Idea   A good beginning to any first draft is a strong topic sentence. Remember that in an explanatory paragraph that defines, your topic sentence must do three things. It must give the subject being defined, put the subject into its general class, and show some of the particular characteristics of the subject.

As you write your first draft, expand the one-sentence definition given in your topic sentence. Use the facts and statistics or specific details and examples you gathered and organized in prewriting to fully develop your definition.

Finish your paragraph with a strong ending sentence. Try to leave your readers with an interesting thought or detail about your subject.

Check It Out   Read the following definition.

A rival is a person or group who competes for the same goal as another person or group. A rival tries to equal or outdo his or her competition. My brother and his friend Don are now rivals for the position of school band leader. The football team from my school, North High, is always anxious to play its rival, the team from South High. My mother, who sells real estate, hopes to do as much business as her rivals. Friendly rivalry is a natural part of everyday life.

• Does each sentence expand the definition in the topic sentence? Explain your answer.

Try Your Skill   Choose one of the words you defined in **Try Your Skill** in the last lesson. Make a list of several specific details you might use to expand the three-part general definition you wrote for that word.

Keep This in Mind

- In an explanatory paragraph that defines, the topic sentence defines the subject.
- The body expands the definition with facts and figures or specific details and examples.
- A strong ending sentence should leave the reader with an interesting thought or detail about the subject.

Now Write Write the first draft of your explanatory paragraph. Include a strong topic sentence that presents a good general definition of your subject. Write an ending sentence that leaves the reader with an interesting thought or detail about your subject. Save your paragraph in your folder.

Extending the Lesson

Using the same paragraphs from **Optional Practice,** have students determine which method of organization was used in their paragraph. Discuss their answers. Explain that studying these paragraphs will help them to write their first drafts.

Objective

To revise a paragraph that states a definition

Presenting the Lesson

1. Read aloud **Here's the Idea.** Have students discuss each of the guideline questions.
2. Read and discuss the revised paragraph from **Check It Out.**
3. Assign **Try Your Skill.**
4. Read aloud **Keep This in Mind** and then assign **Now Write.**

Individualizing the Lesson

Less-Advanced Students

Work closely with students as they revise their paragraphs. Have them pay special attention to their topic sentences.

Advanced Students

Have students work in pairs on their revisions. Suggest that each student in the group be responsible for certain parts of the revision process. For example, one student could be the proofreader, checking for errors in spelling, grammar, and mechanics, while the other student could be responsible for making sure the topic sentence contains the necessary elements.

Optional Practice

Divide the class into five groups. Assign each group one of the guidelines for revising. Have them reread the paragraph from **Try Your Skill** and apply their guideline to the paragraph to help revise it properly.

Another Chance

Revising Your Definition

Here's the Idea   Your reader should have a perfectly clear understanding of the subject you have defined. Read your first draft thoroughly to be sure that the content and the presentation are absolutely clear. Be sure that your writing style suits your purpose and is appropriate to your audience. Answer these questions as you revise your paragraph.

1. Does my topic sentence give a clear three-part definition?
2. Have I included enough details to fully develop my topic?
3. Did I organize the details logically?
4. Have I used transitional words and phrases where needed?
5. Did I write a strong ending sentence?

After you have revised your paragraph, proofread it for errors in grammar, usage, and mechanics.

Check It Out   Notice how this paragraph was revised.

The papaya is a large fruit that grows on trees. The papaya goes from yellow to orange in color and is shaped like a pear. Its taste is like a cantaloupe. In central America, it is eaten as breakfast. And is also used for pies and sherberts. It's too bad it can't be shipped over long distances because of a space in its middle. This space causes it to come apart when it is soft. That is why many people will never get to eat this fruit.

- How has this paragraph been improved through revision?

Try Your Skill   Revise the following paragraph. Compare your revision with those of your classmates.

A wolf looks like a German shepherd dog. They avoid human beings. It is very powerful, and can run for hours in search of prey. Some people think that wolfs live only in Canada. But they also live in Europe, Asia and in Northern United States. It has a long bushy tail and ears, that are always standing up. Farmers and ranchers used to offer rewards for wolf skins because wolfs sometimes steal livestock. And many people fear them. They seldom attack people. Most male wolves weigh over 100 pounds. Females are lighter. They can be white, black, gray, or brown, and there fur is very valuable because it is so beautiful. But I think wolfs should be protected.

Keep This in Mind

- Revise your explanatory paragraph to be sure it is clear and exact. The development of the definition should be well organized.

Now Write   Revise your explanatory paragraph that states a definition, following the guidelines in this lesson. When you are satisfied that your ideas are clear and well organized, and that you have chosen interesting and suitable language, proofread your paragraph for errors in grammar, usage, and mechanics. Then make a final copy of your paragraph. Save your revised paragraph in your folder.

When students have finished revising their part, have the whole class rewrite the revised paragraph.

Extending the Lesson

Bring to class art books which illustrate the process of revision. Point out that all artists—painters, writers, musicians—go through revisions before they feel that their work is finished. Explain that it is an important part of all processes—artistic, scientific, business—to examine what has been done and to try to improve it through revision.

Section **14** Objectives

1. To know that a composition consists of a group of paragraphs that develops one main idea and that is organized into an introduction, a body, and a conclusion

2. To choose and narrow a topic for a composition

3. To gather and organize details to develop a topic

4. To write a first draft of a composition that has an introduction, a body, and a conclusion

5. To revise a composition, improving the content and organization

6. To improve the word choice of a composition and to proofread for errors

7. To write an interesting and appropriate title

8. To review the process of writing

9. To know the guidelines for writing a composition

Preparing the Students

Ask for volunteers to read aloud one complete composition and two brief paragraphs. You may want to use paragraphs that students wrote for earlier Sections. Ask students to discuss the similarities and differences between the composition and the paragraphs. Have a student list these on the chalkboard. Explain that students will learn to write compositions in this Section.

Additional Resources

Mastery Test — pages 28–29 in the test booklet

Practice Book — pages 68–74

Duplicating Masters — pages 68–74

Writing a Composition

Teaching Special Populations

LD See **Teaching Special Populations,** pages 82–83. Longer compositions will pose a considerable challenge for many LD students. Help students individually as they tackle these writing assignments. Allow some assignments to be completed in groups or in pairs.

ESL Be sure students understand what is meant by *introduction, body,* and *conclusion.* Define unfamiliar words students encounter as they read and discuss this Section.

Review with students the methods of organization listed on page 96.

Check students' first drafts before they revise, and suggest improvements in content and language.

NSD See **Teaching Special Populations,** pages 82–83. Remind students that they do not have to worry about their language in the first draft, but that they must use standard, formal English when they revise.

Objective

To know that a composition consists of a group of paragraphs that develops one main idea and that is organized into an introduction, a body, and a conclusion

Presenting the Lesson

1. Read aloud **Here's the Idea.** On the chalkboard, write *introduction*, *body*, and *conclusion*. Define these terms.

2. Ask for a student to read aloud the composition from **Check It Out.** Have the class answer the questions.

3. Read aloud **Try Your Skill.** Do this exercise aloud with students.

4. Read aloud **Keep This in Mind** and assign **Now Write.**

Individualizing the Lesson

Less-Advanced Students

Have students reread **Here's the Idea.** Ask them to begin a composition dictionary. It should contain the important terms and concepts associated with writing compositions. The first entries might be *composition, introduction, body,* and *conclusion.*

Advanced Students

Divide students into two small groups. Ask them to reread the paragraphs they wrote in earlier Sections, and discuss how those topics could or could not be developed into compositions.

Three-Part Harmony

What Is a Composition?

Here's the Idea   A **composition** is a group of paragraphs dealing with a single main idea. A composition, like a paragraph, can be a narrative, a description, or an explanation. It also has a definite beginning, middle, and end. These parts are called the introduction, the body, and the conclusion.

The **introduction** is a single paragraph. It presents the topic of the composition. It also captures the interest of the audience.

The **body** is made up of several paragraphs. These paragraphs support and develop the main idea presented in the introduction. The body may contain the events of a story or the sensory details of a description. It may also contain the step-by-step details of a process or a group of facts used to support an opinion.

The **conclusion** is the last part of the composition. The conclusion gives the reader the feeling that the composition is over. It often restates the main idea of the composition. It may also summarize or draw a lesson from the ideas in the body.

Check It Out   Read this composition.

An Unusual Trip

Last summer, I was a ranch hand at the Lazy K, and my girlfriend Janie was waitressing ninety miles away. We wrote or phoned each other almost every day, but I still missed Janie. Early one morning, my boss said that I could have the day off.

I did not have a minute to spare, so I saddled up Panhandler and raced him to Seven Corners. I was told at the bus station that the bus had come through town just moments before I had. Luckily a rancher driving a load of hogs into the city said that I was welcome to ride along if I didn't mind riding with his livestock. I hopped in among the pigs, and off we went.

Two hours later, I caught sight of Janie's restaurant. Then I saw Janie coming up the street.

"Janie!" I shouted.

"Willie! What are you doing here? I'm on my way to the bus stop," Janie replied. "My boss gave me the afternoon off, so I planned to take a little trip."

"Where?" I asked miserably.

"Some ranch called the Lazy K," she teased, grabbing my arm and tugging me along behind her.

- What kind of composition is this? How do you know?
- Does the introduction capture your interest?
- Does the conclusion signal an end to the composition?

Try Your Skill   Which part of a composition does this paragraph come from? Write a brief explanation for your answer.

Introduction or Conclusion

We are living in the age of the computer. Computers are used in every area of life from big business to small business, from supermarkets to super trains, from space stations to the home. To help young people cope with this new technology, computer science must become an important part of the course of studies in every high school.

Keep This in Mind

- A composition is a group of paragraphs that present and develop one main idea.
- A composition has an introduction, a body, and a conclusion.
- A composition may be narrative, descriptive, or explanatory.

Now Write   Read a brief article in one of your favorite magazines. Notice that it has an introduction, a body, and a conclusion. On a piece of paper, write the title of the article. Tell whether it is narrative, descriptive, or explanatory. Write the sentence that serves as the topic sentence. Save your work.

Have students bring in a brief article from a magazine or newspaper. Have them determine what type of composition it is (a narrative, a description, an explanation).

Extending the Lesson

Have students bring in one example for each type of composition. Ask them to write the topic sentence, and indicate the introduction, the body paragraphs, and the conclusion.

Objective

To choose and narrow a topic for a composition

Presenting the Lesson

1. Read aloud **Here's the Idea.** Point out that choosing a topic requires serious thinking. A good place for students to start is with things that are familiar or important to them.

After choosing a topic, it must be narrowed. Instruct students to ask *who? what? where? when? why?* or *how?* about their topic.

2. Have students look over the pre-writing notes from **Check It Out.** Have students discuss the questions.

3. Read aloud and assign **Try Your Skill.**

4. Read aloud **Keep This in Mind** and assign **Now Write.**

Individualizing the Lesson

Less-Advanced Students

1. Have students reread **Here's the Idea.** Ask them to add *topic* and *narrowed topic* to their composition dictionaries.

2. Before assigning **Try Your Skill,** suggest these students work in small groups.

Advanced Students

Have students review pre-writing techniques from earlier Sections. Suggest they divide into small groups and brainstorm for ideas to help choose and narrow their topics. Work with students to make

The Main Idea

Pre-Writing: Choosing a Topic

Here's the Idea   Good compositions are full of details that appeal to the senses and interests of readers. Finding enough details to fill a composition will be easier if you choose a topic you already know something about.

To choose a good topic, think about the important people, places, things, and events in your life. What sports, hobbies, or other activities do you enjoy? Who are the most interesting people you've met? What people or events have influenced you most? What opinions, beliefs, or values do you have? What subjects in school do you find most interesting? Asking such questions will help you to find a topic you will enjoy.

You can also arrive at a topic by looking through your journal, watching television, or reading magazines, newspapers, and books. Brainstorming, clustering, class discussions, and interviews are also excellent sources of topics.

Once you choose a topic, narrow it to fit your composition. In other words, if your topic is very general, make it more specific. Do this by asking questions about the topic. Begin these questions with *who, what, where, when, why,* or *how.* For more information on narrowing a topic, see pages 88–89.

Check It Out   Read the following list of topics:

a description of a football
the Civil War
learning to drive a car
New York City
how to apply for a job

a definition of *triangle*
the blue whale
a history of the Marine Corps
why seat belts should be
    mandatory
marine life of the Pacific

- Which of these topics are too broad for a five-paragraph composition? too narrow? just right? Explain your answers.

Try Your Skill   Below is a list of general subjects. Choose one that interests you. Ask *who, what, where, when, why,* and *how* questions about it. Narrow the general subject until you have a specific topic that you could cover well in a five-paragraph composition. Write whether your composition would be a narrative, a description, or an explanation.

sporting events	brothers and sisters
July 4th	acts of courage
biology class	city adventures
the beach	hobbies

Keep This in Mind

- Choose a topic that you know something about and that interests you.
- Discover topics by reading your journal, books, magazines, and newspapers. Also try brainstorming, clustering, class discussions, and interviews.
- Narrow your topic to make it more specific.

Now Write   Follow the guidelines in this lesson as you choose and narrow a topic. Be sure your topic is specific enough to be covered well in several paragraphs. You may want to use the topic you developed in **Try Your Skill.** Save your topic in your folder.

sure that their topics are manageable. Ask for volunteers to write their ideas on the chalkboard.

Optional Practice

Ask the class to narrow the following topics until each one is suitable for a five-paragraph composition: medicine, space, jobs.

Extending the Lesson

Suggest to students that they should invite a professional newswriter to class. Have students prepare a list of questions asking how the newswriter discovers and narrows topics for feature articles.

Objective

To gather and organize details to develop a topic

Presenting the Lesson

1. Read aloud **Here's the Idea.** On the chalkboard, list the six methods of organization from page 172. Point out that the kinds of details gathered and the method of organization used are both determined by the type of composition being written.

2. Read aloud the pre-writing notes from **Check It Out.** Ask students what kinds of details the writer has gathered.

3. Assign **Try Your Skill.**

4. Read aloud **Keep This in Mind** and assign **Now Write.**

Individualizing the Lesson

Less-Advanced Students

Have students include in their composition dictionary the six methods of organization. Before assigning **Try Your Skill,** suggest that students work in small groups.

Advanced Students

Ask students to read a composition of the type that they have chosen to write. Have them explain how the writer has gathered details and what method of organization was used to develop the composition.

Optional Practice

Using an overhead projector, display a well-written composition.

Picking up the Pieces

Pre-Writing: Organizing Your Ideas

Here's the Idea   The first step in writing a composition is to choose and narrow a topic. The next step is to select details to develop that topic. You may gather sensory details, specific examples, facts and statistics, or incidents or anecdotes.

The type of details you gather will depend upon the type of composition you are writing. For example, you could gather facts and statistics if you were writing a composition to support an opinion. If you were writing a descriptive composition, you would gather mostly sensory details. Sometimes you will gather more than one kind of detail to support and develop a topic.

Once you have gathered the details you will use in your composition, you must organize these details logically. Begin by getting rid of any details that are not related to your main idea. Then, decide which of the remaining details go together. Try to discover two or three major ideas to which the other details are related. Group your details around each of these major ideas. If you do not have enough information to support or develop a major idea, gather more details. Each of these groups of details will become a paragraph in your final composition.

The next step is to organize the idea groups and the details within each group. Do this as you would for any paragraph. Use any of the following methods of organization.

chronological order	spatial order
order of importance	general to specific order
most familiar to least familiar order	comparison and contrast

For more information about methods of organization, see pages 96–97.

Check It Out   Read these notes for a descriptive composition.

Topic: the old Marine and Hardware Store
Details: kitchen items, straw brooms
fishing lures (feathers, brightly colored thread)
fishing rods/tackle boxes
sail cloth—white, yellow, blue
muffin tins (black, cast iron)
fishers/boaters paradise
row boats—small electric motors
hardware for do-it-yourselfers
shiny copper food molds
hammers, nails, screwdrivers, saws
bright-orange life preservers
plumbing supplies, fix-it manuals

• What kinds of details has the writer gathered?

Try Your Skill   Group the pre-writing notes in **Check It Out** around three main ideas.

Keep This in Mind

• Gather specific examples, sensory details, facts and statistics, or incidents or anecdotes to support and develop the main idea of a composition.
• Group similar details around several main ideas.
• Organize main ideas and the details grouped around them into one of the following orders: chronological, spatial, order of importance, general to specific, most familiar to least familiar, or comparison and contrast.

Now Write   Gather details to support and develop the topic you have chosen. Organize your details into idea groups. Arrange the idea groups and the details within them into an order that suits the purpose of your composition. Save your notes.

Have students discuss the topic, the specific details, and the method of organization.

Extending the Lesson

Point out that writers do not always see the same idea from the same perspective. Ask students to find the same story in two different newspapers. Have them write down the differences in specific details and notice if the method of organization is also different.

Objective

To write a first draft of a composition that has an introduction, a body, and a conclusion

Presenting the Lesson

1. Read aloud **Here's the Idea.** Stress that at this point students should not be concerned with the correctness of their writing. Their objective here is to put down in sentence form their organized pre-writing notes.

Instruct them to use transitional words and phrases to show how the paragraphs are related and to help the reader move easily from one idea to the next.

2. Read aloud the first draft of the composition from **Check It Out.** Have students discuss the questions.

3. Assign **Try Your Skill.**

4. Read aloud **Keep This in Mind** and assign **Now Write.**

Individualizing the Lesson

Less-Advanced Students

Have students reread **Here's the Idea.** Before assigning **Try Your Skill,** divide students into small discussion groups. Have one student act as the secretary and write down the ideas generated from the discussion.

Advanced Students

Ask students to reread **Here's the Idea** before they begin **Now Write.**

Have students read two compositions from a newspaper or magazine. Ask them to pay special attention to the introductions. Have

174

Explorations

Writing the First Draft

Here's the Idea   Writing the first draft of a composition is a process of exploration and discovery. At this stage you should not worry about the details of grammar, punctuation, capitalization, and spelling. Simply follow your organized list of pre-writing notes, and get your ideas down on paper.

Remember that your composition must have three parts: an introduction, a body, and a conclusion. When writing the introduction, be sure to state your topic clearly and directly. Try various ways of introducing the composition until you hit upon one that will capture the attention of your readers.

When writing the paragraphs of the body, make sure that each has a strong topic sentence. Present in a logical order the details that support this sentence. Use transitional words and phrases to show how these details are related.

When writing the conclusion, you have several choices. These depend upon the type of composition you are writing. You may simply tell the last event in a story. You may restate your main idea in different words and summarize your major points. You may also draw a moral from the material presented in the body. In any case, make sure that your reader is left with the feeling that the composition is over.

Check It Out   Read this first draft. It was written from the pre-writing notes in the last lesson.

What I'm going to write about is this old general store in town. It's called the Marine and Hardware Store. It's been they're since 1910. That's a long time ago. The store has something for everyone. Seafarers and landlubbers alike.

174

In the center of it is all kinds of stuff for the kitchen. You can get straw brooms, black cast iron muffin pans, shinny copper molds, and pots and pans.

Along one wall are all kinds of hardware items for do-it-yourself projects. There are hammers, nails, and screwdrivers. Also saws, both regular and power. Plumbing supplies sit on long display shelves. There's even a book section with how-to-do-it manuals for home improvement projects.

In the back of the store is a large section called the Marina. There are many supplies for boaters and people who like to fish. You can get small row boats, electric motors, sail cloth, and bright-orange life preservers. There are also fishing rods, fancy fishing lures, and tackle boxes.

Whatever you want to buy they've got it. From outboard motors to food processors to electric cable, this is the store to find it. It's the most interesting store in town.

- Does this composition have an introduction, a body, and a conclusion? Identify each part. Does each part fulfill its purpose? Explain your answer.

Try Your Skill   Discuss with your classmates the strengths and weaknesses of the composition in **Check It Out.** Talk about some specific ways you could improve the composition.

Keep This in Mind

- Your first draft should have an introduction, a body, and a conclusion.
- Follow your organized pre-writing notes as you write.

Now Write   Using your pre-writing notes as a writing plan, write the first draft of your composition. Follow the guidelines in this lesson. Save your first draft in your folder.

them make a list of the particular elements that make an interesting and attention-getting introduction.

Optional Practice

Have students read a composition of their choice that is either narrative, descriptive, or explanatory. Ask them to do the following.

1. write the title
2. write the kind of composition it is
3. label the introduction, body, and conclusion
4. list the kinds of details and the method of organization
5. explain what they liked or disliked about the composition

Extending the Lesson

Have students work in pairs for this exercise. Using the compositions from **Optional Practice** along with the students' work, have partners exchange material and discuss their reactions to the compositions. Not only will this give students an additional composition to read and study, but it also will provide them with valuable peer feedback.

Part 5

Getting It Right

Objective

To revise a composition, improving the content and organization

Presenting the Lesson

1. Read aloud **Here's the Idea.** On the chalkboard write and define *content* and *organization.* Instruct students to refer to the questions in **Here's the Idea** when they revise their first drafts.

2. Have students study the paragraphs from **Check It Out.** Discuss how the writer has improved these paragraphs.

3. Read aloud and assign **Try Your Skill.**

4. Read aloud **Keep This in Mind** and assign **Now Write.**

Individualizing the Lesson

Less-Advanced Students

Have students add *content* and *organization* to their composition dictionaries. Hold individual conferences with students as they go through the process of revising their compositions.

Advanced Students

After students have completed **Now Write,** have them answer each question under *Content* and *Organization.* Point out that an answer of "yes" is not satisfactory; instead, have them give concrete examples for each question. For example, to answer the question "Is my main idea clearly expressed," each student should state his or her main idea and show how it introduces the subject of the composition.

Revising: Content and Organization

Here's the Idea   Good writing is almost always the result of good rewriting. This is why professional journalists, novelists, screenwriters, and playwrights usually revise their work thoroughly. Revising allows them to improve their work.

Revising is no less important when you write compositions. Once you have finished a first draft, look for ways to improve it. Read your composition several times. Pay special attention to the content, the organization, and the language. In this lesson, you will concentrate on the first two: content and organization.

Content refers to the ideas and the details you have used to develop your main idea. Ask yourself these questions about the content of your composition.

1. Is my main idea clearly expressed?

2. Have I included enough details to develop my main idea?

3. Have I chosen the right kinds of details for the type of composition I am writing?

4. Does my composition have unity? That is, do all my details help to support and develop my main idea?

Organization refers to the structure of your composition. Ask these questions to help check the organization of your work.

1. Does my composition have an introduction, a body, and a conclusion?

2. Does each paragraph have an interesting and informative topic sentence? Is this sentence supported by details?

3. Is my composition coherent? That is, are all of my ideas arranged in a clear, logical order?

4. Have I chosen a suitable method of organization?

Check It Out Look at these paragraphs.

Christopher Columbus, ~~was a sailor and navigator,~~ *is well known as the discoverer of America.* He was born in Genoa, *a port city on the northwest coast of Italy.* Altho the date of his birth isnt known, he was probably born sometime between August and October in 1451. ~~Genoa was once a Capital City in Italy.~~ Christopher was the first of five children who were born to Domenico and Susanna Colombo.

Not a lot is known about his youth. He always wanted to go to sea. He didn't go to school much. Most of what he knew he learned himself. He helped his father, a weaver, at the loom. ~~His mother's father had been a weaver.~~

- How has the writer improved these paragraphs?

Try Your Skill Reread the composition about the Marine and Hardware Store. As a class, revise the content and organization. Add and take out details. Reorganize the details if you wish. Use the questions in this lesson to guide your revision. Save your work so that you can complete it in the next lesson.

Keep This in Mind

- When you revise, try to improve the content and organization of your work.

Now Write Revise the content and organization of the composition you have been writing. Use the questions in this lesson to guide you. Save your work in your folder.

After students have completed revising their compositions, have them exchange papers. Have each partner determine the main idea and the method of organization. Have partners discuss the strengths and weaknesses of one another's work and make suggestions for improvement.

Extending the lesson

Find examples of the revised rough drafts of famous authors. Bring these to class to demonstrate that all good writers rework their material in order to find the most effective way of presenting it.

Objective

To improve the word choice of a composition and to proofread for errors

Presenting the Lesson

1. Read aloud **Here's the Idea.** Stress that revising for content and organization is only part of the process of revision. Checking for the right language and correcting errors in grammar, usage, and mechanics completes the process. Spend time discussing with students how language can say the same thing in many different ways. Suggest to students that it is language which makes their ideas come to life.

2. Have students read the revised paragraphs from **Check It Out.** Discuss how the revision has improved the writing.

3. Assign **Try Your Skill.**

4. Read aloud **Keep This in Mind** and assign **Now Write.**

Individualizing the Lesson

Less-Advanced Students

Have students reread **Here's the Idea.** Have them add *mood, sensory details, dialogue, dialogue tags, transitional words and phrases,* and *proofreading* to their composition dictionary.

Have students refer to the earlier Sections which discussed word choice in order to strengthen their understanding of this part of the process of writing.

It's Your Choice

Revising: Word Choice and Proofreading

Here's the Idea   You have learned that it is important to check the content and organization of your writing when you revise. It is equally important to check the language you have used. Choosing the right words can transform dull, flat sentences and paragraphs into lively, interesting ones.

Word choice affects all aspects of your writing. In a description, carefully chosen nouns, adjectives, verbs, and adverbs can help you to suggest **mood. Sensory details** can also benefit from good word choice. The phrase "a lit pumpkin" is a sensory detail. However, the phrase "a pumpkin glowing in soft orange light" is a better expressed sensory detail.

Dialogue can be improved in two ways through careful selection of language. First, choosing the right words will make your characters believable. That is, teenagers will sound like teenagers, frightened children will sound frightened, and so on. Second, you can say more with a **dialogue tag** when the words are right. You can replace "he said" with more expressive tags, such as "he whispered" or "she yelled."

Appropriate **transitional words and phrases** can also improve your writing. They lead your readers from one idea to the next. They show how your ideas are related. They can help you to express chronological and spatial order.

In general, try to replace vague, general language when you revise. Look for specific nouns, adjectives, verbs, and adverbs that say exactly what you mean.

The final step in revising is **proofreading.** When you proofread, you look for and correct any errors you have made in grammar, usage, capitalization, punctuation, and spelling.

Check It Out   Notice this further revision.

Christopher Columbus was a sailor and navigator. *is well known as the great discoverer of America.* He was born in Genoa, *a port city on the northwest coast of Italy.* Altho~~ugh~~, the date of his birth isn't known, he was probably born sometime between August and October in 1451. ~~Genoa was once a Capital City in Italy.~~ Christopher was the first of five children ~~who were~~ born to Domenico and Susanna Colombo.

~~Not a lot~~ *Little* is known about his ~~youth.~~ *childhood.* ~~He always wanted to go to sea.~~ *However, longed* ~~He didn't go to school much.~~ Most of what he knew he ~~learned himself.~~ *self-taught.* *his knowledge was have formal education.* He helped his father, a weaver, at the loom, ~~His mother's father had been a weaver.~~

- How have these paragraphs been improved through further revision?

Try Your Skill   As a class, continue revising the Marine and Hardware Store composition. Work to improve the word choice. Then, proofread the composition. When you are finished, discuss how you have made the composition better.

Keep This in Mind

- When you revise, replace vague, general words with strong, specific ones.
- Proofread to find and correct errors in grammar, usage, and mechanics.

Now Write   Finish revising your composition. Try to improve your word choice. Don't forget to proofread your work. When you are finished, make a final copy of your work. Save your composition in your folder.

179

Advanced Students

Ask students to make a separate copy of their introductory paragraph. Discuss with them how they have expressed their main idea. Have them closely examine their language. Ask students to point out the strengths and the weaknesses of this paragraph. Remind the class that the introduction is where they want to get their reader's attention, so their language should be lively and informative.

Optional Practice

Duplicate a paragraph which needs revision. Have students proofread it and use the correct proofreader's marks to indicate the necessary changes.

Extending the Lesson

Explain to students that no matter what they write, they always will be revising their work. Suggest that it will be easier for them to revise if they are familiar with all of the usual proofreader's marks. Suggest they go to the library and look through the *Chicago Manual of Style,* which is an authority and guide for all editorial and publishing rules of style and format.

Objective

To write an interesting and appropriate title

Presenting the Lesson

1. Read aloud **Here's the Idea.** Point out that a successful title does more than simply inform. Like the introductory paragraph, a good title must capture the reader's attention. Have students offer titles that they particularly like.

2. Read aloud the titles from **Check It Out.** Have students discuss whether these are good titles and why.

3. Assign **Try Your Skill.**

4. Read aloud **Keep This in Mind** and assign **Now Write.**

Individualizing the Lesson

Less-Advanced Students

Ask students to reread **Here's the Idea.** Have them complete their composition dictionaries by adding *title.* Ask them to revise their dictionary by arranging all the terms and concepts in alphabetical order, and checking for errors in spelling.

Advanced Students

Have students work in pairs for this exercise. After they have chosen several possible titles for their compositions, have them exchange papers with their partners. After reading each other's compositions, have students discuss the suggested titles. Have each partner try to point out what is successful and what does not work for each of the possible titles.

What's Its Name?

Choosing a Title

Here's the Idea   Whenever you write, you make many decisions. You decide whether to write a narrative, a description, or an explanation. You choose and narrow a topic. You also choose the details you want to include and the method of organization you want to use. Finally, you select the particular words with which to put your ideas down onto paper. Each of these decisions is important to producing interesting, effective writing.

Sometimes you must make yet another important decision. This decision concerns your title. Titles are usually not required for short pieces of writing such as paragraphs. However, longer pieces of writing such as compositions generally do have titles.

The title of a composition is often a simple phrase that suggests what the composition is about. "Learning to Surf" and "My Earliest Memory" are titles of this kind. They serve the purpose of introducing the composition to the reader, but they are not very interesting.

The best titles do more than just suggest the subject. They also capture the attention of the reader. There are many techniques that writers use to do this. Some writers create titles that use puns or clichés. Others use rhyming words or repeated sounds in their titles. Still others try to write titles that express odd or unusual ideas.

The best way to learn how to write titles is to examine the titles that you read in everyday life. When you come across a title that seems particularly good, ask yourself why. Soon, you will learn many of the tricks that writers use when creating titles. Then, when you have to write a title of your own, you will be able to draw upon a model from your own experience.

Check It Out Read the following titles of stories you may have read.

"The Red-Headed League"   "Jingle Bells"
"By the North Gate"   "The Stone Boy"
"The Circus"   "Evening Flight"
"The Fan Club"   "Happy Birthday"
"See How They Run"   "Strawberry Ice Cream Soda"

- Are these good titles? Why?

Try Your Skill Choose four of the following possible topics for longer pieces of writing. For each topic, write two titles that might work. Try to express the idea of each topic in simple or surprising titles.

1. a story about a trip you took
2. a description of your neighborhood
3. a report on nutritious breakfast foods
4. an explanation of how to frame a picture
5. an explanation of why space travel is important
6. a story about an imaginary character
7. a report on a famous bridge
8. an explanation of what a hurricane is
9. a description of a beach you like
10. a report on a United States President

Keep This in Mind

- Use a title for longer pieces of writing. A good title should suggest the main idea of your writing. A good title should also attract a reader's interest.

Now Write Write several titles for the composition you are working on. Each title should be interesting and should suggest the main idea of your composition. Choose the title you like the best. Write it at the top of your revised composition.

181

Part 8

Just a Reminder

Guidelines for Writing a Composition

In the next few sections of this book, you will be writing many different kinds of compositions. Whatever type of composition you write, however, the process of writing will remain the same. Below is a list of guidelines to follow when you write a composition. Refer to them often as you write your compositions.

Guidelines for Writing a Composition

Pre-Writing

- Choose a topic that interests you and that you know something about. Narrow the topic so that you can cover it well in the assigned length of your composition.
- Identify your purpose and your audience.
- Gather details to develop your topic.
- Group similar details around two or three main ideas.
- Organize your details into an order that suits the type of composition you are writing.

Writing the First Draft

- Begin your composition with an interesting introductory paragraph that tells your reader what your composition is about.
- After your introduction, write the body of your composition. Use your organized details to develop your topic. Each group of details will become a paragraph in the body of your composition.
- Use transitional words and phrases to lead your readers from one idea to the next.

- Add, take out, and reorganize your ideas if you need to.
- End your first draft with a concluding paragraph that sums up your ideas.
- Add an interesting title to your composition.

Revising

- Be sure your composition has an introduction, a body, and a conclusion.
- Check to see that you have included enough details to develop your topic.
- Organize the paragraphs and the ideas within them logically.
- Be sure the topic sentence of each paragraph presents the main idea of that paragraph.
- Use effective transitional words to make your ideas flow smoothly.
- Make sure you have used vivid language. Use language that suits the audience you are writing for.
- Proofread to find and correct errors in grammar, capitalization, punctuation, and spelling.

Final Copy

- Rewrite your composition neatly in ink on white, lined paper. Or, type your composition, double spaced, on plain white paper.
- Write your name, subject, and the date in the upper right-hand corner of your paper.
- Proofread your final copy one last time. Neatly correct any errors you find.

Section 15 Objectives

1. To know the basic elements of a narrative composition: setting, characters, and a plot with conflict

2. To learn to explain the conflict through a chronological ordering of the plot

3. To understand how to use a flashback

4. To recognize the four points of view and to use them appropriately

5. To write the first draft using an introduction, body, and conclusion

6. To use dialogue and dialogue tags to develop characters

7. To use transitions between and within paragraphs to show chronological order

8. To revise the narrative composition

Preparing the Students

Tell students that the paragraph that they have already studied is the basic building block of writing. However, if they want to tell a long or complicated story, a paragraph would not be adequate. Explain that the narrative composition is the form to use for telling a story that can't be told in one paragraph. Then emphasize that the process of writing remains the same no matter what is being written.

Additional Resources

Practice Book — pages 75–81
Duplicating Masters — pages 75–81

The Narrative Composition

Teaching Special Populations

LD See **Teaching Special Populations,** pages 82–83. Read the samples presented in the text aloud, and have students identify the point of view of each sample. Ask students to briefly retell, in their own words, each passage.

ESL Have students relate stories from their homelands, or from movies they know well, and ask them to identify the narrative elements of character, plot, and conflict.

Provide students with additional point of view exercises that require students to tell stories from first one and then another point of view.

Allow time for students to learn correct punctuation of dialogue. Assign Handbook Section 14, pages 683–687 for practice.

NSD See **Teaching Special Populations,** pages 82–83. Duplicate and discuss with students narratives in which nonstandard dialogue is effectively presented. Encourage students to try to write a dialogue in dialect.

Start Your Engines

Pre-Writing: Planning a Narrative

Part 1

Objective

To know the basic elements of a narrative composition: setting, characters, and a plot with conflict

Presenting the Lesson

1. Write the word *narrative* on the chalkboard and have students define it. Then read aloud and discuss **Here's the Idea.** Go over each paragraph separately, making sure students understand why the questions to ask for each element of the composition are important.

2. Read **Check It Out.** Ask students why it is important to write out the pre-writing notes before they begin to write the first draft.

3. Have a volunteer read aloud the paragraph in **Try Your Skill** and then have the class discuss the questions.

4. Read **Keep This in Mind** and then assign **Now Write.** Have students set up their pre-writing notes like those in **Check It Out.**

Individualizing the Lesson

Less-Advanced Students

1. Compare the explanatory paragraph and the explanatory composition, having students refer to pages 113–123 to review what they have learned about the paragraph.

2. Help the students narrow their topics to incidents that can be narrated in five paragraphs.

Advanced Students

Discuss with students the difference between a brief personal experience narrative and a short

Here's the Idea   A narrative composition is a story. Stories come in many different forms. However, all share a few elements in common. These elements are the parts of a story—setting, characters, plot, and conflict. To plan a narrative composition, make pre-writing notes on each of these parts.

The **setting** is the background of the story. It tells when and where the action takes place. To plan the setting, choose the time and place of the action. Then, ask questions to fill in the details. Does the story take place in the past, present, or future? Does it take place in the country or the city? Is it set inside or outside? What time of year is it? What time of day?

The **characters** are the people or animals in the story. In a short narrative, the number of characters is small. Ask the following questions when planning characters for a story: What people or animals do I want to write about? Will they be real or imaginary? How will they look, act, and speak? What is important to them? What makes them different from one another?

The **plot** is the series of events in the story. The first events in the story introduce a conflict. The **conflict** is a problem or difficulty faced by the main character. The events that follow show how the main character deals with and finally solves the conflict. When planning the plot of a story, ask these questions: Will the events in the story be real or imaginary? What conflict will my main character face? What events will create this conflict? What events will take place after the conflict is introduced? How will my main character solve this conflict?

Check It Out   Read these pre-writing notes.

Setting: Caliphstan, a nation in another world
Characters: Kyril, a young woman; Arius, Kyril's uncle

Plot: Kyril faces an important decision about her future

Conflict: Kyril's desire to please her family versus her need to be true to herself

- Do these pre-writing notes contain all of the important elements of a narrative?

Try Your Skill   Read this opening for an imaginary narrative.

The letter Kyril held in her trembling hands was brief and to the point.

> Her Eminence, the Exeter of Caliph, is pleased to announce your appointment to the Guardians of Caliphstan. Present yourself to the captain of the Guardians at dawn on the first day of Janius.

Kyril could hardly believe her eyes. An appointment to the Guardians was the dream of every young citizen. The Guardians were the elite defenders of Caliphstan. It was the Guardians who had finally defeated the cruel Voss warriors during the War of the Ages. The Guardians had put down the Illyrian insurrection and freed the Bliss people. Indeed, the Guardians' history was a catalog of the glories of the nation of Caliphstan. And now their history was to become Kyril's history. She felt tears well up in her eyes; not tears of joy or relief, however, but tears of sadness and frustration. Kyril had no real desire to become a Guardian. She wanted a much different life.

How does this opening set the scene? What do you learn about the main character? How is the conflict suggested?

Keep This in Mind

- A narrative has a setting, characters, a plot, and a conflict.

Now Write   Think of a story you would like to tell. It might be something that happened to you or to someone you know. It might be the product of your imagination. Write down story ideas and details as they occur to you. Save your notes.

story they have studied recently. Guide students to an understanding of how much more complex the short story is, and in what ways (emphasis on character development, more detailed plot, complicated conflict, etc.).

Optional Practice

Have students create a detailed "biography" for one or two imaginary characters. Explain that this is what they should also do for their narrative compositions, because the more detailed a character is in their own minds, the more effectively they will be able to create the character for their readers.

Extending the Lesson

Select a short narrative to read aloud to the class. Have students identify the setting, characters, plot, and conflict.

Know the Course

Part 2

Objectives

1. To learn to explain the conflict through a chronological ordering of the plot

2. To understand how to use a flashback

Presenting the Lesson

1. Write the words *internal* and *external* on the chalkboard and have students define them. Then read the first two paragraphs in **Here's the Idea.** Ask students for examples of each kind of conflict. Remind students that a conflict should create suspense; that the reader should want to find out how it is resolved.

2. Read and discuss the last two paragraphs in **Here's the Idea.** Make sure students understand that *chronological* refers to time sequence. Ask students why an author might want to use a flashback.

3. Read **Check It Out.** Make sure that students understand that they will be reading and discussing this narrative throughout this Section. Ask students if the conflict presented is internal or external.

4. Assign **Try Your Skill.** Ask volunteers to share their paragraphs with the class.

5. Read **Keep This in Mind** and then assign **Now Write.** Remind students that they are doing the first steps in the process of writing that they have learned before.

Individualizing the Lesson

Less-Advanced Students

Have students begin their pre-writing in class.

Pre-Writing: Developing a Plot

Here's the Idea   As you learned in Part 1, every story is about a series of events called the plot. To develop a plot, you must first decide what your central conflict will be.

The conflict may be internal or external. An **internal conflict** takes place in the mind of a character. For instance, a character might have to choose between being wrongly accused and betraying a friend. An **external conflict** takes place between a character and some outside force. This force can be something in nature, another character, or a social custom or rule. For example, a character might be in conflict with a raging forest fire.

After choosing a conflict, you can begin to develop your plot. The pre-writing notes for your plot will be a list of events. First, list the events that suggest the conflict. Then, list the events that take place as the main character deals with the conflict. Finally, decide what event ends the conflict. As you list these events, put them in chronological order.

If you wish to, you may vary the order of your events by inserting a flashback. A **flashback** is a description of something that happened in the past, before the first event in the story. You can use a flashback to explain how certain things in your story came to be. For example, you might use a flashback to explain a young boy's fear of water. You could describe how, years before, the boy almost drowned in a boating accident.

Check It Out   Continue reading this narrative.

Kyril stared out the window. She remembered how, as a child, her father and mother would tell her stories about the adventures of the Guardians. Kyril and her friends would often play at being Guardians, defending the fields around their homes against invisible Voss warriors and imaginary Illyrian slavemasters. Kyril's uncle, Arius, was a much-decorated

Guardian who had offered Kyril his counsel as she had prepared for the rigorous mental and physical tests that led to becoming a Guardian. Indeed, much of her young life had been influenced by the legends of the Guardians and her parents' strong desire that she should join this elite group.

Kyril remembered another incident from her past. When she was ten star years, her mother had taken her on a voyage to the floating cities of New Caliphstan. Kyril was awestruck as the giant starcruiser approached the first city, gleaming in the reflected light from the sun.

"Whose dream were these places, Mother?" Kyril asked, her face pressed against the cruiser's observation window.

"The Builders have prepared them," her mother replied. "They designed them and built them."

As the cruiser maneuvered for docking, Kyril decided deep in her heart that one day she would help to build the floating cities that her children's children would call home.

Now, Kyril thought, *I must choose my future.* It was a choice Kyril wished she didn't have to make.

- How does the flashback help explain the present conflict?

Try Your Skill   Think about an event from your past that has had an influence on the person you are today. Write a brief narrative paragraph telling about this event.

Keep This in Mind

- In a narrative, the conflict is explained through the plot, a chronological series of events.
- A flashback is an event from the past that explains something about the present.

Now Write   Choose a story to tell. Make some notes about setting, characters, plot, and conflict. Then develop the plot by making a chronological list of the events that will tell your story. Save these pre-writing notes in your folder.

189

Advanced Students

Because students tend to emphasize plot above all other elements of a narrative, monitor their writing carefully. Remind them to deal fully with character development, setting, and conflict. Encourage their use of the flashback.

Optional Practice

Have each student create a character, deciding on his or her appearance, personality, hobbies, etc. (or they may use the biography they developed for **Optional Practice** in Part 1). Then give them an external and an internal conflict and have them write how their character would handle these situations. The conflicts can be funny (ending up with two dates for the prom) or serious (an illness). Make sure the events are presented in chronological order.

Extending the Lesson

Using nonfiction sources (essays, biography, autobiography, etc.), have students find simple narratives that describe different kinds of conflict.

Objective

To recognize the four points of view and to use them appropriately

Presenting the Lesson

1. Review the definition of *point of view*. Refer students to pages 118–119.

2. Read and discuss **Here's the Idea.** Ask students which pronouns are usually used for different points of view. Give students specific examples of the difference between third-person limited and third-person omniscient.

   a. I looked around the room and knew immediately who the thief was. first-person

   b. The detective looked around the room and then pointed his finger at the thief. third-person limited

   c. The world-famous detective, having used his remarkable powers of deduction, looked around the room and pointed at the thief. third-person omniscient

3. Read and discuss **Check It Out.** Ask students what they would need to do to change this passage to first-person point of view. Then assign **Try Your Skill.** Have students read their revised passages aloud.

4. Read **Keep This in Mind** and then assign **Now Write.** Have students indicate which pronouns they would use for the point of view they have chosen.

Individualizing the Lesson

Less-Advanced Students

Prepare copies of a narrative composition. Have students identify whether the composition is written in

Choosing Your Lane

Pre-Writing: Developing a Point of View

Here's the Idea   Before you write a narrative, you must choose a narrator. A narrator is the person who tells your story. You may choose a narrator who is a character in the story, or one who is not. Your choice will determine the point of view of your story. **Point of view** refers to the eyes and mind through which the story is told.

If you choose a narrator who is a character in the story, you will be using the **first-person point of view.** In stories told from this point of view, the narrator takes part in the events of the story. The narrator tells about these events using the pronouns *I*, *me*, and *we*. The reader learns about only what this one character, the narrator, sees and knows.

If you choose a narrator who is not a character in the story, you will be using the **third-person point of view.** In stories told from this point of view, the narrator is an outsider. The narrator tells about the events of the story using pronouns such as *he*, *she*, *it*, and *they*.

There are two kinds of third-person point of view that you can use. One is called **third-person limited.** In stories told in this way, the narrator reports only what the characters say and do. The other third-person point of view is called **third-person omniscient.** The word *omniscient* means "all knowing." In a story told in this way, the narrator knows everything about the characters. The narrator reports not only what the characters say and do, but also what they think and feel.

Check It Out   Read this passage.

Kyril's parents were ecstatic when she told them the news. "Imagine, Rana," her father enthused, "our daughter a Guardian."

"She trained hard, Elech," her mother said. "She knew how much this meant to us."

Kyril turned away, feeling sick at heart. How could she possibly turn down the appointment? Her parents' disappointment would be too much to bear. Still, her dream was, as it had always been, to become a Builder. Kyril knew she needed help, and she knew just whom she must seek it from.

"Mother, Father," Kyril said, "I have much to prepare myself for. Do you suppose I might visit Uncle Arius, to gain his counsel?"

"A splendid idea," her father said. "Arius has much to tell you. I shall contact him this evening."

- Is the narrator a character in the story or an outsider?
- What point of view has the writer chosen for this story? Explain how you know.

Try Your Skill   Imagine that you are Kyril, the central character in the narrative you have been reading. Imagine that you are telling your own story. Rewrite the paragraphs in **Check It Out** using the first-person point of view.

Keep This in Mind

- Point of view is the eyes and mind through which a story is told.
- A story can be told from the first-person, third-person limited, or third-person omniscient point of view.

Now Write   Choose a point of view that suits the story you are telling. Add your choice to your pre-writing notes. Save your notes in your folder.

the first person or third person and circle the pronouns that indicate the point of view.

Advanced Students

Have students experiment with changing the point of view of a narrative. Have each student find a short news story in a newspaper or magazine and rewrite the account, using the same facts, but with a different point of view.

Optional Practice

Remind students that readers can not always trust the narrator in first-person point of view narrations. Tell them to think of an emotional situation (an accident, an argument, a surprise, etc.) and write an account of that incident from the point of view of first one participant and then another.

Extending the Lesson

Have students turn to the short story section of their literature anthologies. Ask them to identify the point of view of each story by reading the first paragraph of the story. Ask them to explain their choices.

Objective

To write the first draft using an introduction, body, and conclusion

Presenting the Lesson

1. Write the words *introduction, body,* and *conclusion* on the chalkboard. Have students define each word.

2. Read and discuss **Here's the Idea.** Make sure students understand what is meant by *showing* rather than *telling about* the action. Ask students for examples of the differences.

3. Read **Check It Out.** Point out the use of italics rather than quotation marks in the passage to indicate thoughts rather than speech.

4. Assign **Try Your Skill.** If possible, duplicate the different paragraphs so the class can compare their work.

5. Read **Keep This in Mind.**

6. Assign **Now Write.**

Individualizing the Lesson

Less-Advanced Students

Work individually with students to make sure they have enough details and a real conflict before they begin writing their first draft for **Now Write.**

Advanced Students

Have students exchange their introductions from **Now Write.** Ask them to offer suggestions for improvement in showing the conflict rather than telling about it.

Moving into the Lead

Writing the First Draft

Here's the Idea After choosing a point of view, you are ready to write your first draft. This draft should have three parts: an introduction, a body, and a conclusion. Use your pre-writing notes as you write each part. Feel free to add or change details as they occur to you. However, stick to one point of view and to one central conflict.

Begin with the introductory paragraph. In this paragraph, describe the setting and introduce your characters. The beginning of a narrative should also suggest the conflict.

Next, write the paragraphs of the body. Use the list of events given in your pre-writing notes. Start by developing the conflict. Do not simply *tell* your readers what the conflict is. Instead, *show* your readers the conflict through the actions, speech, and thoughts of your characters. In the rest of the body, describe the events that further develop the conflict. Show how the main character struggles with his or her major problem or difficulty.

In the concluding paragraph, describe the event that settles the conflict. Remember that this event is usually a decision or action on the part of the main character. Do not simply tell your readers how the conflict is settled. Instead, show the conflict being settled by describing what the main character does to end it.

Check It Out Read this paragraph from the body of a narrative.

During the brief flight to Nutrus, home base of the Guardians, Kyril was beset by doubts. *Perhaps I'm being foolish,* she thought. *Anyone else would give a fortune for an appointment to the Guardians. Besides, if I don't accept the ap-*

pointment, my parents will be furious. They've done so much for me, and seeing me become a Guardian would please them so. Still Kyril could not forget her dream. Remembering the floating cities of New Caliphstan and the vow she made as a young girl seemed to strengthen her resolve. *Why shouldn't I become a builder,* she reasoned. *It's my life, after all. I should be free to pursue my own dreams.* Yet, as the shuttle craft eased into the landing bay, Kyril remained undecided. Seeing her uncle in the arrival lounge, dressed in the striking silvers of a Guardian general, only added to her confusion.

- Does this body paragraph further develop the conflict of the narrative? Explain your answer.

Try Your Skill   Imagine you are writing a story about a character's struggle for survival after his light plane crashes into a dense rain forest. Write an opening paragraph or two that sets the story in motion by introducing the main character and describing the event that begins his struggles. Compare your opening with those of your classmates.

Keep This in Mind

- In a narrative, the introduction presents the setting and the characters. It also suggests the conflict.
- The body develops the plot and the conflict.
- The conclusion settles the conflict and ends the story.

Now Write   Use your pre-writing notes to write the first draft of the introduction to your narrative composition. Be sure your introduction sets the scene, introduces the characters, and suggests a conflict. Save your work in your folder.

Have students read a short narrative from their literature text. Discuss the story in terms of introduction, body, and conclusion as well as how the author shows the conflict through the action, speech, and thoughts of his or her characters.

Extending the Lesson

Bring in some examples of famous conclusions from literature (*Huckleberry Finn, The Legend of Sleepy Hollow,* etc.). Be sure that students understand that the conclusion must do more than just repeat the introduction. Explain that it is in the conclusion that the author may surprise the reader, or explain the main idea of the narrative.

Part 5

Picking up the Pace

The First Draft: Dialogue

Objective

To use dialogue and dialogue tags to develop characters

Presenting the Lesson

1. Read and discuss **Here's the Idea.** Emphasize the difference between a direct and indirect quotation. Discuss the importance of writing dialogue as realistically as possible.

2. Read and discuss **Check It Out.** Have students cite specific words that tell about the characters' personalities and feelings.

3. Assign **Try Your Skill.** Remind students to start a new paragraph for each new speaker.

4. Read **Keep This in Mind** and then assign **Now Write.** Remind students that dialogue not only moves the narrative along, but makes a story more interesting.

Individualizing the Lesson

Less-Advanced Students

1. Go over the rules for writing dialogue correctly in Handbook Section 14, pages 683–687.

2. Do **Try Your Skill** in class. Have students first identify where each speaker begins talking and ends talking. Then have students identify the dialogue tags and decide which dialogue they describe. Then have them add the proper punctuation.

Advanced Students

Have students work in groups to develop a script for a play based on

Here's the Idea   Many narratives about people include dialogue. Dialogue is simply conversation between characters. Writers use dialogue to communicate important information to their readers.

You can use dialogue to reveal the personalities of your characters. Through dialogue, you can show what your characters think and feel about themselves, about events, and about other characters. You can also use dialogue to tell what events are happening in a story.

When writing dialogue, keep in mind the way people actually speak. Try to make your dialogue as realistic as possible. Use dialogue tags to tell who is speaking and how the words are spoken. A dialogue tag is an expression such as *Laurie replied* or *Carlos whispered*. You can use dialogue tags to show how a character is feeling. For instance, instead of writing *Carlotta said*, you can write *Carlotta shouted*, or *Carlotta whimpered*.

When you give the exact words of a speaker, use quotation marks around them. Begin a new paragraph each time a different character speaks. For more information on writing dialogue correctly, see pages 683–687 in the Handbook.

Check It Out   Read this dialogue.

After dinner on her first night in Nutrus, Kyril explained her problem to Arius.

"What?" Arius exploded. "Not accept your appointment to the Guardians? It's preposterous! Unheard of! An insult to Her Eminence, the Exeter. Have you taken leave of your senses, Kyril?"

"No," Kyril replied softly, "In fact, in some ways I've never been more sure of myself."

"Why did you train so long and hard?" Arius demanded.

"Because I wanted to please Rana and Elech," Kyril answered. "I never thought I'd actually make it."

"Not make it?" Arius sputtered. "You've a brilliant mind, Kyril. A strong body. You were born to be a Guardian."

"I was born to be Kyril," she said simply. "And Kyril's dream is to be a Builder. Have you never pursued a dream, Arius?"

"Of course I have," Arius replied gruffly. "That's why I am a Guardian general today."

"Then help me to have my dream, Arius. Show me the way," Kyril pleaded.

- What does this dialogue reveal about Kyril and Arius?
- Do the dialogue tags explain how each character is feeling? Explain your answer.

Try Your Skill   Write the following dialogue correctly. To check your work, see pages 683–687 in the Handbook.

Answers in Teacher's Notes.

My tooth hurts so much moaned Joan who was holding her jaw I know how it must ache said Dr. Goldberg gently this won't hurt a bit is that a promise asked Joan Dr. Goldberg reassured her all right said Joan with a sigh let's get on with it.

Keep This in Mind

- Dialogue is conversation between two characters.
- Dialogue can reveal the thoughts and feelings of your characters. It can also advance the action of a story.

Now Write   Continue writing the first draft of the narrative you began in the previous lesson. Add dialogue in appropriate places. Follow the rules for writing dialogue correctly. Save your work in your folder.

one of the narratives in their literature book. Show them how dialogue is presented in a script and how dialogue tags become stage directions.

Optional Practice

Ask students to write a sentence for each of the following situations. Tell them to include interesting and revealing dialogue tags.

1. a witch asking a small child to come into her gingerbread house
2. a teenager asking her mother for the car keys
3. a grandmother asking her grandson to clean his room
4. an alien creature asking a passerby for directions

Extending the Lesson

To encourage students to use dialogue in their narratives, have them present their stories orally as if they were radio dramas. They could include sound effects also. Have them tape the presentation.

"My tooth hurts so much," moaned Joan who was holding her jaw.

"I know how it must ache," said Dr. Goldberg gently. "This won't hurt a bit."

"Is that a promise?" asked Joan.

Dr. Goldberg reassured her.

"All right," said Joan with a sigh, "Let's get on with it."

Objective

To use transitions between and within paragraphs to show chronological order

Presenting the Lesson

1. Read and discuss **Here's the Idea.** Review the purpose of transitions in a narrative to show chronological order. If necessary, refer students to the definition of a flashback on page 188.

2. Discuss **Check It Out.** Ask students if any flashback is included in this passage.

3. Assign **Try Your Skill.** Have students make up a master list of transitional words and phrases to refer to when writing narratives.

4. Read **Keep This in Mind** and then assign **Now Write.** Have students include a minimum of five transitions in their narratives.

Individualizing the Lesson

Less-Advanced Students

Go over the first drafts from **Now Write** with the students on an individual basis. Allow time in class for writing the first draft, as well as for revising.

Advanced Students

Duplicate a short narrative composition and distribute copies to the class. Have students underline the transitions used within the paragraphs and to circle the transitions used between paragraphs.

One Lap To Go

The First Draft: Transitions

Here's the Idea   As you know, the events in a story should be told in chronological order. If the order of the events is not clear, the reader will become confused. When writing the first draft of a story, keep the order of events clear by using transitions.

In a story, use transitional words and phrases that tell *when* events occur. They are used within paragraphs and between paragraphs. Notice how such words and phrases are used in the following paragraph.

> *While* Felicidad filled the tank with fresh water, I changed the filter. *Soon*, the aquarium was ready for its new occupants. *First*, we poured in the water containing the neon tetras. These were the smallest of our fish. *Then*, we added the angel fish and the pearl gouramis. *Only later* did we realize that the tiny tetras might be in danger of becoming some larger fish's seafood dinner.

You must be particularly careful to use transitions whenever you write flashbacks. A sudden change in time can confuse your readers unless the change is signaled by a transition. Always use transitions, such as *a while before* or *earlier that morning*, to let your readers know what is happening. Then, when you want to return to the present time in your story, use another transition, such as *now* or *at present*.

Check It Out   Read these paragraphs.

> Two days after her dinner with Arius, Kyril left for home. True to his word, Arius had helped Kyril formulate a plan. First she would contact the personal emissary to the Exeter of Cal-

iph. Kyril would thank the Exeter for her kind consideration, express her disappointment at having to decline the appointment, and petition Her Eminence to release her from the Guardians. Next, she would apply for admission to the Builder's Institute. Finally, and this was the part Kyril dreaded, she would inform her parents of her decision. Arius had promised to help with this task.

When the starcruiser was safely in dock, Kyril walked out to meet her waiting parents. She spied them in a corner of the arrival lounge. It was clear from their faces that Arius had already done his work.

"Mother, Father, I am pleased to see you," Kyril said.

"And we to see you," her father said stiffly.

Rana smiled warmly at her daughter.

"Come Kyril, Elech. We have much to talk over," she said.

- Which transitional words and phrases within the first paragraph tell *when?*
- What transitional phrase links the first paragraph with what has come before it? the second paragraph with the first?

Try Your Skill   Look at the list of transitional words and phrases on pages 120–121. See how many words and phrases you can add to this list. Try to add at least ten. Compare your additions with those of your classmates.

> ### Keep This in Mind
>
> - Use transitional words and phrases to show the order of time within and between paragraphs.

Now Write   Finish writing the first draft of your story. Add transitional words and phrases wherever they are needed. Be sure to solve the conflict at the end of your narrative. Save your work in your folder.

Have students write a paragraph about their day in school. Have them keep the order of events clear by using transitional words and phrases that tell when events occur.

Extending the Lesson

Tell students to imagine they are reporters interviewing eyewitnesses to the landing of the first flying saucer. Divide the class into groups, and have each group make up a news story about the interview, using transitions that help tell what each eyewitness saw first, second, etc.

Objective

To revise the narrative composition

Presenting the Lesson

1. Read and discuss **Here's the Idea.** Explain that students will have to read through their compositions a few times in order to think about all the guidelines for revision. Remind them that they will probably want to revise their work more than once.

2. Discuss **Check It Out.** Make sure students understand that parts of their compositions can be moved around or left out if necessary.

3. Assign **Try Your Skill.** It is suggested that this exercise be done in class.

4. Read **Keep This in Mind** and then assign **Now Write.** Tell students to be especially careful when checking the punctuation of their dialogue.

Individualizing the Lesson

Less-Advanced Students

Help the students set up a checklist of things to look for when proofreading and revising. Then as they go over their narratives, they can check off each item they have looked for in their own work. Ask them to hand in their checklists when they give you their final copy of their narrative composition.

Advanced Students

Read several short stories with surprise endings to the class. Discuss the effectiveness of the endings. Ask students how they might

198

The Checkered Flag

Revising Your Narrative Composition

Here's the Idea   You have heard and read many stories. Use this experience to identify strengths and weaknesses when you revise your own narrative composition.

Once you have completed your rough draft, read your story several times. Pretend that you are reading the story in a magazine. If you were just a reader of the story, not its author, would you find the story interesting? Would you like some parts of the story and not like other parts? If so, which parts do you think could be improved? Use the following questions to find ways to make your story better.

1.   Does the story have a point? Is that point clear?

2.   Does the introduction set the scene and introduce the characters? Does it suggest the conflict?

3.   Does the story seem complete? Do more events need to be added to complete the story? Do more details need to be added to keep the reader interested?

4.   Are the events arranged in chronological order?

5.   If any flashbacks are used, are they effective?

6.   Is the conflict clear? Does the body of the story develop the conflict in an interesting way?

7.   Does the story use a single point of view throughout?

8.   Does the story use dialogue to relate events and to reveal the thoughts and feelings of characters? Does it use dialogue tags to tell who is speaking?

9.   Does the story use transitions effectively?

10.   Does the conclusion show how the conflict is solved? Is the conclusion effective and interesting?

When you are satisfied with your story, proofread it. Find and correct any errors in grammar, usage, and mechanics.

198

Check It Out   Notice how this narrative has been revised.

> *¶ Back at home,*
> ^Kyril and her parents ~~talked about~~ *discussed* the future.
>
> "I took the tests ^*only* to make you ^*please* ~~happy~~ Kyril said. "I knew how much it meant to you."
>
> "It did mean a ^*great deal* ~~lot~~ to us," Elech said. "But your happiness is more important to us than ^*our own desires."* ~~we are.~~
>
> "Kyril," Rana said, "the decisions you make ^*now* about your future are very important. You ^*must* ~~should not~~ ^*compromise* ~~change~~ your ideals. Be- come a Builder, Kyril, ^The best builder you can be. That ~~would~~ *will* make us happy."

- How has this first draft been improved?

Try Your Skill   Here is the ending of the narrative you have been reading. Use your revising skills to improve it.

Kyril lay in bed. She thought about her parents. How won- derful they were. How understanding. She thought about the floating cities. She wanted to take her daughter their one day. She hoped her daughter would say "Mother, whose dream was this place."

"Mine" Kyril would reply softly. "All mine".

Keep This in Mind

- Revise your narrative so that it is the best story you can tell.

Now Write   Use the guidelines in this lesson to revise the first draft of your narrative. Proofread it for errors in grammar, usage, and mechanics. Make a final copy. Save your story.

use a surprise ending in their **Now Write** compositions.

Optional Practice

Divide students into groups and have them read their revised com- positions aloud to their groups. Ask them if they found anything in their compositions they would like to re- vise or correct after reading their work aloud. Explain that authors often use this technique to help them revise their writing.

Extending the Lesson

Have students compile their com- positions into "books" with illustra- tions, table of contents, etc. Present these storybooks to some younger classes in a nearby grammar school, or to a local children's hos- pital. You might also have volun- teers from your class read these stories aloud to some of these groups.

Section 16 Objectives

1. To gather and organize sensory details to develop a descriptive composition

2. To group details around main ideas and to use spatial order to organize those details and ideas

3. To write the first draft using an introduction, body, and conclusion

4. To use transitions between sentences and paragraphs to make spatial order clear

5. To write a conclusion that summarizes the main ideas and shows the writer's feelings about a subject

6. To revise the descriptive composition

Preparing the Students

Ask students to close their eyes and think about an experience they remember vividly. Ask them what details their memory makes them see. Explain that this Section will help them make other people clearly see what they see through their writing.

Additional Resources

Practice Book — pages 82–85
Duplicating Masters — pages 82–85

The Descriptive Composition

Teaching Special Populations

LD See **Teaching Special Populations,** pages 82–83.

ESL Help students choose appropriate topics for their descriptive compositions. Refer them to the list of sensory words on pages 20–21. Be sure students understand the vocabulary presented in each of the examples.

NSD See **Teaching Special Populations,** pages 82–83.

Objectives

1. To gather and organize sensory details to develop a descriptive composition

2. To group details around main ideas and to use spatial order to organize those details and ideas

Presenting the Lesson

1. Review what students have learned about a descriptive paragraph (Section 10). Then read and discuss **Here's the Idea.** On the chalkboard list the steps for planning a descriptive composition: choosing a subject that appeals to the senses, gathering sensory details, grouping the details together, and presenting the groups of details in spatial order.

2. Read and discuss **Check It Out.** Ask students what sort of spatial order these notes might use.

3. Assign **Try Your Skill.** It is suggested that this exercise be done in class.

4. Write **Keep This in Mind** on the board and review each part with the class before assigning **Now Write.**

5. Assign **Now Write.** Remind students that they can ask the questions *who, what, where, when* and *how* to help them think of details.

Individualizing the Lesson

Less-Advanced Students

Hold a brainstorming session to help students choose and narrow a topic for **Now Write.** Have each student tell the class what topics he or she has been considering, and

A Sensible Approach

Pre-Writing: Using Sensory Details

Here's the Idea   A descriptive composition is much like a picture. It presents a portrait of a person, place, or thing. Like a picture, a descriptive composition can communicate both information and feelings about the subject.

When planning a descriptive composition, you should choose a subject that appeals to several senses. A song, for example, would not be a good subject. It appeals only to the sense of hearing. However, a rock concert would be a good subject. It appeals to several senses at once.

Once you have chosen a subject, your next step is to gather sensory details. These are details that tell how your subject looks, sounds, smells, feels, and tastes. Not every subject can be described with all five senses. However, you should try to gather many different sensory details about your subject. Gather these details through observation or by using your memory.

When you have finished gathering your details, look them over carefully. All of the details should be about your subject. For example, suppose you were writing about a concert. All of the details would be about the concert. Some details might be about the crowd. Others might be about the atmosphere, the group that was performing, or the music itself. By grouping like details together, you can create idea groups that will become paragraphs in your composition.

After you organize your details into groups, you must decide in what order to present them. Most descriptive compositions are organized according to spatial order. **Spatial order** shows how details are related to each other in space. If your details do not lend themselves to spatial order, you may want to arrange them in whatever order you want the reader to notice them. To learn more about organizing a description, see pages 126–129.

Check It Out   Read these pre-writing notes.

Topic: Greenleaf Beach

air mattress bobbing on waves
hot dogs, chips, candy, ice cream
concession stand (bright red roof)
little kids splashing each other in shallow water
volleyball game in progress ("slap" of ball)
refreshing lemonade, colas, iced tea
lifeguard rowing yellow patrol boat
water cold but not unbearable
kids building sand sculptures
long lines for snacks

• What senses do these pre-writing notes appeal to?

Try Your Skill   The notes in **Check It Out** can be divided into three idea groups. Decide what those idea groups are. Then, on a piece of paper, write a word or phrase to describe each idea group. Under each word or phrase, list the details from the pre-writing notes that belong in that group. Save these notes.

Keep This in Mind

• Develop a descriptive composition with sensory details.
• Organize like details into idea groups.
• Organize your idea groups and the details within them according to spatial order or in the order that you want the reader to notice them.

Now Write   Choose a topic for a descriptive composition. Make a list of sensory details. Organize like details into idea groups. Arrange the idea groups and the details within them in spatial order or in the order that you want your readers to notice them. Save your organized notes in your folder.

have the others ask questions to help the student recall the details that are needed.

Advanced Students

Have students make a list of sensory details that they might hear, feel, taste, see, or smell when swimming underwater. Then have them make a list of the sensory details they would experience when riding on a boat on the water.

Optional Practice

Have students write a list of sensory details that they experience when doing a hobby or favorite job (painting, fixing a car, baking bread, working in the garden, etc.). Then have them group these details and put them into spatial order.

Extending the Lesson

Bring in different objects that appeal to the senses: perfume, spices, vinegar, cotton, sandpaper, etc. Ask students to think of words that would describe these sensory objects.

Make the Scene

Writing the First Draft

Part 2

Objectives

1. To write the first draft using an introduction, body, and conclusion

2. To use transitions between sentences and paragraphs to make spatial order clear

Presenting the Lesson

1. Read and discuss **Here's the Idea.** Write *spatial order* on the board and ask students for its definition. Remind them that spatial order can start anywhere, depending on what they are trying to describe. Then discuss mood and why it is important in a description.

2. Read and discuss **Check It Out.** Ask students what the spatial order of details is based on (view from a distance outside the crater to close up inside the crater).

3. Assign **Try Your Skill.** Have students underline the transitional words and phrases they use in their paragraph.

4. Read **Keep This in Mind** and then assign **Now Write.**

Individualizing the Lesson

Less-Advanced Students

Have students do **Try Your Skill** with a partner.

Advanced Students

Ask students to choose one of the following topics and write a paragraph about it, conveying first one mood and then a second paragraph describing an opposite mood.

1. a hot summer afternoon
2. a large dog

Here's the Idea   When you write the first draft of your descriptive composition, try to picture your subject clearly in your mind. The clearer this picture is, the more vivid your description will be.

Begin your first draft with an introduction. Try to capture the interest and imagination of your readers. State the specific subject of your description in one sentence of the introduction.

Develop the description of your subject in the body of the composition. Each group of ideas in your pre-writing notes will become a paragraph in the body of your composition.

End your composition with a strong conclusion. This paragraph should sum up the feelings and ideas in the composition.

Don't forget to show the reader where things are in your description by using transitional words and phrases. Examples of words and phrases you can use include *on top of, behind, above, below, to the left, to the right, near,* and *far.*

Try to create a specific mood with your description. Choose nouns, verbs, adjectives, and adverbs that will suggest a certain feeling. To learn more about mood, see pages 130–131.

Check It Out   Read the introduction and body of this descriptive composition.

Volcanoes have always fascinated me. I have seen color photographs of the Hawaiian volcano Kilauea shooting flames and molten, glowing lava. I have seen other pictures showing the volcanic island Surtsey with dense clouds of dust pouring from the summit. I thought I knew exactly what it would be like to stare into the crater of a volcano. However, my mental image was changed forever by the surprising appearance of Haleakala Crater on the island of Maui in Hawaii.

The towering Haleakala was much bigger than I had expected. The crater itself, which we were allowed to enter, is seven and a half miles long, two and a half miles wide, and more than two thousand feet deep. We could see that the crater formed a bowl-shaped depression dotted with powdery black cones sticking up from its surface. These cones appeared from a distance to be about as tall as a person. As we approached them, though, we realized that they were actually about ten stories tall.

The name *Haleakala* means "House of the Sun," but from its depths, the crater resembled photographs I had seen of the surface of the moon. Everywhere we saw reddish dust and cinders. It was also strangely quiet. The crunching of cinders underfoot was the only sound. The air felt hot and dry, and the gritty dust rose everywhere until I could taste it.

- Does the introduction present the subject?
- Is the body developed with vivid sensory details? What senses do the details appeal to?

Try Your Skill   Reread the pre-writing notes you organized in **Try Your Skill** in Part 1. Select one of the three idea groups you developed. Use the notes from this idea group to write a descriptive paragraph. Be sure the paragraph has a strong topic sentence and that the details are well organized. Compare your paragraph with those of your classmates.

Keep This in Mind

- In a descriptive composition, use transitional words and phrases that tell *where* to show the order of your details.

Now Write   Begin writing the first draft of your descriptive composition. For now, just write the introduction and the body of your composition. Save your work in your folder.

3. a grade on a composition
4. a move to a new city

Optional Practice

Create a still-life setting in the classroom. Have students write a short description of the setting, using transitional words and phrases to make the spatial order clear. Have them compare their finished descriptions.

Extending the Lesson

Have students bring in examples of descriptions and read them aloud. Have the rest of the class try to draw what is being described from the details that are read. Ask students which descriptions they found the easiest to draw and what that tells them about the description.

The End in Sight

The First Draft: Ending a Description

Objective

To write a conclusion that summarizes the main ideas and shows the writer's feelings about a subject

Presenting the Lesson

1. Read and discuss **Here's the Idea.** Stress that a conclusion does not suddenly change in feeling from the total impression given in the introduction and body. Mention surprise endings, and how they too must follow logically from what has gone before.

2. Read and discuss **Check It Out.** Have students reread the introduction and body of the composition on pages 204–205 while thinking of what points should be brought out in the conclusion.

3. Assign **Try Your Skill.** This exercise could be done with in-class writing groups.

4. Read **Keep This in Mind** and then assign **Now Write.**

Individualizing the Lesson

Less-Advanced Students

Have students first list the main ideas from their descriptive composition before they begin to write the conclusion for **Try Your Skill.**

Advanced Students

Duplicate descriptive compositions from your files. Analyze the sample conclusions; have the students identify key ideas in the introductions that are repeated in the conclusions. Have them discuss what makes a good conclusion.

Here's the Idea   Suppose that you are listening to your favorite song on the radio. You are really enjoying the music when, suddenly, the disc jockey interrupts the song for a commercial. How would this make you feel? Of course, you would feel cheated. To be completely satisfying, a song must have a conclusion.

A good conclusion is also important in a descriptive composition. The conclusion of a descriptive composition should be a single paragraph. The paragraph should tie together the ideas presented in the rest of the composition. It should also tell the reader how you feel about your subject.

To write the conclusion of a description, think about the ideas and details you have presented. What is the mood created by these details? How can you summarize your feelings about them? What lasting impression about your subject do you want to leave with your readers?

Always make sure that the conclusion follows naturally from what has come before it. For instance, if the composition is light and cheery, the conclusion should not be sad or gloomy. Only if you keep the same mood will the conclusion of your composition make sense.

Check It Out   Review the descriptive composition about Haleakala Crater that is shown in the last lesson. Notice how the description is organized. Then read the following conclusion.

> After our return climb up one of the trails within the crater, I thought about my previous images of volcanoes. I thought of the stories I had read about Stromboli and Vesuvius and Krakatoa and their violent eruptions. I realized that quiet, colorful

Haleakala had impressed me because it was so different. In fact, Haleakala Crater was so unexpected that I think I shall never forget it.

- Does the conclusion summarize the ideas presented in the composition?
- How does the writer feel about the subject? How do you know?

Try Your Skill Imagine you have written the composition about Haleakala. What kind of conclusion would you write? Draft a concluding paragraph for this composition. Sum up the ideas in the composition. Leave the reader with some lasting impression of the subject. Compare your conclusion with those of your classmates.

Keep This in Mind

- In the conclusion, summarize your ideas and show your feelings about the subject.

Now Write Review the introduction and body of the descriptive composition you have been writing. Then write the conclusion. Summarize your ideas and your feelings in the conclusion. Save your first draft in your folder.

Objective

To revise the descriptive composition

Presenting the Lesson

1. Read and discuss **Here's the Idea.** List the questions for revision on the board as you discuss them. Ask students if they can think of anything else to look for when they revise (strong verbs and adjectives, clear and specific details, etc.).

2. Read and discuss **Check It Out.** Ask students if they would have made the same revisions and why. Explain that there are many ways to revise.

3. Read and assign **Try Your Skill.** Ask volunteers to read their revisions aloud.

4. Read **Keep This in Mind** and then assign **Now Write.**

Individualizing the Lesson

Less-Advanced Students

Do **Try Your Skill** with students as a class exercise. Use any mistakes that they do not see or understand as the basis for a review lesson.

Advanced Students

Have students bring in examples of descriptions from literature or the travel sections of newspapers or magazines. Discuss the descriptions using the questions on page 208 as a guide.

Optional Practice

Set up peer-editing groups. Have students follow the guidelines for revision in this Part as their model for

208

The Final View

Revising Your Descriptive Paragraph

Here's the Idea   The last step in writing a descriptive composition is revising. When you revise, keep in mind that your purpose is to describe your subject as clearly as possible. As you read your first draft, ask yourself whether your composition achieves this goal.

Here are some other questions to ask yourself as you revise your work.

1. Does the introductory paragraph tell the reader what my subject is?

2. Does each paragraph in the body have a good topic sentence?

3. Did I include enough sensory details to develop my description completely?

4. Did I arrange my details in a logical order?

5. Did I use transitional words and phrases to make the order of the details clear?

6. Does the description create a single strong mood or feeling? Did I use specific language to create this mood?

7. Does the conclusion sum up the ideas in my composition? Does it tell the reader how I feel about my subject?

After you have revised the content, organization, and language of your description, proofread the composition carefully. Check for errors in grammar, capitalization, punctuation, and spelling. Correct any errors that you find.

Check It Out   Notice how this introduction to a descriptive composition has been revised.

- How has the topic sentence been improved?
- What kinds of details have been added during revision?
- What errors in grammar and mechanics were corrected?

Try Your Skill   Revise the following paragraph from the same composition.

In the basement the floor is made with cobblestone bricks. Their is an old coal cellar. Its really neat inside it. The walls have all been blackened with coal dust. The basement also got a wine cellar. There is metal racks against the wall where wine bottles were. Because the ground has shifted over the years, the floor is very uneven. Its funny how it seems to roll along.

Keep This in Mind

- Revise your descriptive composition so that your subject is described clearly and completely.

Now Write   Using the guidelines in this lesson, revise your descriptive composition. Proofread your work. Give your composition a title. Then, make a clean, neat final copy. Proofread this copy one last time and neatly correct any errors you find. Save your composition in your folder.

editing. Be sure to make yourself available to help resolve any problems that might come up and to direct discussions from just finding errors to also finding writing techniques to emulate.

Extending the Lesson

Work with the art teacher to encourage students to illustrate their descriptive compositions using different art media. Display the compositions and art projects together.

Section **17** Objectives

1. To learn to explain a process
2. To organize an explanation in step-by-step order
3. To use appropriate transitions that tell *when*
4. To revise an explanatory composition explaining a process

Preparing the Students

Review Section 11 with the students. Point out that an explanatory composition explaining a process differs from an explanatory paragraph explaining a process in length only. Explain that explanatory compositions are written about subjects that are too long or complicated to be covered in a single paragraph. Tell students that this Section will teach them to write an explanatory composition that explains a process.

Additional Resources

Mastery Test — pages 28–29 in the test booklet
Practice Book — pages 86–89
Duplicating Masters — page 86–89

The Explanatory Composition

Explaining a Process

Teaching Special Populations

LD See **Teaching Special Populations,** pages 82–83. Help students to choose and narrow appropriate topics.

ESL Review with students transitional words and phrases that help indicate time sequence, and that act to bridge ideas. Provide additional exercises based on these words.

Have students read their papers to a group, and ask members of the group to suggest additional revisions that would make the process being explained even clearer.

NSD See **Teaching Special Populations,** pages 82–83.

Objective

To learn to explain a process

Presenting the Lesson

1. Read and discuss **Here's the Idea.** Ask students for specific examples of topics for both kinds of explanatory compositions that explain a process. Then, write on the chalkboard the three steps in planning an explanatory composition.

2. Read and discuss **Check It Out.** Ask students if all the materials required in this process are listed in the pre-writing notes.

3. Assign **Try Your Skill.** It is suggested that this exercise be done as a class discussion.

4. Read **Keep This in Mind** aloud.

5. Assign **Now Write.** Go over some of the topics chosen for **Try Your Skill** and discuss their suitability for a composition of this length.

Individualizing the Lesson

Less-Advanced Students

Have the class work together to assemble pre-writing notes for a simple process such as preparing dinner or planning a party. Write students' suggestions on the chalkboard, making sure they include materials necessary for the process.

Advanced Students

Have students make a set of pre-writing notes for one of the following topics. Make sure they include all the steps to the process and list any necessary tools, ingredients, or materials needed.

212

The Way It's Done

Pre-Writing: Planning an Explanation

Here's the Idea   Everyone has given directions at one time or another. You may have given directions explaining how to make something, such as scrambled eggs or a model rocket. You may have given directions explaining how to do something, such as lift weights or paint with watercolors.

One type of explanatory composition that explains a process includes a set of directions. The directions tell how to do something. Another composition that explains a process might tell how things work or happen. A composition of this type might explain how a car muffler works or how earthquakes happen.

Both types of explanatory compositions explain the steps in a process. When writing such a composition, you must explain each step simply and clearly. You start with the first step and proceed through all the steps in the order in which they happen or should be done.

The first step in writing your explanatory composition is to choose and narrow a topic. The best ideas come from personal experience. For example, if you have played football, you may be able to explain the process of getting prepared for a game. If you have repaired bicycles, you may be able to explain how bicycle gears operate. Always choose a process that you know well so that you can explain it thoroughly.

When you gather details for your pre-writing notes, be sure to include all of the steps in the process you want to explain. If you leave out an important step, your readers may not be able to understand the process. Also be sure to explain the process clearly and directly. List any tools, ingredients, or materials required in the process. Add this list to your pre-writing notes.

212

Check It Out   Read these pre-writing notes.

How To Take Good Photographs

1. Get to know your camera
    no need for expensive camera
    study manual
    learn use of all dials, buttons, and rings
    practice with camera
2. Learn about types of film
    black and white or color
    indoor, outdoor films
3. Take pictures
    subject must be in focus
    hold camera steady
    press shutter-release smoothly

- Do the notes clearly list the steps in a process?

Try Your Skill   Do some brainstorming about processes. Make a list of ten processes that would make good topics for an explanatory composition. Save your list.

Keep This in Mind

- When you want to explain a process, write an explanatory composition.
- In your pre-writing notes, include all of the important steps in the process. List any tools, ingredients, or materials that are needed.
- Explain each step in the process simply and clearly.

Now Write   Choose a process that you would like to explain. You may want to choose one of the topics you developed in **Try Your Skill.** Narrow your topic. Make a set of pre-writing notes to explain your topic. Be sure to include all of the important steps in the process. List any necessary tools, ingredients, or materials. Save your notes in your folder.

1. how to budget your money
2. how to clean an aquarium
3. how to make soup
4. how to fly-cast
5. how clouds are formed

Optional Practice

Demonstrate for the class a process that has clearly defined steps (packing a suitcase, how to record on a tape recorder, etc.). Have students list the steps of the process as you demonstrate. Remind them to make the first step a statement of the materials needed.

Extending the Lesson

Have students bring in "how to" books and magazine articles for a classroom display. Point out to the class the characteristics shared by their examples (specific directions, illustrations, time sequence used for organizing material, etc.).

Objective

To organize an explanation in step-by-step order

Presenting the Lesson

1. Read and discuss **Here's the Idea.** Point out to students that this explanation is written as a composition explaining a process. Make sure they understand that the step-by-step order is the order in which the composition is written: introduction, body, and conclusion.

2. Read and discuss **Check It Out.** Compare the body of the composition with its pre-writing notes on page 213. If necessary, have students list the steps being explained.

3. Assign **Try Your Skill.**

4. Read **Keep This in Mind** and then assign **Now Write.** Tell students that it helps to read their notes aloud to find steps that they might have left out.

Individualizing the Lesson

Less-Advanced Students

1. Do **Try Your Skill** with students in class.

2. Go over students' pre-writing notes for **Now Write** to make sure they are organized correctly and that all the steps are included.

Advanced Students

Have students think of a game they play or played when younger. Tell them to write down the steps for playing this game in step-by-step order. Students can exchange papers to check the thoroughness and clarity of the directions.

214

Stepping Ahead

Pre-Writing: Using Step-by-Step Order

Here's the Idea   In your pre-writing notes for an explanatory composition, you will have a topic and a list of steps. Before you can begin to write, you must organize these steps logically.

The best way to organize an explanatory composition that explains a process, is to follow **step-by-step order.** This is the order in which the steps in a process happen or are done.

First, organize the details you will use in your introduction. Start with a topic sentence that tells what process you will explain. Follow this sentence with any details that might interest your readers in learning about your topic.

Next, organize the details for the body of your composition. Each paragraph in the body will explain one main step and the smaller steps that are part of this main step. Find the first main step in the process. Group the smaller steps that are part of it around it. Then, find the second main step. Group its smaller steps around it. Continue in this way.

If you wish to do so, you may explain the last step and describe the end result of the process in your conclusion. You may also use the conclusion to summarize or review the process as a whole. Another possibility is to use the conclusion to tell your readers why learning about this process is valuable.

Check It Out   Read the body of an explanatory composition about the process of taking good photographs.

Your first step must be to get to know your camera. You do not need an expensive camera to take good pictures. It is more important to know what your camera can or cannot do. You will probably begin by studying the instruction manual. Then practice with the camera itself. Get to know what every dial, button, and ring on your camera is used for.

214

A second necessary step is to learn about the different kinds of film available. You may want to ask a clerk at a camera store for help. You may choose black and white film for certain kinds of photographs. You may choose color film, which is more expensive, for other kinds of pictures.

At last, you are ready to take photographs. Through constant use of a camera you will develop your skills. Be sure the subject of your photograph is in focus. Hold the camera steady. Focus on your subject, and press the shutter-release button smoothly.

- What steps are explained in the body of this composition?
- Has the writer used step-by-step order?

Try Your Skill   Here are some jumbled notes that explain a process. Copy the title and list the steps in the correct order.

How To Wax a Car

4 Apply wax with damp cloth

5 Wipe off excess, polishing to a bright shine

3 Remove any old wax with clean, dry cloth

1 First, wash car

2 Dry car with chamois or lint-free cloth

Keep This in Mind

- In an explanatory composition that explains a process, use step-by-step order to organize your material.

Now Write   Read the pre-writing notes you made in the previous lesson. Organize the steps according to the guidelines in this lesson. Plan to represent your topic in the introduction. In the body, plan to give a step-by-step explanation of the process. In the conclusion, plan to sum up the process, explain the final step of the process, or tell why the process is important. Save your organized notes in your folder.

Have students arrange the following steps in a step-by-step order.

How To Make Popcorn Balls

5 Melt six marshmallows in two tablespoons of butter.

1 You need popcorn kernels, marshmallows, butter, and corn oil for making the popcorn balls.

3 Begin by popping two tablespoons of popcorn kernels in a teaspoon of corn oil.

9 Finally, wrap the balls in the plastic wrap.

2 You will also need clear plastic wrap and a large bowl.

4 Then, put the popped corn in a large bowl while you prepare the syrup.

6 Stir the melted marshmallows and butter into the popcorn.

8 Let the popcorn balls harden overnight.

7 Shape the popcorn and syrup into balls the size of apples.

Extending the Lesson

Divide students into groups and have each group work together to write and organize the pre-writing notes for a composition explaining a process that is important to all students. Topics can be serious or humorous (how to get good grades, how to study for a test, etc.).

First to Last

Writing the First Draft

Part 3

Objective

To use appropriate transitions that tell *when*

Presenting the Lesson

1. Read aloud and discuss **Here's the Idea.** Remind students they have already used some of these transitional words and phrases within paragraphs, but now they should also use them to link paragraphs together.

2. Read and discuss **Check It Out.** Point out that a variety of transitions are used for interest and clarity.

3. Assign **Try Your Skill.** Have volunteers read their revised paragraphs aloud.

4. Read **Keep This in Mind** and then assign **Now Write.** Emphasize that clarity is one of the most important qualities of this kind of composition.

Individualizing the Lesson

Less-Advanced Students

Make sure students do not fall into the habit of numbering each step in their process (*first*, *second*, *third*, etc.). Have them study sample paragraphs from this Section to see how different transitions can be used.

Advanced Students

Have students exchange their first drafts with a partner who should read the paper to see if the step-by-step order is clear and whether enough transitions have been used for coherence.

Here's the Idea   When you write the first draft of your explanatory composition, begin with the introduction. Make sure that this introduction states your topic and captures the interest of your readers. Then, in the body of your composition, present all the steps in the process. Tell about each step in step-by-step order. To make the order of the steps clear, use transitional words and phrases that tell *when*. Here are some examples of these transitions:

first	the next step	when	finally
second	at the same time	before	as soon as
after	after one hour	later	then

Transitions should be used within each paragraph to show the order of each step. Transitions should also be used between paragraphs. They work like bridges to carry the reader from the main idea of one paragraph to the main idea of the next.

Check It Out   Note the transitional words and phrases in the introduction and conclusion of the composition on taking photographs. Review the transitions used in the body of the explanation.

Introduction

What is the best way to recall the most important experience of our lives? Our memories can hold the details of recent experiences with little difficulty. However, most of us need a little help in remembering details about past experiences. The best reminders of special moments are photographs, which capture them forever. With practice, you can take memorable photographs of the special times in your life.

Conclusion

After you shoot a roll of film, it is important to have it developed as soon as possible. Old film will not produce the clearest pictures. When you receive your developed pictures, store the best of them in a photo album or suitable container. Arrange the photographs in a logical order for viewing. As your skill with a camera improves, you will be glad you took the time to take photographs.

- What transitions are used?

Try Your Skill   Read the following explanation of the process of repairing walls. The steps are presented in the correct step-by-step order, but the paragraph is missing transitions. Rewrite the paragraph and add transitional words and phrases to make the order clear. Combine steps whenever it makes sense.

Force the spackling mixture into all cracks or holes. Scrape any excess mixture from the surface of the wall. Let the spackling mixture dry. Add more if any spot is not completely filled. Sand the dry spackling mixture. Wipe off dust. Put on one coat of primer. Let it dry. Paint over primer with paint.

Keep This in Mind

- In an explanatory composition that explains a process, use transitional words and phrases to help make step-by-step order clear.

Now Write   Write the first draft of an explanatory composition explaining a process. Include a topic sentence in your introduction that states the main idea of your composition. Also, be sure that each paragraph in the body of your composition has a topic sentence. Use transitional words and phrases within and between paragraphs. Explain each step clearly. When you are finished with your first draft, save it.

217

Clearly the Best

Objective

To revise an explanatory composition explaining a process

Presenting the Lesson

1. Read and discuss **Here's the Idea.** Outline the revision checklist on the chalkboard as you discuss each point.

2. Read and discuss **Check It Out.** Point out to students how sentences can be moved around during the revision process, and that revision doesn't just mean taking out or putting in new words.

3. Assign **Try Your Skill.** This exercise can be done in class.

4. Read **Keep This in Mind** and then assign **Now Write.** Discuss how to title a composition; students may find a simple, straightforward title the best for an explanatory composition.

Individualizing the Lesson

Less-Advanced Students

Have students work with a partner to revise the paragraph in **Try Your Skill.**

Advanced Students

Encourage these students to think in terms of mental as well as physical processes to write about. Have them write an explanatory composition telling how to overcome fear, how to make a difficult choice, etc.

Optional Practice

Have students revise the following paragraph from the body of a

Revising Your Explanation

Here's the Idea Have you ever tried to follow an explanation that has some steps missing, out of order, or poorly explained? This can be very frustrating. To avoid causing your readers the same kind of frustration, you must revise your explanatory composition carefully.

When revising, try to make your explanation as clear and as simple as possible. To do this, pay close attention to step-by-step order. Make sure you have included *all* the steps in the process. Also make sure that each step is explained completely.

Here are some questions to ask yourself as you revise your composition explaining a process.

1. Does my introduction tell what process the composition will explain? Does it capture the interest of the reader?

2. Have I included *all* the steps in the process I am explaining?

3. Are my details presented in step-by-step order?

4. Does each body paragraph contain a main idea and supporting details?

5. Have I used transitional words and phrases that tell *when* within and between paragraphs?

6. Does the conclusion tell the final step in the process, summarize the process, or tell the reader why learning the process is important or valuable?

When you have revised the content, organization, and language of your composition, proofread it carefully. Check for errors in grammar, capitalization, punctuation, and spelling.

Check It Out Notice how the following paragraph from an explanatory composition has been revised.

- How has this introduction been improved?
- Has this paragraph been proofread? How do you know?

Try Your Skill   Here is a body paragraph from a composition on driving a car with a manual transmission. Use your revising skills to improve it. Compare your revision with those of your classmates.

> The clutch pedal is the one way on the left. You have to step on it. Shift the lever and put the car in gear. Take your foot off the clutch then you can go. Don't step on the break pedal by mistake. Every time you shift the gears you step on this pedal.

Keep This in Mind

- When revising an explanatory composition, your goal is to make it clear and easy for your readers to understand.

Now Write   Following the guidelines in this lesson, revise your explanatory composition. Make sure you have included *all* the steps in the process you chose to explain. Make sure your explanation is clear and correct. When your revision is complete, proofread your composition. Give your work a title. Then, save your finished composition in your folder.

composition on how animals communicate. Answers will vary.

Animals send messages for manny resons. To defend there homes. To find a mate and to warn of danger. They sure cant talk the way we can, but other animals understand them. They make sounds and use smell and touch and colors, and body movements and even make faces to communicate.

Extending the Lesson

Make a class *How-to* book by duplicating the students' revised compositions and assembling them in book form.

Section 18 Objectives

1. To know the elements of an explanatory composition which presents an opinion

2. To write an effective topic sentence which clearly expresses an opinion

3. To use logical reasons and accurate facts to support an opinion

4. To organize reasons in order of importance from least important to most important

5. To write the first draft of an explanatory composition presenting an opinion

6. To revise an explanatory composition which presents an opinion

Preparing the Students

Review with students the difference between a fact and an opinion. Review the ways in which facts can support opinions.

Read aloud one or two editorials from the newspaper, and one or two essays by Andy Rooney. His "Old Clothes," or "Letter Writing" from *And More by Andy Rooney* would be appropriate and interesting selections. Have students discuss how different writers express their opinions. Ask if students prefer a serious or humorous style of writing. Point out that this Section will instruct students how to write effective explanatory compositions which present opinions.

Additional Resources

Practice Book — pages 90–93
Duplicating Masters — pages 90–93

The Explanatory Composition

Presenting an Opinion

Teaching Special Populations

LD See **Teaching Special Populations,** pages 82–83.

ESL Give students practice in stating opinions in class. Suggest mild topics such as sports, weather, or music for a start. Have the class debate these topics, and then list supporting and/or opposing evidence on the board. Show students that one opinion can be both supported and refuted.

Work with students individually as they complete the exercises presented in this Section. Be sure they understand the methods necessary for stating an opinion.

NSD See **Teaching Special Populations,** pages 82–83.

221

I Believe

Objectives

1. To know the elements of an explanatory composition which presents an opinion

2. To write an effective topic sentence which clearly expresses an opinion

3. To use logical reasons and accurate facts to support an opinion

Presenting the Lesson

1. Read and discuss **Here's the Idea**. Stress the importance of having opinions, and learning how to share them.

Tell students that their opinions should be stated clearly in a topic sentence in the introduction. In the body of the composition, students will develop their opinions with logical reasons and accurate facts.

2. Read and discuss **Check It Out**. Have students notice how the pre-writing notes clearly state the writer's opinion, and also include supporting facts and reasons.

3. Discuss and assign **Try Your Skill**.

4. Read aloud **Keep This in Mind** and then assign **Now Write**.

Individualizing the Lesson

Less-Advanced Students

Have students work in small groups to do the exercise from **Try Your Skill**. Stress again that facts can be checked while opinions are neither right nor wrong, but depend on the point of view of the person making the statement.

Pre-Writing: Developing an Opinion

Here's the Idea   Your opinions tell who you are. They tell what you like and don't like. They tell what is important to you and what is not. Your opinions make you unique and interesting. In fact, your opinions make you an individual.

At times you may wish to share an opinion with others. One way to do this is to write an explanatory composition that presents an opinion. In a composition of this kind, you state an opinion. You also support or defend it. In other words, you let your readers know why you feel as you do about a subject.

To find a topic for an explanatory composition, think about your life. Think about your neighborhood, your school, your city, your nation. What do you believe in? What do you think should be started or stopped or changed? What do you approve of, dislike, enjoy, or hate? Any opinion that you hold strongly is likely to be a good composition topic.

Once you have chosen a topic, write a sentence clearly stating your opinion. This sentence will be the topic sentence of the introductory paragraph of your composition. The rest of your composition will tell why you hold the opinion you stated in the first paragraph.

To explain your opinion, you must offer logical reasons. Gather specific facts and accurate statistics to support your opinion. You may also use a personal example or an anecdote. There are several possible sources for supporting facts, statistics, and anecdotes. These include personal experiences, books, reference works, and magazine or newspaper articles.

Check It Out   Examine these notes for a student's explanatory composition expressing a personal opinion.

Topic: Professional athletes deserve to be paid well.

Supporting
Details: good reasons for high earnings
1. talented athletes work hard
   men and women train long hours, face tough competition
2. athletes deserve compensation for risks, injuries—head, back, broken bones—which may be a problem for a long time
3. short careers
   athletes perform best when young—family life suffers

- Is an opinion stated clearly and directly?
- What kind of support has the writer gathered to support the opinion?

Try Your Skill   Make a list of five subjects about which you have strong opinions. Choose three of your subjects, and for each write a sentence that clearly and directly states how you feel.

> ## Keep This in Mind
>
> - An explanatory composition that presents an opinion should be clear and direct.
> - Support an opinion with logical reasons that include specific facts, accurate statistics, or personal examples or anecdotes.

Now Write   Think of several opinions that you hold. Choose one opinion that you would like to present in an explanatory composition. Write a sentence that states your opinion clearly and directly. You may want to choose an opinion and sentence that you developed in **Try Your Skill.** Then list the reasons that you will use to support your opinion. Save your notes.

223

Objective

To organize reasons in order of importance from least important to most important

Presenting the Lesson

1. Read aloud **Here's the Idea.** Discuss why the most important reason should be stated last. Stress that each major supporting idea will become a separate paragraph in the body of the composition.

2. Read and discuss **Check It Out.** Note how the pre-writing notes from the last lesson were developed into body paragraphs. Ask the class to identify the topic sentence of each paragraph as well as the supporting reasons and facts.

3. Assign **Try Your Skill.** After they have completed this exercise, group students who have written on the same opinion and have them compare their supporting reasons and facts.

4. Read aloud **Keep This in Mind** and then assign **Now Write.**

Individualizing the Lesson

Less-Advanced Students

Have students complete **Try Your Skill** in groups of five. Discuss each group's work with the class.

Advanced Students

Using the editorials from **Optional Practice** in Part 1, have students state the opinion and list the supporting reasons. Have them also examine how the opinion has been organized.

Part 2 # The Reasons Why

Pre-Writing: Organizing an Opinion

Here's the Idea   When political candidates debate one another, they do not simply give their opinions. They give reasons, facts, and statistics that support their opinions. They know that to be effective, these ideas must be properly organized.

One way to organize supporting ideas in a composition is by order of importance. Compositions organized in this way start with the weakest supporting idea and end with the strongest. To organize a composition in this way, first study your pre-writing notes. Your notes should contain supporting facts, statistics, and anecdotes. Then, follow these steps:

1. Find two or three major supporting ideas. Write sentences stating each of these ideas. These sentences will serve as topic sentences for paragraphs in the body of your composition.

2. Organize your topic sentences in order of importance, from least important to most important.

3. Find facts, statistics, or anecdotes in your pre-writing notes to support each of your topic sentences. Place these under the topic sentences to which they belong. Then, organize, in order of importance, these supporting ideas for each paragraph.

Check It Out   Read the body of a student's composition.

First of all, hundreds of thousands of fans each season are entertained by outstanding athletes. Talented men and women have earned the opportunity to play through continual tough competition with other athletes. Why should spectators begrudge these hardworking athletes their high salaries? Players deserve to be paid well for their performances. In fact, athletes' salaries represent not only their performance in public, but also all their lengthy practice times. Since practice is a professional requirement, athletes should be compensated for it.

More important, athletes need some benefit to compensate for the physical abuse they suffer in certain sports, such as boxing or hockey. Athletes sometimes risk major physical injuries. They may injure their heads or their backs. They may pull tendons, break bones, or lose teeth. As a result of their careers, they may suffer for the rest of their lives. How many people would face such risks without financial reward?

The most important reason athletes should be paid well is based on simple arithmetic. Most athletes are young and have only a short time to perform at their peak. As a result, athletes must spend a great deal of time away from their families in order to work. In addition, when most other people are firmly settled in their careers, athletes may be out of a job. In fact, money earned early may be needed in leaner years ahead.

- Is an opinion supported by specific reasons or facts and figures? Is the evidence given in order of importance, from the least important to the most important?

Try Your Skill Choose one of the following opinions to support. List at least three supporting reasons or facts and figures. Organize your support according to the order of importance.

1. Everyone should learn basic first aid.
2. A good education is necessary for everyone.
3. Everyone should learn how to cook.
4. Spectators at sports events should be more courteous.

Keep This in Mind

- In an explanatory composition that presents an opinion, organize your supporting evidence according to the order of importance.

Now Write Review the pre-writing notes you have made for your composition. Organize the support for your opinion in a logical way. Save your notes in your folder.

When students have completed **Now Write,** have each student choose a partner and exchange papers. Instead of trading pre-writing notes which have been properly organized from least important point to most important, have students mix-up the order. Have each partner try to reorganize the notes correctly, and explain their reasons why.

Extending the Lesson

Lead a discussion with students about why least important to most important order is the most effective way to organize a composition that presents an opinion.

Objective

To write the first draft of an explanatory composition presenting an opinion

Presenting the Lesson

1. Read aloud **Here's the Idea.** Point out that the introduction is an important part of the composition because it is where the writer first states his or her opinion. Discuss the purpose of the conclusion and the need for useful transitional words and phrases.

2. Read aloud the introduction and conclusion from **Check It Out.** Review with students the elements of effective introductions and strong conclusions. Ask students if these two paragraphs contain those elements.

3. Assign **Try Your Skill.** Tell students to underline each transitional word and phrase they use.

4. Read aloud **Keep This in Mind** and then assign **Now Write.**

Individualizing the Lesson

Less-Advanced Students

Make sure students understand that each major idea in their composition must be developed with supporting facts and reasons.

Have students compare and discuss their work from **Try Your Skill.**

Advanced Students

After students complete **Now Write,** have them divide into small groups in order to discuss their first drafts. Point out that constructive

---

Take One

Writing the First Draft

Here's the Idea   When you write your first draft, do not worry about grammar, usage, and mechanics. Instead, simply write.

Begin your first draft with a one-paragraph introduction that states your opinion and tries to capture your readers' interest. Each paragraph in the body should contain one major idea and its supporting details. Your conclusion should be one paragraph long. It should restate your opinion. It should also summarize your reasons for believing as you do.

As you write, use transitional words and phrases. These will show how your ideas are related and the order of your ideas.

first   the second reason   more importantly   finally

You can also use the following transitions to present reasons and facts.

because   since   if   therefore   as a result

Use transitional words and phrases within and between paragraphs to improve the flow of your ideas.

Check It Out   Read this introduction and conclusion.

Introduction

Professional sports is big business. The public must pay for expensive tickets to sporting events. Many of the athletes involved make huge salaries. All of this moneymaking has led some fans to complain that overpaid athletes are the cause of problems in many sports. These angry fans feel that love of the sport should be what motivates athletes. However, I believe that professional athletes deserve to be paid well.

Conclusion

Therefore, the next time someone complains about the extraordinary salaries of athletes, consider the price they pay.

Athletes work long hours and risk serious injuries. They must often give up family life. It is easy to sit in the stands and criticize professional athletes. However, would you be willing to be on the field doing what they do? I believe professional athletes deserve to be paid well for their effort and dedication.

- Does the introduction clearly state an opinion?
- Does the conclusion summarize the argument?
- Which transitions help to state the reasons or facts?

Try Your Skill   Each group of sentences below begins with a topic sentence and is followed by two supporting reasons. Add details that will strengthen the supporting evidence. Then re-write each group of sentences, adding transitions that state reasons or facts and that show the order of importance.

1. More jobs should be made available to teenagers.
   Teenagers need to learn how to manage their own money.
   Teenagers need work experience to prepare themselves for life after graduation.
2. The city is a good place to live.
   Public transportation is better than it is in the suburbs.
   There is more to see and do in the city.

Keep This in Mind

- In the introduction, clearly state your opinion.
- In the body, present your supporting evidence.
- In the conclusion, summarize your opinion.
- Use transitional words and phrases to help present supporting evidence in the order of importance and to help state reasons or facts.

Now Write   Write the first draft of your explanatory composition. Use transitional words and phrases to present your opinion and to make the order of your idea clear. Save your first draft.

criticism will give them a more ob-jective eye when they are ready to revise their compositions.

Optional Practice

Have students find one editorial in a newspaper that they disagree with. Have them write a letter-to-the-editor expressing their own opinion. Stress the need for a good introduc-tion, and be sure students have or-ganized their reasons from least important to most important.

Extending the Lesson

Discuss with students the need for an effective introduction to a composition that presents an opin-ion. Guide students to discover that the introduction should not only in-troduce the writer's opinion but also hint at the reasons why the writer holds that opinion. These reasons will be developed in the body of the composition.

Objective

To revise an explanantory composition which presents an opinion

Presenting the Lesson

1. Read and discuss **Here's the Idea.** Have students copy the list of questions and ask them to keep it with their notes, so that it will be available when they revise their compositions.

2. Have students study the revised paragraph from **Check It Out.** Discuss specific revisions that make the paragraph better.

3. Assign and discuss **Try Your Skill.** Compare revisions in class.

4. Read aloud **Keep This in Mind** and then assign **Now Write.**

Individualizing the Lesson

Less-Advanced Students

After students complete **Now Write,** have them work in pairs to ask each other the questions from **Here's the Idea.**

Advanced Students

Divide the class into four "revision teams" to complete **Try Your Skill.** Discuss the revisions and decide which is the most effective and why.

Optional Practice

As a class, add three or four additional questions to the six listed on page 228. Have students use these questions to help them when they revise their compositions.

The End of the Road

Revising Your Opinion

Here's the Idea   A movie director may have to shoot a scene ten or twenty times to get it just right. To get your compositions just right, you may have to revise them again and again.

When you revise your explanatory composition, remember that your purpose is to present and support an opinion. Make sure that your evidence is convincing. Also make sure that your reasons, facts, and statistics are in a logical order. You want your audience to be convinced by your evidence. You also want readers to be able to see the logical relationships between your ideas.

When you revise your composition, ask yourself these questions:

1. Did I express my opinion clearly in my introduction?
2. Have I used strong, specific reasons, facts, and statistics to support my opinion?
3. Did I support my main ideas with enough details?
4. Did I use transitional words and phrases both between and within paragraphs?
5. Are my major ideas and the details supporting them arranged logically?
6. Does my conclusion restate my opinion and summarize my reasons for holding it?

Once you have checked your organization and content, proofread your composition. Find and correct all errors in grammar, capitalization, punctuation, and spelling.

Check It Out   Notice how this paragraph from an explanatory paragraph has been revised.

> The National Parks are important for too reasons. They give *w*
> *in its natural beauty.*
> americans the chance to see the country as it was. It also serves
> *species* *The parks*
> to protect many animals and plants that would have died. This
> *american and foreign* *become extinct.*
> second reason is often forgotten by visitors. We must control
> the overcrowding in our Parks if we want to save our wildlife.

Try Your Skill   Here is another paragraph from the composition about the national parks. Use your revising skills to improve it.

In recent years there have been an increase in the number of visitors. This has meant more traffic, and more roads. The air is being polluted. And also many of the timider animals have been scared away from there old, nesting areas. Animals that are not so shy have become a nuisance because people feed them, like bears.

Keep This in Mind

- When revising an explanatory composition that presents on opinion, you want to convince your readers that your opinion is sound and based on good judgment.

Now Write   Revise your explanatory composition. Follow the guidelines in this lesson. When you are satisfied that your composition is the best it can be, make a final copy and save it in your folder.

Extending the Lesson

Bring in an effective editorial from a local newspaper. Analyze it with the students, pointing out what makes it effective. Discuss the introduction, the organization, and the conclusion. Note transitions used to highlight organization and to present reasons.

Section **19** Objectives

1. To plan an explanatory composition, beginning with a short one-sentence definition of a word or term

2. To organize the pre-writing notes for a definition in general to specific order

3. To write the first draft of an explanatory composition

4. To revise an explanatory composition

Preparing the Students

Divide the class into two groups. Tell the students that you have a list of words that you want them to guess by asking questions. Each student from a group can ask one question until the word is discovered. All questions must be phrased to have a "yes" or "no" answer. See which group can guess the greatest number of words.

After the game, explain to students that the process they used to discover the word—moving from general questions to more specific questions—is similar to the process they will use to define words and ideas in an explanatory composition.

The following is a list of suggested words to use.

pomegranate	French horn
castle	croissant
bat	silo
hacksaw	

Additional Resources

Practice Book — pages 94–97
Duplicating Masters — pages 94–97

The Explanatory Composition

Stating a Definition

Teaching Special Populations

LD See **Teaching Special Populations,** pages 82–83.

ESL Define for students any words in the text with which they are unfamiliar. Work with them individually to define terms clearly and completely. Be sure students understand what is meant by *class, term* and *particular characteristics*.

Students may have difficulty organizing their material. Suggest that they list the facts they want to include, and group them according to the guidelines in Part 2. Remind students that they cannot include all facts about a topic in a composition that defines.

NSD See **Teaching Special Populations,** pages 82–83.

Objective

To plan an explanatory composition, beginning with a short, one-sentence definition of a word or term

Presenting the Lesson

1. Read and discuss **Here's the Idea.** Review the three types of explanatory compositions, and discuss what each one does. As you discuss the explanatory composition that defines, emphasize the different ways that details can be gathered for this type of composition.

2. Read and discuss **Check It Out.** Ask several volunteers to read their one-sentence definitions for each word. Try to decide which sentence best defines each word.

3. Read aloud and assign **Try Your Skill.**

4. Read aloud **Keep This in Mind** and assign **Now Write.**

Individualizing the Lesson

Less-Advanced Students

Have students read brief encyclopedia articles for additional examples of explanatory compositions that define.

Work with students as they develop their pre-writing notes.

Advanced Students

Add the following words to **Try Your Skill:** courage, mercy, freedom.

Optional Practice

Have students bring their literature and history books to class.

Happiness Is

Pre-Writing: Developing a Definition

Here's the Idea   In an explanatory composition that states a definition, your goal is to define something as clearly and completely as possible. Your topic may be a real object, such as a computer or a subway. It may also be an idea, such as *trust* or *genius.*

After you have chosen a topic for your explanatory composition, write a sentence that defines the term you have chosen. This one-sentence definition should do three things. First, it should tell what term is being defined. Second, it should put the subject into a general class. Third, it should show the particular characteristics of the subject. In other words, it should show how the subject differs from other members of its class. This one-sentence definition can become the topic sentence of your introductory paragraph. Here is an example of a good one-sentence definition. Try to identify the subject being defined, its general class, and its particular characteristics.

> An electric eel is a slender, tube-shaped fish that can give a strong electric shock.

To develop your definition, you must gather specific details. If you are defining an object, a dictionary, encyclopedia, or other reference work can supply you with facts and statistics. If you are defining a word that stands for an idea, you may want to use specific examples or anecdotes. These come from research, from interviews, or from your own experience.

As you gather facts, examples, and other details for your pre-writing notes, keep your audience in mind. Your audience may not be familiar with your topic. If so, you will have to keep your explanation simple. On the other hand, your audience may already be very familiar with your topic. In this case, you will be able to provide more detailed or complex information.

Check It Out   Read the following pre-writing notes.

Topic: bagels

Introduction: Americans' new interest in food: buying woks, crêpe pans, pasta machines; eating in small, ethnic restaurants but overlooking simple food—bread, especially bagels

Body: bread: most widely eaten food in the world; quick breads—muffins, biscuits, corn bread; flat breads—tortillas, pita bread; yeast breads—white, rye, rolls, bagels

bagels: doughnut-shaped; shiny, crusty outer surface; dense, chewy middle

breakfast food: toasted, warm; good with cream cheese, salmon

Conclusion: bagels are simple, delicious, more popular now

- Do these notes include details or facts and figures that will define the subject clearly?

Try Your Skill   Choose three of the following subjects and write a one-sentence definition of each. Be sure the definition presents the subject to be defined, puts the subject in its general class, and shows how the subject differs from others of its class.

catcher   moped   monarchy   patience   nurse

Keep This in Mind

- In an explanatory composition that states a definition, your goal is to define something as clearly and completely as possible.

Now Write   Choose and narrow a topic to define in your explanatory composition. Write a one-sentence definition of your subject. Then, gather facts and figures or specific examples to develop your definition. Save your pre-writing notes.

Ask them to find three words which are unfamiliar to them. Have them write one-sentence definitions for each word. Point out that they should be sure to include the subject to be defined, its general class, and the specific characteristics which reveal how the subject differs from others in its class.

Extending the Lesson

Have students use the words they defined in **Optional Practice.** Ask them to write five specific details for each word. Have students save their work in their folders.

Part 2

Objective

To organize the pre-writing notes for a definition in general to specific order

Presenting the Lesson

1. Read aloud **Here's the Idea.** On the chalkboard write *general to specific order.* Explain that this is the organizational method used in explanatory compositions that define. Be sure students understand this organizational concept.

2. Ask for a volunteer to read the paragraph in **Check It Out.** Discuss with students the way the writer has developed the definition by providing more specific details about the dulcimer.

3. Read and discuss **Try Your Skill.** Do this exercise orally with the class.

4. Read aloud **Keep This in Mind** and assign **Now Write.**

Individualizing the Lesson

Less-Advanced Students

Work with students as they organize their pre-writing notes. Refer back to the bagel notes on page 233. Point out to the students how these notes move from a very general discussion of food fads to a specific food (breads) to a more specific type of bread (bagels) to a very specific way to enjoy bagels. Tell students that as the definition becomes more specific, the reader learns more about the subject.

Advanced Students

Ask students to bring to class a

Generally Speaking

Pre-Writing: Organizing a Definition

Here's the Idea Suppose you are writing to a friend in another country. You want to tell your friend about where you live. You start by telling about your city or town. Next, you tell about your neighborhood. Then, you tell about your house or apartment. Finally, you tell about your room and the things in it. If you did this, you would be using **general to specific order.** This is the method of organization that is used for an explanatory composition that states a definition. Such compositions begin with an introductory paragraph. This paragraph gives a general definition of the subject. The introduction is followed by several body paragraphs. The body paragraphs develop the general definition by presenting specific details.

Start by organizing the information for your introduction. Place the one sentence definition of your topic first. Follow this definition with any details you can use to interest your readers.

Next, organize the specific details you will use in the paragraphs of the body. Look at your pre-writing notes. Find two or three main ideas that help to define your topic. Group the rest of your details under these main ideas. Each resulting idea group will become a paragraph in the body of your composition.

Check It Out Read the following paragraph.

A dulcimer is a wooden, stringed instrument that sounds like a cross between a guitar and a banjo. Dulcimers were introduced in Persia nearly five thousand years ago. There are two types of dulcimers. One type is called a *hammered dulcimer.* The hammered dulcimer is a trapezoid-shaped box with two or more strings stretched across it. This type of dulcimer is played by striking the strings with curved wooden hammers. The second type of dulcimer is called the *plucked* or *Appalachian dulcimer.* This dulcimer is shaped like an hourglass with three or four strings stretched across it. It is played by plucking or strumming the strings. Although dulcimers have their origins in antiquity, they remain popular musical instruments today.

- Explain how this definition moves from the general to the specific.

Try Your Skill Below are some pre-writing notes for an explanatory composition that defines. The subject being defined is *swamp.* Read the notes carefully. Then group the notes around the three most obvious main ideas.

General Definition: A swamp is an area of muddy land, often covered with water, that supports a variety of plant and animal life.

Details:
deep-water swamps (fresh water)
bald cypress, juniper, pine trees
bear, deer, swamp birds
snakes, raccoons
mangrove swamps (salt water)
wax myrtles, willows, Spanish moss
alligators, crocodiles, turtles
manatees
orchids, palm trees
shallow-water swamps (fresh water)

Keep This in Mind

- Use general to specific order to organize the details for an explanatory composition that states a definition.

Now Write Organize the pre-writing notes for your explanatory composition. First identify two or three main ideas that help you to define your topic. Then group your remaining details around these ideas. Save your pre-writing notes.

brief encyclopedia article. Have them indicate the main ideas and explain how the writer organized the details.

Optional Practice

Have students explain what is wrong with the organization in this paragraph. Details are out of order.

Also known as the bends, or altitude sickness, it affects divers, airplane pilots, and other people breathing compressed air. This was a major problem during the building of the Brooklyn Bridge, causing great delay and even resulting in the death of some of the workers. Decompression sickness is a physiological disorder caused by a rapid decrease in the atmospheric pressure. It results in the release of nitrogen bubbles into the body tissues. These bubbles cut off the necessary supply of oxygen to the body, causing nausea, severe pain in the joints, and in extreme cases, decompression sickness can cause paralysis and death.

Extending the Lesson

Have students rewrite the paragraph from **Optional Practice** using the correct method for organization—general to specific order.

Famous First Words

Writing the First Draft

Presenting the Lesson

1. Read aloud **Here's the Idea.** Review with students the function of each part of an explanatory composition that defines.

2. Have four volunteers read the introduction and body paragraphs from **Check It Out.** Have students discuss the questions. Have them compare these paragraphs with the pre-writing notes from Part 1.

3. Assign **Try Your Skill.**

4. Read aloud **Keep This in Mind** and assign **Now Write.**

Individualizing the Lesson

Less-Advanced Students

Before assigning **Try Your Skill,** divide students into small groups to brainstorm for ideas.

Advanced Students

Remind students that their audience may not be familiar with their topic. It is therefore important for students to write clear, well-developed compositions so that anyone who reads them will get a clear picture of what is being defined.

After students have completed **Now Write,** have them exchange papers. Have each partner offer suggestions about the presentation of the definition in the first draft.

Optional Practice

Have students write an introductory paragraph to an explanatory

Here's the Idea Like any composition, your explanatory composition should have three parts: an introduction, a body, and a conclusion. Working from your pre-writing notes, write a first draft. Try to write sentences and paragraphs that present your ideas clearly and completely.

Begin with your introduction. The first sentence of this paragraph should present a clear, brief definition of your topic. This will be the topic sentence of your introductory paragraph. Then add some interesting details to capture the interest of your readers.

In the body of your composition, present two or three main ideas that help to define your subject specifically. Present each of these main ideas in a separate paragraph. Use the details from your organized pre-writing notes to develop each main idea.

End your composition with a conclusion. This paragraph should summarize the main ideas of your definition.

Check It Out Read this introduction and body.

Recently, many Americans have become more interested in favorite foods from other lands. Many busy cooks are buying Chinese woks, French crêpe pans, and Italian pasta machines. Many adventurous diners are seeking out small ethnic restaurants that serve tasty dishes. In their search for specialty foods, however, many people have been overlooking a basic and delicious food—bread. One of the tastiest ethnic varieties of bread is the bagel, a dense, chewy, ring-shaped roll.

In fact, bread is the most widely eaten food in the world. Combinations of flour and water have existed in some form since the beginning of history. There are quick breads which include an enormous variety of muffins and biscuits, as well as corn bread and gingerbread. There are flat breads, including

Mexican *tortillas* and Middle Eastern *pita*. Most common in the United States are yeast breads. Bagels are a kind of yeast bread, unique because they are boiled and then baked.

Bagels are doughnut-shaped, brown, and shiny. Their outer surface looks like smooth, polished wood. Sometimes it is dotted with tangy black onion flakes. The inside of a bagel is dense, heavy, and quite chewy. Bagels are like no other bread, because of their unique texture.

Bagels are usually served for breakfast. They are particularly good when they are served warm or toasted. However, bagels may be eaten any time. They are a perfect companion to cream cheese or smoked salmon.

- Does the introductory paragraph contain a one-sentence definition of the subject?
- Does each body paragraph talk about just one main idea?
- Do the details in each paragraph relate to its main idea?

Try Your Skill Reread the composition **Check It Out.** Then use the pre-writing notes on page 233 as well as details from your own imagination, to write a conclusion to the composition.

Keep This in Mind

- In an explanatory composition that states a definition, the introduction includes a general, one-sentence definition of the subject.
- The body develops the definition with specific details.
- The conclusion sums up the main ideas of the definition.

Now Write Write the first draft of your explanatory composition. Follow your organized pre-writing notes as you write. Save your first draft in your folder.

composition on one of the following topics. Be sure the introduction includes a complete one-sentence definition.

> biofeedback
> hypnosis
> raquetball

Extending the Lesson

Collect the introductory paragraphs from students when they have finished **Optional Practice.** Read them to the class without the one-sentence definition. Ask students to guess what is being defined. Point out the importance of the topic sentence.

A Definite Improvement

Revising Your Definition

Part 4

Objective

To revise an explanatory composition

Presenting the Lesson

1. Read aloud **Here's the Idea.** Have students study the list of questions and discuss with students any concerns they have about revising.

2. Have students read **Check It Out.** Make sure they understand how the revised paragraph has been improved.

3. Assign **Try Your Skill.**

4. Read aloud **Keep This in Mind** and assign **Now Write.**

Individualizing the Lesson

Less-Advanced Students

Have students work in pairs. Have each partner read one guideline question and have the other partner answer with supporting evidence from his or her revised composition.

Advanced Students

Working in pairs, have students exchange revised compositions. Ask them to examine the introduction and the organization carefully, and to make suggestions for improvement.

Optional Practice

Duplicate a paragraph from an explanatory composition that needs to be revised. Have students revise it and indicate corrections with proofreader's marks. Examine the revisions in class.

Here's the Idea   Revising is a vital step in the process of writing. It is during revision that the careful writer is separated from the careless writer. To make your explanatory composition that states a definition the best it can be, take the time to revise your work thoroughly. Read your composition several times. Make sure that your organization is clear and that your ideas are fully developed.

Here is a list of questions to ask yourself as you revise your composition.

1. Does the topic sentence in my introduction define my subject?

2. Does my one-sentence definition name the subject? Does it place the subject in a general class? Does it name some characteristics that make the subject different from other things in its class?

3. Do the paragraphs of the body develop my definition with enough specific details, facts, statistics, examples, or anecdotes?

4. Does my composition follow general to specific order?

5. Does the conclusion summarize my definition?

6. Is my language interesting, clear, and simple? Will the audience be able to follow my ideas?

After you have checked your ideas, organization, and language, proofread your composition carefully. Correct any errors in grammar, capitalization, punctuation, and spelling.

Check It Out   Notice how this conclusion to the composition about bagels has been revised.

First Draft: Bagels are simple food. You can get them frozen in some stores. They might turn up one day on your table. Have a bagel!

Revision: Bagels are a simple but delicious food. They have become so popular that they can now be found in the frozen food sections of many grocery stores. Soon they may turn up on your family's breakfast table. If so, enjoy! Start your day with a bagel.

- Explain why the revised conclusion is better than the first draft.
- Do you see why it is sometimes necessary to rewrite a paragraph in order to improve it?

Try Your Skill   Below are five poorly written general, one-sentence definitions. Each one was taken from the first draft of an introductory paragraph. Decide what is wrong with each definition and then revise it.

1. A *shark* has several rows of sharp teeth.
2. *Pride* is a feeling that you have.
3. An *avocado* is a fruit that is green.
4. *Orchids* can be found in tropical countries.
5. A *quarterback* is a football player.

> ### Keep This in Mind
>
> - Revise your explanatory composition that states a definition to be sure that you have clearly and completely defined your subject.

Now Write   Following the guidelines in this lesson, revise your explanatory paragraph. Make your definition clear and complete. Proofread your composition for errors in grammar and mechanics. When you are finished revising, make a final copy of your composition and save it in your folder.

Explain to students that they are going to write a part of the classified section of a newspaper. Each ad will include a one-sentence definition of each item to be sold, as well as three specific facts or details about the item. Here are the items to be sold.

steel guitar
anaconda
barometer
scimitar
obi
puttees
quetzal

Section **20** Objectives

1. To choose a subject and find reference sources for a research paper

2. To write bibliography and note cards correctly

3. To recognize and avoid plagiarism

4. To learn to organize note cards

5. To use organized notes to write an outline

6. To write the introduction of a research paper

7. To write the body and conclusion of a research paper

8. To revise and proofread a research paper

9. To prepare footnotes and a bibliography for a research paper

Preparing the Students

Ask students if they have ever written a research paper or a report. Ask how such pieces of writing differ from descriptions and narratives. Point out that research papers are based on information from sources other than personal experience. Explain that this Section will explain the steps to follow when preparing a research paper. Note that the process they will learn in this Section can be used when they write research papers for other classes.

Additional Resources

Mastery Test — page 30 in the test booklet

Practice Book — pages 98–105

Duplicating Masters — pages 98–105

240

The Research Paper

241

Teaching Special Populations

LD See **Teaching Special Populations,** pages 82–83. Help students choose appropriate topics for their reports. Guide students step-by-step through the process described in this Section.

ESL Provide students with simplified reference materials, or steer them toward appropriate books in the library. Help students individually with their reports.

Encourage students to select topics about which they or people they know are familiar, such as the history of a custom or the description of a holiday.

NSD See **Teaching Special Populations,** pages 82–83.

Objectives

To choose a subject and find reference sources for a research paper

Presenting the Lesson

1. Read and discuss **Here's the Idea.** List the various ways of narrowing a topic on the chalkboard. Stress the importance of recording each source of information.

Refer students to Section 22, **Using the Library,** or teach it in conjunction with this Section. Make sure students are familiar with the various kinds of reference materials available to them, both in their school and neighborhood libraries.

2. Read and discuss **Check It Out.** Have students use this list of sources as a model for recording their own sources. Make sure students know where each of these kinds of sources can be located in their own libraries.

3. Assign **Try Your Skill.** Narrow one topic with the class and show them how to locate sources for it before they do the exercise on their own.

4. List **Keep This in Mind** on the chalkboard and have students refer to it as they begin their pre-writing.

5. Assign **Now Write.** If students are having trouble choosing a career to write about, have them use one of the career areas listed in **Try Your Skill.**

To the Source

Developing a Research Paper

Here's the Idea   Students in high school are often asked to write a special type of composition called a **research paper.** Research papers, like compositions, are made of several paragraphs that deal with a single topic. However, research papers differ from compositions in one important respect. All the information in a research paper comes from outside sources. These sources may be books, newspapers, or magazines. They may be reference works, such as encyclopedias, atlases, and almanacs. They may even be non-print materials, such as films or interviews.

The first pre-writing step for a research paper is choosing and narrowing a topic. Suppose you are given the subject of careers. This assignment gives you a general subject. You need to find information from which you can select a specific topic.

Begin your research in the library. Look through the card catalog for the subject card *Careers.* Look in the nonfiction section that contains books on careers. Check encyclopedias in the reference section for information on the general subject of careers. Look in the *Readers' Guide to Periodical Literature* for magazine articles relating to careers. Pamphlets found in the vertical file are also good sources.

Another valuable source of information about careers is the guidance counselor or vocational guidance department at your school. Your counselor may have on hand the latest information about careers. He or she will be able to tell you where to look or to write to get that information.

Here is a list of possible sources you might check to find general information about careers.

1. *Occupational Outlook Handbook*, from the U.S. Dept. of Labor

2. "Careers" in *The World Book Encyclopedia*.

3. *Encyclopedia of Careers and Vocational Guidance*, 1981 ed.

As you read, you will undoubtedly find several careers that you find appealing. Choose one that you would like to investigate further. Remember you will write your best paper on a career that really interests you.

When you have chosen a particular career to investigate, search again for specific information. Check all the sources already mentioned. If possible, talk to someone in the field of your choice. You can also write to the U.S. Department of Labor, Washington, D.C. Record each source of your information in your notebook. Write the titles of books, encyclopedias, pamphlets, and magazine articles in your notebook. Also write the volume and page number of the encyclopedias you may want to use and the dates of the magazines. This will give you a list of sources that contain information about your topic.

Check It Out Look at this list of sources for a research paper about a career in the hotel industry.

1. *Occupational Outlook Handbook,* 1985-86, U.S. Dept. of Labor

2. *Hotel Keeping and Catering as a Career* a book by John Fuller

3. *Opportunities in the Hotel and Motel Industry,* a book by Shepard Henkin

4. *Encyclopedia of Careers and Vocational Guidance,* 1981 ed.

5. *Working Woman* magazine, April, 1978, pages 18-19

- How would you have located the second source? the fifth?
- Is this a varied and specific list of sources for a research paper?

243

Less-Advanced Students

When students have brought their possible topics to class, hold a class discussion in which you ask volunteers to talk about their general topics. Work through the process of limiting a subject with several students, using other students' suggestions whenever possible. When students feel confident that they can narrow their topics, let them work independently to complete **Now Write.** Offer individual help to those who need it.

Advanced Students

Have students find at least ten different sources for **Now Write.** Discuss the fact that it is always better to have more information than necessary when writing a report.

Optional Practice

Have each student help a partner by finding three more sources about his or her partner's topic.

Extending the Lesson

Have students look at textbooks in history, biology, computers, health, etc. Tell them to look through the table of contents in these texts to see how the material in the book is divided into specific topics. Point out that these topics can be used for research or suggest other topics for a research paper.

Try Your Skill   Choose one of these general career areas to research in the library. Narrow, to a specific career, the career area you have chosen. Then list three different sources where you could find information for a research paper about this career.

manufacturing	health	construction	business
communications	fine arts	public service	recreation

Keep This in Mind

- A research paper is a composition developed with information gathered from outside sources.
- With a general subject in mind, search through books, magazines, and other reference works to find a specific, limited topic for a report.
- With a specific subject chosen, begin research for a report by examining all possible sources. Keep a list of the sources.

Now Write   Choose a career to investigate for a report. Go to the library with a general idea of what you will write about and look for a specific career. Check the reference shelves, the card catalog, the *Readers' Guide,* and the vertical file. Talk to a career counselor and, if possible, to someone working in the career that interests you. Find as many sources of information as you can about your career. Keep a list of these sources in your folder. Note the call numbers, the book titles, the magazine issues, or the vertical file references.

Shortcuts

Taking Notes

Here's the Idea   As you know, the ideas in a research paper are not your own. They come from outside sources. You will have to keep a record of the sources you use. Whenever you take notes from a source, make a **bibliography card.** This card will contain information about the source. You will need the information on your bibliography cards when you list your sources at the end of your paper. Bibliography cards for different kinds of sources contain different types of information, as follows:

Book: author, title, publisher, date published
Magazine: author of article (if there is one), title of article, name of magazine, date published, page number of article
Encyclopedia: name of article, name of encyclopedia, date published
Newspaper: author of article (if there is one), title of article, name of newspaper, date published, section, page, and column number of article

When you make bibliography cards, number each source. These numbers will be helpful when you write your note cards.

As you read about your topic, write the important information on **note cards.** Follow these guidelines for making notecards.

1. Use a separate 3" × 5" note card for each fact or idea.
2. Write a key phrase at the top of each card that tells the main idea of the note. Keep cards with similar key phrases grouped together. This will help you to organize your notes later.
3. Label each note card with the number given to that source on its bibliography card. Include the exact page reference so you can check out a fact or a specific quotation.
4. Take notes in your own words. Copying another writer's

Part 2

Objectives

1. To write bibliography and note cards correctly
2. To recognize and avoid plagiarism

Presenting the Lesson

1. Read and discuss the first paragraph of **Here's the Idea.** Make sure that students understand how important it is to have full information about every source written on their bibliography cards. Explain that these cards are necessary when students write their footnotes and bibliography later; that if their information is not complete now, they will have to find their original sources again for the information.

2. Carefully go over the discussion of note cards in **Here's the Idea.** Emphasize to students that only one idea should be placed on a card, even if the paragraph they're reading contains many ideas. Explain how students can use the numbering system from their bibliography cards when writing their note cards as a shorthand for themselves.

3. Finally discuss the word *plagiarism*, which is defined in the last guideline in **Here's the Idea.** Make sure students understand that plagiarism is a serious form of cheating. State your school's penalty for plagiarism. Tell students that if they copy a writer's words directly from a source, they must put quotation marks around the words to indicate they are quoting someone else's exact words.

4. Read and discuss **Check It Out.** Point out that each bibliography card indicates *where* the source was found. Ask students why this may become important to them.

5. Assign **Try Your Skill.** Make sure students write only one fact on the note card they write.

6. Read **Keep This in Mind** and then assign **Now Write.**

Individualizing the Lesson

Less-Advanced Students

Have these students work on their **Now Write** assignment in the school library so they can get individual assistance from the teacher and librarian.

Advanced Students

Instruct students to use at least two direct quotations when writing their note cards.

Optional Practice

Have students write a bibliography card and two note cards based on the following information.

The era of the woodcut passed with the beginning of the seventeenth century and etching and line-engraving came into fashion. The two processes have often been used together on the same plate, but are quite distinct. In etching the design is eaten into the copper plate by acid while in line-engraving a tool called a burin is used to cut lines on the metal.

—from a book called *Botanical Illustration* by Ronald King. It was published by Clarkson N. Potter, Inc., New York, in 1978, and was on page 7.

Note cards will vary.
Bibliography card on page 247.

work is called **plagiarism.** Plagiarism is a serious offense. To avoid plagiarism, jot down information in your own words. To quote a source directly, use quotation marks to show that you have copied a statement. Copy direct quotations exactly as they are. Use direct quotations only for important or unusual ideas.

Check It Out   Look at the sample cards on page 247.

· Which are bibliography cards?
· Which is a note card? What is its source?

Try Your Skill   Read the following information. Make a bibliography card and a note card based on it.   Note card will vary. Bibliography card on page 247.

Personal service jobs are as old as civilization. Some jobs fill essential needs. Others provide luxuries. Some personal service workers keep our lives running smoothly. Others help us to feel better about ourselves or our belongings. Jane Thomas is a rehabilitation counselor. John Glover repairs typewriters. John Glover and Jane Thomas have entirely different jobs, but both perform a personal service.

—from *Jobs in Personal Services*, by Beatrice and Calvin Criner, Lothrop, Lee & Shepard Company, New York, 1974, 13.

Keep This in Mind

· Make bibliography cards that contain basic information about all sources for your report.
· Write note cards. Each card should contain one idea.
· Take notes in your own words. Avoid plagiarism.

Now Write   Take your list of sources and a stack of 3" × 5" note cards to your library. Make bibliography cards for all suitable sources. Read through those sources and make note cards about the information you find. Save the cards in your folder.

Henkin, Shepard
Opportunities in the Hotel and
   Motel Industry
Lincolnwood, Illinois, National
Textbook Company, 1978

371.42
H 832 he
rev. ed

public library

①

"Hotel Occupations"
Occupational Outlook Handbook,
   1985-86 edition
U.S. Department of Labor
   Bureau of Labor Statistics, 1985

guidance counselor

②

Hopke, William E.

"Hotel and Motel Managers,"
The Encyclopedia of Careers and
Vocational Guidance, 1981 ed.

school library

③

---

opportunities in hotel work

"The hotel industry is one of the
few wherein a young person can
secure a position without too much
formal education, and work his
way through the various departments to an executive capacity."

page 27

①

King, Ronald
Botanical Illustration
New York, Clarkson N. Potter, Inc., 1978
page 7

Extending the Lesson

1. Give students practice in note-taking by distributing brief encyclopedia entries, magazine articles, etc. Ask students to make note cards. Remind them to use their own words whenever possible, and to use quotation marks when they use a direct quote.

2. Introduce students to the *ellipsis,* which is used to indicate that words have been left out of a direct quotation.

Criner, Beatrice and Calvin
Jobs in Personal Services
New York, Lothrop, Lee & Shepard
  Company, 1974
page 13

247

Part 3

Pileup

Objective

To learn to organize note cards

Organizing Information

Presenting the Lesson

1. Remind students again that only one idea goes on each note card; then read and discuss **Here's the Idea.** List the steps for organizing the note cards on the chalkboard.

2. Read and discuss **Check It Out.** Ask students which sort of facts would go under each of these main ideas.

3. Assign **Try Your Skill.** Have volunteers write their groups and main ideas on the chalkboard. Discuss the answers.

4. Read **Keep This in Mind.**

5. Assign **Now Write.** Tell students that organizing notes may be difficult, but that once it is done, the remaining work for the paper will become easier. Caution students that if they have more than five or six piles of cards, their papers may become too long.

Individualizing the Lesson

Less-Advanced Students

These students may need extra individual help in organizing the material they have gathered for their papers. Have them work on **Now Write** in class, and offer assistance.

Advanced Students

When students have organized their notes and written their main ideas for each group of notes, have them write down what method of organization they have used for each group.

Here's the Idea Before you can begin to write a research paper, you must organize your information. Start with your note cards. Read your cards and try to find four or five main ideas running through them. The key phrases on your notecards will help you to complete this step. Then separate your cards into piles. Each pile should contain cards dealing with one main idea.

If you were writing about a career in the hotel-motel industry, your information could be organized into four categories: the variety of jobs within this industry, the range of training required, personal traits required, and the benefits of the jobs.

You may find that some cards do not fit into any of your main idea groups. If so, you may decide not to use these ideas in your paper. However, save the cards. They may contain information that you can use in the introduction or conclusion of your paper.

The next step is to write a topic sentence for each of your piles of cards. This topic sentence should state the main idea of the cards in each pile. You will end up with a few topic sentences that you can use when you write the body of your paper.

The last step is to put your notes in order. First, place the piles of cards in the order in which you want to write about them. Then, put the notes in each pile in a sensible order. See pages 96–97 for information on different types of organization. Try several different methods of organization. Find the method or combination of methods that best suits your material.

Check It Out Read these sentences. They were written to describe the main ideas of the research paper on careers in the hotel-motel industry.

1. The hotel-motel industry consists of a variety of separate operations, those related to the "front of the house" and those related to the "back of the house".

2. Hotel work can be skilled or unskilled so there is a broad range of training required.

3. Certain character traits, such as patience and the ability to get along with people, are also required in this personal service industry.

4. There are many benefits to careers in hotel work.

- Is one main idea stated clearly in each sentence?

Try Your Skill Organize the following careers into five groups. For each group write one sentence that expresses the main idea of the career field represented by the various jobs.
Sentences will vary.

a dancer	c police officer	c railroad engineer
b chef	c bus driver	d licensed practical nurse
a actor	d X-ray technician	b bus boy
c firefighter	c airline pilot	b maitre d'
a musician	b waiter	d medical records clerk

Keep This in Mind

- Organize your note cards. Group together cards with the same main idea. Write one sentence stating the main idea of each group. Arrange the piles and the cards within them into a logical order.

Now Write Read your note cards. Organize them into four or five main groups. Make a list of sentences expressing the main idea of each group. Then arrange the sentences and the cards that go with them into a logical order. Save your work.

249

Optional Practice

Have students organize the following notes into two groups. For each group they should write one sentence expressing the main idea of the group. Then have them put the notes in each group into an appropriate order.

1A hard to see stars clearly, even on clear night

2A scientists now use satellites that carry telescopes

1C city lights interfere with view of space

1D atmosphere (thick layer of air around earth) also interferes

2B satellites go above atmosphere

2C satellite telescopes can use mirrors, x-rays, or use ultraviolet light

2D can now see many things about objects in space never seen before

1B telescopes usually on high mountains but still couldn't see enough

Extending the Lesson

Have students research and then report back to the class about the various mechanical ways offered to make storage and organization of note cards easier. This can include everything from using a small file box to using computers.

249

Objective

To use organized notes to write an outline

Presenting the Lesson

1. Read and discuss **Here's the Idea.** Ask students why it is important to write an outline before they write their first drafts. Point out that a well-written outline is like a table of contents for the research paper because it tells the exact organization of the paper.

2. Read and discuss **Check It Out.** Point out the numbering and lettering system and the fact that periods are not used at the end of each line but only after letters and numbers.

3. Assign **Try Your Skill.** Have volunteers write their outlines on the chalkboard.

4. Read **Keep This in Mind** and then assign **Now Write.** Remind students that if they have their note cards well organized, the outline follows in order from their note cards.

Individualizing the Lesson

Less-Advanced Students

1. Discuss how the factual details under each main heading in **Check It Out** logically support and develop the heading.

2. Help students individually with their outlines.

Advanced Students

After organizing their notes and writing their outlines, students may find they need more facts or exam-

---

The Bare Essentials

Making an Outline

Here's the Idea   Once you have listed the main ideas of your research paper, make an **outline.** In an outline, you organize the ideas from your notes in a more detailed way. You decide where each individual note card with its one idea fits into your paper. The outline thus provides you with a plan to follow when you write your rough draft.

To write your outline, use your organized groups of note cards. Each main idea will become a main topic in your outline. The related facts on your note cards will become the subtopics and details of the outline. Each main idea, subtopic, and detail will be stated in a word or phrase.

All outlines follow the same form. You must follow this form whenever you make an outline. An outline begins with a title. Below that, first in importance, are main ideas shown by Roman numerals. Under the main ideas, next in importance, are subtopics, shown by capital letters. Under subtopics, details are shown by Arabic numerals. If more specific details must be shown, small letters are used. You must have no fewer than two main topics or subtopics in an outline.

Each part of an outline is indented from the part above. However, each symbol is in a straight line with the others like it. Each kind of symbol is followed by a period, although the words of the outline are not followed by periods. In a completed outline, the first word and all important words are capitalized in every line, as well as in the title.

Check It Out   Examine the outline on the following page. It is based on notes about a career in the hotel-motel industry.

I. Introduction
  A. Function of hotel-motel industry
    1. A personal services industry
    2. Provides sleeping rooms and meals
  B. Range of services offered
    1. Small inns with few employees
    2. Large complexes with many services

II. Variety of skilled and unskilled occupations
  A. Front of the house
    1. Management
    2. Uniformed service staff
    3. Front office
    4. Accounting and sales
  B. Back of the house
    1. Housekeeping and laundry
    2. Food preparation
    3. Engineering and security

III. Training for a career in hotel industry
  A. Short on-the-job training
    1. Entry-level positions
    2. Part-time work available
  B. Specialty training
    1. Long on-the-job training
    2. Vocational education
    3. Leads to advancement

IV. Personal qualifications
  A. Ability to get along with people
  B. Patience and courtesy
  C. Neatness
  D. Attention to detail

V. Benefits of hotel-motel careers
  A. Flexible schedules, many locations
  B. Promotion, personal growth

ples. Give them one class period in the library to find additional information to add to their outlines.

Optional Practice

Duplicate a clearly written three or four paragraph essay, and ask students to outline it.

Extending the Lesson

Have students select one article or chapter from a book or magazine that pertains to the subject of their report. Ask them to write an outline for the chapter that clearly shows the organization of ideas used by the author.

- What subtopics and details explain a career in the hotel-motel industry?
- Point out how the form for outlining has been followed correctly.

Try Your Skill   Make an outline of the following paragraph of information taken from *The Guide to Career Education* by Muriel Lederer.

In order to be a computer technician you need to have good vision because you work with small parts. You also need normal color perception because wires are color coded. Normal hearing is also a requirement because machine breakdowns are sometimes detected by sound. A pleasant manner is an asset, as well as the ability to cope with other people, since you will be dealing with customers. Last, but by no means least, you should be resourceful and able to work independently with little or no supervision.

Keep This in Mind

- Use your notes to write an outline of the ideas and details to be presented in your research paper.
- Follow the correct form for making an outline.

Now Write   Take out your organized note cards. Make an outline, using your list of main ideas and your note cards. Save your work in your folder.

Take the Plunge

Writing the Introduction

Here's the Idea   After you have finished the outline for your paper, most of your next steps will be familiar. Writing the first draft of a research paper is much like writing the first draft of a composition. Both have three parts—an introduction, a body, and a conclusion. The introduction presents your main idea. The body develops the main idea with supporting ideas and details. The conclusion restates the topic and summarizes the important information presented in the body.

However, research papers differ from compositions in one important respect. In some compositions, you can use the first-person point of view. In other words, you can use the pronouns *I*, *me*, and *my*. You can also include your own opinions. You cannot do these things in a research paper. Research papers are never written using the first-person point of view. They also never include personal observations or opinions. Remember, the ideas in a research paper come from outside sources, not from personal experience.

When you write the introduction to a research paper, be sure to state what the paper will be about. Sometimes you will want to present some of your facts in the introduction. At other times you will want to keep the introduction short and general.

Check It Out   On the following page are the introduction and the first paragraph of the body of the report on a career in hotel work. They are shown as you might have written them after working on a first draft.

- How does this first draft use the information shown in the outline?
- What main idea is presented in the introduction?

253

Part 5

Objective

To write the introduction of a research paper

Presenting the Lesson

1. Read and discuss **Here's the idea.** Stress that students can not use the first (*I*) or second (*you*) person in their research papers, and that they should never begin with a statement like *This paper is about the parts of an airplane.* Define *thesis statement* (a statement about the purpose of a paper) and discuss interesting ways to present it in the introduction.

2. Read **Check It Out.** Have students compare the introduction of the paper with the outline on page 251. Ask students how much of the outline is included in the introduction and first paragraph of the body.

3. Assign **Try Your Skill.** Have volunteers share their introductions.

4. Read **Keep This in Mind** and then assign **Now Write.**

Individualizing the Lesson

Less-Advanced Students

Work individually with students as they do each part of their research papers. Reassure them that they will have plenty of time to correct their introductions when they revise their work.

Advanced Students

Have students specifically work on an interesting introduction that will make their readers want to read their whole paper.

253

Optional Practice

Have students experiment with writing more than one introduction for their papers. Have them discuss their different introductions in groups to determine the most effective paragraph.

Extending the Lesson

Bring in several introductions to research papers from your files. Ask students which ones make them want to go on to read the whole paper. Discuss generally what makes an introduction interesting and what makes it dull.

¶ Many people choose a career in the field of personal service. That is, they choose jobs in which they attend to the needs of other individuals. One of the largest personal service industries is the hotel-motel business. Basically, The function of this business is to provide sleeping (acomodations) [sp?] and meals. However, Hotels and motels range from those simple country inns with a few rooms and employees to those elaborate city skyscrapers with more than 1,000 rooms and hundreds of employees. The largest of these businesses offer many additional conveniences for their guests. The services may include gift shops, recreational facilities, and banquet and convention facilities.

To provide this range of services, the hotel industry employs workers in a wide variety of skilled and unskilled occupations. These various occupations can be divided into those related to the "front of the house" and those related to the "back of the house." The "front of the house" is a hotel term for means the operations that deal directly and are seen by with the guests. These operations are those of management the front office, the uniformed service staff, and the accounting and sales departments. The "back of the house" refers to hotel operations that are seldom not seen by guests. These include housekeeping, food preparation, security, laundry, and engineering.

Try Your Skill   Here is part of an outline for a report on dental assistants. Some of this information would fit nicely into the introduction to such a report. Using the information from the outline, write an introductory paragraph. Compare your introduction with those of your classmates.

I. Nature of the work
   A. Work along with a dentist
      1. Prepare patient for treatment
      2. Hand dentist proper instruments and materials
      3. Keep patient's mouth clear
   B. Work independently
      1. Provide oral health instruction
      2. Make casts of teeth and mouth
      3. Order dental supplies

Keep This in Mind

- Use your outline and note cards to write the first draft of your research paper.
- A research paper, like a composition, has an introduction, a body, and a conclusion.
- In the introduction, state the topic clearly.

Now Write   Take out your outline and note cards. Review them and think about whether to introduce the career you have researched in a general or a detailed way. Decide how you will state the main idea of your information about this career in the introduction.

Using both your outline and your note cards, write the introduction to your paper. Try to present your ideas clearly. However, in this first draft, don't worry about grammar, usage, and mechanics. Save your work in your folder.

Part 6

Objective

To write the body and conclusion of a research paper

Presenting the Lesson

1. Read and discuss **Here's the Idea.** Emphasize that each paragraph in the research paper must still be developed just like any other paragraph: with a topic sentence, supporting details, and logical organization. Ask students the purpose of the conclusion in a research paper.

2. Read and discuss **Check It Out.** As students read the sample paper, have them pay attention to transitions that are used that keep the facts from being strung together monotonously. Also point out the use of interesting, specific examples which keep the paper from being just a list of dry facts and statistics.

3. Assign **Try Your Skill.** Have volunteers read their conclusions to the class.

4. Read **Keep This in Mind** and then assign **Now Write.**

Individualizing the Lesson

Less-Advanced Students

Assist the students individually with **Now Write.** Schedule conferences to discuss the body and conclusion of each student's paper. Use the Handbook Section to help students with specific usage problems.

Go the Distance

Writing the Body and Conclusion

Here's the Idea   As you write the body of a research paper, follow your outline and your note cards. The topic sentence of each paragraph in the body will correspond to a main topic in your outline. The note cards will supply the details. Use those details, examples, and quotations that will add the most to your report.

Use quotation marks when you use the words of another writer. When you prepare your final copy, you will give that writer credit in the correct way. You will learn how to give proper credit in Part 8. To keep track of information that must be credited, use the source numbers on your note cards. Write the source number in the margin next to any sentence that contains a direct quote or any information that must be credited.

Keep reading and reviewing your work as you write. Are your ideas clearly expressed? Are they organized logically? Is your writing detailed and interesting? Take time to think about how you can best express your information.

A research paper must come to a logical ending. A research paper should have a clear conclusion in which you tie ideas together naturally. You may include additional facts about the topic. Your most important purposes are to restate your main idea and to summarize the information you have presented.

Check It Out   On the next page is the rest of the first draft of the research paper on a career in the hotel industry.

- Compare this first draft with the outline. What details, examples, or quotations are used to develop the body?
- Does the conclusion sum up the information presented in the paper?

Because
~~Since~~ the hotel industry ^employs^ ~~contains~~ such a
broad range of occupations, there is ^no single type^ ~~not one~~
^of training^ ~~schedule of preparation~~ necessary. Many
entry-level positions require only a short
period of on-the-job training. ^Entry-level^ ~~Such~~ jobs
are often available on a part-time basis for
students, to (aquaint) them with hotel work.
   sp?
These jobs include waiter, maid, clerk, porter,
bellhop, and elevator operator. However,
longer on-the-job training ^or vocational education^ may lead to
other ^higher-paying^ positions.[1] For instance, those who have
completed programs in cooking, accounting, or
maintenance and repair work may ^eventually^ become
department heads. "The hotel industry is
one of the few wherein a young person can
secure a position without too much formal
education, and work his way through the
various departments to an executive capacity."[2]
   To be successful ^in any position^ in the hotel business, several
basic personal qualifications are required. A
person must be able to ~~get along~~ ^deal^ with all
kinds of people in any situation. Courtesy
and patience are ^essential^ ~~necessary~~ when serving ^guests^ ~~people~~.
In addition to a neat appearance, a pleasant
manner is also important. Finally, ^constant^ careful
attention to detail is called for in ^all aspects of^ hotel work.

257

Advanced Students

Have the students read a model research paper, looking for effective uses of transitional words and phrases. Tell them to be alert to techniques that they can use in their own papers.

Optional Practice

Pair students to read each other's first drafts. Ask each student to comment on what he or she liked about the other person's research paper.

Extending the Lesson

Read the conclusions to some chapters in a history textbook, or to an encyclopedia article. Discuss the techniques used in the conclusion to summarize the main idea of the chapter or article.

There are many benefits for those who choose a career in the hotel industry. The first advantage is a flexible schedule, since hotels and motels operate twenty-four hours a day with three shifts. Other benefits include the choice of part-time, full-time, or seasonal work, and a wide selection of geographic locations. At present The industry is also looking for capable women and members of minority groups to train as managers. A career in the hotel industry offers many opportunities for personal and professional growth.

Try Your Skill   Write a conclusion for a research paper on dental assistants based on information from this outline.

  V. Benefits of the career
    A. Personal growth by helping others
    B. Pleasant work environment
      1. Quiet and relaxed atmosphere
      2. Usually short hours, flexible schedule

Keep This in Mind

- Use the ideas, details, examples, and direct quotations from your outline and note cards to develop the body of a research paper.
- Write a conclusion that summarizes the information presented in the paper.

Now Write   Review your outline and notes, and then write the body and conclusion of your research paper. Use quotation marks if you use another writers' words. Save your first draft.

Better Than Ever

Revising a Research Paper

Here's the Idea   Once you have completed your first draft, you can begin to revise your research paper.

Read your work several times. Is it interesting as well as informative? Is there a beginning, a middle, and an end? Are your dates, statistics, and other facts accurate? Are unusual names or words spelled correctly? You will probably need to make some changes. All successful writers spend a great deal of time revising. Here are some questions to help you remember what to look for as you revise your research paper.

1.   Does my introduction state what my paper will be about? Is it informative and interesting?

2.   Does the paper follow my outline?

3.   Are my facts accurate and clearly presented? Are enough facts included to develop my topic thoroughly?

4.   Have I used quotation marks when copying a writer's words directly?

5.   Does each paragraph deal with one main idea? Do the facts and ideas in each paragraph support the main idea?

6.   Have I followed a logical order in presenting my ideas?

7.   Did I make sure not to include any personal opinions?

8.   Have I used transitions between sentences and paragraphs?

9.   Does my conclusion summarize the main ideas?

After checking your organization and content, be sure to proofread your research paper carefully.

Check It Out   Notice how this conclusion to a research paper about cameras has been revised.

259

Part 7

Objective

To revise and proofread the research paper

Presenting the Lesson

1. Read and discuss **Here's the Idea.** Outline the revision questions on the chalkboard as you discuss them.

2. Have students examine the revised paragraph in **Check It Out.** Point out to the class that the changes made add more specific details.

3. Assign **Try Your Skill.** Ask volunteers to write their revised paragraphs on the chalkboard. Remind students that there is no one way to revise a paragraph correctly.

4. Read **Keep This in Mind.** Stress the second point, which is specific to research papers.

5. Assign **Now Write.** Discuss how to choose a good title for a paper.

Individualizing the Lesson

Less-Advanced Students

After students have made revisions, devote one or more class periods to proofreading for errors in grammar and mechanics. List on the chalkboard those types of mistakes that students in the class have been making, and urge students to watch for these errors in their own papers. Make sure they have access to a dictionary, and help them find those sections in the Handbook that they should use. Have students exchange papers and help their partners proofread.

259

Advanced Students

Have students locate specific parts of their papers that they think need to be substantially revised. Schedule individual conferences with each student, going over these sections with them in detail.

Optional Practice

Duplicate a sample first draft from your files. Have students revise it individually, and then go over the paper in class with the whole class offering revision suggestions.

Extending the Lesson

Devote class time to allow students to read each other's research papers for pleasure. Have each student hand in one extra copy of his or her paper to you for this purpose. After all the papers have been read, hold a general critique about them.

It is true that the electronic
Like I said, new cameras have some advantages over older *the less sophisticated*
ones. *manual.* For one thing, they need alot less skill, And they give you *The electronic cameras require much to operate, a photo-grapher*
more freedom. *On the other hand   tend to   more often than manuals.* The thing is, they break down a lot. And can't
be fixed. *Also, the new cameras are usually plastic.* Who wants to buy a new camera all the time? For
strength, quality, and durbility, I say buy a manual camera. *The older manuals were made of brass.*
it's hard to top a good manual camera.

- Why has the writer taken out all of the references to "I"?
- In what specific ways has the paragraph been improved?

Try Your Skill   Revise this introduction to a research paper about the art of mask making. Be sure the introduction clearly states a main idea. Remember also to proofread the paragraph.

Mask making is an art practised by people all over the world. Sometimes mask are made for fun, like holloween. Sometimes mask are made for religous reasons like in different tribes in south America, Africa and Asia. I like the masks made by the hopi indians. Called Kachinas. Masks have a long history which I will talk about in my paper.

Keep This in Mind

- When you revise your research paper, try to improve your ideas, organization, and language.
- Check your facts, figures, and dates for accuracy.
- Proofread your paper.

Now Write   Follow the guidelines in this lesson and use the other revising skills you have learned to revise your research paper. Give your paper a good title. Save your revised paper.

Final Details

Footnotes and Bibliography

Here's the Idea   As you know, a research paper is based on information gathered from outside sources. When you prepare your final copy, you must be careful to give these sources credit for their ideas. To credit your sources, you must write footnotes and a bibliography.

A footnote gives credit to a writer whose words, facts, or ideas you have used. A direct quotation requires a footnote. So does a statistic. So do any ideas from a writer that are not common knowledge or that are clearly the writer's personal opinion.

To prepare proper footnotes, follow these steps:

1. Look through your paper for any material that needs to be footnoted. Follow each direct quote, statistic, or idea with a number. The number should be written slightly above the line, like this: [1]. The numbers should run in order, with the first piece of text to be footnoted numbered *1*, the second piece numbered *2*, and so on.

2. On a separate page at the end of your paper, make a list of the sources from which your footnoted material was taken. The order in which the footnotes appear in your paper and the order of the footnotes on the footnote page should be the same.

3. To write your footnotes, look for the source number you wrote after each piece of text you wanted to footnote. If you didn't write these source numbers when you wrote your first draft, look through your note cards for the card that contains the information you are footnoting. That note card should contain the proper source number. Then locate the bibliography card with the same number. This bibliography card, together with the page number from the note card, will give you all of the

261

Part 8

Objective

To prepare footnotes and a bibliography for a research paper

Presenting the Lesson

1. Write the words *footnotes* and *bibliography* on the chalkboard. Then read and discuss **Here's the Idea.** List the differences between footnotes and bibliography; it may take more than one discussion for the class to understand these concepts, or why they are needed. Go over the steps for preparing footnotes slowly and carefully; if necessary, have extra examples on hand to illustrate each step.

2. Read **Check It Out.** Go over the examples carefully, pointing out the difference in form and punctuation for the same source in the footnotes and in the bibliography. Make sure students know what the number in front of each footnote means.

3. Assign **Try Your Skill.** If students are unsure about this exercise, take time to go over pages 264–267 with them before they begin. Have volunteers write their footnotes and bibliographies on the board.

4. Read **Keep This in Mind.**

5. Assign **Now Write.** Go over the sample copy of a research paper on pages 268–271 before students complete **Now Write.** Check each step of **Now Write** as students do it, to make sure they understand what they are supposed to do.

261

Individualizing the Lesson

Less-Advanced Students

Students may not have included any direct quotations needing footnotes in their research papers. Have them write one sample footnote entry using one of the sources in their bibliographies.

Advanced Students

Point out to students how professional the typewritten paper beginning on page 268 looks. Encourage those students who can to type the final copy of their research paper.

Optional Practice

Teach students abbreviations that can be used in bibliographies.

ed. (editor), *et al.* (and others), *l.* (line), *ll.* (lines), *n.d.* (no date of publication given), *rev.* (revised), *ms.* (manuscript)

Extending the Lesson

1. Bring to class various pamphlets and books written about the acceptable form for research papers. Point out that although there are slight variations among the books regarding minor points of placement of periods and commas in footnotes and bibliographies, most authors use the same guidelines that the class has been studying.

2. Encourage students to make and use appropriate illustrations, charts, and graphs to accompany their reports.

---

information you need to write your footnote.

Each kind of source has its own special footnote form. To find the proper footnote form for the kind of source you are footnoting, see pages 264–267.

Finally, prepare your **bibliography,** which is a complete list of sources you used to prepare your research paper. A bibliography usually appears on a separate, final page. Each entry contains the information from your bibliography cards, except for the source number and library location. The form for a bibliography entry differs slightly for books, magazines, encyclopedias, and other sources. See pages 264–267 for the proper bibliography forms.

Check It Out　Study the form of a footnote and bibliography for a report on a career in the hotel industry.

Footnote

[1]William E. Hopke, "Hotel and Motel Managers," *The Encyclopedia of Careers and Vocational Guidance,* 1981 ed.

[2]Shepard Henkin, *Opportunities in the Hotel and Motel Industry* (Lincolnwood, Illinois: National Textbook Company, 1978), p. 27.

Bibliography

Henkin, Shepard. *Opportunities in the Hotel and Motel Industry.* Lincolnwood, Illinois: National Textbook Company, 1978.

Hopke, William E. "Hotel and Motel Managers." *The Encyclopedia of Careers and Vocational Guidance.* 1981 ed.

Occupational Outlook Handbook. 1985–86 ed. Washington, D.C.: U.S. Department of Labor, Bureau of Labor Statistics, 1985.

Try Your Skill　Read the following quotation about choosing a career. Notice its source. Write a footnote and a bibliography entry based on this information.

People differ in what they want from a career. Many people desire a high income. Some hope for fame. Others want much leisure time or a life of adventure. Still others want to serve people and help make the world a better place. Before you begin to explore career fields, you should determine (1) your values, or goals in life; (2) your interests; and (3) your abilities. Most people are happiest in occupations that meet their values, interests, and abilities.

from page 172e of an article titled "Careers" by Edwin L. Herr in *The World Book Encyclopedia*, Volume 3 (1979), pages 172d-174 [1]Edwin L. Herr. "Careers." *The World Book Encyclopedia.* 1979 ed., p. 172e.

Herr, Edwin L. "Careers." *The World Book Encyclopedia.* 1979 ed. Pages 172d-174.

Keep This in Mind

- Use footnotes to give credit to writers whose words or ideas you include in a research paper.
- Prepare a bibliography to show the sources of information you used in writing your research paper.

Now Write   Make a final copy of your research paper and include your footnotes and bibliography. First, insert the numbers for your footnotes into the first draft of your research paper. Next, find the information you need for your footnotes on your source cards. Copy it in the correct form on a separate page labeled *Footnotes*.

Then take out your bibliography cards and write a bibliography entry for each source you used in your research paper. Copy the entries in alphabetical order onto a separate page labeled *Bibliography*. Be sure to use the correct form.

Neatly copy your paper in final form.

For help in preparing the final copy of your paper, see Handbook Section 16, **The Correct Form for Writing.**

Also, examine the final copy of the research paper on a career in the hotel industry shown at the end of this section.

Parenthetical Documentation of Sources

The 1984 edition of the *MLA Handbook for Writers of Research Papers* suggests a simplified method for citing sources. When using this method, known as **parenthetical documentation,** list the author's name and the page number of the source in parentheses after the paraphrased or quoted material.

> Most children will have watched 20,000 hours of television and seen 350,000 commercials while growing up (Mayer 128).

At the end of the paper, include a list of "Works Cited" containing complete bibliography entries for all the sources you have referred to.

Note that some sources will require special forms for parenthetical citations:

1. If the bibliography entry in "Works Cited" lists more than one author, include all the last names or one last name followed by "et al." (Bertram Linder et al. 28).

2. If the bibliography entry in "Works Cited" is listed by title, include the title, or a shortened version of it, and the page number (*Literary Market Place* 128).

3. If the "Works Cited" lists more than one work by the same author, include the title, or a shortened version of it, after the author's last name (Hawthorne, *Scarlet Letter* 86).

Basic Forms for Footnotes

A. A book with an author:

^{1}Peter Mansfield, <u>The Arab World</u> (New York: Crowell, 1976), p. 123

B. A book with no author:

^{2}<u>Images of South Africa</u> (Cape Town: C. Struik, 1983), p. 21.

C. A book with an editor:

^{3}John Lahr, ed., <u>Grove Press Modern Drama</u> (New York: Grove Press, Inc., 1975), pp. 93–101.

D. An encyclopedia article:

^{4}"Naval Ships and Crafts," <u>Encyclopedia Britannica</u>, 1981 ed.

E. A magazine article with an author:

^{5}Pico Iyer, "Some Reluctant Friends," <u>Time</u>, 16 July 1984, p. 38.

F. A magazine article without an author:

^{6}"Sleuthing Is the Fun," <u>Time</u>, 4 July 1983, pp. 52–53.

G. A newspaper article:

^{7}Gail Sheehy, "America's Great Awakening," <u>Chicago Tribune</u>, 6 August 1984, Sec. 5, p. 1, col. 1–3.

H. A report or a pamphlet:

^{8}American Medical Association, <u>Medical Relations Under Workmen's Compensation</u> (Chicago: American Medical Association, 1976), p. 3.

If the report is by an individual author rather than by an association or committee, begin with the author's name.

I. A film:

[9]Richard Attenborough, dir., <u>Gandhi</u>, with Ben Kingsley, Columbia Pictures, 1982.

J. A television or radio program:

[10]"A Desert Blooming," writ. Marshall Riggan, <u>Living Wild</u>, dir. Harry L. Gorden, prod. Peter Argentine, PBS, 29 April 1984.

K. An interview:

[11]Personal interview with Robert Hughes, Director, New Playwright's Workshop, University of Washington, Bellingham, Washington, 6 Feb. 1984.

Sources Already Footnoted

To refer to sources already listed in previous complete footnotes, use a shortened form.

A. In most cases, the author's last name, followed by the relevant page numbers, is sufficent.

[12]Robyn Davidson, <u>Tracks</u> (New York: Pantheon Books, 1980), p. 62

[13]Davidson, p. 74.

B. If more than one work by the same author has been referred to, then you should write the author's last name and the title. The title may be in shortened form.

[14]John C. Gardner, <u>Grendel</u> (New York: Alfred A. Knopf, 1971), p. 24.

[15]John C. Gardner, <u>Dragon, Dragon and Other Timeless Tales</u> (New York: Alfred A. Knopf, 1975), p. 6.

[16]Gardner, <u>Dragon, Dragon</u> p. 91.

Basic Forms for a Bibliography

The entries in a bibliography are arranged alphabetically according to the author's last name. When there is no author, use the first important word of the entry to determine the correct place in the bibliography for that entry.

A. A book with an author:

Mansfield, Peter. <u>The Arab World</u>. New York: Crowell, 1976.

B. A book with no author:

<u>Images of South Africa</u>. Cape Town: C. Struik, 1983.

C. A book with an editor:

Lahr, John, ed. <u>Grove Press Modern Drama</u>. New York: Grove Press, Inc., 1975.

D. An encyclopedia article:

"Naval Ships and Crafts." <u>Encyclopedia Britannica</u>. 1981 ed.

E. A magazine article with an author:

Iyer, Pico. "Some Reluctant Friends." <u>Time</u>, 16 July 1984, p. 38.

F. A magazine article without an author:

"Sleuthing Is the Fun." <u>Time</u>, 4 July 1983, pp. 52-53.

G. A newspaper article:

Sheehy, Gail. "America's Great Awakening." <u>Chicago Tribune</u>, 6 August 1984, Sec. 5, p. 1, col. 1-3.

H. A report or a pamphlet:

American Medical Association. <u>Medical Re-</u>
<u>lations under Workmen's Compensa-</u>
<u>tion</u>. Chicago: American Medical
Association, 1976.

If the report is by an individual author rather than by an association or committee, begin with the author's name.

I. A film:

Richard, Attenborough, dir., <u>Gandhi</u>, with
Ben Kingsley, Columbia Pictures,
1982.

J. A television or radio program:

"A Desert Blooming." Writ. Marshall Riggan. <u>Living Wild</u>. Dir. Harry L.
Gorden. Prod. Peter Argentine. PBS,
29 April 1984.

K. An interview:

Hughes, Robert. Director, New Play-
wright's Workshop, University of
Washington. Personal interview.
Bellingham, Washington. 6 Feb. 1984.

267

Chris Adams

English III

March 8, 1985

Reserve a Future in the Hotel Industry

Many people choose a career in the field of personal
services. That is, they choose jobs in which they attend to the
needs of other individuals. One of the largest personal
service industries is the hotel—motel business. Basically, the
function of this business is to provide sleeping
accommodations and meals. However, hotels and motels range
from simple country inns with a few rooms and employees to
elaborate city skyscrapers with more than 1,000 rooms and
hundreds of employees. The largest of these businesses offer
many additional conveniences for their guests. The services
may include gift shops, recreational facilities, and banquet
and convention facilities.

To provide this range of services, the hotel industry
employs workers in a wide variety of skilled and unskilled
occupations. These various occupations can be divided into
those related to the "front of the house" and those related to
the "back of the house." The "front of the house" is a hotel
term for the operations that deal directly with, and are seen
by, the guests. These operations are those of management, the
front office, the uniformed service staff, and the accounting
and sales departments. The "back of the house" refers to hotel

operations that are seldom seen by guests. These include housekeeping, food preparation, security, laundry, and engineering.

Because the hotel industry employs such a broad range of occupations, no single type of training is necessary. Many entry-level positions require only a short period of on-the-job training. Entry-level jobs are often available on a part-time basis for students, to acquaint them with hotel work. These jobs include waiter, maid, clerk, porter, bellhop, and elevator operator. However, longer on-the-job training or vocational education may lead to other, higher-paying positions.[1] For instance, those who have completed programs in cooking, accounting, or maintenance and repair work may eventually become department heads. "The hotel industry is one of the few wherein a young person can secure a position without too much formal education, and work his way through the various departments to an executive capacity."[2]

To be successful in any position in the hotel business, several basic personal qualifications are required. A person must be able to deal with all kinds of people in any situation. Courtesy and patience are essential when serving guests. In addition to a pleasant manner, a neat appearance is important. Finally, constant attention to detail is called for in all aspects of hotel work.

There are many benefits for those who choose a career in the hotel industry. The first advantage is a flexible schedule, since hotels and motels operate twenty-four hours a

269

day with three shifts. Other benefits include the choice of part-time, full-time, or seasonal work, and a wide selection of geographic locations. At present, the industry is also looking for capable women and members of minority groups to train as managers. A career in the hotel industry offers many opportunities for personal and professional growth.

Footnotes

[1]William E. Hopke, "Hotel and Motel Managers." The Encyclopedia of Careers and Vocational Guidance. 1981 ed.

[2]Shepard Henkin, Opportunities in the Hotel and Motel Industry (Lincolnwood, Illinois: National Textbook Company, 1978), p. 27.

Bibliography

Henkin, Shepard. Opportunities in the Hotel and Motel Industry. Lincolnwood, Illinois: National Textbook Company, 1978.

Hopke, William E. "Hotel and Motel Managers." The Encyclopedia of Careers and Vocational Guidance. 1981 ed.

Occupational Outlook Handbook. 1985—86 ed. Washington, D.C.: U.S. Department of Labor, Bureau of Labor Statistics, 1985.

Section **21** Objectives

1. To check statements of fact by using fair, up-to-date, reliable sources

2. To recognize opinions and support them with facts

3. To recognize the three types of opinions: judgments, predictions, and statements of obligation

4. To recognize and avoid loaded language

5. To recognize and avoid over-generalizations, stereotypes, band-wagon, and snob appeal

6. To recognize and avoid false-cause reasoning and only-cause reasoning

7. To learn that conclusions are drawn by first observing a group of facts and then determining how the facts are related

8. To recognize the difference between synonyms and antonyms

9. To learn that analogies are comparisons of two similar but un-like things

10. To learn to answer analogy questions on standardized tests

11. To learn to recognize rela-tionships between words in a sen-tence

Preparing the Students

Bring to class several different advertisements, and ask students to read them carefully. Discuss with students their reactions to the ad-vertisements. What did they like and dislike about them? Did the adver-tisement make them interested in the product? Ask them if they felt the advertisements were "honest."

Point out that the ability to evalu-ate what is read and heard is called critical thinking. Emphasize that

Critical Thinking

273

thinking critically about different ideas is important in making sound decisions.

Explain that this Section presents the elements of sound critical thinking. This Section will not only help students understand new ideas, but also help them present their own ideas more clearly and effectively.

Additional Resources

Mastery Test — page 31 in the test booklet

Practice Book — pages 106–114

Duplicating Masters — pages 106–114

Teaching Special Populations

LD Give students additional practice in identifying facts and opinions. Alter or delete exercises in reasoning that are too difficult for your students.

ESL Help students differentiate between *fact* and *opinion*. Give many examples of both based on the same subject.

Have students find examples of facts and opinions in magazines and newspapers. Ask them to bring these in for discussion.

Students may have difficulty understanding why loaded language should not support opinions. Discuss the text examples in depth.

Discuss with students how stereotyping and snob appeal might differ from culture to culture.

Objectives

1. To check statements of fact by using fair, up-to-date, reliable sources

2. To recognize opinions and support them with facts

Presenting the Lesson

1. Read and discuss **Here's the Idea.** Give students examples of facts that must be checked in a verifiable source, and those that can be checked through personal observation. Point out that opinions cannot be verified.

Explain that recognizing the difference between facts and opinions is the first important step toward critical thinking.

2. Read aloud and discuss **Check It Out.**

3. Read aloud and then assign **Try Your Skill.**

4. Read aloud **Keep This in Mind** and assign **Now Write.**

Individualizing the Lesson

Less-Advanced Students

Have students begin a dictionary about critical thinking. The first entries should be *fact, opinion, sound opinion,* and *unsound opinion.*

For extra practice, have students provide two facts taken from a reliable source, and two taken from personal experience.

Advanced Students

Have students compose a list of five statements of fact similar to

In Fact

Facts and Opinions

Here's the Idea   Critical thinking skills are important tools for learning and presenting new ideas. They can be used in school as you gather information, write papers, and take tests. They can also be used on the job and in making decisions.

Every day you read or hear hundreds of facts and opinions. These come from many sources. Television, books, newspapers, magazines, and other people are just a few of these sources. You must learn to separate facts from opinions. You must also learn how to test facts and opinions to see if they are reliable.

A **fact** is a statement that can be proved true. You can prove a fact in any of the following ways:

1. You can make a personal observation.
2. You can ask an expert.
3. You can check the fact in a reference work (a dictionary, encyclopedia, almanac, or book written by an expert).

The statement "The cheetah is the fastest land animal" is a fact. You can prove it by observing how fast different land animals can run. You can ask an expert on animals. You can also read about the cheetah in an encyclopedia. Whenever you read or hear a statement that is supposed to be a fact, ask yourself whether it can be proved. If it *cannot* be proved, it is *not* a fact.

A statement that cannot be proved is an **opinion.** An example of an opinion is the statement "Michael Jackson is the greatest singer alive." A statement such as this cannot be proved.

Even though opinions cannot be proved, they can be supported. **Sound opinions** are ones that are supported by facts. **Unsound opinions** are ones that are not supported by facts. Whenever you read, hear, or write about an opinion, ask yourself whether it can be supported by facts.

Check It Out   Read the following statements.

Many people enjoy science fiction films.
Science fiction films are really entertaining.

- Which of these statements is a fact? Which is an opinion? How do you know?

Try Your Skill   Check the following statements of fact. Using the reference works listed in parentheses, tell whether each statement is true or false.

1. Franklin D. Roosevelt was President when World War II began. (textbook or encyclopedia)
2. Chad is the largest country in Africa. (atlas)
3. The word *hippopotamus* comes from two words that mean "river horse." (dictionary)
4. Theodore Roethke is a famous American poet. (textbook or encyclopedia)
5. *Thursday* was named after the Norse god Thor. (dictionary)

Keep This in Mind

- A fact is a statement that can be proved true.
- Facts can be checked by observation, by asking an expert, or by reading in a reference work.
- An opinion is a statement that cannot be proved true.
- Sound opinions can be supported with facts. Be sure to support your opinions whenever you speak or write.

Now Write   Write one statement of opinion about each of the following subjects. Then write one statement of fact to support each opinion.

football   music   conservation

Optional Practice

To illustrate that facts change, have students consult reference materials such as almanacs, encyclopedias, or newspapers to find five statements of fact that are out-of-date. Have them then find the current information and compare the differences.

Extending the Lesson

Point out to students that it is important to consider if a verifiable source is biased or unbiased. Ask students which sources they would examine if they were buying a new bicycle, planning a vacation to New York City, selecting a college, or voting for a public official.

Objective

To recognize the three types of opinions: judgments, predictions, and statements of obligation

Presenting the Lesson

1. Read aloud and discuss **Here's the Idea.** On the chalkboard have a student write *judgment, prediction,* and *statements of obligation.* Ask the class to suggest examples of each type of opinion.

2. Read aloud and discuss the statements from **Check It Out.** Have students decide which opinion is a judgment, which is a prediction, and which is a statement of obligation.

3. Read aloud and assign **Try Your Skill.**

4. Read **Keep This in Mind** and assign **Now Write.**

Individualizing the Lesson

Less-Advanced Students

Have students add *judgment, prediction,* and *statements of obligation* to their dictionary. Have students divide into small groups to complete **Try Your Skill.** If students have difficulty with this exercise, point out which words signal the type of opinion in each statement.

Advanced Students

Have students write five pairs of sentences, each pair containing one fact and one opinion. When students have completed this exercise, have them exchange papers and indicate the type of opinion in each sentence.

It Takes All Kinds

Types of Opinions

Here's the Idea   As you learned in Part 1, an opinion is a statement that cannot be proved. There are three main types of opinions. These are judgments, predictions, and statements of obligation.

A **judgment** is a statement that tells how the speaker or writer feels about a subject. The statement "History class is very interesting" is a judgment because it tells how the speaker feels about history class. This type of opinion often includes judgment words, such as *bad, fine, interesting, lovely,* and *excellent.*

A **prediction** is a statement about the future. It tells about something that has not yet happened. Therefore it cannot be proved. The statement "The Greyhawks will win the regional championship this year" is a prediction.

A **statement of obligation** tells what one should or should not do. Such statements usually include one of the following words or phrases: *should, must,* or *ought to.* The statement "You should exercise every day" is a statement of obligation.

Remember that all opinions must be supported by facts. If an opinion can be supported by facts, it is sound. If it cannot be supported by facts, it is unsound.

Check It Out   Read the following statements.

1. The audience should listen politely when a speaker is talking.

2. By the year 2000, robots will be used in most industries.

3. The novels of Stephen King are terrifying.

· Which of these opinions is a judgment? Which is a prediction? Which is a statement of obligation?

Try Your Skill Tell whether the following opinions are judgments, predictions, or statements of obligation.

J 1. Shakespeare was the greatest playwright who ever lived.

P 2. During the next century, mining will take place on the moon.

SO 3. People who drive should learn a little about automotive repair.

J 4. Spring is the nicest season of all.

SO 5. Campers ought to be careful not to leave trash at their campsites.

P 6. The road repairs will be completed by fall.

Keep This in Mind

- A judgment tells how a speaker or writer feels about a subject.
- A prediction is a statement about the future.
- A statement of obligation tells what should or should not be done.

Now Write Read the following paragraph. Identify the two opinions in this paragraph. Tell what types of opinions they are. Also tell whether these opinions are supported by facts.

In the future we will have to find other sources of energy. There is a limited amount of oil and gas in the ground. These fuels are rapidly being used up. We must begin now to find other methods for creating the energy we need.

Overloaded

Objective

To recognize and avoid loaded language

Presenting the Lesson

1. Read aloud **Here's the Idea.** Explain to students that appealing to emotions is not in itself wrong. Our emotions are an important part of the way we think, and should not be disregarded when forming opinions and making decisions. What is wrong, however, is appealing to emotions through bias and misrepresentation. The use of purr words and snarl words are often used in place of facts to influence the opinions of the listener. Students should be aware of their use, and know that purr words and snarl words are not to be used to replace facts.

2. Read and discuss **Check It Out.**

3. Assign **Try Your Skill.**

4. Read aloud **Keep This in Mind** and assign **Now Write.**

Individualizing the Lesson

Less-Advanced Students

Have students add *persuasion, snarl words,* and *purr words* to their dictionaries. Have students work in pairs to complete **Now Write.** Stress that people who are aware of improper appeals to emotion are not likely to be taken advantage of.

Advanced Students

Ask students to bring to class examples of advertising that uses purr words to sell products. Particular examples would include Eastern

Avoiding Loaded Language

Here's the Idea   Even though they cannot be proved, opinions are still very important. They express how we feel about things. They tell what we expect of the future. They show what actions we believe are right and wrong. In fact, many of the most important ideas that we have about the world are opinions. You probably have many opinions of your own about which you feel very strongly. Sometimes you may even attempt to convince other people to adopt these opinions. When you do this, you are practicing the art of **persuasion.**

Whenever you present an argument, always support your opinion with facts. By doing this, you give the other person reasons to see things the way you do. Do not make the mistake of simply stating your opinion and expecting someone to accept it. Also avoid using highly emotional, or loaded, language.

Loaded language is language that appeals to a person's emotions. Such language is often used in place of facts to sway the opinions of readers and listeners. There are two types of loaded language: snarl words and purr words. A **snarl word** is one that creates a negative feeling. A **purr word** is one that creates a positive feeling. Read the following examples.

You are a *miser.*
I am *thrifty.*

You are *overbearing.*
I am *forceful.*

The sentences in each pair mean almost the same thing. However, the first sentence in each pair seems negative. This is due to the snarl words *miser* and *overbearing.* The second sentence in each pair seems more positive. This is due to the purr words *thrifty* and *forceful*. Be alert to the use of snarl and purr words when you listen to the ideas of others. Also be careful when you use them yourself. They should never be used in place of facts.

Check It Out   Read the following pairs of statements.

1. Life in the country is simpler and more peaceful than life in the city.
2. Life in the country is more dull and routine than life in the city.

- In what ways are these two statements alike? How do they differ? What snarl words and purr words do they contain?

Try Your Skill   Find the snarl words and purr words in the following sentences.

1. Many actors and actresses are <u>fabulously wealthy</u>. purr
2. Many actors and actresses are <u>filthy rich</u>. snarl
3. Marietta dresses <u>fashionably</u>. purr
4. Marietta dresses <u>according to every passing fad</u>. snarl

Keep This in Mind

- Loaded language contains snarl words and purr words.
- Snarl words create negative feelings.
- Purr words create positive feelings.
- When supporting opinions, do not use loaded language in place of facts.

Now Write   Choose a topic about which you feel strongly. Write three statements of opinion on this topic. In the first, use snarl words. In the second, use purr words. In the third, avoid loaded language altogether.

Airlines' "The Wings of Man"; Snuggle fabric softener; and Almost Home cookies.

Optional Practice

Have students find a movie or book review from a major magazine or newspaper. Ask students to determine the author's opinion of the work being reviewed. Then have them list the facts used to support the opinion, and the use of persuasive methods—purr words and snarl words.

Extending the Lesson

Have each student create his or her own advertising campaign for an imaginary product. Each advertisement should contain at least one example of a snarl word or a purr word. Put students' ads on the bulletin board and invite other classes in to "shop."

Part 4 Out on a Limb

Errors in Reasoning

Objective

To recognize and avoid overgeneralizations, stereotypes, bandwagon, and snob appeal

Presenting the Lesson

1. Read aloud **Here's the Idea.** On the chalkboard write the word *overgeneralization,* and discuss the example. Ask students for other examples of overgeneralization. Point out that stereotyping, bandwagon, and snob appeal are specific forms of overgeneralization.

2. Read and discuss the examples from **Check It Out.**

3. Read aloud and assign **Try Your Skill.**

4. Have students read **Keep This in Mind** and assign **Now Write.**

Individualizing the Lesson

Less-Advanced Students

Have students add *overgeneralization, stereotyping, bandwagon,* and *snob appeal* to their dictionaries. Be sure they have a sound understanding of the concept of overgeneralization. Suggest that students do **Try Your Skill** in small groups.

Advanced Students

When students have completed **Now Write,** divide them into pairs. Ask them to exchange their papers, and have each student indicate the errors in reasoning for each advertisement. Then have students discuss their answers.

Here's the Idea   Some unsound opinions result from errors in reasoning. A few of these errors have been given names.

Overgeneralization occurs when a person makes a statement about an entire group based on too few examples. Read the following example of an overgeneralization.

> Mr. Gomez was sent to New York on business. The hotel in which he stayed was terrible. When he returned, he told a friend, "Hotels in New York are awful."

This is an overgeneralization because it is based on too few examples. Mr. Gomez would have to stay in many hotels in New York before he could make such a general statement about their quality. Avoid making overgeneralizations yourself. Use **qualifying words** instead of **absolute words.** Here are some examples.

Absolute Words	Qualifying Words
all	most
everyone	many
nobody	few
never	rarely

A **stereotype** is an overgeneralization about an entire group of people. Suppose that you go to a department store and are served by a woman who is extremely rude. If you decide that all female salespeople are rude, you are guilty of stereotyping. Stereotypes are illogical and unreasonable. They are often directed against members of entire racial, ethnic, political, or religious groups. In such cases, stereotypes can be harmful.

Bandwagon is the error of supposing that an action is right simply because a lot of people are doing it. For example, a clothing company may say that you should buy their jeans because everybody is wearing them.

Snob appeal encourages you to take some action because fashionable, or rich people do it. The advertisement "Dine at Des's—where the elite meet" is an example of snob appeal.

Become familiar with these common errors. Learn to recognize them and to avoid them.

Check It Out   Read the following unsound opinions.

All teenagers are irresponsible.
That movie must be great; everyone's going to see it.

• What is wrong with these opinions?

Try Your Skill   Each of the following statements contains an error in reasoning. Choose the name of the error from those given in parentheses.

1. You are one of the few who can appreciate the finer things in life. Don't settle for anything less than a Stellar Electronics stereo system. (bandwagon, overgeneralization, snob appeal)

2. All politicians are dishonest. (snob appeal, stereotyping, bandwagon)

3. Don't be the last person on your block to have a Smokey Jones gas barbecue grill! (stereotyping, bandwagon, snob appeal)

> **Keep This in Mind**
> • Unsound opinions often result from errors in reasoning.
> • Common errors in reasoning include overgeneralization, stereotyping, bandwagon, and snob appeal.

Now Write   Errors in reasoning often appear in advertisements and in television commercials. Using these sources, find an example of each of the four errors in reasoning discussed in this lesson. Describe each error in a paragraph.

281

Point out to students that overgeneralizations and the use of absolutes is not restricted to advertisements and commercials. Ask them to change the following famous quotations from absolute and overgeneralized statements into statements that are not simply "black" or "white."

April is the cruelest month.
All happy families are alike.
Every cloud has a silver lining.
A man works from sun to sun;
    a woman's work is never done.

Extending the Lesson

Have students compose a class letter to an advertising agency. Be sure they include questions about how an ad is written, how the writers know what appeals to customers, and what kind of logic is used in an advertisement.

Part 5 — **Further Out**

Objective

To recognize and avoid false-cause reasoning and only-cause reasoning

Presenting the Lesson

1. Read aloud **Here's the Idea.** On the chalkboard write *false-cause reasoning* and *only-cause reasoning*. Discuss each error in reasoning, and ask students to provide additional examples.

2. Ask for a student volunteer to read the paragraph from **Check It Out.** Have students discuss the questions following the paragraph.

3. Read aloud and assign **Try Your Skill.**

4. Read aloud **Keep This in Mind** and assign **Now Write.**

Individualizing the Lesson

Less-Advanced Students

Have students add *false-cause reasoning* and *only-cause reasoning* to their dictionaries.

Before assigning **Try Your Skill,** ask students to divide into small groups. Have them discuss their answers with each other.

Advanced Students

Have students rewrite the sentences from **Try Your Skill** correcting the faulty reasoning.

Example: Jim lost his ring because he broke a mirror two weeks ago. It was only a coincidence that Jim broke a mirror and also lost his ring. The two events are unrelated.

More Faulty Reasoning

Here's the Idea   People often use reasoning to figure out why something is or why something has happened. Doctors look for the causes of illnesses. Auto mechanics look for the causes of car trouble. All people look for the causes of events in their personal lives. Whenever you reason about causes, you must be careful to avoid two common errors. These errors are called **false-cause reasoning** and **only-cause reasoning.**

When one event happens after another event, people sometimes decide that the first event caused the second one. They may draw this conclusion even though there is no proof that the two events are related. This is an example of **false-cause** reasoning. Many superstitions are based on just such reasoning. For example, suppose a person spills salt and then has bad luck. This person might conclude that spilling salt causes bad luck. However, the two events would actually be unrelated.

Only-cause reasoning is a second type of error. Suppose, for example, that you read the statement "Crime is caused by poverty." This statement is only partly true. Some crime is caused by poverty. However, there are also many other causes that lead to crime, such as greed or anger.

Check It Out   Read the following passages.

Luis is going to junior college full-time. He also works a full-time job in the evenings. Because of his schedule, he doesn't eat well. Lately, he has been complaining of feeling tired all the time. If he would simply start eating when he is supposed to, he wouldn't feel tired any more.

Last week, a house in our neighborhood burned down. The firefighters couldn't determine the cause of the fire. However, I know that the house must have been hit by lightning. After all, there was a thunderstorm just before the fire.

- Which of these passages contains the false-cause error?
- Which contains the only-cause error?

Try Your Skill   Identify the following statements as examples of false-cause or only-cause reasoning.

1. Jim lost his ring because he broke a mirror two weeks ago.
2. Traffic accidents are caused by carelessness.
3. I won a prize at the carnival because I played the games in booth number seven. Seven is my lucky number.
4. Milk must be good for a cold. I know because I drank two glasses of milk. A few days later, I was better.
5. There has been an increase in violence on TV. There has also been an increase in violent crimes. Therefore, TV violence leads to violent crime.

Keep This in Mind

- *False cause* is the error of mistaking an unrelated event for a cause.
- *Only cause* is the error of assuming that an event has only one cause when it actually has many.
- Avoid these errors whenever you reason about causes and effects.

Now Write   Make up several sentences such as those in **Try Your Skill.** Describe the error in reasoning in each sentence. Then write a more logical statement.

Objective

To learn that conclusions are drawn by first observing a group of facts and then determining how the facts are related

Presenting the Lesson

1. Have students read **Here's the Idea.** Discuss the concept of a conclusion. Have students discuss what they attempted to do in the conclusions they wrote for their paragraphs and their compositions. Explain to students that drawing conclusions from facts or events is the same process as drawing a conclusion in a paragraph or composition.

2. Read aloud **Check It Out.** Discuss the two paragraphs with the class.

3. Have students study the graph from **Try Your Skill.** Ask students to answer the three questions on their own, and then discuss their answers with the rest of the class.

4. Read aloud **Keep This in Mind** and assign **Now Write.**

Individualizing the Lesson

Less-Advanced Students

Have students add *conclusion* to their dictionaries. Then have students discuss the conclusions they drew from **Now Write.**

Advanced Students

Have students bring to class several graphs. Have them study the graphs and then write a paragraph explaining the conclusions they drew from each graph.

To Sum It All Up

Drawing Conclusions

Here's the Idea   Every day of your life, you will be drawing conclusions. A **conclusion** is a judgment, interpretation, or decision. You reach a conclusion after observing a group of facts.

To draw a conclusion, you must look for relationships between the facts you observe. Imagine that you hear a Senator speaking on television. She says that she supports tougher air pollution laws. Later, you read that she has introduced a bill to control the disposal of waste. In both cases, the Senator has supported anti-pollution measures. You can draw a general conclusion. The Senator is concerned with controlling pollution.

In school and in your personal life, do not simply take in information without thinking about it. Try at all times to look for the connections between things. In this way, you can build on facts to develop new ideas.

Check It Out   Read the following passages.

Every registered voter in our city voted in the last election. Ms. Lupico is a registered voter. She lives in our city. Therefore, she voted in the last election.

House cats, lions, tigers, mountain lions, and cheetahs all have sharp teeth and claws. Therefore, felines must have sharp teeth and claws.

- What facts are presented in these passages?
- What conclusions are drawn from these facts?

Try Your Skill   Study the graph on the next page. Then, answer the questions that follow. Draw conclusions from the facts presented.

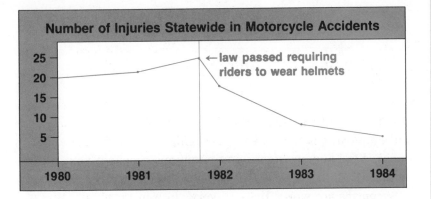

Number of Injuries Statewide in Motorcycle Accidents

← law passed requiring riders to wear helmets

1. What was the trend in motorcycle injuries before the law was passed in November of 1981?

2. What was the trend in injuries after the law was passed?

3. Is it likely that the passage of the law reduced the number of injuries? Why or why not?

Keep This in Mind

- To draw conclusions, you must first observe a group of facts.
- After observing the group of facts, you must determine how the facts are related.
- When you state the relationship between the facts, you have drawn a conclusion.

Now Write   Read the following passage from a short story. Notice the facts presented in the passage. Make a list of the conclusions that you can draw about the character described.

> When Mark returned the first day, he was tired, more tired than he had ever been. His legs and arms ached unbearably. His skin, now a brilliant red, burned and burned. Perhaps, he thought, I'll get used to it. At least the pay is good. As he settled down in bed, he thought once again of the motorcycle. Three months and he would have it.

285

Objective

To recognize the difference between synonyms and antonyms

Presenting the Lesson

1. Read aloud and discuss **Here's
the Idea.** On the chalkboard write
synonym and *antonym*. Have students provide additional examples
of both.

Discuss with students the method
used to answer antonym questions.

2. Read aloud **Check It Out.** Have
students determine which pairs of
words are synonyms and which are
antonyms.

3. Assign **Try Your Skill.**

4. Read aloud **Keep This in Mind**
and assign **Now Write.**

Individualizing the Lesson

Less-Advanced Students

Have students add *synonym* and
antonym to their dictionaries.

When necessary, help students
complete **Now Write.**

Advanced Students

Point out to students that it is
important for them to understand
synonyms and antonyms in their
reading as well as when they take a
test. Very often they will come
across words that are unfamiliar yet
mean the same as words that are
more common. Ask students to find
the synonyms for the following
words: *victuals, parsimonious, fatu-
ous,* and *frenetic.*

Like It or Not

Synonyms and Antonyms

Here's the Idea   One critical thinking skill tested by colleges
and employers is the ability to recognize similarities and differences. Studying synonyms and antonyms can help you to develop this skill.

Synonyms are words that are very close in meaning. Pairs of
words such as *big* and *large, close* and *near,* and *vague* and
unclear are examples of synonyms. To tell whether two words
are synonyms, use one of the words in a sentence. Then, substitute the other word in the same sentence. If both sentences
make sense, and if the meaning of the sentence does not change,
the words are synonyms.

Antonyms are words that have opposite meanings. Word pairs
such as *tall* and *short, dirty* and *clean,* and *patience* and *impa-
tience* are examples of antonyms. Antonym questions are found
on the SAT (Scholastic Aptitude Test). These questions test your
vocabulary. They also test your ability to recognize opposites.
An antonym question begins by giving you a single word. It then
asks you to choose from a list of words the one that is most
opposite in meaning. An antonym question looks like this:

ORDINARY: **(A)** wonderful   **(B)** funny   **(C)** unusual
              (D) common   **(E)** exciting

To answer an antonym question, use this method:

1. Find the meaning of the given word. Think of how it is used
in various sentences.

2. Place the word *not* before the given word. (Example: *not
ordinary*)

3. Find the word from the list that means the same as *not* plus
the given word. For example, *unusual* is the correct answer to
the sample question because it means *not ordinary.*

Check It Out   Read the following pairs of words.

A 1. hot   cold   A 3. light   heavy   S 5. cat   feline
A 2. sharp   dull   S 4. test   examination   S 6. rock   stone

- Which of these pairs of words are antonyms? Which are synonyms?

Try Your Skill   The following questions are like the antonym questions found on the SAT. You are given a word in capital letters. This word is followed by five choices in lower-case letters. Choose the word in lower-case letters that is most nearly opposite the first word.

1. HIT: (A) miss   (B) sit   (C) succeed   (D) mistake
        (E) think
2. LEGALLY: (A) gracefully   (B) suddenly   (C) honestly
        (D) badly   (E) unlawfully
3. INSULT: (A) deny   (B) annoy   (C) compliment
        (D) answer   (E) understand

Keep This in Mind

- The ability to recognize similarities and differences is an important thinking skill.
- Synonyms are words that are similar in meaning.
- Antonyms are words that are opposite in meaning.

Now Write   Choose the correct antonym for each word given in capital letters. Use each antonym in a sentence.

1. COMEDY: (A) story   (B) play   (C) sadness   (D) joke
        (E) tragedy
2. DISGRACE: (A) honor   (B) shame   (C) rumor
        (D) gossip   (E) fame
3. NIMBLE: (A) awkward   (B) clever   (C) quick
        (D) excellent   (E) prompt

Have students determine which word pairs are synonyms, and which are antonyms.

S quixotic/idealistic
A grimace/laugh
S cargo/freight
S premature/early
A cosmopolitan/provincial
S larder/pantry

Extending the Lesson

Have students write to the College Entrance Examination Board for sample questions from the SAT and ACT tests. Use these questions for additional practice and study.

Objectives

1. To learn that analogies are comparisons of two similar but unlike things

2. To learn to answer analogy questions on standardized tests

Presenting the Lesson

1. Read aloud **Here's the Idea.** On the chalkboard write the word *analogy*. Ask students to provide additional examples of analogies.

Explain to students the proper method for answering analogy test questions.

2. Read aloud **Check It Out.** Discuss with students how writing sentences makes clear the relationship between the two words.

3. Assign **Try Your Skill.** Suggest to students that if they are having difficulty, they should make a sentence using the first pair of words.

4. Read aloud **Keep This in Mind** and assign **Now Write.**

Individualizing the Lesson

Less-Advanced Students

Have students add *analogy* to their dictionaries. Then have them study the method for answering analogy test questions. Suggest to students that they work in pairs to complete **Now Write.**

Advanced Students

Have students write five sentences that contain analogies. For example: Receiving an education is like planting a garden.

Close Relations

Analogies

Here's the Idea   Another important critical thinking skill involves the ability to see relationships. Working with analogies can help you to develop this skill.

An **analogy** is a comparison of two things that are not exactly alike. Read the following example.

> Writing is like getting dressed in the morning. You can keep on changing things until you get them just right.

Writing and getting dressed are very different activities. However, they share at least one quality in common. Therefore, an analogy or comparison can be made between them.

SAT tests have sections on analogies. In an analogy question, you are given two words. You must decide how the two words are related. Then, you must choose a second pair of words that are related in the same way. An analogy question looks like this:

CAT: KITTEN   (A) bull: cow   (B) ape: chimpanzee (C) tabby: cat   (D) herd: elephant (E) horse: colt

Use the following method to answer analogy questions.

1. Study the first pair of words. Find the relationship between them by using both in a sentence. (A *cat* is an adult *kitten*.)

2. Next, find a second pair of words that you can put in place of the first pair. (A *horse* is an adult *colt*.)

Check It Out   Read the following pairs of words. Also read the sentence next to each one.

1. strike: hammer   A *hammer* is used to *strike* things.
2. virus: cold   A *cold* is caused by a *virus*.
3. bobwhite: bird   A *bobwhite* is a type of *bird*.
4. roof: house   A *roof* is a part of a *house*.

5. soon: now   *Soon* refers to a time later than *now*.
6. weightlifter: strong   Being *strong* is a characteristic of a *weightlifter*.

- Do you see how sentences can help you to see how words are related?

Try Your Skill   Complete these analogies. Find the word pair that is related in the same way as the first pair of words.

1. AIRPLANE: PILOT::   (A) ship: anchor   (B) car: chauffeur (C) truck: trailer   (D) glider: wood   (E) rocket: space
2. WORD: LETTERS::   (A) night: day   (B) team: players (C) judge: sentence   (D) watch: time   (E) forest: trails
3. LENGTH: RULER::   (A) temperature: thermometer (B) weight: heavy   (C) scale: pounds   (D) yardstick: measure   (E) shadow: sun

Keep This in Mind

- An analogy is a comparison between things that are not exactly alike.
- To answer analogy questions, use the first pair of words in a sentence. Then find another pair that you can substitute for the first pair.

Now Write   Find the pair of words that best completes each analogy. Then choose three pairs of words from your answers. Write three sentences that show how the words are related.

1. EARLY: LATE::   (A) saw: wood   (B) hot: cold   (C) dog: master   (D) true: honest   (E) present: gift
2. STUDENT: CLASS::   (A) bull: steer   (B) chemicals: chemist   (C) fruit: vegetables   (D) actor: cast
3. SQUIRREL: TREE::   (A) fish: trout   (B) worm: ground (C) army: navy   (D) leaf: stem   (E) strawberry: jam
4. BIRD: FEATHERS::   (A) kangaroo: Australia   (B) dogs: paws   (C) male: female   (D) cat: fur   (E) winter: cold

289

Have students study the following types of analogies, and provide one example of each. Do this exercise orally.

—part to whole
—cause to effect
—object to its material
—type to characteristic
—word to synonym
—word to antonym
—object to its purpose

Extending the Lesson

Divide the class into two groups. Using the examples students provided for each type of analogy, have each group prepare its own analogy test. Have students add four additional analogies for each multiple choice question. For example:

Tine:Fork::   A) tooth:comb B) knife:spoon C) thread:button D) key:lock

Have each group take the test prepared by the other group. Have students compare their answers.

Objective

To learn to recognize relationships between words in a sentence

Presenting the Lesson

1. Read aloud **Here's the Idea.** Point out that sentence completion questions require students to use vocabulary words as well as to see relationships among parts of a sentence. In many ways, sentence completion tests students' ability to recognize analogies, synonyms, antonyms, and draw conclusions.

Explain to students the method for answering sentence completion questions.

2. Read aloud the sentences from **Check It Out.** Have students discuss their answers.

3. Assign **Try Your Skill.** This exercise can also be done orally.

4. Read aloud **Keep This in Mind** and assign **Now Write.**

Individualizing the Lesson

Less-Advanced Students

Have students add sentence completion to their dictionaries. Have students revise their dictionaries making sure that all entries are in alphabetical order, each entry is neatly written, and all words are spelled correctly.

Provide students with additional examples of sentence completion.

Advanced Students

Have students work in small groups to complete **Now Write.** Have

---

The Missing Pieces

Sentence Completion

Here's the Idea   You have practiced recognizing relationships between words. Now you will practice recognizing relationships between words in sentences. This will help you to be aware of less obvious meanings in sentences.

The **sentence completion** questions in SAT tests require you to use this skill. In these questions, you are given a sentence from which one or two words have been removed. You must choose the word or pair of words that best complete the sentence. A typical sentence completion question looks like this:

> The audience seemed not to _____ that the music was loud enough to cause _____ damage to their hearing.
>
> (A) care—funny   (B) wonder—valuable   (C) notice—serious   (D) mention—temporary   (E) hope—fine

To answer sentence completion questions, use this method:

1. Read the incomplete sentence carefully. Note any key words. Look for words that state contrasts (*however, but*). Also look for words that signal similarities (*another, the same as*).

2. Try each choice in the sentence. Do not be misled by answers that have only one word that fits well into the sentence. Answer C is the only choice in which both words make sense in the sample incomplete sentence above.

Check It Out   Read the following incomplete sentences.

1. The fog was too _____ for us to _____ across the lake.
2. The actor threatened to _____ the newspaper for its _____ story about him.
3. Because the ancient Greeks admired athletic _____, they treated champion _____ like heroes.

• What words could you use to complete these sentences?

Try Your Skill   Choose the pair of words that best completes the meaning of each of the following sentences.

1. I can vouch for Dan's _____; he always tells the _____.
   (A) honesty—truth   (B) ability—story   (C) hypocrisy—sound   (D) education—tests   (E) happiness—story
2. The _____ child very nearly lost _____ of himself.
   (A) older—pictures   (B) hysterical—control   (C) lazy—comments   (D) uninterested—most   (E) shy—friends
3. In many _____ humans have been _____ by robots.
   (A) actions—seen   (B) books—built   (C) evenings—valued   (D) factories—replaced   (E) ways—lent

Keep This in Mind

- Words in sentences have particular relationships to one another.
- Sentence completion questions require you to recognize relationships between words in sentences.
- When answering sentence completion questions, make sure that both words make sense.

Now Write   Write the pairs of words that best complete the meaning of each of the following sentences.

1. The doctor _____ penicillin for the _____ ear.
   (A) bought—well   (B) left—tiny   (C) prescribed—infected   (D) injected—healed   (E) diagnosed—symptom
2. The accident _____ was knocked _____ by the blow.
   (A) victim—unconscious   (B) report—underground   (C) later—out   (D) simply—everywhere
3. _____ athletes cannot compete in the _____.
   (A) Good—major leagues   (B) Some—contract   (C) Professional—Olympics   (D) Powerful—style

Section 22 Objectives

1. To understand the library system for arranging and shelving fiction and nonfiction books

2. To use the library's card catalog to locate books

3. To understand the organization and content of encyclopedias

4. To know how to use specific types of reference books

Preparing the Students

Ask students where they would find the following materials in a library.

a record album of folksongs
a mystery novel
a book about U.F.O's
a scientific encyclopedia

Discuss with students how often they use the library and how familiar they are with its layout. Also discuss how they can make full use of what the library has to offer.

Provide students with an unlabeled map of the school library. Take the class to the library and have them label their maps with the different parts of the library, including the card catalog, vertical file, periodicals, fiction and nonfiction books, and the check-out desk.

Tell students that this Section will help them to find and use material located in the library.

Additional Resources

Mastery Test — pages 32–33 in the test booklet

Practice Book — pages 115–118

Duplicating Masters — pages 115–118

Using the Library

Teaching Special Populations

LD Take the class to the library for "hands on" explanations of this material. Explain and demonstrate the concepts thoroughly and slowly.

ESL If possible, schedule several library days for ESL students. Explain to students the range of materials made available by the library. Show them, for example, the materials relating to their specific cultures. Encourage students to explore the library's holdings.

Part 1

Shelf by Shelf

Objective

To understand the library system for arranging and shelving fiction and nonfiction books

Presenting the Lesson

1. Read aloud **Here's the Idea.** Discuss the difference between fiction and nonfiction books, and have students provide examples of each. Review where fiction and nonfiction books are located in the library.

Have students study the Dewey Decimal System, as well as the information on the spine of the example book.

2. Read and discuss **Check It Out.**

3. Discuss and assign **Try Your Skill.**

4. Read aloud **Keep This in Mind** and assign **Now Write.**

Individualizing the Lesson

Less-Advanced Students

Have students bring in a library book for comparison with the example book at the top of page 295. Have them work in pairs as they do **Try Your Skill.**

Advanced Students

Ask students under which letter or in which Dewey Decimal category the following books would be found:

1. James P. Barry, *The Fate of the Lakes: A Portrait of the Great Lakes* 500-599

2. Kurt Vonnegut, *Jailbird* V

3. Bill Bentsen, *The Yacht Racing Rules Today* 700-799

4. Carl Sandburg, *Complete Poems* 800-899

5. Nancy Milford, *Zelda: A Biography* 900-999

Finding What You Need

Here's the Idea   A library serves the needs of people because of the variety of factual materials and information it has available. You will also find books and magazines that relate unusual imaginary adventures and experiences. To find whatever you need easily, you need to learn how your school or public library is organized.

You will find that all library books are classified into two general groups, fiction and nonfiction. **Fiction** books are arranged alphabetically according to the author's last name. For example, the novel *A Tale of Two Cities*, by Charles Dickens, would be filed under *D*.

Nonfiction books are arranged according to their subjects on a separate section of shelves. Many libraries use a system called the **Dewey Decimal System.** This system groups nonfiction books into ten numbered categories.

000-099	**General Works**	(encyclopedias, almanacs)
100-199	**Philosophy**	(ethics, psychology, occult)
200-299	**Religion**	(the Bible, mythology)
300-399	**Social Science**	(economics, law, education, government)
400-499	**Language**	(languages, grammar, dictionaries)
500-599	**Science**	(mathematics, biology, chemistry)
600-699	**Useful Arts**	(farming, cooking, sewing, television, business)
700-799	**Fine Arts**	(music, photography, dance, sports)
800-899	**Literature**	(poetry, plays)
900-999	**History**	(biography, travel, geography)

Every nonfiction book has a **call number** written on the spine. This call number includes the Dewey Decimal number and other information. A call number identifies a book. Some libraries add the letter *B* to the spine of a biography or the letter *R* to the spine of a reference work, such as an encyclopedia.

Look at this example of a nonfiction book.

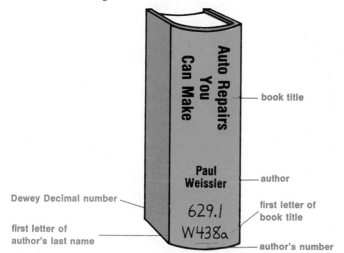

book title

author

Dewey Decimal number

first letter of author's last name

first letter of book title

author's number

Check It Out Examine the spines of the books represented here.

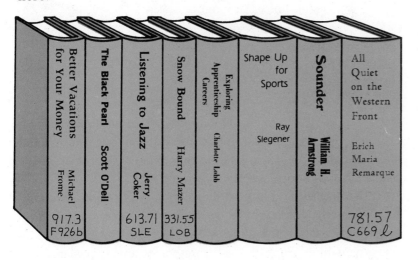

- Which books are fiction and which are nonfiction?
- What is the general category of each nonfiction book?

295

6. Ken Kesey, *One Flew Over the Cuckoo's Nest* K

7. Richard Condon, *The Manchurian Candidate* C

8. Charles M. Evans, *Rx for Ailing House Plants* 500–599

Optional Practice

Have students make up book titles for each of the Dewey Decimal categories. Collect titles, and as you read them aloud to the class, ask students to identify the corresponding Dewey Decimal category.

Extending the Lesson

Ask students to visit another library in their area, such as a law library, a medical library, or the library of a large company. Ask students to walk through the library and study the way it is arranged. Have them speak with the librarian to find out how this library is organized and something about its history. Students can work in groups on this project.

Using Books Effectively

Explain to your students that knowing how to use books effectively can help them to get more out of their studying and research. Then introduce them to these important parts of books.

The Table of Contents The table of contents is a list of all of the chapters or sections of a book along with the page numbers on which these chapters or sections can be found. Urge students to consult the table of contents whenever they want a broad overview of the material a book contains.

The Index The index is a detailed, alphabetical list of all of the important subjects a book contains along with appropriate page references. Tell students that the index will help them to discover whether or not a book contains information on a specific topic or person.

The Appendix Some books may contain an appendix. An appendix is a special section of a book, often placed toward the end, that gives important information that supplements or supports the material presented in the book. An appendix may contain graphs, charts, or statistics.

The Bibliography A book may contain a bibliography. A bibliography is a list of books the writer used to prepare his or her book or that the writer feels will be helpful to any one who wants more information about the subject of the book. Tell your students that whenever they want or need more information about the subject of a book, they should check to see if the author has provided a bibliography.

Special Reference Books Many reference books have a special section in the front of the book called "How to Use This Book." This section explains how the book is organized, and the easiest and fastest way to find information in the book. Encourage your students to look for this section whenever they use reference books.

Try Your Skill Write the answers to these questions.

1. Under what letter on the library shelves would you find the following fiction books?

M *Dragonsinger* by Anne McCaffrey
A *Watership Down* by Richard Adams
C *The Clown* by Barbara Corcoran
E *Incident at Hawk's Hill* by Allan W. Eckert
G *The Good-Luck Bogie Hat* by Constance C. Greene

2. In which categories of the Dewey Decimal System would you find information on these subjects?

a play about Thanksgiving 800–899
directions for making furniture 600–699
a biography of Martin Luther King 900–999
teaching pre-school children 300–399
the Civil War in the U.S. 900–999

Keep This in Mind

- In the library, fiction books are filed alphabetically by the author's last name.
- Nonfiction books may be classified in ten major categories of the Dewey Decimal System. Each nonfiction book has a call number.

Now Write As your teacher directs, learn how materials are arranged in your school or public library. Find out where fiction and nonfiction books are. Find out where reference books, magazines, and special collections are.

In the library, find at least four fiction books and four nonfiction books that you might enjoy reading. You may want to check one out for your own reading. Write the titles and authors of the books you find. Copy the call number of any special marking written on the spine of any of the books. Label your paper **Shelf by Shelf**. Keep it in your folder.

On the Track

Using the Card Catalog

Here's the Idea In every library there is a file called the card catalog. This file organizes information about all the books in that library. Every book is listed in the catalog at least three times—by its author, by its title, and by its subject.

All three cards—author card, title card, and subject card—contain the same information. This information is arranged under different headings so that you will be able to find a book in several ways. All three cards give the call number of a nonfiction book in the upper left corner. This is the same number that appears on the book.

All three cards list the author, title, publisher, date of publication, and the number of pages in the book. There is a notation if the book has illustrations or maps. There may also be a description of the book or a list of related books.

On an **author card,** the author's name is given at the top, last name first. Author cards are filed alphabetically by the author's last name. If there is more than one author, the card is filed by the name of the author whose name is shown first in the book.

On a **title card,** the title appears on the top line, with only the first word of the title capitalized. Title cards are filed alphabetically by the first word of the title. However, if *A, An,* or *The* appears as the first word in a title, look for the card under the first letter of the second word in the title.

On a **subject card,** the subject appears on the top line. The subject may be written in capital letters or in red. Subject cards are filed alphabetically by the first letter of the subject.

You will find some cards that say *See* or *See also.* These **cross reference cards** refer you to other subject headings that are related to the one that you want.

297

Part 2

Objective

To use the library's card catalog to locate books

Presenting the Lesson

1. Read aloud **Here's the Idea.** Explain the purpose of the card catalog, and discuss the function of each type of card.

2. Read aloud and discuss **Check It Out.** Have students read aloud the author card to be sure they understand the abbreviations on the card. Have students discuss their familiarity with using the card catalog and have them explain what problems they have had using it.

3. Assign **Try Your Skill.**

4. Read aloud **Keep This in Mind** and assign **Now Write.**

Individualizing the Lesson

Less-Advanced Students

Point out that understanding how the card catalog works is basic to using the library to its fullest extent.

Have students work in pairs to do **Try Your Skill.** After students have finished, have them exchange papers and compare cards.

Advanced Students

Ask students to use the card catalog in the school library to find the following.

the title of a book about stereos
the author of the novel *To Kill a Mockingbird* Harper Lee
the title of a book by F. Scott Fitzgerald
the name of a book beginning with *Over*

Optional Practice

Have students use the school library's card catalog to find the title, author, call number and publication date of the following books.

a book on gold mining in the U.S.
a book on Chinese brush painting
a book explaining the history of the English language
a collection of Civil War photographs
a book by Robert Frost

Extending the Lesson

Have students return to the specialized library they visited. Ask them to choose a subject that interests them and find three books on it. Have them copy the important information from each subject card and bring it to class. Have students compare the subject cards from their school library with the subject cards from the specialized library.

Using the card catalog is simpler if you check the **guide cards.** These blank cards have tabs on which general subject headings are written. These headings will help you to follow the alphabetical arrangement of the card catalog.

author card

650.14
SOU

Souerwine, Andrew H.
    Career strategies : planning for
personal achievement / Andrew H.
Souerwine. — New York : AMACOM,
© 1978.
    xii, 292 p. : ill. ; 24 cm.

    Includes index.
    Bibliography: p. 280-284.
    ISBN 0-8144-5454-2 : $14.75

title card

650.14
SOU

Career Strategies: Planning for Personal Achievement
    Career strategies : planning for
personal achievement / Andrew H.
Souerwine. — New York : AMACOM,
© 1978.
    xii, 292 p. : ill. ; 24 cm.

    Includes index.
    Bibliography: p. 280-284.
    ISBN 0-8144-5454-2 : $14.75

subject card

650.14
SOU

JOB SATISFACTION
    Career strategies : planning for
personal achievement / Andrew H.
Souerwine. — New York : AMACOM,
© 1978.
    xii, 292 p. : ill. ; 24 cm.

    includes index.
    Bibliography: p. 280-284.
    ISBN 0-8144-5454-2 : $14.75

Check It Out   Examine the three sample cards.

- Under what letter would each card be filed? Where would you look to find more books by Andrew H. Souerwine? Where would you look to see if there are other books about job satisfaction?

Try Your Skill   Here are the authors, titles, and call numbers for three books about careers. Choose one of the books. Draw three rectangles to represent cards in the card catalog. Use the information given about the book you choose to make an author card, title card, and subject card. Make up the other necessary details for the cards. Compare your sample cards with those in the card catalog.

1. Ruth Lembeck, *Teenage Jobs*, 371.425 L542t
2. Joseph L. Norton, *On the Job*, 371.425 N824o
3. Sarah Splaver, *Nontraditional Careers for Women*, 331.702 Sp5ln

Keep This in Mind

- Every book in a library is listed in the card catalog on at least three different cards—author, title, and subject. Each card shows the author, title, publisher, number of pages, and other useful information. Cards for a nonfiction book also list its call number.

Now Write   Choose a subject that interests you and that you can research at the library. Using the card catalog, find at least three nonfiction books about your subject. Copy the important information from the author, title, and subject cards. Label your paper **On the Track,** and keep it in your folder. Also, select the most interesting book you find, and sign it out of the library. Bring the book to class.

Objective

To understand the organization and content of encyclopedias

Presenting the Lesson

1. Read aloud and discuss **Here's the Idea.** Point out to students that the information contained in an encyclopedia can be very useful as source material for a research paper, or if students want general information about a particular subject. Also, explain that encyclopedias usually suggest additional sources for more detailed information. Have students visit the library to see the different kinds of encyclopedias and how a full set is organized.

2. Read aloud and discuss the questions from **Check It Out.** Explain how to identify the key word in a topic.

3. Assign **Try Your Skill.**

4. Read aloud **Keep This in Mind** and assign **Now Write.**

Individualizing the Lesson

Less-Advanced Students

Ask how many students have a set of encyclopedias at home, and if they have been useful for their schoolwork.

Have students work in pairs for **Try Your Skill.** When they have completed the exercise, have students compare sources.

Advanced Students

Have students make a study of the different types of encyclopedias in their school library. Ask students

300

There's One for You

Using an Encyclopedia

Here's the Idea An encyclopedia is a general reference work that contains information on a great many different subjects. The articles are arranged in alphabetical order by subject, from the first volume through the last. On the spine of each volume is either a single letter or a set of guide letters indicating what is included.

A large library will have several sets of encyclopedias. You will find that they have different reading levels. When you want to use an encyclopedia, be sure to choose one that you can read easily. Select an encyclopedia suitable for your work by skimming through several. You may want to ask a librarian for help with your selection.

Suppose you wanted information about education. You might select *The World Book Encyclopedia, Collier's Encyclopedia,* or the *Encyclopaedia Britannica,* for example. Find the appropriate volume and look up "Education." The guide words at the top of the page will help you find the subject quickly.

An encyclopedia article on an important subject, education, for example, is usually presented in several parts with subtitles. The article may include such parts as "Kinds of Education," "Education in the United States," "Education Around the World," "The Educative Process," "History," and "Current Issues in U.S. Education." Depending on your purpose, you may need to read all of the article or only parts of it.

At the end of a major article you will find other helpful information. At the end of an article on education, for example, you may find a list of related articles in the same encyclopedia. These might be about people connected with education, educational institutions, and educational programs and agencies. In addition, you may find an outline of the information in the

300

article, books for further reading on the subject, or a research guide to the subject.

Most encyclopedias also include an index. This is usually the first or last volume of the set. Use the index to find information under related subjects in different articles. Some encyclopedias also publish yearbooks, which contain up-to-date information.

Whenever you research a subject, check more than one source of information. Use several encyclopedias as well as other reference books. If you find different information in different sources, try to use the most recent or most reliable reference.

In addition to the general encyclopedias, there are others that provide information only on a single subject. For example, you may find encyclopedias about sports, music, or careers. These encyclopedias will usually be located in the reference room or area of the library.

Check It Out   Look at the encyclopedias shown below.

- In what volume, and under what key word, would you find information about canoeing? modern painting? the Panama Canal? William Shakespeare? heredity?

to find the specialized encyclopedias, such as those on music, sports, science, and arts. Have students write the titles of each different encyclopedia and a summary of the information each contains.

Optional Practice

Assign each student a topic beginning with a different letter of the alphabet. Have students make a comparative study of encyclopedias by looking up their topic in three different encyclopedias and drawing conclusions about the following.

differences in information covered
differences in writing style
differences in illustrations

Extending the Lesson

Have students write a letter to the publisher of a major encyclopedia. Letters should include questions about how articles are researched, how long it takes to complete an encyclopedia, how often encyclopedias are revised and updated, who writes the articles, and where writers find their information.

Try Your Skill   As your teacher directs, use an encyclopedia to answer the following questions. Answers may vary.

1. Who was the first governor of Virginia? Patrick Henry

Blenheim Palace, Oxfordshire, England
2. What was the birthplace of Sir Winston Churchill?

3. Name an award won by Jane Addams, who founded Hull House. Nobel peace prize.

4. What languages were spoken by the American Algonquin Indians? Macro-Algonkian

5. What are the principal agricultural exports of Colombia, South America? bananas, cacao, coffee

Little Women
6. What is the most famous novel by Louisa May Alcott?

crocodile's snout comes to a point
7. What is the difference between a crocodile and an alligator?

Frank Lloyd Wright; Louis Sullivan
8. Name two twentieth-century American architects.

Hera
9. In Greek mythology, who was the wife of the god Zeus?

Allies invaded Europe
10. What was the importance of D-Day to World War II?

Keep This in Mind

- An encyclopedia is a general reference work that contains information on many different subjects. Articles are arranged alphabetically in numbered volumes. Examine a variety of encyclopedias. Select one that is suitable for your purpose.

Now Write   Write the name of the subject that you researched in the card catalog in the last lesson. Look up that subject in two encyclopedias. List a few of the most interesting facts that you find in each, and compare them. Also, name which encyclopedia you prefer and briefly explain your answer. Be sure to list all important information about your sources: names of the encyclopedias, numbers of the volumes, page numbers of the articles, and titles of other related articles or books on the subject. Label your paper **There's One for You** and put it into your folder.

Did You Know That?

Using Reference Words

Here's the Idea Usually, a library has an entire room or special section containing reference works. Many of these cannot be taken from the library because they are such useful sources of information for so many people. In addition to such general references as dictionaries and encyclopedias, other references provide information about specific areas of interest.

Atlases are books of maps. Many atlases contain information about population, weather, and places throughout the world. Among the most widely used atlases are the *National Geographic Atlas of the World, The International Atlas from Rand McNally*, and the *Atlas of World History.*

Almanacs and **yearbooks** are published every year. In these references you will find current information about world events, governments, population, and sports. You may want to use the *Guinness Book of World Records*, the *World Almanac and Book of Facts*, the *Information Please Almanac, Atlas, and Yearbook*, or the *Statesman's Yearbook.*

Biographical references contain information about important people. Useful reference books include *The Book of Presidents, Current Biography, Who's Who, Twentieth Century Authors*, and the *Dictionary of American Biography.*

A **vertical file** is the library's collection of pamphlets, handbooks, catalogs, and clippings. Usually kept in a file cabinet, this collection varies from library to library. It often includes special information about local events, travel, and careers.

Magazines are valuable sources of information about a great many subjects. A library may subscribe to any number of the leading magazines published in the United States. In order to find specific information in magazine articles, learn to use the

303

Part 4

Objective

To know how to use specific types of reference books

Presenting the Lesson

1. Read aloud **Here's the Idea.** Discuss with students each of the references described, and if possible, display an example of each one. Also, explain where in the library each reference work is located. When discussing the *Readers' Guide to Periodical Literature*, explain how long the library keeps its current magazines. Explain to students how they can find out which magazines their library has.

If possible, arrange with the school librarian for a tour of the reference section.

2. Read and discuss **Check It Out.**

3. Read aloud the instructions for **Try Your Skill.** Divide the class into groups of four to complete this exercise.

4. Read aloud **Keep This in Mind** and assign **Now Write.**

Individualizing the Lesson

Less-Advanced Students

Suggest that students work in pairs to do **Now Write.**

Advanced Students

Have students use the *Readers' Guide to Periodical Literature* to find three articles on a subject of their choosing. Have them write down the title, author (if the article has one), name of magazine, volume, issue, page numbers, and date for each article.

303

Optional Practice

Have students find the following information.

average yearly rainfall in Burma 40 in.
President Martin Van Buren's Vice-
    President Richard M. Johnson
total cheese production in France in
    1981 1,185,000 metric tons
which five countries have the largest
    population see current encyclopedias
British poet laureate in 1670 John Dryden
the lowest point on the moon Imbrium
Basin in the Sea of Rains

Extending the Lesson

Have students form five groups, and give each group one reference work from the five types examined in **Here's the Idea**. Have the group think of five questions that are answered in their reference work. Then have the groups exchange questions and reference works. See if the groups can answer all the questions.

Readers' Guide to Periodical Literature. The *Readers' Guide* contains the titles of articles, stories, and poems published in more than a hundred leading magazines. One hardcover volume of the *Readers' Guide* covers material published during the entire year. Smaller paperback volumes cover material over shorter time periods. Once you learn to use the abbreviated format, you will find the *Readers' Guide* a useful reference.

Each of these specialized references contains an explanation of how its information is arranged, of the abbreviations that are used, and a sample entry. When you use a reference book for the first time, study these explanations.

Check It Out   Examine this portion of a page from the *Readers' Guide to Periodical Literature.*

Earthworms
    A reel man's guide to bassin' and wormin'. R. Gerlach. il

name of magazine _____ |*Outdoor Life*| 172:66-7 + O '83

Anecdotes, facetiae, satire, etc.

title of article _____ |All about worms!| E. Zern. il *Field Stream* 88:130 D '83

Easels
    Easy-to-make, easy-to-store easels for young artists. il
        Sunset 171:114 + D '83

Easley, Marie B.
    In the service. *Work Woman* 8:204 N '83

East, Ben
                            about

author _____ Tribute to Ben East.| V. T. Sparano.| il pors *Outdoor Life*
                172:110 O '83

East Berlin *See* Berlin (Germany: East)

cross reference _____ **East Germany** |*See*| Germany (East)

East Timor *See* Timor

Easter

Greece
    Eternal Easter in a Greek village [Olimpos] M. Nic-

volume number _____ olaidis-Karanikolas. il maps *Natl Geogr* |164|768-77 D
                        '83

Easterbrook, Gregg
    Examining a media myth. il *Atlantic* 252:10 + O '83

Eastern Air Lines, Inc.
    The airline confusion has travel agents flying blind. il
        Bus Week p43 O 17 '83
    Eastern Air Lines on the brink. S. P. Sherman. il por

page reference _____ *Fortune* 108:102-4 + O 17 '83
    Eastern chief tells employees payroll concessions are vital
        [F. Borman] E. H. Kolcum. *Aviat Week Space Technol*

date of magazine _____ 119:30-1| O 3 '83|

- Read through one unmarked listing in this sample and explain all the information given. Where is the *Readers' Guide* located in your school or public library? What other kinds of references are in the reference section of your library?

Try Your Skill   Write the name of a reference work in which you would be likely to find an answer to each of the following questions. If magazines would be the best reference, write *Readers' Guide.*

1. Japan consists of how many major islands? encyclopedia
2. What foods might be discussed in a pamphlet called "Eating for Good Health"? vertical file
3. What is the present population of California? atlas
4. Name two well-known twentieth-century authors. biographical ref.
5. What baseball team won the 1975 World Series? almanac
6. How was President Franklin Roosevelt related to President Theodore Roosevelt? biographical ref.
7. How many countries are members of the United Nations? almanac
8. What was General Custer's full name? biographical ref.
9. What are some arguments for and against nuclear energy? Readers' Guide
10. What is the average yearly rainfall in Michigan? atlas

Keep This in Mind

- There are several kinds of useful specialized references. Learn to use those available in your own library.

Now Write   Choose a well-known person or place that you like. Use several specialized references to find information on your topic. Skim each source and jot down several of the interesting facts. List the titles, call numbers, and volume and page numbers of the sources you find most useful. Label your paper **Did You Know That?** and put it into your folder.

Section 23 Objectives

1. To understand and accurately record assignments

2. To learn and use the SQ3R study method

3. To take notes efficiently on readings, lectures, and class discussions

4. To use different types of reading for different purposes

5. To recognize and use graphic aids

6. To know how to prepare for and take tests

7. To know how to take objective and written tests

8. To know how to prepare for standardized tests

9. To know how to take standardized tests

Preparing the Students

Discuss with students the need for a personal study area. Ask students if they were to design a place to do their school work what it would be like. Point out the need for good lighting, quiet, and order. Also, their study area should be personalized so that they feel comfortable there. Explain that a study area should be a place where students can clear their minds of all other thoughts, and prepare to think hard about school work.

This Section will teach students useful ways to organize their assignments, develop effective study habits, and prepare for test-taking.

Additional Resources

Practice Book — pages 119–127
Duplicating Masters — pages 119–127

Study and Research Skills

Teaching Special Populations

LD This Section contains extremely important information for the LD student. Tailor the readings and the exercises to the abilities and needs of your students.

Require students to keep assignment notebooks. Emphasize the exercises on following directions.

Give students additional practice in answering test questions.

ESL Explain that these study skills will be useful in all classes and can be applied in any language. Provide as much time as necessary for students to complete the exercises successfully.

NSD Tell students to treat test answers like compositions. They should be answered in formal, standard language.

Objective

To understand and accurately record assignments

Presenting the Lesson

1. Read aloud **Here's the Idea.** Discuss how to effectively record assignments in a notebook or journal. Point out that students must remember to check their assignment book daily.

Tell students that learning to follow directions is the first step for successfully completing any job.

2. Read and discuss the sample assignment entry in **Check It Out** and have students answer the questions orally.

3. Read and assign **Try Your Skill.**

4. Read aloud **Keep This in Mind** and assign **Now Write.**

Individualizing the Lesson

Less-Advanced Students

Emphasize neatness and thoroughness as students prepare their assignment notebooks.

Advanced Students

Ask students to prepare a study schedule for each week. Have them include personal as well as employment commitments. Have students mark the times they will use for studying and completing assignments.

Optional Practice

Have students read the following assignment and answer the questions that follow.

Know It All

Understanding Your Assignments

Here's the Idea   One secret to success in high school is understanding exactly what is expected of you. This involves recording your assignments carefully and following directions.

Recording Your Assignments   Whenever you are given an assignment, listen closely to all the details. Then, write the assignment carefully in an assignment notebook. Record the subject or class, the date the assignment is given, and the date it is due. Write any specific directions for the assignment. Include the page numbers of reading assignments. Also include any materials you will need and the form your final product should take.

Following Directions   If the directions are spoken, listen carefully. Write the directions as you hear them. Note the steps involved in the assignment and the order of these steps. Listen for key words, such as *read, answer,* or *explain,* that tell you what to do. If you have questions about the directions, ask your teacher.

If the directions are written, read them carefully. Divide the assignment into steps. Put these steps in a logical order. Ask your teacher to explain any steps that you don't understand. Before you begin to work, gather any materials you will need to complete the assignment.

Check It Out   Read the following entry from an assignment notebook.

- What does this assignment ask you to do?
- What materials will you need?
- What will the final product be?
- When is the assignment due?

Subject	Assignment	Date Given	Date Due
Health	Write a public-service radio commercial. One minute long. 150 words. Type.	March 21	March 23

Try Your Skill   Read the sample home economics assignment below. Then, answer the questions that follow.

Using a red marker, make seven columns on a sheet of paper. Label these columns for the days of the week. Then, using a black pen, prepare menus for a family of four for one week. Write each menu in the appropriate column. Decide what you would have to buy to make these meals. Write a grocery list on a separate sheet of paper. Then, go to a grocery store. Write the price next to each item on your list. At the bottom of the list, tell how much your meal plan would cost. Turn in your plan and your list on Tuesday.

1. What steps are included in this assignment?
2. What materials will you need?
3. What will the final product be? When is the assignment due?

Keep This in Mind

- Record all assignments in an assignment notebook.
- Listen to or read all directions carefully before you begin an assignment.

Now Write   Begin your own assignment notebook. Divide the notebook into separate sections. Label each section for a different class. Record your assignments in this notebook.

Collect ten letters-to-the-editor from a major newspaper. Five of the letters should express well-thought-out opinions supported by sound reasons. Five letters should be poor examples that do not state a definite opinion or that fail to include reasons. Identify the opinions and reasons from each good letter. Then write a few sentences for each letter explaining what is wrong with the poor examples. This exercise should be typed, and bound into a notebook. It is due on Friday.

—What does this assignment require?
—What materials will you need?
—What will the final product be?
—When is the assignment due?

Extending the Lesson

Tell students that in two weeks they are going to have a class discussion on the usefulness of their assignment notebooks. Students should be prepared to discuss how their assignment notebooks helped organize and prepare them for each subject's assignments. Also ask students to talk about any changes or improvements they made to their notebooks to make them more effective.

Part 2

Objective

To learn and use the SQ3R study method

Presenting the Lesson

1. Read and discuss **Here's the Idea.** Point out that SQ3R is a highly effective study method for written material. Discuss each step in detail with students.

2. Read and discuss **Check It Out.**

3. Read aloud and assign **Try Your Skill.**

4. Read aloud **Keep This in Mind** and assign **Now Write.**

Individualizing the Lesson

Less-Advanced Students

Have students work in pairs to complete the exercise from **Try Your Skill.** Point out that it is important for students to follow the correct order when using SQ3R.

Advanced Students

Be sure students understand each step of SQ3R thoroughly, and how each step reinforces each preceding step.

Ask students to work as a group to prepare an SQ3R handout for the entire class.

Optional Practice

Using their SQ3R handout, have students apply the study method to the rest of the Section.

According to Plan

Using SQ3R

Here's the Idea   One plan that you can use to study written materials is the SQ3R study method. The method consists of five steps: **S**urvey, **Q**uestion, **R**ead, **R**ecite, and **R**eview.

Survey the reading assignment.

1. Look over the material to get a general idea of its content.
2. Read the titles and subtitles. Notice the illustrations.
3. Read the introduction and summary.

Question.

1. List any questions that you should be able to answer after your reading.
2. Use any study questions provided by your teacher or at the end of the chapter.
3. Turn titles, topic sentences, and headings into questions.
4. Make questions based upon any illustrations, maps, tables, charts, or graphs.

Read the selection.

1. As you read, look for answers to your questions.
2. Look for main ideas and supporting details.
3. Pay particular attention to definitions, topic sentences, and chapter headings.

Recite the answers to your questions.

1. Recite your answers aloud.
2. Make brief notes to help you remember the answers.
3. Also make notes on important points from the material.

Review the selection.

1. Try to answer each of your original questions without looking at your notes.
2. If necessary, look over the selection to find the answers.
3. Read your notes again to impress the material on your mind.

Check It Out   Read the questions that can be made from these chapter headings.

Chapter Heading	Questions
Using SQ3R	a. What does "SQ3R" mean?
	b. How is SQ3R used?
Preparing for and Taking Tests	a. How can I prepare for tests?
	b. What should I do when taking a test?

- How can such questions help you to study the material under each heading?

Try Your Skill   Study the following selection. Use the SQ3R study method. Write your questions and answers.

The Edsel: A Car That Had Promise

The 1958–59 Edsel, or "E Car," was introduced by a heavy advertising campaign. The car was intended to be a milestone in automotive history.

Costly Mistakes. Unfortunately, the Edsel was plagued with problems from the beginning. Consumers felt that the car cost too much. In addition, the car had noisy gears, hoods that stuck, hubcaps that fell off, and doors that refused to stay shut. By 1959, Ford had produced 110,000 Edsels. Most of them remained unsold. The name "Edsel" came to mean "a loser."

Keep This in Mind

- The SQ3R study method is made up of five steps: *Survey, Question, Read, Recite,* and *Review.*
- Use the SQ3R method for your reading assignments.

Now Write   Using the SQ3R method, complete a class reading assignment. Write down your questions, answers, and any other notes. Label your paper **Using SQ3R.** Save your work.

311

The Long and Short

Objective

To take notes efficiently on readings, lectures, and class discussions

Presenting the Lesson

1. Read aloud **Here's the Idea.** Point out that the physical act of writing forces students to concentrate on what they are reading or listening to.

Discuss each of the guidelines for notetaking with students. Give students an opportunity to talk about their notetaking habits.

2. Read and discuss the notes from **Check It Out.** Ask students if the notes refer to one main idea.

3. Assign **Try Your Skill.**

4. Read aloud **Keep This in Mind** and assign **Now Write.**

Individualizing the Lesson

Less-Advanced Students

Have students make a copy of the notetaking guidelines to keep in their folders. Then have students work in pairs to complete the exercise from **Try Your Skill.**

Advanced Students

Have students find a brief article in a magazine or newspaper that interests them. Tell them to take notes on the article following the guidelines from **Here's the Idea.**

Optional Practice

Tell students to read the following paragraph and to take two sets of notes on it. The first set should not

Taking Notes

Here's the Idea It isn't enough just to listen in class or to read your assignments. You must also take notes on what you read and hear. You can then use these notes when you review for tests and quizzes. Taking good notes is a skill that can be learned. The following guidelines will help you.

1. **Keep your notes in a notebook.** Divide your notebook into sections. Label each section for a specific class. Write the date and the name of the class at the top of each page of notes. Make notes on the main ideas presented in class or in your reading. Include any details related to these main ideas.

2. **Take notes as you read.** Include notes on key words, definitions, and main ideas. Also include any questions and answers that you develop while using the SQ3R method.

3. **Take notes as you listen.** Pay particular attention to clues that tell you what information is important. Such clues include phrases like *the result was*, *the main reason is*, *most importantly*, and *remember this*. A speaker provides other clues by repeating an idea or pausing to emphasize a point.

4. **Write neatly.** Make sure that you will be able to read your notes several days or weeks later.

5. **Use phrases, abbreviations, and symbols.** Do not write your notes in complete sentences. This will take too much time. Use short phrases and abbreviations, and symbols.

w/	with	info.	information
w/o	without	→	becomes
+	and	tho.	though
*	important information	def:	definition
M	memorize this	=	equals
Amer.	American	ex:	example

6. **Record your notes in rough outline form.** Write main ideas at the left margin. Begin each idea with a capital letter. Write any examples or details under these main ideas.

Check It Out Read the following notes.

> Amer. Lit.
> April 12
>
> Robert Frost
>
> Life
> — Lived most of life in New England
> — Wrote about New England life
> — Highly successful poet
> — 4 Pulitzer prizes
> — Many honorary degrees

- What main idea has the student used when taking these notes?

Try Your Skill Take notes on the selection on the Edsel given in Part 2. Use the guidelines given in this lesson.

Keep This in Mind

- Take notes on material presented in class and in your reading.
- Keep your notes in a notebook.
- Use phrases, abbreviations, and symbols.
- Use a rough outline form.

Now Write Begin a notebook for use in your classes. Divide the notebook into separate sections for each class. Take notes, following the guidelines presented in this lesson.

313

include any abbreviations, phrases, or symbols, and should not be written out in outline form. The second set should contain phrases, abbreviations, and symbols, and be written in outline form. Have students discuss the effectiveness of both methods.

George Washington Carver was a black American agricultural chemist. Although he was born a slave, he became the director of agricultural research at Tuskegee Institute in 1896, serving in this capacity until his death in 1943.

Carver dedicated his life to bettering the position of blacks, and to improving the economy of the South through soil improvement techniques and crop diversification. Among his many accomplishments, he found hundreds of different uses for the peanut and found effective ways to use cotton waste.

Extending the Lesson

Have students attend a school lecture, assembly, or community meeting and take notes in rough outline form. Make copies of students' notes to pass out to the rest of the class. Discuss with students how effectively they took notes in this situation.

Objective

To use different types of reading for different purposes

Presenting the Lesson

1. Read aloud and discuss **Here's the Idea.** Point out to students that they should change their reading speed for different kinds of materials as well as for different reading purposes.

Discuss with students the three reading rates: in-depth, skimming, scanning.

2. Read aloud **Check It Out.** Discuss the two separate reading tasks for this assignment, and which reading rates are appropriate for each.

3. Assign **Try Your Skill.** This exercise can be done orally.

4. Read aloud **Keep This in Mind** and assign **Now Write.**

Individualizing the Lesson

Less-Advanced Students

Have students discuss which reading rate they use most often and why.

Advanced Students

Have students work in pairs for the following exercise. Ask one student to skim the passage and have the other student read the passage in depth. Have both students answer the questions that follow it. Then have them compare their answers to the questions to illustrate how reading speed and information retention are related.

In Greek mythology, Laocoön was the Trojan priest of Apollo who warned

Part 4

Speed Zone

Adjusting Your Reading Rate

Here's the Idea   When you page through a magazine in a doctor's office, you read quickly. When you read material that you will be tested on, you read more slowly. You vary your reading speed to suit your purpose.

In-depth reading is used to study material that is new or difficult. Use the SQ3R study method. Survey the selection. Make a list of questions. Then, move your eyes slowly across each line, reading every word. Pay particular attention to definitions, topic sentences, key words, and titles. Look for main ideas and for any details or examples to support them.

Fast reading is used for several different purposes. It is especially useful for surveying or reviewing written material. There are two types of fast reading: skimming and scanning.

Skimming involves moving your eyes quickly over the material. Do not read every word. Glance at titles, subtitles, headings, pictures, and graphic aids. Also look at the first and last sentences of paragraphs. When you are looking at a book, glance at the table of contents. Use skimming to survey material as the first step in the SQ3R study method. Also use it whenever you need to get a general idea of the content of a selection.

Scanning involves moving your eyes quickly across each line or down each page. Use scanning to find specific information. Look for words or phrases that are related to the information that you need. When you spot such a key word or phrase, stop scanning and read more slowly.

Check It Out   Look at the following directions.

Go to the library. Look through several novels. Find one that interests you. Then, check to see if the author of this novel is listed in *Contemporary Authors*.

- What two reading tasks are called for in this assignment?
- Which task involves skimming? Which involves scanning?

Try Your Skill

Would you use skimming, scanning, or in-depth reading for these situations?

1. Reading a textbook chapter to master the material in-depth
2. Studying material on a handout in preparation for a test in-depth
3. Surveying as part of the SQ3R study method scanning
4. Flipping through a book to see if it contains material about whales skimming
5. Looking through a chapter to find the answer to a study guide question scanning
6. Looking for a definition of "enzyme" in a biology text scanning

Keep This in Mind

- Adjust your reading rate to suit your purpose.
- Read in-depth to study new or difficult material.
- Skim to survey material.
- Scan to look for specific information.

Now Write

Scan the following passage for answers to these questions:

1. What method of advertising was used in ancient Rome?
2. What changes took place in advertising in the 17th century?

Write your answers on a piece of paper. Label it **Speed Zone.**

The Early History of Advertising

Printed advertisements have been around for more than three thousand years. In early Rome, circuses and gladiator matches were advertised on posters. In the Middle Ages, handbills and signs advertised items for sale. By the middle of the 17th century, newspaper ads were common.

315

the Trojans not to touch the wooden horse made by the Greeks during the Trojan War. Laocoön and his two sons were crushed by sea serpents as they made a sacrifice to the god of the sea, Poseidon, and the Trojans brought the horse into the city of Troy. Because of the Trojans' failure to heed the warnings of Laocoön, they ended up losing the war.

—Who was Laocoön?
—How was he killed?
—Who died with him?
—Who won the Trojan War?
—Was Laocoön a Greek or a Trojan?

315

Between the Lines

Drawing Conclusions from Graphic Aids

Objective

To recognize and use graphic aids

Presenting the Lesson

1. Read aloud **Here's the Idea.** Discuss the four guidelines for studying a graphic aid.
2. Have students study the graphs in **Check It Out.** Discuss with them the information contained in each graph. Ask which graph is easier to read and why.
3. Assign **Try Your Skill.**
4. Read aloud **Keep This in Mind** and assign **Now Write.**

Individualizing the Lesson

Less-Advanced Students

Before assigning **Try Your Skill,** divide students into small groups. Have them refer to the guidelines from **Here's the Idea** as they answer the questions.

Advanced Students

Divide students into groups of three or four. Have each group select a topic concerning their school and prepare a chart or graph explaining the information they found. Example topics could include: how students get to school; the percentage of students involved in more than one extracurricular activity; how well each sports team has done in competition.

Optional Practice

Have students find a graph or a chart from a major newspaper or magazine. Ask them to draw three

Here's the Idea   Sometimes information is presented in the form of graphic aids. Graphic aids include diagrams and illustrations. They also include maps, tables, charts, and graphs. When studying a graphic aid, follow these guidelines.

1. Read any titles, captions, legends, or labels given.
2. Ask yourself what facts are presented by the graphic aid.
3. Look for relationships between the facts presented.
4. See if you can draw any conclusions about the facts.

Check It Out   Study the following graphs.

1

2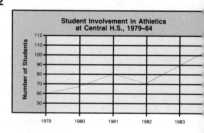

- What is the caption of each graphic aid?
- What two sets of facts does each graphic aid present?
- Which language has the most speakers?

Try Your Skill   Study the following graphic aids. Then, answer the questions that follow.

Robots in Use Worldwide 2

Sources of Income in the U.S.

conclusions based on the information it contains. Have students discuss what kind of graphic aid they found and their conclusions.

Extending the Lesson

Have students select a major business which interests them. Tell students to write a letter to the company requesting an annual report. Have students examine the graphic aids contaned in the report and prepare a brief report explaining the conclusions they were able to draw. If time permits, students can present their reports to the class.

1. What facts are being compared in Graph 1?

2. How does the use of robots in Japan compare to the use of robots in the other three countries?

3. Look at Graph 2. How much income in the United States comes from farming?

4. Manufacturing and trade, taken together, account for what percent of income in the United States?

Keep This in Mind

- Read any titles, captions, legends, or labels given with a graphic aid.
- Decide what facts are presented by the graphic aid. Look for relationships between these facts.
- Draw any conclusions that you can from the facts presented by the graphic aid.

Now Write   List the facts presented by graphic aid 2 in **Check It Out.** (Example: 80 students were involved in athletics at Central High School in 1981.) Then, write at least three conclusions that you can draw based on these facts (Example: Between 1981 and 1982 membership in Central High's athletic teams dropped by about ten students.) Label your paper **Between the Lines.** Save it in your folder.

317

Objective

To know how to prepare and take tests

Presenting the Lesson

1. Read aloud **Here's the Idea.** On the chalkboard write the six guidelines for test preparation, and discuss each one with students. Point out that reviewing notes and assignment notebook entries are important first steps for their test-taking preparation.

Explain that preparing for the test is not in itself enough to ensure that students will do well. They must also use their time wisely during the test. Make sure students prepare and follow their test-taking strategy.

2. Read aloud **Check It Out.** Point out that Enrico did not fully prepare for his test. Ask students what he omitted from his preparation.

3. Assign **Try Your Skill.**

4. Read aloud **Keep This in Mind** and assign **Now Write.**

Individualizing the Lesson

Less-Advanced Students

Have students make a personal copy of the six test preparation guidelines to keep in their folders.

Have students work in small groups to complete the exercise from **Try Your Skill.**

Advanced Students

Explain to students that the use of acronyms or phrases can often help them remember information. For example, "In 1492 Columbus sailed the ocean blue" is a way to re-

---

Test Run

Preparing for and Taking Tests

Here's the Idea   Success in high school depends largely upon the ability to do well on tests. You can learn a few simple guidelines that can improve your test scores tremendously.

Preparing for Tests   Before a test, always make sure that you know what material the test will cover. If you have any questions about this, ask your teacher. Then, allow yourself enough time to review the materials you will be tested on. Try to review the material several times. Follow these guidelines:

1. **Make a list of study questions.**   Include any questions that you wrote while using the SQ3R study method. Also include any study questions given in your textbook or by your teacher.

2. **Review the materials covered by the test.**   Skim your notes, textbook chapters, and other reading materials. Write the answers to your study questions.

3. **Find a study coach.**   Give your list of study questions to a relative or friend. Ask this person to quiz you. Make a note about each question that you cannot answer correctly.

4. **Review in problem areas.**   Go over the questions that you missed when being quizzed by your relative or friend.

5. **Make a list of important names, dates, definitions, events, or formulas.**   Quiz yourself on these, or ask someone to quiz you. You may want to use flashcards.

6. **Eat and sleep properly before the test.**

Taking the Test   Skim the test to see what types of questions it includes. Read all directions and test questions carefully. Do not answer any question before you understand the directions. After looking at the test questions, decide on the order in which you will answer them. Begin with the easiest questions on the test. Save the most difficult questions for last.

Budget your time carefully. Do not spend too long on any one part of the test. Allow plenty of time to answer any long or complicated questions. When you are finished, read over the test. Make sure you have not left out any answers. Try to answer any questions that you skipped the first time through. Check any answers that you are not certain about.

Check It Out   Read the following passage.

Enrico had to study for a test in his computer class. The test covered the following materials:
1. Chapters 1–3 of his textbook.
2. Material presented in class discussions and lectures during the previous three weeks.

Enrico first made a list of study questions. Some came from his teacher. Some were questions that he wrote in his notes when he first studied the three chapters in his textbook. Enrico skimmed his notes and the three textbook chapters. Then, he wrote answers to his study questions.

- How well did Enrico prepare for his test?
- What else could he have done?

Try Your Skill   Imagine that you are going to be tested on the material given under **Try Your Skill** in Part 5. Make a list of study questions that you could use to prepare for your test.

> ### Keep This in Mind
>
> - Before a test, review your materials carefully.
> - When taking the test, read all the directions first. Budget your time, and save time to check answers.

Now Write   Choose a chapter from one of your textbooks. Study it by using the SQ3R method. Make a list of study questions. Also make a list of important names, dates, definitions, events, or formulas. Label these lists **Test Run.** Save them.

member the year Columbus sailed to the New World; or FACE is a useful acronym for remembering the spaces on a musical scale. Have students devise sayings and acronyms to help them remember the information from **Try Your Skill** in Part 5.

Optional Practice

Have students meet in small groups to discuss study questions, memory aids and problem areas for **Now Write** and **Try Your Skill** from Part 5.

Extending the Lesson

Have students form study groups to practice and discuss the study and test-preparation methods from this Section.

Objective

To know how to take objective and written tests

Presenting the Lesson

1. Read aloud **Here's the Idea.** On the chalkboard, write the six types of test questions, and discuss each type.

Point out to students that each type of test question requires a specific strategy for answering it correctly.

2. Have the class answer the questions from **Check It Out.** Ask students to identify each type of question, and explain what strategy they used to answer them.

3. Assign **Try Your Skill.** This can be done in conjunction with **Check It Out.**

4. Read aloud **Keep This in Mind** and assign **Now Write.**

Individualizing the Lesson

Less-Advanced Students

Explain to students that essay questions require the same steps they use in the Process of Writing. For the pre-writing stage, students should clarify the question and write a few notes. When they begin writing their answers, they should plan to have a good topic sentence, an introduction, body, and conclusion for their essay. After they have finished, students should spend a few minutes reviewing what they have written, checking for clarity and spelling errors.

Test Types

Answering Test Questions

Here's the Idea In your classes, you take many different types of tests. Sometimes you take **objective tests.** These tests contain true/false, matching, or multiple-choice questions. At other times you take **written tests.** These tests contain completion, short answer, or essay questions. The following rules will help you to answer each of these types of test questions.

True/False Remember that if any part of a statement is false, the entire statement is false. Also remember that words like *all, always, only, never,* and *everyone* often appear in false statements. Words like *some, often, a few, most,* and *usually* often appear in true statements.

Matching First, check the directions. See if each item is used only once. Also check to see if some are not used at all. Read all items in both columns before starting. Match those you know first. Cross out items as you use them.

Multiple choice Read all of the choices before answering. Eliminate any obviously incorrect answers first. Then choose the answer that is most complete or accurate. Pay particular attention to choices such as "all of the above."

Completion, or Fill-in-the-Blank If several words are required, give them all. Write neatly. Use good grammar and punctuation.

Short Answer Use complete sentences. Answer the question completely. Use correct grammar, capitalization, punctuation, and spelling.

Essay Look for action words like *explain* and *compare.* These are words that tell you what to do. Make a list of the details you will need to answer the question. Make a rough outline of your essay on separate paper. Be sure each paragraph contains a topic sentence. Finally, proofread your work.

Check It Out   Read the following test questions.

1. Write a paragraph explaining the differences between skimming and scanning.
2. The "S" in SQ3R stands for _____ .
3. Which of the following is *not* a type of graphic aid?
    a. picture   b. textbook   c. map   d. graph
4. Notes should *not* be written in complete sentences. (true or false) _____
5. Match the following question types with their guidelines.

a. true/false _____   b. essay _____   c. multiple choice _____

1) Make a rough outline.
2) Pay particular attention to choices such as *none of the above.*
3) Remember that words like *all*, *only*, and *never* often appear in false statements.

• Can you identify each type of test question above?

Try Your Skill   Copy the questions given in **Check It Out** onto your own paper. Then, answer each question.

Keep This in Mind

• Objective tests contain true/false, matching, and multiple choice questions.
• Written tests contain completion, short answer, and essay questions.
• Follow the guidelines in **Here's the Idea** when answering test questions.

Now Write   Review the material in Part 3, **The Long and Short.** Copy the following essay question onto a piece of notebook paper. Circle the key words that tell you what to do. Plan your answer carefully. Then, write and proofread it. Save your work.

ESSAY QUESTION: In your own words, describe how to use a rough outline to take notes. Include a discussion of the use of symbols and abbreviations in note-taking.

321

Standard Procedure

Objective

To know how to prepare for standardized tests

Presenting the Lesson

1. Read aloud **Here's the Idea.** Discuss with students the different types of standardized tests: aptitude, achievement, ACT, SAT.

Explain that most colleges require high school students to take the ACT or SAT prior to admission. Although students cannot study for these tests, there are strategies they can learn which will improve their performance.

2. Read aloud and discuss **Check It Out.** Point out that Coretta prepared herself well for taking the SAT test.

3. Read aloud and assign **Try Your Skill.**

4. Read aloud **Keep This in Mind** and assign **Now Write.**

Individualizing the Lesson

Less-Advanced Students

Before assigning **Now Write,** have students choose a partner for this exercise. Suggest to students that they make a list of resources for information about the occupational field they have selected. Have students refer to Section 22 to help them find what they will need from the library.

Advanced Students

Have students write a letter to the agency that issues the test for the occupational field they selected from **Now Write.** Students' letters

322

Preparing for Standardized Tests

Here's the Idea   Many job fields require you to pass a standardized entry test. Tests are also required by many colleges, vocational schools, and apprenticeship programs. A **standardized test** is a type of objective test. Some measure knowledge of a specific subject such as electronics or auto mechanics.

There are two common standardized tests that you will probably take. One is the SAT (Scholastic Aptitude Test). The other is the ACT (American College Testing Program Assessment Test). These tests are required for admission to many colleges. If you wish to attend college, see your guidance counselor. Ask if you must take one of these tests. Your counselor will explain how to sign up for the test and will help you prepare for it.

When you take a standardized test, follow these guidelines:

1. Find out what types of questions will be included on the test. Also find out what material will be covered by the test.

2. Make use of any practice materials supplied by the testing organization. Also make use of the test-taking manuals available in many libraries and bookstores.

3. Study the types of questions included in the test that you plan to take. Learn specific guidelines for answering questions of these types (See Part 9).

4. Rest and eat well before the test.

5. Try not to become nervous before the test. If possible, do some light exercise an hour or so before the test begins. This will clear your mind. It will also relieve tension.

Check It Out   Read the following passage.

Coretta decided to enroll in night classes at a local junior college. According to the college catalog, she had to take the SAT before she could be admitted. Therefore, she went to her

322

guidance counselor. Her counselor signed her up for the PSAT and the SAT. The PSAT is a practice SAT test. It helped Coretta to prepare for the SAT. In addition, Coretta studied the sample questions that were sent to her in the mail by the makers of the SAT test. On the night before the SAT, Coretta ate well and got plenty of sleep.

- What did Coretta do to prepare for her test?
- What else could she have done?

Try Your Skill   You are planning to apply for a summer office job. You are told that when you come to the interview, you will have to take a standardized test. The first part of the test will cover grammar, capitalization, punctuation, and spelling. The second part will cover proper form for business letters. The third part will cover basic office procedures. Make a list of the steps that you would take to prepare for this test.

Keep This in Mind

- Many employers, colleges, vocational schools, and other organizations require standardized tests.
- To prepare for standardized tests, make use of the available practice materials.
- Also study the types of questions asked on the test that you plan to take.

Now Write   In many states, you must take a standardized test before you can enter any of the following fields.

Radiology	Accounting
Physical therapy	Airplane and power plant mechanics
Stock brokerage	Electronics

Choose one of the above professions. Do some research to find out what sort of test must be taken to enter this field. Write a paragraph explaining how you could prepare for this test.

should include requests for information about length of test, material covered, cost of test, testing places, and a sample test if it is available. Have students explain to the rest of the class the information they have received.

Optional Practice

Ask students to present their research from **Now Write** to the rest of the class. Afterward, have students discuss the similarities and differences among the different standardized tests.

Extending the Lesson

Explain to students that there are many professional organizations that teach effective methods for preparing for and taking standardized tests. Have students write a letter to one of these organizations requesting information about their programs. Have students discuss the information they receive.

Objective

To know how to take standardized tests

Presenting the Lesson

1. Read aloud **Here's the Idea.** Explain to students that sentence correction and reading comprehension questions complete the verbal skills questions contained in the ACT or SAT tests. Have students refer to Section 21, **Critical Thinking,** for a review of antonyms, analogies, and sentence completion questions.

Discuss with students the guidelines for answering sentence correction and reading comprehension questions.

2. Read aloud **Check It Out.** Discuss how students should answer these antonym and analogy questions.

3. Read aloud **Try Your Skill.** Have students answer these questions orally.

4. Read aloud **Keep This in Mind** and then assign **Now Write.**

Individualizing the Lesson

Less-Advanced Students

Have students review Parts 7–9 of Section 21. Remind students that before answering a sentence correction question, they first have to identify the error.

Ask students to write two additional reading comprehension questions based on the passage from **Here's the Idea.**

You've Got the Answer

Answering Standardized Test Questions

Here's the Idea   The SAT and the ACT both contain special types of test questions. Three of these types of questions were discussed in Parts 7–9 of Section 21, **Critical Thinking.** These questions involved antonyms, analogies, and sentence completion. Now, you will learn about two other types of questions.

1. **Sentence Correction.** A sentence correction question tests your ability to find an error in a sentence. If the underlined material in the sentence does not contain an error, mark, "A". "A" repeats the underlined material. If the underlined material does contain an error, choose the answer that corrects the error.

Though Jim has moved, he still <u>be</u> my best friend.

(A) be   (B) are   (C) is   (D) had been

Follow these guidelines when answering sentence corrections:

a. Find the error, if there is one, before looking at the answers. Look for errors in grammar, usage, and mechanics.
b. Check your answer by placing it into the sentence.

2. **Reading Comprehension.** Reading comprehension questions measure your understanding of short reading passages. Read the passage carefully. Look for main ideas and supporting details. Look for relationships. Read the question and all the choices before answering. Base your answer on information contained in the passage, not on your own opinion.

In A.D. 986 Bjarni Herjulfson sailed for Iceland to join his father, Herjulf. On arriving and learning that Herjulf had moved to Greenland, Bjarni and his crew set out to follow them. Sailing west, they missed Greenland. Eventually, they sighted lands no one recognized. These lands are now part of Canada. The Norse sailors turned their boats eastward and finally reached Greenland.

About the year 1000, Leif Ericson set out from Greenland with thirty-five sailors to seek the land Bjarni had described. On finding the land, he called it *Markland*.

The land that Bjarni sighted is now called

(A) Markland   (B) The United States   (C) Norway
(D) Canada

Check It Out   Review the test questions covered in Parts 7–9 of 2, **Critical Thinking.** Then, read the following questions:

1. WORK: (A) job   (B) play   (C) business   (D) labor
2. FOREST: TREE   (A) vacation: travel   (B) musician: guitarist   (C) class: student   (D) afternoon: evening

• What steps would you take to answer these questions?

Try Your Skill   Answer the following questions based on the reading passage given in **Here's the Idea.**

1. The first Europeans to reach the New World were
   (A) English   (B) Portuguese   (C) Norse
2. Bjarni Herjulfson reached the new world
   (A) by accident   (B) by plane   (C) after Leif Ericson

Keep This in Mind

• Before taking a standardized test, study the various types of standardized test questions.
• Questions found on standardized tests include antonyms, analogies, sentence completion, sentence correction, and comprehension questions.

Now Write   Choose a short passage from a textbook. Copy the passage. Then, write five reading comprehension questions dealing with the passage. Exchange your paper with a classmate. Complete each other's questions.

Ask students to write five sentence correction questions like the sample from **Here's the Idea.** Have them exchange papers with their partner from **Now Write** and complete each other's questions.

Optional Practice

Ask students to read the following passage and write five reading comprehension questions based on the passage. Have students discuss their questions with the rest of the class.

The *Titanic,* was a British luxury ocean liner which sank on the night of April 14, 1912, after striking an iceberg in the North Atlantic. The disaster, which occured on the ship's maiden voyage, claimed the lives of more than 1,500 of the ship's 2,200 passengers and crew members. Many people died because of a shortage of lifeboats. As a consequence, more stringent safety rules for ships were enacted.

Extending the Lesson

Have students use the sample test questions they received from the College Entrance Examination Board to further practice their skills in answering sentence correction and reading comprehension questions.

Section 24 Objectives

1. To know the five parts of a personal letter

2. To know the different types of personal letters

3. To know how to prepare letters for the mail

4. To know the correct form for a business letter

5. To know the correct form for letters of request

Preparing the Students

Discuss with students letters they have received and written. Ask students why they send letters, and what they can accomplish. Be sure to cover the following reasons for writing letters.

letters help writers organize thoughts
letters provide a lasting record
letters can encourage specific action
letters are more economical than phone calls or visits
letters can build strong relationships between people

Tell students that Section 24 will teach them to write effective letters.

Additional Resources

Mastery Test — pages 34–35 in the test booklet

Practice Book — pages 128–131

Duplicating Masters — pages 128–131

Writing Letters

Teaching Special Populations

LD Show students each step involved in preparing letters for the mail. Give students individual guidance as they write and prepare their letters.

ESL Discuss with students letter-writing conventions that are not universally followed, such as business block form, date form, and greetings. Check students' letters for errors.

NSD Remind students that business letters and letters of request require formal language. Assign additional letters for students to write and prepare.

Keep in Touch

Writing Personal Letters

Presenting the Lesson

1. Read aloud **Here's the Idea.** On the chalkboard list the five parts of a personal letter. Discuss with students the purpose of each part.

Discuss the different types of personal letters. Have students discuss occasions when they have sent out invitations and thank-you notes.

2. Read and discuss the personal letter in **Check It Out.** Point out the friendly tone and neatness of the letter.

3. Discuss and assign **Try Your Skill.** Have students refer to the letter in **Check It Out** as a model.

4. Read aloud **Keep This in Mind** and then assign **Now Write.**

Individualizing the Lesson

Less-Advanced Students

Have students study the model letter from **Check It Out.** Emphasize neatness and adherence to the correct form of personal letters.

Advanced Students

Ask students to look over personal letters they have received. Have them compare the way those letters were written to the model letter from **Check It Out.** Do their letters contain all five parts? Are they neatly written?

Here's the Idea   The term **personal letter** includes all letters not written to businesses. Writing personal letters is a way of keeping in touch with absent friends or of expressing your feelings in certain social situations. Personal letters, which are usually handwritten, have five main parts.

The **heading** contains three lines: one line for the writer's street address, one for the city, state, and ZIP code, and one for the date. None of this information should be abbreviated. The heading appears at the top right corner of your letter.

The **salutation** is the greeting. Usually beginning with *Dear*, it is written on the next line below the heading. It starts at the left margin of the page and is followed by a comma.

The **body** of the letter is the main part. There you write what you want to say in a detailed and conversational way. The body begins on the line following the salutation. Each paragraph of the body should be indented.

The **closing** is your way of saying "goodbye." You may say *Love,* or *Your friend,* for instance. The closing is written on the line below the last line of the body and is followed by a comma. The first word of the closing should align with the first words of the heading.

Your **signature** is the last part of a letter. Skip a line after the closing and sign your name in line with the first word of the closing. Usually, only your first name is needed.

Some forms of personal letters are written only for special occasions. These social notes include invitations and thank-you notes. The notes also have five main parts, but the heading may be shortened to the date only.

If you send an **invitation,** include all information about the event. If you receive an invitation, reply at once.

Sometimes you will send **thank-you** notes. One kind of thank-you note is written to thank someone for a gift you have received. Another kind of thank-you thanks someone for his or her hospitality. You would write this kind of note if you stayed overnight as a guest in someone's house.

Check It Out   Read this personal letter.

1315 Albion Drive
St. Paul, Minnesota 55105
April 19, 1985

Dear Susan,

I am sorry to hear about your broken ankle. I know you're as disappointed as I am that we have to postpone our hiking trip. However, resting for two weeks will give you the perfect chance to catch up on all the reading that you said you had to do — not to mention the letter writing!

How about rescheduling your visit for the weekend of June 8? You plan whatever will be best for you. I'm looking forward to seeing you soon.

Love,
Chris

- Identify the five parts of this personal letter.
- Is this a well-written letter? Why or why not?

Suggest to students that they research the name of an international pen pal organization. Have students join the organization and write letters to their pen pals. Ask students to share their responses with the class.

Extending the Lesson

Have students use the library to find collections of letters written by famous people. Have students bring examples of these letters to class.

Try Your Skill Arrange the following information in the correct form for a personal letter. Add any other information or details that you think might be included in the letter. Be sure to add capital letters and correct punctuation wherever necessary.

31 Forest Street, Fairfield, Iowa 52556, October 23, 1984 dear randy Shortly after you left, I discovered your notebook under the stack of newspapers you had been reading. The notebook is in the mail already, so you should get it in time to finish your English assignment next week. Remember, we have plans to watch more football together on Thanksgiving. until then george

Keep This in Mind

- Write personal letters that are conversational, detailed, and neat. Be sure that the heading, salutation, body, closing, and signature follow the correct form.
- Social notes are short forms of personal letters. Write invitations that are specific and thank-you notes that express your appreciation.

Now Write Write a personal letter to a friend or relative. You may want to write a social note. Use your own address and today's date in the heading. The body of your letter may be based on either real or imaginary events. Make sure that all parts of your letter follow the correct form. Label your paper **Keep in Touch** and put it into your folder. Make a copy of the letter that you could send and save that also.

Special Delivery

Preparing Letters for the Mail

Here's the Idea   Once you have written a letter, you must prepare it correctly for mailing. Begin by folding the letter neatly and choosing an envelope that matches the width of the stationery. Insert the folded letter and seal the envelope.

To make sure that your letter reaches its destination without delay, take extra care to address the envelope accurately and neatly. Follow these steps.

1. Address the envelope. Add your return address.
2. Check all numbers to make sure that they are correct.
3. Include the correct ZIP code. To learn the correct use of ZIP codes and state abbreviations, turn to page 333.
4. Put a stamp on the envelope. Be sure that you have used enough postage for the letter or package.

Check It Out   Look at the envelope below.

> Dee Wendell
> 162 Exeter Street
> Kansas City, MO 64108
>
>   Jim Shortelle
>   2178 Broadway
>   New Haven, CT 06510

- Who wrote the letter? Who will receive it? What state abbreviations are used? How could you check all the information?

331

Part 2

Objective

To know how to prepare letters for the mail

Presenting the Lesson

1. Read aloud and discuss **Here's the Idea.** List the four steps for correctly addressing an envelope.

2. Have students study the sample envelope from **Check It Out.** Discuss the questions. Point out to students that the state abbreviations do not require periods, but must be accompanied by a ZIP code.

3. Assign **Try Your Skill.**

4. Read aloud **Keep This in Mind** and then assign **Now Write.**

Individualizing the Lesson

Less-Advanced Students

Have students make their own personal list of the four steps for addressing an envelope correctly. Then have them work in pairs for the exercise in **Try Your Skill.**

Advanced Students

Have students make a poster of the correct form for addressing an envelope, including all four necessary steps. Put the finished poster on the bulletin board.

Optional Practice

Have students address envelopes to the following people.

the President of the United States
an aunt or uncle
the head of the department of tourism
  in a foreign country

331

a doctor

the chairman of the Spanish department of an American university

Extending the Lesson

Ask volunteers to visit their local post office. Have them discuss postal regulations about addressing envelopes and packages with a postal employee. Have students report their findings to the class. Also, if literature is available, have students request samples to bring back to class.

Try Your Skill Write each of these jumbled addresses as it should appear on an envelope. Also write a return address. Refer to the list of correct state abbreviations on the next page.

1. Mike Ruddy, 31 Sullivan Street, Livingston, New Jersey 07039

2. 580 Rosewood Avenue, Phoenix, Arizona 85002, Maria Cordova

3. Philadelphia, Pennsylvania 19101, 122 Salem Lane, Robert Bernstein

4. 179 Foster Street, Frankfort, Kentucky 40601, Joe Leone

5. Susan Kim, Des Moines, Iowa 50306, 14 Briar Road

6. Enrico Sanchez, 259 Bennett Road, Falls Church, Virginia 22046

7. Christine Sobel, Atlanta, Georgia 30302, 3871 Beacon Boulevard

8. Whitinsville, Maryland 01588, Dr. Jonathan Schmitt, 644 Eastern Parkway

9. 22 Lyndon Terrace, Chapel Hill, North Carolina 27514, Ellie Johannson

10. Ms. Susan Lindahl, 2002 Oceanview Drive, Santa Monica, California 90405

Keep This in Mind

- Prepare letters for the mail carefully. Check all information for accuracy.

Now Write Find your personal letter labeled **Keep in Touch.** On the other side of the paper, add the title of this lesson **Special Delivery.** Draw a rectangle to represent an envelope. Address it as if you were going to mail it to your friend or relative. Keep this paper in your folder.

Copy your work on a real envelope. Fold the copy of the letter that you can send, and put it into the envelope. Put a stamp on your letter and mail it.

ZIP Codes and State Abbreviations

In order to make sure that your letter reaches its destination, check the address, including the ZIP code. The ZIP code is very important today. It enables the postal department to sort your letter for delivery as rapidly as possible. If you don't know a particular ZIP code, call your local post office. Someone will give you the correct ZIP for any address in the United States.

The United States Postal Service has a list of approved state abbreviations to be used on all envelopes and packages. You must use the ZIP code with these abbreviations.

Abbreviations of State Names

State	Abbr.	State	Abbr.
Alabama	AL	Montana	MT
Alaska	AK	Nebraska	NE
Arizona	AZ	Nevada	NV
Arkansas	AR	New Hampshire	NH
American Samoa	AS	New Jersey	NJ
California	CA	New Mexico	NM
Canal Zone	CZ	New York	NY
Colorado	CO	North Carolina	NC
Connecticut	CT	North Dakota	ND
Delaware	DE	Ohio	OH
District of Columbia	DC	Oklahoma	OK
Florida	FL	Oregon	OR
Georgia	GA	Pennsylvania	PA
Guam	GU	Puerto Rico	PR
Hawaii	HI	Rhode Island	RI
Idaho	ID	South Carolina	SC
Illinois	IL	South Dakota	SD
Indiana	IN	Tennessee	TN
Iowa	IA	Trust Territories	TT
Kansas	KS	Texas	TX
Kentucky	KY	Utah	UT
Louisiana	LA	Vermont	VT
Maine	ME	Virginia	VA
Maryland	MD	Virgin Islands	VI
Massachusetts	MA	Washington	WA
Michigan	MI	West Virginia	WV
Minnesota	MN	Wisconsin	WI
Mississippi	MS	Wyoming	WY
Missouri	MO		

Part 3

Writing Business Letters

Objective

To know the correct form for a business letter

Presenting the Lesson

1. Read aloud **Here's the Idea.** Point out that unlike personal letters, business letters are usually typed, and the language of a business letter is more formal than that of a personal letter.

On the chalkboard, draw the two forms: block form and modified block form.

Point out that in addition to the five parts of a personal letter, a business letter has a sixth part, known as the inside address.

2. Read the business letter in **Check It Out** and discuss the questions.

3. Assign and discuss **Try Your Skill.** After students have completed the exercise, have them compare their letters.

4. Read aloud **Keep This in Mind** and then assign **Now Write.**

Individualizing the Lesson

Less-Advanced Students

Have students work as a group to make a poster of the business letter on page 335. Be sure they label each of the six parts of the business letter.

Advanced Students

Have students work in pairs to edit and proofread their business letters from **Now Write.** Have students check for clarity, neatness, and proper form.

Here's the Idea   In addition to writing personal letters, you will also be writing **business letters.** Learning to write business letters is a useful, practical skill. There will be times when you need to write to a company regarding its products. There will be times when you will want to write to a school or college. In seeking employment you may need to write letters and résumés and to complete application forms. In all of these situations, you will be likely to meet with more success if you follow the correct form for business letters.

In order to make the best impression, you must make your business letters neat. Plain white paper, 8-1/2 × 11 inches, is considered standard, and typing is considered an advantage. It is not required that you type any of your business letters. However, most businesses type letters and reports.

Any business letter that you write may take one of two forms. One form is the **block** form, which should be used only if you type a letter. In the block form, begin every part of a letter at the left margin. Leave two lines of space between paragraphs and do not indent them. Another form, the **modified block** form, may be used either for handwritten or typewritten letters. In this form, place the heading, closing, and signature at the right side of the page. Indent the paragraphs and do not leave extra space between them.

Every business letter has six parts—the five parts of a personal letter, plus an **inside address.** The inside address is the name and address of the company to which you are writing. If possible, the inside address should include the name of an employee or department within the firm. Place an inside address at the left margin between the heading and the salutation.

More formal language is used in business letters than in personal letters. For the greeting use *Dear Mr., Mrs., Miss,* or *Ms.* before the person's name. Or, use a general greeting, like *Dear Sir or Madam.* Place the salutation two lines below the inside address and use a colon (:) after it.

For the more formal closing, write *Sincerely, Yours truly,* or *Very truly yours,* followed by a comma. If you type a letter, leave four lines of space between the closing and your typed signature. Then, write your signature in the space.

Always make a business letter polite, specific, and neat. Keep a copy of each business letter that you write.

Check It Out Read this business letter.

```
        317 Grantly Boulevard
        Los Angeles, California   90017
        September 8, 1985


        Power Products, Incorporated
        1105 Moore Street
        Reston, Virginia   22091


        Dear Sir or Madam:


        Recently I bought a PPI amplifier, Model 217,
        at The Sound Store in Los Angeles.  The package
        was factory sealed, but when I opened it I found
        no instructions and no schematic diagrams.  The
        salesperson had assured me that I would find
        both of them inside the package.


        Please send me a copy of each as soon as possible.


        Yours truly,

        Edward McKenna

        Edward McKenna
```

335

335

- What is the purpose of this business letter?
- In what form is this letter?

Try Your Skill   Write a letter from Gina Hampton, president of Power Products Incorporated, to Edward McKenna. Have Ms. Hampton apologize to Edward for any inconvenience, and have her assure him that the papers he requested are on their way. For the purpose of this exercise, use the block form, even though your letter will be handwritten.

Keep This in Mind

- You may write a business letter to request information, to order a product, to apply to a school, or to seek employment. Whether you write or type a business letter, be polite, specific, and neat. Keep a copy of every business letter.
- Use either the *block* or *modified block* form for a business letter. Either form has six parts, including an inside address.

Now Write   Write or type a letter to a real organization regarding a real product. Also, draw an envelope and address it. Label your paper **The World of Business** and put it into your folder.

What Do You Need?

Writing Letters of Request

Here's the Idea   Often you will write a business letter because you would like something from a company or an organization. You may need information for a report. You may want tourist information about a place that you plan to visit. You may want to order a product.

Letters of request are business letters. Therefore, they should contain the six parts of a business letter, and they should follow either the *block* or *modified block* form. However, you must keep two additional points in mind when you write a letter of request.

First, be specific. Provide all the information that the other person needs in order to fill your request. If you want information, state exactly what information you need. If you are placing an order, be sure to state exactly what you want and where it is to be sent. Also include any necessary details about the size, color, cost, or identification number of the product you want. Most businesses and organizations can fill your request promptly if it is precise and complete.

Second, remember that you are asking another person to take time to fill your request. Therefore, be especially sure that your letter is courteous, clear, and to the point.

Check It Out   Read the letter of request on page 338.

- Is this letter of request courteous, specific, and to the point? Which form does this business letter have?

337

Part 4

Objective

To know the correct form for letters of request

Presenting the Lesson

1. Read aloud **Here's the Idea**. Point out that letters of request should be specific and courteous, since students are asking someone to take time to accommodate their requests.

Ask students if they have ever written letters of request and what kind of response they have received.

2. Read aloud the letter from **Check It Out.** Ask students if this letter has all the important parts of a letter of request. Have students point out what makes this letter courteous and precise.

3. Assign **Try Your Skill.**

4. Read aloud **Keep This in Mind** and then assign **Now Write.**

Individualizing the Lesson

Less-Advanced Students

Have students work in pairs to do the exercise from **Try Your Skill.**

Advanced Students

Have students work in pairs to edit and proofread their letters from **Now Write.** Have one student be the manufacturer and one student be the consumer. This should help them gain perspective on the quality of their letters. Afterward, have students switch roles.

Optional Practice

Ask students to rewrite the following letter, correcting the form and making it more courteous and specific. Answers will vary.

Office of Financial Aid
Roosevelt Art School
1001 South Second Street
Ithaca, New York 14850

Dear Sir (or Madam,)

I go to Westview High School and have taken many art courses. I like photography.
I heard that your school is pretty good, and I'd like to attend. I need to know more about financial aid. Send me some information right away.

Sincerely,

Jeff Judson

Extending the Lesson

Ask students to use the library to find a list of U.S. government publications. Have each student write a letter requesting one of the publications that interests him or her.

Have them use their home address as their mailing address. When the publications arrive, ask students to bring them to class.

```
                    28 Plainview Road
                    Greenfield, Wisconsin  53220
                    December 3, 1985


                    Chamber of Commerce
                    1122 West Main Street
                    Petersburg, Virginia  23803


                    Dear Sir or Madam:


                    I am a junior in high school, and I am working
                    on a report on Tiffany stained glass.  Through
                    my research I have discovered that the Blanford
                    Church in Petersburg has windows designed by
                    Louis Tiffany.  I need to know the year the
                    windows were installed, the dimensions of the
                    windows, and their original cost.  Could you
                    provide me with this information or give me the
                    name of someone in town who can?


                    I also understand that there are free picture
                    post cards available through your office that
                    feature the windows.  May I have a copy of such
                    a post card?


                    This information, plus any additional facts you
                    might have about the windows, will be very useful
                    for my report and will be greatly appreciated.


                    Yours truly,

                    Frances Russell

                    Frances Russell
```

Try Your Skill Write a letter to the United States Soccer Federation, 350 Fifth Avenue, New York, New York 10001, asking for information about where regulation soccer balls may be purchased locally. Use your home address and today's date.

Keep This in Mind

- Write a letter of request that is courteous, specific, and to the point. You may use either the *block* or *modified block* form for this business letter.

Now Write Write to the manufacturer of a product that you would like to know more about. You may write to a mail order company that you have seen advertised, or to the manufacturer of a product that is made in your town. Use the phone book or printed advertisements to help you find the address.

Use the modified block form for your handwritten letter. Be sure that you ask for specific information. Write the title of this lesson, **What Do You Need?** on your paper. Put your work into your folder. You may want to make a copy of your letter of request and send it.

Section 25 Objectives

1. To gain skill in identifying interests and skills

2. To know which references are useful sources of information about career choices

3. To know how to prepare a well-organized and informative résumé

4. To know which sources can provide information about job opportunities

5. To gain skill in writing letters to seek employment

6. To gain skill in preparing for a job interview

7. To gain skill in participating in a job interview

8. To know how to complete an employment application

9. To know how to write letters of inquiry to schools

Preparing the Students

Ask how many students currently have or have ever had a part-time job. Have these students tell the class how they found their jobs, and whether or not they had to write a résumé.

Ask the students what kinds of careers interest them and what skills they already have which could help them to be successful in those fields.

Ask students if they know what a seismologist, a geneticist, an art therapist, and a curator do. Point out that there are hundreds of career choices available to them, but first students need to find out what the jobs are and what their specific educational and vocational requirements are.

Explain that this Section will help students to identify and learn about

Skills for Your Future

341

their career interests. Students will also learn how to write a useful résumé, prepare for a job interview, and gain skill in writing letters seeking employment and information about schools.

Additional Resources

Mastery Test — page 36 in the test booklet

Practice Book — pages 132–142

Duplicating Masters — pages 132–142

Teaching Special Populations

LD Help students read the abbreviations in Help Wanted ads. Provide extensive help for students writing letters to employers.

Help students individually as they complete job applications. Require them to write the important information down for later reference.

Read and correct the students' letters to schools. Discuss with them how schools might respond to their particular letters.

ESL Write on the chalkboard common abbreviations in Help Wanted ads, and discuss these with students. Have a counselor talk to the students about legal working papers they may need if they are not citizens.

Explain each of the categories listed on the job application.

NSD Stress that letters to employers and to schools must be written in formal English.

Got Your Interest?

Assessing Your Interests and Skills

Objective

To gain skill in identifying interests and skills

Presenting the Lesson

1. Read and discuss **Here's the Idea.** Point out that before students can make meaningful decisions about school or their careers, it is necessary for them to evaluate their interests and skills.

2. As a class, read and discuss **Check It Out.**

3. Assign **Try Your Skill.**

4. Read aloud **Keep This in Mind** and then assign **Now Write.**

Individualizing the Lesson

Less-Advanced Students

As students complete **Try Your Skill,** point out that it is important for them to be as honest and realistic as possible. Have students give specific examples for the questions in **Check It Out.**

Advanced Students

Ask students to find four employment ads that interest them. Have them write a few sentences for each job explaining what specific skills and interests they have that would suit the job description.

Optional Practice

The following is a list of personality characteristics that are valued by employers. Ask students to indicate which characteristics they demonstrate often, and which they demonstrate less frequently.

Here's the Idea   Before long you will begin to make decisions about your future. Choosing the right college or career is, of course, very important. After all, you are likely to spend much of your adult life at work. If you choose work that is personally satisfying, you are more likely to be happy. This is why you should begin your career search by looking at your interests and skills. The following exercises will help you to learn more about yourself. You can then look for a career or a course of study that is suited to you.

Check It Out   Read the following list of job skills.

Acting	Driving	Proving
Building	Entertaining	Questioning
Calculating	Leading	Reading
Computing	Managing	Remembering
Counseling	Measuring	Repairing
Dancing	Organizing	Speaking
Decorating	Operating	Teaching
Designing	Painting	Typing
Drawing	Persuading	Writing

- Which of these skills have you used in the past? On what occasions did you use them?
- Which of these skills are you particularly good at?

Try Your Skill   The following questions will help you to decide what kinds of jobs are right for you. Answer these questions. Then, study your answers. Tell what they reveal about the kinds of jobs you would prefer.

1. Have you had any special training in job skills, such as typing or automotive repair?

2. Do any of your hobbies or other activities involve job skills? Describe any that do.

3. Do you prefer mental work or physical work?

4. Do you prefer working with words or with numbers?

5. Do you prefer working outdoors or indoors?

6. Do you prefer working with people or with machines?

7. Do you prefer working alone or with other people?

8. Are you willing to take additional training or schooling after high school?

9. In what part of the country do you want to live? Would you prefer living in a city or in a rural area?

10. How much money will you have to make to meet your needs?

punctual	reliable
imaginative	neat
good listener	disciplined
assertive	organized
determined	goal oriented
open-minded	careful

Have students save their notes in their folders.

Extending the Lesson

Discuss with the class how and why you decided to become a school teacher. Explaining your experiences can help students to understand that choosing a career or a specific education is a difficult but rewarding process.

Keep This in Mind

- Before making a career choice, identify your interests and skills. This will help you to find work that is suited to you.

Now Write   Choose a career possibility that matches the skills and interests that you identified in **Check It Out** and **Try Your Skill.** Write a paragraph explaining why you chose this particular job.

The World of Work

Exploring Careers

Objective

To know which references are useful sources of information about career choices

Presenting the Lesson

1. Read aloud and discuss **Here's the Idea.** Point out to students that the next step in selecting a career is to find out what type of careers exist, where they exist, and what special skills they require.

2. Read and discuss with students the list of occupational fields from **Check It Out.**

3. Assign **Try Your Skill.**

4. Read aloud **Keep This in Mind** and then assign **Now Write.**

Individualizing the Lesson

Less-Advanced Students

Ask students to use their self-assessment notes from Part 1 to determine which two occupational fields from **Check It Out** they would best be suited for.

Advanced Students

Ask students to use their self-assessment notes from Part 1 to determine which two occupational fields from the list in **Check It Out** they would best be suited for as well as two that would not suit them. Have students explain their reasons with specific examples of their interests, skills, and personality characteristics.

Optional Practice

Have students interview one or two adults about their occupations.

Here's the Idea   Once you understand your own interests and skills, you can begin to search for careers to which you are well suited. Sources of information about careers include the following:

1. Reference works, including encyclopedias and almanacs
2. Counselors, teachers, relatives, and employers
3. Books
   a. *Occupational Outlook Handbook.* This book is published by the U.S. Department of Labor. It is available in many guidance offices and public libraries.
   b. *Dictionary of Occupational Titles.* This book is also published by the Department of Labor and is available in guidance offices and libraries.

These sources can tell you about working conditions, job duties, possible earnings, and training or special skills required. They can also tell you about the many sources of job training, including the following:

1. Technical or trade schools
2. Community and junior colleges
3. Apprenticeships
4. Training programs offered by the armed services
5. Colleges and universities
6. On-the-job training programs

Check It Out   The following is a list of the fifteen major job fields and some particular jobs in each field. Read this list.

1. **Agriculture/Natural Resources** (farmer, gardener, forest ranger, fisherman, miner)

2. **Business and Office** (clerk, secretary, bank teller, real estate salesman, bookkeeper)

3. **Communications and Media** (projectionist, telephone line worker, proofreader, reporter, photographer, disc jockey)

4. **Construction** (carpenter, mason, electrician, heavy equipment operator, drafter, surveyor, plumber, civil engineer)

5. **Environment** (sewage disposal worker, fire warden, park maintenance worker, pest control worker, safety inspector)

6. **Fine Arts/Humanities** (stagehand, interior designer, writer)

7. **Health** (nurse, ambulance driver, medical records clerk)

8. **Home Economics** (dry-cleaning machine operator, food service worker, nursing home or child-care aide, chef)

9. **Hospitality/Recreation** (travel agent, hotel desk clerk, lifeguard, tour guide, railroad ticket clerk, usher)

10. **Manufacturing** (cannery worker, machinist, mill worker)

11. **Marine Science** (hatchery worker, marine biologist, sailor)

12. **Marketing** (cashier, shipping clerk, auctioneer)

13. **Personal Services** (beautician, kennel worker, barber, janitor)

14. **Public Service** (teacher, teacher's aide, police officer, soldier, post office clerk, customs inspector)

15. **Transportation** (truck or bus driver, dispatcher)

- Which of these job fields is most appealing to you? Why?

Try Your Skill   Choose any five of the job fields listed in **Check It Out.** For each job field, list one job title not mentioned.

> ## Keep This in Mind
> - There are many sources of information about possible careers.
> - Use these sources to identify careers that suit your interests and skills.

Now Write   Choose any occupation that interests you. Do some research. You might check the dictionary of occupational titles. Write a paragraph describing the following:

the job title	training required	chances of employment
job duties	skills required	possible earnings

Ask them to find out the following information for use in a class career discussion.

    job title
    duties
    employment opportunities
    training required
    skills required
    entry level salary

Extending the Lesson

Have students select one of the two occupational fields which suited them from the list in **Check It Out.** Ask them to write a letter to a specific business requesting information about a career in that field.

For information about writing letters of request, students should re-read Part 4 from Writing Section 24.

Have students share their responses with the class.

Part 3

Experience Counts

Writing a Résumé

Objective

To know how to prepare a well-organized and informative résumé

Presenting the Lesson

1. Read and discuss **Here's the Idea.** On the chalkboard write the word *résumé.* Ask students if they have ever written a résumé. Discuss the different types of information a résumé should contain and the guidelines for writing a résumé.

2. Read aloud the résumé from **Check It Out.** Ask students if it contains all the important and necessary information, and if it is well-organized and easy to read.

3. Read aloud and discuss **Try Your Skill.** This exercise can be done orally.

4. Read aloud **Keep This in Mind** and then assign **Now Write.**

Individualizing the Lesson

Less-Advanced Students

Work individually with these students as they write their own résumés. Be sure they use the guidelines listed in **Here's the Idea.** Suggest to students that they look over their self-assessment notes before beginning their résumés.

Advanced Students

Emphasize to students the importance of using active and positive language in their résumés. Explain that a résumé is their first chance to show an employer why they are special. Be sure students include information that illustrates their special skills and achievements. Have

Here's the Idea When the time comes for you to look for a job, you will have to prepare materials to send to possible employers. Usually you apply for a job by sending a brief letter and a résumé. A **résumé** (rez′•oo•mā′) summarizes your life in relation to work. A résumé contains basic information about you, your education, your work experience, and your special skills.

No two résumés are exactly the same. However, most are one page long and typewritten. All résumés contain brief phrases that summarize information. Use these guidelines:

1. State your name, address, and telephone number, including the area code.

2. State your job objective. What kind of position or general area of work are you seeking?

3. Summarize your education. List your high school, its address, your expected date of graduation, and any special subjects helpful for a particular job. If you have attended more than one school, list the most recent first.

4. Summarize your job experience. State the beginning and ending dates of your employment, the name and address of your employer, the position you held, and your duties. Again, list your most recent jobs first. If you have had any related volunteer experience, also include it here.

5. Mention any meaningful personal achievements. Include special skills such as knowledge of computer language or a foreign language, office skills, or community work. Also include awards, hobbies, special interests, and offices held in societies or clubs.

6. Mention at least two or three references. You may list the names of several adults—teachers or employers, for example—who can give you good character or employment references. It

is also standard practice to say that you will supply references on request. If you decide to list references on your résumé, make sure to contact these people before including their names. Only list those people who have agreed to supply written recommendations for you.

As your life and work change, so should your résumé. Revise your résumé so that it is accurate and up to date.

Check It Out   Examine the résumé on page 348.

- Is this résumé well organized and easy to read? Does it include all the necessary information?

Try Your Skill   Which of the following items should be added to the résumé shown in this lesson? Explain why the information is appropriate for the résumé.

1. broke arm, sophomore year, while ice-skating
2. won school attendance medals for freshman and sophomore years
3. won first-place speed certificate in typing class
4. studied Spanish for two years
5. played role in school play

Keep This in Mind

- A résumé summarizes basic information about your life in relation to work.
- Write a résumé that is well organized, easy to read, and up to date.
- Include all information that shows your special experiences and skills.
- Contact the people whom you wish to list as references before putting their names on your résumé.

Now Write   Write your own résumé. Follow the model given on page 348.

students review their self-assessment notes to help them write their résumés.

Optional Practice

Have students use the library to find books that contain sample résumés. Have students study a few of the résumés contained in the book before they begin writing their own.

Extending the Lesson

Invite an employment representative from a local company or from an employment agency to discuss with students the ways to write an effective résumé.

Elizabeth Ann O'Brien

257 Walker Road
Memphis, Tennessee   38104
(901) 555-3650

OBJECTIVE   A summer job as a cashier in
                   a supermarket.

EDUCATION   Central High School
                   Memphis, Tennessee
                   Member of Junior class graduating in
                   June, 1985, with courses in business
                   math and office skills.

WORK EXPERIENCE   Cashier
        Present   Dan's Market
                   522 Sherman Street
                   Memphis, Tennessee
                   On part-time basis.

Summer, 1983   Stock clerk, bagger
                   Dan's Market
                   Full time.

PERSONAL   Able to operate calculator, adding
                   machine, and cash register. Secretary,
                   Junior Chamber of Commerce, 1978-79.
                   Member of glee club and volleyball team.

REFERENCES   Will be provided upon request.

Classified Information

Discovering Job Opportunities

Here's the Idea   Once you have written a résumé, you are ready to look for a job. The following are some of the sources that you can use to find out what jobs are available:

Counselors.   One source of information about jobs is the counseling department in your school. A guidance counselor can give you advice about what jobs are right for you. He or she may be able to suggest particular job opportunities in your area.

Help-Wanted Ads.   These ads appear in most newspapers. They are arranged alphabetically according to job title. Full-time jobs are usually listed separately from part-time jobs. Help-wanted ads may contain all or part of the following information: job title, job description, skills or experience required, number of hours per week, days or shifts to be worked, salary or wages, and how to contact the employer.

Employment Agencies.   Employers sometimes list job openings with employment agencies. The addresses and telephone numbers of these agencies may be found in your telephone directory.

Telephone Directories.   Looking through the yellow pages of your local telephone directory may suggest some places where you might work. Using such a directory, you can make a list of possible employers. Then you can call them to see if any openings exist.

Personal Contacts.   One excellent source for information on job opportunities is your family and friends. Let these people know that you are looking for a job. They may be able to suggest some places where you can apply.

349

Part 4

Objective

To know which sources can provide information about job opportunities

Presenting the Lesson

1. Read aloud **Here's the Idea.** Discuss with students what can be gained by using each of the sources for job information. Have students talk about their experiences using these sources for finding a job. Which were most helpful? Why?

2. Have students read the help-wanted ads from **Check It Out.** Have them explain why the first ad would not be appropriate for high school students.

3. Assign **Try Your Skill.**

4. Read aloud **Keep This in Mind** and then assign **Now Write.**

Individualizing the Lesson

Less-Advanced Students

Have students work in small groups to complete **Now Write.** For students interested in similar jobs, this will increase their resources of people to contact.

Advanced Students

Explain to students what a Situations Wanted ad is. Have them study these ads in a major newspaper, and write one for a job for which they would be suited. Have them review their self-assessments notes before they begin writing. Ask students to share their ads with the class.

349

Optional Practice

Using their occupational selection from **Extending the Lesson** in Part 3, have students find as many newspaper ads for this kind of work as they can. For each ad, ask students to qualify the job by asking the following questions.

1. Is the job full or part time?
2. What are the job's duties?
3. Is experience required for the job?
4. Is it a daytime or evening job?

Extending the Lesson

Another source of job information students should familiarize themselves with is trade journals. Have students find a trade journal in their school or public library. Ask them to copy down any ads for which they would be suited or would like more information.

Have students share their findings with the class.

Check It Out Read the following help-wanted ads.

DELIVERY PERSON–Social welfare agency. Full-time, days. Delivering meals to elderly and handicapped persons. Must be responsible, punctual. Must have own transportation and valid driver's license. Call 555-3867 for further info. Ask for Pat.

COOK/DISHWASHER–Part-time, evenings. Some weekends. Exper. pref., but will train right person. Minimum wage to start. Apply in person, Rick's Place, 230 Casablanca Blvd.

• Which of these jobs might be appropriate for a high school student? Why?

Try Your Skill Reread the want ads in **Check It Out.** For each ad, answer the following questions.

1. Is the job full-time or part-time?
2. What are the job duties?
3. Does the ad specify that experience is required?
4. Is this a daytime or an evening job?

Keep This in Mind

• The following sources can supply information about job openings: counselors, help-wanted ads, employment agencies, telephone directories, and friends.

Now Write Using a telephone directory, make a list of businesses in your area that may hire teens. Give the name, address, and telephone number of each business. Tell what sorts of jobs each business might offer to teenagers.

On the Job

Writing Letters to Employers

Here's the Idea   Once you have found a job for which you would like to apply, you will have to contact the employer. One way to do this is to send the employer a letter, along with your résumé.

When you write a letter seeking employment, you need to be clear and direct. Follow these guidelines:

1. State the title of the job you are seeking.
2. Be specific about the kind of job you are looking for. Indicate whether you are looking for full-time, part-time, or temporary employment.
3. Include a brief statement about yourself. Also include your age and grade level in school.
4. Include a brief statement about your qualifications. Be sure to mention any related work experience or courses taken in school.
5. Be specific about your availability for work. Mention particular days or hours you will be available. Always include a starting date.
6. Include a request for an interview if the job is in your area.

If you are sending your letter to a large company, write to the personnel department. If you are writing to a small company, write to the owner or manager. If you answer a newspaper advertisement, look carefully for information telling you how to reply. Many ads will give you a box number to write to in care of the newspaper. Others may contain an address.

Make sure that your letter follows the correct form for business letters. It should be informative, neat, and polite. Also, be sure to proofread your letter carefully. Your attention to detail may lead to a job offer.

Part 5

Objective

To gain skill in writing letters to seek employment

Presenting the Lesson

1. Read aloud **Here's the Idea.** Ask students how they think an employer would respond to a disorganized and carelessly written letter. Discuss the six guidelines for writing letters to employers. Stress the importance of accuracy and neatness in these letters.

2. Read and discuss the letter in **Check It Out.** Ask students if the letter contains all the information listed on page 351. Have students identify each part of the business letter.

3. Assign **Try Your Skill.** Have students use the letter on page 352 as a guideline.

4. Read aloud **Keep This in Mind** and then assign **Now Write.**

Individualizing the Lesson

Less-Advanced Students

Have students review Parts 3 and 4 from Writing Section 24. Point out that a letter is the first impression a prospective employer will have of the applicant. Students should take special care to proofread their letters to make sure they are free of errors.

Advanced Students

Emphasize that students should make a positive presentation of themselves in their letters. Self-confidence and goal orientation are always appreciated by employers.

After students have completed **Now Write,** have them work in pairs to proofread each other's letters. Be sure they check for neatness, completeness, and errors in mechanics.

Optional Practice

Using the same occupational topic from **Optional Practice** in Part 4, have students select one company and write a letter seeking employment. Have students find out the name of the person to whom the letter should be addressed. Have students read their letters aloud to the class.

Extending the Lesson

Invite a local businessperson to visit the class. Have students prepare questions about writing letters seeking employment. If time permits, students could discuss one or two of their letters with the businessperson.

Check It Out   Read this letter.

257 Walker Road
Memphis, Tennessee 38104
March 18, 1985

Mr. Ralph Owens, Manager
First Federal Food Stores
31 State Street
Memphis, Tennessee 38104

Dear Mr. Owens:

I am interested in working full time this summer as a cashier in any of the First Federal Food Stores. I am currently a junior at Central High School. I have taken several business courses. Last summer I worked as a stock clerk and bagger at Dan's Market, 522 Sherman Street. I am working part time on weekends during this school year at the same job. I have had experience at checking stock, operating a cash register, and bagging.

I will be available for full-time work on June 6, although I can also be available part time before that date for any training that is required. I will be able to continue until August 28. I am willing to work any schedule, including weekends.

I will apply in person next week. I will also be available for an interview at your convenience.

Yours truly,

Elizabeth O'Brien

Elizabeth O'Brien

- Does this letter include all the necessary information?
- Is it courteous and neat?

Try Your Skill   Imagine that you are interested in one of the following jobs. Write a letter seeking employment. Mention your related experiences, including any job experiences you have had.

1. Wanted: Part-time, year-round help for telephone sales. Good spelling and some typing required. Write Advertising Department, *Suburban Tribune*, 425 Warren Street, Northbrook, Illinois 60062.

2. Wanted: Experienced kitchen help for summer. Write The Summit Inn, Pine Crest Road, Boulder, Colorado 80303.

3. Wanted: Part-time clerks in sales and stock during Christmas season. Write Personnel Manager, Lacy's Department Store, 1890 Grant Avenue, Manchester, Connecticut 06040.

Keep This in Mind

- A letter to an employer should create a good impression.
- The letter should be informative, polite, and neat.
- Include specific information about yourself and the job you want.

Now Write   Write a letter seeking employment at a supermarket, restaurant, department store, or other business in your town. Ask to be considered for a particular job. Be sure to include all necessary information. Revise and proofread your letter carefully.

All in a Day's Work

Objective

To gain skill in preparing for a job interview

Presenting the Lesson

1. Read aloud **Here's the Idea.** Discuss the importance of the résumé and how to keep it current. Discuss the questions on page 354 about students' backgrounds.

Point out that researching the company is an important part of preparing for an interview.

2. Read aloud **Check It Out,** and discuss the preparations Carrie made for her interview. Also, discuss how Carrie could find out information about the auto parts store and what questions she could ask during her interview.

3. Assign **Try Your Skill.**

4. Read aloud **Keep This in Mind** and then assign **Now Write.**

Individualizing the Lesson

Less-Advanced Students

Before assigning **Try Your Skill,** have students divide into small groups. Have them refer to the list in **Here's the Idea** to make certain they have included all the steps.

Advanced Students

Have students design and prepare a class checklist poster to be used in preparing for a job interview. Be sure students include the questions about personal background as well as methods for researching a company, and important questions to ask during the interview.

354

Here's the Idea   A job interview is a speaking situation. You must be prepared to talk with a prospective employer.

The first step in your preparation is to be sure your résumé is up to date. Sometimes you may want to send it in with a letter seeking employment. At other times, you may want to bring it with you to an interview. In any case, be sure you can talk easily about everything you have included.

It is often helpful to ask yourself some questions about the background information you have included on your résumé. For example, you might practice answering the following questions.

1. What are my strongest assets as an employee?

2. What experience do I have that helps qualify me for this particular job?

3. What personal attributes do I have that will make me valuable to this company?

If your résumé shows a weak area—for example, if you were dismissed from a previous job—be prepared to talk about it. You do not want to stumble if asked a difficult question. Simply explain what happened, emphasizing why you think you will be successful this time.

Before you go to your interview, find out as much as you can about the company and the job you want. Perhaps you can talk to someone who is working there now. If not, try to visit the company. For example, if you want a job as a cashier in a supermarket, shop in the store several times. Watch the cashiers. What seem to be their responsibilities? Of course, you should observe quietly and not talk with employees while they are on the job.

Having done this, you will probably have some questions of your own to ask at the interview. Think about them ahead of time. One or two good questions will show the employer that you are thinking and that you have initiative.

It is also important when you go to an interview to give some thought to your personal appearance. Wear clothes that help you feel good about yourself. It is best to dress neatly and appropriately.

Check It Out   Consider the following situation.

Carrie wanted to apply for a job as an office clerk in a nearby auto-parts store. Her résumé was ready, and when she studied it, she discovered this information:

1. My strongest assets are my typing speed and my ability to keep good records.

2. I have two experiences that help qualify me for this job. I worked last summer as a clerk in City Hall. I am now working at school as Ms. Tandy's assistant.

3. My personal attributes include promptness and an ability to get along well with other employees.

Carrie thought of a weakness that could hurt her chances. She was a poor speller. She decided not to mention this problem unless asked. She also planned to explain, if necessary, that her spelling suffered because of a poor beginning in reading. Carrie knew how to use a dictionary, however, and she could promise an employer that she would be careful about looking up words. Carrie had asked Ms. Tandy for a reference. Ms. Tandy had agreed to write a letter for Carrie to take with her.

On the day of her interview, Carrie dressed in her favorite skirt and blouse. She also wore low-heeled shoes that she had cleaned that morning.

- What preparations did Carrie make for her interview?
- What else could Carrie have done to get ready?

Try Your Skill   Tom wants a job at a service station. He would like to work after school and on weekends. He sent in a

Using the company students selected for writing their letter seeking employment, have students find out as much information about this company as they can. Suggest they visit and observe what specific employees do, discuss with employees what it is like working there, and research the company in the library for more information.

Extending the Lesson

Have students speak with the school principal requesting him or her to speak to the class about interviewing prospective employees. Have students prepare a list of questions they can ask about appearance, résumés, and questions employers like to hear.

résumé and has been offered an interview. Write out and number the steps that Tom should take in getting ready for his interview.

Keep This in Mind

- Before you go to a job interview, review your résumé.
- Be prepared to talk about yourself.
- Learn as much as you can about the company and about the job. Think of questions that you might like to ask at the interview.
- Dress neatly and appropriately.

Now Write Select a job that interests you. The company and job may be real or imaginary. Make a list of the skills and experience that qualify you for this job. Also list your strongest personal qualities. Finally make a list of questions you might want to ask at your interview.

At Your Best

Having an Interview

Here's the Idea   A job interview will be much easier for you if you have prepared carefully. Get off to a good start by taking with you everything you might need: several copies of your résumé, a pad of paper, a pen or pencil, and identification that includes your social security number. Allow yourself plenty of time in order to be prompt for the interview.

Once you arrive, you will need to introduce yourself. When you meet your interviewer, stand up. It's best to be informal but polite. Perhaps you will say, "Hello, Mr. Logan. I'm Terry Robbins from Jackson High School." Always shake hands if the interviewer extends a hand to you. Look directly at your interviewer.

Be direct and say your name clearly. You should be sure you catch the name of the interviewer. If you don't hear it, ask the interviewer to repeat it.

If you haven't already sent the interviewer a copy of your résumé, offer it now. While the interviewer reads it, sit quietly. Be thinking about what you are going to say.

Once the interview begins, listen carefully. Try not to be distracted by your unfamiliar surroundings. Keep your mind on the interview so that you can answer questions well.

If the interviewer asks a question that is difficult or surprising, remain calm. It is perfectly all right to say, "Let me think about that for a moment." Don't be afraid to pause while you get your ideas together.

In addition, try to avoid some of the common pitfalls in interviewing. For example, if the interviewer asks you a hard question, don't give a negative, dead-end answer, such as "I don't know." Also, the interview is usually not the time for you

357

Part 7

Objective

To gain skill in participating in a job interview

Presenting the Lesson

1. As you read **Here's the Idea,** discuss the specifics with the class. For example, talk about having proper identification, and paper and a pen for writing down important information during the interview. Stress punctuality; lateness is a sign of inconsideration and neglect. Remind students of the importance of listening and establishing eye contact with the interviewer. Ask students who have had interviews to discuss their experiences.

2. Read and discuss **Check It Out.** Point out that it was not inappropriate for the interviewer to ask Adam about being late. Note that Adam responded honestly and directly. Point out, too, that Adam gave excellent explanations of his qualifications and why he needed the job. Point out that Adam's answers clearly show that he prepared thoroughly for his interview.

3. Assign **Try Your Skill.**

4. Read aloud **Keep This in Mind** and then assign **Now Write.**

Individualizing the Lesson

Less-Advanced Students

Suggest that students work in pairs to do the exercise in **Try Your Skill.** Have students alternate being the interviewer and the applicant.

357

Optional Practice

Divide students into five groups. Have each group prepare a skit illustrating one effective and one ineffective interview. After students have practiced their skits, have them perform them for the rest of the class.

Extending the Lesson

1. Invite a personnel director to visit the class and hold several interviews with student volunteers. Request the interviewer to explain how to make a good impression at an interview, and what students should do after the interview is over.

2. If any students have had interviews, ask them to report to the class on the questions they were asked and how they felt during the interview. These students should be able to provide valuable first-hand information about the interviewing process.

to ask about salary or advancement opportunities. If the interviewer offers information on these subjects, you should feel free to discuss them. Otherwise, wait until you get a job offer. Finally, all prospective employers want to see evidence of self-control. Let your hands rest quietly in your lap or on the arms of your chair. Don't smoke or chew gum. Keep your voice at a reasonable pitch and volume.

The interviewer will let you know when the interview is over. Before leaving, show your interest in the job. Ask when you can expect to hear something from the company. As you leave, check to be sure you have all your belongings. Thank the interviewer for his or her time. Then shake hands and leave. Don't linger to look around or to talk to employees.

Check It Out   Consider the following situation.

Adam had an interview scheduled for 10:00 Friday morning at a citrus fruit processing plant. He was applying for a summer job in the canning department.

Adam arrived at 10:05. Traffic had been heavy, and he was nervous about being late.

His interviewer greeted him, "Good morning, Adam. I'm John Clark, the foreman."

They shook hands, and Adam said, "Hello, Mr. Clark. I'm Adam Stern. I'm sorry I'm late. The bus was slow."

Adam's interview went well. Here are some of the interviewer's questions and the answers that Adam gave.

Mr. Clark: I see that you worked during the school year. Did you usually get to work on time?

Adam: Yes, I did. I was late only once, and that was the day we had a fire alarm drill at school.

Mr. Clark: What makes you think you could stand the grind of factory work?

Adam: I have a lot of patience. I sometimes spend hours working on wood carvings. My job last year gave me experience, too. I spent most of the time repairing motors on lawnmowers.

Mr. Clark: Why do you want this job?

Adam: I know the plant is good to its employees. I have several friends who have worked here and liked it. There's also the fact that I need the money. My family expects me to earn my own spending money.

- How well did Adam handle this interview? Give specific reasons and details to explain your answer.

Try Your Skill   Imagine that you work at a summer camp. You have been asked to interview students for jobs as groundskeepers and crafts teachers. Make a list of questions that you would ask applicants for each job.

Keep This in Mind

- Introduce yourself to your interviewer.
- Answer all questions completely and thoughtfully.
- Let your interviewer see your best assets.

Now Write   Choose a job that you would like to have. Imagine that you are the employer. Make a list of questions that you would ask applicants for this job. Then, write the answers you would give if asked these questions.

Objective

To know how to complete an employment application

Presenting the Lesson

1. Read aloud **Here's the Idea.** As you discuss the guidelines, point out that students should write some of the information they need to complete the application on a separate sheet of paper. Certain information about references, business addresses, phone numbers, and specific dates can be prepared in advance. This will insure that students will have all the correct information, and that their application will be complete.

2. Read and discuss the completed job application in **Check It Out.** Remind students not to leave any blank spaces; if a question does not apply to them, they should write "does not apply" in the blank.

3. Assign **Try Your Skill.**

4. Read aloud **Keep This in Mind** and then assign **Now Write.**

Individualizing the Lesson

Less-Advanced Students

Have students reread **Here's the Idea.** Ask students to make a list of references and important dates that they would need to fill out an employment application. Tell students to save this list for future reference.

Advanced Students

Have students work in pairs for this exercise. Have each student fill

Part 8   **A Work Sheet**

Completing a Job Application

Here's the Idea   Whenever you apply for a job, you will probably be asked to complete a job application. The form of the application will vary from company to company. However, there are certain guidelines you should always follow.

1. Be prepared to answer several standard questions. You will be asked to state your address, telephone number, date of birth, social security number, and your citizenship. You will be asked about your education, special skills, and any past work experience. You will also be asked to name references. In other words, you will be asked to name two or three people not related to you who have known you for some time and who would be willing to discuss your strengths and abilities. A reference may be a former employer, a teacher, or a clergyman, for example.

2. Be neat. Print your answers carefully. You are being judged on your ability to follow directions and to work neatly. Use a good pen with blue or black ink. Because there is never enough space for the information requested, plan your answers before you print them. Read all instructions carefully, especially those in fine print. For example, you may be asked to give your last name first.

3. Complete every item. There may be questions that you cannot answer, such as a question about military service or home ownership. However, you should never leave any space blank on an application. Leaving a blank space only causes confusion. If an item does not apply to you, write "does not apply."

4. Be honest. You will be asked to sign your name to a statement that all information is correct.

Check It Out   Examine the completed job application on page 361.

FEDERAL FOOD STORES

APPLICATION FOR EMPLOYMENT

Date _March 25, 1985_

Name _O'Brien,   Elizabeth   Ann_   Tel. No. _555-3650_
    Last   First   Middle

Present Address _257 Walker Road,   Memphis,   Tenn.   38104_
        Street   City   State   Zip

Do you rent? ☐   Own your home? ☐   Live with parents? ☑

Previous Address _Does not Apply_
        Street   City   State   Zip

Soc. Sec. No. _986-77-2166_ Date of Birth _6/15/68_ Are you a citizen? Yes ☑ No ☐

Person to be notified in case of accident or emergency _Francis O'Brien_

Address _same as above_   Phone _same_

Position applied for _cashier_   Date available for work? _June 16, 1981_

RECORD OF EDUCATION

School	Name and Address of School	Years Attended	Circle last year completed
Elementary	Columbus Elementary School Memphis, Tennessee	1974-1982	5 6 7 ⑧
High	Central High School Memphis, Tennessee	1982-Present	1 2 ③ 4
College	Does not Apply		1 2 3 4

Did you serve in the military? Yes ☐   No ☑   Which branch? _Does not Apply_

Rank _Does not Apply_   Date of discharge _Does not Apply_

RECORD OF EMPLOYMENT   (List your last two employers, starting with the more recent one)

Dates	Name and Address of Employer	Salary	Position	Reason for Leaving
Sept. 1984	Dan's Market, 522 Sherman, Memphis	$3.50/hr.	cashier	
Summer 1984	Dan's Market, 522 Sherman, Memphis	$3.10/hr.	stockclerk, bagger	

Check the following office operations with which you have had experience

☐ Adding Machine   ☐ Switchboard   ☐ Shorthand   ☐ Addressograph   Other _cash register_
☐ Proof Machine (IBM)   ☐ Dictaphone   ☐ Typewriter   ☐ Bookkeeping Machine

PERSONAL REFERENCES   (Not former employers or relatives)

Name and Occupation	Address	Phone No.
Ruth Watson, M.D.	12 Elm Rd., Memphis, Tenn. 38104	555-8611
Michael Simpson (teacher)	Central High, Memphis, Tenn. 38104	555-3274
Rev. John Bucci	St. Mary's Church, Memphis, Tenn. 38104	555-4337

I hereby affirm that my answers to the foregoing questions are true and correct and that I have not knowingly withheld any information which would, if disclosed, be considered sufficient cause for dismissal.

In the event of my employment, I promise to comply faithfully with all the rules and regulations presently in effect, or which may hereafter become effective, relating to the conduct and performance of the employees of Federal Food Stores.

Applicant's Signature _Elizabeth Ann O'Brien_

---

out an employment application, then trade applications to correct any errors.

Optional Practice

Have students write a letter of request to the business they have been using for the previous **Optional Practice** asking for an employment application. Have students fill out the application following the guidelines they have learned.

Extending the Lesson

Invite an employment counselor or personnel director to speak to the class about job applications. Have students prepare questions concerning references, salary, and how best to display their qualifications. Have students write a letter of thanks to the businessperson.

- Have all items on the form been completed? How might an employer check that the information is correct?
- Has the application been filled in neatly? Have all of the instructions been followed carefully?

Try Your Skill Suppose that you are applying to First Federal Food Stores for a part-time job as a cashier. You are interested in working after school or on weekends. Refer to the application for employment on page 361. On a separate sheet of paper, list the information as you would write it on the application. Your teacher may give you a copy of the actual application to complete.

Keep This in Mind

- Answer all items on an application form honestly, correctly, and completely.
- Fill in the items on the application by printing neatly, using ink. Work carefully. Read all instructions.

Now Write Complete an actual employment application. Use a form given to you by your teacher or one from a business in your community. Complete the form honestly and neatly, following the guidelines you have learned.

To Your Knowledge

Writing Letters to Schools

Here's the Idea   After high school, you may decide to take additional schooling before starting a career. You can learn a great deal about various schools and colleges from your guidance department and from the school or public library. Usually, these sources have catalogs for you to look through, as well as some scholarship information. You will also find valuable information about our nation's schools, including their addresses, in such references as *Barron's Profiles of American Colleges*.

However, the best way to get specific information about a particular school that interests you is to write to the school itself. A letter to a vocational school or college is a business letter. Address it to the Admissions Office of the school and follow either of the standard business forms described on pages 334–336. Briefly give the school the information it needs in order to supply you with the information you need.

The school that you might attend will want to know about you. Include information about the name of your school, your grade level, and the date of your graduation. State your main area of interest. Also, you want to know about the school. Request information about entrance requirements, special programs offered, the size and location of the school, tuition costs, and scholarships. Also request a copy of the college catalog.

Because the cost of education is often high, you may also be interested in information about student loans and scholarships. If so, write directly to the Office of Financial Aid. Ask about financial assistance available for the year you plan to enter. The school will send you information about its programs and the necessary forms to be completed.

363

Part 9

Objective

To know how to write letters of inquiry to schools

Presenting the Lesson

1. Read aloud **Here's the Idea.** Ask students how many intend to go to a college or vocational school. Point out that letters of inquiry can help them find out the specific information they will need about each school. Explain that students can find out about facilities, programs, housing, and financial assistance by writing letters.

2. Read aloud and discuss the letter in **Check It Out.** Ask students if the letter contains all the necessary information. Point out that this letter uses block form and is written clearly and courteously.

3. Assign **Try Your Skill.** Remind students that since this letter will not be mailed, they may invent details. However, if students are interested in hospital work, they may want to send their letters to this institute. Have volunteers read their letters to the class.

4. Read aloud **Keep This in Mind** and then assign **Now Write.**

Individualizing the Lesson

Less-Advanced Students

Have students work in pairs to do **Now Write.** Suggest that each student proofread his or her partner's letter, checking for correct form, requests for specific information, and errors in mechanics and spelling.

363

Advanced Students

Have students look through *Barron's Profiles of American Colleges* or a similar reference book to find the addresses of two schools that interest them. Ask students to write a letter to both schools requesting a general catalog and information about a specific program.

Optional Practice

On the chalkboard write a brief letter to a college or vocational school requesting information. This letter should not be specific or use proper form. Have students discuss the letter, suggesting how it can be improved.

Extending the Lesson

Suggest to students that they begin a filing system to keep current records of all their correspondence. They should include a copy of their résumé, copies of letters sent to schools and places of employment, as well as responses to these letters. Have them divide their filing system according to the type of correspondence, and to arrange their letters and responses alphabetically.

Deciding to continue your education is an important decision. You need to compare several schools in order to make the best choice. Writing letters to schools is a good way to start.

Check It Out   Read the following letter.

32 Meyer Road
Galveston, Texas 77550
February 16, 1985

Admissions Office
Texas College of Arts and Industries
Kingsville, Texas 78363

Dear Sir or Madam:

I am a junior and will graduate from Galveston West High School in the spring of 1986. I am interested in continuing my education in the field of data processing, and I am particularly interested in the program you offer. Do you anticipate many openings in your program for the fall of 1986, or will there be a limited enrollment?

I would also like to know what subjects you advise potential students to take during their senior year in high school. Also, is job experience required of applicants? If so, what type of experience is preferred?

Please send me a copy of your catalog so that I may examine the tuition costs, entrance requirements, and the specific courses offered in the data processing program.

Very truly yours,

Jessica Roberts

Jessica Roberts

- What specific information does this business letter include? What specific information does it request?

Try Your Skill   Suppose you are a high school senior interested in hospital work. You are considering a career as an emergency medical technician. Write a letter to the Admissions Office of Midwest Vocational Institute, 3527 Western Avenue, Chicago, Illinois 60604. Request a catalog and other important information about the program offered by the school. Include the important information about yourself described in **Here's the Idea.**

Keep This in Mind

- When you write to vocational schools and colleges, use the correct business letter form.
- Include specific information about yourself and request specific information from the school.

Now Write   Write a letter to a real vocational school or college that interests you. Use either correct business letter form. Ask about various aspects of a program in the field of your choice. Request a catalog. Be sure to revise and proofread the letter carefully.

Section 26 Objectives

1. To know how to present oneself when speaking before an audience

2. To develop listening skills that show politeness and attention

3. To prepare an informal talk

4. To write a formal speech

5. To practice the presentation of a speech

6. To understand how group discussions are organized and how they operate

7. To learn the duties of the chairperson and participants in a group discussion

Preparing the Students

Give students a written copy of a short speech, such as Lincoln's *Gettysburg Address,* Martin Luther King's *I Have a Dream,* or John Kennedy's Inaugural Address and ask them to read it. Have students discuss their reaction to it. Then play a recording of the same speech. Discuss with students the effect hearing the speech made on them. Have students list on the chalkboard the differences between hearing and reading the speech. Talk with students about what speech contributes to the process of communication.

Point out to students that this Section will develop the necessary skills for speaking formally and informally in front of groups of people. Also, students will learn how to participate more effectively in group discussions.

Additional Resources

Mastery Test — page 37 in the test booklet

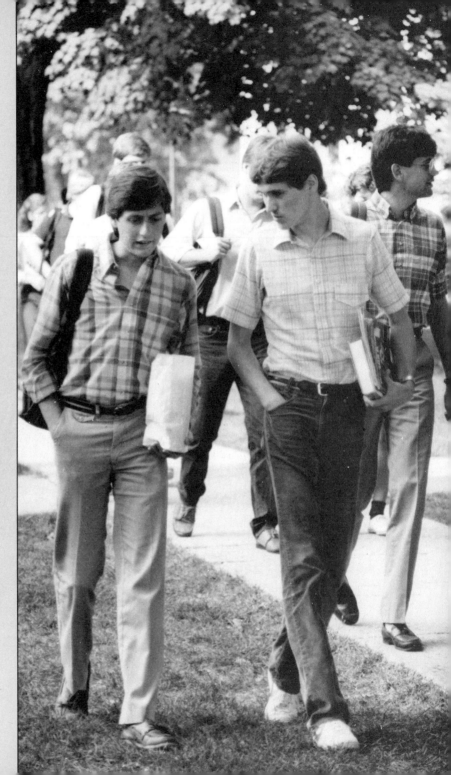

Speaking and Listening

Practice Book — pages 143–149
Duplicating Masters — pages 143–149

Teaching Special Populations

LD Some students with learning disabilities should be exempt from participating in these exercises. Others may be more successful if you allow them to record their speeches on a tape recorder instead of presenting them in front of the class.

ESL ESL students may be very self-conscious about their speech skills. Help students with their pronunciation and grammar as they prepare their speeches, and emphasize good listening skills to your class before students begin presenting their speeches.

Discuss with students differences in body language (especially gestures and eye contact) of different cultures.

Help ESL students gain confidence in speech-giving. Have students present their speeches first to partners, then to a small group, and finally in front of the entire class.

NSD Remind students to prepare their speeches in standard English. Help them individually with their pronunciation.

Objective

To know how to present oneself when speaking before an audience

Presenting the Lesson

1. Read aloud **Here's the Idea.** Discuss the importance of appearance, eye contact, voice quality, and natural expressions. Ask students to provide examples of people they have seen or heard who have good speaking skills and those who have poor speaking skills.

2. Read aloud **Check It Out** and discuss how each person's performance could be improved.

3. Assign **Try Your Skill.** Have students work in pairs for this exercise.

4. Read aloud **Keep This in Mind** and assign **Now Write.**

Individualizing the Lesson

Less-Advanced Students

Have students work in pairs to complete the following. Ask them to pay close attention to a news-reporter who is "live" rather than reading the news in the newsroom. Ask students to make notes about the reporter's eye contact with the camera, his or her posture, and any gestures or expressions the reporter uses. Have them bring their notes to class for discussion.

Advanced Students

Have students work in pairs for this lesson. Ask each student to spend a few minutes thinking about his or her favorite food, hobby, season, sport, music, or anything else

368

Your Public Awaits

Developing Speaking Skills

Here's the Idea Both in school and in later life, the ability to speak well is a key to success. Good speaking skills are important when you take part in a discussion or give an oral report. These skills are also important when you meet new people or interview for a job. The following guidelines will help you to make a good impression whenever you speak.

1. Appearance. Stand up straight. Try to look confident and relaxed. Make sure that your clothes suit the occasion.

2. Eye Contact. Look directly at your listeners. This will help you to keep their attention. Never stare at your notes or at any one person.

3. Voice. Speak loudly enough for your listeners to hear you without difficulty. Do not speak so loudly that your listeners become uncomfortable. Pronounce your words clearly. Do not rush or speak too slowly. Make sure that your tone of voice fits what you are saying. Vary your volume, tone, pitch, and pace. Pause for emphasis, especially before important points.

4. Gestures and Facial Expressions. Use natural gestures and facial expressions. These will help you to appear relaxed and confident. They will also help your audience to understand how you feel. For example, if you are talking about an important problem, you can show its importance by looking concerned. If you are talking about an exciting event, you can show your feelings by looking excited.

Check It Out Read the following descriptions. Think about how each speaker presents his or her ideas.

1. Margaret saw a *Help Wanted* sign in a bakery window. She went into the shop and asked for the manager. "I see you need

368

help," she said in a low voice while looking out the window. "Maybe I could work here."

2. Andy was asked to represent the ski team at the opening day assembly. He was very nervous. His legs shook, and his hands trembled. He stared at his notes and spoke quickly so he could get the speech over with.

- How could the performance of each speaker be improved?

Try Your Skill Read the following sentences aloud. Practice pronouncing each word clearly.

1. A tiny toddler came tumbling down the slope.
2. Arthur, the author, read his guest his best stories.
3. Darlene cleaned these kitchen cabinets, didn't she?
4. My sister Sarah sings sensationally.
5. The clouds now looked like billowy, downy, pillows.

Keep This in Mind

- Whenever you speak in public, stand up straight and look at your audience.
- Speak loudly enough to be heard. Pronounce your words clearly. Vary your volume, pitch, pace, and tone. Pause when necessary.
- Use natural gestures and facial expressions to communicate your feelings.

Now Write Think of a time when you heard a really interesting speaker. This speaker may have been a teacher, another student, or a politician on television. Write a paragraph telling why this speaker's performance was effective. Share your paragraph with your classmates.

they would like to talk about with the other student. Have each student talk for about three minutes on his or her topic. Ask the other student to pay attention to the speaker's voice quality, gestures, and eye contact. When both students have finished, have them discuss their talks.

Optional Practice

Have students practice speaking by using a tape recorder. Have them read a few pages from a story, history book, or from a speech they find in the library. Have them make notes about how they could improve the quality of their speaking voices.

Extending the Lesson

For examples of excellent vocal presentation, have students listen to recordings by Vincent Price, Orson Welles, or Martin Luther King, Jr. Ask students to write down what they like about the way these people speak. Have them pay special attention to tone of voice, expressiveness, pace, enunciation, and pauses.

Objective

To develop listening skills that show politeness and attention

Presenting the Lesson

1. Read aloud **Here's the Idea.** On the chalkboard write the five "Guidelines for Good Listening." Have students make a copy to keep in their folder.

2. Read aloud **Check It Out** and discuss the question following it.

3. Read aloud the directions for **Try Your Skill** and assign the exercise.

4. Read aloud **Keep This in Mind** and assign **Now Write.**

Individualizing the Lesson

Less-Advanced Students

Have students work in pairs to do the exercise from **Try Your Skill.** Have students discuss their answers. Have them discuss times when other people did not listen to them, and explain how they felt.

Advanced Students

Explain to students that listening is a very important skill. Being a good listener will help them understand concepts better and enable them to make better decisions. Ask students to listen to a recorded speech. When the speech is over, have them make notes of the important points. Have them listen to the speech again, and make a second set of notes. Have them compare their notes to see how much more they understood after the second listening.

370

Listen to This!

Developing Listening Skills

Here's the Idea   Listening is a skill that you use every day. In school you listen to lectures, speeches, and class discussions. Outside of school, you listen to the conversation of people around you. Developing good listening skills will increase your understanding of materials presented in your classes. In addition, these skills will help you to communicate better with others. The following guidelines will help you to develop good listening skills.

Guidelines for Good Listening

1. When someone is speaking, give the speaker your full attention.

2. Try to make the speaker feel comfortable. Let your eyes and expression show that you are interested in what the speaker is saying.

3. Do not make distracting noises or movements. Never speak when someone else is speaking.

4. Think about what the speaker is saying. Listen for main ideas and supporting details. In some situations, you may wish to take notes.

5. Be open-minded. Do not judge the speaker's ideas before you hear how they are supported.

Check It Out   Rolanda went to hear a speech by a Senator who was running for President. The audience was very excited.

370

Several people clapped and cheered throughout the speech. They were so loud that Rolanda couldn't hear a word.

- How could the Senator's audience have been more considerate?

Try Your Skill   Read the following descriptions of poor listening. Tell what each listener could do to improve his or her listening skills.

1. Marietta won first place in a speech contest. When she returned home, she ran to tell her brother about it. She found her brother watching television. She told him all about the contest. Her brother said, "That's nice," and continued watching TV.

2. A guest speaker visited Bill's United States history class. Bill listened to the first couple of sentences. Then, he decided that he wasn't interested. For the rest of the class period, Bill did his mathematics homework.

Keep This in Mind

- Always be polite when listening to a speaker. Show your interest. Do not make distracting movements or noises.
- Think about what the speaker is saying. Listen for main ideas and supporting details.

Now Write   Think of a time when you had difficulty hearing a speaker. Write a paragraph describing this situation. Label your paper **Listen to This!** Save it in your folder.

Objective

To prepare an informal talk

Presenting the Lesson

1. On the chalkboard list the four types of informal talks. Discuss each type with students and ask them for their experiences with these informal talks.

2. Read and discuss **Check It Out.** Ask if any student has ever changed a tire on a car. Ask students if after reading the directions on changing a tire they would know exactly how to do it themselves.

3. Assign **Try Your Skill.**

4. Read aloud **Keep This in Mind** and assign **Now Write.**

Individualizing the Lesson

Less-Advanced Students

Have students work in pairs to do the exercise in **Try Your Skill.** Point out that many of these informal talks can happen every day, such as giving directions or making announcements. To help students, ask them to think of situations when they gave directions to a friend, or explained how to do something.

Advanced Students

For **Now Write,** ask students to prepare an introduction. Have them select one of the following people to introduce. Have students research this person to find two interesting and important facts to use in their presentation.

Small Talk

Preparing an Informal Talk

Here's the Idea   On many occasions you will be required to give an informal talk. An informal talk is a short talk used to present information quickly. There are four types of informal talks.

1. **Announcements** tell about an event that has happened or will happen.
2. **Introductions** present people to audiences.
3. **Demonstrations** show how something is done.
4. **Directions** tell how to do something.

To prepare an informal talk, decide what facts you need to present. Then, gather these facts and put them in a logical order. The facts you include depend on the type of talk you want to give.

1. **Announcements** should answer the questions *who? what? when? where?* and *why?* Keep your announcement short and simple. Leave out any unnecessary details.

2. **Introductions** should provide information about the person you are introducing. Make sure that you have something interesting to say about this person. You may have to interview the person beforehand to gather this information. Be enthusiastic and polite.

3. **Demonstrations** should present the activity you wish to demonstrate in separate steps. Perform each step for your audience. Explain each step as you perform it. Suppose you wanted to demonstrate how to prepare a new aquarium. To do so, you would actually set up an aquarium in front of your audience. During each step, you would explain what you are doing and why. If you wish to use props in a demonstration, practice using

these props before your talk. When giving the talk, keep your props where your audience can see them.

4. **Directions** should include all necessary or helpful details. Arrange these details in step-by-step order. Make sure that each step is presented in the right order.

Check It Out   Read the following talk.

To change a tire on a car, loosen the lug nuts. Take off the tire. Then, put on the new tire.

- What type of informal talk is this?
- What is wrong with this talk? How could it be improved?

Try Your Skill   Write an informal talk on one of these topics.

1. A demonstration of a craft or hobby
2. An introduction presenting one of your teachers to a group of parents
3. An announcement telling about a special event at your school (Include details that would make people want to attend.)
4. Directions explaining how to get from your school to a local movie theater

Keep This in Mind

- An informal talk is a short talk used to present information quickly.
- Informal talks include announcements, introductions, demonstrations, and directions.
- To prepare an informal talk, gather all the necessary information. Then, place this information in a logical order.

Now Write   Choose a second topic from the list given in **Try Your Skill**. Write another informal talk. If your teacher directs you to do so, deliver your talk to your class.

373

Part 4

Objective

To write a formal speech

Presenting the Lesson

1. Ask students if they have ever given a formal speech.

On the chalkboard list all the pre-writing, writing, and revising steps for preparing a formal speech. Discuss with students the importance of each step. Point out that these steps are similar to the stages of the process of writing.

2. Read the passage from **Check It Out.** Discuss with students what sources Sarah should check for information.

3. Assign **Try Your Skill.**

4. Read aloud **Keep This in Mind** and assign **Now Write.**

Individualizing the Lesson

Less-Advanced Students

Have students compare Part 8 from Writing Section 14 with the guidelines for preparing a formal speech. For students having difficulty with **Now Write** and **Try Your Skill,** suggest they work in small groups and brainstorm for ideas.

Advanced Students

Emphasize to students that keeping their audience in mind when they prepare their speeches is very important. Have them rewrite their introduction from **Check It Out,** addressing it to a different audience. For example, the speech on athletics could be addressed to junior high school students or to parents at a town meeting.

In Good Form

Preparing a Formal Speech

Here's the Idea   Formal speeches require more preparation than informal talks. A formal speech is longer and presents a subject in detail. Book reports, lectures, sermons, and campaign speeches are all types of formal speeches. When preparing a formal speech, follow these steps:

Pre-Writing

1. **Choose your topic.** Narrow it to fit the time available.
2. **Define your purpose.** Your purpose may be to explain, to persuade, or to entertain.
3. **Identify your audience.** Think about your audience. Make sure that your topic is one that they will enjoy.
4. **Determine your main idea.** Write a sentence stating this idea.
5. **Gather supporting information.** Use sources such as personal experience, other people, and reference works.
6. **Organize your information.** A speech may be organized in any of these ways: spatial order, chronological order, the order of importance, or order of familiarity.

Writing

1. Write an introduction that states your main idea and gains the attention of your audience.
2. Write the body of the speech. Develop your main idea using facts, details, and examples.
3. Write a conclusion that "wraps up" your speech. If your purpose is to entertain, end on a note of amusement or interest. If your purpose is to explain or persuade, end in one of these ways:
   a. Repeat the main idea in different words. Then, summarize the major points made in the speech.
   b. Draw a lesson or moral from the ideas presented.

c. Make an appeal for some sort of action on the part of your listeners.

Revising

1. See that all the material relates to your main idea.
2. Check your speech for errors in grammar and usage.

Check It Out Read the following passage.

Sarah was asked to give a speech in her social studies class. She remembered seeing an old silver certificate in her uncle's coin collection. She began to wonder what other types of money had been used in the past. She thought this would make a good subject for her speech. Her teacher agreed. He said that United States currency has gone through several changes.

· What sources could Sarah check for information?

Try Your Skill Choose one of the following topics for a five-minute speech. Narrow the topic. Then write an interesting introduction, that states the main idea.

athletics   the Old West   famous scientists

Keep This in Mind

· When preparing a speech, narrow your topic. Identify your purpose and audience. State your main idea. Organize your information.
· Make sure that your speech has an introduction, a body, and a conclusion.
· Make sure that your ideas are all related to your main idea. Proofread your rough draft.

Now Write Write the body and conclusion of the speech that you began in **Try Your Skill.** Make sure that your information is organized logically. Revise and proofread your final draft.

375

Objective

To practice the presentation of a speech

Presenting the Lesson

1. Point out to students the importance of practice in order to perfect any skill. Read aloud **Here's the Idea.** Discuss with students their experiences with practicing. Do they practice a musical instrument, a sport, or an artistic skill? Explain to students that before they can be "expert" speakers, they have to practice this skill too. Discuss whether or not to memorize parts of a speech. Point out that it is not necessary to memorize an entire speech. What counts most when delivering a good speech is familiarity with the material and self-confidence.

2. Read aloud and discuss **Check It Out.**

3. Assign **Try Your Skill.** Have students work in pairs or small groups to do this exercise.

4. Read aloud **Keep This in Mind** and assign **Now Write.**

Individualizing the Lesson

Less-Advanced Students

Once students have memorized the introduction and conclusion to their speeches, have them work in pairs or small groups to practice their delivery. Have students make notes on each speaker. Have students discuss what they did well and also what areas still need improvement.

Part 5 # Down Pat

Practicing and Presenting a Speech

Here's the Idea   What would happen if no one on the U.S. Olympic Team ever practiced? Of course, the team would lose every event. Practice is necessary in order to perfect any skill. Speakers, like athletes, must practice in order to do their best.

Before practicing a speech, decide how much of the speech you wish to memorize. You can memorize the entire speech. You can also memorize just the introduction and conclusion. Notes or an outline can then be used for the body of the speech. If you do decide to use notes or an outline, practice with these beforehand. When giving the speech, try not to look at your notes or outline too often.

Use the following method to memorize all or part of a speech:

1. Read one sentence.
2. Recite the sentence several times without looking at it.
3. Read the next sentence.
4. Recite both sentences without looking.
5. Go through all the material in this manner. When you miss a sentence, start all over again.

When you practice, say your speech aloud several times. If possible, make a tape recording of your presentation. Then, play back this tape to check your voice. Practice before a mirror at least once. Check your posture, facial expressions, and gestures. Ask friends or relatives to listen to your speech. See if they have suggestions for improvements.

When you deliver your speech, keep in mind the guidelines for effective speaking given in Part 1, **Your Public Awaits.** Try to appear relaxed and confident. Look at your audience. Speak loudly enough to be heard. Use natural gestures and facial expressions.

Check It Out   Arthur wrote a speech for his science class on how batteries work. He memorized the entire speech. Then, he practiced his speech several times. First, he made a tape recording of the speech. He noticed that he was talking too fast, so he slowed the speech down. Second, he practiced his speech in front of a mirror. He noticed that he wasn't standing up straight, so he corrected this problem, too. Finally, he practiced his speech for two of his friends. They suggested that he use a drawing of a battery as a visual aid. Arthur did this. Then, he practiced the speech again using the drawing.

- How thoroughly did Arthur practice his speech?

Try Your Skill   Practice giving one of the informal talks that you wrote for Part 3, **Small Talk.** As you practice, make a list of problems that you notice in your delivery. Then list the improvements that you make as you practice.

Keep This in Mind

- Memorize your entire talk, or memorize just the introduction and the conclusion. If you use notes or an outline, practice with these.
- Practice your talk several times. Use a tape recorder and a mirror, if possible.
- Ask your friends or relatives to listen to your speech. Listen to their suggestions.
- When you deliver your talk, follow the guidelines given in Part 1, **Your Public Awaits.**

Now Write   Practice the speech you wrote for Part 4, **In Good Form.** Memorize the introduction and conclusion. Use note cards or an outline for the body. Practice the speech yourself and in front of other people. List any improvements that you make as you practice. Label this list **Down Pat.** Save it.

377

Part 6

Objective

To understand how group discussions are organized and how they work

Presenting the Lesson

1. Read aloud **Here's the Idea.** Ask students to discuss times when they have participated in group discussions. Have students point out the difficulties as well as the advantages of group discussions. Did the chairperson maintain order and recognize all participants who wanted to speak? Were agreements and decisions reached smoothly, or was it difficult for people to compromise?

Discuss with students the procedure for group discussions: statement of topic and purpose, definition of key terms, narrowing the topic, discussion of topic, summary.

2. Read aloud **Check It Out.** Have students discuss the problems encountered by this group.

3. Assign **Try Your Skill.**

4. Read aloud **Keep This in Mind** and assign **Now Write.**

Individualizing the Lesson

Less-Advanced Students

Make sure students understand the responsibilities of each member of a discussion group, as well as the procedures they must follow.

For students having difficulty with **Try Your Skill,** point out that they should include important information, ideas for solving the problem, and possible courses of action.

United We Stand

Organizing a Group Discussion

Here's the Idea   You have probably heard the expression "Two heads are better than one." Like many old sayings, this one contains a great deal of truth. Groups can often accomplish much more than one person acting alone. This is why group discussion is so widely used in businesses and schools.

Every group discussion should have a **chairperson.** This person's duty is to keep order and to lead the discussion. In addition, a discussion group may choose a **secretary.** This person takes notes on what is said. The other members of the group act as **participants.** They discuss the topic under the guidance of the chairperson.

The chairperson should begin by stating the topic and purpose. The purpose may be to explore an idea or to exchange information. It may also be to solve a problem or to plan a course of action. The participants then define any key terms that will be used in the discussion. By doing this, members of the group can be certain that they are talking about the same things. A group may also decide to narrow their discussion topic before continuing. Doing this will keep the group from getting off the subject.

During a discussion, members of the group should ask to be recognized by the chairperson. Then, they should offer their ideas and opinions. They may also wish to question other group members. What happens during the discussion will vary, depending on the subject being discussed.

At the end of the discussion, the chairperson or the secretary should summarize what has been said. The summary should include any agreements or decisions arrived at during the discussion.

Check It Out   Read the following description of a discussion.

A group of students at Central High School decided to start a computer club. Six of these students got together one day after school to discuss forming this club. They hoped to receive official approval and support from their school.

The group decided not to choose a chairperson because they wanted everyone to be on an equal footing. Two of the students spent most of the time talking about a new computer game. One of the students told the group about the new computer terminals being purchased by the school. A fourth student said that she thought the club would teach people how to use computers. At the end of an hour, everyone realized that the group had not discussed their initial topic.

- What went wrong in this discussion?

Try Your Skill   Imagine that your state is considering a bill to raise the legal age for obtaining a driver's license. You have been elected chairperson of a group of students who will discuss this question on a local cable television station. Write an introduction to the discussion. In your introduction, state the topic and purpose of the discussion.

Keep This in Mind

- The chairperson, secretary, and participants all have important roles to play in a discussion.
- A discussion should begin with an explanation of the topic and purpose and end with a summary.

Now Write   Think of an interesting or successful discussion in which you have taken part. This may be a discussion from one of your classes. It may also be from a club or team meeting. Write a paragraph describing this discussion. Tell who led the discussion and describe its topic and purpose. Label your paper **United We Stand.** Save it in your folder.

Part 7

Objective

To learn the duties of the chairperson and participants in a group discussion

Presenting the Lesson

1. Read and discuss the duties of the chairperson and the participants. On the chalkboard briefly outline the duties of each.

2. Ask three students to read the parts of the chairperson and the two participants from **Check It Out.**

Ask students if the chairperson is fulfilling his or her job, and if the comments of Luis and Erica are appropriate.

3. Read and assign **Try Your Skill.**

4. Read aloud **Keep This in Mind** and assign **Now Write.**

Individualizing the Lesson

Less-Advanced Students

Have students reread the duties of the chairperson and the duties of the participants. Ask them to rewrite the selection from **Check It Out** changing the comments that are inappropriate. Have students meet in small groups to discuss their changes.

Advanced Students

Before assigning **Now Write,** have students prepare an introduction to the discussion. Be sure students state the topic and purpose of the discussion.

Participating in a Discussion

Here's the Idea   Each person in a discussion group has specific duties. If you understand what these duties are, you can help a discussion to flow smoothly.

Duties of a Chairperson

1. Prepare for the discussion by researching the topic.
2. Introduce the topic and purpose of the discussion.
3. Allow time for the introduction, the discussion, and the summary.
4. Keep order in the discussion group.
    a. Allow only one person to speak at a time.
    b. Insist that members of the group ask to be recognized before they speak.
5. Encourage everyone in the group to participate.
6. Ask questions to keep the group interested in the topic.
7. Keep the discussion on the topic.
8. Take notes in order to summarize what has been said.

Each participant can also affect the success of a discussion.

Duties of a Participant

1. Speak only when the chairperson recognizes you.
2. Take part in the discussion.
3. Support your statements with facts. (See Chapter 21, **Critical Thinking.**)
4. Listen carefully, following the guidelines for good listening given in Part 2, **Listen to This!**
5. Be polite, especially when disagreeing with another member of the group. Use phrases such as "You've made a good point, but don't you think that . . . ?"
6. Be open-minded. Try to understand the views of other group members. Ask questions if you do not understand a point.

Check It Out   Read the following selection from a discussion.

CHAIRPERSON: Our topic for today is "Should students be allowed to drive their automobiles to school?" As you know, the school administration is considering . . .

ERICA: (Interrupting) Who cares? I don't drive.

CHAIRPERSON: Excuse me, Erica. Please wait to be recognized. Also, please give me a moment to introduce the topic. Then you will have a chance to voice your opinion.

As you know, the school administration is considering banning student-driven vehicles from school property. Our purpose for meeting today is to decide what recommendation we should make to the school board. Yes, Luis?

LUIS: Don't you think we ought to talk about getting some new basketball uniforms instead?

- Is the chairperson in this group doing his or her job?
- Are the comments of Erica and Luis appropriate?

Try Your Skill   You have been asked to lead a discussion on a short story or poem of your choice. Write a list of five questions that you could ask to keep the discussion going.

Keep This in Mind

- The chairperson should introduce the topic and purpose. This person should also keep order and keep the discussion on the topic.
- A participant in a discussion group should take part in the discussion, listen carefully, and be polite.

Now Speak   If your teacher directs you to do so, join a small group. Elect a chairperson to lead your group. Also elect a secretary to take notes. Discuss this question.

What new courses should be taught at this school?

Choose someone to report your group's conclusions.

381

381

Handbook

A detailed Table of Contents for the Handbook appears in the front of this book.

Section Objectives

1. To distinguish between complete sentences and fragments

2. To identify subjects and predicates and to understand how these two parts make a complete sentence

3. To identify the verb and its simple subject

4. To identify main verbs, helping verbs, and separated parts of a verb

5. To identify the subject in sentences with unusual word order, sentences beginning with *there*, and sentences giving commands

6. To identify and understand the functions of direct objects and indirect objects

7. To differentiate between transitive and intransitive verbs

8. To recognize linking verbs

9. To recognize predicate words: predicate nouns, predicate pronouns, and predicate adjectives

10. To distinguish between predicate words and direct objects

11. To identify and form compound sentence parts

12. To recognize the four kinds of sentences and to use the proper end punctuation with each

13. To recognize and form sentences using the five basic sentence patterns

Preparing the Students

Explain to students that the purpose of this Handbook is to teach students how to write and speak more effectively.

Read the introduction on page 385.

The Sentence and Its Parts

Additional Resources

Mastery Test — pages 38–41 in the test booklet

Additional Exercises — pages 413–421 in the student text

Practice Book — pages 153–165

Duplicating Masters — pages 153–165

Special Populations — See special section at the front of this Teacher's Edition.

Clear communication is the purpose of language. Once small children learn a number of words, they start putting them together to express their needs. Soon they are speaking in simple sentences.

Milk. (One word)
More milk. (Two words)
I want more milk. (Sentence)

The sentence is the basic unit of communication. In order to write good sentences, it is helpful to know the parts of the sentence—subjects, verbs, objects, modifiers, and more.

In this section you will learn about the parts of a sentence and how they are put into working order.

385

Part 1

Objective

To distinguish between complete sentences and fragments

Presenting the Lesson

1. Read page 386. Go over the definitions and examples of complete sentences and sentence fragments. Stress that a sentence fragment is incomplete because a part of an idea is missing from it.

2. Do Exercise A on pages 386–387 as an oral exercise with the class. Have individual students read the items aloud and then identify them as a complete sentence or a fragment. For each fragment, have students tell what part of the idea is missing.

3. Assign and discuss Exercise B on page 387.

Individualizing the Lesson

Less-Advanced Students

1. Help students complete each sentence fragment in Exercise A, page 386.

2. Have students complete each sentence fragment in Exercise B, page 387, on their own. Then have students write what part of the sentence they added to complete each fragment (*who* accepted the collect phone call or *what about* the exhaust fumes from the cars).

Advanced Students

Have the students complete each sentence fragment in Exercises A and B, pages 386–387. Then have the students write what part of the sentence they added (*who* sang a

In everyday speech, you sometimes use only parts of sentences. For example, you might answer a question with one or two words:

Tomorrow.   No.   Maggie's house.

In writing, however, complete sentences are important. With them, your ideas are clear and understandable.

A sentence is a group of words that expresses a complete thought. A sentence makes sense because it is a whole idea, not just part of one.

These groups of words are sentences:

Paul caught a bass.
Our soccer team won the match.
The car skidded into a snowbank.

Sometimes part of an idea is missing from a sentence. Then the group of words is a sentence fragment. A **sentence fragment** is a group of words that does not express a complete thought. For example, these are sentence fragments:

Caught a bass. (Who caught a bass?)
Our soccer team. (What about the team?)
Into a snowbank. (What happened?)

Exercise A   Number your paper from 1 to 10. For each group of words that is a sentence, write *S*. For each group of words that is a sentence fragment, write *F*.

F 1. Sang a duet.

S 2. The horses raced around the track.

F 3. A mysterious stranger.

F 4. Completed the jigsaw puzzle.

S 5. Mom drove through the car wash.

F 6. The smell of cinnamon.

S 7. Ben waited patiently.

F 8. Ads in the school newspaper.

S 9. Eric planted the seeds.

S 10. Where did Mildred go?

Exercise B   Follow the directions for Exercise A.

F 1. Scratched the paint on the fender.

S 2. Andrea won the tennis match.

S 3. The referee called a foul.

F 4. Drives a brown van.

F 5. A conference of senior citizens.

S 6. What made that noise?

F 7. Exhaust fumes from the cars.

F 8. Accepted the collect phone call.

S 9. Lee signed the receipt.

S 10. The wind whipped the trees.

Part 2 The Subject and the Predicate

Every sentence is made up of two basic parts: the subject and the predicate. The **subject** tells *who* or *what* the sentence is about. The **predicate** tells *what is done* or *what happens*.

Subject (Who or what)	Predicate (What is done or what happens)
A hurricane	hit Miami.
The teller at the desk	sounded the alarm.
Our track team	won the trophy.

Each of these sentences expresses a complete thought.

There is an easy way to remember the parts of a sentence. Think of the sentence as telling who did something or what happened. The subject tells *who* or *what*. The predicate tells *did* or *happened*.

387

duet or *what about* a conference of senior citizens).

Optional Practice

Present the following sentences and fragments, either on the chalkboard or on a worksheet. Have students write *S* or *F* to indicate whether each is a sentence or a fragment.

F 1. Entered the study hall

F 2. Jerry and his sisters

S 3. A button fell off your coat

F 4. The candidate for county clerk

F 5. Ate steak and salad

S 6. Bonnie is visiting a friend

S 7. The line for the movie was too long

F 8. Have three children in college now

F 9. All of Woody Allen's movies

F 10. Is already leaving for work

Extending the Lesson

Have students identify sentence fragments in a conversation from a short story or play. Have students identify what part of the sentence is missing, then complete each fragment.

Part 2

Objective

To identify subjects and predicates and to understand how these two parts make a complete sentence

Presenting the Lesson

1. Read and discuss pages 387–388. Go over the explanations of the

387

subject and the predicate on page 387. Study examples of sentences divided into subjects and predicates. Emphasize the definitions of the subject and the predicate on page 388.

2. Read the following sentences aloud. For each sentence, have students tell which part of the sentence tells *who or what did something*. Write those sentence parts in a column on the chalkboard. Then, ask students to tell which part of the sentence tells *what is done or what happened*. Write those sentence parts in a column at the right of the other one. When both columns are completed, ask students what title should appear above each column. Write *subject* and *predicate* at the top of the columns.

1. The wet <u>snow</u> <u>soaked</u> through my boots.
2. Bright <u>sunshine</u> <u>poured</u> in the windows.
3. <u>Everyone</u> in the bleachers <u>cheered</u>.
4. <u>Terry</u> <u>put</u> three scoops of ice cream in his dish.
5. The brilliant <u>ring</u> <u>flashed</u> on her finger.

3. Do Exercise A on page 388 orally with the class.

4. Assign and discuss Exercise B on pages 388–389.

Individualizing the Lesson

Less-Advanced Students

Have students copy ten sentences from a short story. Tell them to draw a line between the subject and the predicate.

Advanced Students

Have each student write five sentences about one of their favorite

Who or What	Did or Happened
The members of our band	led the parade.
The shortstop	tagged the runner.
That car	conserves gas.

The subject of the sentence tells *who* or *what* did something, or what the sentence is about.

The predicate of the sentence tells what is done or what happens.

Exercise A   Head two columns *Subject* and *Predicate*. Write the proper words from each sentence in the columns.

Example: My brother paints houses.

Subject	Predicate
My brother	paints houses.

1. A dozen jets| lined the runway.
2. Our coach| distributed information about scholarships.
3. Marsha| wears a digital watch.
4. Those trucks| carry produce to the city.
5. The surf| pounded the reef.
6. A lovely garden| surrounds the old hotel.
7. Today's newspaper| ran a story about the street fair.
8. Canoes| glided down the canal.
9. Ned| lost his wool mittens.
10. Auditions for the play| begin today.

Exercise B   Follow the directions for Exercise A.

1. Mindy's kite| soared over our heads.
2. The workers| poured new sidewalks.
3. Some animals| hibernate during the winter.
4. Steve| designed the set for our play.
5. That horror film| frightens many people.

388

6. A spring blizzard_S| blanketed_P the Midwest with snow.
7. The litter of puppies_S| whined_P all night.
8. Three of my friends_S| joined_P the volunteer group.
9. The rescue helicopter_S| landed_P in the jungle.
10. Karen_S| munched_P popcorn during the movie.

Part 3 Simple Subjects and Verbs

In every sentence, certain words are more important than the others. These words are the basic framework of the sentence. Look at these sentences once again:

Subject	Predicate
A **hurricane**	**hit** Miami.
The **teller** at the desk	**sounded** the alarm.
Our track **team**	**won** the trophy.

All the words in the subject part of the sentence are called the **complete subject.** Within the complete subject is a key word, the **simple subject.** In the last example above, *our track team* is the complete subject. *Team* is the simple subject.

The **complete predicate** is all the words that tell what was done or what happened. The key word within the complete predicate is the **simple predicate.** In the sentence about the track team, the complete predicate is *won the trophy.* The key word is *won.* *Won* is the simple predicate.

The key word in the subject of a sentence is called the simple subject. It is also called the *subject* of the verb.

The key word in the predicate is the simple predicate. The simple predicate is the verb.

Verbs that tell about an action are called **action verbs.** Some verbs tell about an action that can be seen.

The wheel *fell* off.   Jack *painted* my portrait.

Other action verbs tell of an action that cannot be seen.

389

Optional Practice

Place the following sentence parts on the board or on a worksheet. Have students identify each as a subject or a predicate. Have students add an appropriate subject or predicate to make a complete sentence out of each part.
Answers may vary.

P 1. finished the task in two hours

S 2. a jacket

S 3. some small towns on the coast

P 4. splattered the windshield

P 5. dribbled the ball across the court

Part 3

Objective

To identify the verb and its simple subject

Presenting the Lesson

1. Review the method learned in Part 2 for dividing a sentence into the subject and the predicate. Use the following sentences as examples.

The newly modernized building sold quickly.
The representative voted for higher taxes.

Divide these sentences into subjects and predicates and put them on the chalkboard.

2. Read page 389. Go over definitions of *complete subject, simple subject, complete predicate,* and *simple predicate.* Stress that when the words *subject* and *verb* are used, they refer to the simple subject and the simple predicate.

3. Read page 390. Go through the steps used to find the verb and its subject. Have students find the simple subjects and verbs in the two sentences on the board. Underline the verbs twice and the subject once.

4. Read pages 390–391 showing how to diagram subjects and predicates. Use the two sentences on the board to demonstrate how the subject and verb should be diagramed.

5. Do Exercise A on page 391 orally with the class.

6. Assign and discuss Exercise B on page 391.

Individualizing the Lesson

Less-Advanced Students

1. After students study page 389, have them write a brief explanation of the difference between a *complete subject* and a *simple subject*. Then have them write an explanation of the difference between a *complete predicate* and a *simple predicate*, or *verb*.

2. For Exercise B, page 391, have students follow the steps on page 390 in writing out their answers. Students should copy each sentence and write the verb separately on the next line. Then they should write *who* or *what* before the verb to identify the subject, and then write the subject.

Advanced Students

Have students write ten original sentences about anything they choose. Have students put parentheses around the complete subject

---

They *remembered* the answer.   Steven *thought* about the question.

Another kind of verb tells that something *is* or *exists*. These verbs are called **state-of-being verbs.**

The puppy *is* a dalmation.   The water *seemed* warm.

A verb is a word that shows action or state of being.

Finding the Verb and Its Subject

In any sentence, the verb and its subject are the most important words. Other words in the sentence tell more about these key words. To find the key words in any sentence, first find the verb. It tells what was done or what happened. Then ask *who* or *what* before the verb. That answer will give you the subject of the verb.

> The pilot of the plane signaled the tower.
> *Verb:* signaled
> *Who signaled?* pilot
> The subject is *pilot*.
> The boat sailed into the harbor.
> *Verb:* sailed
> *What sailed?* boat
> The subject is *boat*.

Diagraming Subjects and Verbs

A sentence diagram is a drawing of the parts of a sentence. It shows how the parts fit together.

A sentence diagram shows the importance of the subject and the verb. These key parts are placed on a horizontal main line. They are separated by a vertical line that crosses the main line. The subject appears before the verb. Later you will learn how every other word in the sentence has its own place in the diagram, too.

In diagraming, only words capitalized in the sentence are capitalized in the diagram. No punctuation is used.

Eric walked quickly.

Eric	walked

Lorraine studied the problem.

Lorraine	studied

Exercise A   Label two columns *Verb* and *Subject*. Number your paper from 1 to 10. For each sentence, write the verb and its subject.

1. George sealed the packages.
2. Some dancers practiced all afternoon.
3. Our tour of the museum includes a stop for lunch.
4. The Army nurses worked double shifts.
5. This stew needs onions.
6. Cary's sister plays racquetball twice a week.
7. Bright red spots covered the child's face.
8. A heart specialist performed the surgery.
9. This porch light attracts insects.
10. That ladder collapses easily.

Exercise B   Follow the directions for Exercise A.

1. The waiter took our dinner order.
2. Barbara Mandrell sang at the state fair.
3. Severe floods forced residents from their homes.
4. The bells in that tower ring every hour.
5. Two ducks swam across the lake.
6. The attendant at the gas station gave us a road map.
7. This restaurant serves lunch outdoors.
8. The sound of the alarm startled me.
9. Ice on the runway created a hazard.
10. A vendor at the gate sold balloons.

and complete predicate in each sentence; then have them underline the simple subject and verb.

Optional Practice

Place the following sentences on a worksheet. Have students underline the verbs twice and the subjects once.

1. The felt-tipped pen leaked in my pocket.
2. A Greek ocean liner cruised past the islands.
3. Many new medicines prevent serious epidemics.
4. The new passenger trains are quite luxurious.
5. Our newspaper landed in our neighbor's yard.
6. The leather on my boots scuffs easily.
7. The seniors at that school have their prom in May.
8. Drab, gray curtains blocked the beautiful view from the windows.
9. The players on the team practice daily.
10. The boys planted tomatoes in the garden.

Extending the Lesson

Do this exercise orally with the class. Challenge students to come up with as many sayings, expressions, or other phrases they use in everyday conversation as they can. Write each expression on the board; have students identify whether it is a sentence or fragment. If it is a sentence, have them find the complete subject, complete predicate, simple subject, and verb in each expression.

To identify main verbs, helping verbs, and separated parts of a verb

Presenting the Lesson

1. Read page 392. Go over the list of words frequently used as helping verbs and show how these may be used with main verbs. Stress that verbs often consist of more than one word. Read the explanation of separated parts of a verb and contractions. Study examples carefully.

2. Do Exercise A on page 393 orally. In identifying verbs, have students tell which are helping verbs and which are main verbs.

3. Assign and discuss Exercise B on page 393.

Individualizing the Lesson

Less-Advanced Students

1. Have students study the list of helping verbs on page 392, then have them close their books. Quiz the students—either orally or with a written test—on the list of helping verbs.

2. Have students go through their answers in Exercises A and B again, circling each helping verb.

Advanced Students

1. Have students write five sentences about a recent movie or television program. Tell them to be sure to use helping verbs in each sentence.

2. Have students circle all helping verbs and underline all main verbs in the sentences they wrote.

392

Part 4   The Parts of a Verb

A verb may consist of one word or several words. The verb may be composed of a **main verb** and one or more **helping verbs.**

Helping Verbs	+	Main Verb	=	Verb
shall		leave		shall leave
should		go		should go
is		talking		is talking
could have		found		could have found

To name the verb in any sentence, you must name all the words that make up the verb.

These words are frequently used as helping verbs:

am	are	have	will	may
is	be	do	would	might
was	has	does	can	shall
were	had	did	could	should

Separated Parts of a Verb

At times you will find words inserted between the parts of a verb. These words are not included in the verb. Look at the following sentences. The parts of the verb are in bold print.

> Laura **had** never **flown** before.
> My car **would** not **start** during the blizzard.
> This frame **will** easily **fit** that picture.

Some verbs are joined with other words to make contractions. In naming verbs that appear in contractions, pick out only the verb. The word *not* and its contraction *n't* are adverbs. They are never verb parts.

> Mark **did**n't **attend** the meeting. (*Did attend* is the verb.)
> Ms. Vernon **has**n't **ordered** the costumes yet. (*Has ordered* is the verb.)

392

Exercise A Number your paper from 1 to 10. List the verbs in the following sentences.

1. Several riders have not practiced their jumps.
2. The program hasn't begun yet.
3. I will never finish this project on time.
4. Sue has often attended council meetings.
5. They shouldn't arrive for at least another hour.
6. Larry will probably go to the concert.
7. This train has never been late.
8. Sara can usually do the algebra homework.
9. Marty can't go to the beach this afternoon.
10. I am still reading *The Scarlet Letter.*

Exercise B Follow the directions for Exercise A.

1. The artist was carefully cleaning her brushes.
2. The baseball season hasn't started yet.
3. Our dog doesn't usually bark at neighbors.
4. We couldn't even see the mountains through the fog.
5. The trailer was safely hitched to the car.
6. Jill could not remember the address.
7. Troops are sometimes stationed at this border.
8. George did not understand the chemistry experiment.
9. That store has never accepted credit cards.
10. Laura didn't really enjoy that movie.

Part 5 Subjects in Unusual Positions

The subject of a sentence usually comes before the verb. In some sentences, however, part or all of the verb comes before the subject.

To find the subject in any sentence, first find the verb. Then ask *who* or *what* before it. The answer will be the subject.

393

393

Presenting the Lesson

1. Ask students to look again at the sentences in Exercises A and B on page 393. Ask students in what order the subject and verb appear in each sentence. Stress that the usual word order is the subject first, followed by the verb. Tell students that now they will work with sentences in which the subject occurs in an unusual position.

2. Read pages 393–394. Study examples of each type of sentence beginning with *there*. Make certain that students understand the difference between the use of *there* as an introductory word and *there* used to explain the verb. Point out the difference in diagram positions of *there* when used in these two ways.

3. Do Exercise A on page 395 orally. Encourage students to follow the procedure suggested on page 393: 1) find the verb   2) ask *who* or *what* before it. The answer will be the subject.

4. Assign and discuss Exercise B on page 395.

5. Read pages 395–396. Go over examples of sentences beginning with *here*, questions, and sentences starting with phrases or other words. Note that unusual word order does not change the sentence diagram.

6. Read pages 396–397. Make sure that students understand the concept of the subject (*you*) understood.

7. Assign and discuss Exercises A and B on page 397.

Individualizing the Lesson

Less-Advanced Students

1. Make sure students understand the concept of *you under-*

Sentences Beginning with *There*

In sentences beginning with *there*, the verb often comes before the subject.

There is used in two ways. It may be used to tell something about the verb. It tells *where* something is.

> There are my boots. (*Boots* is the subject; *are* is the verb. *There* tells where the boots are.)

> There is the elevator. (*Elevator* is the subject; *is* is the verb. *There* tells where the elevator is.)

Sometimes *there* is used simply as an introductory word to get a sentence started.

> There was an air controllers' strike. (*Strike* is the subject; *was* is the verb.)

> There is an error in this article. (*Error* is the subject; *is* is the verb.)

To diagram sentences beginning with *there*, you must know if *there* tells *where* or is an introductory word. If *there* tells *where*, it belongs on a slanted line below the verb. If *there* is an introductory word, it belongs on a horizontal line above the subject.

There are the dancers.

There has been an accident.

Exercise A Write the <u>subject</u> and the <u>verb</u> in each sentence. Tell whether *there* is used to tell *where* or as an *introductory* word.

w 1. There <u>is</u> the stage <u>door</u>.

I 2. There <u>weren't</u> any <u>messages</u> for you.

w 3. There <u>is</u> the <u>Sears Tower</u>.

I 4. There <u>was</u> a <u>freeze</u> in Florida.

w 5. There <u>are</u> my new roller <u>skates</u>.

I 6. There <u>was</u> an <u>epidemic</u> of cholera.

w 7. There <u>is</u> the reptile <u>house</u>.

I 8. There <u>will be</u> cash <u>prizes</u>.

I 9. There <u>aren't</u> any <u>napkins</u> left.

I 10. There <u>will be</u> <u>rain</u> later today.

Exercise B Follow the directions for Exercise A.

I 1. There <u>was</u> an <u>elephant</u> in the parade.

w 2. There <u>is</u> the <u>exit</u>.

I 3. There <u>was</u> a <u>party</u> for my brother.

I 4. There <u>must have been</u> some <u>mistake</u>.

I 5. There <u>should have been</u> some <u>mail</u>.

w 6. There <u>are</u> my tennis <u>shoes</u>.

w 7. There <u>is</u> the grocery <u>store</u>.

I 8. There <u>is</u> never enough <u>ice</u>.

I 9. There <u>was</u> an <u>avalanche</u> near the ski resort.

w 10. There <u>is</u> the <u>key</u> to the mailbox.

Other Sentences with Unusual Word Order

Sentences beginning with *there* are just one kind of sentence with unusual word order. Here are some others.

1. **Sentences beginning with *here***

   Here comes the sun. (*Sun* is the subject; *comes* is the verb.)

   Here is the bus. (*Bus* is the subject; *is* is the verb.)

stood. Have them apply the concept to the following sentences.

1. Eat more slowly.
2. Save me an apple for dessert.
3. Down poured the rain.

2. Have students copy each sentence when doing Exercises A and B, page 395. Then have them write each verb beneath the sentence and the *who* or *what* question that helps them identify the subject. Then have them write the subject.

Advanced Students

Have students suggest as many sentences using the word *there* as they can. *There* can be in any position in the sentence. Write the sentences on the board. Have the students decide if *there* is *introductory* or if it explains the verb, and why.

Optional Practice

Have students locate the subjects and verbs in the following sentences. Students should underline the verb twice and the subject once.

1. Into the alley <u>darted</u> the <u>runner</u>.
2. There <u>is</u> a <u>crowd</u> in the auditorium.
(You) 3. <u>Eat</u> your spinach right now.
4. Across the field <u>ran</u> the <u>children</u>.
5. Here <u>is</u> my favorite picnic <u>spot</u>.
6. There <u>was</u> a severe <u>thunderstorm</u> last night.
(You) 7. <u>Bring</u> your finished work up to the desk.
8. Here <u>is</u> a <u>basket</u> of fresh eggs.
9. Eagerly <u>flocked</u> the hungry <u>birds</u>.
10. There <u>can be</u> no <u>exceptions</u> to the rules.

Have students write ten sentences following the directions listed below. Students should underline the verbs twice and the subjects once in each sentence.

1. two sentences beginning with *there*
2. two sentences beginning with *here*
3. two questions
4. two sentences giving commands
5. two sentences beginning with phrases or other words

The word *here* always tells *where* about the verb. It is not used as an introductory word.

2. Questions

Have you eaten? (*You* is the subject; *have eaten* is the verb.)

Will Mike be waiting for us? (*Mike* is the subject; *will be waiting* is the verb.)

3. Sentences starting with phrases or other words

Up the hill lurched the old car. (*Car* is the subject; *lurched* is the verb.)

Gently flows the river. (*River* is the subject; *flows* is the verb.)

When you are looking for the subject in a sentence with unusual word order, first find the verb. Then ask *who* or *what* before the verb.

Here are the tools.
Verb: are
Who or what are? tools
Subject: tools

Unusual word order in a sentence does not change the sentence diagram. The verb and the subject are still placed on the horizontal main line with the subject first and then the verb.

Around the bend raced the cyclist.

cyclist	raced

Sentences Giving Commands

In sentences that give commands, the subject is usually not stated. Since commands are always given to the person spoken to, the subject is *you*. The word *you* is not stated, but it is *understood*.

Help yourself. (*You* is the subject of *help*.)

Turn right at the corner. (*You* is the subject of *turn*.)

To diagram a sentence giving a command, place the subject *you* in parentheses.

Write soon.

Exercise A Label two columns *Subject* and *Verb*. Number your paper from 1 to 10. Write the <u>subject</u> and <u>verb</u> for each sentence.

1. Here <u>is</u> an extension <u>cord</u>.
(You)2. <u>Open</u> all the windows.
3. <u>Are</u> the <u>roads</u> icy?
4. Here <u>is</u> the paperback book <u>section</u>.
5. Out of the bag <u>tumbled</u> the <u>groceries</u>.
6. <u>Can</u> <u>you</u> <u>hear</u> the crickets?
(You)7. <u>Plant</u> the marigolds near the porch.
8. Here <u>comes</u> <u>Jim</u> on his bicycle.
(You)9. Into the water <u>fell</u> my <u>sunglasses</u>.
10. <u>Try</u> some of this chili.

Exercise B Follow the directions for Exercise A.

(You)1. <u>Look</u> at this gift from my dad.
2. Where <u>is</u> <u>Julia</u>?
3. Out of the sky <u>dropped</u> a <u>parachute</u>.
4. Into the cave <u>walked</u> the <u>explorers</u>.
5. Here <u>is</u> my ticket <u>stub</u>.
(You)6. Don't <u>forget</u> your plane tickets.
7. <u>Have</u> the <u>scissors</u> been <u>found</u> yet?
8. Through the dark tunnel <u>raced</u> the <u>roller</u> coaster.
9. Here <u>is</u> the last <u>piece</u> of the puzzle.
10. <u>May</u> <u>Elizabeth</u> <u>go</u> to the art fair?

Part 6

Objectives

1. To identify and understand the functions of direct objects and indirect objects

2. To differentiate between transitive and intransitive verbs

Presenting the Lesson

1. Review with students the definition of a *complete sentence*. Remind students that although a sentence must have a subject and a verb, it must also express a complete thought. Use the following examples to point out that sometimes a subject and verb alone are not enough to express a complete thought.

> Maria prepared _____
> Greg wanted _____
> The worker lifted _____

Explain that sometimes the action of the verb is incomplete without another word or words to complete the meaning. Ask students to offer words to complete the three sentences above.

2. Read page 398 and discuss how a direct object completes the meaning of a sentence by completing the action of the verb. Be sure that students understand how to locate direct objects.

3. Read the discussion of *transitive* and *intransitive verbs* on page 399. Spend some time discussing the meaning of the words *transitive* and *intransitive*. Ask students what a transit system does. Students will probably relate *transit* to the movement or carrying of people on buses and trains. Explain that *transit* is

Some verbs do not need other words to complete their meaning in a sentence. The action they describe is complete.

> The team *cheered*.   The car usually *starts*.
> Craig *was leaving*.   The storm *will end*.

There are other verbs that do not express a complete action by themselves. These verbs need other words to complete their meaning.

> Lisa tossed _____. (Tossed what?)
> Mr. Wright mailed _____. (Mailed what?)

Direct Objects

One kind of word that completes the meaning of a verb is the direct object. A **direct object** receives the action of the verb.

> Lisa tossed the *salad*.
> Mr. Wright mailed the *package*.

In the sentences above, *salad* receives the action of *tossed*. *Package* receives the action of *mailed*.

A direct object can also tell the *result* of an action.

> The farmer raised *soybeans*.
> Robert Cormier wrote a *book*.

When you are looking for a direct object, first find the verb. Then ask *whom* or *what* after it.

> Martha telephoned Amy.
> *Verb:* telephoned
> *Telephoned whom?* Amy
> *Direct object:* Amy

> Matt ordered a sandwich.
> *Verb:* ordered
> *Ordered what?* sandwich
> *Direct object:* sandwich

When a verb has a direct object, the verb is a **transitive verb.** When a verb does not have a direct object, the verb is an **intransitive verb.** Notice the difference in these sentences:

> The ice cream melted. (*Melted* is intransitive. It has no direct object.)

> Bert discovered the solution. (*Discovered* is transitive. It has a direct object, *solution.*)

Some verbs may be intransitive in one sentence and transitive in another.

> Intransitive: The police officer stopped.
> Transitive: The police officer stopped the car.

Transitive or Intransitive?

Look at the following sentences. Are the verbs transitive or intransitive?

> Dick *sang* softly.
> Dick *sang* in the variety show.
> Dick *sang* a solo.

In the first two examples, the verb *sang* has no direct object. In those sentences, *sang* is intransitive. However, in the third sentence, if you ask *whom* or *what* after the verb, you find that *solo* is the direct object. In that sentence, *sang* is a transitive verb.

> Dick sang a solo.
> *Verb:* sang
> *Sang what?* solo
> *Direct object:* solo

Exercise A Number your paper from 1 to 10. For each sentence, write the direct object of the verb.

1. A clown walked the tightrope.
2. Mr. Benson donated a turkey for the raffle.

399

from Latin, meaning "to go across, or pass." A transitive verb is one whose action goes across or is passed to an object. Make certain that students understand the meaning of *intransitive*, especially its prefix *in-*, meaning *not*. Carefully study examples of verbs which can be transitive or intransitive, depending upon their context.

4. Assign and discuss Exercises A and B on pages 399–400. In Exercise B, have students identify the direct objects in all sentences containing transitive verbs.

5. Read pages 400–401. Discuss the function and position of indirect objects, and the way to identify them in sentences. Study the examples of diagrams of direct and indirect objects.

6. Assign and discuss Exercises A and B on pages 401–402.

Individualizing the Lesson

Less-Advanced Students

1. Review both direct and indirect objects with the students.

2. Have students write a brief paragraph explaining the difference between a transitive and an intransitive verb.

3. Work through Exercise A, pages 401–402, orally with the students. Then have them complete Exercise B, page 402, on their own.

Advanced Students

1. Have each student write ten sentences—five with direct objects and five with indirect objects.

2. Have students underline each direct object once and each indirect object twice. Then have them circle transitive verbs and put intransitive verbs in brackets.

Optional Practice

Have students complete the action of the verbs in the following sentences according to the directions in parentheses. Answers will vary.

1. Sam won _____. (transitive with direct object)
2. In an interview, reporters asked _____. (transitive with direct object and indirect object)
3. The firemen rescued _____. (transitive with direct object)
4. The alarm clock tells _____. (transitive with direct object and indirect object)
5. For lunch, Mom serves _____. (transitive with direct object)

Extending the Lesson

Have students diagram the following sentences. Students need to position only the subject, verb, and object in the diagram.

1. Marty wrote letters.
2. Ken served us dinner.
3. Barbara brought us Cokes.
4. Everyone thanked her.
5. The bus has arrived.

3. Mary Jo has accepted the <u>award</u> for the team.
4. Chris usually brings the <u>volleyball</u>.
5. After dinner, I will finish my <u>project</u>.
6. Play another <u>song</u> on the juke box.
7. Mom appreciated the <u>flowers</u>.
8. I forgot the <u>coupons</u>.
9. Michele answered the <u>question</u> thoughtfully.
10. Jeff studies <u>business</u> in college.

Exercise B   Number your paper from 1 to 10. Decide whether the verb in each sentence is *Transitive* or *Intransitive*.

T 1. Ann can speak Chinese.
I 2. The auctioneer speaks rapidly.
I 3. Sam ate early today.
T 4. Hank ate lunch at noon.
I 5. The electrician climbed to the top of the tower.
T 6. Marcy climbed the ladder.
I 7. The sunbathers roasted in the tropical sun.
T 8. The boys roasted the corn on the grill.
T 9. Mike drives a Fiat.
I 10. Gayle drives carefully.

Indirect Objects

In addition to direct objects, some sentences also have **indirect objects** of the verb. Indirect objects sometimes tell *to whom* or *to what* about the verb. At other times they tell *for whom* or *for what* about the verb.

> Sue gave **Len** the *gift*. (gave *to* Len)
>
> The guide showed **us** the *landmarks*. (showed *to* us)
>
> Linda made **me** a hot fudge *sundae*. (made *for* me)

The words *Len, us,* and *me* are indirect objects. The direct objects are in italics. Indirect objects appear only in sentences with direct objects. Indirect objects are found between the verb and direct object. Never use the words *to* or *for* with an indirect object.

> Mark showed the driver his bus pass. (*Driver* is the indirect object of *showed.*)
>
> Mark showed his bus pass to the driver. (*Driver* is not an indirect object.)

In a diagram, place a direct object on the main line after the verb. The vertical line between the verb and object does not go below the main line.

> Marilyn wrote a letter.

The indirect object belongs on a horizontal line attached below the verb.

> Marilyn wrote the newspaper a letter.

Exercise A   Number your paper from 1 to 10. Label three columns *Verb,* *Indirect Object,* and *Direct Object*. For each of the following sentences list those parts. Not all sentences will have all three parts.

Example: The waitress brought me the check.

Verb	Indirect Object	Direct Object
brought	me	check

1. The artist <u>drew</u> (us) a <u>sketch</u>.
2. Joe <u>tossed</u> (Jill) the <u>Frisbee</u>.

3. Pay the (manager) the <u>rent</u> on the first of the month.
4. Grace <u>prepared</u> <u>chicken</u> for lunch.
5. Max <u>told</u> (us) the bad <u>news</u>.
6. Someone <u>handed</u> (Rose) a free <u>sample</u> of pizza.
7. <u>Send</u> (Bob) a <u>postcard</u> from Florida.
8. Peggy <u>practiced</u> her <u>serve</u> all afternoon.
9. The nurse <u>gave</u> the (patient) a <u>shot</u>.
10. The audience <u>gave</u> the (speaker) a warm <u>round</u> of applause.

Exercise B Follow the directions for Exercise A.

1. The police officer <u>wrote</u> (Bill) a <u>ticket</u>.
2. Marty <u>left</u> his <u>pole</u> on the boat.
3. Carrie <u>called</u> <u>me</u> from a phone booth.
4. Collin <u>read</u> (us) the <u>review</u>.
5. <u>Give</u> the (plants) some <u>water</u>.
6. That bakery <u>makes</u> delicious rye <u>bread</u>.
7. The quarterback <u>passed</u> the <u>football</u>.
8. <u>Bring</u> (me) the <u>saucepan</u>.
9. The golfer <u>chipped</u> his <u>ball</u> onto the green.
10. Did Mom <u>save</u> (me) a <u>piece</u> of pie?

Objectives

1. To recognize linking verbs
2. To recognize predicate words: predicate nouns, predicate pronouns, and predicate adjectives
3. To distinguish between predicate words and direct objects

Presenting the Lesson

1. Read pages 402–403. Go over the definition and examples of linking verbs. Point out how they differ

Part 7 Linking Verbs and Predicate Words

Not all verbs express action. Some tell of a state of being. These verbs link the subject with a word or group of words in the predicate. Verbs that link the subject with another word are called **linking verbs.**

Luke *is* a tenor.   Charlotte *must be* upset.
We *are* the losers.   The children *were* happy.

The verb *be* is the most commonly used linking verb and has many forms. This list will help you to become familiar with them.

be   been   is   was
being   am   are   were

The verbs *be*, *being*, and *been* can also be used with helping verbs. These are examples:

should be   were being   had been
may be   was being   could have been
will be   is being   might have been

Words that are linked to the subject by linking verbs are called **predicate words.** The three kinds of predicate words are **predicate nouns, predicate pronouns,** and **predicate adjectives.** Predicate words tell something about the subject.

Nancy is a *drummer*. (predicate noun)

That was *she*. (predicate pronoun)

Warren was *calm*. (predicate adjective)

In the above sentences, the subjects and predicate words are linked by the verbs *is* and *was*.

Here are some other common linking verbs.

appear   seem   sound   grow
feel   look   taste   become

Like *be*, these linking verbs have various forms (*grew, looked, tastes*). Linking verbs can also be used with helping verbs (*will become, can seem, might have sounded*).

The record *sounded* scratchy.

The juice *tasted* fresh.

Fran *has become* a fine swimmer.

In a sentence diagram, place a predicate word on the main line after the verb. A slanted line above the main line separates the verb from the predicate word. That line, like the predicate word, points back to the subject.

from action verbs dealt with in Part 6. Go over the definition and examples of predicate words. Stress the difference between predicate words, which rename or describe the subject, and objects, which complete the action of the verb.

2. Read pages 403–404. Go over examples of diagrams of sentences with linking verbs and predicate words.

3. Read pages 404–405. Go over the differences between action verbs with direct objects and linking verbs with predicate words.

4. Assign and discuss Exercise A on page 405. Have students tell whether each predicate word is a predicate noun or pronoun (renaming the subject) or a predicate adjective (describing the subject).

5. Assign and discuss Exercise B on page 405.

Individualizing the Lesson

Less-Advanced Students

1. Review with students the difference between a direct object and a predicate word.

2. Have students write five sentences containing a linking verb and a predicate word. Students should circle the linking verb and underline the predicate word.

3. Have students write five sentences containing a direct object. Students should circle each direct object.

Advanced Students

1. Have students write ten sentences—five containing direct objects and five containing predicate words.

2. Then have students circle each direct object and bracket each predicate word. Students should then draw an arrow to the verb (in the case of a direct object) and to the subject (in the case of a predicate word).

Optional Practice

Have students underline verbs in the following sentences and label them *Linking Verb* or *Action Verb*. Students should mark *DO* over direct objects and *PW* over predicate words.

1. The book was very realistic. (L, PW)
2. Mothers give advice. (A, DO)
3. The winner appeared shocked. (L, PW)
4. Hugh is playing drums in the band. (A, DO)
5. He will become a professional musician. (L, PW)
6. Andrea is a loyal friend. (L, PW)
7. Mr. Harris was my math teacher. (L, PW)
8. Gail found the missing letter. (A, DO)
9. Tim read the sports pages. (A, DO)
10. Chris took first place in the contest. (A, DO)

Extending the Lesson

Have students write sentences using the following linking verbs.

1. will be
2. appeared
3. became
4. felt
5. sounds
6. looks

Dr. Weaver is a surgeon.

That bus looks empty.

Direct Object or Predicate Word?

A verb may be completed in one of two ways. It may have a direct object, or it may have a predicate word. How can you tell the difference between a predicate word and a direct object?

The verb is the key word. Decide whether the verb is an action verb. If it is, the word following the verb that tells *whom* or *what* is a direct object.

> The florist arranged the flowers. (*Arranged* is an action verb. *Flowers* is its direct object.)

> The dog chewed my slipper. (*Chewed* is an action verb. *Slipper* is its direct object.)

Is the verb a linking verb? If it is, the word following the verb that tells about the subject is a predicate word.

> Alexander Godunov is a *dancer*. (*Is* is a linking verb. *Dancer* is a predicate word.)

> These potatoes seem *dry*. (*Seem* is a linking verb. *Dry* is a predicate word.)

Read the following sentences.

> Ms. Edwards is a lawyer.

> Ms. Edwards called a lawyer.

The first sentence contains a linking verb, *is*. The word *lawyer* follows the linking verb and tells about the subject. *Lawyer* is a predicate word. In the second sentence, *called* is an action verb. In this sentence, *lawyer* tells *whom* about the action verb. *Lawyer* is a direct object.

Exercise A   Label three columns *Subject, Linking Verb,* and *(Predicate Word.)* Find these parts in the following sentences and write them in the proper columns.

1. These boots are (warm.)
2. The crew looked (weary.)
3. Parents were the (sponsors.)
4. Those puzzles were (easy.)
5. The yogurt tasted (tart.)
6. The ocean seems (rough.)
7. Lance must be (nervous.)
8. The winner is (he.)
9. Judy will become (captain.)
10. These old chairs are (antiques.)

Exercise B   Make four columns. Head the columns *Subject, Verb, Direct Object,* and *Predicate Word.* Find these parts in the following sentences and place them in the proper columns. Remember, no sentence can contain a direct object *and* a predicate word.

1. The Bears are a football team. [PW]
2. Their home is Chicago. [PW]
3. They were finalists in 1977. [PW]
4. They lost the play-off game. [DO]
5. The team has had several unsuccessful seasons. [DO]
6. However, their fans are loyal. [PW]
7. They support the Bears every year. [DO]
8. Most games are sellouts. [PW]
9. The Bears beat San Diego in overtime in 1981. [DO]
10. Someday the Bears will be champions. [PW]

Objective

To identify and form compound sentence parts

Presenting the Lesson

1. Review the sentence parts covered thus far: subject, verb, direct object, indirect object, and predicate word. Explain that any of these sentence parts may be compound. Read page 406. Be sure that students understand the meaning of *compound* and *conjunction*.

2. Put the following sentences on the board. Have students identify the sentence part indicated in parentheses.

1. Jane Fonda and Robert Redford starred in the movie. (subject)
2. The birds chirped and warbled all night. (verb)
3. Joe ordered tacos, a tamale, and a burrito. (direct object)
4. Mr. Downs offered Ryan and me a job. (indirect object)
5. Mike looks tall and handsome in his new suit. (predicate word)

3. Read and discuss pages 406–407, studying diagrams carefully.

4. Assign and discuss Exercises A and B on page 408.

Individualizing the Lesson

Less-Advanced Students

Work through Exercise A, page 408, orally with the students.

Advanced Students

Have students choose one sentence from each of the previous exercises on verbs, direct objects,

Part 8 Compound Parts in a Sentence

Compound means "made up of two or more parts."

Each of the sentence parts described so far in this section can be compound—subjects, verbs, direct objects, indirect objects, and predicate words.

Join the two parts of a compound construction with a conjunction (*and, or, but*). If a compound construction has three or more parts, the conjunction comes between the last two parts.

Compound Subject:	Jan, Ramon, and Lisa will arrive soon.
Compound Verb:	They will sing and dance for us.
Direct Object:	Jan will bring the guitars and castanets.
Indirect Object:	Maybe Ramon will show you and me how to use castanets.
Predicate Words:	Those three are the best Spanish dancers and singers I've ever seen.

Diagraming Compound Subjects

To diagram compound subjects, split the subject line. Place the conjunction on a dotted line connecting the subjects.

Bottles, cans, and papers littered the park.

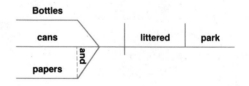

Diagraming Compound Verbs

To diagram compound verbs, split the verb line in the same way.

The tourist waved, whistled, and shouted for a taxi.

Diagraming Compound Objects

To diagram compound direct objects or indirect objects, split the object line.

Clara bought a watermelon and some peaches. (compound direct object)

Mr. Maltas gave Chuck and Bob a catalog.

Diagraming Compound Predicate Words

To diagram compound predicate words, split the predicate word line.

The new co-captains are Kirsten and Claudia. (compound predicate word)

indirect objects, subjects, and predicate words. Have them add a conjunction and a word of their choice to turn these parts into compounds.

Optional Practice

Have students write ten original sentences, two with compound subjects, two with compound verbs, two with compound direct objects, two with compound indirect objects, and two with compound predicate words.

Extending the Lesson

Have students find one published example of a use of each of the compound sentence parts.

407

Exercise A As your teacher directs, show the compound parts in the following sentences. Tell whether they are compound subjects, verbs, objects, or predicate words.

1. Boston and Philadelphia were two stops on our trip.
   <small>S   S</small>
2. Lee cut and raked the lawn.
   <small>V   V</small>
3. Joshua is the secretary and treasurer of the tennis club.
   <small>PW   PW</small>
4. Kelly put raisins and cinnamon into the bread.
   <small>DO   DO</small>
5. Mr. Simmons wrote and directed the play.
   <small>V   V</small>
6. Dad planted maples, elms, and lilacs in the yard.
   <small>DO   DO   DO</small>
7. Spring and fall are her favorite seasons.
   <small>S   S</small>
8. The decorators painted the kitchen, the hallway, and the porch.
   <small>DO   DO   DO</small>
9. The carpet was soft and thick.
   <small>S   PW   PW</small>
10. Dancers and musicians from many different countries entertained us.
    <small>S   S</small>

Exercise B For each of the following sentences, make the part noted in parentheses compound. Write the new sentences. <small>Sentences will vary.</small>

  Example: The parakeet whistled all afternoon. (*verb*)
  The parakeet whistled and chattered all afternoon.

1. Marilyn wrote several songs for the musical. (*subject*)
2. The cook tasted the stew. (*verb*)
3. Brian bought some new jeans. (*direct object*)
4. The apples were crisp. (*predicate adjective*)
5. The coach congratulated the players. (*subject*)
6. Dave sang in the variety show. (*verb*)
7. The day was chilly. (*predicate word*)
8. Liz brought the badminton set. (*subject*)
9. The fire chief gave the students a talk on fire prevention. (*indirect object*)
10. Nellie toasted the muffins. (*direct object*)

Part 9 Kinds of Sentences

There are several different reasons for using sentences. Sometimes you want to state something. Sometimes you want to ask a question. At other times, you want to give a command. There are also times when you want to express strong feeling. In each case, you use a different kind of sentence.

A **declarative sentence** makes a statement. It ends with a period (.).

> The guard patrolled the grounds.
> We saw that movie on TV.

An **interrogative sentence** asks a question. It ends with a question mark (?).

> Have the guests arrived?   When is the test?

An **imperative sentence** gives a command. It usually ends with a period.

> Turn left at the stoplight.   Please pass the pepper.

An **exclamatory sentence** expresses strong emotion. It ends with an exclamation point (!).

> You saved the day!   What a great game that was!

Exercise A   For each of the following sentences, write *Declarative, Interrogative, Imperative,* or *Exclamatory* to show what kind each is. Add the proper punctuation mark.

D 1. John paints with watercolors.
Ex 2. What a surprise this is!
Int 3. Was the pizza delivered on time?
Imp 4. Rewind the tape, please.
Int 5. Which picture do you prefer?
D 6. Debby finished the crossword puzzle.
Imp 7. Don't take too long.
Imp 8. Go out the back way.

Part 9

Objective

To recognize the four kinds of sentences (declarative, interrogative, imperative, and exclamatory) and to use the proper end punctuation with each

Presenting the Lesson

1. Read and discuss page 409. Go over the definitions and examples of the four kinds of sentences. Stress the purpose of each. In discussing imperative sentences, refer students to pages 396–397.

Review the subjects (*you*) understood in imperative sentences. Ask students to give several examples of each kind of sentence and the end punctuation required.

2. Assign and discuss Exercises A and B on pages 409–410.

Individualizing the Lesson

Less-Advanced Students

Have students find one published example of each kind of sentence.

Advanced Students

Have students write a paragraph about a recent school event. Tell them to include at least one example of each kind of sentence in the paragraph.

Optional Practice

Have students identify the kind of sentence for each of the following, adding the proper end punctuation.

Imp 1. Close your books now.
Int 2. Have you finished?
D 3. Lunch is ready.

409

Int 4. Who called?
Imp 5. Take two aspirin and rest.
E 6. Do I feel awful!
D 7. My family is taking a vacation.
D 8. Elizabeth is finishing her homework.
E 9. What a storm we had!
Int 10. Is that the final question?

Extending the Lesson

Have students rewrite the following sentences to make them the kind indicated in parentheses.

1. All of the papers are soaked. (interrogative)
2. Will you please stand? (imperative)
3. Have the ballots been counted? (declarative)
4. Please stop talking. (interrogative)
5. What a mess we have made! (declarative)

1. Are all of the papers soaked?
2. Please stand.
3. The ballots have been counted.
4. Will you please stop talking?
5. We have made a mess.

Part 10

Objective

To recognize and form sentences using the five basic sentence patterns

Presenting the Lesson

1. Write the following pairs of sentences on the board.

Sandy and Paul sing well together.
The senior class graduated in June.
Birds eat worms.
The fire did much damage.
Carlotta became the manager.

410

Int 9. Does Harry play tennis?
D 10. Carol fed the goldfish.

Exercise B   Follow the directions for Exercise A.

Ex 1. What a ride that was!
D 2. The parrot squawked at the visitors.
Int 3. Is that your umbrella?
D 4. The storm damaged the crops.
Imp 5. Be ready for anything.
Ex 6. What a team we have!
Int 7. When does the bank open?
D 8. Jane filed the documents.
D 9. Roger typed his report.
Int 10. Does anyone need a pen?

Part 10   Basic Sentence Patterns

Words can be organized into sentences in an endless number of ways. However, most sentences follow certain basic **sentence patterns.** The five patterns that follow are the most common ones.

Study each sentence pattern carefully. Try to think of an example of your own for each pattern.

Pattern One

This is the simplest type of sentence. It has a subject and a verb. The subject is usually a noun or pronoun. In this chart, N stands for the noun (or pronoun) in the complete subject. V stands for the verb in the complete predicate.

N	V
Time	flies.
She	studied hard.
Our neighbor	runs daily.

410

Pattern Two

In this pattern, the noun (or pronoun) that follows the verb is a direct object.

N	V	N
The detective	solved	the crime.
Laura	lost	her favorite ring.
The tutor	helped	us.

Pattern Three

Two nouns follow the verb in this pattern. The first is an *indirect object*. The second is a *direct object*.

N	V	N	N
Kathy	told	me	a joke.
Nobody	would give	us	information.
The jockey	gave	the horse	an apple.

Pattern Four

The verb in this pattern is a *linking verb* (LV). The noun that follows it is a *predicate noun* (or predicate pronoun).

N	LV	N
That notebook	is	yours.
The play	was	a success.

Pattern Five

In this sentence pattern, a linking verb is followed by a *predicate adjective* (Adj).

N	LV	Adj
Ballet	is	graceful.
The water	was	icy.
The test	will be	complicated.

Rocky is the champion.

Tell students that while the subject matter or meaning of the two sentences in each pair is quite different, the two sentences in each pair are similar in the way they are constructed. The two sentences in each pair follow the same pattern.

In each sentence on the board, underline the subject once, the verb twice, circle the direct objects, and place a box around predicate words. Ask students if they can now see the similarity between the sentences in each pair. Explain that this Section will acquaint students with five common sentence patterns.

2. Read pages 410–411. For each pattern, study the examples and have students offer additional examples. Point out that a basic pattern is not affected by compound sentence parts, helping verbs, or modifiers.

3. Do Exercise A on page 412 together as a class activity. Send students to the board to answer each item. Have students write the sentences on the chalkboard, separating it into parts and labeling them.

4. Assign and discuss Exercise B on page 412.

Individualizing the Lesson

Less-Advanced Students

Complete Exercise A, page 412, with the class. Then have students complete Exercise B on their own.

Advanced Students

Have students find a published example of each kind of sentence pattern.

Optional Practice

Present the following sentences on a worksheet, leaving space between sentences. Have students mark the sentence patterns above the appropriate parts.

    1. Mom repaired the broken table.
          N   V   N

    2. Beth cried after the race.
         N   V

    3. Heavy rain and floods spoiled our vacation.
           N   N   V

    4. Nancy's coat is purple and black.
         N   LV Adj   Adj

    5. A volunteer gave us hot soup.
         N   V N   N

    6. Ms. Reyes is the chairperson.
  N   N

(You) 7. Close the window.
        V   N

    8. Jonas Salk developed the polio vaccine.
       N   N

    9. The frightened dog dashed into the street.
              N   V

  10. My sister knitted me a warm sweater.
      N   V   N   N

Extending the Lesson

Have students write two sentences for each of the five sentence patterns. All ten sentences should be labeled according to the sentence patterns.

Exercise A   Tell which sentence pattern is used in each sentence.

1. The gardener trimmed the hedge. N V N
2. The Cubs were the winners. N LV N
3. Food was plentiful. N LV Adj
4. Sean talks softly. N V
5. The oysters are raw. N LV Adj
6. Martha waxed her surfboard. N V N
7. Ralph showed us his experiment. N V N N
8. The valley flooded. N V
9. These shoes seem tight. N LV Adj
10. Those flowers are geraniums. N LV N

Exercise B   Follow the directions for Exercise A.

1. The milk tastes sour. N LV Adj
2. The train left already. N V
3. Elliott collects toy soldiers. N V N
4. Maggie gave Dirk a souvenir. N V N N
5. Japan is an island. N LV N
6. Paul gave Andy some advice. N V N N
7. These vegetables are fresh. N LV Adj
8. The book was a biography. N LV N
9. James left early. N V
10. Ed signed Mary's cast. N V N

ADDITIONAL EXERCISES

The Sentence and Its Parts

A. Sentences and Fragments Number your paper from 1 to 10. For each group of words that is a sentence, write *S*. For each sentence fragment, write *F*. In class, be ready to add words to change fragments into sentences.

S 1. Rachel floated on her back.

F 2. Tossed the mitt into the air.

S 3. The glass of water is too full.

F 4. Large, lazy flakes of snow.

S 5. Derrick took the engine out of the car.

S 6. Speed is important in soccer.

S 7. Are the top bleachers full?

F 8. Are moving to Texas.

F 9. Several old exercise mats.

S 10. Stephanie answered.

B. Complete Subjects and Complete Predicates Number your paper from 1 to 10. Label two columns *Complete Subject* and *Complete Predicate*. Write the proper words in each column.

1. One passenger|would not move from the doorway.

2. Contact lenses|can be a nuisance.

3. Sam's best friends|go to a different school.

4. Truckers from all over|gathered at Mel's.

5. The Navy|was recruiting here.

6. Goats|will eat almost anything.

7. The pens without caps|dried up.

8. This street|is noisy in summer.

9. Those small radios|are also popular.

10. Natives of Peru|are called Peruvians.

413

Additional Exercises

These Additional Exercises may be used for additional practice of the concepts presented in this Section. Each exercise focuses on a single concept, and should be used after the page number indicated in parentheses.

Review

If you have not assigned these Additional Exercises before this time, you can also use them as an excellent Section Review.

C. Verbs and Simple Subjects Number your paper from 1 to 10. Write the simple subject and the verb in each sentence.

1. The big race is at Indianapolis.
2. The two trainers disagreed.
3. Dirty grease coated the machine.
4. Wet towels belong in the bin by the showers.
5. A red bandana hung from his pocket.
6. Few words begin with *x*.
7. An inspector from city hall visited the building.
8. The plumber parked her truck in front of the house.
9. A fire in the tunnel delayed the trains.
10. Caroline oiled the chains of her bike.

D. The Parts of a Verb Number your paper from 1 to 10. Write the verb in each sentence. Include helping verbs.

1. Tony had recently sold his car.
2. You may certainly react differently.
3. The disc jockey was reading a list of dedications.
4. Vacation has finally begun.
5. The manager did not return Jeff's call.
6. Someone is standing by the window.
7. Most dentists have used high-speed drills for years.
8. I can't really explain that.
9. The class lists have been printed.
10. Plastic would probably have melted.

E. Subjects and Verbs in Sentences with *There* Number your paper from 1 to 10. Write the subject and verb in each sentence. Tell whether *there* tells *where* or is an introductory word.

I 1. There will be several new courses.
I 2. There is no more salad.
W 3. There are your skates under the bench.
W 4. There is a good place for the tent.

l 5. There was a quiz in history this morning.

l 6. There is a conflict in your schedule.

l 7. There was not enough time for warm-up exercises.

w 8. There is the opener.

l 9. There have been many floods this spring.

w 10. There goes Jody.

F. Sentences with Unusual Order   Number your paper from
1 to 10. Label two columns *Subject* and *Verb*. Write the subject and
verb for each sentence.

   1. Here is a secret compartment.

   2. Has Amy proved her point?

   3. Beside our house sits a tractor.

(You) 4. Fry the eggs for five minutes.

   5. In the last row sat Heidi.

   6. Can you read blueprints?

   7. Here are the attendance sheets.

(You) 8. Hold your hand out.

   9. Finally came the sports announcements.

   10. Into the street ran the child.

G.   Direct Objects   Number your paper from 1 to 10. If a sentence has a direct object, write the direct object. If a sentence has
no direct object, write *Intransitive Verb*.

   1. Tamara asked good questions.

   2. The coach threw a party after the victory.

l 3. The clock had stopped.

   4. Clean the brushes in soapy water.

l 5. Aaron dodged.

   6. Kenny dodged the ball too late.

   7. The Davises have adopted another child.

   8. Nina needs some encouragement.

l 9. Act quickly.

   10. The carpenters have finished the new porch.

415

H. Sentence Parts Label three columns *Verb,* *(Indirect Object,)* and *Object*. For each of the following sentences fill in those parts that you find. After each verb write *Transitive* or *Intransitive*.

T 1. The bank gave (Lyle) a loan.

T 2. The teacher handed each (student) a newspaper.

T 3. The painters trampled the garden.

T 4. Bud gave the (table) a coat of lavender paint.

T 5. Some drugstores sell food.

T 6. A door-to-door salesperson sold (Al) a vacuum.

I 7. Betsy walks quickly.

T 8. I wrote the (President) a letter.

I 9. He has not answered yet.

T 10. Julia gave (Dave) a subscription to that magazine.

I. Direct Object or Predicate Word? Number your paper from 1 to 10. Label four columns *Subject, Verb, Direct Object,* and *Predicate Word*. Fill in the parts that you find for each sentence. You will find either a direct object or a predicate word in each sentence.

1. Your teeth are very straight.
2. This station sounds clear.
3. Rainy days seem long.
4. Jason's pulse felt too fast.
5. Laura is the best bowler on our team.
6. Nancy has perfect pitch.
7. Some gym shoes are washable.
8. Linda hid the rowboat in the reeds.
9. The path looked dangerous.
10. Vince bought an old piano with his first paycheck.

J. Compound Parts As your teacher directs, show the compound parts in the following sentences. Tell whether they are compound subjects, verbs, objects, or predicate words.

1. Their truck makes pick-ups and deliveries.
2. Ice and snow covered the sidewalk.

3. We washed and dried clothes at the laundromat.
   <small>V   V</small>
4. The horror movie was funny but scary.
   <small>PW   PW</small>
5. We had a parade and fireworks on Independence Day.
   <small>DO   DO</small>
6. Delia or Joanne will go with you to the nurse's office.
   <small>S   S</small>
7. That company is small but successful.
   <small>PW   PW</small>
8. Jamaica and Dominica are independent countries.
   <small>S   S</small>
9. The Harts celebrate Christmas and Hanuka.
   <small>DO   DO</small>
10. The wind howled, hissed, and whistled all night.
    <small>V   V   V</small>

K. Kinds of Sentences Write whether the following sentences are *Declarative, Interrogative, Imperative,* or *Exclamatory.* Add the correct punctuation.

Int 1. What does this code mean?

Imp 2. Please fill this order.

Ex 3. What a gossip he is!

D 4. Plumbers charge an hourly rate.

Imp 5. Move with the music.

Ex 6. How she has changed!

Int 7. How has she changed?

Int 8. Does the high school offer business courses?

Imp 9. Call the emergency room first.

D 10. Ms. Rojac recommended thermal window shades.

L. Sentence Patterns Write which sentence pattern is used in each of the following sentences. Each sentence follows one of these patterns: **N V, N V N, N V N N, N LV N, N LV Adj.**

1. Hal photographs sunsets. NVN
2. Allison finally relaxed. NV
3. Maria wore her uniform. NVN
4. The neighbors were watching. NV
5. The largest island in the world is Greenland. NLVN
6. The work was not easy. NLV Adj
7. Sandra gave Chet her chair. NVNN
8. Her shoelaces had rainbows on them. NVN

Mixed Review

These exercises provide re-view of the concepts pre-sented in this Section. Each exercise challenges the stu-dents to apply several of the skills they have acquired dur-ing previous study. Because the "mixed" feature of these activities makes them more difficult, the teacher may wish to have less-advanced stu-dents do them orally or in small groups.

MIXED REVIEW

The Sentence and Its Parts

A. Finding subjects and predicates and identifying fragments Decide whether the following groups of words are sentences or fragments. Copy each sentence and underline the subject once and the predicate twice. Then write *Declarative, Interrogative, Imperative,* or *Exclamatory* to show what kind of sentence it is. Add the correct punctuation. If a group of words is not a sentence, write *Fragment.*

F   1. Rolled her sleeves up

(*You*) 2. Roll your sleeves up Imp

   3. What a nightmare I had Ex

   4. What is the title? Int

   5. Clouds hid the mountains. D

F   6. A long white scar above his left eyebrow

(*You*) 7. Inflate the soccer ball to twenty-eight inches.

F   8. Faded slowly away

   9. Who laughed? Int

  10. Where is the tape? Int

B. Finding helping verbs, main verbs, and simple subjects Number your paper from 1 to 10. Label three columns *Helping Verbs, Main Verbs,* and *Simple Subjects.* For each sentence, write the parts in the proper columns.

            HV   MV
1. Sandra does know Julie.
          HV   MV
2. The plane was flying too low.
        HV   MV
3. The band had finally arrived.
              HV   MV
4. Across the highway was limping a dog.
           HV   MV
5. Maybe he couldn't think clearly.
         HV   MV
6. There might be a few problems.
   HV   MV
7. Did you check the spark plugs?
   HV   MV
8. Will your family watch the game on television?

9. A huge brown spider was building a web. [HV MV]

10. After all, Jerome hasn't often been wrong. [HV MV]

C. Finding sentence parts Number your paper from 1 to 10. Label five columns on your paper *Subject, Verb, Predicate Word, Indirect Object,* and *Direct Object.* Fill in the parts that you find in each sentence. No sentence will have every part.

1. The ladder was too short. [PW]
2. Alison never skips lunch. [DO]
3. The company sent Martin a refund. [IO DO]
4. The leaves are yellow now. [PW]
5. The usher handed me a program. [IO DO]
6. Marcus Dupree plays football. [DO]
7. This instrument is a trumpet. [PW]
8. Ms. Hammond found Simon another textbook. [IO DO]
9. I found my cat at the animal shelter. [DO]
10. Jeff was slicing onions in the kitchen. [DO]

D. Finding compound sentence parts Number your paper from 1 to 10. Write the compound parts for the following sentences. Write whether each is a compound subject, verb, direct object, indirect object, or predicate word.

1. The ground rumbled and cracked. [V V]
2. The mornings and evenings grew darker. [S S]
3. Ms. Sands took Mary and Loretta to Williamsburg. [DO DO]
4. You can use an orange or a lemon. [DO DO]
5. The attic was dusty, hot, and dark. [PW PW PW]
6. The best volleyball servers are Pam and Kristy. [PW PW]
7. Darryl has an atlas, an almanac, an encyclopedia, and a dictionary. [DO DO DO DO]
8. The acorns and foliage of the oak are poisonous. [S S]
9. Dr. Alvarez will give Franklin or Stacy the job. [IO IO]
10. The skater wobbled but stayed on her feet. [V V]

E. Finding sentence patterns Write the pattern for each of the following sentences.

1. A computer broke the code. NVN
2. Winter arrived. NV
3. The goalie was alert. N LV Adj
4. This car is almost an antique. N LV N
5. Some viruses give people colds. NVNN
6. The sun bleached the wood. NVN
7. The fever tree has yellow bark. NVN
8. The muffler fell onto the road. NV
9. She sounded cheerful. N LV Adj
10. The guard spotted the open window. NVN

F. Using sentence patterns Write two original sentences for each of the following sentence patterns. Sentences will vary.

1. N V
2. N V N
3. N V N N
4. N LV N
5. N LV Adj

USING GRAMMAR IN WRITING
The Sentence and Its Parts

A. Upon returning home from school one day, you are surprised to find a special-delivery letter. The envelope is marked URGENT. You tear the envelope open and find a computer-written letter. Unfortunately, a malfunction of the computer's printer has left gaps in the message. Below are the fragments that were printed. Supply the missing sentence parts.

You have been chosen for _____. _____ that you will accept the mission. We must receive _____. Your country _____. Of course, you _____. _____ the thanks and admiration of your friends.

B. Imagine that you have just set a world record for staying awake. At a press conference, reporters ask you questions about the experience. Complete the following interview. Write an answer to each reporter's question. For each statement, write the question that might have been asked.

Q: How long have you been awake?

A: _____

Q: _____

A: My sense of balance was poor, and I had trouble focusing my eyes.

Q: In what ways did your appetite change?

A: _____

Q: _____

A: I felt colder and colder as time went by.

Q: If your record is broken, will you try again?

A: _____

Using Grammar in Writing

These challenging and enjoyable activities allow the students to see how the concepts of grammar, usage, and mechanics may be applied in actual writing situations. Each exercise is designed to allow students practice in several of the skills they have acquired in this Section. The activities also provide opportunities for students to write creatively about a wide variety of interesting and unusual subjects.

Section Objectives

1. To avoid and correct sentence fragments

2. To avoid and correct run-on sentences

Preparing the Students

Explain to students that the purpose of communication is to get your ideas across to someone else. When you communicate by writing, sentences are your vehicle for expressing ideas. Even if it is clear to you what you intend to say, you must be certain that your sentences express all of your ideas completely and logically. Two common errors in writing can interfere with communication and cause a reader to not understand the writer's ideas.

Have students read the introduction to the two types of sentence errors on page 422.

Additional Resources

Diagnostic Test — page 1 in the test booklet

Mastery Test — pages 42–43 in the test booklet

Additional Exercises — pages 427–430 in the student text

Practice Book — pages 166–168

Duplicating Masters — pages 166–168

Special Populations — See special section at the front of this Teacher's Edition.

Using Complete Sentences

Sentences express thoughts and feelings. When they are clear, sentences communicate the speaker's message. When sentences are not clear, the message is lost.

One common problem in writing is omitting part of a sentence. An incomplete sentence is called a **sentence fragment**. Another common problem is writing two or more sentences as one. The result is called a **run-on sentence**.

Sentence fragments and run-on sentences weaken communication. In this section you will learn how to avoid them.

Part 1   What Is a Sentence Fragment?

A group of words that is only part of a sentence is a **sentence fragment**. A sentence fragment does not express a complete thought.

A fragment is confusing because something is missing from the sentence. Sometimes the subject is left out. Then the reader wonders *who* or *what* the sentence is about. At other times the verb is left out. Then the reader wonders *what happened?* or *what about it?*

Fragment: Raced to the finish line. (Who raced? The subject is missing.)

Sentence: The sprinter raced to the finish line.

Fragment: The trombone player in the back. (What happened? The verb is missing.)

Sentence: The trombone player in the back dropped her music.

Fragments Due to Incomplete Thoughts

Sometimes when you write, you are in a hurry. You jot down only bits of ideas. What you write are incomplete thoughts. Your pen doesn't keep up with the flow of your ideas.

Maybe you can understand these pieces of ideas. However, to a reader they will probably seem unclear.

Here is an example of a series of fragments:

Solar energy an alternative. Solar collectors expensive. Will reduce gas and electric bills.

These complete sentences show what the writer meant:

Solar energy is an alternative energy source. The solar collectors are expensive. However, using solar energy will reduce gas and electric bills.

Part 1

Objective

To avoid and correct sentence fragments

Presenting the Lesson

1. Review with students the requirements of a complete sentence: 1) it has a subject, 2) it has a predicate, and 3) it expresses a complete thought. Tell students that a fragment is not a complete sentence because it fails to fulfill at least one of these three requirements.

2. Read the explanation of fragments on pages 423–424. Go over all examples of fragments and note what has been added to correct them. Point out how incorrect punctuation can create fragments by separating sentence parts incorrectly.

3. Do Exercise A on page 424 orally. For each fragment, have students tell what sentence part is missing. Have students add words as necessary to make each fragment into a complete sentence.

4. Assign and discuss Exercise B on pages 424–425.

Individualizing the Lesson

Less-Advanced Students

1. Have students complete each fragment in Exercises A and B, pages 424–425. Have them indicate whether each fragment is the result of incomplete punctuation or an incomplete thought.

2. Have each student write ten sentence fragments; then have students exchange papers to complete each fragment.

423

Fragments Due to Incorrect Punctuation

Every sentence ends with a punctuation mark. The mark may be a period, a question mark, or an exclamation point. If you use one of these marks before your idea is complete, a sentence fragment results.

Fragment: Long distance runners. Gathered from all over the country.

Sentence: Long distance runners gathered from all over the country.

Fragment: On a clear, cold day. Skiers dotted the hills.

Sentence: On a clear, cold day skiers dotted the hills.

Fragment: The magician pulled a rabbit. From her hat.

Sentence: The magician pulled a rabbit from her hat.

Exercise A   For each group of words that is a sentence, write *S* on your paper. For each sentence fragment, write *F*. Be ready to add words to change the fragments into sentences.

S   1. The line was busy
F   2. The juggler in the program
F   3. Asked for some help
S   4. Ask Linda for some help
F   5. Came in second place
F   6. Landed on an island in the Caribbean
S   7. Cindy caught up with us
S   8. The clock on the mantel ticks loudly
S   9. What was that
F 10. Fell off the ladder

Exercise B   Follow the directions for Exercise A.

S   1. Betsy mailed the entry form
F   2. Included three box tops in the envelope

S 3. The grand prize is a trip to Europe

F 4. All expenses paid

S 5. The odds of winning are slim

F 6. Millions of entrants

S 7. Second prize is a television set.

F 8. A self-addressed, stamped envelope

S 9. Winners will be notified

S 10. Prizes must be claimed by June 1

Part 2   What Is a Run-on Sentence?

A **run-on sentence** is two or more sentences written incorrectly as one.

A run-on confuses the reader. It does not show where the first idea ends and the second one begins. The sentences need a period or other punctuation mark to signal the end of each complete thought. Here are some examples:

Run-on: The pistol shot rang out it signaled the start of the race.

Correct: The pistol shot rang out. It signaled the start of the race.

Run-on: Carl ate spaghetti Jack ate lasagna.

Correct: Carl ate spaghetti. Jack ate lasagna.

Sometimes writers make the mistake of using a comma instead of a period. Again, the result is a run-on.

Run-on: The center tossed the ball from mid-court, she made a basket.

Correct: The center tossed the ball from mid-court. She made a basket.

Run-on: The car is ready, we can leave now.

Correct: The car is ready. We can leave now.

425

Part 2

Objective

To avoid and correct run-on sentences

Presenting the Lesson

1. Read page 425, studying the definition of run-on sentences, the examples of run-ons, and their corrections. Review with students the four types of sentences and the proper end punctuation for each. Stress that a comma is never used as an end punctuation mark.

2. Assign and discuss Exercises A and B on page 426.

Individualizing the Lesson

Less-Advanced Students

Do Exercise A, page 426, orally with the students.

Advanced Students

Explain to students that there are ways of correcting a run-on sentence other than dividing it into two separate sentences. Have students correct the following run-on sentences in ways other than creating two separate sentences. Answers will vary.

425

1. The bridge collapsed we were stranded.
2. I want to go to college, my family can't afford it.
3. I missed the bus, I was late for work.
4. Jean saw that movie, she didn't enjoy it.
5. The fog is lifting we can see the mountain.

Optional Practice

Have students correct the following run-on sentences

1. The sun came out, we went on the picnic.
2. I read that book I also saw the movie.
3. The cat slept; he had been active all day.
4. She played the piano for us; last time she played the violin.
5. The girls won the volleyball game the score was 15 to 12.

Extending the Lesson

Have students rewrite the following paragraph, correcting run-on sentences in a variety of ways. Answers will vary.

Arizona is known as the Grand Canyon State, it is well known for its delightful climate and beautiful scenery. You can see signs of both past and future in the state of Arizona there are still active Indian villages, there is also the Lowell Observatory in Flagstaff where scientists use the most modern equipment to study the moon. The population of Arizona is growing rapidly, older people enjoy their retirement there young families enjoy raising their children there.

426

Exercise A Correct the following run-on sentences.

1. The days grew longer, we knew that spring would be here soon.
2. The beagle ran down the steps; it was chasing a rabbit.
3. Jan looked through the catalogs; she selected hiking boots and some books.
4. The scouts are collecting newspapers this week; Dad put out four big bundles.
5. I received a letter from my cousin in Oregon; I hadn't heard from him in months.
6. Air controllers direct air traffic; they use radios.
7. I placed the plant in the window; it can get light.
8. We rode our horses down the trail in the forest preserve, we stopped to eat our lunch by a stream.
9. Storms swept the West Coast; many homes were destroyed in the floods.
10. Put the milk and cheese in the refrigerator; put the canned goods on the shelves.

Exercise B Follow the directions for Exercise A.

1. Steve is very talented; he plays the piano.
2. Microwave ovens are different from conventional ovens; in microwave ovens, no metal pans can be used.
3. Corn has many uses; it can be used for animal feed.
4. I like oranges; they are good for you.
5. Frost can damage a citrus crop; growers use heaters called smudge pots.
6. Some poisonous snakes have triangular-shaped heads; the rattlesnake is poisonous.
7. Drifting snow closed the road; people were stranded.
8. Snakes have jaws that can unhinge; a snake can swallow a mouse whole.
9. The play was about to begin; the lights dimmed.
10. Preheat the oven to 350 degrees; bake for one hour.

426

ADDITIONAL EXERCISES

Using Complete Sentences

A. Sentences and Fragments Number your paper from 1 to 10. Write *Fragment* or *Sentence* for each of the following groups of words to show what each group is.

s 1. Rachel repairs cars in her spare time
s 2. An overturned truck blocked traffic
F 3. A nationally known cartoonist
s 4. Steve types at a fast pace
F 5. Draws sketches with charcoal
s 6. The cook grilled two hamburgers
F 7. The apartment on the fourth floor
s 8. A subway train sped past
F 9. Led the group in exercises to the music
s 10. A German neighborhood held a fall festival

B. Sentences and Run-ons Number your paper from 1 to 10. Write *Sentence* or *Run-on* for each of the following groups of words to show what each group is.

R 1. Ray Charles sometimes uses back-up singers they are usually the Rayettes
R 2. Tony tried to skate, he ended up with a sprained arm
s 3. We attended the opening of the football season
R 4. Larry was trained as a welder, he learned the skills quickly
s 5. Add some powdered milk to the batter
s 6. Alligators, crocodiles, and lizards descended from dinosaurs
R 7. A pipe burst water flooded the basement
s 8. Sunlight streamed through the window

427

Additional Exercises

These Additional Exercises may be used for additional practice of the concepts presented in this Section. Each exercise focuses on a single concept, and should be used after the page number indicated in parentheses.

Review

If you have not assigned these Additional Exercises before this time, you can also use them as an excellent Section Review.

S 9. Six squad cars, an ambulance, and a fire truck sped by

R 10. The school district sponsors adult classes, many courses are offered

C. Sentences, Fragments, and Run-ons   Number your paper from 1 to 10. Write *Fragment, Sentence,* or *Run-on* for each of the following groups of words to show what each group is.

F 1. A part-time job at the grocery store

F 2. A movie with a surprise ending

R 3. The lights went out everyone lit candles

S 4. The antique clock on the mantel is a gift from Aunt Helen

R 5. All the gym students climbed the rope, only Holly got to the ceiling

S 6. Crews piled sandbags along the river banks

F 7. The horoscope in the daily newspaper

S 8. Styles change

F 9. Rice, tomatoes, onions, green peppers, and spices

R 10. Sean sang Maureen clapped

MIXED REVIEW

Using Complete Sentences

A. Identifying sentences, fragments, and run-ons   Write *Fragment, Sentence,* or *Run-on* for each of the following groups of words to show what each one is. Then correct fragments by adding words to make complete sentences. Correct run-ons by using the correct capitalization and punctuation. Corrected fragments will vary.

F 1. Tomato sauce, vinegar, and chili powder.

R 2. The ball dropped through the net, ^Eeverybody cheered.

S 3. Balloons and buttons carried the slogan.

S 4. Kate listened.

F 5. Finally read the instructions.

S 6. Finally the wasp landed.

F 7. Turned the radio off during my favorite song.

R 8. The wind was brisk. Joachim pulled his collar up.

S 9. The coach shouted and waved a towel.

R 10. The telephone had no dial, ^Tthere were pushbuttons on the receiver.

B. Correcting fragments and run-on   The following paragraph contains fragments and run-on sentences. Rewrite the paragraph, correcting the fragments and run-ons.

     The tight space between the seat cushion and the frame of our armchair. Is a little like a personal safe. All kinds of objects are hidden there. push your hand down into the chair and pick out a surprise. Almost anything small can be wedged in our safe. we have found pencils, coins, pocket mirrors, scissors, old birthday cards, And even an overdue library book. There is one big difference between our armchair safe and an ordinary safe. the owners of a regular home safe usually know its contents. Our safe gets filled by chance.

429

Mixed Review

   These exercises provide review of the concepts presented in this Section. Each exercise challenges the students to apply several of the skills they have acquired during previous study. Because the "mixed" feature of these activities makes them more difficult, the teacher may wish to have less-advanced students do them orally or in small groups.

USING GRAMMAR IN WRITING
Using Complete Sentences

A. You awaken in the night to find your room flooded with pale green light. You go to the window and find a small object hovering in the air outside your window. You call the police and excitedly deliver this description to the desk sergeant.

> You're going to think I'm crazy I think there's an alien space ship right outside my window. Just hanging in the air. A small thing, about the size of a football. I always thought that an alien ship would be enormous didn't you think it would take a lot of fuel to travel from another solar system? Better get over here fast. 1280 14th Street.

Your call was recorded at the station. A newspaper reporter corrected the run-on sentences and completed the fragments. Write the statement as it appeared in the newspaper.

B. Imagine that you have overslept. You race to get to school. You dash into your first class to find that a surprise quiz is in progress. Here is what you say:

> I'm sorry that I'm late, it really wasn't my fault. You see it all started when the cat knocked the fish tank. Onto the floor, of course. The water spilled onto a lamp cord the next thing we knew all the lights were out Not only was our power off. But every apartment in our building had no power. The power company finally repaired the damage at midnight, by then I was asleep. I never reset my clock, that's why I was late.

Your teacher agrees to give you a make-up quiz if you put your story in writing. Rewrite the explanation, correcting the sentence fragments and run-on sentences.

Using Nouns

Section Objectives

1. To identify nouns and distinguish between common nouns and proper nouns

2. To identify and understand the function of nouns used as subjects, direct objects, indirect objects, and predicate nouns

3. To form the plurals of nouns correctly

4. To form and use the possessives of nouns correctly

Preparing the Students

Ask students if any of them have studied a foreign language in school. Ask those students who have what the first words they learned were; no doubt students will list the names of many things. Explain that most language-learning does begin with learning names—or nouns.

Read the introduction on page 431.

Additional Resources

Diagnostic Test — page 2 in the test booklet

Mastery Test — pages 44–45 in the test booklet

Additional Exercises — pages 443–446 in the student text

Practice Book — pages 169–176

Duplicating Masters — pages 169–176

Special Populations — See special section at the front of this Teacher's Edition.

Words are the building blocks of communication. Putting words together correctly to create good, clear sentences is something that you do every day.

The words used in sentences fall into certain groups called the parts of speech. You can talk and write without knowing the names of the parts of speech. However, skilled speakers and writers recognize the different parts of speech and use them properly.

In this section you will learn about one of the eight parts of speech: nouns.

Objective

To identify nouns and distinguish between common nouns and proper nouns

Presenting the Lesson

1. Read page 432, emphasizing the definition of a noun. Look at the examples of nouns. Ask students to name at least five additional nouns for each category—persons, places, and things.

2. Assign and discuss the Exercise on page 432.

3. Read pages 432–433. Study the definitions and examples of common nouns and proper nouns.

4. Assign and discuss Exercises A and B on page 433.

Individualizing the Lesson

Less-Advanced Students

1. Work with students to develop a list of ten common nouns. Have students write the list on their papers. Then have students write one proper noun that fits each category of common noun. For example:

book   *The Jungle*
relative   Aunt Mary

2. Have students write five sentences using common nouns from the list and five sentences using proper nouns from the list.

Advanced Students

1. Have students write a brief travelogue of a recent trip they've taken. The trip can be a vacation, trip into the city, shopping, etc. Tell students *not* to capitalize any words except

Part 1   What Are Nouns?

You use words to name the people, places, and things around you. Words that name are called **nouns**.

A noun is a word used to name a person, place, or thing.

Nouns name things that you can see, like cities, streets, furniture, and books. They also name things you cannot see, such as feelings, ideas, and beliefs.

Persons: plumber, Sally, Christopher Reeves, singer
Places: Alabama, hospital, Denver, restaurant
Things: towel, brush, spirit, kindness

Exercise   Make three columns on a sheet of paper. Label them *Names of Persons, Names of Places,* and *Names of Things.* Find the nouns in the following paragraph. List each one in the proper column.

The *Double Eagle V*, a large balloon filled with helium, made a historic flight across the Pacific Ocean. The balloon lifted off in Japan and touched down in California. The trip was almost 6,000 miles. Four men flew in the gondola. One problem during the trip was ice forming on the balloon. Another problem was a storm off the coast of California. Ben Abruzzo, the captain, feels that teamwork carried the *Double Eagle V* to victory.

Proper Nouns and Common Nouns

How do these two italicized nouns differ?

Mary Cassatt, an American *artist*, lived in France.

The word *artist* is a general term. It refers to many people. It is a **common noun**. A common noun is a general name.

The noun *Mary Cassatt*, on the other hand, refers to only one person. It is a **proper noun**. A proper noun is a specific name.

A common noun is the name of a whole class of persons, places, or things. It is a name that is common to the class.

A proper noun is the name of a particular person, place, or thing. Proper nouns are capitalized.

Look at the following examples of common nouns and proper nouns. As you can see, some nouns are made up of more than one word.

Common Nouns	Proper Nouns
movie	*Casablanca*
river	Danube River
columnist	Ann Landers
week	Fire Prevention Week
country	France
state	Ohio
governor	Governor Henderson

Exercise A   Make two columns on your paper. Label one column *Common Nouns* and the other *Proper Nouns*. Place each of the following nouns in the correct column. Capitalize all proper nouns.

1. snack bar, mc donald's, restaurant, taco bell
2. al's body shop, gas station, standard oil, garage
3. josé feliciano, guitar, chuck mangione, trumpet, brass
4. nashville, capital, city, frankfort, town
5. park, zoo, san diego zoo, animals, milwaukee zoo
6. mexico, country, border, texas, river
7. chevrolet, ford, chrysler, automobile, car
8. st. francis hospital, clinic, hospital, maryhaven nursing home, nurse
9. store, sears, catalog, j. c. penney, clerk
10. new york mets, baseball, team, manager, sport

Exercise B: Writing   Write five sentences of your own, using at least one proper noun in each sentence. Sentences will vary.

for the first word in each sentence. Then have students exchange papers.

2. Have students capitalize all proper nouns on the paper they receive.

Optional Practice

Have students list five proper nouns for each of the following common nouns. Answers will vary.

1. athlete   4. school
2. river   5. book
3. newscaster   6. film

Extending the Lesson

1. Give students a copy of a brief newspaper or magazine article. Tell them to circle all common nouns and underline all proper nouns.

2. Have students write five sentences using five common nouns from the article and five sentences using five proper nouns from the article.

To identify and understand the function of nouns used as subjects, direct objects, indirect objects, and predicate words

Presenting the Lesson

1. Read page 434. Study the examples of nouns used as subjects.

2. Assign and discuss Exercises A and B on pages 434–435. You may wish to have students indicate whether each subject is a common noun or a proper noun.

3. Read page 435. Remind students how to find the direct object in a sentence. (Refer to page 398 in the text.)

4. Assign and discuss Exercises A and B on pages 435–436.

5. Read pages 436–437. Review the way indirect objects are identified. (Refer to pages 400–401 in the text.)

6. Assign and discuss Exercises A and B on page 437.

7. Read page 437. Study the examples of nouns used as predicate words. Review linking verbs and predicate words. (Refer to pages 402–405.) Stress that a predicate noun renames the subject.

8. Assign and discuss Exercises A and B on page 438.

Individualizing the Lesson

Less-Advanced Students

1. To assist students with this part of the Section, have them write a brief explanation of how to tell the difference among *subject, direct*

Part 2 How Are Nouns Used?

Nouns Used as Subjects

As you learned in Section 1, the **subject** of a sentence tells who or what is being talked about. Nouns are frequently used as subjects.

> *Fish* stole the bait from my hook. (The noun *fish* is the subject of the verb *stole*.)

> My *uncle* from Ohio writes me often. (The noun *uncle* is the subject of the verb *writes*. Notice that in this sentence, the subject is not next to the verb.)

Two or more nouns may form a compound subject.

> *Dennis* and *Joshua* competed for the title. (The nouns *Dennis* and *Joshua* are the subject of the verb *competed*.)

> *Diamonds* and *emeralds* adorned the crown. (The nouns *diamonds* and *emeralds* are the subject of the verb *adorned*.)

Exercise A   Number your paper from 1 to 10. Write the nouns used as the subjects of these sentences.

1. Raccoons raided the trash cans.
2. The singer crooned lovely ballads.
3. The girls won the soccer game.
4. That rumor is spreading all over town.
5. Lawyers and accountants provide services.
6. Some secretaries take shorthand.
7. Marge and Kent planned the party.
8. Prices have gone up each year.
9. Mel has been writing a story for the creative writing contest.
10. Many neighborhoods are having block parties to celebrate the holiday.

1. The smell of popcorn filled the theater.
2. Mark painted the neighbor's garage.
3. Many students eat at the snack bar.
4. Travelers shopped for souvenirs at the market.
5. The nurse checked the patient's blood pressure.
6. A flock of geese flew overhead.
7. The magician mystified the audience.
8. Anwar Sadat was an Egyptian leader.
9. Kevin and Fred are good salesmen.
10. Paris is the capital of France.

Nouns Used as Direct Objects

A **direct object** completes the action of a verb. It answers *whom* or *what* about the verb. Nouns are frequently used as direct objects.

> The clown entertained the *children.* (The noun *children* tells *whom* about the verb *entertained.*)
>
> Dean took *slides* during his vacation. (The noun *slides* tells *what* about the verb *took.*)
>
> Beth made a *belt* and a *wallet* from the leather. (Both the nouns *belt* and *wallet* are the compound direct object. They tell *what* about the verb *made.*)

Exercise A   As your teacher directs, write the nouns used as direct objects in the following sentences.

1. A player dunked the basketball through the hoop.
2. Colleen has a good attitude.
3. Tennis built Ken's endurance.
4. Children like opera, too.
5. Heather reads her horoscope every day.
6. Those shoes have long laces.
7. John heaped spaghetti onto his plate.

object, indirect object, and *predicate word.*

2. Have students write an original example of each type of noun use.

Advanced Students

Have students write five original sentences for each type of noun use—subject, direct object, indirect object, and predicate word. Tell students to circle the noun and indicate the specific noun use in each sentence.

Optional Practice

Have students underline the nouns in the following sentences. Above each noun, students should mark *S* (subject), *DO* (direct object), *IO* (indirect object), or *PN* (predicate noun) to indicate how the noun is used.

1. This pen is a Paper-Mate.
2. The doves flew away.
3. Jenny gave David a record.
4. Today is Friday.
5. The noise and music gave Gina a headache.
6. My grandmother enjoys tennis.
7. Our class bought the school a gift.
8. Coach Hayes gave Buck and Glen their letters.
9. Can Mark bring Carol and Robbie?
10. The Tercel is a nice little car.

Extending the Lesson

Have students write original sentences using the following nouns in the ways indicated. Answers will vary.

house	(subject)
Mr. Davis	(subject)
shoes	(direct object)
family	(indirect object)
candidate	(predicate noun)

8. Judy cut her own <u>hair</u>.
9. Artists brought their <u>crafts</u> to the fair.
10. Brett plays <u>chess</u> and <u>backgammon</u>.

Exercise B   Follow the directions for Exercise A.

1. Josh rode a <u>bicycle</u> through the park.
2. The lawyer interviewed her <u>client</u>.
3. The doctor hired a <u>receptionist</u>.
4. Most companies have <u>insurance</u>.
5. Lifeguards usually wear <u>whistles</u>.
6. That restaurant serves <u>lunch</u> and <u>dinner</u>.
7. Lee ordered a <u>jacket</u> from the catalog.
8. Mosquitoes bit my <u>wrists</u> and <u>ankles</u>.
9. Max tutored his younger <u>brother</u>.
10. A stream borders the <u>property</u>.

Nouns Used as Indirect Objects

Another use of the noun is as an **indirect object**. The indirect object tells *to whom* or *for whom* or *to what* or *for what* about the verb.

> The guide showed the *tourists* the monument. (The noun *tourists* is the indirect object. It tells *to whom* about the verb *showed*.)
>
> Angela gave the *beagle* and the *terrier* a bath. (The nouns *beagle* and *terrier* are the compound indirect object, telling *to what* about the verb *gave*.)

An indirect object is used only with a direct object. The indirect object appears before the direct object in the sentence.

Subject	Verb	Indirect Object(s)	Direct Object
Jan	gave	the driver	directions.
Mom	fixed	the guests	a snack.
Allen	showed	Curt and Bill	the play.

The words *to* or *for* are never used with an indirect object.

Exercise A   Find the nouns used as indirect objects in the following sentences.

1. Tanya gave the waiter our order.
2. Larry paid Mr. Crane the rent.
3. The electrician sent the company a bill.
4. Mr. Jackson gave Toni some advice.
5. J.C. Penney sent the Dawsons a catalog.
6. Dad handed Chuck a dish towel.
7. Rose showed Alex the photo album.
8. Leo gave the walls and the ceiling a fresh coat of paint.
9. Kelly saved Susan a seat.
10. Mickey told Jerry a secret.

Exercise B   Follow the directions for Exercise A.

1. The lawyer asked the witness a question.
2. John passed Tracy the hamburgers.
3. Dr. Phillips gave Carol some vitamins.
4. Jackie mixed her friends some lemonade.
5. Kate loaned Kim her navy sweatshirt.
6. Don owes Luke a favor.
7. Loud music gives Casey a headache.
8. Ann made Judy a promise.
9. Bill handed the checker a coupon.
10. The actor gave the magazine an exclusive interview.

Nouns Used as Predicate Words

Sometimes a noun in the complete predicate of a sentence is linked to the subject. That noun is called a **predicate noun**. It always follows a linking verb. The predicate noun usually means the same thing as the subject.

Marilyn is a dental *hygienist.*

The workers were all *volunteers.*

The flowers in the vase are *roses* and *carnations.*

The nouns *hygienist, volunteers, roses,* and *carnations* are predicate nouns.

Exercise A   Find the nouns used as predicate nouns in the following sentences.

1. Al is an excellent golfer.
2. Russia was an ally during World War II.
3. Friday is the day of the history test.
4. The symptoms of the illness are fever and a rash.
5. Mabel's choice for dinner is shrimp.
6. Albany is the capital of New York.
7. Mr. Allen became the assistant principal.
8. Denise's brother is a pilot in the Air Force.
9. The winners of the contest are Mike, Sally, and Kim.
10. The opponents were Jimmy Connors and John McEnroe.

Exercise B   Follow the directions for Exercise A.

1. Some teachers become school administrators.
2. David Letterman is the host of the program.
3. Brooklyn is a borough of New York City.
4. Homework can be a problem for students with part-time jobs.
5. The luncheon specials were chicken and ham.
6. Oak Street Beach is a popular spot for sunbathers.
7. That house is the home of the mayor.
8. Jack Benny was a famous comedian.
9. The President was a former governor.
10. The ducks in the pond are mallards.

Part 3 The Plurals of Nouns

When a noun names one thing, it is singular. When a noun names more than one thing, it is plural.

Here are some rules for forming the plurals of nouns.

1. To form the plural of most nouns, just add -s:

juices   actors   squares   nations

2. When a singular noun ends in s, sh, ch, x, or z, add -es:

dresses   ashes   churches   foxes   buzzes

3. When a singular noun ends in o, add -s:

trios   halos   radios   photos   stereos

For a few words ending in *o*, add *-es*:

heroes   tomatoes   potatoes   echoes   cargoes

4. When a singular noun ends in y with a consonant before it, change the y to i and add -es:

story—stories   lady—ladies   hobby—hobbies

When a vowel (*a, e, i, o, u*) comes before the *y*, do not change the *y* to *i*. Just add *-s*:

toy—toys   bay—bays   monkey—monkeys

5. For some nouns ending in f, add -s to make the plural:

roofs   chiefs   reefs   beliefs

For many nouns ending in *f* or *fe*, change the *f* to *v* and add *-s* or *-es*. Since there is no rule to follow, you will have to memorize such words. Here are some examples:

leaf—leaves   loaf—loaves   calf—calves
shelf—shelves   thief—thieves   knife—knives

6. Some nouns have the same form for both singular and plural. They must be memorized.

deer   sheep   moose   salmon   trout

Part 3

Objective

To form the plurals of nouns correctly

Presenting the Lesson

1. Read pages 439–440. Go over rules for forming plurals carefully, especially noting the examples given.

2. Assign and discuss Exercises A and B on pages 440–441.

Individualizing the Lesson

Less-Advanced Students

For Exercise A, page 440, have students write the correct plural of each word. Then have them write the number of the rule that applies to the forming of each plural. If students misspell a plural, have them use the correct spelling in a sentence.

Advanced Students

1. Have students find fifteen different plural words in a newspaper or magazine article. Have them write the words in a column on their paper. Then have them write the singular of each word next to the plural. Students should then check the spellings of both singular and plural words in the dictionary.

2. If students misspell a plural word, have them write the correct spelling of the word as well as the rule that applies to making it plural.

Optional Practice

Have students copy the following sentences, using the plural forms of the nouns in parentheses.

1. The (brush) ~brushes~ at the carwash scratched my car.
2. Jon ate three (sandwich). ~sandwiches~
3. The (alto) ~altos~ and the (soprano) ~sopranos~ sang together.
4. Wash the (potato) ~potatoes~ and the (tomato). ~tomatoes~
5. Many of our (hero) ~heroes~ are no longer living.
6. In the forest we saw (deer), ~deer~ but (moose) ~moose~ are rarely seen in this area.
7. Three (lady) ~ladies~ bought the (piano). ~pianos~
8. The (waitress) ~waitresses~ brought steak (knife) ~knives~ to the customers.
9. Dad got three (handkerchief) ~handkerchiefs~ for Christmas.
10. The (shelf) ~shelves~ with the toys of the (child) ~children~ are loose.

Extending the Lesson

Tell students that a large part of being a good speller is memorizing which words follow specific spelling rules and which do not. Encourage students to keep a running list of plural words they find difficult to spell. From the students' lists compile a master list from which to give spelling quizzes covering plurals.

7. Some nouns form their plurals in special ways. They, too, must be memorized.

man—men	tooth—teeth	ox—oxen
woman—women	mouse—mice	foot—feet
goose—geese	child—children	louse—lice

Dictionaries show the plural of a word if it is formed in an unusual way. Here is a dictionary entry for the noun *knife*. The entry shows the plural, *knives*.

knife (nīf) *n., pl.* **knives** [OE. *cnif:* for IE. base see KNEAD] **1.** a cutting or stabbing instrument with a sharp blade, single-edged or double-edged, set in a handle **2.** a cutting blade, as in a machine —*vt.* **knifed, knif′ing 1.** to cut or stab with a knife ☆**2.** [Colloq.] to use underhanded methods in order to hurt, defeat, or betray —☆*vi.* to pass into or through something quickly, like a sharp knife —☆**under the knife** [Colloq.] undergoing surgery —**knife′like′** *adj.*

Use the dictionary if you have a question about plurals.

Exercise A   Write the plural of each of these nouns. Then use your dictionary to see if you are correct.

1. life ~lives~
2. fear ~fears~
3. salmon ~salmon~
4. jockey ~jockeys~
5. waitress ~waitresses~
6. baby ~babies~
7. leaf ~leaves~
8. moose ~moose~
9. studio ~studios~
10. ax ~axes~
11. hero ~heroes~
12. goose ~geese~
13. ditch ~ditches~
14. hoof ~hooves~
15. tooth ~teeth~
16. fly ~flies~
17. potato ~potatoes~
18. door ~doors~
19. dish ~dishes~
20. reply ~replies~

Exercise B   Write each sentence. Correct the errors in plural forms of nouns.

1. The womans ~women~ will meet in these roomes. ~rooms~
2. The churchs ~churches~ planned the Easter services together.
3. The deeres ~deer~ ran across the fieldes. ~fields~
4. Cut the loafes ~loaves~ of bread with these knifes. ~knives~
5. The babys ~babies~ are both twenty-one inchs ~inches~ long.

6. Each of the studioes has at least two pianoes. ^(studios) ^(pianos)
7. The mans discussed their believes. ^(men) ^(beliefs)
8. Two kinds of fishes are salmons and tunas. ^(fish) ^(salmon) ^(tuna)
9. Many countrys sponsor Olympic teames. ^(countries) ^(teams)
10. The climbers heard echos. ^(echoes)

Part 4   The Possessives of Nouns

Nouns can indicate possession or ownership.

Dad's camera   a tourist's suitcase   Larry's paper

Nouns can show that something is part of a person.

Jan's personality   Dr. Feldman's smile

The *'s* makes the above nouns show ownership. Words like *Dad's*, *tourist's*, and *Larry's* are called **possessive nouns**.

Usually, people and animals possess things. Sometimes, however, things are also in the possessive. Some examples are *a week's wages, a day's work,* or *a city's growth.*

Forming Possessives

There are three rules for forming the possessive of nouns.

1. If the noun is singular, add an apostrophe (') and s.

Ralph—Ralph's dog
Emma—Emma's sweater

2. If the noun is plural and ends in s, add just the apostrophe.

bankers—bankers' hours
Russells—Russells' cottage

3. If the noun is plural but does not end in s, add an apostrophe and s.

gentlemen—gentlemen's agreement
people—people's vote

441

Objective

To form and use the possessives of nouns correctly

Presenting the Lesson

1. Read page 441 and discuss the meaning of *possession* or *ownership*. Study the examples of possessives, pointing especially to the use of things (such as *week* and *day*) in the possessive.

2. Read page 441. Go over the rules for forming possessives. Ask students for additional examples for each rule.

3. Assign and discuss Exercises A and B on page 442. Correct answers should be written on the board so that students can see correctly formed plurals.

4. Assign and discuss Exercise C on page 442.

Individualizing the Lesson

Less-Advanced Students

1. Have students write the rule that applies to the formation of each possessive in Exercises A and B, page 442.

2. Have students use five words from Exercise A and five words from Exercise B in ten different sentences.

Exercise A   Write the possessive form of each of these nouns.

1. senator's	6. branch's	11. bike's	16. general's
2. Peg's	7. girl's	12. James's	17. Donny's
3. city's	8. runner's	13. jogger's	18. librarian's
4. realtor's	9. Mary's	14. guide's	19. secretary's
5. yesterday's	10. guest's	15. boss's	20. Carla's

Exercise B   Follow the directions for Exercise A.

1. pans'	6. hosts'	11. knives'	16. armies'
2. people's	7. students'	12. geese's	17. children's
3. sisters'	8. men's	13. players'	18. states'
4. birds'	9. dentists'	14. deer's	19. deserts'
5. engineers'	10. lawyers'	15. Johnsons'	20. ladies'

Exercise C   Write the possessive form for each italicized word.

1. *Wednesday's* meeting is important.
2. *Terry's* bike needs a new chain.
3. The *Cardinals'* pitcher was injured.
4. The *winners'* comments were in the paper.
5. The *golfers'* scores were high because of the wind.
6. *Lois's* appointment was at five o'clock.
7. That was the space *shuttle's* third trip.
8. Dale broke the *men's* track record.
9. Coffee spilled on the *nurse's* uniform.
10. *Amanda's* relatives live in England.

ADDITIONAL EXERCISES

Using Nouns

A. Common and Proper Nouns Label two columns _Common Nouns_ and _Proper Nouns_. Decide whether the following nouns are common or proper. Place each in the correct column. Capitalize the proper nouns.

1. basketball, net, [C]celtics, [J]julius [E]erving, referee
2. [A]africa, land, continent, island, [P]philippines
3. students, [P]priscilla, employees, [A]andrew, people
4. newspaper, magazine, _[D]detroit [F]free [P]press_, [N]newsweek
5. pioneer, [C]chisholm [T]trail, wagons, trapper, [R]rocky [M]mountains
6. [A]arctic [O]ocean, [R]red [S]sea, ocean, sea, [C]cape [C]cod
7. movie, play, _[A]annie_, characters, script
8. [T]tammy [W]wynette, music, [D]diana [R]ross, [K]kenny [R]rogers, radio
9. automobile, convertible, [J]jeep, [C]chevy [C]citation, [C]chrysler
10. store, clothes, [T]thompson's [H]hardware [S]store, customer, [C]carson, [P]pirie, [S]scott and [C]co.

B. How Nouns Are Used Decide how each italicized noun is used in the following sentences. Write the word and label it _Subject, Direct Object, Indirect Object,_ or _Predicate Noun._

1. Jody received a _telegram_ [DO] on her birthday.
2. Bill showed his _friends_ [IO] the winning lottery _ticket_ [DO].
3. _Kara_ [S] took movies at the ceremony.
4. The accident was a head-on _collision_ [PN].
5. The _Yankees_ [S] made four _runs_ [DO] in the fifth inning.
6. The _hurricane_ [S] tore through Cuba and Haiti.
7. After a tour of the lake, the _boat_ [S] docked in Milwaukee.
8. Mr. Rodriguez identified the _thief_ [DO] from a photograph.
9. On Monday, _Lee_ [S] polished the _chrome_ [DO] on her bike.
10. The _police_ [S] gave the _firefighters_ [IO] some _help_ [DO].

Additional Exercises

These Additional Exercises may be used for additional practice of the concepts presented in this Section. Each exercise focuses on a single concept, and should be used after the page number indicated in parentheses.

Review

If you have not assigned these Additional Exercises before this time, you can also use them as an excellent Section Review.

443

C. Plurals of Nouns   Write the plural of each of these nouns.

1. match~es~
2. life *(lives)*
3. class~es~
4. time~s~
5. rodeo~s~
6. story *(stories)*
7. trout *(trout)*
8. cargo~s~
9. victory *(victories)*
10. ax~es~
11. thief *(thieves)*
12. studio~s~
13. pony *(ponies)*
14. half *(halves)*
15. joy~s~
16. woman *(women)*
17. belief~s~
18. potato~es~
19. key~s~
20. dash~es~

D. Possessives of Nouns   Write the possessive form in the singular or plural as indicated.

Example: the officer (singular) message
          the officer's message

1. Roberta~'s~ (singular) tour of duty
2. the scientist~s'~ (plural) reports
3. the pitcher~s'~ (plural) styles
4. a captain~'s~ (singular) job
5. Nicholas~'s~ (singular) answer
6. some driver~s'~ (plural) licenses
7. the critic~'s~ (singular) favorable review
8. an actress~'s~ (singular) career
9. two grandchild *(grandchildren's)* (plural) pictures
10. several company *(companies')* (plural) personnel offices
11. March~'s~ (singular) cold weather
12. the waitress *(waitresses')* (plural) uniforms
13. the runner~'s~ (singular) speed
14. the woman *(women's)* (plural) shoe department
15. the Jarvis *(Jarvises')* (plural) house
16. Wes~'s~ (singular) idea
17. the sky~'s~ (singular) odd color
18. the fish~'s~ (singular) gills
19. the brush *(es')* (plural) handles
20. the deer~s'~ (plural) habitat

MIXED REVIEW

Using Nouns

A. Identifying nouns and their uses   Copy the <u>nouns</u> from these sentences. After each, write *Subject, Direct Object, Indirect Object,* or *Predicate Noun* to show how it is used.

1. That <u>insect</u> [S] is a <u>cricket</u> [PN].
2. A <u>neighbor</u> [S] takes my <u>grandfather</u> [IO] a hot <u>lunch</u> [DO].
3. The <u>motorcycle</u> [S] needs new <u>cylinders</u> [DO].
4. <u>Mary Shelley</u> [S] created <u>Frankenstein</u> [DO].
5. <u>Nolan</u> [S] showed <u>Marvin</u> [IO] the <u>blueprints</u> [DO].
6. <u>Rosita</u> [S] was watching the <u>Super</u> [DO] Bowl.
7. Your <u>friend</u> [S] is certainly a <u>character</u> [PN].
8. <u>Russell</u> [S] dialed the <u>number</u> [DO] again.
9. Her older <u>brother</u> [S] joined the <u>Marines</u> [DO].
10. A <u>dingo</u> [S] is a wild <u>dog</u> [PN].

B. Using plural and possessive forms correctly   Rewrite these sentences, correcting the errors in the plural and possessive forms of nouns. If a sentence is correct, write *Correct.*

1. A thoroughbred horses [horse's] lungs and nostrils are unusually large.
2. White mouses [mice] are often used in laboratories.
3. Bess [Bess's] bookshelves were the best in the carpentry class.
4. The two dogs' owners untangled the leashes.
^C 5. Mr. Curtis's car had two flat tires.
6. Patchs [Patches] of sunlight fell on the living room floor.
7. Ann's four friends have the same hobbies.
^C 8. These photos show the baby's new teeth.
^C 9. The men's watches had alarms.
^C 10. The knives go to the right of the dishes.

445

Using Grammar in Writing

These challenging and enjoyable activities allow the students to see how the concepts of grammar, usage, and mechanics may be applied in actual writing situations. Each exercise is designed to allow students practice in several of the skills they have acquired in this Section. The activities also provide opportunities for students to write creatively about a wide variety of interesting and unusual subjects.

USING GRAMMAR IN WRITING
Using Nouns

A. A close friend of yours is going to move to a distant city. The friend has invited you and some other close friends to a goodbye party. The friend has asked you and the other guests to promise to meet again in ten years. At the party, each of you will give to your friend a sealed envelope containing written predictions about what you and the others will be doing ten years from today. Choose several friends and write predictions for them. Where will each be living? What work will each be doing? Will there be a family? Write your predictions in paragraph form. Underline every noun. Underline proper nouns twice.

B. You work as a courier for a famous art museum. Your job is to see that an important and valuable painting reaches London safely. Rumors have been circulating that a gang of international art thieves will try to steal the painting somewhere between the airport and the National Gallery in London. Cautiously, you study the people waiting to board the plane with you.

Choose four of the people to describe. Describe each in a short paragraph. First describe what the person looks like. Then tell what the person is wearing. Finally, describe the person's attitude and actions. When you have finished your descriptions, underline the nouns. Label each one *S* (subject), *DO* (direct object), *IO* (indirect object), or *PN* (predicate noun).

C. Your family will be away from home for two weeks. You have made arrangements for a neighbor to take care of the pets, collect mail, and water the plants. Write a paragraph of instructions for the neighbor. When you refer to the things that the neighbor is to do, use at least three plural nouns (such as *guppies* and *ferns*) and three possessive nouns (such as *cats'* food, *Jean's* letters, and *Rowdy's* leash).

Using Pronouns

Nouns name people, places, and things. However, using too many nouns can make a sentence sound awkward and repetitious. Read this example:

Beth wrote Beth's report and then typed the report.

Sentences like this can be improved by using another part of speech, the **pronoun.** A pronoun is a word that takes the place of a noun.

Beth wrote *her* report and then typed *it.*

Her takes the place of the noun *Beth,* and *it* takes the place of the noun *report.*

In this section you will learn to identify and use pronouns correctly.

447

Section Objectives

1. To recognize personal pronouns in both singular and plural form and to understand their function

2. To recognize and use pronouns correctly in subject, object, and possessive form

3. To use the correct pronoun form in compound sentence parts

4. To use pronouns that agree in number with their antecedents

5. To use compound demonstrative, interrogative, and personal pronouns correctly

6. To differentiate between singular and plural indefinite pronouns

7. To use indefinite pronouns with possessive pronouns that agree with them in number

8. To use pronouns correctly in situations often causing problems: 1) contractions and possessives, 2) *who* and *whom,* 3) *we* and *us* with nouns, 4) *them* and *those*

Preparing the Students

Read the following paragraph to the class.

Mary is a college student. Mary goes to Northwestern University. Mary earns money by baby-sitting.

Point out that pronouns are words that can make our writing and speaking less repetitive. Read the introduction on page 447.

Additional Resources

Diagnostic Test — page 2 in the test booklet

Mastery Test — pages 46–47 in the test booklet

Additional Exercises — pages 468–474 in the student text

Practice Book — pages 177–187

Part 1

Objective

To recognize personal pronouns in both singular and plural form and to understand their function

Presenting the Lesson

1. Read page 448. Discuss the three situations in which pronouns may be used—first, second, and third person. Be sure students understand why these are called personal pronouns. Study the list of personal pronouns in both singular and plural form.

2. Assign and discuss Exercises A and B on page 449.

Individualizing the Lesson

Less-Advanced Students

Do the first five sentences in Exercise A, page 449, orally with students.

Advanced Students

Have students write a paragraph or two about their favorite person. Then have them circle all personal pronouns in the paragraph.

Optional Practice

Have students fill the blanks in the following sentences with personal pronouns. Answers will vary.

448

Part 1 Personal Pronouns

A pronoun is a word used in place of a noun. Pronouns are very helpful words. They may be used in three situations:

1. They may refer to the person speaking.

   I jog.   *We* bought the tickets.

2. They may refer to the person spoken to.

   You plant *your* own garden, don't *you*?

3. They may refer to other people, places, or things.

   He gave *her* a hand.   *They* ate *their* lunch outside.

The examples above show that a pronoun often refers to a person. For that reason, these pronouns are called **personal pronouns.**

There are many forms of personal pronouns. Like nouns, personal pronouns may be singular or plural. In the following chart, see how personal pronouns change from singular to plural.

Singular:	I	me	my, mine
	you	you	your, yours
	he, she, it	him, her, it	his, her, hers, its
Plural:	we	us	our, ours
	you	you	your, yours
	they	them	their, theirs

As the chart shows, most plural pronouns are totally different from their singular forms. Notice these examples:

Singular	Plural
I forgot.	*We* forgot.
Help *him!*	Help *them!*
It broke.	*They* broke.

448

Exercise A Number your paper from 1 to 10. Write the <u>pronouns</u> used in place of nouns in these sentences. After each pronoun, write the noun or nouns it stands for.

1. Sue looks at magazines while <u>she</u> watches TV. [Sue]
2. Amy and Jo cleaned <u>their</u> typewriters. [Amy and Jo]
3. The drummers played as <u>they</u> marched. [drummers]
4. Fred recorded <u>his</u> speech for practice. [Fred]
5. "<u>We</u> have a surprise for <u>you</u>," announced the twins. [twins] [person spoken to]
6. The elephant grabbed the tent pole and lifted <u>it</u>. [pole]
7. The students displayed <u>their</u> art projects. [students]
8. When the workers arrived, <u>they</u> repaired the roof. [workers]
9. Dean, did <u>you</u> feed the dog? [Dean]
10. The egg broke when <u>it</u> rolled off the counter. [egg]

Exercise B Follow the directions for Exercise A.

1. Sam and Hy sold <u>their</u> deli. [Sam and Hy]
2. The scientist wrote <u>her</u> autobiography. [scientist]
3. Julie planted the tree and watered <u>it</u>. [tree]
4. Flo waited for the bus at <u>her</u> corner. [Flo]
5. Lenny checked the air in <u>his</u> bicycle tires. [Lenny]
6. Some tourists lost <u>their</u> traveler's checks. [tourists]
7. Brendon and Mike brought flashlights with <u>them</u>. [Brendon and Mike]
8. The cashier gave Pat <u>his</u> receipt. [Pat]
9. "Do <u>you</u> like sunflower seeds?" Doris asked Rob. [Rob]
10. Jeff bought roses and gave <u>them</u> to <u>his</u> mom. [roses] [Jeff]

Part 2 The Forms of Pronouns

Pronouns can be used in all the ways that nouns are used. Personal pronouns can be subjects, objects, predicate words, and possessives.

However, a personal pronoun changes form as its use in a sentence changes. Look at these sentences:

449

---

1. I took _____ dog to the vet this morning.
2. The President met with _____ advisors.
3. The governor visited each city; _____ received a warm welcome.
4. The boys made pizza, but _____ didn't bake _____ long enough.
5. Ginny went to the doctor and _____ gave _____ some cough medicine.
6. Dan, David wants to know if _____ will help _____ study for _____ test.
7. Bobby played _____ guitar for the guests.
8. Bert and Bernie found _____ cat in a tree.
9. Girls, close _____ lockers quietly.
10. Our school has _____ football games on Friday nights.

Extending the Lesson

Have students read a brief newspaper or magazine article. Have them circle each personal pronoun in the article; then have them write each personal pronoun on a sheet of paper. Next to the pronoun, have them write the noun that each personal pronoun replaces.

Part 2

Objective

To recognize and use pronouns correctly in subject, object, and possessive form

449

Presenting the Lesson

1. Review the ways in which nouns can be used: subject, objects, predicate words, and possessives. Read page 449, noting that pronouns can be used in the same ways as nouns.

2. Read page 450, pointing out the three forms of pronouns—subject, object, possessive—and how each is used. Go over the complete list of personal pronouns, divided into the subject, object, and possessive forms.

3. Do the Exercise on page 450 orally. Have students tell whether each pronoun is in the subject, object, or possessive form.

4. Read the discussion of the subject form of pronouns on page 451. Go over the list of subject pronouns. Stress that the subject form of pronouns is used for both the subject of a sentence and the predicate pronoun. Have students read aloud the examples in order to hear the correct usage.

5. Read the discussion of the object form of personal pronouns on page 452. Go over the list of the object form of pronouns. Study the examples of the object form of pronouns used as direct objects, indirect objects, and objects of prepositions.

6. Read the discussion of the possessive form of pronouns on pages 452–453. Go over the list of possessive pronouns. Study the examples of possessive pronouns used by themselves (as subject, direct object, predicate pronoun, indirect object, or object of preposition) and those used with a noun.

She missed. (*She* is the subject.)
Kathy fouled *her*. (*Her* is the direct object.)
Her free throw was good. (*Her* shows possession.)

The three pronouns in these examples all refer to the same person. The forms, though, are different.

The three forms of a personal pronoun are **subject form, object form,** and **possessive form.** Here are the forms for all the personal pronouns:

	Subject	Object	Possessive
Singular:	I	me	my, mine
	you	you	your, yours
	he, she, it	him, her, it	his, her, hers, its
Plural:	we	us	our, ours
	you	you	your, yours
	they	them	their, theirs

Exercise   The following sentences use different forms of pronouns correctly. Read each sentence aloud.

1. *We* accepted the package.
2. Did *you* receive *your* paycheck?
3. The guard dog frightened *us*.
4. Mr. Daley and *she* gave *their* permission.
5. This is *he*.
6. The smoke detector warned *me* of the fire.
7. That locker is *his*.
8. *They* visited the Orient.
9. *I* went hiking with Max and *him*.
10. *Our* dog chases *their* cat.
11. The robin flew to *its* nest.
12. Marty buys old cars and rebuilds *them*.
13. This album is *yours*.
14. The doctor gave *him* some medication.
15. The error was *mine*.

The Subject Form of Pronouns

Subject Pronouns

I	we
you	you
he, she, it	they

For the subject of a sentence, the subject form of the personal pronoun is used. The following sentences use the subject form for the subject:

> *They* plotted and planned.   *He* created a monster.
> *She* did the experiment.   *I* called the police.

Using pronouns as subjects usually causes few problems. A more troublesome use, though, is the predicate pronoun. A **predicate pronoun** is a pronoun that is linked with the subject. It follows a linking verb, just as a predicate noun does.

Look at these examples of predicate pronouns:

> The winner was *she*. (*She* is a predicate pronoun used after the linking verb *was.*)
>
> That must be *he*. (*He* is a predicate pronoun used after the linking verb *must be.*)

As you see, the subject forms of pronouns are used for predicate pronouns. This may not sound natural at first. If you are in doubt about which form to use, reverse the subject and the predicate pronoun. The sentence should still sound correct.

> The coach was *he*.
> *He* was the coach.

Here are more examples of the correct use of the subject form for predicate pronouns:

> That was *she* in the car.
> Was it *he* on the phone?
> The announcer was *she*.

Always use the subject form for subjects and predicate pronouns.

451

7. Assign and discuss Exercises A and B on pages 453–454.

8. Assign and discuss Exercise C on page 454.

Individualizing the Lesson

Less-Advanced Students

After students have completed Exercises A and B, pages 453–454, have them go back through the exercises and indicate how each personal pronoun is used—subject, object, or possessive form.
Answers will vary.

Advanced Students

Have students find five examples of different forms of personal pronouns in a newspaper article.

Optional Practice

Have students supply a correct pronoun in each of the following sentences and label it *subject form*, *object form*, or *possessive form*.

1. My cousin brought <u>his/her</u> camera to the party. possessive
2. All of the teachers park <u>their</u> cars behind the gym. possessive
3. Please remain in <u>your</u> seats until the program is over. possessive
4. We call <u>him</u> Charlie. object
5. Gayle was pleased that the winner of the writing contest was <u>she</u>. subject
6. The dog rubbed <u>its</u> nose against my leg. possessive
7. After school I do <u>my</u> homework and then go to work. possessive
8. The volunteers gave <u>their</u> best efforts to the project. possessive
9. The children brought <u>her/him</u> some flowers. objective
10. Did <u>you</u> return the library books? subject

451

Have students write sentences using the following pronouns in the ways indicated. Answers will vary.

1. she (subject)
2. she (predicate pronoun)
3. our (possessive)
4. theirs (possessive)
5. him (direct object)
6. him (indirect object)
7. him (object of preposition)
8. hers (possessive)
9. her (direct object)
10. us (indirect object)

The Object Form of Pronouns

Object Pronouns

me	us
you	you
him, her, it	them

When personal pronouns are used as objects, the object form of the pronoun is used. There are three kinds of objects: direct objects, indirect objects, and objects of prepositions.

In these sentences the object form of the pronoun is used for direct objects.

Darrell avoided *them*.   The puzzle fascinated *me*.
Carol led *us*.   The paramedics revived *her*.

These sentences use the object form for indirect objects:

Ms. Abbott gave *me* a job.   Tracy promised *them* a reward.

Ned fixed *us* some popcorn.   Cole lent *him* a jacket.

The third kind of object is the object of a preposition. Prepositions are short connecting words like *to*, *for*, and *with*. The pronouns that follow such words are the objects. For more explanation of prepositions, see Handbook Section 7.

These sentences use the object form for objects of prepositions:

They rehearsed with *us*.
Vicki made a promise to *her*.
Craig brought the information to *me*.
The cashier wrapped the gift for *them*.

The Possessive Form of Pronouns

Possessive Pronouns

my, mine	our, ours
your, yours	your, yours
his, her, hers, its	their, theirs

Possessive pronouns show possession or ownership. Many times, possessive pronouns are used by themselves. Then, like a noun, a possessive pronoun has one of these uses: subject, object, or predicate word. Read these examples:

That bicycle is *his*. (predicate pronoun)
Hers is in the garage. (subject)
Paul and Ron are riding *theirs*. (direct object)
Sean gave *his* a push. (indirect object)
This bike looks like *mine*. (object of preposition)

At other times, possessive pronouns are not used alone. Instead, they are used to tell about nouns. Look at these sentences:

Sally brushed *her* Siamese cat.
Each university has *its* strengths.
The students scheduled *their* field trip.
It is *your* turn now.

Exercise A Choose the correct pronoun from the two given in parentheses. Write it. Read the sentence to yourself.

1. (They, Them) competed in the Olympics.
2. The results astonished (we, us).
3. That taxi splashed mud on (I, me).
4. Was that (she, her)?
5. The usher handed (he, him) the ticket stubs.
6. Most of (we, us) like cheese pizza.
7. The painting is (my mine).
8. Jack received (him, his) invitation today.
9. Nora sent (he, him) a singing telegram.
10. The audience applauded (we, us).

Exercise B Follow the directions for Exercise A.

1. Is that radio (your, yours)?
2. The mosquitoes bothered (we, us).
3. The sitter is (she, her).

Part 3

Objective

To use the correct pronoun form in compound sentence parts

Presenting the Lesson

1. Review with students the three forms of pronouns—subject, object, and possessive. Ask for examples of subject and object forms from students.

2. Read pages 454–455. Read aloud sample sentences using pronouns correctly. Go over the suggested way to determine which pronoun form to use.

3. Assign and discuss Exercises A and B on pages 455–456.

Individualizing the Lesson

Less-Advanced Students

Have students indicate whether the pronouns in each sentence in Exercises A and B, pages 455–456, are used as a subject, object, or indirect object. Explain to students that doing this will help them determine which pronoun in parentheses is correct.

Advanced Students

Students should write fifteen sentences using pronouns in compound constructions. Five sentences should use pronouns as subjects, five should use pronouns as objects and five should use pronouns as indirect objects.

4. Usually (I, me) run a mile each day.

5. Soon (we, us) will choose a new uniform.

6. It was (he, him) in the photograph.

7. A heavy fog enveloped (they, them).

8. Dan handed a letter to (I, me).

9. Ken checked (him, his) watch.

10. The music was composed by (she, her).

Exercise C   The personal pronouns in the following sentences are in italics. Write each pronoun and label it *Subject Form, Object Form,* or *Possessive Form.*

s   1. *She* arranged the flowers in a vase.

o   2. Kurt wrestled with *him*.

s   3. Is it *they?*

o   4. That comment annoyed *us*.

s   5. For once *I* finished on time.

o   6. Jane gave *him* a campaign button.

p   7. The most original idea was *hers*.

p   8. Tim was nervous during *his* interview.

s   9. *We* devoured the tacos.

o 10. Ms. Valenti showed *me* the blueprints.

Part 3 Pronouns in Compound Constructions

Compound sentence parts, or **compound constructions,** in a sentence have more than one part. The parts are joined by *and, or,* or *nor,* as in *Ned and me.* A pronoun may be one or both of these parts.

You may wonder which pronoun form to use in a compound construction. Here are sentences with pronouns used correctly as compound parts:

Jesse and *I* studied for the exam. (*Jesse* and *I* are both subjects. The subject form *I* is used.)

Mr. Justice gave *him* and *me* the programs. (*Him* and *me* are both indirect objects. The object forms are used.)

This secret is between *you* and *me*. (*You* and *me* are both objects of the preposition *between*. The object forms are used.)

You can avoid problems with compound parts if you think of each part separately. For instance, in the first example above, omit the words *Jesse and*. Should the sentence read *I studied for the exam* or *Me studied for the exam?* The pronoun *I* is correct.

Here is another example:

Scott offered Heather and (I, me) a suggestion.
Scott offered *me* a suggestion.

Exercise A   Choose the right pronoun from the two given.

1. Vera and (<u>he</u>, him) are working this evening.
2. Mr. Olivera gave (we, <u>us</u>) the test results.
3. Cancel the orders for Judd and (I, <u>me</u>).
4. The performance was given by Erin and (they, <u>them</u>).
5. The argument was between Chris and (I, <u>me</u>).
6. Kate's partners were Ralph and (her, <u>she</u>).
7. The manager fired Susan and (he, <u>him</u>).
8. Todd and (<u>he</u>, him) share a locker.
9. Just between you and (I, <u>me</u>), I'm worried.
10. The refreshments were provided by (she, <u>her</u>) and (I, <u>me</u>).

Exercise B   Follow the directions for Exercise A.

1. Save seats for Jenny and (he, <u>him</u>).
2. The directors are Louis and (<u>she</u>, her).
3. Meg and (<u>I</u>, me) prefer math to science.

Put the following sentences on the chalkboard or on a worksheet. Have students read the sentences. If all pronouns are used correctly, students should mark C after the sentence. Any errors in pronoun usage should be corrected. Students should be prepared to explain why corrections are needed.

1. ^{He} Him and his brother pushed their car out of the snow drift.
C 2. May she and I sit with you?
3. A policeman questioned my Dad and I about the suspect.
4. The principal met with the teachers and they. ^{them}
5. Her and Sally work well together. ^{She}
6. Mark and me tackled the ball carrier. ^I
C 7. He bumped into Ed and me.
8. A package arrived for you and I. ^{me}
9. Return the finished work to her or I. ^{me}
10. Me and her will take first prize. ^{She and I}

Extending the Lesson

Have students write sentences using the following phrases.

1. them and their parents
2. My cousin and I
3. my cousin and me
4. she and he
5. them and us
6. he and they

4. Heidi reminded Gayle and (she, <u>her</u>).
5. Mark and (<u>he</u>, him) played cards.
6. The dog barked at Terry and (I, <u>me</u>).
7. The nurse gave Lon and (I, <u>me</u>) ice packs.
8. Marsha waved at Gary and (he, <u>him</u>).
9. Carl waited for (they, <u>them</u>) and (we, <u>us</u>).
10. The McMahons and (<u>we</u>, us) planted a vegetable garden.

Part 4   Pronouns and Antecedents

A pronoun is a word used in place of a noun. The noun that the pronoun replaces is called the **antecedent.** A pronoun refers to its antecedent.

> Joan reviewed *her* notes.
> (*Her* takes the place of the noun *Joan. Joan* is the antecedent.)

> The silver lost *its* shine.
> (*Its* refers to the noun *silver. Silver* is the antecedent.)

The antecedent usually appears before the pronoun. The antecedent may appear in the same sentence or in the preceding sentence, as in this example:

> The space shuttle landed this morning. *It* had made another successful trip.
> (*It* stands for the antecedent *shuttle.*)

Pronouns may be the antecedents of other pronouns:

> You forgot *your* newspaper.
> (*You* is the antecedent of *your*).

A pronoun must be like its antecedent in one important way. A pronoun must have the same number as its antecedent. If the antecedent is singular, the pronoun must be singular. If the antecedent is plural, then the pronoun must be plural.

A pronoun must agree with its antecedent in number.

The swimmers grabbed *their* towels.
  (*Swimmers* is plural; *their* is plural.)

The actress read *her* script.
  (*Actress* is singular; *her* is singular.)

The children have *their* own playroom.
  (*Children* is plural; *their* is plural.)

Exercise A Write each personal pronoun that is italicized. Then write its antecedent.

1. Ms. Landen waxed *her* car.
2. Tom finished the puzzle and glued *it* together.
3. Ann and I discussed *our* plans.
4. The conductor gave the violinists *their* music.
5. Lois dropped the coins into *her* pocket.
6. DePaul lost *its* chance to win the championship.
7. The boys put *their* sleeping bags into the trunk.
8. Sally set the record in the broad jump and then broke *it*.
9. Marty forgot *his* lines.
10. Water the plants when *they* get dry.

Exercise B Follow the directions for Exercise A.

1. The hawk flew from *its* perch.
2. Some people invest *their* money in gold.
3. The spy decoded *her* instructions.
4. I have outlined *my* project.
5. The carpenter measured the wood and cut *it*.
6. Those trees have Spanish moss on *them*.
7. Janet practiced *her* serve.
8. Rhonda and I placed the game between *us*.
9. Can you remember *your* way home?
10. Did Eric check the stores near *him*?

457

Individualizing the Lesson

Less-Advanced Students

Discuss with students why an antecedent must agree in number with its pronoun. Then have the students write five sentences using pronouns with antecedents. Tell students to make sure the pronoun and antecedent agree in number.

Advanced Students

Have students write a story using as many personal pronouns as they can. Then have them underline the antecedents. Have them check to make sure the pronouns and antecedents agree in number.

Optional Practice

Put the following sentences on the chalkboard or on a worksheet. If the pronoun used is correct, students should write a *C*. If the pronoun does not agree with its antecedent, students should correct it and be prepared to explain why.

1. The cowboy wore their white hat. [his]
2. The cars on the expressway honked its horns. [their]
3. A child cried for his mother. [C]
4. The batteries in your radio are losing its power. [their]
5. I love pretzels. It's my favorite snack. [They're]

Extending the Lesson

Have students find five examples of sentences containing a personal pronoun. Students should copy each sentence, circle the pronoun and underline the antecedent. If any antecedent is unclear, discuss with students how the sentence can be improved.

457

Objective

To use compound personal pronouns correctly

Presenting the Lesson

1. Read page 458, going over the list of compound personal pronouns and examples of their use.

2. Assign and discuss Exercises A and B on pages 458–459.

Individualizing the Lesson

Less-Advanced Students

Work through Exercise A, page 458, orally with the students.

Advanced Students

Have students use each compound personal pronoun from each sentence in Exercises A and B, pages 458–459, in an original sentence.

Optional Practice

1. Have students correct the compound personal pronouns in the following sentences. One sentence is already correct.

1. Mario and I did the shopping *ourselves* ~~*our-self*~~.
2. I painted the kitchen *myself* ~~*myselves*~~.
3. Help *yourself* ~~*yourselves*~~ to a glass of milk, Sandi.
C 4. Andrea went to the concert by *herself*.
5. The story was interesting, but the book *itself* ~~*itselves*~~ was poorly written.

2. Have students explain what was wrong with the pronouns they changed.

458

Part 5 Compound Personal Pronouns

A **compound personal pronoun** is a pronoun with *-self* or *-selves* added.

myself	ourselves
yourself	yourselves
himself, herself, itself	themselves

Notice how compound personal pronouns are used for emphasis:

The President *himself* presented the award.
Tina *herself* wallpapered the room.
I mowed the lawn *myself*.
They moved the piano *themselves*.

Exercise A Number your paper from 1 to 10. Beside each number write the correct compound personal pronoun for each of the following sentences. After it, write its <u>antecedent</u>.

Example: Our dog Bob thinks of (pronoun) as a person.
himself, dog

1. <u>Donna and I</u> cleaned the fish by (pronoun). *ourselves*
2. The <u>students</u> (pronoun) supervise the study hall at our school. *themselves*
3. <u>Kathy</u> (pronoun) prepared the report. *herself*
4. The <u>mayor</u> (pronoun) led the parade. *himself or herself*
5. <u>I</u> wrote this story by (pronoun). *myself*
6. The <u>children</u> (pronoun) planned the trip. *themselves*
7. <u>We</u> yelled (pronoun) hoarse at the game. *ourselves*
8. The <u>workers</u> (pronoun) were not allowed to vote on the new hours. *themselves*
9. <u>We</u> made (pronoun) a snack. *ourselves*
10. Help (pronoun) to some lunch, <u>Gordon</u>. *yourself*

458

Exercise B Follow the directions for Exercise A.

1. <u>Carole King</u> (pronoun) *herself* appeared at the rally.
2. <u>Ed and Adam</u> helped (pronoun) *themselves* to the strawberries.
3. The <u>dentist</u> (pronoun) *himself/herself* cleaned my teeth.
4. <u>Bridget</u> studied (pronoun) *herself* in the mirror.
5. Give (pronoun) *yourself* credit, <u>Luke</u>.
6. <u>Mario</u> programed the computer by (pronoun) *himself*.
7. <u>Fran</u> (pronoun) *herself* flew the plane.
8. The <u>brush fire</u> burned (pronoun) *itself* out.
9. The <u>problem</u> (pronoun) *itself* remains unsolved.
10. <u>Pam and I</u> warmed (pronoun) *ourselves* by the fire.

Part 6 Demonstrative Pronouns

The pronouns *this, that, these,* and *those* point out people or things. They are called **demonstrative pronouns**.

This and *these* point to people or things that are near in space or time. *That* and *those* point to people or things that are farther away in space or time.

This makes a good shelter.   *These* are fake furs.
That was a compliment.   *Those* were funny cartoons.

Exercise Number your paper from 1 to 10. Write the correct demonstrative pronoun for the blank space in each sentence.

1. _____These_____ are better than those.
2. _____That_____ was a close golf match yesterday.
3. _____Those_____ are your snapshots, not these.
4. _____Those_____ are valuable gems in that necklace.
5. _____This_____ is my sister beside me.
6. _____That_____ must be our moving van over there.
7. _____That_____ is my dog chasing the ducks.
8. _____This_____ is a wonderful view here.
9. _____That_____ is the ocean out there.
10. _____Those_____ are the old dishes in that box.

459

Part 7

To recognize and use inter-rogative pronouns correctly

Presenting the Lesson

Read page 460. Stress that to be considered an interrogative pro-noun, the pronoun must be used alone and not before a noun.

Individualizing the Lesson

Less-Advanced Students

Have students write a definition of the interrogative pronoun; then have them list the interrogative pronouns.

Advanced Students

Have students write a sentence for each interrogative pronoun.

Optional Practice

Have students write sentences using interrogative pronouns. Write the sentences on the chalkboard. Have them correct any sentences without interrogative pronouns.

Extending the Lesson

Have students find one example of each interrogative pronoun.

Part **8**

Objectives

1. To differentiate between sin-gular and plural indefinite pronouns

460

Part 7 Interrogative Pronouns

Certain pronouns are used to ask questions. They are called **interrogative pronouns**. The interrogative pronouns are *who*, *whom*, *whose*, *which*, and *what*.

Who parked a car in the alley?   *Which* is the best buy?
Whom did Bonny ask?   *What* cured your cold?
Whose is this suitcase?

Exercise   Number your paper from 1 to 10. Write all the pronouns in these sentences. After each pronoun, write *Demonstrative* or *Interrogative* to show what kind it is.

Example: Who brought the apple pie?
Who—Interrogative

1. That is confusing.
2. Who has seen Jason?
3. Which is the more expensive?
4. These are unusual doorknobs.
5. Is that Betty's signature?
6. Whom does Mr. Price tutor?
7. These are the overdue books.
8. Are those the party decorations?
9. Whose are those?
10. What makes this chili so spicy?

Part 8 Indefinite Pronouns

Some pronouns do not refer to a definite person or thing. Such pronouns are called **indefinite pronouns**.

The following are indefinite pronouns. They are singular. Because they are singular, these pronouns are used with the singular possessive pronouns *his*, *her*, and *its*.

460

another	each	everything	one
anybody	either	neither	somebody
anyone	everybody	nobody	someone
anything	everyone	no one	

Each of the apartments has *its* own fireplace.
Nobody ate *his* dinner.
Nobody ate *his* or *her* dinner.

The last example uses the phrase *his or her* instead of simply *his*. That phrase shows that the indefinite pronoun may refer to a male or female. Many people prefer such a phrase.

Although most indefinite pronouns are singular, some are plural. They refer to more than one person or thing. The following indefinite pronouns are plural. They are used with the plural possessive *their*. Study these examples.

both   many   few   several

Several of the dancers practiced *their* routines.
Few of the tenants knew *their* neighbors.
Many of my friends sew *their* own clothes.
Both of the dogs broke *their* leashes.

A few indefinite pronouns can be either singular or plural, depending on their meaning in a sentence. Read these examples:

all   none   some

All of the drinking water has flouride in *it*.
All of the ribs have barbeque sauce on *them*.
None of the music had life in *it*.
None of the politicians wrote *their* own speeches.
Some of the ice cream has strawberries in *it*.
Some of the dancers changed *their* costumes.

Exercise A   Number your paper from 1 to 10. For each sentence write the indefinite pronoun.

1. No one brought a can opener.
2. Where is everyone going?

461

2. To use indefinite pronouns with possessive pronouns that agree with them in number

Presenting the Lesson

1. Read pages 460–461. Go over the list of singular indefinite pronouns. Study the sample sentences showing singular indefinite pronouns used correctly with singular possessive pronouns. If necessary, refer to the list of singular and plural possessive pronouns on page 452.

2. Go over the list of the four plural indefinite pronouns. Stress that only these four are always plural. Again, study sample sentences showing plural indefinite pronouns correctly used with plural possessive pronouns.

3. Read page 461, studying the examples of indefinite pronouns which may be singular or plural, depending on the context in which they are used.

4. Assign and discuss Exercises A and B on pages 461–462.

5. Assign and discuss Exercise C on pages 462–463. Stress that the subject of a sentence is never found in a prepositional phrase.

Individualizing the Lesson

Less-Advanced Students

Have students write two sentences for each indefinite pronoun that can be either singular or plural. Tell students to make sure the pronoun agrees in number with its antecedent.

Advanced Students

Have students use the incorrect verbs from Exercise C, page 462, in a new exercise. Students should

461

write original sentences using the incorrect verb from Exercise C and matching that verb with a properly used pronoun.

Have students study the list of indefinite pronouns on page 461.

Optional Practice

Have students choose the correct pronoun from the two in parentheses.

1. None of the workers wore (his or her, their) uniforms.
2. Both of my shoes were soaked through to (its, their) soles.
3. Neither of the artists sold (his or her, their) pictures.
4. All of the students brought (his or her, their) notes from home.
5. Can't anyone offer (his or her, their) help?
6. Some of the cookies spilled out of (its, their) box.
7. Each of my socks has a hole in (its, their) toe.
8. Everyone should have (his or her, their) eyes checked once a year.
9. Some of the roses lost (its, their) petals.
10. Either of the girls can bring (her, their) guest.

Extending the Lesson

Have students study the list of indefinite pronouns on page 461. Then give students a quiz on indefinite pronouns. Just as in a spelling test, say the indefinite pronoun, have students write the word, and then have them use the indefinite pronoun in a sentence. Along with indefinite pronouns include other types of pronouns as well. Tell students *not* to write any word that is not an indefinite pronoun.

3. None of us missed the bus.
4. Did anyone write down the address?
5. Karen found all the Easter eggs.
6. Many of the tourists photographed the view.
7. Tim walked both of the dogs.
8. Why is everybody upset?
9. Several of the bulbs were broken.
10. Only one of the trees died.

Exercise B   Choose the correct pronoun from the two given.

1. Some of the musicians forgot (his or her, their) music.
2. Neither of the men brought (his, their) briefcase.
3. If anyone arrives early, have (him, them) wait for me.
4. Everybody introduced (his or her, their) guests.
5. Somebody left (his or her, their) picnic basket.
6. All of the rookies have completed (his or her, their) training program.
7. One of the eagles spread (its, their) wings.
8. Did somebody forget (his or her, their) newspaper?
9. All of the drivers adjusted (his or her, their) face masks.
10. Each of these Indian tribes has (its, their) own special customs.

Exercise C   Number your paper from 1 to 10. For each of the following sentences write the indefinite pronoun and the correct verb from the two in parentheses.

1. Everyone (take, takes) chances.
2. Nobody (confuse, confuses) me with my sister.
3. All of these melons (is, are) ripe.
4. Neither of the towns (has, have) a daily newspaper.
5. One of my cats (has, have) an infection.
6. Many of the magazines (is, are) printed here.
7. Some of the shows (is, are) reruns.

8. <u>Many</u> of the athletes (is, <u>are</u>) becoming celebrities.

9. <u>Each</u> of the mechanics (use, <u>uses</u>) his or her own tools.

10. <u>Some</u> of the butter (<u>is</u>, are) salt-free.

Part 9 Special Problems with Pronouns

Contractions and Possessive Pronouns

Certain contractions are sometimes confused with possessive pronouns.

Contractions are formed by joining two words and omitting one or more letters. An apostrophe shows where letters are left out.

it's = it + is   they're = they + are
you're = you + are   who's = who + is

The above contractions are sometimes confused with the possessive pronouns *its, your, their,* and *whose.* The words sound alike but are spelled differently.

Incorrect: Who's turn is it?
Correct: Whose turn is it?

If you can't decide which word is correct, substitute the words the contraction stands for. If the sentence sounds right, then the contraction is correct.

Exercise A Choose the right word from the two in parentheses.

1. (<u>Whose</u>, Who's) pen is this?

2. (Your, <u>You're</u>) new here, aren't you?

3. The divers left (<u>their</u>, they're) gear in the boat.

4. (Their, <u>They're</u>) lost in the crowd of people.

5. (Its, <u>It's</u>) time for the kickoff.

6. (Whose, <u>Who's</u>) the anchor for the news on channel 5?

463

Part 9

Objective

To use pronouns correctly in situations often causing problems: 1) contractions and possessives, 2) *who* and *whom,* 3) *we* and *us* with nouns, 4) *them* and *those*

Presenting the Lesson

1. Read page 463. Be certain that students understand what contractions are. Point out the similarity in sound, but difference in spelling and meaning between the possessive pronouns and the contractions. Pay special attention to the suggested way to determine if a contraction or pronoun should be used.

2. Assign and discuss Exercises A and B on pages 463–464.

3. Read page 464. Stress that *who* is the subject form and that *whom* is the object form.

4. Assign and discuss Exercises A and B on pages 464–465.

5. Read page 465 discussing the way to determine whether *we* or *us* should be used, by omitting the noun. Remind students that *we* is the subject form and *us* is the object form.

6. Read page 466, discussing when to use *them* and when to use *those.* Stress that *them* is always a pronoun.

7. Assign and discuss Exercises A and B on pages 466–467.

463

Less-Advanced Students

1. Tell students that the easiest way to remember how to use special problem pronouns is to memorize how and when each problem pronoun is used. Have students study pages 463–466 again.

2. Have students write brief explanations of the differences between *who* and *whom,* between *we* and *us,* and between *them* and *those.* Have them use each word in a sentence.

Advanced Students

Have students write a sentence using each problem pronoun.

Optional Practice

Put the following sentences on the chalkboard or on a worksheet. Have students read the sentences. If the sentence is correct, students should mark *C* after the sentence. If there are any errors, students should correct them. Students should be prepared to explain why the corrections were needed. Answers may vary.

1. Us students are entering the track meet.
   We
2. Put them life preservers on them children.
   these/those   *these/those*
3. Those are the presents from we girls.
   These   *us*
4. Whom put those books here? Whose are they?
   Who   *these*
C 5. For whom is the message?
C 6. Who gave us boys permission to leave?
7. Them chairs are yours.
   These/Those
8. It's hard for we teen-agers to earn money.
   us

---

7. (Your, You're) name was in the paper.
8. That cat has lost (its, it's) collar.
9. Is that (your, you're) wallet?
10. (Whose, Who's) the gentleman on the stage?

Exercise B   Write the words each contraction below stands for.

1. Who's going to the concert in the park? *Who is*
2. They've volunteered for the clean-up committee. *They have*
3. She's shoveling the snow on the sidewalk. *She is*
4. You're the first guest to arrive. *You are*
5. We'll organize the meeting. *We will*
6. I'd like a glass of water. *I would*
7. They're waiting for us at the theater. *They are*
8. What's on the menu? *What is*
9. I'm allergic to milk. *I am*
10. We'd better leave early. *We had*

Who and *Whom*

Many people have problems with the pronouns *who* and *whom.*

Who sounds natural in most questions. Use *who* as the subject of a sentence.

> *Who* wound the clock?   *Who* is that?

Whom is harder to get used to. *Whom* is used as an object.

> *Whom* did you invite?
> > (direct object of the verb *did invite*)
>
> To *whom* are the applications given?
> > (object of the preposition *to*)

Exercise A   Choose the right pronoun from the two in parentheses.

1. (Who, Whom) can reach that shelf?
2. (Who, Whom) won the game?

3. (Who, <u>Whom</u>) did you videotape?
4. (Who, <u>Whom</u>) were you helping?
5. (<u>Who</u>, Whom) is the newspaper reporter?
6. (<u>Who</u>, Whom) fixed your TV?
7. (<u>Who</u>, Whom) directed that movie?
8. With (who, <u>whom</u>) will you meet?
9. (Who, <u>Whom</u>) did the committee select?
10. (Who, <u>Whom</u>) do you support?

Exercise B   Follow the directions for Exercise A.

1. (<u>Who</u>, Whom) programs the computer?
2. (Who, <u>Whom</u>) did the lawyer question?
3. To (who, <u>whom</u>) were the flowers sent?
4. (Who, <u>Whom</u>) were they expecting?
5. (Who, <u>Whom</u>) did the voters elect?
6. (<u>Who</u>, Whom) rehearsed last night?
7. To (who, <u>whom</u>) was the building dedicated?
8. (<u>Who</u>, Whom) cultivated the field?
9. With (who, <u>whom</u>) did you meet?
10. (<u>Who</u>, Whom) needs a daily vitamin?

We and Us with Nouns

The pronouns *we* and *us* are often used with nouns, as in the phrases *we girls* or *us players*. Such phrases can cause problems.

To decide whether to use *we* or *us*, omit the noun. Say the sentence with *we* and then with *us*. You will then probably be able to choose the correct pronoun.

Problem: (We, Us) divers practice daily.
Correct: We practice daily.
Correct: We divers practice daily.

Problem: Low grain prices hurt (we, us) farmers.
Correct: Low grain prices hurt us.
Correct: Low grain prices hurt us farmers.

c 9. Your car has a scratch in its paint.
10. Who's going to rake ~~them~~ leaves?
^{these/those}

Extending the Lesson

Have students write sentences using the following phrases.

1. it's easy   4. we boys
2. their helmets   5. from whom
3. they're ready   6. with those

Them and *Those*

Them and *those* are sometimes confused. To use the words correctly, remember that *them* is always a pronoun. It takes the place of a noun.

> The state trooper helped *them*. (In this sentence, *them* is used as the direct object.)

Them is never used to tell about or describe a noun. *Those* should be used.

> Incorrect: Lorraine baked them muffins.
>
> Correct: Lorraine baked those muffins.

Exercise A Choose the correct pronoun from the two given in parentheses.

1. The mayor thanked (we, us) volunteers.
2. Did you find (them, those) pliers?
3. (Them, Those) foods are nutritious.
4. Exchange (them, those) gloves for the right size.
5. (We, Us) bowlers formed a summer league.
6. (Them, Those) plants look healthy.
7. The coach congratulated (we, us) winners.
8. (We, Us) campers enjoy peace and quiet.
9. Bill bought one of (them, those) radios.
10. The monkey made faces at (we, us) tourists.

Exercise B Follow the directions for Exercise A.

1. (We, Us) girls organized the picnic.
2. Are (them, those) ski vests warm?
3. (Them, Those) peppers are hot.
4. The photographer snapped a picture of (we, us) graduates.
5. I prefer (them, those) boots.

6. Do you like (them, <u>those</u>) alfalfa sprouts in your sand-wich?

7. (<u>We</u>, Us) bookworms should start a book exchange.

8. Should (them, <u>those</u>) pants be dry-cleaned?

9. The power failure in the store gave (we, <u>us</u>) shoppers a fright.

10. Today (<u>we</u>, us) gymnasts face our toughest rivals.

Exercise C   In the sentences that follow, there are some errors in the use of pronouns. If a sentence is incorrect, correct it. If it is correct, write *Correct*.

   1. She will lend the book to we girls when she is through with it.
  us

   2. Bring them pictures of the team with you.
  those

   3. Us cyclists are hoping to win the race next Thursday.
  We

   4. Did Henry bring them peaches, or did Marla?
  those

C 5. We students are going to visit Taos Pueblo this summer.

   6. André saw them skaters in his home town.
  those

C 7. Those shoes were left here by mistake.

   8. Us three split the cost of the album.
  We

C 9. Will you play Monopoly with us if it rains?

 10. Who talked to them strangers?
  those

ADDITIONAL EXERCISES

Using Pronouns

A. Nouns and Pronouns Number your paper from 1 to 10. Write the pronouns you find in each of the following sentences. After each pronoun, write the noun or nouns it stands for.

1. The zipper had gone off its track. [zipper]
2. Ian took his time. [Ian]
3. The Oak Ridge Boys sang their most recent hit. [Oak Ridge Boys]
4. Are you in training, Amy? [Amy]
5. Turtles never leave their shells. [Turtles]
6. Ms. Neff rewired her stereo. [Ms. Neff]
7. "My guitar needs tuning," said Judi. [Judi]
8. "Here we are!" shouted the children. [children]
9. Wendy was the first to call Mark on his new phone. [Mark]
10. Tamara and Chuck were reading from their scripts. [Tamara and Chuck]

B. The Use of Pronouns Choose the correct pronoun from the two given in parentheses. Be ready to explain how it is used in the sentence.

1. (They, Them) put new shingles on the roof.
2. Does (she, her) work in a lab?
3. The alderman asked (she, her) for help.
4. Jackson tossed the ball to (she, her) for the third out.
5. A chunk of plaster landed on (him, his) head.
6. The tenants discussed (they, their) requests with the landlord.
7. The newest recruit was (he, him).
8. The chef for the evening is (I, me).
9. The class sent (she, her) a get-well card.
10. Maybe (we, us) should hold a block party.

C. Pronouns in Compound Constructions Choose the correct pronoun from the two given in parentheses.

1. Julia and (<u>he</u>, him) work in a sporting goods shop.
2. Alec took Nancy and (I, <u>me</u>) to a roller derby.
3. Todd and (<u>I</u>, me) dug holes for the fence posts.
4. The trail was too rough for Matthew and (she, <u>her</u>).
5. The McCoys and (<u>they</u>, them) take vacations together.
6. Chandra and (<u>we</u>, us) designed the mural.
7. Don't give Sam and (he, <u>him</u>) all the credit.
8. The farmer hired Billie and (we, <u>us</u>) to harvest the hay.
9. Just between you and (I, <u>me</u>), I should have won that race.
10. The vice-principals are Mr. Guiterrez and (<u>she</u>, her).

D. Pronouns and Antecedents Write the <u>antecedent</u> for each italicized pronoun.

1. <u>Betsy</u> put *her* lunchbag into the backpack.
2. Tony bought the <u>groceries</u> and had *them* delivered.
3. Fran found some <u>change</u> under the cushions and pocketed *it*.
4. May <u>I</u> give *my* report first, Mr. Byers?
5. <u>You</u> seem angry about *your* mistake.
6. Gina realigned the <u>drainpipe</u> and fastened *it*.
7. <u>Ronnie</u> has a habit of rubbing *his* forehead.
8. James photographed the <u>does</u> and *their* fawns.
9. The <u>shop</u> has burglar bars on *its* windows.
10. <u>We</u> strapped suitcases and boxes onto *our* luggage rack.

E. Compound Personal Pronouns Number your paper from 1 to 10. Beside each number write a correct compound personal pronoun for each of the following sentences. After it, write the <u>noun or pronoun</u> to which it refers.

1. Don't hurt (pronoun)^{yourself} with that blade, <u>Mike</u>.

469

2. Some <u>men</u> shave (pronoun) *themselves* without using a mirror.
3. <u>Rachel</u> treated (pronoun) *herself* to a pizza.
4. <u>Andy</u> is too young to cross the street by (pronoun) *himself*.
5. <u>We</u> serve (pronoun) *ourselves* at the salad bar.
6. The <u>alarm</u> turns (pronoun) *itself* off too soon.
7. The <u>tourists</u> found (pronoun) *themselves* stranded in a strange town.
8. <u>I</u> (pronoun) *myself* prefer swimming in a pool.
9. Please grade (pronoun) *yourselves*, <u>students</u>.
10. <u>He</u> soon found (pronoun) *himself* friendless.

F. Different Kinds of Pronouns Number your paper from 1 to 10. Write all the <u>pronouns</u> in each sentence. After each pronoun, write *Indefinite*, *Demostrative*, or *Interrogative* to show what kind it is.

1. <u>That</u>ᴰ is Mt. Rainier off in the distance.
2. <u>Everything</u>ᴵⁿᵈ went smoothly until the last act.
3. <u>What</u>ᴵⁿᵗ is bothering Jonathan?
4. <u>This</u>ᴰ has been a long day.
5. Has anybody ever tried <u>that</u>ᴰ before?
6. <u>Whom</u>ᴵⁿᵗ are those for?
7. <u>Which</u>ᴵⁿᵗ are the left-handed scissors?
8. Please give <u>each</u>ᴵⁿᵈ of the patients one of <u>these</u>ᴰ.
9. <u>Who</u>ᴵⁿᵗ is playing the saxophone upstairs?
10. <u>Neither</u>ᴵⁿᵈ of the suspects admitted <u>anything</u>ᴵⁿᵈ.

G. Indefinite Pronouns Number your paper from 1 to 10. For each sentence write the <u>indefinite pronoun</u>. Then, write the word that agrees with the indefinite pronoun.

1. Has <u>anyone</u> ever had (<u>his or her</u>, their) fortune told?
2. <u>Some</u> of the gymnasts have (her, <u>their</u>) own warm-up exercises.
3. <u>Each</u> of the parking lots has (<u>its</u>, their) own rates.
4. <u>Few</u> of the players had signed (his, <u>their</u>) contracts yet.

5. Both of the runners broke (her, their) own records.
6. Nobody (knows, know) the cause of the crash.
7. Neither of them (works, work) at the gas station.
8. One of these medicine bottles is missing (its, their) label.
9. Everything (depends, depend) on the weather.
10. None of the food had salt in (it, them).

H. Special Pronoun Problems Choose the correct word from the two given in parentheses.

1. The bikers loaded (their, they're) backpacks with food for the trip.
2. Does (your, you're) car use unleaded fuel?
3. (Who, Whom) did she sign a contract with?
4. (Who, Whom) brought the FM radio?
5. (We, Us) city dwellers are used to noise.
6. Have you tried one of (them, those) egg rolls?
7. (It's, Its) rude to call at dinner time.
8. That mountain is not for (we, us) amateur climbers.
9. The computer terminal prints (it's, its) message on this screen.
10. (Whose, Who's) using the gym on Thursday night?

Mixed Review

These exercises provide review of the concepts pre-
sented in this Section. Each
exercise challenges the students to apply several of the
skills they have acquired during previous study. Because
the "mixed" feature of these
activities makes them more
difficult, the teacher may wish
to have less-advanced students do them orally or in
small groups.

MIXED REVIEW

Using Pronouns

A. Using personal pronouns Write the correct pronoun for
each of the following sentences. After each one, write its antecedent.

1. An arctic fox changes (its, their) color in winter.
2. "Is the backpack (your, yours)?" Elam asked Rich.
3. Judy said, "The person in charge is (I, me)."
4. Polish the shoes and then buff (it, them, they).
5. Natalie, have (you, your) seen Kelly?
6. Mark pointed to Carl and said, "The boss asked
   (he, him)."
7. Shirley forgot (her, hers, she) pen.
8. Both coaches praised (his, their, they) teams.
9. Melissa and Tony saw the accident. (Them, They) will
   testify.
10. Ms. Chen smiled at Lisa and gave (her, she) the card.

**B. Using compound pronouns and pronouns in com-
pound parts correctly** Some of the following sentences use
pronouns incorrectly. Rewrite correctly any sentences that do. If a
sentence is correct, write *Correct*.

1. The players themself insist on proper equipment. [themselves]
2. Angela and you will solve the problem by yourself. [yourselves]
3. I was waving to Ginger and him. [C]
4. The Wilsons and them have Thanksgiving dinner with [they]
   us.
5. Sara and me talked ourselves out of the idea. [I]
6. A fire can burn themselves out. [itself]
7. The thunder scared Junior and she. [her]
8. The principal handed Martha and he their science fair [him]
   ribbons.

9. Just between you and ~~I~~, Ron and he made the same
mistake themselves.

c 10. The high scorers in the game between Eastern and us
were Jo and she.

C. Using the correct form of pronouns Write the correct
pronoun from those given in parentheses.

1. (This, <u>That</u>) must be Paula on the other side of the
gym.
2. Nobody forgot (<u>his or her</u>, their) coat today.
3. (<u>Who</u>, Whose) is at the door?
4. (<u>This</u>, That) is the shallow end right here.
5. Neither of the dogs has had (<u>its</u>, their) rabies shot.
6. (Who, <u>Whose</u>) are the black skates?
7. Everyone wore (<u>her</u>, their) corsage to the dance.
8. Each of the students has (<u>his or her</u>, their) own locker.
9. Few of the students have (his or her, <u>their</u>) own
computers.
10. None of the soldiers remembered (<u>his or her</u>, their)
orders.

D. Using pronouns correctly Write the correct pronoun
from those given in parentheses.

1. The taxicab had one of (them, <u>those</u>) glass partitions.
2. (<u>Who</u>, Whom) is running with the ball?
3. (Us, <u>We</u>) people in wheelchairs can't get into that
building.
4. I checked the wires; (their, <u>they're</u>) fine.
5. (<u>Who's</u>, Whose) wearing a beeper?
6. The gusts of wind were losing (<u>their</u>, they're) force.
7. (Who, <u>Whom</u>) have you told?
8. Maybe (their, <u>they're</u>) invisible.
9. Did the cashier put the change on (<u>your</u>, you're) tray?
10. The bird builds (it's, <u>its</u>) nest by instinct.

These challenging and enjoyable activities allow the students to see how the concepts of grammar, usage, and mechanics may be applied in actual writing situations. Each exercise is designed to allow students practice in several of the skills they have acquired in this Section. The activities also provide opportunities for students to write creatively about a wide variety of interesting and unusual subjects.

USING GRAMMAR IN WRITING
Using Pronouns

The following poem has been rewritten incorrectly with few pronouns. Correct the poem by replacing the underlined words with pronouns. You may choose *he, she,* or *it,* but be consistent throughout the poem.

The Fox and the Grapes
A Moral Tale for Those Who Fail

One summer's day a Fox was passing through
An orchard; faint <u>the Fox</u> was and hungry, too.
When suddenly <u>the Fox's</u> keen eye chanced to fall
Upon a bunch of grapes above the wall.
"Ha! Just the thing!" <u>the Fox</u> said. "Who could resist
  <u>the bunch of grapes</u>!'"
<u>The Fox</u> eyed the purple cluster—jumped—and missed
  <u>the purple cluster</u>.
"Ahem!" <u>the Fox</u> coughed. "I'll take more careful aim,"
And sprang again. Results were much the same,
Although <u>the Fox's</u> leaps were desperate and high.
At length <u>the Fox</u> paused to wipe a tearful eye,
And shrug a shoulder. "I am not so dry,
And lunch is bound to come within the hour . . .
Besides," <u>the Fox</u> said, "I'm sure those grapes are
  sour."

THE MORAL is: We somehow want the peach
That always dangles just beyond our reach;
Until we learn never to be upset
With what we find too difficult to get.
—JOSEPH LAUREN

Using Verbs

Section Objectives

1. To identify verbs and distinguish between action verbs and linking verbs

2. To differentiate between transitive and intransitive verbs

3. To recognize main verbs and helping verbs, even when verb parts are separated

4. To recognize and form the six main verb tenses and to understand the purpose of each tense

5. To recognize the principal parts of regular verbs

6. To recognize the principal parts of irregular verbs, and to use the dictionary to check the parts

7. To distinguish between active and passive verbs

Preparing the Students

Remind students that verbs, which will be dealt with in detail in this Section, are the driving force of the sentence—they bring action and life to a sentence. Read the introduction on page 475.

Additional Resources

Diagnostic Test — page 3 in the test booklet

Mastery Test — pages 48–51 in the test booklet

Additional Exercises — pages 493–499 in the student text

Practice Book — pages 188–197

Duplicating Masters — pages 188–197

Special Populations — See special section at the front of this Teacher's Edition.

You already know something about the verb. It is the most important part of a sentence. A verb tells of an action or a state of being.

The verb is another one of the parts of speech. In this section you will find out more about verbs and how they are used.

1. To identify verbs and distinguish between action verbs and linking verbs

2. To differentiate between transitive verbs and intransitive verbs

Presenting the Lesson

1. Review with students the main parts of a sentence—the subject and the verb. Remind them that the verb tells what happened or tells something about the subject.

2. Read page 476. Study the definition and examples of action verbs. Stress that not all "actions" can be seen. Go over the definition and examples of linking verbs. Pay special attention to verbs that can be either linking verbs or action verbs. Point out the link between the subject and the predicate word when the verb expresses a state of being.

3. Read page 477. Stress that the designation as transitive or intransitive refers only to action verbs and not to linking verbs. Go over explanations and examples of transitive and intransitive verbs. Pay special attention to verbs which can be either transitive or intransitive.

4. Assign and discuss Exercises A and B on pages 477–478.

5. Assign and discuss Exercise C on page 478.

Individualizing the Lesson

Less-Advanced Students

Have students write five original sentences containing a linking verb,

476

Part 1   What Is a Verb?

A verb tells of an action or a state of being.

Action Verbs

One kind of verb indicates action, even if the action is unseen.

Ella *frowned*.   Mary *organized* her thoughts.
The train *stopped*.   Craig *has* a cold.

An **action verb** tells that something is happening, has happened, or will happen.

Linking Verbs

Some verbs simply tell that something exists. Such verbs express a state of being rather than action.

The assembly *is* tomorrow.   Lee *was* anxious.
Lynn *seems* upset.   The paint *feels* tacky.

These verbs are called **linking verbs**. They link the subject with some other word or words in the sentence.

Here are the most common linking verbs:

be (am, are, is, was,	look	smell	seem
were, been, being)	appear	taste	sound
become	feel	grow	

Some linking verbs can also be used as action verbs.

Linking Verbs	Action Verbs
The bread *tasted* dry.	Kate *tasted* the chili.
The children *grew* sleepy.	Larry *grew* vegetables.

When you look at the verb in a sentence, see how it is used. Decide whether it expresses action or simply links the subject with a word in the predicate.

476

Transitive and Intransitive Verbs

In many sentences an action verb expresses an idea by itself. In other sentences a direct object completes the action of the verb. The direct object, as you have learned, answers *whom* or *what* about the verb.

Verbs that have direct objects are **transitive verbs**.

> Myra *examined* the envelope.
> (The direct object *envelope* completes the meaning of the verb *examined*.)
> The car *towed* a trailer.
> (The direct object *trailer* completes the meaning of the verb *towed*.)

Verbs that do not have direct objects are another kind of verb. They are called **intransitive verbs**.

> The audience *rose*.
> (The verb *rose* has no direct object.)
> Warren *swam* in the stream.
> (The verb *swam* has no direct object.)

Some action verbs are always transitive or always intransitive. Other verbs change. The same verb may be transitive in one sentence and intransitive in another. Compare these examples.

Transitive Verbs	Intransitive Verbs
The chorus *sang* a medley.	The chorus *sang* at the assembly.
The fans *shouted* a cheer.	The fans *shouted*.
Pam *parked* the car.	Pam *parked* near the library.

Exercise A Write the verb in each sentence. After each verb write *Action* or *Linking* to show what kind it is.

A 1. The general issued a statement.
L 2. Iowa farm land is fertile.
A 3. The judge called for order in the courtroom.

477

Advanced Students

Have students write a paragraph about a chosen topic. Tell them to make sure they use both transitive and intransitive verbs in their sentences. Have them leave a space after each sentence. Then have students exchange papers and identify whether the verbs are transitive or intransitive. Have them write their answers in the space after each sentence.

Optional Practice

Have students identify the verb in each of the following sentences, telling whether it is a linking verb or an action verb. For each action verb, have students tell whether the verb is transitive or intransitive.

T 1. Julie always sings pretty songs.
L 2. Our classroom clock is slow.
T 3. I wrote a three-page book report.
L 4. The newscast was late tonight.
L 5. Dana feels sorry for Lindsey.
T 6. The doctor checked Vera's temperature.
T 7. I have a stone in my shoe.
L 8. Meryl Streep is a fine actress.
I 9. We ate early during our vacation.
T 10. Everyone ate cake and ice cream.

Extending the Lesson

Have students write sentences using the following verbs in the way indicated. Answers will vary.

1. grew (linking)
2. grew (action-transitive)
3. became (linking)
4. planted (action-transitive)
5. swam (action-intransitive)

L 4. That jingle is catchy.
A 5. The critic praised the performance.
L 6. A resort was down in the valley.
L 7. The banker seemed confident.
A 8. Joe daydreamed about his vacation.
L 9. Gasoline became scarce during the oil embargo.
A 10. We saw a three-ring circus.

Exercise B Follow the directions for Exercise A.

A 1. A tornado destroyed the town.
A 2. The WPA created jobs during the Depression.
A 3. The turtles basked in the sun.
L 4. The Bedouins are nomads.
L 5. This collar feels stiff.
A 6. Can you leave a message for the doctor?
L 7. The DC–10 is a jumbo jet.
A 8. Milton Friedman won a Nobel Prize in economics.
A 9. Wreckers demolished the building.
L 10. The faces of the firefighters were grim.

Exercise C Write the action verb in each sentence. After it write *Transitive* or *Intransitive* to show what kind it is.

I   1. The hound howled at the moon.
I   2. Every year new fads appear.
T   3. That radio station only plays rock music.
T   4. The scientist checked the test tubes.
I   5. Paramedics arrived on the scene.
I   6. Our houseguests finally left.
T   7. Clare rarely drinks milk.
I   8. During the winter the pool closes.
T   9. Lou made bacon and eggs.
T 10. Some cars have diesel engines.

Part 2 The Parts of a Verb

Many verbs are made up of a **main verb** plus one or more **helping verbs**.

The most common helping verbs are forms of *be, have,* and *do*. They may also be used as main verbs. Here are their forms:

be—am, is, are, was, were, be, being, been
have—has, have, had
do—does, do, did

Used as Main Verb	Used as Helping Verb
I *was* happy.	I *was baking* a pizza.
Nick *has* a headache.	Nick *has ordered* the tickets.
We *did* the laundry.	We *did receive* invitations.

Here are other frequently used helping verbs:

can	will	shall	may	must
could	would	should	might	

Helping verbs combine with the main verb to become part of the verb.

Helping Verb(s) +	Main Verb =	Verb
will	play	will play
had	played	had played
should have	played	should have played
must	walk	must walk
has	walked	has walked

Sometimes the parts of the verb are separated. The words that come between them are not part of the verb. Study these examples.

Baseball *has* always *been* a popular sport.
The kite *was* barely *staying* aloft.
When *will* the senator *give* her speech?
Did the catalog order *arrive?*
Our puppy *will* not *eat* dog food.

479

Part 2

Objective

To recognize main verbs and helping verbs, even when verb parts are separated

Presenting the Lesson

1. Read page 479. Go over forms of *be, have,* and *do,* and the examples showing them as main verbs and as helping verbs. Go over the list of other frequently used helping verbs.

2. Assign and discuss Exercises A and B on page 480.

Individualizing the Lesson

Less-Advanced Students

1. Have students study the list of frequently used helping verbs.

2. Have students identify the helping verbs and main verbs in a newspaper article.

3. Have students write five sentences using five different helping verbs.

Advanced Students

Have students use each helping verb in a sentence. Tell students to circle each helping verb and underline each main verb.

Optional Practice

Have students identify main verbs and any helping verbs in the following sentences.

1. We have tried every flavor of ice cream in that store.
   HV   MV
2. The cost of living has been going up every month.
   HV   HV   MV
3. Can anyone see the exit ramp?
   HV   MV

479

4. Barbara has always been a good
   skier. (HV: has, MV: been)
5. Our family rented a beach house
   for the weekend. (MV: rented)
6. We were watching *Hill Street Blues*. (HV: were, MV: watching)
7. When were you planning your va-
   cation? (HV: were, MV: planning)
8. Why does it always rain on Saturday? (HV: does, MV: rain)
9. Janette does her homework in
   study hall. (MV: does)
10. Ethan has suddenly changed his
    mind about tomorrow. (HV: has, MV: changed)

Extending the Lesson

Have students write sentences
using the following verbs as indicated. Answers will vary.

1. *has* (helping verb) + *been* (main
   verb)
2. *had been* + main verb
3. *might have* + main verb
4. *did* as main verb
5. *could have been* + main verb

Part 3

Objective

To recognize and form the six
main verb tenses and to understand
the purpose of each tense

Exercise A Make two columns. Label them *Helping Verb* and
Main Verb. Find the parts of the verb in each sentence. Write them in
the proper columns.

1. The pool was overflowing.
2. The neighborhood grocery has closed.
3. The burglars could not hear the silent alarm.
4. The chef will dice the vegetables.
5. Has the test been postponed?
6. The piano should be tuned occasionally.
7. Did you win a prize in the raffle?
8. Kelly had never met my sister.
9. Newspaper reporters must often work odd hours.
10. A bulletproof vest would have protected the police
    officer.

Exercise B Follow the directions for Exercise A.

1. The ambulance had been called by a bystander.
2. Dee is rehearsing her lines.
3. David has read that story before.
4. Will Mr. Langan consider our offer?
5. Molly should have taken the make-up test.
6. Can Ginny find the map?
7. The river has nearly reached flood level.
8. Have you ever camped in the desert?
9. Your cousin will certainly call you from the airport.
10. This floor must be waxed regularly.

Part 3   Verb Tenses

Verbs indicate time. They tell when an action or state of being
occurs. Verbs can indicate past time, present time, or future
time by changing form.

These changes in form to show time are called **tenses**. The
changes are usually made in these ways:

1. Change in spelling

   sit ⟶ sat   cry ⟶ cried   walk ⟶ walked

2. Use of helping verbs

   had shown   will compete   has taken

This list shows examples of the six main tenses for the verbs *listen* and *skate*.

Present Tense	I listen.	She skates.
Past Tense	I listened.	She skated.
Future Tense	I will listen.	She will skate.
Present Perfect Tense	I have listened.	She has skated.
Past Perfect Tense	I had listened.	She had skated.
Future Perfect Tense	I will have listened.	She will have skated.

Simple Tenses

The **present tense** shows time in the present. The present tense form is usually the same as the name of the verb. For verbs used with most singular subjects, an *-s* is added to the verb.

   I swim.   David swims.   My brother swims.

The **past tense** shows past time. Most verbs form the past tense by adding *-d* or *-ed*.

   Ron cooked.   Sue phoned.   He chuckled.

Some verbs form the past tense in different ways.

   They swam.   Marge went to the movies.   Eve thought.

The **future tense** shows time in the future. In this tense, use *shall* or *will* with the verb.

   Ed will finish.   I shall continue.   Annette will try.

The three tenses just described are called the **simple tenses**.

481

1. Have students write one original sentence using each verb tense. Tell students to leave at least five lines between sentences.

2. After the original sentences have been written, have students adapt each original sentence using all the other verb tenses. Students should end up with five additional sentences for each original sentence.

Optional Practice

Have students identify the verbs in the following sentences and tell the tense of each.

1. Our dog, Coco, follows me everywhere. present
2. The orchestra has begun its program. present perfect
3. Bert planted tomatoes near the fence. past
4. The candidates will have a debate. future
5. By graduation you will have learned all of this information. future perfect
6. By noon the sun had gone behind the clouds. past perfect
7. Peter fell in the mud along the river bank. past
8. The roses will be in bloom soon. future
9. Birds gather around the fountain. present
10. Dinner will be ready at six o'clock. future

Extending the Lesson

Have students write an essay about any subject they choose. Tell students to use each verb tense—past, present, future, present perfect, past perfect, and future perfect—at least once in the essay.

Perfect Tenses

The **perfect tenses** are used when you speak of two different times, one earlier than the other. The perfect tenses are formed by using the helping verbs *has, have,* and *had.*

The **present perfect tense** tells of an action or state of being in some indefinite time before the present. The helping verb *has* or *have* is used.

> Louis has skied often.   Joan has won.
> They have finished   Terry and Bill have left already.
>   their work.

The **past perfect tense** tells of a time *before* another time in the past. The helping verb *had* is used.

> Mother *had* not *been* nervous before she *went* for the test.
> Wayne *had filled* the tire with air, but it *leaked.*
> We *had* just *arrived* at the airport when the plane *landed.*

The **future perfect tense** tells of a time in the future *before* some other time in the future.

> By midnight tonight, you *will have missed* the deadline.
> When the class is over, we *will have read* ten books.

Exercise A   Find the verbs in the following sentences. Tell the tense of each.

1. Jesse aimed the bow and arrow. Past
2. Two schools in this district have closed. Present Perfect
3. The team has won the play-off game. Present Perfect
4. Andrea plays the clarinet. Present
5. Your speech will conclude the program. Future
6. The nurses will change shifts at eleven. Future
7. Most colas contain caffeine. Present
8. By July the temperature will have risen. Future Perfect
9. The exterminators sprayed the apartment. Past
10. The bloodhounds had almost lost the trail. Past Perfect

Exercise B: Writing Write a sentence for each of the verbs below. Use the tense indicated. Sentences will vary.

1. plant (past)
2. copy (present)
3. walk (present perfect)
4. fly (future)
5. wait (past perfect)
6. sing (present)
7. borrow (past)
8. cook (present perfect)
9. repair (future)
10. run (future perfect)

Part 4   The Principal Parts of a Verb

The **principal parts** of a verb are its basic forms. By combining these forms with helping verbs, you can make all tenses.

The principal parts of a verb are the **present tense**, the **past tense**, and the **past participle**. They are usually written in that order.

Most verbs form the past tense and past participle by adding -*d* or -*ed* to the present form. These verbs are called **regular verbs**. They are called regular verbs because they form the past tense and past participle in regular ways.

Present	Past	Past Participle
work	worked	(have) worked
talk	talked	(have) talked
march	marched	(have) marched
repeat	repeated	(have) repeated

Some regular verbs change their spelling when the -*d* or -*ed* is added. Study the examples on the next page.

483

Part 4

Objective

To recognize the principal parts of regular verbs

Presenting the Lesson

1. Read pages 483–484. Study the examples of the principal parts of the four verbs. Be sure students understand how each part is formed. Ask students for the principal parts of *plant, save,* and *clean.*

Individualizing the Lesson

Less-Advanced Students

Have students write the principal parts of ten regular verbs not listed in the lesson.

Advanced Students

Have students write the principal parts of ten regular verbs; then have them write ten sentences using some of the principal parts of the verbs. Students should use present tense three times, past tense four times, and past participle four times.

Optional Practice

Have students supply the verb form indicated in each of the following sentences.

1. We *hurry* to the ticket window. (past) hurried
2. The children *play* in the park every morning. (present) play
3. The faucets *drip* ever since we moved in. (past participle) have dripped
4. Brenda *drop* her books off before class. (past) dropped

483

5. The farmers *fill* their trucks with fruits and vegetables. (past participle) have filled

Extending the Lesson

Have students write original sentences using the following verb parts.

1. spill (past)
2. stay (past participle)
3. erase (present)
4. shout (past participle)
5. jump (past participle)

Part 5

Objective

To recognize the principal parts of irregular verbs, and to use the dictionary to check the parts

Presenting the Lesson

1. Review with students the way principal parts of regular verbs are formed.

2. Read pages 484–485. Be certain that students understand how irregular verbs differ from regular verbs. Point out that -*d* or -*ed* are not added to form the past and that there may be one, two, or three different forms. Study the examples of

484

Present	Past	Past Participle
cry	cried	(have) cried
blot	blotted	(have) blotted
drop	dropped	(have) dropped
plan	planned	(have) planned

The past participle is used for perfect tenses. It must have a helping verb.

They have worked.   Mimi has written to us.
Tony must have eaten.   They have planned it.

Exercise Make three columns on your paper. Label them *Present, Past,* and *Past Participle.* List the principle parts of these verbs in the proper columns.

1. **wash** washed, have washed
2. **carry** carried, have carried
3. **close** closed, have closed
4. **own** owned, have owned
5. **push** pushed, have pushed
6. **reply** replied, have replied
7. **occur** occured, have occured
8. **rip** ripped, have ripped
9. **juggle** juggled, have juggled
10. **tug** tugged, have tugged

Part 5 Irregular Verbs

You have learned the principal parts for regular verbs. Many verbs, though, do not follow the regular pattern. They do not add -*d* or -*ed* to form the past tense and past participle. They are called irregular verbs. Here are some examples:

Present	Past	Past Participle
break	broke	(have) broken
bring	brought	(have) brought
ring	rang	(have) rung
see	saw	(have) seen
put	put	(have) put

You will notice that some of the verbs have one or two different forms. Others have three different forms.

484

If you do not know the principal parts of a verb, look up the verb in a dictionary. If no parts are listed, the verb is regular. If the verb is irregular, the dictionary will list the irregular forms. It will give two forms if both the past and past participle are the same, as in *catch*, *caught*, for example. It will give three forms if all principal parts are different, as in *ring*, *rang*, *rung*, for example.

Using Irregular Verbs

There are two ways to be sure of the forms of irregular verbs. One way is to look up the verbs in the dictionary. The other way is to learn the principal parts of commonly used irregular verbs.

Once you know the principal parts, keep these rules in mind: Use the past participle with *have* and *be* helping verbs. The past participle is used for present perfect and past perfect tenses. The past form is not used with helping verbs.

The principal parts of irregular verbs can be confusing. They may seem simpler if you learn the following five patterns.

Group 1 Some irregular verbs keep the same form for all three principal parts. These are easy to remember.

Present	Past	Past Participle
burst	burst	(have) burst
cost	cost	(have) cost
cut	cut	(have) cut
let	let	(have) let
put	put	(have) put
read	read	(have) read
set	set	(have) set

Here are some sentences using verbs from this group:

Carl's mother *lets* him use the car. (present)
Martin *set* the table. (past)
That mistake *has cost* us time. (past participle)

irregular verbs shown on page 484. Have students note how many different forms each verb has.

3. Read page 485. Have students practice looking up principal parts of irregular verbs in the dictionary.

4. Begin studying the groups of irregular verbs. Pace the remainder of the lessons according to students' ability to assimilate material. Study Groups 1 and 2 on pages 485–486. Be certain students understand why the verbs are grouped together as they are.

5. Assign and discuss Exercises A and B on pages 486–487. For additional practice, students can tell whether the correct verb form is present, past, or past participle. Have students practice using principal parts in sentences.

6. Continue studying the groups of verbs and assigning and discussing the exercises that accompany each group until this part is completed.

Individualizing the Lesson

Less-Advanced Students

Have students copy the various groups of verbs on paper or in a notebook they will keep. Have the students write the characteristics of each verb group beneath the group.

Advanced Students

Have students choose three irregular verbs from each group. Tell students to use all the principal parts of each verb chosen in sentences.

Optional Practice

Have students supply the correct form of the verb in parentheses for each of the following sentences.

1. How long have you (know) about the leak? *known*
2. Bernie has (cut) the ribbon to start the race. *cut*
3. The baby has (drink) his milk. *drunk*
4. The game (begin) an hour ago. *began*
5. Danita must have (wear) her new jacket. *worn*
6. Someone must have (steal) Ralph's bicycle. *stolen*
7. The mayor (speak) at the convention next week. *spoke*
8. Parents have (let) their children swim here. *let*
9. The police (catch) the vandals. *caught*
10. I have always (say) you were a good sport. *said*

Extending the Lesson

Have students use the dictionary to look up the principal parts of the following verbs. Students should write sentences using the principal parts of each verb. **Answers will vary.**

1. drive — *drove, driven*
2. bend — *bent, bent*
3. take — *took, taken*
4. rise — *rose, risen*
5. eat — *ate, eaten*
6. try — *tried, tried*

Group 2 Another group of irregular verbs changes form only once. The past and the past participle are the same.

Present	Past	Past Participle
bring	brought	(have) brought
catch	caught	(have) caught
lead	led	(have) led
lend	lent	(have) lent
lose	lost	(have) lost
say	said	(have) said
sit	sat	(have) sat

These sentences use irregular verbs from Group 2:

Tim usually *catches* with his right hand. (present)
Marla *lost* her purse. (past)
The scouts *have brought* a compass. (past participle)

Exercise A   Choose the correct form of the verb.

1. The hen (sat, sitted) on the eggs.
2. Tina (said, sayed) her name softly.
3. Greg has (lost, losed) his keys.
4. Mark has (lent, lended) me his tent.
5. Lewis and Clark (leaded, led) the expedition.
6. Myra has (catched, caught) the flu.
7. The campers (brought, brang) a lantern.
8. The floodwaters (burst, bursted) the dam.
9. The auto repairs (costed, cost) Al $700.53.
10. The barber (cut, cutted) my hair.

Exercise B   Follow the directions for Exercise A.

1. Mom has (let, letted) Dad choose the wallpaper.
2. Fido (put, putted) my slippers in his doghouse.
3. Tom and Jim have (set, setted) the timer for twenty minutes.
4. Mandy has (brung, brought) her pictures from the trip.

5. Detective Thorpe (catched, <u>caught</u>) the mugger.
6. Megan has (<u>lost</u>, losed) her place in line.
7. The runners have (setted, <u>set</u>) a new record.
8. The guide (leaded, <u>led</u>) the climbers to the peak.
9. Carol has (<u>put</u>, putted) her savings in the bank.
10. That toy helicopter (costed, <u>cost</u>) $2.98.

Group 3 Verbs in this group add *-n* or *-en* to the past tense to form the past participle.

Present	Past	Past Participle
break	broke	(have) broken
choose	chose	(have) chosen
freeze	froze	(have) frozen
speak	spoke	(have) spoken
steal	stole	(have) stolen
tear	tore	(have) torn
wear	wore	(have) worn

Here are three sentences using Group 3 verbs:

Break the eggs into a bowl. (present)
The UN delegates *spoke* different languages. (past)
Thieves *have stolen* the jewels. (past participle)

Exercise A Choose the correct form of the verb from those given.

1. Matt (<u>chose</u>, chosen) the blue stone for his class ring.
2. Carrie has (broke, <u>broken</u>) the school high jump record.
3. Much of the orange crop (<u>froze</u>, frozen) last winter.
4. Someone has (stole, <u>stolen</u>) my wallet!
5. Liz has (wore, <u>worn</u>) contact lenses for years.
6. The principal (<u>spoke</u>, spoken) to the students at the assembly.
7. Tom has (chose, <u>chosen</u>) a topic for his term paper.
8. The milk has (froze, <u>frozen</u>) on the back porch.
9. The football team (<u>wore</u>, worn) new jerseys.
10. The fish (<u>stole</u>, stolen) the bait from my hook.

Exercise B Follow the directions for Exercise A.

1. Julie (broke, broken) the candy bar in half.
2. The witnesses have (spoke, spoken) to the detective.
3. Chris had been (chose, chosen) by the class.
4. A tornado (tore, torn) through the countryside.
5. Spies have (stole, stolen) the secret documents.
6. Mom has (froze, frozen) the extra spaghetti sauce.
7. Craig (wore, worn) a tuxedo to the dance.
8. Melissa has (tore, torn) the article from the newspaper.
9. Ken (chose, chosen) a blue plaid shirt.
10. Mr. Ross has (wore, worn) a neck brace since the accident.

Group 4 The irregular verbs in this group change their final vowels. The vowel changes from *i* in the present tense to *a* in the past tense and *u* in the past participle.

Present	Past	Past Participle
begin	began	(have) begun
drink	drank	(have) drunk
ring	rang	(have) rung
sing	sang	(have) sung
swim	swam	(have) swum

Here are examples of irregular verbs from Group 4:

I *drink* root beer. (present)
The mother *sang* softly. (past)
Gary *has swum* in the new pool. (past participle)

Exercise A Choose the correct verb form.

1. Someone must have (rang, rung) our doorbell by mistake.
2. Class (began, begun) at nine o'clock.
3. Mark Spitz (swam, swum) in the Olympics.
4. The school choir has (sang, sung) at many civic events.
5. Ms. Silva (drank, drunk) her coffee black.

6. The baby must have (drank, **drunk**) his bottle.
7. Our school has (began, **begun**) a new admission policy.
8. The phone (**rang**, rung) ten times.
9. Cindy has already (swam, **swum**) fifty laps.
10. Diana Ross (**sang**, sung) a medley of her hits.

Exercise B   Follow the directions for Exercise A.

1. Carl (**drank**, drunk) three glasses of lemonade.
2. Mr. Evans has (rang, **rung**) the church bells for years.
3. Laura (**swam**, swum) in the water ballet.
4. Local farmers have (began, **begun**) the harvest.
5. Martha (**sang**, sung) a solo in the musical.
6. The hospital patient (**rang**, rung) for the nurse.
7. That child has (swam, **swum**) four lengths of the pool.
8. The kittens have (drank, **drunk**) all of the milk.
9. Dad has (sang, **sung**) with a barbershop quartet.
10. Nora (**began**, begun) her driving lessons today.

Group 5 For some irregular verbs the past participle is formed from the present tense. The past participle looks more like the present tense than the past tense.

Present	Past	Past Participle
come	came	(have) come
do	did	(have) done
eat	ate	(have) eaten
fall	fell	(have) fallen
give	gave	(have) given
go	went	(have) gone
grow	grew	(have) grown
know	knew	(have) known
ride	rode	(have) ridden
run	ran	(have) run
see	saw	(have) seen
take	took	(have) taken
throw	threw	(have) thrown
write	wrote	(have) written

Here are sentences using Group 5 verbs:

I *know* the address. (present)
Marty *gave* a speech. (past)
The leaves *have fallen*. (past participle)

Exercise A Choose the correct verb form from the two given.

1. Crowds of people (came, come) to the grand opening of the new department store.
2. Michele has (did, done) the assignment thoroughly and is prepared for the test.
3. Mr. Price (gave, given) the class a quiz.
4. Jean (knew, known) the algebra equation.
5. We (rode, ridden) the subway downtown.
6. The nest has (fell, fallen) from the tree.
7. That horse has (ran, run) its last race.
8. Terry has (went, gone) on vacation.
9. Bob and Jim have (saw, seen) all of the *Star Wars* movies four times.
10. Clara has never (ate, eaten) Mexican food.

Exercise B Follow the directions for Exercise A.

1. We (saw, seen) Vicky at the carnival.
2. My brother has (grew, grown) a beard.
3. John (ran, run) to the finish line.
4. The pitcher has (threw, thrown) a curve ball.
5. Jan has (rode, ridden) in horse shows.
6. The police have (come, came) to the same conclusion.
7. Our class (took, taken) the exam yesterday.
8. Bonny has already (wrote, written) a letter to the travel agency.
9. My ring (fell, fallen) down the drain.
10. Pat (did, done) her homework at the library before she came home.

Part 6 Active and Passive Verbs

You have seen how the tenses of verbs indicate time. There is another way that verbs help you say exactly what you mean.

Suppose that a package was delivered. If you knew who delivered it, you could say:

Beth delivered the package today.

However, if you don't know who delivered the package, you might say:

The package was delivered today.

In the first sentence, the subject, *Beth*, tells who performed the action. If the subject performs the action, the verb is **active**.

In the second sentence, the subject, *package*, tells what received the action. If the subject names the receiver or the result of the action, the verb is **passive**. The word **passive** means "acted upon."

Forming the Passive

The passive form of the verb is made with the past participle. A form of *be* is the helping verb.

Active	Passive
That store *sells* furniture.	Furniture *is sold* by that store.
Luke *has built* the model.	The model *has been built* by Luke.
The janitor *will paint* the hallway.	The hallway *will be painted* by the janitor.
Gayle *baked* the pie.	The pie *was baked* by Gayle.

Read the direct objects in the sentences in the first column above. You can see that the direct objects have become the subjects of the sentences in the second column. Only verbs that have objects (transitive verbs) can be changed from active to passive.

491

Part 6

Objective

To distinguish between active and passive verbs

Presenting the Lesson

1. Read page 491. Discuss the differences in meaning between active and passive. Study the examples of how the passive form is made. Stress that only transitive verbs can be changed from active to passive. Read the definitions of active and passive on page 492.

2. Assign and discuss Exercises A and B on page 492.

Individualizing the Lesson

Less-Advanced Students

1. Have students study, then copy, the definitions of active and passive verbs on page 492.

2. Have students write five original sentences containing active verbs. Then have students change the active verbs to passive verbs and rewrite the sentences.

Advanced Students

Have students write ten original sentences using active verbs and ten sentences using passive verbs.

Optional Practice

Have students rewrite the following sentences. If the verb is active, it should be rewritten as passive. If the verb is passive, it should be rewritten as active. Answers on page 492.

1. This picture was drawn by Henry.

2. Gabriel watered the plants.

491

3. A jackrabbit ate our vegetables.
4. The leaves have been raked by Randi.
5. The telephone call was placed by the operator.

1. Henry drew this picture.
2. The plants were watered by Gabriel.
3. Our vegetables were eaten by a jackrabbit.
4. Randi raked the leaves.
5. The operator placed the telephone call.

Extending the Lesson

Have students write sentences with passive verbs using the following subjects.

1. dishes
2. motorcycle
3. horses
4. basketball
5. spaghetti

A verb is active when its subject performs the action stated by the verb.

A verb is passive when its subject names the receiver or result of the action stated by the verb.

Exercise A Write the verb in each sentence. After each, write *Active* or *Passive* to tell what kind it is.

P 1. Secret talks were arranged by the Secretary of State.

A 2. The electrician repaired the wiring.

P 3. The patient was referred to a specialist.

P 4. A survey had been taken by the student council.

A 5. Judge Blackwell gave the jury instructions.

A 6. The Garden Club sponsored a plant sale.

P 7. The walk-a-thon was organized by our school.

A 8. Paul fed the stray kitten.

A 9. Jason compared the two novels in his term paper.

P 10. Prizes for the raffle were provided by local merchants.

Exercise B Change the verbs in the following sentences from passive to active. Rewrite the sentences.

1. The barn was demolished by the tornado.
   The tornado demolished the barn.
2. Larry was given a sedative by the doctor.
   The doctor gave Larry a sedative.
3. No information on the case has been released by the police.
   The police have released no information on the case.
4. The door was answered by Mr. Scott.
   Mr. Scott answered the door.
5. The invitation was written by Lisa.
   Lisa wrote the invitation.
6. Ten thousand dollars was given by an anonymous donor.
   An anonymous donor gave ten thousand dollars.
7. Thunderstorms were predicted by the weather reporter.
   The weather reporter predicted thunderstorms.
8. The letters were filed by the secretary.
   The secretary filed the letters.
9. An interview had been arranged by the personnel manager.
   The personnel manager had arranged an interview.
10. Refreshments will be provided by a catering service.
    A catering service will provide refreshments.

ADDITIONAL EXERCISES

Using Verbs

A. Action and Linking Verbs Make three columns on your paper. Label them *Action—Transitive*, *Action—Intransitive*, and *Linking*. Find the verb in each sentence. Write the verb in the correct column.

AI 1. We climbed into the rowboat.

AT 2. The Navy plane patrolled the North Pacific.

L 3. The rapids were dangerous.

AI 4. The helicopter landed in a field.

L 5. Are mouthpieces optional in football?

AT 6. One dancer lost the beat.

AT 7. Eric accompanied the radio with his bongo drums.

AI 8. Ken studied for the history quiz.

L 9. The clouds seemed motionless.

AI 10. Polly looked at each picture for a long time.

B. Parts of the Verb Find the parts of the verb in each sentence. Write them in two columns labeled *Helping Verbs* and *Main Verbs*.

  1. The pilot should have radioed the tower.

  2. Nancy must be rehearsing for the play.

  3. The countdown will soon begin.

  4. Poisonous gases had leaked into the air.

  5. By tomorrow the fog will have cleared.

  6. The flight to Miami was canceled.

  7. Residents have often been told about the danger.

  8. A penalty was called on that play.

  9. Stan will certainly be removed from the game by the end of the quarter.

10. The divers have thoroughly searched the river and parts of the lake.

493

Additional Exercises

These Additional Exercises may be used for additional practice of the concepts presented in this Section. Each exercise focuses on a single concept, and should be used after the page number indicated in parentheses.

Review

If you have not assigned these Additional Exercises before this time, you can also use them as an excellent Section Review.

C. Verb Tenses Write each verb and its tense.

1. Yolanda now **belongs** to several of the school clubs. present
2. The physical fitness tests **will start** early tomorrow morning. future
3. We **will have graduated** by then. future perfect
4. The carton of milk **dripped**. past
5. Jerome **has** no locker. present
6. Satchel Paige **had earned** his place in sports history as a great baseball pitcher. past perfect
7. Ms. Deer **has complained** to the Better Business Bureau. present perfect
8. He **laughed** for no apparent reason. past
9. I **shall see** you then. future
10. **Has** Frances ever **used** a mimeograph machine or an overhead projector before? present perfect

D. Principal Parts of the Verb Write the italicized verbs in the form stated in parentheses. If the sentence is already in the form stated in parentheses, write *Correct*.

Example: I *like* those styles. (past)

I liked those styles.

1. Sam had *mist* the plants with a sprayer. (past participle) [had misted]
2. Jessica *brand* the calf. (past) [branded]
3. Ronnie has *apply* for officer's training school. (past participle) [had applied]
C 4. Most drivers *obey* the crossing guard. (present)
5. Mud *splatter* over our boots. (past) [splattered]
6. Aaron should have *block* that pass. (past participle) [had blocked]
7. The hikers had *blaze* a trail. (past participle) [had blazed]
C 8. Slush can *harden* into ice. (present)
C 9. Surgeons *work* quickly and carefully. (present)
10. Should Lee have *enter* the contest sooner? (past participle) [have entered]

494

E. Irregular Verbs: Groups 1 and 2   Number your paper from 1 to 10. Write the correct verb.

1. Jon had (put, putted) the maps in the car.
2. Medical care has never (cost, costed) more.
3. The raft (brang, brought) us to safety.
4. The Lakers (lost, losed) by one point.
5. The Eskimo (cutted, cut) a circle in the ice.
6. The dentist finally (set, setted) her drill down.
7. Karen (lended, lent) me her radio.
8. Without a glove, Robin (catched, caught) the ball.
9. You have (sayed, said, saided) too much already.
10. We (sat, sitted) in the front row and craned our necks.

F. Irregular Verbs: Group 3   Number your paper from 1 to 10. Write the correct verb.

1. Dad and I (torn, tore) down the old wallpaper.
2. Has anyone (spoke, spoken) to the career counselor?
3. Stephanie has (broke, broken) her glasses.
4. Somebody had (stole, stolen) the portable television.
5. Amanda (chose, choosed, chosen) bright yellow paint.
6. The windows had all (froze, frozen) shut.
7. Should the bandage be (tore, torn) off quickly?
8. Grover (stealed, stole) a look at the price tag.
9. The children (speaked, spoke, spoken) Polish at home.
10. Luke had never (wore, worn) a tuxedo before.

G. Irregular Verbs: Group 4   Number your paper from 1 to 10. Write the correct verb.

1. The actress had (began, begun) with only bit parts.
2. The hikers (drank, drunk) from their canteens.
3. Smokey Robinson (sang, sung) the first song.
4. The camp chef (rang, rung) the dinner bell.
5. A snapping turtle (swam, swum) right past my foot.

495

6. Nobody had (rang, <u>rung</u>) the fire alarm.

7. Christina had (swam, <u>swum</u>) to the island.

8. I (<u>began</u>, begun) the work in a cheerful mood.

9. Everyone with stomach pains had (drank, <u>drunk</u>) the eggnog.

10. She could have (sang, <u>sung</u>) that song in her sleep.

H. Irregular Verbs: Group 5 Number your paper from 1 to 10. Write the correct verb.

1. That bakery has (went, <u>gone</u>) out of business.

2. Eliza (<u>saw</u>, seen) the filming of a movie.

3. Tom's contact lens had (fell, <u>fallen</u>) into the snow.

4. Melissa Mathison (<u>wrote</u>, written) the script for *E. T.*

5. The roses (<u>grew</u>, grown) near the back porch.

6. Benita has (took, <u>taken</u>) the civil service exam.

7. A path (<u>ran</u>, run) across the cornfield.

8. I hadn't (knew, <u>known</u>) about the law against jaywalking.

9. Earl (<u>did</u>, done) better last season.

10. The coach has (gave, <u>given</u>) Celeste an ice pack.

I. Passive and Active Verbs Change the verbs in the following sentences from passive to active. Rewrite the sentences.

1. Night crawlers are sold by the Rod and Reel Shop.

The Rod and Reel Shop sells night crawlers.

2. The home run was made by Gussie.

Gussie made the homerun.

3. Spanish is spoken by the hospital admissions clerk.

The hospital admissions clerk speaks Spanish.

4. A refugee family has been sponsored by our church.

Our church sponsored a refugee family.

5. "Diamonds and Rust" was written by Joan Baez.

Joan Baez wrote "Diamonds and Rust."

6. A soccer stadium was built by Indiana University.

Indiana University built a soccer stadium.

7. Static had been picked up by the computer.

The computer had picked up static.

8. The fire department was called by Ms. Slawek.

Ms. Slawek called the fire department.

9. The holes in this sweater were made by moths.

Moths made the holes in this sweater.

10. The sense of hearing can be damaged by noise.

Noise can damage the sense of hearing.

MIXED REVIEW

Using Verbs

A. Finding action verbs and linking verbs
Write the verbs from each sentence. Next, write whether they are *Action* or *Linking Verbs*. If a verb is an action verb, write whether it is *Transitive* or *Intransitive*.

AT 1. The cow licked the salt block.

AT 2. Rosemary has some good ideas.

L 3. The sky looks mean.

AI 4. Mr. Vargo looked at the engine.

L 5. This old sweatshirt feels comfortable.

AT 6. The firefighter carefully felt the hot wall.

AT 7. The vet lifted the dog from the table.

L 8. Jake is in your science class.

L 9. Nancy is a good sport.

AT10. After a few minutes, Joachim and his friends left the movie theater.

B. Helping verbs and main verbs
Label two columns on your paper *Helping Verbs* and *Main Verbs*. Fill in the parts from each of the following sentences.

1. That restaurant has been closed all month.
2. The marathon has already started.
3. I might see the movie tomorrow.
4. Did you miss your bus?
5. Have you been working on weekends?
6. Aunt Ruth is still looking for a better job.
7. Craig might yet change his mind.
8. Stacey will probably never change.
9. Should I use cold water?
10. Somebody must have been using this cabin recently.

497

Mixed Review

These exercises provide re-view of the concepts pre-sented in this Section. Each exercise challenges the stu-dents to apply several of the skills they have acquired dur-ing previous study. Because the "mixed" feature of these activities makes them more difficult, the teacher may wish to have less-advanced stu-dents do them orally or in small groups.

C. Using verb forms correctly Write each of the following sentences, using the verb and the verb form given in parentheses.

Example: The spoon (*fall*, past perfect) into the soup.
The spoon had fallen into the soup.

1. Gene (*swim*, past) underwater. swam
2. Molly (*ride*, present perfect) a dirt bike. has ridden
3. Who (*let*, past) the cat out? let
4. The players (*put*, past) their mouthpieces in before the game. put
5. The bus driver (*say*, past) nothing to the passengers. said
6. Martin (*sing*, past perfect) despite his sore throat. had sung
7. The car (*turn*, past) into the alley. turned
8. I (*do*, future perfect) most of the research by Monday. will have done
9. The ducks (*go*, future) south in a few weeks. will go
10. My cousin never (*write*, past) back. wrote

D. Recognizing active and passive verbs Write the verb in each sentence. Write *Active* or *Passive* to tell what kind it is. Then rewrite each sentence. Change each passive verb to an active verb. Change each active verb to a passive verb.

P 1. The basement was flooded by the rain.
The rain flooded the basement.

P 2. The emergency brake was used by the driver.
The driver used the emergency brake.

P 3. Several video games were played by Terry.
Terry played several video games.

A 4. The weather changed our plans.
Our plans were changed by the weather.

A 5. A small plane carried the mail.
The mail was carried by a small plane.

A 6. Cold water soothes a burn.
A burn is soothed by cold water.

P 7. That role was played by James Earl Jones.
James Earl Jones played that role.

A 8. This generator supplies our electricity.
Our electricity is supplied by this generator.

A 9. The Coast Guard patrols the lake.
The lake is patrolled by the Coast Guard.

P 10. The test was completed by everyone.
Everyone completed the test.

USING GRAMMAR IN WRITING
Using Verbs

A. Verbs power sentences. A strong sentence usually has a strong verb; a weak sentence usually has a weak verb. Pay special attention to verbs as you complete the following writing assignment.

Last weekend, you attended a concert. In the middle of the concert, all electrical power in the building failed. What happened next? Did an emergency lighting system come on automatically? Did the performers help calm the audience? What did you do? How did the other people in the audience react? How did people make their way to the exits? How did you get home? Write a paragraph about the experience. Use vivid verbs that capture the tension and describe people's actions. Circle each verb.

B. You are applying for a very special scholarship. This scholarship allows a student to follow any course of study whatsoever. It can be used for flying lessons, college, art school, clown school, computer programing courses, or any other kind of training. As part of the application, you must write three paragraphs about yourself. These paragraphs should help explain your interest in the field you will choose.

First, write a paragraph about yourself as you were five years ago. Use past tenses for the verbs in this paragraph.

Next, write a paragraph about yourself as you are now. Use present tenses for the verbs in this paragraph.

Finally, write a paragraph about yourself as you hope to be in five years. Use future tenses for the verbs in this paragraph.

These challenging and enjoyable activities allow the students to see how the concepts of grammar, usage, and mechanics may be applied in actual writing situations. Each exercise is designed to allow students practice in several of the skills they have acquired in this Section. The activities also provide opportunities for students to write creatively about a wide variety of interesting and unusual subjects.

Section Objectives

1. To recognize adjectives and understand their functions

2. To recognize and use proper adjectives correctly

3. To recognize and use predicate adjectives correctly

4. To recognize and use articles correctly

5. To form and use correctly the comparative and superlative forms of adjectives

6. To recognize adverbs and understand their functions

7. To form and use correctly the comparative and superlative forms of adverbs

8. To avoid confusion between the use of adjectives and adverbs

9. To use certain troublesome modifiers correctly: *them* and *those*, *here* and *there*, *kind* and *sort*, *good* and *well*

10. To avoid the use of double negatives

Preparing the Students

Ask students to comment on the following sentences.

The catcher reached for the ball.
The nervous rookie catcher reached awkwardly for the ball.

Ask students which sentence conveys a clearer, more interesting picture. Explain that modifiers make communication more specific and help create vivid pictures.

Additional Resources

Diagnostic Test — page 4 in the test booklet

Mastery Test — pages 52–55 in the test booklet

Using Modifiers

When you try to describe someone or something, you have to use specific words. Then your listeners will be able to picture in their minds exactly what you are describing.

Look at these sentences:

The cafeteria served chicken.
The cafeteria served *crispy*, *fried* chicken.

The second sentence is more specific. It uses **modifiers. Modifiers are words that modify, or change, other words.**

In the example above, the modifiers describe a noun. Modifiers can also be used with verbs. Look at these sentences:

Hikers climb this path.
Hikers *usually* climb this path *quickly*.

Modifiers help make your writing more lively and interesting. There are two kinds of modifiers—adjectives and adverbs. Both of them are parts of speech. In this section you will learn to identify and use modifiers.

Part 1 Using Adjectives

One kind of modifier is an **adjective**.

An adjective is a word that modifies a noun or pronoun.

Adjectives can tell three different kinds of things about nouns or pronouns.

Which one or ones?

this cup, *that* hat, *these* gloves, *those* papers

What kind?

black sand, *muddy* shoes, *sad* news, *brilliant* light

How many or how much?

five days, *much* love, *several* opinions, *few* comments

Proper Adjectives

One special kind of adjective is the **proper adjective**.

A proper adjective is formed from a proper noun. Therefore, it refers to a specific person, place, or thing. This kind of adjective is always capitalized. Here are some examples:

Swiss cheese   a Ford car
the French language   a Mediterranean port

Predicate Adjectives

Most adjectives come before the words they modify:

Mom handed me a *cool, refreshing* drink.
(*Cool* and *refreshing* modify *drink*.)

A **predicate adjective**, though, comes after the word it modifies. A predicate adjective follows a linking verb and modifies the subject of the sentence.

Albert seemed *confused*.
(*Confused* modifies the subject, *Albert*.)

501

Additional Exercises — pages 521–526 in the student text

Practice Book — pages 198–205

Duplicating Masters — pages 198–205

Special Populations — See special section at the front of this Teacher's Edition.

Part 1

Objectives

1. To recognize adjectives and understand their functions

2. To recognize and use proper adjectives correctly

3. To recognize and use predicate adjectives correctly

4. To recognize and use articles correctly

Presenting the Lesson

1. Read page 501, going over the definition of an adjective and the three ways in which adjectives modify nouns or pronouns.

2. Read page 501, studying the explanation and examples of proper adjectives. Have students form proper adjectives from these words.

Mexican   Greek
Mexico   Greece
English   Russian
England   Russia

3. Read pages 501–502. Stress the position and function of a predicate adjective. Remind students that a predicate adjective describes the subject, but does not rename it. Use the following examples to help students distinguish between predicate adjectives and predicate nouns.

501

The car is *yellow*. (predicate adjective)
The car is a *Toyota*. (predicate noun)

Marla is *intelligent*. (predicate adjective)
Marla is a *genius*. (predicate noun)

4. Read page 502 regarding articles.

5. Read pages 502–503. Study examples of diagrams of adjectives, predicate adjectives, and compound predicate adjectives.

6. Assign and discuss Exercise A on page 503. Have students say what each adjective tells about the noun or pronoun it modifies.

7. Assign and discuss Exercise B on pages 503–504.

Individualizing the Lesson

Less-Advanced Students

Have students find five published examples of each type of adjective, including proper adjectives, predicate adjectives, and articles. Have students copy each sentence, circle each adjective, and write the word the adjective modifies at the end of the sentence.

Advanced Students

Have students make up ten simple sentences using action verbs and linking verbs. Write them on the board. Have students add different kinds of adjectives to each sentence and compare the results. Discuss how adjectives can change the meanings of sentences.

Optional Practice

Have students add at least three adjectives to each of the following sentences. Answers will vary.

502

The instructions were *clear*.
(*Clear* modifies the subject, *instructions*.)

As you can see, here *confused* and *clear* are predicate adjectives. They follow linking verbs, *seemed* and *were*. Each one also modifies the subject of the sentence.

Articles

The adjectives *a*, *an*, and *the* are called **articles**.

The is the **definite article**. It points out a specific person, place, or thing.

Guard *the* secret carefully. (a particular secret)

A and *an* are **indefinite articles**.

Do you know *a* secret? (any secret)
I would like *an* egg. (any egg)

Notice that *a* is used before a consonant sound (*a* rock, *a* book, *a* meal). *An* is used before a vowel sound (*an* ear, *an* orange, *an* urn).

Pay attention to the sound, not the spelling. You would say *a* hero, but *an* honor.

Diagraming Adjectives

In a sentence diagram, an adjective appears below the word it modifies. It is placed on a slanted line.

This car has a rebuilt engine.

Predicate adjectives are diagramed differently. Like predicate nouns and pronouns, they are placed on the main line. A slanted

502

line goes between the verb and the predicate adjective.

These tires are bald.

A compound predicate adjective appears on a split line.

The upholstery is old and worn.

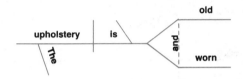

Exercise A   Number your paper from 1 to 10. Write the adjectives in each sentence. After each adjective, write the word it modifies. Do not include articles.

1. The bridal bouquet contained white roses, pink carnations, and blue cornflowers.
2. Several mysterious footprints were found in the soft mud by the old shack.
3. Georgina painted green stripes on that old wagon.
4. Mr. Marks wears a rumpled raincoat and a plaid cap.
5. Several political figures attended the public meeting.
6. The physicians disagreed on the proper treatment.
7. Two kites were caught in the old elm tree.
8. Some employees at that bank speak foreign languages.
9. Frank sprinkled a little salt on the tasteless meatloaf.
10. The chilly rain pelted the new flowers in the garden.

Exercise B   Number your paper from 1 to 10. Write the predicate adjectives in these sentences.

1. The tennis court is free.
2. The wound looks serious.

1. The boy walked the dog.
2. The rain spoiled the party.
3. My shirt goes with these pants.
4. A bird nested in the tree.
5. We had a sandwich in that restaurant.

Extending the Lesson

Have each student write a paragraph describing a book, movie, magazine, painting or activity they recently enjoyed (or didn't enjoy). Tell them to concentrate on effective use of adjectives in the paragraph.

3. Power steering is <u>helpful</u> for parking.
4. The vicinity of the trash dump smelled <u>foul</u>.
5. Reservations are <u>necessary</u>.
6. The team felt <u>certain</u> of victory.
7. Interest rates are <u>high</u> now.
8. Angie felt <u>proud</u> of herself.
9. That chair is <u>old</u> and <u>uncomfortable</u>.
10. These houses are <u>expensive</u>.

Part 2 Adjectives in Comparisons

You often learn about new things by making comparisons. You compare new things with things you already know. You might describe a movie, for example, as "*more spectacular* than *Star Wars*." Or you might explain that the grapes were *fresher* than the melons.

Adjectives help you to make such comparisons.

The Comparative

Adjectives have special forms for making comparisons. When you compare one person or thing with another, you use the **comparative** form of an adjective. Here are some examples:

> Melissa is *younger* than Meg.
> This is a *funnier* movie than that one.
> Bill is *more studious* than I am.

The comparative is made in two ways:

1. Add *-er* to short adjectives like *tall* and *great*.

> soft + -er = softer   old + -er = older
> pretty + -er = prettier   small + -er = smaller

Notice that the spelling of some adjectives changes in the comparative form.

Objective

To form and use correctly the comparative and superlative forms of adjectives

Presenting the Lesson

1. Read pages 504–505. Be certain that students understand the purpose of the comparative form of adjectives. Go over the two rules for forming comparatives. Have students form the comparative of these words.

1. tired — more tired
2. silly — sillier
3. eager — more eager
4. peaceful — more peaceful
5. noisy — noisier
6. flexible — more flexible

2. Read pages 505–506. Discuss the purpose of the superlative and go over the rules for forming the superlative on page 505. Go over the three points for using adjectives in comparisons.

3. Read page 506, studying examples of irregular comparisons.

4. Assign and discuss Exercises A and B on pages 506–507.

504

2. Use *more* for longer adjectives like *popular*.

more confident   more curious

Most adjectives ending in *-ful* or *-ous* form the comparative with *more*.

more careful   more dangerous

The Superlative

When you compare a person or thing with all others in its class, you use the **superlative** form of the adjective. In addition, use the superlative when you compare a person or thing with two or more others.

Here are some examples:

Mark ate the *largest* piece of pie.
That is the *craziest* idea I've heard yet.
Judy is the *most powerful* swimmer on the team.

The superlative form of an adjective is made by adding *-est* or by using *most*. If an adjective adds *-er* for the comparative, it adds *-est* for the superlative. If an adjective uses *more* for the comparative, it uses *most* for the superlative.

Adjective	Comparative	Superlative
rough	rougher	roughest
light	lighter	lightest
forceful	more forceful	most forceful
terrible	more terrible	most terrible
expensive	more expensive	most expensive

Remember these three points about using adjectives in comparison:

1. To compare two people or things, use the comparative. To compare more than two, use the superlative.

This engine is *more powerful* than that one.
Mel's Market sells the *thickest* steaks in town.

505

7. That candidate is (popular) than his opponent.
8. Mr. Thomas is the (good) teacher at this school.

best

9. Who is the (handsome) actor on television?

most handsome

10. That was the (silly) show I have ever watched.

silliest

Extending the Lesson

Have students form the comparative and superlative of the following adjectives and use each in a sentence.

1. spicy
   spicier, spiciest
2. expensive
   more, most
3. little
   littler, littlest

4. windy
   windier, windiest
5. intelligent
   more, most
6. subdued
   more, most

2. Use the word *other* when you compare something with everything else of its kind.

Incorrect: Jeff is smarter than any student.
(This sentence says that Jeff is not a student.)

Correct: Jeff is smarter than any *other* student.

Incorrect: This statue is *more delicate* than any of the porcelain figures.
(This sentence says that the statue is not a piece of porcelain.)

Correct: This statue is *more delicate* than any of the *other* porcelain figures.

3. Do not use *-er* with *more*, or *-est* with *most*.

Incorrect: Chris is much more smaller than his brother.
Correct: Chris is much *smaller* than his brother.
Incorrect: This is the most ugliest Halloween mask here.
Correct: This is the *ugliest* Halloween mask here.

Irregular Comparisons

Some comparatives and superlatives are formed in unusual ways:

Adjective	Comparative	Superlative
good	better	best
well	better	best
bad	worse	worst
little	less or lesser	least
much	more	most
many	more	most
far	farther	farthest

Exercise A Two of the following comparisons are correct. If a sentence is correct, write *Correct*. If it is incorrect, write it correctly.

1. Saudi Arabia contains the world's ~~most~~ largest sand desert, the Rub al-Khali.

c 2. Riyadh is the largest city in Saudi Arabia.

3. Food is more expensiver in Saudi Arabia than in the United States.

4. Gasoline is the bestest bargain in Saudi Arabia.

C 5. Of all the O.P.E.C. countries, Saudi Arabia has the friendliest relations with the United States.

6. Today the Saudis have a more better standard of living.

7. Saudi Arabia exports more oil than any other nation.

8. The geography in Saudi Arabia is among the most harshest on earth.

9. Of the two kings, King Faisal was the more progressive.

10. In recent years, oil production has become more importanter to the Saudis.

Exercise B   Follow the directions for Exercise A.

1. Pink coral grows in more deeper water than black coral.

2. Of all divers, coral divers are the most courageous.

C 3. Of all coral, shallow water varieties are the most porous.

4. Of black and gold coral, gold is the more valuable.

5. The state of Hawaii is more stricter about managing coral harvests than it used to be.

C 6. Bamboo coral is more expensive than black coral.

C 7. Of the two types, black coral is more plentiful.

8. Is gold coral more harder than ivory?

9. When considering safety and profits, divers' safety should be the greater concern.

10. Pink coral has a more slower growth rate than black coral.

Part 3   Using Adverbs

An **adverb** is another kind of modifier. Adverbs help you to express yourself clearly and vividly. They tell *how, when, where,* or *to what extent* about something.

Adverbs are words that modify verbs, adjectives, and other adverbs.

507

Presenting the Lesson

1. Read pages 507–508. Go over the definition of adverbs and study examples of adverbs used to modify verbs. Study the list of adverbs telling *how, when, where,* and *to what extent.*

2. Read pages 508–509 showing how adverbs modify adjectives and other adverbs. Study the list of adverbs that often modify adjectives or other adverbs.

3. Read pages 509–510 concerning the formation of adverbs from adjectives and noting spelling changes.

4. Read page 509, studying modifiers that can be either adjectives or adverbs. Stress that to determine whether a modifier is an adverb or an adjective, students must determine the part of speech of the word modified.

5. Read page 510, studying how adverbs are diagramed.

6. Assign and discuss Exercises A, B, and C on pages 510–511.

Individualizing the Lesson

Less-Advanced Students

1. For each sentence in Exercises A and B, pages 510–511, have students write what each adverb tells *(how, when, where, to what extent).*

2. Have students find five published examples of adverbs modifying verbs, five examples of adverbs modifying adverbs, and five examples of adverbs modifying adjectives. Have students indicate what each adverb tells in each case.

Advanced Students

Have students write fifteen original sentences. Five sentences should

Using Adverbs with Verbs

Adverbs frequently modify verbs. Adverbs tell *how, when, where,* or *to what extent* something happened.

Adverbs are used with verbs to tell *how:*

Dan *graciously* accepted the award.

The witness answered *completely*.

Adverbs also tell *when* about verbs:

That outdoor cafe opened *recently*.

The dance committee meets *today*.

Adverbs can tell *where* about verbs:

Our car is parked *nearby*.

We eat *here* in the cafeteria.

In addition, adverbs can tell *to what extent:*

Brian *almost* dropped the football.

Study the following list of adverbs.

How?	When?	Where?	To What Extent?
slowly	soon	there	often
happily	then	here	never
speedily	later	nearby	not
carefully	finally	above	seldom

Using Adverbs with Adjectives and Other Adverbs

Besides modifying verbs, adverbs also modify adjectives and other adverbs. Look at these sentences:

Some people are *extremely* nearsighted.
(*Extremely* tells to what extent. It is an adverb modifying the adjective *nearsighted*.)

The pastor spoke *very* softly.

(*Very* tells to what extent. It is an adverb modifying the adverb *softly*.)

Here are other adverbs that often modify adjectives or other adverbs:

| too | quite | rather | most | more | extremely |
| just | nearly | so | really | truly | somewhat |

These adverbs tell *to what extent* something is true.

Forming Adverbs

Many adverbs are formed by adding *-ly* to an adjective.

| dim + -ly = dimly | perfect + -ly = perfectly |
| cautious + -ly = cautiously | rapid + -ly = rapidly |

At times, the addition of *-ly* causes a spelling change in the adjective.

probable + -ly = probably
dainty + -ly = daintily
full + -ly = fully

Some adverbs are not formed from adjectives. *Quite, so, rather*, and *somewhat* are examples.

The post office had never been *so* crowded before.

John is *quite* capable of this work.

Some words can be either adverbs or adjectives. *Late* and *high* are examples of such words.

The warning came too *late*.
(*Late* is an adverb, modifying the verb *came*.)

Chris watched the *late* movie on TV.
(*Late* is an adjective, modifying the noun *movie*.)

509

use adverbs modifying verbs, five should use adverbs modifying adverbs, and five should use adverbs modifying adjectives. Then tell students to indicate what each adverb tells in each case.

Optional Practice

Have students form adverbs from the following adjectives and use each in a sentence.

1. sleepy   sleepily
2. glad   gladly
3. sudden   suddenly
4. usual   usually
5. loud   loudly
6. sly   slyly
7. accurate   accurately
8. immediate   immediately
9. angry   angrily
10. loyal   loyally

Extending the Lesson

Have students form adverbs from the following words. Then have them use each adverb in a sentence.

careful	carefully
powerful	powerfully
nice	nicely
exquisite	exquisitely
definite	definitely

509

The kite flew *high* above the park.
(*High* is an adverb, modifying the verb *flew.*)

Shoppers hate these *high* prices.
(*High* is an adjective, modifying the noun *prices.*)

Diagraming Adverbs

Adverbs are diagramed like adjectives. An adverb is placed on a slanted line attached to the word it modifies. This diagram shows an adverb modifying a verb:

The paramedics worked quickly.

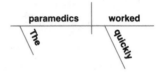

Adverbs that modify adjectives or other adverbs are diagramed like this:

Too few people eat really well.

Exercise A Write the adverbs in these sentences. Then write the word each modifies.

> Example: A new movie opened here today.
> *today* modifies *opened* (tells *when*)
> *here* modifies *opened* (tells *where*)

1. The wind blew fiercely.
2. Bernadette cautiously stepped back from the door.

3. Helen left yesterday for San Francisco.
4. The dog slept peacefully in the sun.
5. Gloria finally answered the phone.
6. The clerk was quite patient with me.
7. We often take the bus home.
8. Mr. Edwards spoke too quickly. (*too* modifies *quickly*)
9. Ink is much neater.
10. The audience was unusually quiet.

Exercise B   Follow the directions for Exercise A.

1. We recently went to the ocean.
2. The water seemed very rough.
3. The pool looked especially inviting.
4. The tide was exceptionally high.
5. Swimmers found the water too cold.
6. Pelicans swooped down gracefully.
7. Bathers very often find unusual shells. (*very* modifies *often*)
8. Sandpipers still hop quickly along the shore.
9. Vendors usually charge very high prices for suntan oil.
10. Tourists frequently come here for vacations.

Exercise C   Change the following adjectives into adverbs by adding *-ly*. Check your spelling in a dictionary.

fearlessly	stiffly	partially	neatly	steadysteadily
nearly	painfully	lazylazily	usually	obviously
happyhappily recently	extremely	formally	nervously

Part 4   Adverbs in Comparisons

You can use adverbs to compare actions. For example, you might say, "This team wins often, but that team wins *more often*." Or you might say, "Of all the players, Erica practices *hardest*." Such comparisons help you to convey ideas clearly. Like adjectives, adverbs have special forms for making comparisons.

Objective

To form and use correctly the comparative and superlative forms of adverbs

1. Review with students the purpose of the comparative and superlative forms of adjectives. Review also how most comparatives and superlatives are formed.

2. Read pages 511–513. Study the explanation and examples showing the use and formation of comparatives and superlatives. Pay special attention to the points about using adverbs in comparisons on pages 512–513.

3. Read page 513 showing adverbs that change completely in the comparative and superlative forms.

4. Assign and discuss Exercises A and B on pages 513–514.

Individualizing the Lesson

Less-Advanced Students

1. Have students study how the comparative and superlative forms of adverbs are formed. Then discuss with them how the comparative and superlative forms of adverbs compare with the comparative and superlative forms of adjectives.

2. Have students choose five comparative adverbs and five superlative adverbs from the ones created in Exercise A, page 513. Have students use each adverb in a sentence.

Advanced Students

Have students use each comparative and superlative created in Exercise A, page 513, in an original sentence. Then have students exchange papers to determine whether or not the adverbs have been used correctly.

The Comparative

The **comparative** form of an adverb compares one action with another. Look at this example:

Your team plays *rougher* than ours.

The comparative is made in two ways:

1. Add *-er* to short adverbs like *hard* and *fast*.

    Kevin works *harder* than his cousin.

2. Use *more* with most adverbs ending in *-ly*.

    Some people write *more neatly* than others.

The Superlative

The **superlative** form of an adverb compares one action with two or more others. Notice these examples:

The night security guard works *latest* of all.
Of all the witnesses, Mr. Lee answered the questions *most completely.*

To form the superlative, either add *-est* or use *most.* If an adverb adds *-er* for the comparative, it adds *-est* for the superlative. If an adverb uses *more* for the comparative, it uses *most* for the superlative.

Adverb	Comparative	Superlative
long	longer	longest
quickly	more quickly	most quickly

Remember these points about adverbs in comparisons:

1. To compare two actions, use the comparative. To compare more than two actions, use the superlative.

Driving will take *longer* than flying.
Biking will take *longest* of all.

2. Use the word *other* when you compare an action with every other action of the same kind.

Incorrect: Mr. Russell tips more generously than any customer.

Correct: Mr. Russell tips more generously than any *other* customer.

3. Do not use *-er* with *more*, or *-est* with *most*.

Incorrect: Some athletes try more harder than others.

Correct: Some athletes try *harder* than others.

Irregular Comparisons

Some adverbs change completely in the comparative and superlative forms. These are examples:

Adverb	Comparative	Superlative
well	better	best
much	more	most
far	farther	farthest

This car goes *far* on a gallon of gas.
That car goes *farther*.
A motorcycle goes *farthest* of all.

Exercise A   Write the comparative and superlative forms.

1. calmly   *more calmly, most calmly*
2. steadily   *more steadily, most steadily*
3. fast   *faster, fastest*
4. rapidly   *more rapidly, most rapidly*
5. late   *later, latest*
5. neatly   *more neatly, most neatly*
7. often   *more often, most often*
8. accurately   *more accurately, most accurately*

Exercise B   If a sentence is correct, write *Correct*. If there is an error in the comparison of adverbs, write the sentence correctly.

1. The students exited ~~quicklier~~ *more quickly* during the fire drill.
2. Televised games take ~~more long~~ *longer*.
C 3. Most people sleep better at night.

513

Have students supply a comparative or superlative form of an adverb to complete each of the following sentences. Answers will vary.

1. Ray swims _____ than any other boy on the team.
2. This radio works _____ than that one.
3. His motorcycle goes _____ on a tank of gas than any car.
4. Enid came in last because she skated _____ of all the racers.
5. Yesterday I worked _____ than today.
6. People cheer _____ at soccer games than at football games.
7. The jeans fit _____ than the shorts.
8. I finished working _____ than my sister did.
9. Of all the babies, this one cries _____.
10. The snow melted _____ on the front lawn than on the back.

Extending the Lesson

Have students write the comparative and superlative forms of the following adverbs and use each in a sentence. Answers will vary.

1. easily   *more easily, most easily*
2. hard   *harder, hardest*
3. much   *more, most*
4. patiently   *more patiently, most patiently*
5. slowly   *more slowly, most slowly*

513

Objective

To avoid confusion between the use of adjectives and adverbs

Presenting the Lesson

1. Read page 514. Study the suggested ways to determine if an adjective or adverb is needed. Study the chart that reviews what adjectives and adverbs tell about the words they modify.

2. Assign and discuss Exercises A and B on page 515.

3. Read pages 515–516. Study examples carefully, stressing that linking verbs can be followed by adjectives and action verbs must be modified by adverbs.

4. Assign and discuss the Exercise on pages 516–517.

Individualizing the Lesson

Less-Advanced Students

1. Work through Exercise A, page 515, orally with the students.

2. Have students identify each adjective, adverb, and predicate adjective in a magazine article. Students should write each word along with the word it modifies.

Advanced Students

Have students find fifteen adjectives, adverbs, or predicate adjectives in a magazine article. Have them write the words they find along with the words modified.

514

c 4. Carpenters worked more steadily last year.

5. We shop here oftenest of all. *most often*

6. Of all the cars, this one runs more smoothly. *most*

7. Cheetahs run fastest than gazelles. *faster*

c 8. Ms. Bell dresses more formally than the students.

9. Barbecued chicken tastes bestest of all.

10. Of all the dance students, Tanya practices more often. *most*

Part 5 Adjective or Adverb?

Read these sentences. Which one sounds right to you?

Sirens screamed *noisy*.
Sirens screamed *noisily*.

If you said the second sentence, you are correct. An adverb (*noisily*), not an adjective (*noisy*), is needed to modify the verb *screamed*.

Sometimes you may have trouble deciding whether to use an adjective or an adverb. To decide, ask yourself:

1. What kind of words does the modifier tell about? If your answer is an action verb, adjective, or adverb, use the adverb. If your answer is a noun or pronoun, use the adjective.

2. What does the modifier tell about the word it goes with? If it tells *how, when, where,* or *to what extent,* use the adverb. If it tells *which one, what kind,* or *how many,* use the adjective.

An adjective tells	An adverb tells
Which one	How
What kind	When
How many	Where
	To what extent
About a noun or pronoun	About a verb, adjective, or adverb

Exercise A List each <u>adjective</u> and <u>adverb</u>, together with the word it modifies. Do not list articles.

1. The four hawks circled overhead.
2. The black ants slowly carried the crumbs away.
3. Copy those numbers very carefully.
4. Lions attack their prey ferociously.
5. Too few movies are comedies.
6. Two great comedians were Jack Benny and Buster Keaton.
7. The golfer hit precisely onto the green.
8. Several birds had somewhat similar markings.
9. That typewriter requires an expensive ribbon.
10. The program moved rather slowly.

Exercise B Choose the correct modifier from the two in parentheses. Tell whether it is an <u>adjective</u> or an <u>adverb</u>.

1. Francie added the figures (accurate, <u>accurately</u>).
2. Dad looked (furious, <u>furiously</u>) at the dented fender.
3. It was (terrible, <u>terribly</u>) dark inside the cave.
4. The dirt bikes raced (quick, <u>quickly</u>) over the hill.
5. Lucy walked (slow, <u>slowly</u>) through the art gallery.
6. These hamburgers taste (terrible, <u>terribly</u>) greasy.
7. The lawyer seemed (<u>confident</u>, confidently) in the courtroom.
8. Kent was (awful, <u>awfully</u>) confused about the computer.
9. (<u>Heavy</u>, Heavily) rains damaged the crops.
10. Nights in the desert are (extreme, <u>extremely</u>) cold.

Adverb or Predicate Adjective?

You have learned that a predicate adjective follows a linking verb and modifies the subject. Besides forms of *be*, other linking verbs are *become, seem, appear, look, sound, feel, taste, smell,* and *grow.*

Optional Practice

Have students choose the correct modifier from the two in parentheses and tell whether it is an adjective or an adverb.

1. Jill washed the vegetables (careful, <u>carefully</u>). Adv
2. Grandpa looks (<u>tired</u>, tiredly) since his operation. Adj
3. Doesn't the food taste (<u>delicious</u>, deliciously)? Adj
4. The baby was wrapped (warm, <u>warmly</u>) in her blanket. Adv
5. Handle the cactus (gentle, <u>gently</u>). Adv
6. Betsy grew (<u>impatient</u>, impatiently) as she waited. Adj
7. The soft rain felt (<u>nice</u>, nicely) on my face. Adj
8. Tina decorated her room (cheerful, <u>cheerfully</u>). Adv
9. Mr. Hayes speaks too (soft, <u>softly</u>) to be heard. Adv
10. The game ended (abrupt, <u>abruptly</u>). Adv

Extending the Lesson

Have students fill in the blanks in the following sentences with a correct modifier. Have them label the modifier *adverb* or *predicate adjective*. Answers will vary.

1. The pizza tasted _____.
2. I ate the pizza _____.
3. The doctor looked _____.
4. Jane looked _____ for her contact lens.
5. The pickles smelled _____.
6. The dog _____ smelled the ground.
7. The flower grew _____ this spring.
8. John grew _____ after an hour's wait.

Mr. Andrews looks angry. (*Angry* modifes *Mr. Andrews*.)

The paint feels tacky. (*Tacky* modifies *paint*.)

The tea tastes bitter. (*Bitter* modifies *tea*.)

The verbs *looks*, *feels*, and *tastes* can also be action verbs. So can *sound*, *appear*, *smells*, and *grew*. When these verbs are action verbs, they are followed by adverbs instead of predicate adjectives. Adverbs tell *how*, *when*, *where*, or *to what extent* about the action verbs.

Here are sentences using the same words as linking verbs and as action verbs.

Linking Verbs with Adjectives	Action Verbs with Adverbs
The sky *looked* clear.	Carol *looked* carefully.
The pilot *appeared* calm.	A train *appeared* suddenly.
The soup *smells* delicious.	A retriever *smells* keenly.
The traffic *sounds* hectic.	The chime *sounds* often.

If you can't decide whether to use an adverb or an adjective in a certain sentence, ask these questions:

1. Can you substitute *is* or *was* for the verb? If so, the modifier is probably an adjective.

2. Does the modifier tell *how*, *when*, *where*, or *to what extent*? If so, the modifier is probably an adverb.

Exercise   Choose the right modifier for the following sentences.

1. The speaker (nervous, <u>nervously</u>) approached the stage.
2. The huge diamond looked (<u>flawless</u>, flawlessly).
3. The robbery suspect appeared (<u>calm</u>, calmly).
4. Detective Burke looked (careful, <u>carefully</u>) for clues.
5. During the show the children grew (<u>quiet</u>, quietly).

6. Mandy did her chores (quick, <u>quickly</u>).
7. That man looks (<u>suspicious</u>, suspiciously).
8. Aunt Jane looked (sad, <u>sadly</u>) at the broken vase.
9. Sandpaper feels (<u>rough</u>, roughly) to the touch.
10. The soldiers retreated (slow, <u>slowly</u>) into the jungle.

Part 6 Troublesome Modifiers

Certain modifiers are frequently used incorrectly.

Them and Those

Those can be used as an adjective.

Who has the combinations for *those* locks?

Them is never an adjective. It cannot substitute for *those*.

Incorrect: We took them snapshots.
Correct: We took *those* snapshots.
Correct: We took *them*.

Here and There

Sometimes people incorrectly say "this here jacket" or "that there room." "This here" and "that there" repeat ideas. The word *this* includes the idea of *here*. The word *that* includes the idea of *there*. Avoid "this here" and "that there."

Kind and Sort

Kind and *sort* are singular. *Kinds* and *sorts* are plural. No matter what words follow, use *this* or *that* with *kind* and *sort*. Use *these* and *those* with *kinds* and *sorts*.

This kind of ink is erasable. (singular)
Those sorts of colas contain caffeine. (plural)

517

Part 6

Objectives

1. To use certain troublesome modifiers correctly: *them* and *those*, *here* and *there*, *knd* and *sort*, *good* and *well*
2. To avoid the use of double negatives

Presenting the Lesson

1. Explain to students that certain modifiers often cause usage problems that they should try to avoid. Read pages 517–518 covering the troublesome modifiers. Go over the examples of each carefully.
2. Read the discussion of double negatives on pages 518–519. Be certain students can distinguish between negative and positive words. Study the examples of negative words on page 519.
3. Assign and discuss Exercises A, B, and C on pages 519–520.

Individualizing the Lesson

Less-Advanced Students

1. Work through Exercise A, page 519, orally with the students
2. Have students find published examples of the uses of *them* and *those*, *here* and *there*, *kind* and *sort*, and *good* and *well*. Students should

517

study the samples they find to make sure they conform to the rules of this lesson.

Advanced Students

Have students write two original sentences using each of the troublesome modifiers in this Part correctly.

Optional Practice

Have students correct errors in the use of modifiers in the following sentences. Not all sentences contain errors.

1. There wasn't hardly any snow left.
2. Emily plays the piano good. *(well)*
3. We don't never eat dinner before 7:00.
4. Where did you find them goggles? *(those)*
5. Do you like these kind of baggy jeans? *(this)*
6. The chef uses this here kind of shortening.
7. Coolidge shot good from the free-throw line. *(well)*
C 8. Have you ever eaten this kind of chili?
9. Them boys don't have no right to be here. *(Those)* *(any)*
C 10. David skated well in the competition.

Extending the Lesson

Have students rewrite the following sentences, making sure to correct any errors.

1. Them records belong to me. *(Those)*
2. I'm not never going to the ballet again.
3. The band played very good. *(well)*
4. She has all sort of books. *(sorts)*
5. I'm sitting in this here desk because that there desk is broken.

518

Good and *Well*

Good and *well* have similar meanings, but the words are not the same. You cannot always substitute one word for the other. Look at the differences in these sentences:

That is a *good* car for you. (The adjective *good* modifies the noun *car.*)

You dance *well*. (The adverb *well* modifies the verb *dance.*)

Good is always an adjective modifying nouns and pronouns. It is never used to describe an action.

Well can be either an adjective or an adverb. In the sentence above, *well* is used as an adverb modifying an action verb. *Well* can also be used after a linking verb to mean "in good health."

Brad doesn't look *well*.
(*Well* is a predicate adjective modifying *Brad.*)

Stacy sings *well*.
(*Well* is an adverb modifying the action verb *sings.*)

If you are describing an action, use *well*.

The Double Negative

The use of two negative words when only one is necessary is called a **double negative**. Avoid using double negatives.

Incorrect: I didn't take no breaks.
Correct: I did*n't* take *any* breaks.

Incorrect: The twins never want no advice.
Correct: The twins *never* want *any* advice.

Incorrect: Richard couldn't do nothing all day.
Correct: Richard could*n't* do *anything* all day.

Contractions like *couldn't* contain a shortened form of the negative *not*. Do not use other negative words after them.

518

Some common negative words are *no, none, not, nothing*, and *never*. Instead of these words, use *any, anything*, or *ever* after negative contractions.

> Jim Thompson has*n't ever* lost an election.
> Jeff could*n't* understand *any* French.
> The storm did*n't* damage *anything*.

Other negative words are *hardly* and *barely*. Don't use them with negative contractions like *hasn't* and *didn't*.

> Incorrect: Anne couldn't barely speak.
>
> Correct: Anne *could barely* speak.
>
> Incorrect: The speaker hadn't scarcely begun.
>
> Correct: The speaker *had scarcely* begun.
>
> Incorrect: The police hardly never patrol the park.
>
> Correct: The police *hardly ever* patrol the park.

Exercise A   Choose the correct word from the two in parentheses.

1. Have (them, those) apples been washed?
2. I prefer (this, these) kind of lotion.
3. How do you cook (them, those) crabs?
4. (That, That there) letter is for Peggy.
5. Evan collects (this, these) kinds of shells.
6. Which store sells (them, those) orange golf balls?
7. Mike drew (that, that there) picture.
8. (This, These) sorts of plants are hardy.
9. The critics raved about (this, this here) movie.
10. Is (this, these) sort of camera easy to use?

Exercise B   Follow the directions for Exercise A.

1. The cook at camp feeds us (good, well).
2. This magazine prints many (good, well) short stories.
3. Mr. Nabor ran very (good, well) in the marathon.

519

4. Most athletes stay in (good, well) health.

5. Tom gave a (good, well) performance at the piano recital.

6. This taco salad tastes (good, well).

7. The horse took the jumps (good, well).

8. Have you read any (good, well) books lately?

9. Bess and I work (good, well) together.

10. Does Joe write (good, well) enough to enter the essay contest?

Exercise C Number your paper from 1 to 10. Correct the double negatives in the following sentences. If a sentence does not contain a double negative, write *Correct*.

1. Our team hasn't played ~~no~~ ^{any} games lately.

2. Haven't you ~~never~~ ^{ever} been to Chinatown?

3. Dan couldn't barely read the tiny print.

C 4. The trapped miners could hardly breathe.

5. Matt didn't want ~~nothing~~ ^{anything} on his hamburger.

6. These fries don't have ~~no~~ ^{any} salt on them.

7. Janet hardly keeps ~~nothing~~ ^{anything} in her purse.

8. Because of the blizzard, we haven't scarcely gone out of the house.

C 9. Nancy hasn't given any time to her studies lately.

10. Bob ~~doesn't have~~ ^{has} hardly any camping equipment.

520

ADDITIONAL EXERCISES

Using Modifiers

A. Adjectives Write the adjectives you find in each sentence. Then write the word each modifies. Do not include *a, an,* or *the.*

1. This film was made on a low budget.
2. Does anyone know the true story?
3. That Italian sports car has a deluxe interior.
4. Dense, black smoke poured out of the tailpipe.
5. One candidate received a special award.
6. Two mysterious strangers appeared at the meeting.
7. No newspaper can print every bit of news.
8. Everyone likes these new wider sidewalks.
9. Some Indian food is cooked in a clay oven.
10. Reggae music is from the tropical island of Jamaica.

B. Predicate Adjectives Write the predicate adjective in each sentence. After each adjective, write the word it modifies.

1. Rebecca seems unusually quiet.
2. That dead tree is hollow.
3. The track team is strong this year.
4. The California sun is intense.
5. That African nation has just become independent.
6. The heat in a sauna is dry.
7. Most puppies are clumsy.
8. Baseball fans can be very rude.
9. The brass doorknob felt sticky.
10. The night buses are almost empty.

C. Adjectives in Comparisons Choose the correct adjective.

1. Have you ever tasted (more spicier, spicier) chili?
2. Who was the (younger, youngest) of all the Presidents?

521

Additional Exercises

These Additional Exercises may be used for additional practice of the concepts presented in this Section. Each exercise focuses on a single concept, and should be used after the page number indicated in parentheses.

Review

If you have not assigned these Additional Exercises before this time, you can also use them as an excellent Section Review.

3. This year the business was (<u>more profitable</u>, most profitable) than last year.
4. Jennifer looks (<u>happier</u>, happiest) than her friend.
5. Of all the paperbacks, this one is the (more enjoyable, <u>most enjoyable</u>).
6. Nardi is the (<u>better</u>, best) of the two trainers.
7. That was the (worse, <u>worst</u>) mistake you ever made.
8. Mr. Katoka had the (<u>most</u>, mostest) customers.
9. Which is the (<u>lesser</u>, least) of the two evils?
10. The top shelf is (<u>dustier</u>, more dustier) than the bottom shelf.

D.   Adverbs and Words They Modify   Number your paper from 1 to 10. Write the <u>adverbs</u> in the following sentences. After each adverb, write the word it modifies.

1. Cindy Nicholas swam the English Channel twice.
2. My grandparents arrived yesterday.
3. A trapdoor slowly opened.
4. Two helicopters hovered overhead.
5. Carrie is too busy.   *(very* modifies *reluctantly)*
6. The union members very reluctantly signed a contract.
7. The skaters practice here quite frequently. *(quite* modifies *frequently)*
8. Furious, Seth stomped out.
9. Congress is seriously considering other budget cuts.
10. That painter usually throws paint wildly at the canvas.

E.   Adverbs in Comparisons   Choose the correct adverb.

1. The hurricane hit (<u>hardest</u>, most hard) in the tropics.
2. Randy can repair appliances (<u>more skillfully</u>, most skillfully) than his brother.
3. Amanda parked (<u>closer</u>, closest) to the curb than I did.
4. Washington played (badder, <u>worse</u>, worst) than usual.
5. The flood waters receded (quicklier, <u>more quickly</u>) than expected.

6. The brakes work (gooder, <u>better</u>, more well) now.

7. Cynthia dances (<u>better</u>, more better) barefoot.

8. Blue-collar workers were hurt (most hardest, <u>hardest</u>).

9. Nina answered the (more, <u>most</u>) thoughtfully of all four candidates.

10. Ty stood (<u>farther</u>, farthest) from the basket than Bo did.

F. Adjectives and Adverbs Choose the correct modifier.

1. The veterans talked (honest, <u>honestly</u>) about their problems.

2. The ice-cold watermelon tasted (<u>sweet</u>, sweetly).

3. Nicole looked (eager, <u>eagerly</u>) at the swimming pool.

4. The lizard's tiny ribs moved (rapid, <u>rapidly</u>) in and out.

5. He had (careless, <u>carelessly</u>) set the tea on the floor.

6. One player felt (real, <u>really</u>) bad about being traded.

7. Vicky felt (<u>sad</u>, sadly) about the loss.

8. The outcome is by no means (<u>certain</u>, certainly).

9. The clean mirrors looked (<u>bright</u>, brightly).

10. You are (certain, <u>certainly</u>) punctual today.

G. Special Problems with Modifiers If there is an error, write the sentence correctly. If it is correct, write *Correct*.

1. The health department inspects restaurants ~~good~~ ^{well}.

2. These kinds of motor bikes use hardly ~~no~~ ^{any} gasoline.

3. The security guard didn't see ~~nobody~~ ^{anybody} on her rounds.

C 4. Sherry brought two bags of laundry and left them here.

5. He hadn't ever seen ~~them~~ ^{those} insects before.

6. "Magic" Johnson ~~didn't~~ hardly ~~touch~~ ^{touched} the basketball.

7. That ~~there~~ hockey stick was autographed by Phil Esposito.

8. These ~~sort~~ ^{sorts} of shirts don't look good with jeans.

9. This bread isn't ~~no~~ ^{any} more nutritious than that.

C 10. The engine runs well, and the body shows hardly any rust.

MIXED REVIEW

Using Modifiers

A. Finding adjectives and adverbs Copy the following sentences. Underline each adjective once and each adverb twice. Then draw an arrow from each modifier to the word it modifies. Do not include articles.

1. The American audience barely understood the Japanese movie.
2. That breakfast was too hearty for me.
3. Those small, simple cars can actually be very expensive.
4. Four new students enrolled today.
5. Many old songs are still popular.
6. The hockey fans were certainly angry about the unfair penalty.
7. Natalie is too patient sometimes.
8. The rough, bumpy oysters most often produce the pearls.
9. The bland rice went well with the spicy chili.
10. The tall woman in the blue dress made the Olympic team.

B. Using modifiers correctly All of these sentences contain errors in the use of modifiers. Rewrite each sentence correctly.

1. China has a ~~more~~ bigger population than India.
2. The singer sounded even worser than the band.
3. A dog will usually wander ~~more~~ farther from home than a cat.
4. Nathan is the _{most obedient} ~~obedientest~~ child on our block.
5. Is a piranha _{more vicious} ~~viciouser~~ than a shark?

6. The first chapter is easier than any ^other part of the math textbook.

7. Sheila performed the bestest of the four gymnasts.

8. The paramedics arrived ~~more~~ faster than the firefighters.

9. Chad smiles ^(more often) ~~oftener~~ than Trisha.

10. Of the two boxers, Liston fought ^(more roughly) ~~roughest~~.

C. Choosing the correct modifier Write the correct word from the two in parentheses.

1. Becky felt (<u>nervous</u>, nervously) about the interview.

2. Ellis looked (nervous, <u>nervously</u>) over his shoulder.

3. (<u>That</u>, That there) mirror makes me look thinner.

4. Night falls (sudden, <u>suddenly</u>) in Africa.

5. Those (kind, <u>kinds</u>) of comments are not helpful.

6. For a beginner, Gus works (good, <u>well</u>).

7. Are you (real, <u>really</u>) certain about your plans?

8. I don't want (no, <u>any</u>) lettuce on my sandwich.

9. (Them, <u>Those</u>) valves are clogged again.

10. The bran muffins tasted very (<u>good</u>, well).

These challenging and enjoyable activities allow the students to see how the concepts of grammar, usage, and mechanics may be applied in actual writing situations. Each exercise is designed to allow students practice in several of the skills they have acquired in this Section. The activities also provide opportunities for students to write creatively about a wide variety of interesting and unusual subjects.

USING GRAMMAR IN WRITING
Using Modifiers

A. You are in charge of publicity for a fund-raising event. All the members of a club contributed items for a yard sale. Following are some of the items.

camera	radio	books
desk	table	tray
pen	game	pitcher

The local paper will give your group a free classified ad, but you may use no more than twenty-five words to describe all of the items. Write the classified ad, describing the items as well as you can within the limit of twenty-five words.

A local radio station has agreed to describe the items to listeners. The people at the station will let you write as much about each item as you wish. Expand the descriptions that you wrote for the classified ad. Use vivid modifiers to help the listeners picture each item.

B. Think of two rides that give a person very different feelings. Write a paragraph about each ride. Use many strong modifiers to make the contrast clear. Use details from your experience, or use your imagination to invent details. You might contrast a merry-go-round and a roller coaster, a rowboat and a sailboard, or a hot-air-balloon ride and a ski lift.

C. Writers of science fiction and fantasy create settings, objects, plants, and creatures that no one has ever seen. To bring their creations to life for a reader, they must describe them especially vividly. They must paint a word picture for the reader. Imagine a setting, plant, or creature for a fantasy that you might write. Describe your imaginary thing vividly enough so that a reader can picture it. Underline each modifier.

Using Prepositions and Conjunctions

Section Objectives

1. To recognize prepositions and prepositional phrases and to understand their functions

2. To distinguish between prepositions and adverbs

3. To identify prepositional phrases as adjective or adverb in function

4. To recognize coordinating and correlative conjunctions and to understand their functions

Preparing the Students

Tell students that good communication must do more than name objects and tell what happened. It must show relationships between things and events. Two useful parts of speech, prepositions and conjunctions, show relationships.

Read the introduction on pages 527–528.

Additional Resources

Diagnostic Test — page 5 in the test booklet

Mastery Test — pages 56–57 in the test booklet

Additional Exercises — pages 538–541 in the student text

Practice Book — pages 206–210

Duplicating Masters — pages 206–210

Special Populations — See special section at the front of this Teacher's Edition.

The purpose of language is to express ideas. With nouns and verbs you can express simple ideas:

> Robert walked.
> The bird eats oranges.

When you add adjectives and adverbs, the sentences become more specific.

> Robert walked briskly.
> The pesky mynah bird eats oranges.

When you want to express relationships, you use words that connect other words. One type of connecting word is a preposition. This sentence shows where Robert walked by using a prepositional phrase.

> Robert walked briskly through the deserted streets.

527

Another type of connecting word is a conjunction. By using a conjunction, this sentence shows other things the bird eats.

The pesky mynah bird eats oranges and apples.

Prepositions and **conjunctions** are parts of speech. In this section you will learn to identify these parts of speech and to use them properly.

Part **1**

Objectives

1. To recognize prepositions and prepositional phrases and to understand their functions
2. To distinguish between prepositions and adverbs

Presenting the Lesson

1. Read pages 528–529. Be sure students understand the meaning of *connective.* Study examples of sentences with prepositions. Go over definitions of *preposition, object of the preposition,* and *prepositional phrase.*
2. Read page 529, going over the list of words often used as prepositions. Go around the classroom and have students give sentences for each preposition.
3. Assign and discuss Exercises A and B on pages 529–530.
4. Read page 530, discussing how to tell the difference between adverbs and prepositions. Stress that a preposition cannot be used alone, and is always part of a phrase.
5. Assign and discuss Exercises A and B on pages 530–531.

Part 1   What Are Prepositions?

Words that join other words or word groups are called **connectives**. One important kind of connective is the **preposition**. Prepositions show relationships. Look at the relationships expressed in the following sentences:

Mary walked *up* the stairs.
Mary walked *down* the stairs.
Mary walked *around* the stairs.

The prepositions *up, down,* and *around* show the relationship between the noun *stairs* and the verb *walked.* In each of the above sentences, *stairs* is the **object of the preposition.** Like all prepositions, *up, down,* and *around* connect their objects to another part of the sentence.

Prepositions do not show relationships all by themselves. They begin a *phrase,* a group of words that does not have a subject or verb. The **prepositional phrase** makes the relationship clear. In the above sentences, *up the stairs, down the stairs,* and *around the stairs* are prepositional phrases. Here are some other sentences with prepositional phrases:

The poster glowed *in the dark.*
During the summer, Ned went *to camp.*
The stack *of napkins* blew *off the table.*

A preposition is a word used with a noun or pronoun, called its _object_, to show the relationship between the noun or pronoun and some other word in the sentence.

A prepositional phrase consists of a preposition, its object, and any modifiers of the object.

The list below shows words often used as prepositions. Many of them, like *above*, *over*, *in*, and *beside*, show location. Others, like *until*, *after*, and *before*, show time. Still others show other kinds of relationships. Look at these prepositions and see if you can tell the relationship each one suggests.

Words Often Used as Prepositions

about	behind	during	off	to
above	below	except	on	toward
across	beneath	for	onto	under
after	beside	from	out	until
against	between	in	outside	up
along	beyond	inside	over	upon
among	but (*except*)	into	past	with
around	by	like	since	within
at	concerning	near	through	without
before	down	of	throughout	

Exercise A Number your paper from 1 to 10. Find the prepositional phrases in the following sentences.

> Example: Sean leaves for school at seven o'clock.
>
> for school, at seven o'clock

1. The train raced through the tunnel.
2. No one worked during the strike.
3. Brian walked toward the ballpark after school.
4. Linda tripped clumsily over the rug.
5. Ask Dad for the keys to the boat.
6. The doorman stands inside the lobby during winter.
7. Have you looked for your umbrella in the closet?

Less-Advanced Students

1. Work through Exercise A, pages 529–530, orally with students.

2. Have students write the object of each preposition in Exercises A and B, pages 529–530.

3. Have students choose ten prepositions from the chart on page 529. Have them use each preposition they choose in an original sentence.

Advanced Students

Have students write an original sentence for twenty-five of the prepositions listed in the chart on page 529. Have them underline the object of each preposition they use.

Optional Practice

Have students identify the prepositional phrases in the following sentences.

1. Colleen marched down State Street in the St. Patrick's Day parade.
2. Put your bike in the garage and come along with us.
3. Guy went to the doctor for his allergy shot on Monday.
4. Throughout the summer our town has special events.
5. Chris Evert-Lloyd jumped over the net when the game was over.
6. The papers fell under the desk.
7. Which candidate won in the primaries in most states across the country?
8. The dancers went through their number before the curtain went up.
9. Jan left for school without his books.
10. The eggs were baked in butter and served with cream.

Have students use the following prepositional phrases in sentences.

1. on the radio
2. between the two trees
3. along the path
4. throught the gym
5. toward the Atlantic Coast
6. with disbelief

8. The signature on the check is a forgery.
9. David drove past the driveway.
10. Without a doubt, this is the best restaurant in town.

Exercise B Follow the directions for Exercise A.

1. The safe is behind the painting on this wall.
2. A flock of geese landed beyond the ridge.
3. An assortment of wildflowers grew in the meadow.
4. You sound like Helen on the phone.
5. A horseshoe was nailed over the door.
6. We parked in the lot near the bank.
7. Without a doubt, Natalie will arrive before us.
8. Cassie has not been in town since last month.
9. Throughout the day, newscasters broke into the regular programs with special bulletins.
10. June sat on a bench against the wall.

Preposition or Adverb?

Many words used as prepositions can also be used as adverbs. How can you tell the difference?

A preposition is never used alone. It is always followed by a noun or pronoun as part of a phrase. If the word is in a phrase, it is probably a preposition. If the word has no object, it is probably an adverb.

> The commuters walked *across* the bridge. (preposition)
> The commuters walked *across*. (adverb)
> Jim went *inside* the garage. (preposition)
> Jim went *inside*. (adverb)

Exercise A Decide whether the italicized words in these sentences are adverbs or prepositions. Write *Adverb* or *Preposition* for each sentence.

A 1. Please turn *off* the stereo.

P 2. The shoe box fell *off* the shelf.

A 3. Turn the lights *on*.

P 4. The trophies were *on* the mantle.

A 5. Fred sang *along*.

P 6. Jean planted flowers *along* the fence.

P 7. The laundry fell *down* the chute.

A 8. The power lines blew *down*.

P 9. Mr. Drew dropped the letters *into* the mailbox.

A 10. The ballerina spun *around* dizzily.

Exercise B   Follow the directions for Exercise A.

A 1. Mario Andretti put his helmet *on*.

P 2. You'll find the map *in* the glove compartment.

P 3. *Without* a sound, the mouse scurried across the room.

P 4. Dick got *on* the wrong bus.

A 5. Is Jason going to tag *along* again?

P 6. Katherine walked *along* the shore.

P 7. Mom put some carrots *into* the stew.

P 8. The jeep drove *through* the snowdrift.

A 9. I tried to drive *through*, but I got stuck.

A 10. Has Lauren been *around* lately?

Part 2 Prepositional Phrases as Modifiers

Single words are often used as modifiers. However, groups of words can also be modifiers. Prepositional phrases can modify different parts of a sentence. They work in the same way that single adjectives or adverbs do.

An adjective phrase is a prepositional phrase that modifies a noun or pronoun. The phrase always includes the preposition, its object, and any modifiers of the object.

531

Part 2

Objective

To identify prepositional phrases as adjective or adverb in function

Presenting the Lesson

1. Review with students the two types of modifiers—adjectives and adverbs—and how they function. Point out that prepositional phrases can be used in the same way as adjectives and adverbs.

2. Read pages 531–532. Study examples of adjective and adverb phrases, noting how each functions. Pay particular attention to the explanation of prepositional phrases in a series.

3. Read page 533, studying the examples of diagrams of prepositional phrases. Remind students that because prepositional phrases are modifiers, they are placed under the words they modify, just as adverbs and adjectives are.

4. Assign and discuss Exercises A and B on pages 533–534.

Individualizing the Lesson

Less-Advanced Students

1. Have students write a brief explanation of how to determine the difference between an adjective phrase and an adverb phrase.

2. Have students make up five prepositional phrases together. Then have them make up sentences using these phrases. Have students tell how the phrases are used in the sentences.

3. Have the class make up five more prepositional phrases. This time have students work individually, first using the phrase in a sentence and then determining how the phrase is used.

Advanced Students

Have students write twenty sentences—ten with adjective phrases and ten with adverb phrases. Students should then circle each prepositional phrase and draw an arrow to the word it modifies.

Optional Practice

Have students identify the prepositional phrases in each of the following sentences. Have students indicate if the phrase is an adjective phrase or an adverb phrase.

1. Gloria put the vase on the shelf [ADV] in her room. [ADJ]
2. Roses bloom throughout the year [ADV] in Arizona. [ADV]
3. Stretch your arms above your head. [ADV]
4. We parked in the lot [ADV] behind the library. [ADJ]
5. Everyone sang to Louis [ADV] on his birthday. [ADV]
6. The key is under the mat [ADV] near the back door. [ADJ]
7. Adam went to the library [ADV] after dinner. [ADV]
8. The judge of the contest [ADJ] chose Michelle and Sara.
9. The child wanted help from his mother and father. [ADJ]
10. The heater in the den [ADJ] can throw heat throughout the room. [ADV]

Extending the Lesson

Have students write sentences using the following prepositional

John has a car *with a sun roof.*
(*With a sun roof* is an adjective phrase, modifying the noun *car.* It tells *what kind* of car.)

The key *on the hook* unlocks the garage.
(*On the hook* is an adjective phrase, modifying the noun *key.* It tells *which one.*)

Some *of the runners* are doing warm-up exercises.
(*Of the runners* is an adjective phrase that modifies the pronoun *some.* It tells *what kind.*)

As you can see, adjective phrases, like adjectives, tell *which one* or *what kind.*

Adverbs tell *how, when, where,* and *to what extent* about verbs. Adverb phrases modify verbs in the same way.

Adverb phrases are prepositional phrases that modify verbs.

The coupons are sent *by mail.*
(*By mail* is an adverb phrase telling *how.* It modifies the verb *are sent.*)

The play will start *at eight o'clock.*
(*At eight o'clock* is an adverb phrase. It tells *when* about the verb *will start.*)

The dog snoozed *by the fireplace.*
(*By the fireplace* is an adverb phrase. It tells *where* about the verb *snoozed.*)

Sometimes one prepositional phrase follows another. Frequently, the second phrase is an adjective phrase modifying the object in the first phrase.

Paula went *to the market on Fifth Street.*
(*To the market* is an adverb phrase modifying the verb *went.* On Fifth Street is an adjective phrase modifying the noun *market.*)

Hansel marked the trail *with crumbs of bread.*
(The adverb phrase *with crumbs* tells *how* about the verb *marked. Of bread* is an adjective phrase describing the noun *crumbs.*)

Diagraming Prepositional Phrases

To diagram a prepositional phrase, place it under the word it modifies.

The students at the rally cheered for their team.

At times a preposition may have two or more nouns or pronouns as objects in the prepositional phrase.

On Saturday Marla shopped for shoes and a purse.

Exercise A Copy these sentences. Circle each prepositional phrase. Draw an arrow from the phrase to the word it modifies. Tell whether the phrase is an adjective phrase or an adverb phrase.

1. Jerry has a Ford with a stick shift. ADJ
2. Carol searched through the stack of photographs. ADV ADJ
3. Do you study on weekends? ADV
4. The two schools have been rivals for dozens of years. ADV ADJ
5. Orange juice is a good source of vitamin C. ADJ
6. We waved to the driver of the truck. ADV ADJ
7. The pool is closed after 9:00 P.M. ADV

phrases. Then have them indicate whether the phrase is an adjective or an adverb phrase.

1. under the table
2. around the corner
3. throughout the country
4. during a thunderstorm
5. at high noon

8. Did you lock your keys in the $\overset{\text{ADV}}{\text{car}}$?

9. We played tennis $\overset{\text{ADV}}{\text{during}}$ the day and danced at $\overset{\text{ADV}}{\text{night}}$.

10. With $\overset{\text{ADV}}{\text{a}}$ little luck, one of the Jets recovered the football.

Exercise B   Follow the directions for Exercise A.

1. Connie is studying in the $\overset{\text{ADV}}{\text{library}}$.
2. The cafe in the $\overset{\text{ADJ}}{\text{park}}$ sells pink lemonade.
3. A neon sign flashed over the $\overset{\text{ADV}}{\text{door}}$.
4. The truck parked near the $\overset{\text{ADV}}{\text{garage}}$ in the $\overset{\text{ADJ}}{\text{alley}}$.
5. Nobody except $\overset{\text{ADJ}}{\text{Angie}}$ wants the notes for $\overset{\text{ADJ}}{\text{that}}$ lecture.
6. The car behind the $\overset{\text{ADJ}}{\text{shop}}$ belongs to $\overset{\text{ADV}}{\text{Darrell}}$.
7. We sailed past the $\overset{\text{ADV}}{\text{canal}}$ and into the $\overset{\text{ADV}}{\text{open}}$ sea.
8. The trainer put a muzzle on the $\overset{\text{ADV}}{\text{dog}}$ in the $\overset{\text{ADJ}}{\text{pen}}$.
9. The woman with the tennis $\overset{\text{ADJ}}{\text{racket}}$ is my mom.
10. Betsy returned the books on the $\overset{\text{ADJ}}{\text{table}}$ to the $\overset{\text{ADV}}{\text{library}}$.

Part 3   Conjunctions

A conjunction is another kind of word that shows relationships.

A conjunction is a word that connects words or groups of words.

Look at the conjunctions in the following sentences:

Doug *and* Tom will trim the hedges.
The weather reporter predicted *either* rain *or* snow.
JoAnne designed *and* made the costumes.
That jacket is warm *but* stylish.
Tickets are on sale *both* at the office *and* in the lounge.

Like prepositions, conjunctions show a relationship between the words they connect. Conjunctions differ from prepositions, however, in two ways. Conjunctions link similar kinds of words, like two nouns or two phrases. Also, conjunctions do not have objects.

Part 3

Objective

To recognize coordinating and correlative conjunctions and to understand their functions

Presenting the Lesson

1. Read page 534. Study the definition of conjunctions and stress how they differ from prepositions. Study examples of conjunctions, noting their functions.

2. Read page 535. Study examples of coordinating conjunctions.

3. Read pages 535–536 and study examples of correlative conjunctions.

4. Assign and discuss Exercises A, B, C, and D on pages 536–537.

Coordinating Conjunctions

Coordinating conjunctions are used to join single words or groups of words of the same kind. *And, but,* and *or* are the most common coordinating conjunctions.

The words joined by coordinating conjunctions are compound constructions. Compound constructions include compound subjects, compound direct objects, and compound verbs, for example.

Students *and* teachers share the same cafeteria.
(*And* links *students* and *teachers*, making them a compound subject of the verb *share*.)
The children ran *and* jumped.
(*And* connects *ran,* and *jumped,* forming a compound verb.)
Ann wanted that dress *but* couldn't afford it.
(*But* connects the two predicates.)
The iced tea looked cool *and* refreshing.
(*And* connects two predicate adjectives.)
The thieves worked quickly *and* quietly.
(*And* connects two adverbs.)
Bob ordered mushrooms, onions, *and* sausage on his pizza.
(*And* connects the three parts of the compound direct object.)
Give Marcy *or* Joe your dues.
(*Or* connects the compound indirect object.)
Kirsten can babysit on Friday *or* Saturday.
(*Or* connects the compound object of a preposition.)

Correlative Conjunctions

Some conjunctions are used in pairs. They are called **correlative conjunctions**. These are correlative conjunctions:

both . . . and	not only . . . but (also)
either . . . or	whether . . . or
neither . . . nor	

535

Extending the Lesson

Have students write a descriptive paragraph that includes at least five coordinating conjunctions. Have students circle and identify the compound parts.

Both Don *and* Sam are on the team.
You may have *either* a sandwich *or* a bowl of soup.
Neither ducklings *nor* baby chicks make good pets.
Dad is grilling *not only* hamburgers, *but also* bratwurst.
The class voted on *whether* Chuck *or* Kim should be the president.

Exercise A   Find the conjunctions in the following sentences. Tell what words or word groups are connected by the conjunction. Give the part of speech of the connected words.

> Example: The 747 banked and turned.
>
>   The verbs *banked* and *turned* are connected by the conjunction *and*.

1. Either Chuck or Marge will introduce us. N
2. Mr. Morton spoke to the children softly but firmly. ADV
3. The locker room was hot and humid. ADJ
4. Sean fell and broke his arm. V
5. Should I wear a sweater or a coat? N
6. Kangaroos and koala bears are natives of Australia. N
7. Gene spends his money on movies and records. N
8. Ann not only designs but also builds furniture. V
9. Mr. Anderson enjoys both classical music and jazz. N
10. The stowaway on the ship had neither a ticket nor the money for one. N

Exercise B   Write the kind of compound construction in each sentence. Write the construction with its conjunction.

1. The farmer plowed and fertilized the field. comp verb
2. The detective knew the identity of the thief but couldn't prove it. comp predicate
3. Zucchini and tomatoes grow in the garden. comp subject
4. The pendulum swung back and forth. comp adverb
5. The letters from the attic were old, brittle, and dusty. comp predicate adjective
6. Take either a taxi or a limousine to the airport. comp direct object

536

7. Gary cleaned not only the basement but also the attic. comp direct object
8. Is Marilyn disappointed or relieved? comp verb
9. Both the walls and the cabinets in the kitchen need painting. comp subject
10. Passengers bought snacks, magazines, and newspapers on the train. comp direct object

Exercise C: **Writing** Write two sentences using *and*, two sentences using *but*, and two sentences using *or*. After each sentence, write the words or groups of words that are joined by the conjunctions.

Exercise D: **Writing** Write one sentence for each of the following pairs of correlative conjunctions:

both . . . and   either . . . or   neither . . .nor

Additional Exercises

These Additional Exercises
may be used for additional
practice of the concepts presented in this Section. Each
exercise focuses on a single
concept, and should be used
after the page number indicated in parentheses.

Review

If you have not assigned
these Additional Exercises
before this time, you can also
use them as an excellent Section Review.

ADDITIONAL EXERCISES

Using Prepositions and Conjunctions

A. Prepositions and Their Objects   Number your paper
from 1 to 10. Write the prepositions in the following sentences. Also,
write the object of each preposition.

1. Both Sonny Rollins and Miles Davis have played at that
    club.
2. Mary searched for the envelope with the address on it.
3. I enjoy games like Monopoly.
4. Jane woke at dawn to the sound of birds outside her
    window.
5. The cables ran along the roof.
6. Since yesterday I have changed my mind about my
    plans.
7. The plane passed through the cluster of clouds.
8. Have you looked under the chair for your shoes?
9. Electric cars might be the autos of the future.
10. Julie left her bike by the tree near the corner.

B. Adverbs and Prepositions   Decide whether the italicized
words in these sentences are adverbs or prepositions. Write *Adverb*
or *Preposition* for each sentence.

P 1. The papers blew *off* the table.
P 2. Eddie ran *toward* the airplane terminal.
P 3. A scar ran *down* his cheek.
A 4. Stand *by*, please.
P 5. There is a pay phone *by* the subway entrance.
A 6. The news is *out*.
P 7. Marilyn grabbed the vine and swung *across* the creek.
A 8. Has the search party given *up*?
P 9. The patient looked *around* the room.
A 10. The trial is not *over* yet.

538

C. Prepositional Phrases as Modifiers Copy these sentences. Circle each prepositional phrase. Draw an arrow from the phrase to the word it modifies. Label each phrase *Adjective* or *Adverb* to tell how it is used.

1. Pat threw the line into the river. ADV
2. Are Volkswagens made in the United States now? ADV
3. A movie about a baseball player is playing here. ADJ
4. Bert hung his hat carefully on the hook. ADV
5. These gloves are lined with fur. ADV
6. The woman with the briefcase is Dr. Sanchez. ADJ
7. A crowd of people swarmed the stage. ADJ
8. The young man in the green jacket is Jake Houston. ADJ
9. The ball landed in the bleachers. ADV
10. Nobody but Rachel understood the question. ADJ

D. Conjunctions Find the conjunctions in the following sentences. Write the words connected by each conjunction.

1. The Pirates and the Steelers are Pittsburgh teams.
2. Father Hidalgo of Mexico was both a priest and a political leader.
3. Gilda Radner talked and joked with the audience.
4. The speaker's voice was quiet but firm.
5. Andrew was not only hungry but also thirsty.
6. Can you tell whether a computer or a person made the mistake?
7. Somebody called for you but left no message.
8. In gym class, we'll play either volleyball or softball.
9. Rugs, drapes, and furniture muffle the noises in a room.
10. Neither Kelley nor Rivera caught the grounder to left field.

Mixed Review

 These exercises provide review of the concepts pre-
sented in this Section. Each
exercise challenges the students to apply several of the
skills they have acquired during previous study. Because
the "mixed" feature of these
activities makes them more
difficult, the teacher may wish
to have less-advanced students do them orally or in
small groups.

MIXED REVIEW

Using Prepositions and Conjunctions

A. Recognizing prepositional phrases Copy these sentences. Circle the prepositional phrases. Draw arrows from each
prepositional phrase to the word it modifies.

 1. Angelo struggled against the dusty wind.
 2. For two years Kyle lived in Florida.
 3. Everybody at the party moved toward the table of food.
 4. The actors in the movie were amateurs.
 5. Don't stand under a tree during a storm.
 6. Nobody except you could have hit that ball.
 7. We drove past a pond with an alligator in it.
 8. From the top of the mountain he could see the ocean.
 9. I cannot speak for anyone but myself.
 10. The coach kept Evans on the bench during the entire
     game.

**B. Recognizing adverbs, prepositions, and conjunc-
tions** Write the italicized words in the following sentences. After
each, write *Adverb, Preposition,* or *Conjunction* to show how it is
used in the sentence.

P 1. The package was delivered *by* UPS.

A 2. Jonathan stood *by.*

C 3. Are you shivering *or* trembling?

P 4. Everybody *but* Emily went on the field trip.

C 5. The road curved *but* then suddenly straightened.

A 6. Talk the situation *over* with Brenda.

P 7. Melissa put a sheet *over* the chair.

C 8. *Either* Atlanta *or* Miami is their destination.

P 9. *Outside* the house, the air felt warmer.

C 10. *Both* Samuel *and* Nancy answered at the same time.

USING GRAMMAR IN WRITING
Using Prepositions and Conjunctions

A. Imagine that you are attending an air show as a reporter for a news magazine. The show will feature acrobatic stunt planes, sky diving, the newest ultralight aircraft, and balloon flights. Write a paragraph describing some of the things that you see. Use prepositional phrases in your paragraph to tell where and when things happen. Underline the prepositional phrases and circle the prepositions. You may want to include the following phrases.

    above the crowd   into the air   with the wind
    into a small circle   on the ground
    under a brilliant yellow parachute

B. The following notes are instructions for assembling a cookbook stand. You are to write the instructions from these notes and add some ideas of your own about how useful the cookbook stand is. Notice how choppy the notes are. Conjunctions can be used to connect related ideas and make a piece of writing flow more smoothly. Use each of the following conjunctions at least once: *and, or, but, either . . . or, both . . . and.*

> Unpack the base. Unpack the rear support. Unpack the bookrest. Slide the bookrest into the slot in the middle of the base. Secure it with two screws. Do not tighten the screws fully. Slide the rear support into the slot at the back of the bookrest. Be sure that it meets the base on the center line. Secure the rear support with one screw through the bookrest. Also secure it with another screw through the base. Tighten all screws. The cookbook stand is now ready.

Using Grammar in Writing

These challenging and enjoyable activities allow the students to see how the concepts of grammar, usage, and mechanics may be applied in actual writing situations. Each exercise is designed to allow students practice in several of the skills they have acquired in this Section. The activities also provide opportunities for students to write creatively about a wide variety of interesting and unusual subjects.

Section Objectives

1. To recognize and understand the function of interjections

2. To review the eight parts of speech

3. To recognize a word that can be used as different parts of speech

Preparing the Students

Review with students the seven parts of speech studied thus far. Tell students that this Section will review the seven parts of speech and present the eighth part of speech.

Additional Resources

Mastery Test — pages 58–59 in the test booklet

Additional Exercises — pages 546–548 in the student text

Practice Book — pages 211–213

Duplicating Masters — pages 211–213

Special Populations — See special section at the front of this Teacher's Edition.

Part 1

Objectives

1. To recognize and understand the function of interjections

2. To review the eight parts of speech

Presenting the Lesson

1. Read page 542. Stress that words are grouped into the eight parts of speech because of the

Review of Parts of Speech

Part 1 The Parts of Speech

You have studied seven **parts of speech** so far—nouns, pronouns, verbs, adjectives, adverbs, prepositions, and conjunctions. There is one more part of speech. It is called the **interjection**.

A word is labeled a particular part of speech depending on how it is used in a sentence. One word may be used as different parts of speech.

You will review all the parts of speech in this section.

What Is an Interjection?

An interjection is a word or group of words used to express strong feeling.

An interjection may be either a phrase or a word. In either case, the interjection shows strong feeling. These feelings might be joy, anger, terror, surprise, disgust, or sadness. Because it conveys strong emotions, an interjection is followed by an exclamation point.

Notice the interjections in the following sentences.

Wow! I like this.
Oh! What a scary mask!
Ugh! There's a dead mouse.

Now you have studied all eight parts of speech:

The Parts of Speech			
nouns	verbs	adverbs	conjunctions
pronouns	adjectives	prepositions	interjections

Exercise A Write each italicized word. Next to it, write what part of speech it is.

V 1. The swimmer *grasped* the life preserver.

I 2. *Wonderful!* I'm glad you'll be there.

Pro 3. Did *anyone* find my locket?

Prep 4. Doris rode *around* the track.

C 5. Dan *or* Greg will introduce the speaker.

Adv 6. We *seldom* attend baseball games.

Adj 7. That parking lot is always *full*.

Adj 8. Susan gave me a *silly* grin.

N 9. Country-western *songs* tell stories.

V 10. The Supreme Court *reversed* the decision.

Exercise B Follow the directions for Exercise A.

C 1. Swenson's serves a variety of soups *and* salads.

543

2. Read page 543, going over the definition and examples of interjections.

3. Review the eight parts of speech, listed on page 543. Ask students to define each.

4. Assign and discuss Exercises A and B on pages 543–544.

Individualizing the Lesson

Less-Advanced Students

Have students write a definition for each part of speech, but tell them not to indicate what part of speech is being defined. Tell them to mix up the order of the parts of speech. Have students exchange papers and write what part of speech is being defined next to its definition.

Advanced Students

Have students write one sentence for each part of speech. Students should identify the part of speech used in each sentence.

Optional Practice

Have students use each of the following words in a sentence and tell its part of speech. Answers will vary.

1. tornado	6. heavily
2. sings	7. yellow
3. too	8. swam
4. good grief!	9. or
5. between	10. himself

Extending the Lesson

Have students read an act from a play, then have them find and copy one example of each part of speech from the play. Have students identify each example they copy.

Section Objective

To recognize words that can be used as different parts of speech

Presenting the Lesson

1. Read page 544. Stress that context determines the part of speech of a word. Study examples of words used as different parts of speech on pages 544–545.

2. Assign and discuss Exercises A and B on page 545.

Individualizing the Lesson

Less-Advanced Students

1. Work with students to come up with a list of ten words that can be used as more than one part of speech. Have students identify which parts of speech each word can be used as; then have students check their answers by using a dictionary.

2. Have students write sentences for each part of speech each word can be used as.

Advanced Students

1. Divide the class into groups of two or three; then have students work together to develop a list of words that can be used as more than one part of speech. Have students check their lists by looking up the words in the dictionary.

2. Have students work independently, using the list they created in the group, to write a sentence for each part of speech the words can be used as. Have them compare their sentences.

544

V   2. Jason hiked and *fished* in the Canadian Rockies.

Prep   3. Please be home *by* seven.

N   4. Shoppers swarmed through *Macy's.*

I   5. *Hurrah!* Superman saved the day!

Pro   6. Jennifer sat next to *him* in the assembly.

Adv   7. Millie danced the tango *clumsily.*

Adj   8. Many airlines serve *light* snacks as well as full meals.

V   9. Samuel Clemens' pen name *was* Mark Twain.

N   10. Collectors shop for *antiques* at farm sales.

Part 2   Using Words as Different Parts of Speech

Very often the same word can be used as different parts of speech. For example, a word might be a noun in one sentence and an adjective in another.

There is only one way to tell what part of speech any word is. You must see how that word is used in a sentence.

Here are some examples of one word used as two different parts of speech:

Mr. Hayakawa pruned the *plant.*
(*Plant* is used as a noun, the direct object of the verb *pruned.*)
Jessica bought a book on *plant* care.
(*Plant* is used as an adjective, modifying *care.*)
Time is the most valuable asset we have.
(*Time* is used as a noun, the subject of the sentence.)
Ms. Ricardo will *time* the test.
(*Time* is used as the main verb.)
Is the bookstore on the *lower* level?
(*Lower* is used as an adjective, modifying the noun *level.*)
The temperature fell *lower.*
(*Lower* is used as an adverb, modifying the verb *fell.*)
What is that noise?
(*What* is used as a pronoun, the subject of the sentence.)

What movies are playing in town?

    (*What* is used as an adjective, modifying the noun *movies*.)

Mr. and Mrs. Lewis went *out*.

    (*Out* is used as an adverb, modifying the verb *went*.)

The canary flew *out* the door.

    (*Out* is used as a preposition.)

Great! I love spaghetti!

    (*Great* is used as an interjection.)

Joy had a *great* idea.

    (*Great* is used as an adjective, modifying the noun *idea*.)

Exercise A   Write each italicized word. Next to it, write what part of speech it is in that sentence.

Adj 1. Wally visited the *wax* museum.

N 2. Crayons are made with *wax*.

V 3. Tim will *wax* the car today.

V 4. *Pass* the mustard, please.

N 5. The mountain *pass* was closed during the blizzard.

I 6. *Ouch!* The stove is still hot.

Adv 7. Those sandwiches were *really* good.

Pro 8. *That* is our new car.

Adj 9. Where did you buy *that* jacket?

N 10. There is a *fire* in the basement!

Exercise B   Follow the directions for Exercise A.

Adv 1. The electrician turned the power *off*.

Prep 2. The ping-pong ball bounced *off* the table.

V 3. That costume doesn't *fool* me.

N 4. He was a *fool* for endangering our safety.

Adj 5. Bring a *light* sweater.

N 6. Turn on the *light*, please.

V 7. *Light* the campfire first.

Adj 8. Put the silverware in *this* drawer.

Pro 9. *This* is my cousin Josh.

V 10. Martha *cut* the pie into six pieces.

545

Have students identify the part of speech of the italicized word in each of the following sentences.

    1. *Cotton* is a natural fiber. [N]

    2. Stacey ate *cotton* candy. [Adj]

    3. *Surprise!* You are the prize winner. [Inter]

    4. There was a *surprise* ending to the play. [Adj]

    5. Joey set a *record* in the 100-yard dash. [N]

    6. The scorekeeper will *record* the times. [V]

    7. A *record* number of people signed up. [Adj]

    8. The weekend is *over*. [Adv]

    9. The eagle flew *over* the peak. [Prep]

  10. A chair fell *over*. [Adv]

Extending the Lesson

Have students use each of the following words in an original sentence as the part of speech indicated.

    1. color (verb)

    2. color (noun)

    3. No! (interjection)

    4. no (adjective)

    5. drip (noun)

    6. drip (verb)

    7. off (preposition)

    8. off (adverb)

    9. this (pronoun)

  10. this (adjective)

Additional Exercises

These Additional Exercises may be used for additional practice of the concepts presented in this Section. Each exercise focuses on a single concept, and should be used after the page number indicated in parentheses.

Review

If you have not assigned these Additional Exercises before this time, you can also use them as an excellent Section Review.

ADDITIONAL EXERCISES

Review of Parts of Speech

The Parts of Speech Copy the italicized word in each sentence. Write what part of speech the word is in that sentence.

Prep 1. It rained every day *for* a week.

Prep 2. That man looks exactly *like* Louis Gossett, Jr.

Pro 3. Did the reporter quote *you* accurately?

I 4. *Ouch!* That really stings.

N 5. We planned a *visit* to the space center.

C 6. Jim talks too fast *and* too much.

V 7. Laura *dances* to any kind of music.

N 8. The police officer examined the skid *marks*.

Pro 9. *This* is Randy's birthday.

Adv 10. Do you feel better *now*?

N 11. *Americans* drink more than one-third of the world's coffee.

Adj 12. Ghana and Zaire are *African* countries.

Adj 13. The President tossed out the *game* ball.

V 14. Mr. Spence *signs* his papers with a flourish.

V 15. Ben *starches* his collars.

Adj 16. *That* shop specializes in repairs for motorcycles.

N 17. Pueblo Indian *architecture* is very energy-efficient.

Adv 18. The emergency room is *always* crowded.

Pro 19. Did *anyone* pour cool water on the burn?

Adv 20. Here winter begins *early* and ends late.

N 21. The *leaves* of ginkgo trees look like small fans.

V 22. The art class designed and *sold* calendars.

Adj 23. Robert takes his *youngest* sister to the day-care center every morning.

V 24. The California Angels *won* their first pennant in 1979.

I 25. *Phew!* We got here just in time.

MIXED REVIEW

Review of Parts of Speech

Recognizing the parts of speech   Copy the italicized words from these sentences. Write what part of speech each is used as.

I   1. *Well!* What can possibly happen next?

N   2. Frogs got into the farmer's *well*.

Adv   3. My pen isn't working *well*.

N   4. Ginny used a circular *saw* for that wood.

V   5. The hawk *saw* a field mouse in the weeds.

N   6. Without any *thought* of the long way back, the hiker continued.

V   7. He *thought* of a snappy comeback a little too late.

Pro   8. *This* is the entrance.

Adj   9. *This* entrance will take us to the shoe department.

Prep   10. *By* the way, Connie called you.

Adv   11. The weekend flew *by*.

Adv   12. Tom couldn't keep *up* with the other joggers.

Adj   13. An *American* tourist interpreted for me.

N   14. In many countries, an *American* is often the tallest person around.

C   15. Jackie *and* Tonya always have lunch together.

Prep   16. He walked *past* her house.

N   17. In the *past*, fresh fruits were available only in summer.

Adv   18. Twigs and leaves drifted *past*.

Adj   19. This *past* season was not the Lakers' best.

Adj   20. Elephants were hunted for their *ivory* tusks.

N   21. *Ivory* was quite valuable.

N   22. These *lines* are parallel.

V   23. The class *lines* up during fire drills.

Adv   24. The team plays *better* with an audience.

Adj   25. I am *better* now.

547

USING GRAMMAR IN WRITING
Review of Parts of Speech

A. You are on a hike with a small group of your friends. One of your friends has brought a dog along. The dog is especially frisky, and it enjoys running off into the woods to chase birds, chipmunks, and toads. Suddenly, the dog begins digging furiously at a spot just off the trail. All of you gather around the spot, and soon you see that the dog is uncovering a metal box. You lift the box out of the hole. It is locked. What happens next? Write about the events that follow the discovery. You may want to include some dialogue. Use all eight parts of speech. Label each one the first time you use it. Be sure to use strong verbs, vivid modifiers, and prepositional phrases to make your story lively.

B. Each word below can be used as at least two different parts of speech. Write two brief stories, each using all of the words. Use each word as a different part of speech in each story.

Example: light

The light of the candle threw strange shadows. (noun)
We ate a light breakfast. (adjective)
I'm using light blue yarn for the sweater. (adverb)
Wait here while I light the lamp. (verb)

1. shop   4. present
2. cut   5. reverse
3. park   6. turn

Using Verbals

Section Objectives

1. To recognize and understand the function of gerunds and gerund phrases

2. To recognize and understand the function of participles and participial phrases

3. To recognize and understand the function of infinitives and infinitive phrases

4. To avoid split infinitives

Preparing the Students

Remind students that the part of speech of words is determined by how the words are used. Some words are always used as one part of speech, while others can be used in various ways. Tell students that this Section will present three types of words that are formed from the same part of speech—verbs—but are not used as verbs.

Read the introduction on page 549, paying special attention to the definition of verbals.

Additional Resources

Diagnostic Test — page 6 in the test booklet

Mastery Test — pages 60–61 in the test booklet

Additional Exercises — pages 564–569 in the student text

Practice Book — pages 214–217

Duplicating Masters — pages 214–217

Special Populations — See special section at the front of this Teacher's Edition.

In addition to the eight parts of speech, there are three other kinds of words. They are **gerunds, participles,** and **infinitives.** These three kinds of words are made from verbs. They are called **verbals.** Although verbals look like verbs, they are used as other parts of speech.

This section will explain how to identify verbals and how to use them.

549

Objective

To recognize and understand the function of gerunds and gerund phrases

Presenting the Lesson

1. Review with students the main ways in which a noun can be used—as subject, as direct object, and as object of the preposition. Review the definition of a verbal—a word formed from a verb but not used as a verb. Explain that gerunds are verbals. They are formed from verbs but used as nouns.

2. Read page 550, going over the definition of gerunds and examples of gerunds used as subjects, direct objects, and objects of the preposition.

3. Read pages 550–551. Study examples of gerund phrases, gerunds modified by adverbs, and gerunds modified by adjectives.

4. Read pages 551–552. Study diagrams of gerund phrases, noting position of modifiers and objects of gerund phrases.

5. Assign and discuss Exercises A and B on pages 552–553.

Individualizing the Lesson

Less-Advanced Students

1. Have students write a definition of a gerund and explain how a gerund is formed. Then have students explain the relationship between gerunds, verbs, and nouns. (Students should explain that

Part 1   Gerunds

A gerund is a verb form that is used as a noun. A gerund ends in *-ing*. It may be used in any way that a noun is used.

Like a noun, a gerund may be used as a subject.

> *Swimming* is good exercise.
> (*Swimming* is a gerund, the subject of the verb *is*.)

Like a noun, a gerund may be used as a direct object.

> Ron enjoys *skating*.
> (*Skating* is a gerund, the object of the verb *enjoys*.)

Like a noun, a gerund may be used as an object of a preposition.

> Kate relaxes by *reading*.
> (*Reading* is a gerund, the object of the preposition *by*.)

The Gerund Phrase

A gerund is not always used alone. Often a gerund has a modifier or an object or both. Together, they form a **gerund phrase.** The entire gerund phrase is used as a noun.

Because a gerund is formed from a verb, it can have an object.

> Dirk earns extra money by *mowing lawns*.
> (*Mowing* is a gerund; *lawns* is the object of *mowing*. The phrase *mowing lawns* is the object of the preposition *by*.)

Because a gerund is formed from a verb, it can be modified by adverbs.

> The crew began *working again*.
> (*Working* is a gerund; *again* is an adverb modifying *working*. The phrase *working again* is the object of the verb *began*.)

Because a gerund is used as a noun, it can be modified by adjectives.

Careful planning was our main advantage.

> (*Planning* is a gerund; *careful* is an adjective modifying *planning*. The phrase *careful planning* is the subject of the verb *was*.)

Gerunds can also be modified by prepositional phrases.

Standing in line is tiresome.

> (*Standing* is a gerund; *in line* is a prepositional phrase modifying *standing*. The entire gerund phrase is the subject of *is*.)

In these examples you can see that gerunds are used as nouns, even though they look like verbs. *Swimming, skating, reading, mowing, working, planning,* and *standing* all look like verbs but are not used as verbs. Because they are used as nouns, they are gerunds. Modifiers and objects that are used with them form gerund phrases.

Diagraming Gerunds

A gerund or gerund phrase used as a subject or direct object is diagramed on a line above the main line. The gerund belongs on a line drawn as a step. Its modifiers are placed on slanted lines below it. Its object is shown on the horizontal line following the gerund.

Fixing old cars is Jay's hobby.

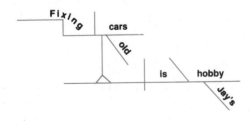

gerunds are formed from verbs but used as nouns.)

2. List five action verbs on the board. Have students change the verbs into gerunds. Then have them make up sentences using the gerunds as nouns. Make sure that students understand how each gerund is used in each sentence. Then list five more verbs for students to turn into gerunds and use in sentences. Have students work individually.

Advanced Students

Have students write a paragraph about a job they perform (mowing the lawn, baby-sitting, cleaning the house). Students should include at least two gerunds used as subjects, two as direct objects, and two as objects of a preposition.

Optional Practice

Have students write the gerunds and gerund phrases in the following sentences and tell how each is used.

S 1. Watching old movies is his hobby.

DO2. Our family enjoys gardening together.

OP3. Scott earned money by washing cars.

S4. Raising animals takes time and effort.

DO5. Mr. Richey teaches creative writing.

Extending the Lesson

Have students use the following gerund phrases in sentences. Students should tell how each gerund phrase is used.

1. cooking the hot dogs
2. writing letters
3. careful searching
4. rehearsing for the play
5. working in the grocery store

The project includes giving an oral report.

A gerund or gerund phrase used as the object of a preposition is diagramed below the main line. The preposition belongs on a slanted line going down from the word modified. Again, the gerund appears on a stepped line.

We were exhausted from cross-country skiing.

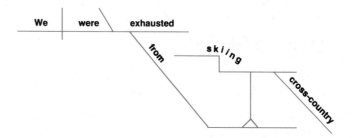

Exercise A Find the gerunds or gerund phrases in these sentences. As your teacher directs, show how each is used.

1. Jack started using gasohol in his car. Object
2. Working in the coal mines is dangerous. Subject
3. Sewing costumes is Jean's job. Subject
4. We were hoarse from cheering so much. Object
5. Shoplifting is a crime. Subject
6. Use this container for watering the plants. Object
7. Everyone appreciates good cooking. Object
8. Following the suspect was difficult. Subject

9. Playing chess requires concentration. _{Subject}
10. Outlining can be the key to a successful paper. _{Subject}

Exercise B   Follow the directions for Exercise A.

1. Jan increased her speed by running daily. _{Object}
2. Stamp collecting is Randy's hobby. _{Subject}
3. Will replacing the furnace be expensive? _{Subject}
4. Mountain climbing can be dangerous. _{Subject}
5. The children were filthy from playing in the mud. _{Object}
6. Scaring away evil spirits is the witch doctor's job. _{Subject}
7. Matching that shade of green will be impossible. _{Subject}
8. The Scotts considered moving to Alaska. _{Object}
9. An hour of swimming burns about five hundred calories. _{Object}
10. David earns extra money by shoveling snow. _{Object}

Part 2   Participles

A participle is a verb form that is used as an adjective.

You learned about the **past participle** as one of the principal parts of a verb. It is formed by adding *-d* or *-ed* to the present tense, as in *wave—waved* or *pass—passed*. The past participles of irregular verbs are formed differently and must be learned separately: *ring—rung, wear—worn.*

There is another kind of participle besides the past participle. It is called the **present participle.** The present participle is always formed by adding *-ing* to the present tense: *wave—waving, pass—passing, ring—ringing, wear—wearing.*

Here are more examples of participles:

Verb	Past Participle	Present Participle
pack	packed	packing
sing	sung	singing
try	tried	trying

553

Presenting the Lesson

1. Review the definition of a verbal—a word formed from a verb but not used as a verb. Remind students that gerunds are verb forms used as nouns.

2. Read pages 553–554. Go over the definition of a participle and the ways to form past participles and present participles. Study the examples of participles at the top of page 554. Stress that to be considered a verbal, the participle form must be used as an adjective. Point out the difference beween these sentences.

Jeremy was watching TV and fell asleep on the couch.

553

Explain that in the first sentence, the
past participle is used with a helping verb and is a verb. In the second
sentence the past participle is used
without a helping verb and is used
as an adjective to describe the subject of the sentence.

3. Read pages 554–555, discussing participial phrases. Study the
examples of participles with objects
and those modified by adverbs and
prepositional phrases.

4. Read the section on page 555
showing how to diagram participles.

5. Assign Exercises A and B on
pages 555–556.

6. Read pages 556–557 stressing
the way to differentiate between
gerunds and participles.

7. Assign the exercise on page
557.

Individualizing the Lesson

Less-Advanced Students

1. Discuss with students the definition of a participle. Have students
write an explanation of how a participle differs from a gerund; then,
have them use each one in a separate sentence.

2. Write on the chalkboard three
words that can be used as either
gerunds or participles. Ask students
for sentences using the words as
either kind of verbal. Have them explain what kind of verbal they have
used. See how many different sentences using these verbals students
can think of.

Advanced Students

Have students find ten examples
of participles or participial phrases

As verbals, participles are always used as adjectives. A participle modifies either a noun or a pronoun.

> *Refreshed*, Mr. Jordan challenged me to another game of
> tennis.
> (*Refreshed* is a past participle modifying the noun
> *Mr. Jordan.*)
> *Running*, she arrived just in time.
> (*Running* is a present participle modifying the pronoun
> *she.*)
> The *sunken* treasure has never been found.
> (*Sunken* is a past participle modifying the noun *treasure.*)
> The *traveling* circus came to our town.
> (*Traveling* is a present participle modifying the noun
> *circus.*)

The Participial Phrase

A participle is not always used alone. Often a participle has a
modifier or an object or both. Together, they form a **participial
phrase.** The entire participial phrase is used as an adjective.

Because a participle is formed from a verb, it may have an
object.

> The girl *selling tickets* is Ben's sister.
> (*Selling tickets* is a participial phrase modifying *girl.*
> *Tickets* is the object of the participle *selling.*)

Because a participle comes from a verb, it may be modified by
adverbs.

> *Laughing hysterically*, Mary Jo tried to tell us the joke.
> (*Laughing hysterically* is a participial phrase modifying
> *Mary Jo. Hysterically* is an adverb modifying the
> participle *laughing.*)
> Children played in the water *spurting from the fire hydrant.*
> (*Spurting from the fire hydrant* is a participial phrase
> modifying *water. From the fire hydrant* is a prepositional
> phrase modifying the participle *spurting.*)

In all of these examples you can see that participles are used as adjectives, even though they look like verbs. *Refreshed, running, sunken, traveling, selling, laughing,* and *spurting* all look like verbs but are not used as verbs. Because they are used as adjectives, they are called participles. Modifiers and objects used with them form participial phrases.

Diagraming Participles

To diagram a participle, place it below the noun or pronoun it modifies. Place the participle on an angled line. Put modifiers of the participle on lines slanted down from it. An object follows the participle on the horizontal line.

Listening carefully, Meg took notes.

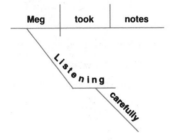

Exercise A Write the participles or participial phrases in these sentences. Show which word the participle or phrase modifies.

Example: Raising her eyebrows, Regina stared at the conductor.
Raising her eyebrows (participial phrase, modifying *Regina*)

1. Running water is a luxury in many countries.
2. Breathing hard, the jogger slowed his pace.
3. The bank returned the canceled checks.
4. Ken stirred the bubbling casserole.
5. Confused, Vinnie checked the instruction sheet.

555

555

6. Adam showed us the <u>refinished</u> <u>furniture</u>.
7. The <u>woman</u> <u>playing the violin</u> is a member of several orchestras.
8. The <u>birds</u> <u>nesting in the garage</u> are swallows.
9. <u>Still proclaiming his innocence</u>, the <u>suspect</u> was led to jail.
10. The house with the lilac <u>bushes</u> <u>surrounding it</u> is my grandmother's.

Exercise B Follow the directions for Exercise A.

1. <u>Twirling a baton</u>, the <u>majorette</u> led the parade.
2. That is a fully <u>grown</u> German <u>shepherd</u>.
3. What is behind the <u>locked</u> <u>door</u>?
4. <u>Turning the key in the lock</u>, <u>Nancy Drew</u> quickly looked around.
5. Many <u>retired</u> senior <u>citizens</u> move to warmer climates.
6. Packages of <u>dried</u> <u>fruit</u> are sold at most grocery stores.
7. A <u>broken</u> <u>mirror</u> means seven years bad luck.
8. <u>Walking fearlessly into the cage</u>, the lion <u>tamer</u> cracked the whip.
9. <u>Baying at the moon</u>, the <u>dog</u> woke up half the neighborhood.
10. <u>Cory</u>, <u>grinning from ear to ear</u>, told us about her raise.

Gerund or Participle?

The two kinds of verbals you have studied, gerunds and participles, often look the same. Gerunds and present participles are both formed by adding *-ing* to the present tense of verbs. How can you avoid confusing them?

To tell whether a word is a gerund or a present participle, look at how it is used. If it is used as a modifier, it is a participle. If it is used as a noun, it is a gerund.

Read the following sentences.

Fishing in a mountain stream is Paul's idea of a vacation.
(The gerund phrase *fishing in a mountain stream* is the subject of the verb *is*.)

Fishing in a mountain stream, Paul enjoyed his vacation.
(The participial phrase *fishing in a mountain stream* modifies the noun *Paul*.)

Exercise For each sentence, write the gerund or participle and say which each is. Be prepared to explain your answer.

P 1. <u>Swimming</u> against the current, Dave was getting tired.

G 2. <u>Swimming</u> against the current is hard work.

G 3. <u>Painting</u> the house will improve its appearance.

P 4. <u>Painting</u> the house, Dan stood on the ladder.

P 5. <u>Eating</u> a taco, Sherry spilled the filling on her blouse.

G 6. <u>Eating</u> a taco can be messy.

G 7. <u>Trimming</u> the bushes is Steve's job.

P 8. <u>Shoveling</u> snow, Dad strained his back.

G 9. Ellen won the contest by <u>spelling</u> *conscience* correctly.

P 10. The official <u>checking</u> the luggage is a customs agent.

Part 3 Infinitives

The third kind of verbal is the **infinitive. An infinitive is a verbal form that usually begins with the word *to*.** *To* is called the **sign of the infinitive.**

to print	to whisper	to win	to remember
to speak	to choose	to quit	to help

Note: You have learned that the word *to* is used as a preposition. *To* is a preposition when it is followed by a noun or pronoun as its object. However, when *to* is followed by a verb, it is the sign of the infinitive. Compare these examples:

Prepositional Phrases

Cathy ran to the door.
Mark wrote to Alex.

Infinitives

The team wanted to win.
The prisoner tried to escape.

Part 3

Objectives

1. To recognize and understand the function of infinitives and infinitive phrases
2. To avoid split infinitives

Presenting the Lesson

1. Again review the definition of a verb. Explain that the infinitive, formed from a verb, may be used as *three* parts of speech.
2. Read page 557, studying the definition and form of the infinitive and stressing the difference between *to* as the sign of the infinitive and *to* as a preposition.

557

3. Read page 558, studying examples of infinitive phrases with objects and modifiers.

4. Read pages 558–559, studying the various uses of infinitives as nouns, adverbs, and adjectives.

5. Read page 559, stressing the way to avoid split infinitives.

6. Study the examples of how to diagram infinitives on page 560.

7. Assign and discuss Exercises A and B on pages 560–561.

8. Read pages 561–562, reviewing the three kinds of verbals. Stress the form and the use of each verbal.

9. Assign and discuss Exercises A and B on pages 562–563.

Individualizing the Lesson

Less-Advanced Students

1. Discuss with students the difference between *to* as part of the infinitive and *to* as a preposition. Have students give examples of each use; then, write the examples on the chalkboard to illustrate the difference.

2. Ask students for five infinitives and write them on the chalkboard. Ask students for sentences using these infinitives, either alone or as part of infinitive phrases. Then, have students write five original sentences using infinitives and infinitive phrases. At least one sentence should use the infinitive as a subject, one as an adjective, and one as an adverb.

Advanced Students

1. Have students write ten original sentences using verbals. Tell students to make sure to use at least two of each type of verbal—gerund,

The Infinitive Phrase

Like gerunds and participles, infinitives are not always used alone.

An infinitive can have modifiers and objects. The infinitive with its modifiers and objects forms an **infinitive phrase.**

Because an infinitive is formed from a verb, it is like a verb in some ways. Like a verb, an infinitive can have an object.

> Karen decided *to attend the concert.*
> (*Concert* is the direct object of the infinitive *to attend.*)
>
> Ms. Abbott wanted *to give us some help.*
> (*Us* is the indirect object and *help* is the direct object of the infinitive *to give.*)

Because an infinitive is formed from a verb, it can be modified by adverbs.

> Marlene wanted *to ride along.*
> (*Along* is an adverb modifying the infinitive *to ride.*)
>
> The committee decided *to meet again tomorrow.*
> (*Again* and *tomorrow* are adverbs modifying the infinitive *to meet.*)

Infinitives may also be modified by prepositional phrases.

> The magician appeared *to pull the scarves from his hat.*
> (*From his hat* is a prepositional phrase modifying the infinitive *to pull.*)
>
> Couples began *to dance to the music.*
> (*To the music* is a prepositional phrase modifying the infinitive *to dance.*)

Uses of the Infinitive Phrase

Unlike gerunds and participles, infinitives can be used as more than one part of speech. An infinitive or infinitive phrase can be used as one of the following: a noun, an adjective, or an adverb.

Infinitives and infinitive phrases can be used in ways that nouns are used. As you know, nouns may be subjects or direct objects.

Subject: *To play professional football* is his goal.
(*To play professional football* is the subject.)

Direct Object: Len remembered *to lock the door*.
(*To lock the door* is the direct object.)

Infinitives and infinitive phrases can also be used as adjectives or adverbs. The infinitive or infinitive phrase is used as an adjective if it modifies a noun or pronoun. It is used as an adverb if it modifies a verb, adjective, or adverb.

Adjective: These are the facts *to remember*.
(*To remember* modifies the noun *facts*.)

Adjective: Craig wants the list of books *to read*.
(*To read* modifies the noun *books*.)

Adverb: The voters came *to cast their ballots*.
(*To cast their ballots* modifies the verb *came*.)

Adverb: The chili is too hot *to eat*.
(*To eat* modifies the adjective *hot*.)

Adverb: The disease spread too quickly *to save the tree*.
(*To save the tree* modifies the adverb *quickly*.)

From all of the examples, you can see that infinitives look like verbs, but are not used as verbs. Infinitives and their phrases are used as nouns, adjectives, and adverbs.

The Split Infinitive

Sometimes a modifier is placed between the word *to* and the verb of an infinitive. A modifier in that position is said to split the infinitive. Usually, a split infinitive sounds awkward and should be avoided.

Awkward: Clay wanted to *immediately* leave.
Better: Clay wanted to leave *immediately*.

559

participle, and infinitive. Then have students exchange papers.

2. Students should underline the verbal in each sentence and identify it as a gerund, participle, or infinitive; then they should write how it is used. If the verbal has modifiers, objects, or serves as a modifier, the students should indicate this.

Optional Practice

Have students identify the infinitive phrases in the following sentences and tell how each is used.

DO 1. I wanted to see *The Bill Cosby Show*.

Adv 2. To earn his allowance, Adam takes care of the yard.

Adj 3. These are the best vitamins to take.

S 4. To sing in the musical was his goal.

Adv 5. My hair is hard to manage.

DO 6. Jeff tried to teach us the game.

DO 7. Mom said to come home at five o'clock.

DO 8. Everyone likes to be popular.

Adv 9. It is too dark to see in this room.

DO10. The President hopes to halt inflation.

Extending the Lesson

After students have completed Exercises A and B, pages 560–561, review the exercises orally and have students explain how each infinitive phrase is used in each sentence.

Diagraming Infinitives

To diagram an infinitive or infinitive phrase used as a noun, place it on a bridge above the main line. *To*, the sign of the infinitive, belongs on a slanted line. The infinitive is shown on a horizontal line. Modifiers appear on lines slanted down from the infinitive. An object is shown on a horizontal line following the infinitive.

Sean wanted to finish his chores quickly.

To diagram an infinitive or infinitive phrase used as a modifier, place it below the word modified. Modifiers and objects of the infinitive appear as explained above.

Insulation helps to cut energy costs.

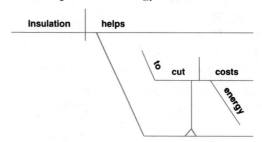

Exercise A Write each infinitive or infinitive phrase. Be prepared to tell how it is used in the sentence.

> Example: Caroline wants to take pictures of us.
> *to take pictures of us* (infinitive phrase, used as direct object)

DO 1. Mr. Johnson forgot to pay his electric bill.

560

Adv 2. The pizza was too large <u>to finish</u>.

Adv 3. Arthur is afraid <u>to enter the talent contest</u>.

DO 4. Craig had planned <u>to visit Pike's Peak</u>.

S 5. <u>To find a new world</u> was the explorers' goal.

DO 6. Does Jason intend <u>to stay late</u>?

Adv 7. Alice went <u>to mail the invitations</u>.

DO 8. Has anyone tried <u>to climb that tree</u>?

DO 9. Does Lisa intend <u>to do all that housework herself</u>?

S 10. <u>To landscape the building</u> is the architect's responsibility.

Exercise B Follow the directions for Exercise A.

Adj 1. Doug bought tools <u>to repair the plumbing</u>.

Adj 2. Celia is the person <u>to represent our class</u>.

DO 3. Do you want <u>to take a picnic lunch</u>?

DO 4. Mr. Drake told us <u>to write a letter to the company president</u>.

S 5. <u>To lose a game in overtime</u> is heartbreaking.

Adv 6. The Indians fought <u>to protect their hunting grounds</u>.

Adv 7. An omelet is easy <u>to make</u>.

S 8. <u>To fly to San Diego for the reunion</u> is their plan.

DO 9. Roger always tries <u>to complete his homework assignments.</u>

DO 10. The union asked its members <u>to take a cut in pay</u>.

A Review of Verbals

Although verbals are verb forms, they are never used as verbs. They are used as other parts of speech.

The three kinds of verbals are gerunds, participles, and infinitives. All three kinds of verbals may be used alone. At times, though, they are used in phrases. These phrases are called gerund phrases, participial phrases, and infinitive phrases. Because they are like verbs, all three kinds of verbals can have objects or modifiers.

Gerunds are the verb forms used as nouns. Gerunds, which end in *-ing*, may be used in all the ways nouns are used.

> *Jogging* is a popular sport. (subject)
> Dick started *jogging* last year. (direct object)
> Dr. Ellis suggested *jogging* to his patient.
>   (direct object)
> Kris keeps in shape by *jogging*. (object of preposition)

Participles are verb forms used as adjectives. Like adjectives, participles modify nouns and pronouns. Present participles end in *-ing*. Past participles of regular verbs end in *-d* or *-ed*.

> *Drying the dishes*, Kate dropped a plate.
> The woman *drying her hair* is Ms. Bell.
> Nancy arranges *dried* flowers.
> *Dried in the sun*, apricots keep well.

Infinitives are the verbals that begin with the word *to*. Infinitives may be used as three different parts of speech. They may be *nouns*, *adjectives*, or *adverbs*.

> *To make the team* was Ed's goal. (noun, subject)
> Lucy asked the girls *to make their own costumes*. (noun, direct object)
> Dr. Matthews has a few comments *to make*. (adjective)
> Everyone moved over *to make room*. (adverb)
> This bread is not difficult *to make*. (adverb)

Exercise A   Find the verbal in each sentence. Write the verbal or verbal phrase. Tell whether the verbal is a gerund, a participle, or an infinitive.

I   1. The vice-principal's job is to handle discipline problems.

P,P   2. You will find canned chili in the prepared foods section.

P   3. Sweet corn sold at roadside stands is really fresh.

I   4. Who taught you to play the harmonica?

P   5. Absorbed in the novel, Judy lost track of time.

G 6. <u>Keeping quiet</u> is difficult for small children.

G 7. <u>Emptying the wastebaskets</u> is Brenda's job.

P 8. Have you ever seen a <u>falling</u> star?

G 9. Mr. Stiles is in charge of <u>organizing the car pool</u> this semester.

I 10. The witness is unable <u>to identify the criminal.</u>

Exercise B Follow the directions for Exercise A.

P 1. The <u>retired</u> admiral lives in Florida.

I 2. Arrange <u>to meet me</u> at the airport.

G 3. <u>Studying hard</u> is easy for Susan.

P 4. <u>Looking out the window</u>, Eric daydreamed about his vacation.

P 5. The suitcase was stuffed with <u>wrinkled</u> clothes.

P 6. <u>Connecting the Atlantic Ocean and the Pacific Ocean,</u> the Panama Canal saves ships time.

G 7. <u>Using dental floss</u> helps prevent cavities.

I 8. Peggy has collected enough leaves <u>to make a display for the science fair.</u>

P 9. <u>Knocking on the door,</u> the realtor waited for the owner of the house.

G 10. <u>Believing in yourself</u> is the key to success.

Additional Exercises

These Additional Exercises may be used for additional practice of the concepts presented in this Section. Each exercise focuses on a single concept, and should be used after the page number indicated in parentheses.

Review

If you have not assigned these Additional Exercises before this time, you can also use them as an excellent Section Review.

ADDITIONAL EXERCISES

Using Verbals

A. Gerunds and Gerund Phrases Write the gerunds and gerund phrases in these sentences.

1. Rabbits survive by running away.
2. Washing those clothes in hot water might shrink or fade them.
3. Gluing the pieces together took several hours.
4. There is an observation deck for viewing the city.
5. Nora suggested returning the carton of sour milk.
6. Tony practiced parallel parking.
7. Stu couldn't keep from arguing with the coach.
8. Stop giggling, Fred.
9. Jeremy has often talked about learning a trade.
10. Sky diving can be a dangerous sport.

B. Participles and Participial Phrases Write the participles and participial phrases in these sentences.

1. Watch out for hidden rocks.
2. Discouraged, the team retreated to the locker room at half-time.
3. Adjusting the wheels, Lee discovered a new problem.
4. The wildflowers growing in the park are goldenrod.
5. Thrusting itself up out of the water, the dolphin sailed through the hoop.
6. Does anybody want this burnt bratwurst?
7. Tapping her white cane, the woman found the curb.
8. Even used clothing has become expensive.
9. The driver's voice wakened the dozing passengers.
10. Occasionally jotting notes, Domenica listened closely.

C. Gerunds and Participles Write the gerund or participle from each sentence. Label it *Gerund* or *Participle*.

P 1. This coat has reinforced pockets.

P 2. Reinforced with steel, the door was almost unbreakable.

P 3. Her hair, parted in the middle, hung straight to her shoulders.

P 4. Recognizing nobody at the party, Jacob left early.

G 5. Check the suspect's alibi by interviewing her friends.

G 6. Getting the ball past Ron wasn't easy.

G 7. I have never enjoyed riding Ferris wheels.

P 8. Using a loudspeaker, the state trooper ordered the driver to the side of the road.

G 9. Using an electric drill would save time.

G 10. On summer nights, the chirping of crickets fills the air.

D. Infinitives and Infinitive Phrases Find the infinitives and infinitive phrases in these sentences.

1. Julie is training to work as a tour guide.
2. I expect to see Mel this afternoon.
3. The government attempts to warn us of health hazards.
4. Did you try to talk to Lena first?
5. This copy is too faint to read.
6. Tricia wants to skate to school.
7. Native Americans used certain plants to cure many illnesses.
8. To keep the wallet seems wrong to me.
9. My grandfather thought of a way to feed the baby bird.
10. Molly absolutely refuses to join us for tennis.

E. The Kinds of Verbals Write the verbal or verbal phrase in each sentence. Label it *Gerund, Participle,* or *Infinitive.*

G 1. Moving West solved many problems in earlier times.

I 2. We had almost persuaded Sandy to stay.

P 3. Forced out of their native country, the refugees sought protection in the United States.

G 4. Is tap-dancing still popular?

P 5. The crowd waiting for the bus grew impatient.

I 6. Trucks take longer to brake than cars.

G 7. Tyler is nervous about speaking in public.

P 8. Chameleons will eat only living prey.

G 9. Getting away from it all is quite impossible.

I 10. Is it too late to order some flowers?

P 11. Whistling bravely, Ilana walked into the principal's office.

I 12. My father wanted to leave at noon, but nobody was ready then.

I 13. It was hard to hear the telephone from outside.

I 14. The twins tried to move the couch and chairs closer to the fireplace.

P 15. Doing a double somersault; the gymnast flipped off the balance beam.

I 16. The bottle cap was labeled *easy to open*.

P 17. The fans, booing loudly, did not agree with the umpire.

G 18. Cooking can be both a hobby and a profession.

I 19. The label on the sweater said to wash it by hand.

P 20. Cindy always draws smiling faces next to her signature.

MIXED REVIEW

Using Verbals

A. Recognizing verbals Write the verbals and verbal phrases from the following sentences. Then write whether the verbal or verbal phrase is a *Gerund*, *Participle*, or an *Infinitive*. A sentence may contain more than one verbal.

G 1. <u>Bragging</u> annoys almost everybody.

G 2. Some football coaches forbid <u>practicing on hot days</u>.

P,I 3. Put the <u>camping</u> gear in the sun <u>to dry</u>.

P,P 4. The <u>flashing</u> lights warned us of a train <u>approaching</u>.

P 5. Thursday morning we took a <u>standardized</u> test.

I 6. Ingrid wants <u>to get Michael Jackson's autograph</u>.

P 7. Holiday shoppers <u>crowding the store</u> barely listened to the carols.

I 8. Mr. Vallina plans <u>to saw the decayed branch off</u>.

P 9. Mr. Calvey makes delicious <u>barbecued</u> ribs.

I 10. Rose told the children not <u>to turn on the hydrant</u>.

B. Identifying verbals and their uses Write the verbals and verbal phrases from the following sentences. If a verbal is used as a noun, write whether it is a *Subject*, an *Object*, or a *Predicate Word*. If it is used as a modifier, write whether it is an *Adjective* or *Adverb*.

Adj 1. Don't put the rug in the <u>washing</u> machine.

S 2. <u>Washing the dog</u> is Jim's responsibility.

O 3. I tried <u>to explain</u> to Maggie.

Adj 4. That is no way <u>to treat a friend</u>.

S 5. <u>Buying a new clutch for the old car</u> is foolish.

Adj 6. <u>Checking her pay stub</u>, June found a mistake.

O 7. Celia has improved her <u>timing</u>.

S 8. <u>To get to Monterey from here</u> takes two hours.

Adv 9. It isn't comfortable <u>to sleep on the floor</u>.

Adj 10. <u>Without knowing it</u>, Ann had hit the wrong button.

567

Mixed Review

  These exercises provide review of the concepts presented in this Section. Each exercise challenges the students to apply several of the skills they have acquired during previous study. Because the "mixed" feature of these activities makes them more difficult, the teacher may wish to have less-advanced students do them orally or in small groups.

USING GRAMMAR IN WRITING
Using Verbals

A. You are writing a celebrity exercise book, such as those put out by Hollywood stars and sports figures. Each chapter will focus on one fitness activity. Gerunds and gerund phrases are especially useful for naming activities. Think about the activities that a person might do to keep fit. Write an opening sentence for each of ten chapters. In each opening sentence, tell how one activity helps a person stay fit. Use a gerund or a gerund phrase in each sentence. You might want to use the following gerund phrases in your sentences.

> walking around the block in the morning or evening
> playing tennis with a friend on weekends
> swimming at a municipal pool

B. Participial phrases are modifiers, but they also give a sense of action. Imagine, or recall, a chase scene in an adventure movie. Describe part of the scene in a paragraph of at least five sentences. Try to include a participial phrase in each sentence. You might want to use some of the following.

> racing through downtown San Francisco
> dashing through the crowds on the sidewalk
> ducking into a highrise office building
> running up the stairs two at a time

C. Imagine a scene from a horror story. The narrator is alone, or is supposed to be alone, in an empty house at night. A storm is beginning. Write a paragraph describing the scene. Include at least five infinitive phrases. Begin your paragraph with the sentence *The wind began to howl*. You might want to include some of the following.

> decided to telephone   afraid to look
> caused me to shiver   tried not to worry

CUMULATIVE REVIEW

The Parts of Speech

Identifying parts of speech   There are twenty underlined words in the following paragraph. Decide what part of speech each word is used as. Number your paper from 1 to 20. Write *Noun, Verb, Pronoun, Adjective, Adverb, Preposition,* or *Conjunction* for each word. Be sure to check *how* the word is used in the sentence.

Many athletes are <u>going</u> "bananas" <u>these</u> days. The [V-1] [Adj-2]

banana is the most popular fruit in the United States.

Americans <u>consume</u> about 12 billion bananas <u>annually.</u> [V-3] [Adv-4]

<u>They</u> are particularly <u>popular</u> with athletes who need a [Pro-5] [Adj-6]

great deal <u>of</u> <u>endurance</u>—cyclists, triathletes, mar- [Prep-7] [N-8]

athoners, and long-distance swimmers. Why are

bananas so valuable? They <u>are</u> an <u>extremely</u> healthy [V-9] [Adv-10]

food. Bananas have no cholesterol <u>and</u> almost no fat. In [Conj-11]

addition, they contain more potassium than any other

fruit <u>except</u> avocados. Potassium is important for ath- [Prep-12]

letes because it <u>controls</u> <u>the</u> amount of water in the [V-13] [Adj-14]

body tissues. <u>It</u> also helps the <u>muscle</u> cells perform [Pro-15] [Adj-16]

<u>well.</u> <u>Eating</u> a banana also provides an athlete with a [Adv-17] [N-18]

supply of sucrose, which supplies <u>energy.</u> Not only are [N-19]

bananas good for <u>you,</u> but, best of all, they taste [Pro-20]

good, too!

569

Cumulative Review

These exercises are designed to cover broad areas of grammar, usage, and mechanics. They require the application of skills taught thus far in the text. The exercises may be used for testing purposes, or as an excellent resource for review.

Section Objectives

1. To use verbs that agree with their subjects in number

2. To use verbs that agree in number with compound subjects

3. To use verbs that agree in number with an indefinite pronoun subject

4. To avoid problems of subject-verb agreement in sentences containing *don't* and *doesn't,* and sentences beginning with *there, here,* or *where*

Preparing the Students

When planning meals, students will recognize that tacos and chop suey do not go together or "agree." When getting dressed, students will recognize that a formal gown and heavy boots do not go together or "agree." This Section will help students avoid using subjects and verbs that do not agree. Read the introduction on page 570.

Additional Resources

Diagnostic Test — page 3 in the test booklet

Mastery Test — pages 62–63 in the test booklet

Additional Exercises — pages 578–582 in the student text

Practice Book — pages 218–222

Duplicating Masters — pages 218–222

Special Populations — See special section at the front of this Teacher's Edition.

Making Subjects and Verbs Agree

The subject and the verb of a sentence must be alike in certain ways. When they are alike, they are said to agree. For example, if the subject of a sentence is plural, the verb must also be plural. Then they agree. In this section you will learn how to make subjects and verbs agree.

Part 1 Making Subjects and Verbs Agree in Number

The **number** of a word refers to whether the word is singular or plural. A word is **singular** when it refers to one thing. A word is **plural** when it refers to more than one thing. If a subject and verb are the same in number, they agree.

A verb must agree in number with its subject.

If a subject is singular, its verb must be singular. If a subject is plural, then its verb must be plural.

Singular	Plural
He *sings*.	They *sing*.
It *falls*.	They *fall*.
She *reads*.	They *read*.

You can see that in the examples, the singular of each verb ends in *s*. In each plural verb, there is no *s*.

Subject and verb agreement usually seems natural. Problems arise, though, when you are not sure which word is the subject of the sentence. Remember that to find the subject, first find the verb. Then ask *who?* or *what?* before it.

The pictures in this album are recent.
Verb: are
What are? pictures
The subject is *pictures*.

The subject of the verb is never found in a prepositional phrase.

When you are trying to make subjects and verbs agree, watch out for phrases. Often a phrase appears between the subject and the verb.

The *apples* in the refrigerator *are* cold.
That *bunch* of bananas *is* green.
The *books* by that author *are* thrillers.
One of the pieces *is* missing.

571

Part 1

Objective

To use verbs that agree with their subjects in number

Presenting the Lesson

1. Remind students that the two basic components of a sentence are its subject and its verb. Subjects may be nouns or pronouns, either of which may be singular or plural.

2. Read page 571, going over the definitions of *number, singular,* and *plural.* Be sure students can differentiate between singular and plural nouns. Have students identify the following nouns and pronouns as either singular or plural.

S person	P children	P geese	P we
P dogs	S woman	S mouse	S she
S sweater	P people	S tooth	S I
S winter	P seasons	P they	S it

3. Read page 571 studying the three rules governing agreement between subject and verb. Stress that the subject is never found in a prepositional phrase. Pay special attention to the phrases on page 572, stressing that they are never part of the subject.

4. Assign and discuss Exercises A and B on pages 572–573. In going over the exercises, have students identify the subject and tell whether it is singular or plural.

Individualizing the Lesson

Less-Advanced Students

Have students write an original sentence for each verb not used in Exercises A and B, pages 572–573. Students should be sure that verbs agree in number with their subjects.

571

Advanced Students

Have students write ten original sentences to illustrate subject/verb agreement. Five of the sentences should contain plural nouns and five sentences should include singular nouns. Students should include prepositional phrases and phrases such as *with, as well as,* and *in addition to* in their sentences.

Optional Practice

Put the following sentences on the chalkboard or a worksheet. Have students decide whether the verb agrees with the subject in number. If the subject and verb agree, students should mark the sentence *Correct.* If the verb does not agree, students should rewrite the sentence, using the correct verb.

C 1. The paper in the boxes is for recycling.

2. The shoes in the closet needs polishing.

3. The children, as well as their teacher, is coming. *are*

C 4. Tons of coal were dumped down the chute.

C 5. Three members of the team have the flu.

6. Money, in addition to gifts, were received. *was*

C 7. Members, including their families, are invited.

8. Senators from our state is voting today. *are*

C 9. The marks on the floor are from your shoes.

C 10. The peninsula, in addition to the islands, has docks for small boats.

Extending the Lesson

Work with students to develop a list of ten plural nouns relating to the

572

Phrases beginning with the words *with, together with, including, as well as,* and *in addition to* are not part of the subject.

> *Aunt Agnes*, in addition to Aunt Rita, *is* here.
> Hard *work*, as well as ambition, *is* necessary.
> The *class*, including our teacher, *takes* a field trip in the spring.

Exercise A Choose the verb that agrees with the subject.

1. Those reports, including the one by Len, (is, are) on the bulletin board.
2. The table, as well as the chairs, (needs, need) polishing.
3. The box of pins (is, are) on the shelf.
4. The strength of chimpanzees (is, are) amazing.
5. Two of the pages from this book (is, are) missing.
6. The quilt on the bed (was, were) made by my great-grandmother.
7. New players for the marching band (is, are) needed.
8. The jockey in the yellow silks (ride, rides) the horse Suncat.
9. The cups, as well as the teapot, (has, have) been washed.
10. Even the worst times (get, gets) better.

Exercise B Follow the directions for Exercise A.

1. That girl with the braids (walk, walks) to school.
2. Fay, as well as the other swimmers, (practice, practices) after school.
3. All of the options on this car (cost, costs) a fortune.
4. A car with weak brakes (is, are) dangerous.
5. The stops on the bus tour (include, includes) Chinatown.
6. The hinges on that trunk (is, are) rusty.
7. Two reporters on the paper (cover, covers) city news.

572

8. The tickets at this booth (<u>cost</u>, costs) half price.
9. All the players on the team (<u>work</u>, works) together.
10. The house, together with the garage, (<u>is</u>, are) freshly painted.

Part 2 Compound Subjects

A compound subject is two or more subjects used with the same verb.

A compound subject joined by *and* is plural. Therefore, it requires a plural verb.

The store *manager* and the *clerks* **are preparing** for the sale.
Laurie and *Jim* **sing** in the choir.

When the parts of a compound subject are joined by *or* or *nor*, the verb should agree with the subject nearer to the verb.

Neither Liz nor her brothers *take* the bus.
Either sandwiches or a salad *is* a good lunch.

Exercise A Choose the verb that agrees with the subject.

1. Mark and Scott (is, <u>are</u>) planning a fishing trip.
2. The oven and the refrigerator (<u>need</u>, needs) cleaning.
3. Egypt and Tunisia (is, <u>are</u>) in Africa.
4. Both the bread and the muffins (<u>seem</u>, seems) to be fresh.
5. Neither dessert nor the beverages (has, <u>have</u>) been included in the price.
6. Neither the beverages nor dessert (<u>has</u>, have) been included in the price.
7. Either Mom or Dad (cook, <u>cooks</u>) dinner.
8. Either the dog or the cats (is, <u>are</u>) in the garage.
9. Both Joan and Kirsten (<u>live</u>, lives) on that block.
10. Neither Dan nor Greg (shop, <u>shops</u>) at that store.

573

same topic (books, shelves, mysteries, libraries). Have students write a paragraph about the topic using ten plural nouns. Students should be sure that the verbs agree in number with their subjects.

Part 2

Objective

To use verbs that agree in number with compound subjects

Presenting the Lesson

1. Read page 573. Study the two rules governing agreement of a verb with a compound subject. Study the examples.
2. Assign and discuss Exercises A and B on pages 573–574.

Individualizing the Lesson

Less-Advanced Students

1. Have students change the subjects in Exercise A, page 573, to correctly use the verbs that were not used the first time.
2. Students should work as a group to write ten sentences—five containing a plural compound subject joined by *and* and five containing correlative conjunctions such as *or* or *nor,*

Advanced Students

1. Have students find several published examples of compound subjects joined by *and* and several joined by *or* or *nor.*
2. Have students work individually and write ten original sentences. Five sentences should

573

contain a compound subject using *and* and five sentences should use a compound subject joined by *or* or *nor*.

Part 3

Objective

To use verbs that agree in number with an indefinite pronoun subject

Exercise B   Follow the directions for Exercise A.

1. Either Sharon or Kim (work, works) tonight.
2. Neither the movie nor the TV show (is, are) as good as the book.
3. Either a diet or medication (is, are) prescribed for diabetes.
4. Neither snow nor icy roads (stop, stops) this little jeep.
5. Suntan oil and sun visors (is, are) sold at the beach.
6. Both the detergent and the bleach (work, works) better in soft water.
7. Ghost stories and monster movies (upset, upsets) me.
8. Neither the sales clerk nor her manager (was, were) very helpful.
9. Hot dogs and baked beans (was, were) on the menu for Tuesday.
10. Either the radio or the TV (get, gets) turned off.

Part 3   Indefinite Pronouns

To make a verb agree with an indefinite pronoun used as the subject, you must know if the pronoun is singular or plural. As you have learned, some indefinite pronouns are singular, and some are plural. Others may be either singular or plural.

The following indefinite pronouns are **singular:**

another	each	everything	one
anybody	either	neither	somebody
anyone	everybody	nobody	someone
anything	everyone	no one	

Nobody there *wants* to go.
Somebody plans the activities.
Each of the students *has* a locker.

The following indefinite pronouns are **plural:**

both   few   many   several

Many of the voters *support* that candidate.
Several of the children *have* chicken pox.

The following indefinite pronouns are **singular** if they refer to one thing. They are **plural** if they refer to several things.

all   any   most   none   some

All of the sugar *is* in the tin.
All of the tools *are* in the garage.

None of the paint *is* red.
None of the pears *are* ripe.

Some of the music *is* Lauren's.
Some of the horses *are* in the barn.

Exercise A   Choose the verb that agrees with the subject.

1. Most of the jackets (is, <u>are</u>) waterproof.
2. (Is, <u>Are</u>) all of the tickets sold?
3. Few of the secretaries (<u>take</u>, takes) shorthand.
4. Each of the boats (<u>has</u>, have) two sails.
5. No one here (<u>has</u>, have) played rugby before.
6. Someone on the elevator (want, <u>wants</u>) to get off.
7. Some of the glue (<u>is</u>, are) stuck on the table.
8. Everything in the kitchen (<u>is</u>, are) unbreakable.
9. Most of those rumors (is, <u>are</u>) not true.
10. Some of the rolls (was, <u>were</u>) burned.

Exercise B   Follow the directions for Exercise A.

1. Some of the hats (has, <u>have</u>) brims.
2. Most of the paint (<u>is</u>, are) peeling.
3. Neither of the dogs (<u>has</u>, have) a collar.
4. Someone (prepare, <u>prepares</u>) the newsletter each month.
5. None of the potato salad (<u>was</u>, were) eaten.
6. Most of the flowers (has, <u>have</u>) been planted.
7. Many of the tomatoes (is, <u>are</u>) ripe.

Presenting the Lesson

Read pages 574–575. Study the list of indefinite pronouns that are always singular. Study the four indefinite pronouns that are always plural. Study the five pronouns that may be singular or plural. Stress that the subject of a sentence is never found in a prepositional phrase.

Individualizing the Lesson

Less-Advanced Students

1. Have students study the lists of indefinite pronouns on pages 574–575. Stress that students should try to remember which pronouns are always plural, which are always singular, and which can be either singular or plural.

2. Give students a closed-book quiz on indefinite pronouns. Have students spell the pronoun properly, and indicate whether it can be used as singular, plural, or either. Then have students use the pronoun correctly in an original sentence.

Advanced Students

Have students write an original sentence for each of the indefinite pronouns. For each pronoun that can be used as either singular or plural, students should write one sentence demonstrating each use.

Optional Practice

Have students read the following sentences. If the subject and verb agree, students should mark the sentence *Correct*. If the verb does not agree, students should rewrite the sentence, using the correct verb.

1. One of my fillings ~~need~~ **needs** to be re-placed.

C 2. All of the shades were down.

3. Several of the players wants a time out.

4. Everything in these drawers ~~are~~ **is** my brother's.

5. All of the cookies ~~is~~ **are** gone.

C 6. Some of the problems are too hard for us.

7. One of the answers ~~are~~ **is** incorrect.

8. Both of the traffic lights ~~is~~ **are** green.

9. Each of the programs ~~last~~ **lasts** an hour.

10. Most of the leaves ~~has~~ **have** fallen.

Extending the Lesson

Have students write sentences using the following as subjects.

1. each of the meetings
2. none of our streets
3. several of the eggs in the carton
4. some of the lemonade
5. either of the coaches

Part 4

Objective

To avoid problems of subject-verb agreement in sentences containing *don't* and *doesn't*, and sentences beginning with *there*, *here*, or *where*

Presenting the Lesson

1. Read page 576, stressing that *doesn't* is singular. Study examples of correct usage of *don't* and *doesn't*.

2. Read the discussion of sentences beginning with *there*, *here*, and *where*. Be sure students can locate the subjects in these sentences.

8. One of the cars (<u>is</u>, are) low on gas.

9. Everyone on vacation (want, <u>wants</u>) pleasant weather.

10. Each of the welders (wear, <u>wears</u>) safety glasses.

Part 4 Other Problems of Agreement

Doesn't and *Don't*

The verb *doesn't* is singular. *Doesn't* is used with the subjects *she, he,* and *it*. All other personal pronouns are used with *don't*.

It *doesn't* please me. They *don't* work nights.
He *doesn't* work nearby. I *don't* play an instrument.
She *doesn't* like squash. We *don't* grow asparagus.

Sentences Beginning with *There*

When sentences begin with *there, here,* or *where*, the subject comes after the verb. You must look ahead to find the subject of the sentence. Then you must use the verb that agrees with that subject.

There *are* several good *songs* on that album.
Here *are* the *plums*.
Where *is* my other *shoe*?

Exercise A Choose the verb that agrees with the subject.

1. Elliot (<u>doesn't</u>, don't) play soccer.

2. It (<u>doesn't</u>, don't) take that long.

3. He (<u>doesn't</u>, don't) enjoy that program.

4. Where (<u>is</u>, are) the ambulance?

5. These shoes (doesn't, <u>don't</u>) fit well.

6. (Doesn't, Don't) Flo play chess?

7. (Doesn't, <u>Don't</u>) egg rolls contain cabbage?

8. There (is, <u>are</u>) some napkins in the pantry.

9. There (goes, <u>go</u>) the ducklings.

10. There (<u>was</u>, were) a snake in the garden.

Exercise B   Follow the directions for Exercise A.

1. Mary Beth (<u>doesn't</u>, don't) eat red meat.

2. Here (<u>is</u>, are) a vegetarian dinner.

3. (<u>Isn't</u>, Aren't) there any meat in this casserole?

4. Where (<u>is</u>, are) the cheese?

5. Sheila (<u>doesn't</u>, don't) enjoy fried foods.

6. Where (is, <u>are</u>) the hard-boiled eggs?

7. Hamburgers (doesn't, <u>don't</u>) taste good without onions.

8. Mr. Fraser (<u>doesn't</u>, don't) agree with me.

9. Here (is, <u>are</u>) the dill pickles.

10. There (is, <u>are</u>) two jars of garlic salt.

3. Assign and discuss Exercises A and B on pages 576–577.

Individualizing the Lesson

Less-Advanced Students

Have students use each verb not used in Exercises A and B, pages 576–577. Have them change the original sentence so the verb is correctly used.

Advanced Students

Have students write five original sentences using *don't* and five using *doesn't*.

Optional Practice

Have students choose the verb that agrees with the subject.

1. Rachel and Frank (<u>don't</u>, doesn't) ever go to movies.

2. She (don't, <u>doesn't</u>) like to spend money.

3. (Don't, <u>Doesn't</u>) anyone have a watch?

4. Where (is, <u>are</u>) your slippers?

5. Here (<u>is</u>, are) the garbage truck.

6. There (wasn't, <u>weren't</u>) any oranges left.

7. (<u>Doesn't</u>, Don't) it look stormy to the west?

8. There (is, <u>are</u>) strawberries for dessert.

Extending the Lesson

Have students make up ten sentences beginning with *there, here,* or *where.* Then have students underline the verb and circle the subject in each sentence.

Additional Exercises

These Additional Exercises may be used for additional practice of the concepts presented in this Section. Each exercise focuses on a single concept, and should be used after the page number indicated in parentheses.

Review

If you have not assigned these Additional Exercises before this time, you can also use them as an excellent Section Review.

578

ADDITIONAL EXERCISES

Making Subjects and Verbs Agree

A. Verbs and Their Subjects   Write the verb that agrees with the subject.

1. Two pieces of pizza (is, are) left.
2. Several people, including Marion, (has, have) a key to that door.
3. Vic, as well as his co-workers, (attends, attend) staff meetings.
4. Noises from the street (drifts, drift) up to my room.
5. Our chances of winning (is, are) better than theirs.
6. The slices of bread in this loaf (isn't, aren't) moldy.
7. Two rooms, in addition to this one, (is, are) not in use.
8. The barn, together with the stables, (is, are) by the dirt road.
9. Rats in a building (endangers, endanger) health.
10. The mood in those classrooms (is, are) peaceful.

B. Verbs and Compound Subjects   Write the verb that agrees with the subject.

1. Privacy and free time (is, are) not always easy to find.
2. The suitcase and the totebag (is, are) both stuffed with clothes.
3. As children, both Thomas Edison and Albert Einstein (was, were) thought to be rather stupid.
4. Farming and ranching (has, have) replaced buffalo hunting for many Plains Indians.
5. Mirrors and water (reflects, reflect) print backwards.
6. Neither white rice nor white bread (provides, provide) as much nutrition as brown rice or whole-grain bread.
7. Both rice and bread (contains, contain) carbohydrates.

8. Neither Katy nor her sister (<u>looks</u>, look) pleased.
9. Either the manager or one of her assistants (<u>handles</u>, handle) complaints.
10. Masking tape or staples (is, <u>are</u>) used to fasten those envelopes.

C. Verbs and Indefinite Pronouns Write the verb that agrees with the subject.

1. Each of the bikes (<u>has</u>, have) been customized.
2. Both of the books (contains, <u>contain</u>) information on the Olympics.
3. Some of the injured players (insists, <u>insist</u>) on returning to the field.
4. Some of the fudge (<u>is</u>, are) for the bake sale.
5. Another of those old war movies (<u>is</u>, are) on tonight.
6. Only one of the hotels (<u>faces</u>, face) the ocean.
7. Few of the factories (hires, <u>hire</u>) summer help.
8. Everybody in the bleachers (<u>was</u>, were) standing.
9. Everything certainly (<u>seems</u>, seem) under control.
10. (<u>Was</u>, Were) all of the money refunded?

D. Problems of Agreement Write the verb that agrees with the subject.

1. He really (<u>doesn't</u>, don't) seem to feel at home.
2. Here (is, <u>are</u>) the rules.
3. There (is, <u>are</u>) several thin sheets of wood in plywood.
4. (Doesn't, <u>Don't</u>) Carol and Ruth have their ticket stubs?
5. Where (<u>was</u>, were) the junior prom held last year?
6. It (don't, <u>doesn't</u>) bother me much.
7. There (<u>is</u>, are) no easy answer to that question.
8. Where (has, <u>have</u>) the flood victims been housed?
9. Those sandwiches in the vending machine (<u>don't</u>, doesn't) look fresh.
10. There (is, <u>are</u>) pedalboats for rent at the lagoon.

Mixed Review

These exercises provide re-view of the concepts pre-sented in this Section. Each exercise challenges the stu-dents to apply several of the skills they have acquired dur-ing previous study. Because the "mixed" feature of these activities makes them more difficult, the teacher may wish to have less-advanced stu-dents do them orally or in small groups.

MIXED REVIEW

Making Subjects and Verbs Agree

A. Choosing the correct verb In each of the following sentences, write the verb that agrees with the subject.

1. Neither his socks nor his gloves (matches, <u>match</u>).
2. Neither gossip nor rumors (belongs, <u>belong</u>) in a news story.
3. Neither the window nor the door (<u>is</u>, are) locked.
4. The jokes in her speech (was, <u>were</u>) funny.
5. One of the doves (<u>coos</u>, coo) every morning.
6. Counties near Chicago (includes, <u>include</u>) Kane and Lake.
7. The greens, as well as the chicken, (needs, <u>need</u>) salt.
8. Both the greens and the chicken (needs, <u>need</u>) some pepper.
9. Eve, together with her friends, (<u>sits</u>, sit) on the porch.
10. Mr. Bensdorf and Mr. Fletcher (works, <u>work</u>) at the same post office.

B. Using the correct verb Some of the following sentences contain errors in subject-verb agreement. If a sentence contains an error, rewrite it correctly. If a sentence is correct, write *Correct*.

1. Neither of those hobbies ^{requires} require much money.
2. Both of those albums ^{are} is available as cassettes.
c 3. Everyone depends on Vincent.
4. Where ^{are} is the vending machines?
5. Sandra ^{doesn't} don't have last year's yearbook.
c 6. Don't parakeets sing?
7. There ^{were} was two notes taped on the classroom door.
8. It ^{does} do bother me sometimes.
c 9. None of the waiters get sick leave.
10. None of the garden ^{gets} gets enough sun.

580

USING GRAMMAR IN WRITING
Making Subjects and Verbs Agree

A. Suppose that you have been given a chance to write an editorial for a local paper. What do you want to say? You might point out a situation that you think is unfair. You might praise someone. You might suggest a way to solve a community problem. Choose a topic that interests you, and then write your editorial. Begin the opening sentence with *There*. This sentence should state the problem or identify the person or situation you are writing about. Also use at least four of the following indefinite pronouns in your editorial. Be certain that all verbs agree with their subjects.

anyone	everyone	nobody	someone	something
each	many	several	none	all

B. You have been asked to take a poll for the school newspaper, magazine, or radio station. What questions will you ask students in your school? You might ask their opinions about political candidates. You might ask about school policies. Assume that you have asked your questions and collected the answers. Write a paragraph summarizing the results. Use the following as subjects for your sentences. Be certain that the verbs you use agree with their subjects.

a handful of students	half of the student population
most	nearly every student
few	students who walk to school
many students and the principal	each of the students

Using Grammar in Writing

These challenging and enjoyable activities allow the students to see how the concepts of grammar, usage, and mechanics may be applied in actual writing situations. Each exercise is designed to allow students practice in several of the skills they have acquired in this Section. The activities also provide opportunities for students to write creatively about a wide variety of interesting and unusual subjects.

CUMULATIVE REVIEW

Usage

Using words correctly   Twenty words are underlined in the following paragraph. Ten of the underlined words contain errors in the use of verbs, nouns, pronouns, adverbs, and adjectives. Ten of the words are correct. Proofread the paragraph. Rewrite it, correcting the errors.

"Let's go ice-skating," said my friend Brenda. Before I knew it, my feet were laced into skates, and I was being led toward the ice. "What kind of a torture is this?" I asked myself. As I got to the edge of the rink, I decided to approach this sport fearless. [fearlessly] I boldly slid into the rink. Then I prompt [promptly] made a three-point landing. Between chuckles Brenda said, "You won't never make the Olympics that way!" As I struggled to my feet, I requested that Brenda learn [teach] me a few basic skills. She mustn't of [have] heard me, because she skated off without me. I decided to learn by watching. "Them [These/Those] skaters seem to be good," I said to myself as I took tiny step [steps] across the ice toward a group of three skaters. Each of them was doing their [his or her] own favorite thing. The nearer [nearest] skater was doing figure eights, and the farthest skater was skating backwards. Since I needed to learn how to go forward, they weren't much help! Gradually, I slipped and slid my way back to the warming house. "Next time I'll plan our activities!" I told Brenda as I removed the skates.

Using Compound and Complex Sentences

1. To review the simple sentence and compound sentence

2. To recognize and construct complex sentences

3. To recognize and identify main clauses and subordinate clauses

4. To identify subordinate adverb clauses, subordinate adjective clauses, and subordinate noun clauses and to understand their functions

5. To recognize relative pronouns and understand their function in introducing adjective clauses

6. To differentiate between noun clauses, adverb clauses, and adjective clauses

7. To avoid using subordinate clauses as sentence fragments

8. To recognize and construct compound-complex sentences

Preparing the Students

Remind students that to help convey meaning most efficiently, use four different types of sentences: simple, compound, complex, and compound-complex. Then read the introduction on page 583.

Additional Resources

Diagnostic Test — page 7 in the test booklet

Mastery Test — pages 64–67 in the test booklet

Additional Exercises — pages 614–624 in the student text

Practice Book — pages 223–235

Duplicating Masters — pages 223–235

Special Populations — See special section at the front of this Teacher's Edition.

There are four kinds of sentences—simple sentences, compound sentences, complex sentences, and compound-complex sentences. You have already studied the simple sentence, and you know how the parts of a sentence work together. In this section you will learn about the other three types of sentences.

583

To review the simple sentence and its possible compound parts

Presenting the Lesson

1. Read page 584. Review the subject and predicate and the function of each.

2. Read page 584. Study examples of compound sentence parts.

3. Read page 585. Study the definition of the simple sentence. Stress that although sentence parts may be compound, a simple sentence expresses only one main idea.

4. Assign and discuss Exercises A and B on pages 585–586.

Individualizing the Lesson

Less-Advanced Students

1. Have students write an original sentence for each of the compounds listed on page 584. Have them underline each compound part.

2. Have students write the compound subjects, verbs, and objects found in each of the sentences in Exercise A, page 585.

Advanced Students

Have students write two original simple sentences for each compound sentence part listed on page 584 (twelve sentences total). Students should underline each compound and identify its use in the sentence.

Optional Practice

Have students read the following simple sentences. Students should

Part 1 Review of the Sentence

The sentence is composed of two basic parts. These key parts are the subject and the predicate.

Subject	Predicate
Birds	sang.
Birds	sang early this morning.
Birds in the trees	sang early this morning.
Several bluebirds in the tree	sang very loudly this morning.

The **subject** tells who or what the sentence is about. The predicate tells what the subject did, what the subject is, or what happens.

The **simple predicate** is called the verb. The simple subject is called the **subject of the verb**.

Within the subject of the sentence are the simple subject and its modifiers. In the predicate of the sentence are the verb, objects, predicate words, and their modifiers.

Compound Parts in a Sentence

You have learned that all parts of the sentence may be **compound**.

Compound subject:	Fresh lemons and limes filled the basket.
Compound verb:	The clown tripped, stumbled, and fell.
Compound predicate:	We went to the pet store and bought a parakeet.
Compound object:	Jenny painted the lawn furniture and the porch swing.
Compound object of the preposition:	During May and June, we plant our garden.
Compound predicate word:	The down comforter is soft and fluffy.

The Simple Sentence

Even though sentences may have compound parts, they still express only one main idea. Such sentences, like all of those you have been studying, are called **simple sentences**.

A simple sentence is a sentence with only one subject and one predicate. The subject and the predicate, along with any part of the subject or predicate, may be compound.

Now you are ready to distinguish simple sentences from other types of sentences.

Exercise A Copy each of the following simple sentences. Then draw a line between the subject and the predicate.

1. Marcy and Joel | work for their dad.
2. The IRS and the FTC | are government agencies.
3. Noreen | put her scarf and her gloves into her locker.
4. The Bee Gees and Men at Work | are both from Australia.
5. Iowa and Indiana | border Illinois.
6. The houses on that block | are old and run-down.
7. Margaret | looked up the phone number and then dialed it.
8. The sales clerk | was both helpful and courteous.
9. Judy | forgot the volleyball and the net.
10. Mr. Kendall | ordered a belt and a sweater through the catalog.

Exercise B Write the compound subjects, verbs, predicates, and objects you find in these simple sentences.

v 1. Dr. Imhof cleaned and examined my teeth.
s 2. Tracy Austin and Andrea Jaeger are both tennis pros.
v 3. Stamp and then mail the letter.
o 4. Tables for the reception were set up in the dining room and living room.

585

divide their papers into four columns, headed *Subject, Verb, Direct Object,* and *Predicate Word.* For each sentence, students should put the sentence parts in the appropriate columns. Not all sentences contain all parts.

1. The tea spilled into the saucer.
2. Dr. Wolf is a surgeon.
3. Bees and wasps swarmed around the hive.
4. Fireworks flared and lighted the sky.
5. Mr. Baggert is elderly but healthy.
6. Dad takes a bus and the subway to work.
7. Bert put the knives, forks, and spoons on the table.
8. Can you play the guitar or drums?
9. Marilyn and Don sang and danced in the show.
10. Tuesday and Wednesday are my days for work.

Extending the Lesson

1. Have students copy ten simple sentences from a children's book. If the sentences include a compound, have students underline the compound and write what part of the sentence it is.

2. Have students rewrite the simple sentences that do not include a compound to include a compound.

586

O 5. The band played <u>either country-western music or gospel songs</u>.

S 6. <u>Meg, Jo, Beth, and Amy</u> are the sisters in *Little Women*.

O 7. The farmer planted <u>corn, soybeans, and wheat</u>.

V 8. Dave <u>washed, waxed, and buffed</u> the tile hallway.

S,P 9. <u>Kate and Anna</u> <u>made a spaghetti dinner</u> and then <u>cleaned up the kitchen</u>.

S,O 10. Did <u>you and Jim</u> borrow the <u>staple gun</u> and the <u>glue</u>?

Part 2

Objective

To review the compound sentence

Presenting the Lesson

1. Review how both the subject and predicate may be compound in a simple sentence.

2. Read page 586, studying the definition of the compound sentence. Stress that the two simple sentences joined into a compound sentence must express related ideas. Study the examples of compound sentences on page 586. Point out how the simple sentences are joined and how each simple sentence has its own subject and verb. Be sure that students can identify the subject and the verb in each simple sentence.

3. Study the passages on pages 586–587 showing the purpose and advantages of using compound sentences.

4. Study the instructions for diagraming compound sentences.

5. Assign and discuss Exercises A and B on pages 588–589.

Part 2 The Compound Sentence

Sometimes two simple sentences express related ideas, and they are joined to form one sentence. The resulting sentence has more than one subject and more than one predicate. It is called a **compound sentence**.

A compound sentence consists of two or more simple sentences joined together. The parts of the compound sentence may be joined by a coordinating conjunction (*and, or, but*) or by a semicolon (;). Look at the following examples.

The sun is out, **and** the temperature is in the 80's.
Our dog sounds ferocious, **but** he is really very friendly.
Pay your dues, **or** you will be dropped from the club.
We visited a college in Wisconsin; my sister wants to attend school there.

Why are compound sentences used? Why don't writers use only simple sentences? This passage will help you to see why.

Many people think that a career in the theater is glamorous. It is really a lot of hard work. You have to be prepared to rehearse at any time of the day or night. You have to memorize moves. You must remember your lines. It is also important that you work well with people. You must be prepared to take instruction from your director.

The series of simple sentences one after another becomes dull and tiresome. Notice how much better the same paragraph sounds with compound sentences.

> Many people think that a career in the theater is glamorous, but it is really a lot of hard work. You have to be prepared to rehearse at any time of the day or night. You have to memorize moves, and you must remember your lines. It is also important that you work well with people, and you must be prepared to take instruction from your director.

Diagraming Compound Sentences

If you can diagram simple sentences, you can diagram compound ones. The diagram simply shows that a compound sentence is two or more simple sentences joined together. The simple sentences are diagramed one under the other. Then the two sentences are connected with a dotted line. The coordinating conjunction sits on a "step" in the line.

> The controller gave the pilot instructions, and the plane taxied down the runway.

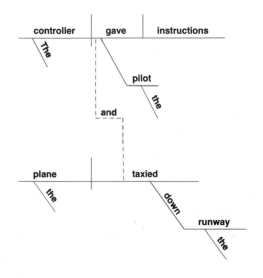

587

6. Read and discuss page 589, explaining how to distinguish between compound sentences and sentences with compound predicates. Study the examples on pages 589–590 showing the difference between compound sentences and simple sentences with compound predicates.

7. Assign and discuss Exercises A and B on pages 590–591. Have students identify all subjects and verbs in each sentence.

8. Read pages 591–592, showing how to punctuate compound sentences. Stress the purpose of the punctuation. Study examples carefully, noting placement of a comma before the conjunction and the placement of the semicolon. Point out the use of a semicolon before a conjunctive adverb. Pay special attention to page 592, showing the difference in punctuation between a compound sentence and a simple sentence with a compound predicate.

9. Assign and discuss Exercises A and B on pages 592–593.

Individualizing the Lesson

Less-Advanced Students

1. Have students write ten compound sentences, leaving out the punctuation. Also tell students to write five simple sentences with compound predicates, also leaving out the punctuation.

2. Have students exchange papers. Then have them insert punctuation in the proper places.

3. Have students pass the paper on to a third person to correct; then have students return the paper to its original owner.

Advanced Students

1. Have students write ten original compound sentences. Five of the sentences should require the use of a comma, and five should require the use of a semicolon.

2. Have students write ten original simple sentences that contain a compound predicate.

3. After all the sentences have been written, have students write brief explanations of when to use a semicolon in a compound sentence and how to tell a compound sentence from a simple sentence with a compound predicate.

Optional Practice

Have students identify the following sentences as *Simple* or *Compound*.

C 1. The flowers wilted, but the plant stayed green.

S 2. Everyone cheered and shouted for an encore.

C 3. Carol ordered a hamburger, but she got a barbecued beef sandwich.

C 4. The sale begins tomorrow; however, not all items will be reduced.

S 5. You should see your doctor or go to the clinic.

C 6. I have to earn $15.00, or I can't go to the football game.

C 7. My feet hurt; these shoes don't fit at all.

S 8. Jack painted the walls and waxed the floor.

C 9. The rain has stopped; nevertheless, the field is too muddy to play.

C 10. The phone rang and the doorbell chimed at the same time.

Exercise A   Number your paper from 1 to 10. Label three columns *Subject/Verb, Conjunction,* and *Subject/Verb*. For each sentence, fill in the columns.

Example: Craig plays backgammon, but Jim and Al prefer chess.

Subject/Verb	Conjunction	Subject/Verb
Craig/plays	but	Jim, Al/prefer

1. The performer sang, and the pianist accompanied her.
2. The examination was long, but it was easy.
3. Uncle Jim built a fire in the fireplace, and then we roasted chestnuts.
4. Alligators were on the endangered species list, but now their number is growing.
5. We can ride our bikes, or we can walk.
6. The drama group won the local contest, and now it will compete at the state level.
7. The movie was terrible, but the theater was packed.
8. Should I call a plumber, or can you fix the leak?
9. The United States Post Office has a package delivery service, but many people use private delivery firms.
10. The tourist checked his map, and then he drove onto the interstate highway.

Exercise B   Follow the directions for Exercise A.

1. Dad sanded the windowsills, and I stained them.
2. The tornado damaged the buildings, but no one was hurt.
3. The letter carrier rang the doorbell, but no one answered.
4. Mom planted roses in the garden, and they bloomed until October.
5. Hokkaido is a Japanese island, and the Ainu people live there.

6. Would you like some water, or should I make tea?
7. Dandelions and clover covered the lawn, and crabgrass grew in the flower bed.
8. Mark and Pam will telephone the members, or nobody will remember the meeting.
9. Acrylic sweaters look like wool, but wool sweaters are warmer.
10. My grandmother made slipcovers for the chairs, and she ordered new drapes for the windows.

Compound Sentence or Compound Predicate?

A **compound predicate** is two verbs within one predicate. The parts of a compound predicate, like the parts of a compound sentence, are joined by a coordinating conjunction.

> Kristi *memorized the poem* and *recited it for me*.
> (This compound predicate is joined by *and*.)

How can you tell whether a sentence is compound or whether it has a compound predicate? If each verb has its own subject, then the sentence is compound. If the verbs share the same subject, then only the predicate is compound.

> s. v. v.
> *Lance walked* to the podium and *gave* his speech.
> (This simple sentence has a compound predicate. Both verbs, *walked* and *gave*, have the same subject, *Lance*.)

> s. v. s. v.
> *Lance walked* to the podium, and *he gave* his speech.
> (This is a compound sentence. The verb *walked* has its own subject, *Lance*. The verb *gave* has its own subject, *he*.)

> s. v. v.
> The *receptionist answers* phones and *types* letters.
> (The conjunction *and* joins the compound predicate of this simple sentence. Both verbs, *answers* and *types*, have the same subject, *receptionist*.)

589

$$\overset{\text{S.}}{\text{The }} \overset{}{\textit{receptionist}} \overset{\text{V.}}{\textit{answers}} \text{ phones, and the } \overset{\text{S.}}{\textit{secretary}} \overset{\text{V.}}{\textit{types}}$$
letters.

(This compound sentence is actually two simple sentences joined by the conjunction *and*.)

Exercise A Number your paper from 1 to 10. Decide whether the following sentences are compound sentences or simple sentences with compound predicates. Write *Compound Sentence* or *Compound Predicate*.

CP 1. Alice does warm-up exercises and then jogs before breakfast.

CP 2. Keith measured the board and sawed it.

CS 3. The Indianapolis 500 time trials are this week, and the unofficial track record is 203.7 mph.

CS 4. Barbra Streisand is the female vocalist, and Andy Gibb is the male vocalist.

CS 5. The lifeguards are on duty, but the beach is not yet open.

CP 6. The children waded in the water and built sand castles.

CS 7. Is that the prince, or is that his cousin?

CS 8. I usually work on Saturdays, but I worked on Sunday this week.

CS 9. Is this plant sick, or did you forget to water it?

CS 10. Has Mike found an apartment, or does he still live at home?

Exercise B Follow the directions for Exercise A.

CP 1. Adam overhauled the engine and then sold the car.

CP 2. Sara looked at the price of a new car and decided to buy a used one instead.

CS 3. Vince was a member of the team, but he sat on the bench all season.

CP 4. Kelly was absent on the day of the test but was given a make-up exam the next day.

cs 5. Amy Koopman made the Olympic gymnastic team, but the team didn't compete in the 1980 Olympics.

cs 6. We get several FM stations, but the reception isn't very good.

cp 7. Did Marla bake the cake or order it from a bakery?

cs 8. Nancy put on her bathing cap and adjusted her swim goggles; then she dove into the pool.

cs 9. Do you want to bring a picnic, or would you rather buy hot dogs there?

cs10. Phil, Greg, and Henry may go to the rock concert, but they have to be home by ten.

Punctuating Compound Sentences

One of two punctuation marks is used in a compound sentence. Either a **comma** before a coordinating conjunction or a **semicolon** is needed to separate the two parts of a compound sentence. The punctuation keeps the two parts separate. It also shows where to pause in reading the sentence.

In a compound sentence, a comma is used before a coordinating conjunction. Notice how the comma is used in these compound sentences:

$\;\;\;\;\;$ s.$\;\;\;\;\;$ v.$\;\;\;\;\;\;\;\;\;\;\;\;\;\;$ s.$\;\;\;\;\;$ v.

The theater was already full, **and** the line stretched around the block.

$\;\;\;\;\;$ s.$\;\;\;\;\;$ v.$\;$ s.

The plane was scheduled for a noon departure, **but** the flight
$\;\;\;$ v.
was delayed.

Instead of a comma and a conjunction, a semicolon may be used in a compound sentence.

$\;\;\;\;\;$ s.$\;\;\;\;\;$ v.$\;\;\;\;\;\;\;\;\;\;$ s. v.

New Orleans is an important city; it is one of the largest ports in the United States.

$\;\;\;\;\;$ s.$\;\;\;\;\;$ v.$\;\;\;\;\;\;\;\;\;$ s.$\;\;\;\;\;$ v.

Scott ordered a turkey sandwich; Lee ordered tuna salad.

A semicolon may also be used with a **conjunctive adverb**. A conjunctive adverb is an adverb like *therefore, however, moreover, consequently,* or *otherwise.* It helps to join the two parts of a compound sentence. It also shows the relationship between them.

s.   v.   s.   v.

Clay parked the car; **however**, he forgot to turn off the lights.

s.   v.   s.   v.

The Dolphins won their last two games; *therefore,* they have a chance for the play-offs.

As you can see, a conjunctive adverb is used after a semicolon. A conjunctive adverb is followed by a comma.

The parts of a compound sentence are separated by either a comma or a semicolon. However, no punctuation is used between the two parts of a compound predicate. Note the following examples:

s.   v.   v.

Nectarines look like peaches but taste different.

s.   v.   v.

The batter swung at the ball and missed it.

In addition, commas are not necessary in very short compound sentences.

Snow flew and the wind howled.
They won and we lost.

Exercise A   Commas and semicolons have been omitted between the parts of the following compound sentences. For each sentence, write the two words between which punctuation belongs. Put in the comma or semicolon. If a sentence needs no punctuation, write *Correct*.

1. The volcano erupted a cloud of smoke and ash filled the air.
2. The orange crop was damaged by the frost therefore the cost of orange juice increased.

3. Dr. Robert Koch isolated the TB bacillus in 1882; however, a drug therapy was not found until 1944.

4. Dr. Shore is the dentist; Ms. Rizzo is the hygienist.

5. Carl went to the art fair, and he bought a watercolor painting.

6. Mr. Jackson hooked a marlin on the deep-sea fishing trip, but it got away.

7. The secretary composed the letter; she typed it on the word processor.

8. The Kentucky Derby is the first race in the Triple Crown, and the Preakness is the second.

9. Mark left a message on the answering machine, but no one returned his call.

c 10. Either you go or I will.

Exercise B Follow the directions for Exercise A.

1. The police questioned a suspect; however, they had to let him go.

c 2. Lightning cracked and thunder roared.

3. Sylvia likes cats, but she is allergic to them.

4. Violet parked in a no-parking zone, and she got a ticket.

5. Mr. Elliott does the bookkeeping for the company; Mr. Fernandes handles the correspondence.

6. Lakes usually contain fresh water; nevertheless, there are some saltwater lakes.

7. Lake Pontchartrain is in New Orleans; Salt Lake is in Salt Lake City.

8. Mudslides are common in California; however, people continue to build houses on hills.

9. The elm tree looks healthy, but it might have Dutch elm disease.

10. You can take a walking tour of the city, or you can take a bus tour.

Part 3

Objectives

1. To recognize and construct complex sentences
2. To recognize and identify main clauses and subordinate clauses

Presenting the Lesson

1. Read and discuss page 594. Study the definition and examples of a clause.
2. Read pages 594–595, showing how to distinguish between phrases and clauses. Be certain that students can tell the difference between clauses and phrases. Use the following for practice in identifying groups of words as phrases or clauses.

since our meeting
during study period
after we met
when the bell rings
before you leave
after the ending

3. Read page 595. Study the definitions and examples of main clauses and subordinate clauses. Remind students of earlier work on sentence fragments. Point out that subordinate clauses by themselves are fragments because although they contain subjects and verbs, they do not express complete thoughts. Discuss the meaning of the words *subordinate, dependent,* and *independent.*
4. Read page 595 and page 596, going over the explanation and examples of subordinating conjunctions. Let students practice forming subordinate clauses with each of the subordinating conjunctions.

You have learned about simple sentences and compound sentences. Another kind of sentence, the **complex sentence,** can also help you to express your thoughts.

Before you can understand the structure of a complex sentence, you must know what a clause is.

A clause is a group of words containing a verb and its subject.

With this definition, you could say that a simple sentence is a clause. It contains a verb and its subject.

s.   v.
The lawyer signed the contract.

s.   v.
Some police officers wear service revolvers.

Your study of sentence structures will be easier, however, if you think of a clause as *part of a sentence.* A clause is *a group of words within a sentence,* containing a subject and verb.

Compound sentences also contain clauses. Compound sentences have two or more groups of words containing a subject and verb. Notice these examples.

s.   v.   s.   v.
The tour stopped in San Francisco, and we visited Fisherman's Wharf.

s.   v.   s.   v.
The air controllers went on strike, but the airlines continued to operate.

Clause or Phrase?

Clauses differ from phrases. Like a clause, a phrase is part of a sentence. However, a clause has a subject and a verb. A phrase does not.

Phrases: after the dance
before breakfast

Clauses: s.   v.
after the music stopped

s.   v.
before she leaves

Subordinate Clauses

The clauses of a compound sentence are actually two separate sentences. Each one can stand alone. Each is a **main clause.** A main clause, or **independent clause,** is a clause that can stand by itself as a sentence.

Subordinate clauses, or **dependent clauses,** cannot stand alone. A subordinate clause is not a complete sentence.

s.   v.
If you enjoyed the play

s.   v.
Unless you start immediately

Both of these subordinate clauses contain subjects and verbs, but neither of them expresses a complete thought. Both leave you wondering *then what?*

The words that begin subordinate clauses have an important function. Words like *if* and *unless* are called **subordinating conjunctions.** They make the clause *dependent* on the main clause to complete its meaning. Many, though not all, subordinate clauses begin with subordinating conjunctions.

Study the following chart.

Words Often Used as Subordinating Conjunctions			
after	because	so that	when
although	before	than	whenever
as	if	though	where
as if	in order that	till	wherever
as long as	provided	unless	while
as though	since	until	

5. Assign and discuss the exercise on page 596.

6. Read and discuss the definition of a complex sentence on page 596. Then assign and discuss Exercises A and B on page 597.

Individualizing the Lesson

Less-Advanced Students

Work with students to develop a list of ten phrases. Write the phrases on the board. Have students copy each phrase, then turn it into a clause. Next have students use each clause in a sentence. Make sure students identify each clause as either a main clause or subordinate clause.

Advanced Students

Have each student write ten complex sentences; then have students underline each main clause once, and underline each subordinate clause twice.

Optional Practice

Have students identify the following clauses as *Main Clause* or *Subordinate Clause.* Students should add another clause to make each clause into a complex sentence.
Answers will vary.

S 1. When we moved into our house
S 2. Because I ran out of money
S 3. Since Jill got her job
M 4. We walked to the grocery store
M 5. Tim ran a mile
S 6. Whoever wants to contribute
S 7. Although I studied hard
S 8. Unless the weather improves
M 9. Mike applied to that school
S10. That we finished yesterday

Have students write a mystery story using the following phrases. First, they should turn each phrase into a clause and write a complex sentence. They may rearrange the order of the phrases. Have them compare their results.

1. behind the grandfather clock
2. in the fireplace
3. a dark, cluttered room
4. a sound of laughter
5. up the attic stairs
6. footprints in the dust
7. a letter on the desk
8. near the open window
9. out the back door
10. thunder and lightning

Note: the words in the chart on page 595 are subordinating conjunctions only when they begin clauses. Many of them can be used in other ways.

Furthermore, not all subordinate clauses begin with subordinating conjunctions. Some clauses begin with words like these:

that	who, whom, whose
what, whatever	whoever, whomever
which	why
how	

Exercise   Using *if, because, when, after,* and *since,* make subordinate clauses out of these sentences. Answers will vary.

1. My ride is early.
2. The towel is damp.
3. Darren enjoys tennis.
4. There is a slow leak in the tire.
5. The boutique sold only handmade items.
6. Fruit is a healthy snack.
7. The seals were sunning on the rocks.
8. Those seats are taken.
9. Peaches are on sale.
10. Estelle shopped at J.C. Penney.

Definition of the Complex Sentence

Now that you know the difference between main clauses and subordinate clauses, you can understand the complex sentence.

A complex sentence is a sentence that contains one main clause and one or more subordinate clauses.

Main Clause	Subordinate Clause
The Lakers will lose	unless Jabbar sinks this basket.
The clambake starts	when the sun goes down.
A pediatrician is a doctor	that specializes in caring for children.

Exercise A Find the (subordinate clause) in these complex sentences. Copy it, underlining the subject once and the verb twice.

1. It rained (while we were in the theater.)
2. Phyllis asked (if I liked artichoke hearts.)
3. Rob read the program (before the show began.)
4. Peggy visits the museum (whenever she gets a chance.)
5. Donna refuses to attend (unless we go.)
6. Let's hurry (before the store closes.)
7. The family posed (while Mr. Valenti focused the camera.)
8. The Mortons are moving (because Mr. Morton has been transferred.)
9. (Although Joan prefers classical music,) she enjoyed the bluegrass band.
10. (Unless it rains,) the picnic will be held at Heritage Park tomorrow.

Exercise B Follow the directions for Exercise A.

1. (Before he fixed the flat tire,) Frank set up the emergency flares.
2. Claudia got a summer job (so that she could earn money for college.)
3. Larry forgot (where he had put the keys.)
4. (When the subway doors opened,) people swarmed out onto the platform.
5. Clara can't remember (where we're supposed to meet.)
6. (Wherever you see a Red Cross flag,) there is a first aid station.
7. Mr. Rogers explained (how a thermostat works.)
8. (As the whistle blew,) the factory workers left the building.
9. Maria feels better now (than she did before lunch.)
10. No one knows (why the bridge collapsed.)

597

Part 4   Adverb Clauses

To identify subordinate adverb clauses and to understand their function

Presenting the Lesson

1. Review the definitions of the complex sentence and the subordinate clause. Stress the difference between phrase and clause, and between main clause and subordinate clause.

2. Read page 598. Go over the definition and examples of adverb clauses, emphasizing what adverb clauses tell, and what kinds of words they modify. Refer to the list of subordinating conjunctions on page 595. Point out that these words are used to introduce adverb clauses, as well as other subordinate clauses.

3. Read page 598, studying the way to diagram an adverb clause.

4. Assign and discuss Exercises A and B on page 599. Have students identify the subordinating conjunction in each sentence.

Individualizing the Lesson

Less-Advanced Students

1. Ask students for examples of an adverb phrase modifying a verb, an adjective, and an adverb.

2. Have students find an example of an adverb clause in a novel, short story, play, or scene directions in a play. Have students copy the sentence containing the clause. Then have them underline the adverb clause and draw an arrow to the word it modifies.

598

Part 4   Adverb Clauses

Subordinate clauses may be one of three kinds. One type is the **adverb clause.** It has the same function as an adverb.

An **adverb** modifies a verb, an adjective, or another adverb. It tells *how, when, where,* or *to what extent.*

>Adverb: Michael studied *diligently.*

An **adverb phrase** is a prepositional phrase used as an adverb.

>Adverb phrase: Michael studied *in the library.*

An adverb clause is a subordinate clause used as an adverb.

>Adverb clause: Michael studied *after he had finished his chores.*
>
>*When the guests arrived,* Mr. Lyons greeted them.

Adverb clauses tell *how, when, where,* and *to what extent.* They modify verbs, adjectives, and adverbs.

Remember that a clause has a subject and a verb.

Diagraming Adverb Clauses

To diagram an adverb clause, place it on a separate horizontal line below the main line. A dotted line connects the adverb clause to the word it modifies in the main clause. The subordinating conjunction is shown on the dotted line.

When the alarm rang, the police responded to the call.

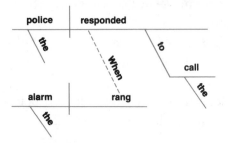

Exercise A   Copy the adverb clause from each sentence.

1. We drove <u>until we reached Kansas City</u>.
2. <u>If Marge wins the poster contest</u>, she will get a fifty dollar savings bond.
3. <u>Although the shot hurt</u>, Nancy did not complain.
4. The bridge was raised <u>as the tall ship sailed out of the harbor</u>.
5. Candy's dog always barks <u>when the telephone rings</u>.
6. We haven't heard from Erin <u>since she moved</u>.
7. The waiter prepared the flaming dessert <u>while we watched</u>.
8. The ground shook <u>as the cement mixers roared by</u>.
9. I couldn't get that book <u>because the library was closed yesterday</u>.
10. Martin said goodbye to us <u>before he left</u>.

Exercise B   Follow the directions for Exercise A.

1. Ms. Paley will substitute for Mr. Johnson <u>until he returns from jury duty</u>.
2. The carpenter measured the wood <u>before he cut it</u>.
3. <u>When the Irish came to America</u>, they were fleeing the potato famine.
4. Eric makes friends <u>wherever he goes</u>.
5. <u>Although the theater opens at noon</u>, the movie does not begin until 12:30.
6. Laura replaced the battery in her car <u>because the old one was dead</u>.
7. <u>If Joe calls</u>, please take a message.
8. <u>Whenever Martha gives a speech</u>, she gets nervous.
9. <u>Because the program started late</u>, the audience grew restless.
10. <u>Since Ned is interested in computers</u>, he is going to a computer camp.

599

599

1. To identify subordinate adjective clauses and to understand their function

2. To recognize relative pronouns and understand their function in introducing adjective clauses

Presenting the Lesson

1. Read page 600. Go over the definition and examples of adjective claues. Explain how adjective clauses function, where they are positioned, and how they are often introduced.

2. Read pages 600–601. Discuss the function of relative pronouns and study the examples carefully.

3. Read pages 601–602, studying the examples of diagrams of adjective clauses.

4. Assign and discuss Exercises A and B on pages 602–603.

Individualizing the Lesson

Less-Advanced Students

1. Have students study the explanation of relative pronouns on pages 600–601. Then have students write, in their own words, a brief explanation of the purpose of relative pronouns.

2. Have students use each relative pronoun listed on page 600 in a sentence to introduce a relative clause. Students should underscore the relative pronoun, circle the clause, and draw an arrow to the word the clause modifies.

Part 5 Adjective Clauses

A second type of subordinate clause is the **adjective clause.** An adjective clause has the same function as an adjective.

An **adjective** modifies a noun or pronoun.

Adjective: The magician wore a *tall black* hat.

An **adjective phrase** is a prepositional phrase that modifies a noun or pronoun.

Adjective phrase: Olivia read the list *of movies.*

An adjective clause is a subordinate clause used as an adjective to modify a noun or pronoun.

Adjective clause: A thesaurus is a book *that lists synonyms for words.*

Anyone *who wants a job* should read the want ads.

Adjective clauses, like adjectives and adjective phrases, tell *what kind* or *which one.* An adjective clause comes directly after the word it modifies. Unlike adjective phrases, adjective clauses have subjects and verbs.

There are several words used to introduce adjective clauses. Two of them are *where* and *when.*

This is the university *where my brother studies.*

June is the time *when schools close for the summer.*

Relative Pronouns

Besides *when* and *where,* the words *who, whom,* and *whose* are also used to begin adjective clauses. *Who, whom,* and *whose* are called **relative pronouns.** They relate a clause, called a **relative clause,** to a noun or pronoun in the sentence. Sometimes *that* and *which* are relative pronouns.

Here are the words used as relative pronouns:

who   whom   whose   that   which

Relative pronouns are special because they have three functions:

1. They introduce adjective clauses.
2. They link the clause to a word in the main clause.
3. They have a function within the clause. They act as subject, object, or predicate pronoun of the verb within the adjective clause. They may also be the object of a preposition in the clause. *Whose* functions as an adjective.

> Doctors *who treat eye diseases* are opthamologists.
> (*Who* is the subject of *treat*.)

> Mexican restaurants serve food *that is spicy*.
> (*That* is the subject of is.)

> The coach *whom we like best* is Mr. Kraus.
> (*Whom* is the direct object of *like*.)

> The partner *with whom I danced* was clumsy.
> (*Whom* is the object of the preposition *with*.)

> Parents *whose children attend that school* are protesting its closing.
> (*Whose* modifies *children*, the subject of the clause.)

Sometimes you may be confused about whether *who* or *whom* is the correct relative pronoun. To decide, see how the pronoun is used within the clause. Keep in mind that *who* is the subject form. *Whom* is the object form.

Diagraming Adjective Clauses

To diagram an adjective clause, use a separate line beneath the main line. A dotted line runs from the relative pronoun to the word in the main clause that the adjective clause modifies.

The manufacturer who makes that part is in Japan.

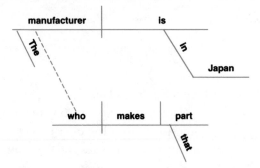

The delivery boy on whom we rely quit yesterday.

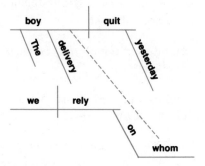

Exercise A Copy the (adjective clause) from each sentence. Underline the subject once and the verb twice. Before the clause, write the word it (modifies.)

Example: He is the author who wrote that novel.

author—who wrote that novel

1. It was the cutest (kitten) (that I had ever ever seen.)
2. The (necklace) (that I am wearing) is an antique.
3. Kirsten is the (girl) who mows our lawn.)
4. One (writer) (whom I enjoy) is Agatha Christie.
5. We bought only the (food) (that was necessary for the trip.)

6. Workers who earn a monthly salary do not get paid for overtime.
7. The personnel manager is the person to whom your application should be sent.
8. The furniture, which belonged to my grandparents, is made of white oak.
9. The house that Mr. Lee bought was built by my dad.
10. This is the brand of jeans that I like best.

Exercise B Follow the directions for Exercise A.

1. One of the prizes that Elaine won was a quartz watch.
2. The waiter who took our order has disappeared.
3. Brad is a shopper who cannot resist a sale.
4. The Oldsmobile *Cutlass*, which is a mid-size car, holds six people comfortably.
5. The room in which we met was cold.
6. Barbie made her own greeting cards, which were silk-screen prints.
7. The teacher read a list of students whose assignments were late.
8. The driver whose car hit the wall escaped without any serious injury.
9. Friday night is the night when we eat out.
10. The price, which included tax and tip, was $25.50.

Part 6 Noun Clauses

The noun clause is the third type of subordinate clause.

A noun clause is a clause used as a noun in a sentence. Like a noun, a noun clause can be used as a subject, an object of the verb, a predicate word, or an object of a preposition. It can be used in any of the ways that nouns are used. Unlike adverb and adjective clauses, noun clauses do not modify other words in the sentence.

Part 6

Objective

To identify subordinate noun clauses and to understand their function

Presenting the Lesson

1. Read pages 603–604. Discuss the construction of noun clauses

603

and their functions. Study the examples of noun clauses, noting the words with which they begin.

2. Read pages 604–605, studying diagrams of noun clauses used as subject, object of the verb, and object of the preposition.

3. Assign and discuss Exercises A and B on page 606.

Individualizing the Lesson

Less-Advanced Students

1. Have students define adverb clause, adjective clause, and noun clause. Then have them illustrate each clause in an original sentence.

2. Have students make up sentences containing noun clauses and write them on the board. Be sure there is at least one example of a noun clause used as a subject, a direct object, an object of a preposition, and a predicate noun. Label each.

Advanced Students

Have students write a letter to a friend—real or imaginary. Students should include at least one example of a noun clause used as a subject, a direct object, an object of a preposition, and a predicate noun.

Optional Practice

Have students write sentences with noun clauses introduced by the words *that, what, whatever, who, whoever, whomever, where, when, how,* and *why.* Answers will vary.

Extending the Lesson

Have students write complex sentences by adding a main clause to

Uses of Noun Clauses

Subject: *Whoever sent these flowers* forgot to sign the card.
What concerns the voters is unemployment.

Direct object: Dan knows *when the game starts.*
Kris told us *that she needed help.*

Object of preposition: The child was frightened by *whatever she saw.*
You can walk to *where we parked the car.*

Predicate noun: History is *what Jack usually reads.*
The message was *that I should call Marnie.*

As you can see from these examples, many noun clauses begin with the words *that* or *what.* The words *whatever, who, whoever,* and *whomever* can also signal noun clauses. *Where, when, how,* and *why* are used, too.

Diagraming Noun Clauses

To diagram a noun clause, extend a bridge from the place where the clause is used in the sentence. If the word that begins the clause functions simply as an introductory word, place it on a line over the clause.

1. Noun clause used as subject

What I really want is a new bike.

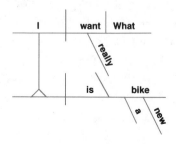

2. Noun clause used as object of the verb

The doctor said that I am in perfect health.

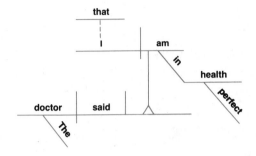

3. Noun clause used as object of a preposition

Mr. Brown will work for whoever will hire him.

4. Noun clause used as a predicate noun

One problem is that I don't have any money.

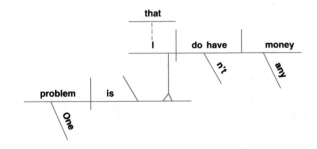

each of the following subordinate clauses. Students should tell how the noun clause functions in each sentence. Answers will vary

1. that it would rain
2. what the owner had hoped for
3. whoever hit the fly ball
4. what was really bothering him
5. whatever the committee decides
6. where the marathon is run
7. why the accident occurred
8. whoever arrives first
9. that the amendment would pass
10. how we planned the magazine

605

Exercise A   Copy the (noun clauses) in these sentences. Underline the subject once and the verb twice. Tell whether the clause is a direct object, subject, predicate noun, or object of a preposition.

DO 1. Lill explained (how the Wankel engine works.)

PN 2. Jackson Square in New Orleans is (where the Louisiana Purchase was signed.)

DO 3. Do you know (why John isn't going to the party?)

PN 4. The reason is (that he dislikes crowds.)

OP 5. We'll make soup with (whatever leftovers we have.)

DO 6. These books will give you (whatever information you need.)

OP 7. That politician gives favors to (whomever he likes.)

S 8. (Whoever planned the science fair) was very well organized.

S 9. (What I forgot) was the map.

DO 10. The truck driver wondered (where the next truck stop could be.)

Exercise B   Follow the directions for Exercise A.

DO 1. Ms. Fischer asked (why we were ten minutes late for class.)

DO 2. Lois explained (that the assembly ran late.)

PN 3. My idea is (that we organize a household help service) for senior citizens.

S 4. (How my parents met) is a funny story.

DO 5. I wonder (what the big secret is.)

S 6. (The date chosen for the junior prom) is the committee's decision.

DO 7. Todd thinks (that the test on the Constitution was difficult.)

DO 8. Freddie said (that he is allergic to milk.)

OP 9. I will lend the album to (whoever wants it.)

S 10. (What you have done in the past) always affects your future.

Part 7 A Review of Subordinate Clauses

You have learned about the three kinds of subordinate clauses. They are the adverb clause, the adjective clause, and the noun clause.

The only way to identify the kind of clause is to look at its use in the sentence. A clause used as a noun is a noun clause. A clause used as a modifier is an adverb or adjective clause, depending on the word modified.

Exercise A   Write the subordinate clause in each sentence. If the clause is used as a noun clause, tell whether it is the subject, direct object, or object of a preposition. If the clause is used as an adjective or adverb clause, tell what it modifies.

DO 1. Sean discovered where Mom had hidden the presents.

Adv 2. When the street musicians started playing, a crowd gathered.

Adj 3. San Francisco is one city where I would like to live.

DO 4. Robert forgot what he was saying.

Adj 5. Harold Washington, who is the mayor of Chicago, led the St. Patrick's Day parade.

DO 6. Emily recognized who was behind the big sunglasses.

OP 7. Mr. Bradstreet waited for whoever needed a ride.

Adj 8. The jewels that were stolen in the robbery were recovered.

Adv 9. Chris watches old movies whenever they are on TV.

Adj 10. Employees who wear uniforms to work save money on clothing.

Exercise B   Follow the directions for Exercise A.

Adv 1. Go to the information booth if you need directions.

Adj 2. The vase, which had been a gift from my aunt, fell and broke.

607

Part 7

Objective

To differentiate between noun clauses, adverb clauses, and adjective clauses

Presenting the Lesson

1. Review the definition of a subordinate clause and the three types of subordinate clauses studied. Be sure students can distinguish between phrases and clauses.

2. Read page 607. Stress that the way to determine the type of clause is to decide on its function. Certain introductory words may be clues, but many words introduce more than one type of clause.

3. Assign and discuss Exercises A and B on pages 607–608. Have students identify the subject and the verb in each subordinate clause.

Individualizing the Lesson

Less-Advanced Students

Have students define each type of subordinate clause and write a sample sentence for each type.

Advanced Students

Have students write five sentences for each type of subordinate clause. For the noun clause, students should tell how each clause is used. For the adjective and adverb clauses, students should identify what the clause modifies.

Optional Practice

Have students identify the subordinate clauses in each of the following and tell how each functions.

607

1. This is the state <u>that will determine the election</u>. Adj
2. <u>When the storm passed</u>, destruction was everywhere. Adv
3. We don't know <u>who left the basket of fruit</u>. Noun
4. <u>As we waited for summer</u>, we thought of the long, warm days ahead. Adv
5. You can do <u>whatever you like</u>. Noun

Extending the Lesson

Have students write a report on a recent book they have read or on a lengthy magazine article. Students should be sure to use each type of subordinate clause in their report.

Part 8

Objective

To avoid using subordinate clauses as sentence fragments

Presenting the Lesson

1. Review with students the definition of a complete sentence. Remind them that it must contain a subject and verb and express a complete thought.
2. Read pages 608–609. Point out that a subordinate or dependent clause must be accompanied by a main clause in order to express its idea completely. Whether a subordinate clause is a noun clause, an adverb clause, or an adjective clause, it must not be written separately from the main clause on which it depends. Students should correct a subordinate clause fragment by connecting it to a main clause.

Adj 3. Cars <u>that use diesel fuel</u> are becoming more common.
S 4. <u>Who wins the car</u> is determined by a contest.
Adj 5. The <u>usher</u> <u>who showed us our seats</u> handed us our programs.
DO 6. Liz could not remember <u>why she had tied a string around her finger</u>.
Adv 7. Ed <u>listens</u> to cassette tapes <u>while he is jogging</u>.
Adv 8. <u>While Amy was practicing her gymnastics routine</u>, she fell off the balance beam.
Adj 9. The garden is the <u>place</u> <u>where Dad spends his free time</u>.
Adv 10. <u>Before Jacqueline writes a paper</u>, she does a lot of thinking.

Part 8   Clauses as Sentence Fragments

You have studied about sentence fragments. You learned about fragments that do not have subjects and verbs.

The cat on the balcony.   Crowded into the bus.

The subordinate clause is a sentence fragment, too, even though it does have a subject and a verb. It still does not express a complete thought. For that reason, a subordinate clause is a sentence fragment. It is only part of a sentence. It is not meant to stand alone.

Notice the difference between these word groups:

The comedian cracked a few jokes.
While the comedian cracked a few jokes.

The first word group is a sentence. The subordinating conjunction *while*, however, makes the second word group a sentence fragment. A subordinate clause is only part of a sentence.

A subordinate clause must not be written as a complete sentence. It must always be joined to a main clause.

Fragment: When the snow melts.

Sentence: When the snow melts, the basement floods.

Fragment: What Mr. Allen did for a living.

Sentence: No one knew what Mr. Allen did for a living.

Fragment: Where we go.

Sentence: Where we go depends on how much time we have.

Exercise A   Number your paper from 1 to 10. Decide whether the groups of words below are sentences or fragments. Write *S* for *Sentence* and *F* for *Fragment*. Add words to make each fragment a complete sentence. Punctuate and capitalize where necessary.

Answers will vary.

F   1. What the messenger brought

S   2. What does Martha want?

S   3. When is the algebra test?

F   4. After the senior class luncheon

S   5. After lunch everyone went home.

S   6. That jingle is catchy.

F   7. The dress that you wanted

F   8. Before the speaker began

F   9. Why the audience is cheering

S 10. Why is Emily laughing?

Exercise B   Follow the directions for Exercise A.

F   1. Why the restaurant is successful

F   2. Since we were too late

S   3. Whose shoes are these?

F   4. When French Club meets in the library

F   5. Before breakfast was served

S   6. Before dinner Alex studies.

S   7. That is the landmark.

S   8. Where is the nearest mailbox?

F   9. If the dog stays in the kennel

F 10. Because Margaret works part time

609

3. Assign and discuss Exercises A and B on page 609.

Individualizing the Lesson

Less-Advanced Students

Work with students to compile a list of subordinate clauses that are sentence fragments. Then have students complete the clauses on their own.

Advanced Students

Have students write ten subordinate clauses. Then have students exchange papers. Students should copy each clause and join it to a main clause. Make sure they punctuate and capitalize where necessary.

Optional Practice

Have students decide whether the following groups of words are sentences or fragments. Have them make each fragment a complete sentence and punctuate as necessary. Answers will vary.

F 1. When he hit a line drive

F 2. While I was eating a box of crackers

S 3. That was the warning bell.

F 4. That the car needs a tune-up

F 5. Whenever the wind howls

Extending the Lesson

Have students revise the following paragraph.

We contacted the telephone company. Because our phone was not working. They sent a worker. Who was unable to find the problem. After two more service calls. The problem was located. A squirrel had upset the wires. That connect our telephone to the main cable.

To recognize and construct compound-complex sentences

Presenting the Lesson

1. Review with students the definitions of compound sentences (Part 2) and complex sentences (Part 3).

2. Read page 610, defining compound-complex sentences. Study the examples, making certain students can differentiate between main clauses and subordinate clauses.

3. Assign and discuss the Exercise on pages 610–611.

Individualizing the Lesson

Less-Advanced Students

Have students find published examples of five compound-complex sentences. Students should underline each subjunctive clause and circle each main clause.

Advanced Students

Give students four subordinate clauses and six main clauses. Have them write as many complex sentences as they can. The sentences may be humorous, but they should make sense.

Optional Practice

Have students identify the two main clauses and the subordinate clause in these compound-complex sentences.

1. Louise looked at her notes, and she suddenly realized what she had forgotten.

610

Part 9 Compound-Complex Sentences

You have already been introduced to simple, compound, and complex sentences. The fourth and final kind of sentence is the **compound-complex sentence.**

A compound-complex sentence consists of two or more main clauses and one or more subordinate clauses.

It may help you to think of a compound-complex sentence as a compound sentence plus a subordinate clause. Actually, the compound-complex sentence joins two sentences, at least one of which has a subordinate clause. The clause may be an adjective, adverb, or noun clause. The main clauses are joined by either a coordinating conjunction or a semicolon.

These are examples of compound-complex sentences:

Main Clause | Main Clause

Doug searched for an hour, but he couldn't find the book

Subordinate Clause

that he wanted.

Subordinate Clause | Main Clause | Main Clause

When the pioneers traveled, they needed salt; it was the only preservative for their food.

Exercise Identify the two main clauses and the subordinate clause in these compound-complex sentences.

1. Dad liked the golf shirt that I gave him, but it didn't fit.

2. Colonial Virginia needed no port cities; plantations were built on rivers that led to the sea.

3. Ms. Brookman showed us how the potter's wheel works, and then we tried it ourselves.

4. The guard dogs are caged during the day, but they are turned loose in the store after it closes.

5. Sacajawea was a sixteen-year-old Shoshone Indian girl; moreover, she was the guide who led the Lewis and Clark Expedition.

6. The tulips that we planted last fall came up beautifully in the spring; this year we'll plant even more.

7. Tracy liked the scarf that I had knitted, so I made one for her, too.

8. Craig realized that he had forgotten his wallet; consequently, he went back for it.

9. Swimming, which has been called the perfect exercise, requires endurance, but it doesn't put stress on the body joints.

10. The child confided to the babysitter that he could not sleep; therefore, the sitter read him a story.

Part 10   A Review of Sentences

There are four basic kinds of sentences.

A **simple sentence** contains one subject and one predicate. Parts of the simple sentence, however, may be a compound. A simple sentence tells one idea.

        s.   v.
The airline cancelled the flight.

    s.   v.   v.
Rod stood in line and bought the tickets.

A **compound sentence** is made up of two simple sentences. These simple sentences are connected by a comma and coordinating conjunction or by a semicolon. Sometimes a conjunctive adverb follows the semicolon. A compound sentence expresses two related ideas.

       s.   v.   s.   v.
The airline cancelled the flight; the ticket agent notified the passengers.

    s.   v.   s.   v.
Rod stood in line, and he bought the tickets.

611

Extending the Lesson

Have students write five compound-complex sentences of their own.

Part 10

Objective

To review the four types of sentences: simple, compound, complex, and compound-complex

Presenting the Lesson

1. Read pages 611–612. Study the definitions and examples of each of the four sentence types. Point out that the subordinate clauses are printed in italics. Have students compare sentence types in terms of how many clauses—both main and subordinate—each has.

2. Do Exercise A on pages 612–613 as a class activity. Have each sentence written on the chalk-

board, and have students mark *s* and *v* over all subjects and verbs. Also, have students underline main clauses once and subordinate clauses twice.

3. Assign and discuss Exercise B on page 613. If the class needs extra guidance, follow the procedure outlined above for Exercise A.

Individualizing the Lesson

Less-Advanced Students

1. Discuss simple, compound, complex, and compound-complex sentences with students. Have students give examples of each type of sentence to be written on the chalkboard. Then have students underline the subordinate clause and circle the main clause in each sentence.

2. Have students find published examples of each type of sentence. Students should copy the sentences, underline the subordinate clauses, and circle the main clauses.

Advanced Students

1. Have students write ten sentences. Tell them to make sure to write at least two of each kind of sentence—simple, compound, complex, and compound-complex. Then have students exchange papers.

2. Students should identify each type of sentence, underscore any subordinate clauses, and circle the main clauses.

Optional Practice

Have students identify the following sentences as simple, compound, complex, or compound-complex.

612

A **complex sentence** contains one main clause and one or more subordinate clauses. The subordinate clauses may be used as adverbs, adjectives, or nouns. A complex sentence expresses one main idea and one or more dependent ideas.

Because the runway was icy, the airline cancelled the flight.

Although the line was long, Rod got the tickets.

A **compound-complex sentence** contains two main clauses and one or more subordinate clauses. The subordinate clauses may be adverb, adjective, or noun clauses. A compound-complex sentence expresses two main ideas, as well as one dependent idea.

The airline cancelled the flight; the ticket agent notified the passengers *that they would be delayed*.

Although the line was long, Rod stood in it, and he got the tickets.

Exercise A Number your paper from 1 to 10. For each sentence, write *Simple, Compound, Complex,* or *Compound-Complex* to show what kind it is.

s 1. Why did Mr. Lawrence go to New Hampshire?

s 2. Mr. Kramer not only designed the house but also built it.

s 3. The picnic basket contained fried chicken, potato salad, and fresh strawberries.

cc 4. Phil asked why the train was late, and the conductor explained.

s 5. What a glorious day this is!

cx 6. When Ms. Flaherty went on vacation, she forgot her travelers' checks but remembered her credit cards.

612

CX 7. George thinks that he did well on the exam.

CX 8. Since time was running short, we took a cab to the concert hall.

CX 9. Anna put some of the sprouts that she had grown from alfalfa seeds into the tomato and avocado salad.

CX 10. Out in the yard sat an old pick-up truck that hadn't run for years.

Exercise B Follow the directions for Exercise A.

CX 1. Mom reads the newspaper while she rides the train to work.

CX 2. Before Bill dove into the pond, he checked its depth.

CC 3. The secretary answered the phone as soon as he could, but the caller had already hung up.

C 4. The waiter brought us water and menus, and then he took our order.

S 5. After skating, we went home and made hot chocolate.

C 6. Did you paint the house, or did you put up aluminum siding?

CX 7. Who said that love is blind?

CX 8. We stacked the wood that we had chopped into a neat pile next to the garage.

CC 9. If it is a nice day, we can go to the zoo, or if it rains, we can go to the museum.

C 10. Mr. Beach, the geography teacher, knew that the students needed a chapter review; therefore, he made a study guide.

S 1. The custodian arrived and fixed the broken desk.

Cx 2. The magazines that you need for your report are in the reference room.

CC 3. Mother lit the candles and Father said the blessing before we ate.

CX 4. Because the book is copyrighted, you must not photocopy it.

S 5. Jessica and Aaron have been rehearsing their dance number for three weeks.

Cx 6. Although they are bad for her posture, Maryann insists on wearing those high heels.

S 7. The highway patrol officer stopped me and asked to see my license.

Cp 8. The concert began and everyone relaxed and enjoyed it.

CC 9. If the winters continue to be cold, we may run out of natural gas; consequently, we must conserve fuel now.

S 10. The tables and chairs were scattered and upset by the crowds.

Extending the Lesson

Read sentences aloud to the class and see how quickly students can identify the sentences as simple, compound, complex, or compound-complex. Have students try to identify the main and subordinate clauses as well. This can also be done spelling-bee style.

Review

ADDITIONAL EXERCISES

Using Compound and Complex Sentences

A. Simple Sentences Label four columns *Subject, Verb, Direct Object,* and *Predicate Word.* Place the parts of the sentence in the appropriate columns. Some parts may be compound.

1. During the winter Jan shoveled snow for her neighbors.
2. The hubcap fell off and clattered down the highway.
3. The emergency room is always open and always full.
4. The Orioles and the Angels have solid pitching staffs.
5. Superman and Batman have amazed children for years.
6. We bought corn and peaches at a roadside stand.
7. The thermos smelled musty and sour.
8. Do you play ice hockey or field hockey?
9. Move your wrists but not your elbows.
10. Gil and Les found spare parts and repaired the bicycle.

B. Simple and Compound Sentences Copy these sentences. Underline each subject once and each verb twice. After each sentence write *Simple* or *Compound* to show what kind it is.

c 1. Some Islamic women wear veils, but others do not.
c 2. The fare increased, but the service was no better.
s 3. Rafael is shy but has a good sense of humor.
s 4. Debra applied for a job at IBM and got it.
c 5. The snow has melted, and soon the trees will bud.
s 6. Dawn set the fishbowl down too hard and cracked it.
c 7. Dawn set the fishbowl down too hard, and it cracked.
s 8. Mel pulled himself up and stood, but again lost his balance.
s 9. Ms. Canchola lengthened the coat, lined it, and replaced the buttons.
s 10. Some vegetarians will not eat eggs or drink milk.

C. Punctuation of Compound Sentences
Number your paper from 1 to 10. Write the last word of the *first* part of each compound sentence. Next write the proper punctuation mark. Then write the first word of the *second* part of the compound sentence.

1. A marshmallow is a spongy candy, but a marsh mallow is a flowering plant.
2. Many players dislike artificial turf; nevertheless, they must play on it.
3. The beanbag chair had a small rip in its cover, and the filling was leaking out.
4. We must catch that train; it's the last one today.
5. Barb added some garlic to the sauce, and the flavor improved.
6. Will you pick an album, or shall I choose one?
7. Ernie will use the bonus for a vacation, or maybe he will save it.
8. The truck weighs three tons, it cannot stop very fast.
9. After the explosion the plant was closed; moreover, the area around it was evacuated.
10. The map is old, but it will serve as a general guide.

D. Adverb Clauses
Copy the (adverb clause) in each sentence. Underline the subject once and the verb twice. Draw a circle around the subordinating conjunction.

1. (Because Ed works after school,) he values his free time. Because
2. The African Emperor Taharga led his armies into battle (when he was sixteen.) when
3. (Since Ian had been benched,) Cal got a chance to play. Since
4. (After the other guests had left,) Danny stayed and helped with the dishwashing. After
5. After her defeat, Natalie trained harder (than she ever had before.) than
6. Since the night before, Tracy had studied (as hard as she could.) as hard as

7. Call me (if you get a chance.) if

8. (If you will clean the grill,) I'll barbecue the ribs. If

9. (After the elm trees died,) the street never looked as pretty. After

10. It looks (as though the snow won't stop before morning.) as though

E. Adjective Clauses Copy the (adjective clause) from each sentence. Underline the subject once and the verb twice. After each clause, write the word it modifies.

1. Ms. Simmons and Mr. Moore are the only choir members (who can do justice to that spiritual.) members

2. The cabinet (where the supplies are kept) is in here. cabinet

3. Where did Karen put the card (that I brought?) card

4. The priest comforted the people (whose relatives had been injured.) people

5. After the wrestling match, we looked for a restaurant (that was still open.) restaurant

6. Red and green are colors (that are opposite each other on a color wheel.) colors

7. The American chameleon, (which is really an anole,) can grow a new tail. chameleon

8. Which are the months (when hurricanes most often occur?) months

9. The woman (for whom Ty worked) gave him a good reference. woman

10. The odds (that we will see you at the festival) are quite good. odds

F. Noun Clauses Copy the noun clause in each sentence. Tell how the clause is used.

DO 1. Rosa said (that she would be here before dinner.)

DO 2. Alice knew (who would get the credit.)

DO 3. In the fog, Liz could hardly see (what was ahead.)

DO 4. How do you know (what happened?)

DO 5. Nicole explained (how an electric car operates.)

S 6. (Why traffic laws are necessary) is obvious.

PN 7. Clyde's worst fault is (that he's always apologizing.)

OP 8. Write about (whatever you know best.)

OP 9. Give the piano to (whoever will haul it away.)

DO 10. (Who) do you think (will win the pennant?)

G. Subordinate Clauses   Write the (subordinate clause) in each sentence. Tell whether it is an *Adverb*, *Adjective*, or *Noun Clause*.

Adj 1. That was the cheese (that I had saved for the pizza.)

N 2. Many people dream (that they can fly.)

Adj 3. Sabrina has dreams (in which she can fly.)

N 4. Weekends are (when the family has breakfast together.)

Adj 5. There were times (when we wanted to turn back.)

Adv 6. Althea practiced only (when she felt like it.)

Adv 7. Stay in the storm cellar (until the tornado siren stops.)

N 8. Who knows (where these pipes lead?)

Adj 9. After that, the cab driver helped passengers (who seemed confused.)

Adv 10. Why doesn't he look at people (when they talk to him?)

H. Sentence Fragments   Decide whether the groups of words below are sentences or fragments. Write *S* for *Sentence* and *F* for *Fragment*.

F 1. The rainbow that the spacecraft left at the end of *E.T.*

F 2. When the awards assembly is

S 3. When is the awards assembly

S 4. After the ice storm the highway was closed

F 5. After Julia had checked the lost and found department

F 6. While the fields are being plowed

S 7. While washing the dishes, Will listens to the radio

S 8. That does not surprise me at all

F 9. That I was right about the address

S 10. Who knows the answer

I. Compound-Complex Sentences Make three columns. Label them (1) *Verb, First Main Clause;* (2) *Verb, Second Main Clause;* and (3) *Verb, Subordinate Clause.* Put the verbs from each sentence into the correct column.

1. Our morale fell when Joey was injured, and we played poorly after that.
2. The fireball that struck Siberia in 1908 exploded with as much force as an H-bomb, but the impact left no crater.
3. Hilary explained how to tie a square knot, and Don muttered that a picture was worth a thousand words.
4. The car was old, but June liked the fact that the mileage was low.
5. Anthony recognized the customer who was wearing dark glasses, and he waited on her with extra courtesy.
6. Do you want to look through the books before I give them away, or have you already seen them?
7. Check the guarantee if the watch doesn't work; maybe the manufacturer will repair it.
8. Because the princess was born at the end of a drought, her original name meant "Little White Cloud"; only later did she become Pocahontas.
9. One of the world's plant or animal species becomes extinct every day, and conservationists worry that a million species may be gone by the year 2000.
10. While Kim was in Atlanta, she rode a roller coaster called the Mindbender; it offered full-circle loops, dark tunnels, and horrifying drops.

J. Kinds of Sentences For each sentence, write *Simple, Compound, Complex,* or *Compound-Complex.*

c 1. Pauline and Laura gathered the pages together, and Matt stapled them.

S 2. Until midnight Jerome rehearsed his speech.

CC 3. Jane steered the jeep down the muddy road to the river, and then she discovered that the bridge had collapsed.

C 4. The callouses on Martina's hands are not from work; they are from climbing the rope in gym.

CX 5. Long ago, soldiers bit on bullets while they were having surgery.

S 6. Why didn't Art applaud after the play?

CX 7. Tina asked why Midsummer's Eve comes in June.

CX 8. The witness who testified was brave.

S 9. Who wants to look around the shopping mall for a while?

C 10. The tide came in and our raft returned.

MIXED REVIEW

Using Compound and Complex Sentences

A.   Identifying sentences and fragments   Decide whether the following groups of words are sentences or fragments. If a group is a sentence, write *S*. If a group is a fragment, write *F*. Then write whether the fragment is a *phrase* or a *clause*.

F   1. If there are living creatures on Mars, Venus, and Pluto ^{clause}

S   2. If I fall, catch me

F   3. Since her birthday party last January _{phrase}

F   4. Since Julia is next in line _{clause}

S   5. Mike has been running daily since he joined the team

S   6. Which switch will turn the computer off

F   7. Which the previous owner did not mention _{clause}

F   8. Until yesterday afternoon _{phrase}

F   9. Because my name is not on the list _{clause}

S 10. Until then Roy had worked

B.   Identifying kinds of sentences   For each of the following sentences write *Simple*, *Compound*, *Complex*, or *Compound-Complex* to tell what kind it is.

CX 1. The team that wins today will play in the Rose Bowl.

C 2. The door was open, and I got up to shut it.

S 3. Quentin and Gil were joking and laughing.

CX 4. Hannibal, who was a general, used elephants in battle.

S 5. That is hardly the point.

S 6. After the long hike, Jody slept deeply and did not wake up until the next morning.

CX 7. When there is a disaster, the Red Cross and other re-lief agencies often work together.

CX 8. When will the pizza that you ordered arrive?

S 9. When does the popcorn counter in the lobby close?

CX 10. That the driver was a beginner became clear.

C. Recognizing subordinate clauses Copy the (subordinate clause.) Underline its subject once and its verb twice. Then write *Adverb, Adjective,* or *Noun* to show what kind of clause it is.

Adv 1. A helicopter can fly much lower (than a plane does.)

Adv 2. (Since the highway was built,) the signs have rusted.

N 3. I wonder (what Cheryl wanted.)

Adj 4. Who is the woman (who is ringing the doorbell?)

Adj 5. The sweatpants (that Frank was wearing) were gray.

N 6. Before long, I sensed (that the undertow was strong.)

Adv 7. Al asked (because he was curious.)

N 8. The reporter asked (where he could find a telephone.)

Adv 9. Why did you swim (where there are sea urchins?)

Adj 10. Put the plant on a windowsill (where it will get sun.)

D. Using subordinate clauses correctly Copy the (subordinate clause) from each of the following sentences. Write *Noun, Adjective,* or *Adverb* to show what kind it is. If the clause is used as a noun, write *Subject, Direct Object, Object of Preposition,* or *Predicate Noun* to show what part of the sentence it is. If the clause is used as an adjective or adverb, write the word it modifies.

Adj 1. A driver (who makes a right turn on red) must give pedestrians the right of way.

Adj 2. Bob Marley was the singer (for whom a monument was put up.)

Adj 3. Egypt is not the only country (where there are pyramids.)

N 4. Where did you say (that you were going?) DO

N 5. (Whoever signs the equipment out) must return it. S

Adj 6. Anybody (who shops here) must pay cash.

Adv 7. Who could study (while that noise was going on?)

Adj 8. (As I have said before,) I prefer wearing jeans.

Adv 9. A pound of lead is no heavier (than a pound of feathers is.)

N 10. Al told us (that he planned to surprise Ed.) DO

USING GRAMMAR IN WRITING
Using Compound and Complex Sentences

A.   Compound sentences joined by *and* are useful for showing that two things are similar. Compound sentences joined by *but* show a contrast. The conjunction *or* in a compound sentence shows a choice. Use these kinds of compound sentences to write a prediction of ways that everyday life will change in the future. For example, you might write:

> Most people will live longer, *but* more of them will need expensive medical care.

At least one compound sentence should show that two of your predictions are similar. Another should show a contrast. A third should show a choice.

B.   You will find complex sentences useful for stating opinions. The subordinate clause can give a reason for the opinion or show the result of an action. Study the following examples.

> People should use automobile seat belts because belts reduce the number of serious injuries in accidents.

> If more people ate meals standing up, the furniture industry would collapse.

Write five complex sentences stating reasons why something should be or would be so. Use one clause to state the thing that should or would be. Use the other to give a reason for it. Your sentences may be serious or humorous.

CUMULATIVE REVIEW

The Sentence

A. Identifying kinds of sentences Copy the following sentences. Insert the correct punctuation. After each sentence, write *D* for declarative, *INT* for interrogative, *IMP* for imperative, or *E* for exclamatory. Underline each subject once and each verb twice.

Imp 1. Put the tractor in the barn. (You)

D 2. Playing cards were first used in China.

D 3. Are those boots waterproof.

Ex 4. What a magnificent view this is!

D 5. Louis XIV was called the Sun King.

B. Understanding agreement in sentences Write the correct word from the two given in parentheses.

1. Either flowers or a plant (make, makes) a nice gift.
2. Some of the job applicants (seem, seems) prepared.
3. Most of the files (is, are) incomplete.
4. One of these diamond bracelets (is, are) a fake.
5. Where (was, were) those old fishing poles?
6. Evie (don't, doesn't) understand that poem.
7. Here (is, are) the shampoo and a towel.
8. Everyone made (his or her, their) own sundae.
9. That box of recipes (is, are) from my grandmother.
10. Where (was, were) the snow shovel?

C. Correcting fragments and run-on sentences The following paragraph contains fragments and run-on sentences. Rewrite the paragraph. Use capitalization and punctuation to correct the fragments and run-ons. Do not add or change any words.

> The bald eagle, our national emblem! Was chosen by our founding fathers in 1782. Not all Americans wanted the bald eagle for a symbol; some wanted the golden eagle. Since the golden eagle was also found on other

623

Cumulative Review

These exercises are designed to cover broad areas of grammar, usage, and mechanics. They require the application of skills taught thus far in the text. The exercises may be used for testing purposes, or as an excellent resource for review.

continents. It was rejected for the national emblem. Although the bald eagle is a distinctive looking bird. Benjamin Franklin wanted the wild turkey as the national emblem. he thought the bald eagle was not a noble bird. And it is cowardly it preys on smaller and weaker osprey. Which are a kind of hawk. The bald eagle. Is truly a controversial bird. It has been killed by Alaskan fishermen. Who thought it was destroying the salmon. It has been killed by hunters. For sport. DDT has harmed the population growth of bald eagles. land development has ruined many nesting and wintering areas. By the 1940's. The bald eagle was in danger. Of extinction. Now, with the Endangered Species Act. The bald eagle is a protected species. The bald eagle will stay a part of the American wilderness.

D. Writing good sentences Rewrite each of the following sentences. Follow the directions in the parentheses. Answers will vary.

1. Ingrid sent the graduation gift by mail. (Add the prepositional phrase *for her cousin*.)
2. Eric is taking karate lessons. Eve is taking them, too. (Combine these two sentences into one with a compound subject.)
3. The mechanic charged the battery. The car still wouldn't start. (Combine these two simple sentences into one compound sentence using **, but.**)
4. Gerald Ford spoke at the museum's fund-raising dinner. He was the 38th president of the United States. (Combine these two simple sentences into one complex sentence using *who*.)
5. Allison has a good voice. She didn't try out for the school musical. (Combine these two simple sentences into one complex sentence using *although*.)
6. Aretha baked for the party. (Change this NV sentence to one with a NVN pattern.)

The Right Word

Section Objectives

1. To understand the difference between standard and nonstandard English and to know the advantage of using standard English

2. To distinguish between words that are often confused, and to use them correclty

3. To use troublesome pairs of verbs correctly

4. To use problem words correctly

Preparing the Students

Explain to students that a person's level of education, background, and social milieu can account for differences in language. Stress that while language is a personal thing, there are still standards that are established to help language do its most important function—to communicate with others.

Read the introduction on page 625.

Additional Resources

Diagnostic Test — page 10 in the test booklet

Mastery Test — pages 68–69 in the test booklet

Additional Exercises — pages 638–641 in the student text

Practice Book — pages 236–242

Duplicating Masters — pages 236–242

Special Populations — See special section at the front of this Teacher's Edition.

There are certain words in the English language that are often used incorrectly. It is important to know how to use these words correctly in order to write clear standard English.

Standard English is the language of educated people. It is the language that would be judged correct by people in most situations. **Non-standard English** is not generally considered correct in all situations.

In this section, you will learn to use certain troublesome words correctly. By learning to use these words correctly, you can improve your use of standard English.

625

Objective

To distinguish between words that are often confused, and to use them correctly

Presenting the Lesson

This part covers twelve sets of homonyms which are often confused. Pace your presentation of the words according to the class's ability to absorb the words. You may want to present three or four sets of words at a time, spreading the lessons over several days. In presenting the words, follow this procedure:

1) Read the words, noting carefully the differences in spelling. It may help students visualize the differences between words if you underline the distinctive parts or use colored chalk to highlight them. 2) Go over the definitions of each word, offering students helpful ways to distinguish the words ("the Capitol has a dome"; "stationery is made of paper".) 3) Go over the sentences that use the words. 4) Ask students to write one or two sentences using each word. 5) Assign and discuss Exercises A and B on pages 628–629.

Individualizing the Lesson

Less-Advanced Students

Give students a spelling test on words often confused using the list on pages 626–628. Have students write the word, then use it in a sentence.

Part 1 Words Often Confused

The words listed in this section are often misused. The pairs of words may look alike or have similar meanings. However, they are not the same. One word cannot be used in place of the other. Study the lists of words often confused. Try to use the right word at the right time.

capital means "most important." It also names the city or town that is the official center of government for a state or country.

capitol refers to the building where a state legislature meets.

the Capitol is the building in Washington, D.C., where the United States Congress meets.

> The *capital* of California is Sacramento.
> Have you ever toured the state *capitol* building in Springfield?
> The newscaster reported the story from the *Capitol* in Washington.

des' ert means "a dry, barren region."

de sert' means "to abandon."

des sert' (note the difference in spelling) is "a sweet food at the end of a meal."

> Camels are called ships of the *desert*.
> Did the mother bird *desert* the babies?
> Kathy made apple crisp for *dessert*.

hear means "to listen to" or "to receive sound by the ear."

here refers to this place.

> You could *hear* the siren for miles.
> The meeting will be *here* in the library.

its is a possessive, meaning "belonging to *it*."

it's is the contraction for *it is* or *it has*.

> Put the typewriter into *its* case.
> *It's* time to go.

loose means either "not tight" or "free and untied."

lose means "to be unable to find or keep." It is also the opposite of *win*.

> The doorknob is *loose*.
> I *lose* my sense of direction in a strange place.
> Did you *lose* the race?

principal means "leading," "chief," or "highest in importance." It also refers to the head of an elementary or high school.

principle refers to a basic truth, rule, or law.

> Ed spoke to the *principal* about his problem.
> San Francisco is one of the *principal* cities of California.
> The *principle* I value most is honesty.

stationary means "not moving, fixed."

stationery refers to writing materials like paper and envelopes.

> The room dividers are *stationary*.
> Clair wrote on yellow *stationery*.

their shows possession by *them*.

there means "in that place."

they're is the contraction for *they are*.

> The twins have *their* own room.
> Put your boots *there* in the hallway.
> *They're* leaving for Dallas tomorrow.

to means "toward" or "as far as."

too means "also" or "extremely."

two is the number 2.

> Kelly wrote a letter *to* Gloria.
> The oven is *too* hot.
> *Two* of the meeting rooms are free.

weather refers to the condition of the atmosphere, such as its heat, cold, wetness, or dryness.

Have students use twenty-five of the words from the list on pages 626–628 in original sentences. Have students exchange papers to be sure the words have been spelled and used correctly.

Optional Practice

Have students read the following sentences, looking for incorrect use of the words presented in this Part. Students should correct errors and be prepared to tell why the corrections are necessary. If a sentence contains no errors, it should be marked *Correct*.

1. We didn't know ~~weather~~ *whether* the ~~whether~~ *weather* would improve.
2. It's so hot in the desert that ~~your~~ *you're* likely to become ill.
3. The principal reason I went out was to buy stationery, but it was ~~to~~ *too* expensive.

C 4. You're foolish not to visit the state capitol during your vacation.

5. ~~Whose~~ *Who's* going to be the winner? I know I will lose.
6. The crew did not want to ~~dessert~~ *desert* the ship, but it became too dangerous to stay on board.
7. The pipe is supposed to be stationary, but ~~its~~ *it's* loose.
8. Do you mean ~~your to~~ *you're too* full for dessert?
9. The protesters remained at the ~~capital~~ *capitol* on principle.
10. The Congress is voting in the Capitol on the issue of capital punishment; ~~their~~ *they're* deciding whether it is ~~to~~ *too* harsh a punishment for any crime.

Extending the Lesson

Have students use the following words in sentences of their own.

1. principal   4. lose
2. you're   5. too
3. their   6. capital

whether indicates a choice between two things.

> Did you listen to the *weather* forecast?
> Dan can't decide *whether* or not to quit his job.

who's is the contraction for *who is* or *who has*.

whose is the possessive form of *who*.

> *Who's* playing the piano?
> *Whose* lunch is this?

your shows possession by *you*.

you're is the contraction for *you are* or *you were*.

> Here are *your* gloves.
> *You're* the winner.

Exercise A   Choose the right word from the words given.

1. The soldier (deserted, desserted) his unit.
2. Cactus plants grow in the (desert, dessert).
3. The Arabs wear (loose, lose) robes.
4. Will they (loose, lose) the game if Payton doesn't play?
5. (Its, It's) snowing in the Rocky Mountains.
6. Put the canary back in (its, it's) cage.
7. The (capital, Capitol, capitol) of Kentucky is Frankfort.
8. The track is (stationary, stationery); the light fixtures are moveable.
9. The country fought for its (principals, principles).
10. Jenny will meet us (hear, here) at noon.

Exercise B   Follow the directions for Exercise A.

1. The water in Lake Michigan was (to, too, two) cold for swimming.
2. The customer complained (to, too, two) the manager.
3. Polly and Sue researched (their, there, they're) topics.
4. When (their, there, they're) through practicing, they will rehearse with Ms. Carlson.

5. The tape recorder is over (their, <u>there</u>, they're).

6. Michele considered (weather, <u>whether</u>) or not to join Pep Club.

7. (<u>Who's</u>, Whose) turn is it?

8. (<u>Who's</u>, Whose) making dinner tonight?

9. (<u>Your</u>, You're) prize is a $25.00 gift certificate.

10. (Your, <u>You're</u>) not feeling well, are you?

Part 2 Troublesome Verbs

These pairs of verbs are often confused. Notice how they differ.

Bring and *Take*

Bring refers to movement toward the person speaking. Example: The pipeline *brings* water here to the desert.

Take refers to motion away from the speaker. Example: Did you *take* those books back to the library?

Here are the principal parts of these verbs:

bring, brought, brought

Present: *Bring* your camera along.

Past: They *brought* too much luggage.

Past Participle: Linda *has brought* the new album.

take, took, taken

Present: *Take* this message to Mr. Gray.

Past: He *took* his brother to the park.

Past Participle: Sara *has taken* my bicycle.

Learn and *Teach*

Learn means "to gain knowledge or skill." Example: When did you *learn* how to cook?

Teach means "to help someone learn." Example: Will you *teach* me that dive?

629

Part 2

Objective

To use troublesome pairs of verbs correctly

Presenting the Lesson

This Part covers seven pairs of verbs that are often confused. Pace your presentation of the verb pairs according to the class's ability to remember them. You may want to present two or three sets of verbs at a time, spreading the lessons over several days. In presenting the verb pairs, follow this procedure: 1) Read the verbs and the definition and usage guidelines given for each. 2) Study the example for each word, pointing out how the use in that sentence fits each definition. 3) Study the principal parts of each verb, and the examples using each of the principal parts. 4) Have students use each of the principal parts in sentences. 5) Assign and discuss Exercises A and B on pages 632–633.

Individualizing the Lesson

Less-Advanced Students

1. Have students write each troublesome verb on pages 629–632 along with its definition.

629

2. Have students use the verbs *not* used in Exercises A and B, pages 632–633, in original sentences.

Advanced Students

Have students find five published examples of the troublesome verbs listed. Students should copy the example sentence, write the applicable definition after the sentence, and write an original sentence for the other verb of the pair.

Optional Practice

Have students read the following sentences, looking for incorrect use of the verbs presented in this Part. Students should correct errors and be prepared to tell why the corrections are necessary. If a sentence contains no errors, it should be marked *Correct*.

C 1. Use the car to bring the books back to the library.
C 2. The sitter let the child stay up past her bedtime.
3. Frank learned me how to play chess. *taught*
C 4. If you lie in the sun too long, you may get burned.
5. At school, we rise the flag every morning. *raise*
6. We set in the fourth row of the bleachers. *sat*
C 7. Ask Mr. Simmons if you may take his chair.
C 8. When the delivery person brings the package, ask him to set it on the porch.
C 9. Lay the notebooks on the table.
10. The trainer is learning the dogs to set. *teaching* *sit*

Here are the principal parts of these verbs:

learn, learned, learned
Present: *Learn* the song by next week.
Past: The children *learned* the multiplication tables.
Past Participle: We *have learned* two magic tricks.

teach, taught, taught
Present: Ms. Stein *teaches* swimming.
Past: Lucy *taught* me about gardening.
Past Participle: This book *has taught* me a lot about the Civil War.

Let and Leave

Let means "to allow or permit." Example: *Let* her go.
Leave means "to go away from" or "to allow something to remain." Example: *Leave* your coats here.
The principal parts of these verbs are as follows:

let, let, let
Present: *Let* the phone ring.
Past: Sylvia *let* her hair grow long.
Past Participle: The mayor *will let* us interview her.

leave, left, left
Present: *Leave* the door open.
Past: Mark *left* on Tuesday.
Past Participle: The taxi *had left* in a hurry.

Lie and Lay

Lie means "to rest in a flat position" or "to be in a certain place." Example: *Lie* still.
Lay means "to place." Example: *Lay* the wreath here.
The principal parts of these verbs are on the next page.

lie, lay, lain

Present:	*Lie* down on your bed.
Past:	Harry *lay* in the hammock all afternoon.
Past Participle:	The dog *has lain* by the fire all night.

lay, laid, laid

Present:	*Lay* the books on the desk.
Past:	The hen *laid* an egg.
Past Participle:	Dad *has laid* the carpeting.

May and Can

May refers to permission. *May* also refers to something that is possible. *Might* is another form of the word.

May we go to the concert?   I *might be* a little late.

Can refers to ability. *Can* means being physically or mentally able to do something. *Could* is another form.

Can you play the piano?   We *could* walk to the beach.

May and *might* and *can* and *could* are helping verbs.

Rise and Raise

Rise means "to go upward." Example: The sun *rises*.
Raise means "to lift or to make something go up." It also means "to grow." Example: *Raise* your right hand.
The principal parts of these verbs are as follows:

rise, rose, risen

Present:	Did you see the moon *rise?*
Past:	Dale *rose* from his chair.
Past Participle:	The temperature *has risen* to 80°.

raise, raised, raised

Present:	Please *raise* the flag.
Past:	Lynn *raised* these tomatoes.
Past Participle:	The school *has raised* its tuition.

631

Sit and *Set*

Sit means "to occupy a seat." Example: *Sit* on this bench.
Set means "to place." Example: *Set* the tools there.
The principal parts of these verbs are as follows:

sit, sat, sat

Present:	*Sit* at the head of the table.
Past:	They *sat* around the pool.
Past Participle:	The candidates *have sat* in the first row.

set, set, set

Present:	*Set* the bottles on the back porch.
Past:	Lois *set* the box on the floor.
Past Participle:	They *have set* the albums on the shelf.

Exercise A   Choose the right verb from the two given.

1. The puppy (lay, laid) in the chair.
2. The price has (raised, risen) to $14.95.
3. We (sat, set) the baby in the stroller.
4. Nat will (bring, take) Karen back here by noon.
5. (May, Can) I ride with you?
6. Carl (sat, set) on Dad's hat.
7. Who (let, left) the ice cream on the counter?
8. The pep club has (raised, risen) money for new uniforms.
9. Pat (learned, taught) us a new dance step.
10. Nancy (let, left) the water out of the tub.

Exercise B   Follow the directions for Exercise A.

1. (Bring, Take) the shovel here, please.
2. Many children (may not, cannot) swim.
3. Who (learned, taught) you about soil conservation?
4. Sherry has (laid, lain) by the pool all afternoon.
5. Who (may, can) lift those boxes?
6. (Let, Leave) the chairs on the patio.

7. The reporters (raised, <u>rose</u>) when the President entered the room.
8. Marnie (lay, <u>laid</u>) the groceries on the counter.
9. Ms. Harris said I (<u>may</u>, can) leave early.
10. Did you (<u>let</u>, leave) Dan borrow your skates?

Part 3   Usage Problems

The words in this section are often used incorrectly. Notice the standard usages for these problem words.

accept means "to agree to something or to receive something willingly."

except means "to leave out." *Except* also means "not including."

> "I will *accept* the call," said Joe to the operator.
> "We will *except* you from the requirement," said the clerk.
> Everyone *except* Todd was there.

agree on means "to come to an understanding." You and others agree *on* a plan.

agree to means "to consent to." You agree *to* do something.

agree with means "to have the same opinion as someone else." You agree *with* somebody. *Agree with* may also refer to something being suitable, as when certain foods don't *agree with* you.

> The committee members *agreed on* a date for the meeting.
> We *agreed to* meet again.
> Laura never *agrees with* Jean.
> The tuna salad didn't *agree with* Bill.

all right is the correct spelling. *Alright* is nonstandard. There are two words.

> *All right*, I'll do the dishes.
> John felt *all right* after the accident.

633

phrases. Be sure to have students check whether each word or phrase has been used correctly.

Advanced Students

Have students use each problem word in an original sentence. Students should exchange papers to check their work.

Optional Practice

Have students read the following sentences, looking for usage errors presented in this Part. Students should correct errors and be prepared to tell why the corrections are necessary. If a sentence contains no errors, it should be marked *Correct*.

1. My parents and I don't always
   with
   agree to one another.
   lend
2. A good friend will always borrow you what you need.
C 3. Just between you and me, I don't think that school will accept me.
4. They worked out a schedule be-
   among
   tween all the volunteers.
5. There were fewer empty seats than
   have
   there should of been.
6. John acted like there was some sort of a problem.
C 7. Everyone filed into the gym except the seniors.
8. Labor Day is a long ways off, somewheres in September.
   All right
9. Alright, we'll divide the prize money among all the winners.
C 10. Party members couldn't agree on a plan to accept the treaty.

Extending the Lesson

This exercise is similar to a spelling bee. Divide the class into two teams. Have one person from one

among refers to a group of more than two people or things.

between refers to two people or things.

> We split up the work *among* the six of us.
> The conversation *between* the two of them ended abruptly.

anywhere, nowhere, somewhere, and **anyway** are standard usages. The words *anywheres, nowheres, somewheres,* and *anyways* are nonstandard. The final *s* should be dropped.

Nonstandard: Cary was nowheres to be found.

Standard: Cary was *nowhere* to be found.

Nonstandard: That note is here somewheres.

Standard: That note is here *somewhere*.

between each, followed by a singular noun, is incorrect. *Between* should not be used with a singular noun.

Nonstandard: Between each speech there was a five-minute break.

Standard: *Between speeches*, there was a five-minute break.

Nonstandard: Carol practiced her dives between every meet.

Standard: Carol practiced her dives *between meets*.

borrow means "to receive something on loan." Don't confuse it with *lend*, meaning "to give out temporarily."

Nonstandard: Will you borrow me your car?

Standard: Will you lend me your car?

Standard: May I borrow your car?

Exercise A Look for sentences with nonstandard usage. Rewrite those sentences, using the right words. If a sentence is correct, write *Correct* after that number.

accepted
1. Bob excepted the award.
C 2. The key is somewhere in my purse.

3. There are file cabinets between ^the each desk^s.

4. Kent will ~~borrow~~ ^lend you his notes.

C   5. Did you agree with Lois about what happened?

6. We divided the cookies ~~between~~ ^among the three of us.

C   7. Put the box down anywhere.

C   8. Toni accepted the award with pleasure.

9. The college basketball coaches agreed ^on ~~to~~ the schedule.

10. Everyone ~~accept~~ ^except Helen had dessert.

Exercise B   Follow the directions for Exercise A.

1. Allison had to choose ^between ~~among~~ the two magazines.

2. The farmer walked between ^the ~~each~~ row^s of beans.

3. ~~Alright~~ ^All right, who has my lunch?

4. Mike and Gayle agreed ^on ~~to~~ the best candidate for mayor.

5. Ben will ~~borrow~~ ^lend me his flashlight.

6. I like all vegetables ~~accept~~ ^except peas.

7. ~~Anyways~~ ^Anyway, I'm busy Saturday night.

C   8. Jessica agrees with me about what to wear.

9. The restaurant did not ~~except~~ ^accept personal checks.

C   10. Betty and Ellen split the reward between them.

fewer refers to numbers or things that can be counted.

less refers to amount or quantity.

> Curt's bike has *fewer* gears than Al's.
> It takes *less* time to take the short cut.

in means "inside something."

into tells of motion from the outside to the inside of something.

> Nonstandard: The security guard went in the bank.
>
> Standard: The security guard went *into* the bank.
>
> Nonstandard: Sam put a dime in the parking meter.
>
> Standard: Sam put a dime *into* the parking meter.

kind of a and **sort of a** are nonstandard. The *a* is not necessary.

Nonstandard: What kind of a car is that?

Standard: What *kind of* car is that?

Nonstandard: There is some sort of a form to fill out.

Standard: There is some *sort of* form to fill out.

like is a preposition. Using *like* as a conjunction before a clause is not fully accepted. Especially in writing, it is better to use *as* or *as if*.

Nonstandard: Like the almanac predicted, it rained today.

Standard: *As* the almanac predicted, it rained today.

Nonstandard: Jake walked like he knew the way there.

Standard: Jake walked *as if* he knew the way there.

of is sometimes incorrectly used in phrases like *could of, shouldn't of,* and *must of.* The correct word is *have* or its contraction: *could have, could've, shouldn't have, must have, might have, might've.*

Nonstandard: Sally should of left earlier.

Standard: Sally *should have* left earlier.

ways does not refer to distance. *Way* is correct.

Nonstandard: It is a short ways to the pool.

Standard: It is a short *way* to the pool.

Exercise A   Correct the sentences with nonstandard usage. If a sentence is correct, write *Correct*.

1. Irma poured the orange juice in the glasses.
   into
2. The grain elevator is a ways down the highway.
   way
3. That kind of a jacket is waterproof.
4. Ginger could of driven you.
   have
5. There are less summer jobs available this year.
   fewer
6. Like the coach said, we have to practice every day.
   As

7. Marge put her boots ^{into} in her locker.

C 8. There are fewer Spanish Club members this year.

9. This cola has ^{fewer} less calories.

10. Betsy acted ^{as if} like she had lost her best friend.

Exercise B Follow the directions for Exercise A.

1. We should ^{have} of done our homework first.

C 2. What ingredients did you put into this barbeque sauce?

C 3. Kelly looks as if she is tired.

4. ^{Fewer} Less people drive downtown.

5. The barn is quite a ^{way} ways from the house.

C 6. Fewer sales clerks are hired after the holidays are over.

7. Jack put his check ^{into} in his savings account.

8. Pete and Al got along ^{as if} like they were old friends.

9. Abby chose this kind of a bike.

10. Jeff looked ^{as if} like he had seen a ghost.

Additional Exercises

These Additional Exercises may be used for additional practice of the concepts presented in this Section. Each exercise focuses on a single concept, and should be used after the page number indicated in parentheses.

Review

If you have not assigned these Additional Exercises before this time, you can also use them as an excellent Section Review.

ADDITIONAL EXERCISES

The Right Word

A. Words Often Confused Choose the correct word from those given in parentheses.

1. Have you claimed (<u>your</u>, you're) prize yet?
2. Did you (loose, <u>lose</u>) your ticket stub?
3. (<u>Who's</u>, Whose) the passenger in the sidecar?
4. (<u>It's</u>, Its) almost time to leave.
5. The fish had jumped out of (it's, <u>its</u>) bowl.
6. I always keep the Turners' mail for them when (there, <u>they're</u>, their) on vacation.
7. Saudi Arabia is a kingdom in the (<u>desert</u>, dessert).
8. (Their, <u>There</u>, They're) is a whistle that only a dog can (<u>hear</u>, here).
9. Erin doesn't go (<u>to</u>, too, two) the youth center (to, <u>too</u>, two) often.
10. The lifeguards put on (<u>their</u>, there, they're) jackets if the (<u>weather</u>, whether) turns chilly.

B. Troublesome Verbs Choose the correct verb from those given in parentheses.

1. Please (<u>bring</u>, take) me a glass of water.
2. (<u>May</u>, Can) we make a U-turn on this street, officer?
3. The trainer has (learned, <u>taught</u>) the boxer proper footwork.
4. A huge crane (<u>raised</u>, rose) steel beams to the upper stories.
5. The tug-of-war ends when one team (<u>lets</u>, leaves) go of the rope.
6. The test pilot (<u>sat</u>, set) at the controls.
7. Meredith (<u>lay</u>, laid) awake and couldn't sleep.

8. The oil has (raised, <u>risen</u>) to the surface of the sea.

9. Jude (lay, <u>laid</u>) cloth over the picnic table.

10. Don't (sit, <u>set</u>) the plastic bowl on the hot stove.

C. Usage Problems   Choose the correct word or phrase from the two given in parentheses.

1. Will you (borrow, <u>lend</u>) me some warmer gloves?

2. (<u>All right</u>, Alright), operator, we'll (<u>accept</u>, except) the charges.

3. Our family divides the work (<u>among</u>, between) the five of us.

4. Trisha ran (in, <u>into</u>) the room (<u>as if</u>, like) she were terribly excited.

5. There is some (<u>sort of</u>, sort of a) curb (<u>between the</u>, between each) parking spaces.

6. I should (<u>have</u>, of) eaten (<u>fewer</u>, less) pretzels and drunk (fewer, <u>less</u>) 7-Up.

7. (<u>Anyway</u>, Anyways), Rick has (<u>nowhere</u>, nowheres) else to go.

8. Has Mr. Roman (agreed on, <u>agreed to</u>, agreed with) let you take Saturday off?

9. The players in the huddle quickly (<u>agreed on</u>, agreed to, agreed with) a strategy.

10. Everyone (accept, <u>except</u>) Bev had biked a long (<u>way</u>, ways).

MIXED REVIEW

The Right Word

A. Using the right word   Correct any errors in spelling or usage. If there is no error, write *Correct.*

C 1. What kind of book is that?

2. He sometimes acts like he can't hear well. [as if]

3. I should not of driven into the desert with so little gas. [have]

4. Your clothes will feel loose after you loose weight. [lose]

5. Pour less batter in the pan for all the pancake except Vi's. [into] [pancakes]

6. The chairs are stationary; the tables are to heavy to move. [too]

7. Let's have fewer arguments; we're getting nowheres. [nowhere]

C 8. I agree with your idea of borrowing Ms. Barber's shovel and dividing the work among the three of us.

9. Between each act their was an intermission. [there]

10. It's a long ways from here to the Capitol, and I don't know whether Congress is still in session. [way]

B. Using troublesome verbs correctly   The verbs in these sentences are used incorrectly. Rewrite each sentence correctly.

1. The cat laid on laundry that I had set on the table. [lay]

2. Can you rise your injured arm? [raise]

3. Can I please lie down for a few minutes? [May]

4. Jan brought the television set to that shop. [took]

5. Please learn that dog not to lie on the bed. [teach]

6. May I take some tea to you while you sit here? [bring]

7. The children in class learned to set and listen. [sit]

8. Nick's voice raised as he asked the boss to raise his salary. [rose]

9. Leave Amanda set the chess pieces on the board. [Let]

10. The paramedics laid the stretcher down and left the victim laying there. [lying]

USING GRAMMAR IN WRITING
The Right Word

A. Imagine that you work on the staff of a local newspaper. You have the job of correcting errors in letters to the editor. Of course, you may not change any of the ideas in a letter. However, you may correct errors of grammar and usage. Following is one of the letters that you must correct. Read the letter to learn what the writer's ideas are. Then rewrite the letter, using standard English.

The city shouldn't of cancelled the summer music program. Hundreds of people came to here the concerts last summer. Did the city council ask they're opinion about cancelling the concerts? No. I think the city should of left the concerts go on for at least another year. If their to expensive, why not charge some kind of a fee? Anyone who went to the concerts would say they liked them. Let's see the city give the music program one more chance.

B. Rewrite the following passage in standard English.

My first day on my first job was almost my last. I thought it would be so fun. Then I missed my bus I got there 5 minutes late and my boss goes "you gotta do better then that." So he gives me a uniform that was to large and I'm holding it up with one hand and trying to hear what hes learning me. And then my friends come in and order hamburgers and I forget the fries. It sure wasn't my best day, no way.

These challenging and enjoyable activities allow the students to see how the concepts of grammar, usage, and mechanics may be applied in actual writing situations. Each exercise is designed to allow students practice in several of the skills they have acquired in this Section. The activities also provide opportunities for students to write creatively about a wide variety of interesting and unusual subjects.

Section Objectives

1. To understand and apply the general rules for capitalizing proper nouns and adjectives, the pronoun *I,* and abbreviations

2. To understand and apply the rules for capitalizing first words in sentences and in poetry, quotations, letter parts, outlines, and titles

Preparing the Students

Tell students that proper capitalization is a way to help writers and readers communicate most effectively. Capital letters tell a reader to be on the alert for new sentences, important words, and names.

Read the introduction on page 642.

Additional Resources

Diagnostic Test — page 8 in the test booklet

Mastery Test — pages 70–71 in the test booklet

Additional Exercises — pages 654–659 in the student text

Practice Book — pages 243–249

Duplicating Masters — pages 243–249

Special Populations — See special section at the front of this Teacher's Edition.

Capitalization

Capital letters are signals. They make the reader aware of certain important words and of the first words in sentences.

This section will show you the specific rules for capitalizing words. You should refer to this section at any time if you are in doubt about whether or not to capitalize a word.

642

Proper Nouns and Adjectives

Capitalize proper nouns and proper adjectives.

A **proper noun** is the name of a particular person, place, or thing. In contrast, a **common noun** is the name of a whole class of people, places, or things. A **proper adjective** is an adjective formed from a proper noun.

Common Noun	Proper Noun	Proper Adjective
king	Edward	Edwardian
country	Spain	Spanish
government	Congress	Congressional

There are many kinds of proper nouns. The following rules will help you decide whether or not a noun is a proper noun.

Names of People

Capitalize people's names. Also capitalize the initials or abbreviations that stand for names.

J.F. Kennedy	John Fitzgerald Kennedy
Louis **C.** Tiffany	Louis Comfort Tiffany

Capitalize the titles used with people's names. Also capitalize the initials or abreviations that stand for those titles.

The titles *Miss, Ms., Mrs.,* and *Mr.* are always capitalized.

Gov. James Thompson	Major Margaret Houlihan
Ms. Marianne Rizzo	Dr. Carlos Rodriguez
Judge Sandra Day O'Connor	Rev. J.L. Bluett

Do not capitalize a title that is used without a name. It is a common noun.

Who is the governor of Missouri?
Richard Posner is a federal judge.

643

Objective

To understand and apply the general rules for capitalizing proper nouns and adjectives, the pronoun *I*, and abbreviations

Presenting the Lesson

1. Read pages 643–644. Go over the definitions and examples of common nouns, proper nouns, and proper adjectives.

2. Go over each of the rules for capitalization printed in bold type on pages 643–644. Study the examples offered below each rule, and ask students to offer several additional examples to which the rule would apply.

3. Assign and discuss Exercises A and B on page 645.

4. Read pages 646–647. Study rules and examples, again asking students to add additional examples to which each rule would apply.

5. Assign and discuss Exercises A and B on pages 647–648.

6. Read pages 648–649, studying rules and examples, and offering additional illustrations of each rule.

7. Assign and discuss Exercises A and B on page 650.

Individualizing the Lesson

Less-Advanced Students

1. Have each student bring in a copy of a weekly newsmagazine. Then have students go through the magazine looking for published examples of each rule of capitalization discussed in this lesson. Students should copy the example sentences they find, underline the letter or letters affected by the specific capitalization rule, and write the specific rule after each sentence.

2. If students cannot find a published example of each rule, have them write an original sentence illustrating the specific rule. Have students underline the letters affected by the rule and have them write the rule after the sentence.

Advanced Students

Have each student write an original sentence illustrating each of the capitalization rules covered in the lesson. Students should underline the capital letter(s) affected by the rule, then write the rule after the sentence.

Optional Practice

Have students capitalize words as necessary in the following sentences.

1. My grandmother died on labor day, september 2, 1978; that was a very sad autumn for us.
2. Cancer research is being conducted at st. jude's hospital in Tennessee.
3. The treaty of versailles, signed when woodrow wilson was president, ended world war I.
4. I cashed my check at sears bank and trust company.
5. The shoreline of lake michigan stretches twelve miles north from downtown chicago to the northern suburbs.
6. The month of july is named after julius caesar, who died in 44 b.c.
7. Aunt etta and uncle fred took *the cincinnati limited* from cleveland to cincinnati.

Capitalize titles of very high importance, even when they are used without names.

the President of the United States
the Chief Justice of the Supreme Court
the Prime Minister of Canada
a Congresswoman
the Pope

Family Relationships

Capitalize such words as *mother, father, aunt,* and *uncle* when they are used as names. If the noun is preceded by a possessive word or by *a* or *the*, it is not capitalized.

My mom will give you a ride home.
Was Dad a good student, Grandpa?
My aunt and uncle have confusing names, Uncle Gene and Aunt Jean.
Do you need any help, Mom?

The Pronoun *I*

Capitalize the pronoun *I*.

She and I played video games.   I study after dinner.

The Supreme Being and Sacred Writings

Capitalize all words referring to God, to the Holy Family, and to religious scriptures.

the Almighty	the Bible	the Son of God
the Lord	the Talmud	the New Testament
the Blessed Virgin	Allah	the Book of Job

Capitalize personal pronouns referring to God.

They thanked the Lord for His bounty.

Exercise A Copy the following sentences. Change small letters to capital letters wherever necessary.

1. The car broke down while ᴹmom and ᴵi were out shopping.
2. The reading at the funeral was from the ᴮbook of ᴾpsalms.
3. My father enjoys the short stories of ᴼo. ᴴhenry.
4. My brother introduced ᴿrev. ˢsmyth to ᴰdr. ˢshores.
5. Did the name on the envelope say ᴹmajor ᴶjean ᴿreilly or ᴹmayor ᴶjean ᴿreilly?
6. The ᴾprime ᴹminister of England is ᴹmargaret ᵀthatcher.
7. My aunt, ᴹmichele ᴱelaine ᴸlevine, is a curator.
8. Did ˢsenator ᴬadlai ˢstevenson resign his position to run for governor?
9. The soldier thanked the ᴸlord for sparing his life.
10. Professor ᶠfriedman shook hands with ᴾprofessor ˢsamuelson before the debate.

Exercise B Follow the directions for Exercise A.

1. Will ᴸlen accompany ᵁuncle ᴿrobert to St. Louis?
2. My sister reads from the ᴮbible every day.
3. The ᴾpresident met with the ᴾpope during his last visit to Europe.
4. Did ᶠflorence write a thank-you note to her grandmother?
5. Mr. ᴹmiller wrote a letter to ˢsen. ᶜcharles ᴾpercy.
6. The ᴿreverend ᴬarthur ᴰdimmesdale is a character in a novel.
7. The ᴮbook of ᴳgenesis in the ᴮbible tells the story of creation.
8. Has ᴹmom met ᴰdr. ᴶjohnson yet?
9. The novelist ᴮbill ᴳgranger also writes under the name of ᵂwilliam ᴳgriffin.
10. Our neighbor, ᴹmr. ᴶj.ᴮb. masters, met the ᴾpresident at a fund-raising dinner.

8. The ᴾpanama ᶜcanal, built during ᵀtheodore ᴿroosevelt's presidency, links the ᴬatlantic and ᴾpacific oceans.
9. Ask ᴹmr. ᴱevans if ᴵi can take drivers ed. in summer school or if ᴵi have to wait until ˢseptember.
10. The ᴹmayor marched in the ˢst. ᴾpatrick's day parade in ᴺnew ʸyork ᶜcity.

Extending the Lesson

1. Discuss with students the importance of capitalization. Have them explain why capital letters are needed; then discuss problems that might occur if capitalization rules were not followed.

2. Have students read and comment on several poems by e.e. cummings. Are the poems harder to read than poems using capital letters? Why or why not? Ask students what they think e.e. cummings is trying to do by ignoring or violating rules of capitalization.

Geographical Names

In a geographical name, capitalize the first letter of each word except articles and prepositions.

If the article *the* appears before a place name, it is not part of the name and is therefore not capitalized.

Continents:	Australia, Africa, South America, Asia
Bodies of Water:	the Indian Ocean, the Sangamon River, the Gulf of Mexico, the Mediterranean Sea, Tampa Bay, the Suez Canal, Lake Erie
Landforms:	Mount Rushmore, the Hawaiian Islands, the Rocky Mountains, the Sahara Desert, Cape Horn, the Grand Canyon
Political Units:	Colorado, Orlando, the Province of Quebec, the Republic of Chad, United Mexican States, Tenth Congressional District
Public Areas:	Yellowstone National Park, Fort Pulaski, the Statue of Liberty, Blackhawk State Park, Arlington House, Custer Battlefield
Roads and Highways:	Route 47, Interstate Highway 75, Glenview Road, Michigan Avenue, Market Street

Directions and Sections

Capitalize names of sections of the country.

The Midwest includes Wisconsin and Minnesota.
Many people retire to the South.
The climate in the Northwest is very different from that in the Southwest.

Capitalize proper adjectives that come from names of sections of the country.

a **M**idwestern farm	a **W**estern resort
Southern hospitality	a **W**est **C**oast fad

Do not capitalize directions of the compass.

San Diego is south of Los Angeles.
The airport is west of the city.

Do not capitalize adjectives that come from words showing direction.

The drug store is on the west side of the street.
The kitchen window has a southern exposure.

Exercise A   Number your paper from 1 to 10. Find the words in the following sentences that should be capitalized. Write the words after the proper number, using the necessary capital letters.

1. They backpacked in glacier national park.
2. We traveled from washington into british columbia.
3. The business center of the south is atlanta, georgia.
4. The mojave desert is in california.
5. The panama canal connects the atlantic ocean with the pacific ocean.
6. The caspian sea is really a lake bordered by the soviet union and iran.
7. Is interstate 55 the same road as route 66?
8. The southeast has a hot, humid climate, and the southwest has a hot, dry climate.
9. The west met the east with the completion of the transcontinental railroad at promontory point, utah.
10. In hong kong many people live on boats.

Exercise B   Follow the directions for Exercise A.

1. Sherry lives south of cleveland, ohio.
2. Don met me on the northeast corner of park drive and morse avenue.

647

^C 3. The north side of the solar home was built into a hill,
and its south side had large windows.

4. Do you sell ^Ssouthern fried chicken and hush-puppies?

5. Craig reported on the ^Iindians of the ^Ssouthwest.

6. The steamboat churned down the ^Mmississippi ^Rriver.

7. Many people vacation in the ^Ssouth to escape harsh ^Mmid-
western winters.

8. A ^Ssouthern drawl differs from a ^Wwestern twang.

9. The ^Hhoover ^Ddam spans the ^Ccolorado ^Rriver in ^Nnevada.

10. The ^Bbering ^Ssea is on the western coast of ^Aalaska.

Names of Organizations and Institutions

Capitalize the names of organizations and institutions, including political parties, governmental bodies or agencies, schools, colleges, churches, hospitals, clubs, businesses, and abbreviations of these names.

Democratic Party	Massachusetts General Hospital
Federal Communications Commission	American Dental Association
	United Nations
Villa Grove High School	A.M.A.
St. Raymond's Church	

Do not capitalize such words as *school, company, church,* and *hospital* when they are not used as parts of names.

That school is between a hospital and a church.

Names of Events, Documents, and Periods of Time

Capitalize the names of historical events, documents, and periods of time.

Battle of Wounded Knee	Webster-Ashburton Treaty
Korean War	the Dark Ages
Bill of Rights	the Industrial Revolution

Months, Days, and Holidays

Capitalize names of months, days, and holidays, but not the names of seasons.

June	Tuesday	fall
Easter	Christmas	spring

Races, Languages, Nationalities, and Religions

Capitalize the names of races, languages, nationalities, and religions. Also capitalize any adjectives that come from these names.

Dutch	Japanese	Catholicism	Protestant
Irish	Buddhism	Cuban	Jewish

School Subjects

Do not capitalize the names of school subjects, except course titles followed by a number.

math	History of Civilization I
home economics	Biology 100

Remember that the names of languages are always capitalized.

French	Spanish	German	English

Ships, Trains, Airplanes, and Automobiles

Capitalize the names of ships, trains, airplanes, and automobiles.

U.S.S. Constitution	Boeing 747	Oldsmobile Cutlass

B.C., A.D.

Capitalize the abbreviations *B.C.* and *A.D.*

The Chou dynasty in China lasted from 770 to 256 **B.C.**
William of Normandy conquered England in **A.D.** 1066.

649

Exercise A Write the words in each sentence that should be capitalized. Use the necessary capital letters.

1. In may, st. francis hospital holds a fund-raising dance.
2. The american economic association convention will be in december.
3. Is there a hospital near glenbrook south high school?
4. Many polish people live in chicago.
5. The jewish new year is called rosh hashana.
6. The flowering of the arts during the late middle ages, a.d. 1300–1600, is called the renaissance.
7. Charles Lindbergh left new york on may 20, 1927, in his plane, the spirit of st. louis.
8. The battle of gettysburg was fought in july of 1863.
9. A phonetic alphabet was developed in phoenicia before 1600 b.c.
10. A chevrolet *chevette* is about the size of a volkswagen *rabbit*.

Exercise B Follow the directions for Exercise A.

1. The fourth thursday in november is celebrated as thanksgiving day.
2. Kevin has advanced art I after his gym class.
3. Both the french and the italians participated in the conference.
4. The fund-raiser for the republican party is on june 24.
5. The illinois education association is part of the national education association.
6. We read about the battle of little big horn in history.
7. Both english and gaelic are spoken in ireland.
8. Many new yorkers escape to the seashore on summer weekends.
9. Dad ordered a new pontiac *firebird*.
10. A graduate of stanford university, susan has worked for the federal reserve bank and also for bank of america.

First Words

Sentences and Poetry

Capitalize the first word of every sentence and the first word of most lines of poetry.

The quarterback was sacked. He lost five yards on the play.

Listen my children, and you shall hear
Of the midnight ride of Paul Revere, . . .
—from "Paul Revere's Ride," HENRY WADSWORTH LONGFELLOW

Sometimes, especially in modern poetry, the lines of a poem do not begin with capital letters.

Quotations

Capitalize the first word of a direct quotation.

A **direct quotation** tells the exact words of a speaker or writer.

Wordsworth said, "The child is father of the man."

In a **divided quotation,** a direct quotation is broken into two parts by words like *he said* or *she explained.* Do not capitalize the first word of the second part unless it starts a new sentence.

"I insist," Mr. Jackson said, "that you join me for dinner."
"I insist," Mr. Jackson said. "Join me for dinner."

Letter Parts

Capitalize the first word in the greeting of a letter. Also capitalize the name of the person addressed, or words like *Sir* and *Madam* that stand for names.

Dear Ms. Takamoto,   Dear Mr. Conn,   Dear Sir or Madam:

In the complimentary close, capitalize only the first word.

Very truly yours,   Sincerely yours,

First Words

Objective

To follow rules for capitalizing first words in sentences and in poetry, quotations, letter parts, outlines, and titles

Presenting the Lesson

1. Read pages 651–652. Read each rule and study the examples that illustrate it. Spend extra time on difficult concepts, such as the difference between direct quotations and indirect quotations, and divided quotations. Supply additional examples as necessary.

2. Assign and discuss Exercises A and B on pages 652–653.

Individualizing the Lesson

Less-Advanced Students

1. Have students write a brief letter telling a friend about a recent conversation they could have had with a third person about a book. Tell students to include the book's title and an excerpt from their conversation in the letter. Also tell students to be sure to use proper letter-writing format. Remind students to use capital letters correctly.

2. Have students exchange papers to check one another's work.

Advanced Students

Have students outline a brief newspaper or magazine article. Remind students to use capital letters correctly.

Have students capitalize words as necessary in the following sentences.

1. the title of loren's speech is "why the future is in our hands."
2. i outlined the chapter as follows:
   caring for houseplants
   I. light
      A. direct light
      B. filtered light
      C. artificial light
   II. moisture
      A. water
      B. misting and spraying
3. our class visited the art institute of chicago to see rembrandt's *night watch.*
4. edgar allen poe's "the raven" begins like this:
   once upon a midnight dreary,
   while i pondered, weak and weary
5. i learned about stereo equipment by reading *consumer reports.*
6. we must read chapter 3, "causes of the civil war," in our american history book.
7. my mother read *the little engine that could* to my little brother.
8. let's sing "for he's a jolly good fellow."
9. "joel," warned phil, "you can't take *newsweek* out of the library."
10. marty asked me how many times i had seen *raiders of the lost ark.*

Extending the Lesson

1. Have students try writing their own poetry. Tell students they don't have to use capital letters, but that they should be able to explain why they didn't use capitals if they choose not to. Remind students that not using capital letters may make the poem more difficult to read.

Outlines

Capitalize the first word of each item in an outline. Also capitalize the letters before each line.

I. Endangered species
   A. Mammals
      1. Florida panther
      2. Utah prairie dog
   B. Reptiles

Titles

Capitalize the first word and all important words in the titles of chapters, magazine articles, short stories, essays, poems, and songs or short pieces of music.

Chapter title:	Chapter 10, "The Industrial Revolution"
Magazine article:	"Improve Your Tennis Game"
Short story:	"The Open Window"
Essay:	"Self-Reliance"
Poem:	"Spring Thunder"
Song:	"Battle Hymn of the Republic"

Capitalize the first word and all important words in titles of books, newspapers, magazines, plays, movies, television programs, works of art, and long musical compositions.

Book title:	*To Kill a Mockingbird*
Newspaper:	*Knoxville News-Sentinel*
Magazine:	*People*
Play:	*The King and I*
Movie:	*Raiders of the Lost Ark*
Television program:	*Today*
Work of art:	*Girl with Braids*
Long musical composition:	*Messiah*

Exercise A Capitalize these sentences correctly.

1. Many people subscribe to *the wall street journal.*
2. both *forbes* and *fortune* are business magazines.

3. ms. appleton read the poem "danny deever" to us.

4. I. major world religions

    a. buddhism

      1. origins

5. billy joel won an award for the song "just the way you are."

6. dear sir or madam:

    i would like to order four mezzanine seats for the *nutcracker suite.* a check is enclosed.

                    sincerely yours,

7. "doris," asked sue, "will you save a place for me?"

8. "my term paper is due next week," said ken. "maybe i'd better go to the library tonight."

9. edgar allan poe wrote "the pit and the pendulum."

10. the painting *at the moulin rouge* is by toulouse lautrec.

Exercise B   Follow the directions for Exercise A.

1. the sportscaster sang "take me out to the ball game."

2. miniver cheevy, child of scorn

    grew lean, while he assailed the seasons;

  he wept that he was ever born

    and he had reasons.

    —from "Miniver Cheevy," EDWIN ARLINGTON ROBINSON

3. our class read chapter two, "how painting began."

4. "if i take the bus," complained howard, "i'll be late."

5. dad watches *the evening news* when he gets home.

6. jason asked, "who has my copy of *life* magazine?"

7. who played the title role in the movie *gandhi?*

8. the article "the two souls of peru" appeared in the march, 1982, *national geographic.*

9. the song "my way" was made famous by frank sinatra.

10. dear ms. schmidt,

    here are the two tickets to the play *west side waltz.*

              yours truly,

2. Duplicate the poems, keeping them anonymous, and pass them out to the class. Discuss the use of capital letters, using the poems as examples.

ADDITIONAL EXERCISES

Capitalization

A. Proper Nouns Number your paper from 1 to 10. Find the words in the following sentences that should be capitalized. Write the words beside the proper numbers. Capitalize the words correctly.

1. Was the soft drink dr. pepper named after an actual doctor?
2. My sister auditioned for the part of lady macbeth.
3. Margaret thatcher became prime minister of england in 1979.
4. This passage from the *bible* was written by st. luke.
5. Reverend elaine jones, rabbi samuel h. gelman, and father edward krause co-teach a course on the *old testament*.
6. Doesn't sgt. hays realize that i am on leave?
7. Your brother called while you were at work, grandpa.
8. Reg dwight changed his name to elton john.
9. Doesn't b. b. king call his guitar lucille?
10. At once, rep. garcia wired the president at the White House.

B. Capital Letters Copy the following sentences. Change small letters to capital letters wherever necessary.

1. the okefenokee swamp is in georgia and florida.
2. We drove south through brown county into kentucky.
3. The southwest can get very hot; its rivers sometimes dry up.
4. the coast of poland is on the baltic sea.

5. Penny worked at $\overset{S}{s}$ix $\overset{F}{f}$lags, a park in $\overset{M}{m}$agic $\overset{M}{m}$ountain, $\overset{C}{c}$alifornia.

6. $\overset{K}{k}$ay was used to swimming in the ocean and was surprised that the $\overset{M}{m}$editerranean had no tides.

7. $\overset{O}{o}$ne island in the $\overset{W}{w}$est $\overset{I}{i}$ndies is $\overset{S}{s}$t. $\overset{V}{v}$incent.

8. The $\overset{S}{s}$wan $\overset{I}{i}$slands are controlled by $\overset{H}{h}$onduras.

9. The $\overset{U}{u}$nited $\overset{S}{s}$tates is on the south bank of $\overset{R}{r}$ainy $\overset{R}{r}$iver; $\overset{C}{c}$anada is on the river's north shore.

10. $\overset{P}{p}$eople who fear heights can ask a guard to drive their cars across $\overset{C}{c}$hesapeake $\overset{B}{b}$ay $\overset{B}{b}$ridge.

C. Proper Nouns and Adjectives Number your paper from 1 to 10. After each number, copy the words from each sentence that should be capitalized. Use the necessary capital letters.

1. Students in $\overset{S}{s}$panish III can earn extra credit by going to special sessions on $\overset{T}{t}$hursdays.

2. The scanners at many food stores are made by $\overset{IBM}{ibm}$.

3. Uncle $\overset{G}{g}$ene owns a '63 $\overset{C}{c}$hevy that is in mint condition.

4. My cousin graduated from $\overset{R}{r}$oberto $\overset{C}{c}$lemente $\overset{H}{h}$igh $\overset{S}{s}$chool last $\overset{J}{j}$une.

5. Since 1800, the $\overset{P}{p}$resident of the $\overset{U}{u}$nited $\overset{S}{s}$tates has lived in the White House, which was rebuilt after the $\overset{W}{w}$ar of 1812.

6. Our $\overset{A}{a}$merican history class toured the headquarters of the $\overset{U}{u}$nited $\overset{N}{n}$ations.

7. The public schools as well as the $\overset{C}{c}$atholic schools are closed on $\overset{G}{g}$ood $\overset{F}{f}$riday.

8. The $\overset{J}{j}$ewish holiday of $\overset{Y}{y}$om $\overset{K}{k}$ippur is celebrated in autumn.

9. Students in $\overset{M}{m}$s. $\overset{H}{h}$olden's $\overset{O}{o}$ffice $\overset{M}{m}$achines II class learn to use a computer.

10. The $\overset{M}{m}$ayans in $\overset{Y}{y}$ucatán devised an extremely accurate calendar around 300 $\overset{B}{b}.\overset{C}{c}.$

D. Titles, Outlines, and Letters   Number your paper from 1 to 10. Find the words in the following sentences that should be capitalized. Write the words after the proper numbers, using the necessary capital letters.

1. the television comedy *after M*A*S*H* is a spinoff from *M*A*S*H*.

2. "*the moonlight sonata* is too difficult for you now," said the piano teacher. "maybe next year you can try it."

3. ms. mihalos assigned an article from *business week*.

4. dear madam or sir:
   have you often asked yourself, "is there any way that i can earn money at home?"

5. for my report, i read *let the circle be unbroken*, a novel by mildred d. taylor.

6. it was the summer of the sequels: *grease 2, rocky III,* and *star trek II: the wrath of khan.*

7. the state song of georgia is "georgia on my mind."

8. "can't you think of a better title for your essay," asked pat, "than 'how to make good pancakes'?"

9. my mother looked through the job ads in the *houston chronicle.*

10. II. superstitions
   a. good-luck charms
      1. rabbit's foot

MIXED REVIEW

Capitalization

A. Using capitalization correctly Number your paper from 1 to 10. Copy the following sentences, using the correct capitalization.

1. the dancer ronald perry trained at the dance theatre of harlem.
2. dear ms. allegretti,
      thank you for the cassette of christmas songs. my sister and i especially like "silent night" and "we three kings."
3. i think that the first woman to fly an aircraft across the english channel was an american, harriet quimby.
4. ross perot, jr. and s. w. coburn were co-pilots of the *spirit of texas*, the first helicopter to fly around the world.
5. my grandfather plays bagpipes with the shannon rovers band.
6. slowly grandfather said, "you may have heard about that battle in your history class."
7. after the battle of yorktown, general cornwallis refused to surrender his sword; the general ordered an irish soldier to do it for him.
8. on monday in world history II, i gave a report on the mali empire.
9. according to *information please almanac*, chief sitting bull was born in the west, on grand river, south dakota.
10. katherine d. ortega became treasurer of the united states on october 3, 1983.

657

Mixed Review

These exercises provide review of the concepts presented in this Section. Each exercise challenges the students to apply several of the skills they have acquired during previous study. Because the "mixed" feature of these activities makes them more difficult, the teacher may wish to have less-advanced students do them orally or in small groups.

657

B. Using capitalization correctly in proofreading Proofread the following paragraph. Rewrite it, using correct capitalization.

"peace" is a word rich in meaning, as a look at some recent recipients of the nobel peace prize will show. rev. dr. martin luther king, jr. was honored for leading a nonviolent movement for equal rights for all people in the united states. the co-winners mairead corrigan and betty williams worked toward a nonviolent solution to the problems between catholics and protestants in northern ireland. a nun, mother teresa of calcutta, won the prize for her care of the poor in india. For their efforts to promote disarmament, alfonsa garcia robles of mexico and alva myrdal of sweden shared the award. a polish labor leader, lech walesa, won for founding a union called *solidarity*, which seeks to achieve fair treatment for workers. the many kinds of work recognized by the nobel committee suggest that peace is much more than the absence of war.

USING MECHANICS IN WRITING
Capitalization

A. Your class has decided to publish a school *Who's Who.* Every student will be included, and each student will write one of the biographies. Interview a friend and then write a paragraph about your friend that could be included in the *Who's Who.* Be sure to include all the following information.

- your friend's full name
- the city and state (or country) of your friend's place of birth
- the names of places where your friend has traveled or would like to travel
- the names of clubs or other organizations to which your friend belongs
- the names of schools that your friend has attended
- the names of your friend's favorite book, movie, television program, and song

Check your work to be sure that the capitalization is correct. Underline each capital letter.

B. You have landed a job at a travel agency. This agency organizes group tours of major cities. Your first job as a trainee is to write a brochure about a city that you would like to visit. What city would you like to visit? How would you convince other people that they would like to visit it?

Write a paragraph that will help attract people to your favorite city. Before you begin writing, do some research to learn more about the city. Be sure to include historic sites, homes of famous people, and other attractions. Mention them by their proper names. Be careful to follow the rules for capitalization.

Section Objectives

1. To use end punctuation marks correctly

2. To use commas, semicolons, colons, dashes, hyphens, apostrophes, and quotation marks correctly

Preparing the Students

Ask students how a speaker helps the listener understand when one idea ends and another begins, when a particular word is very important, or when he or she is quoting someone. Students will no doubt mention voice intonation, volume, pauses, and facial expression. Remind students that the writer is not able to use these communication techniques. However, the writer is able to use punctuation, which serves the same important purpose.

Read the introduction on page 660.

Additional Resources

Diagnostic Test — page 9 in the test booklet

Mastery Test — pages 72–73 in the test booklet

Additional Exercises — pages 690–697 in the student text

Practice Book — pages 250–263

Duplicating Masters — pages 250–263

Special Populations — See special section at the front of this Teacher's Edition.

Punctuation

When you speak, you pause, you stop, and you raise or lower your voice at certain points. However, when you read and write, how do you show where to pause, stop, or raise or lower your voice? **Punctuation marks** serve this purpose. They show how a sentence should be read.

This section will review all the punctuation marks. Refer to these pages whenever you have a question about punctuation.

End Marks

End marks are the punctuation marks that indicate the end of a sentence. The three kinds of end marks are the **period,** the **question mark,** and the **exclamation point.**

The Period

Use a period at the end of a declarative sentence.

A **declarative sentence** is a sentence that makes a statement. You use declarative sentences when you tell something.

The meeting ended at noon.

Use a period at the end of most imperative sentences.

An **imperative sentence** is a sentence that orders or requests someone to do something.

Please pass the mustard.

At times, imperative sentences express strong excitement or emotion. Then an exclamation point, rather than a period, is used at the end of the sentence.

Stop that!   Wake up!

Use a period at the end of an indirect question.

An **indirect question** tells that someone asked a question. However, it does not give the exact words of the question.

The waiter asked if we had enjoyed our dinner.

Notice how a **direct question** differs:

The waiter asked, "Did you enjoy your dinner?"

A direct question shows the exact words of the person asking the question. A direct question ends with a question mark.

661

End Marks

Objective

To use end punctuation marks correctly

Presenting the Lesson

1. Read pages 661–663. Go over all of the rules for the use of periods, question marks, and exclamation points. Study the examples used to illustrate each rule, and supplement with examples from students. Be certain that students understand the terms: *declarative sentence, imperative sentence, indirect question, abbreviation, initial, interrogative sentence, exclamatory sentence,* and *interjection.* While each of these terms is defined within the explanatory material following each rule, further review may be necessary. Fuller explanations of the terms may be found in appropriate text sections.

2. Assign and discuss Exercises A and B on pages 663–664.

Individualizing the Lesson

Less-Advanced Students

1. Have students write a brief account—including excerpts of conversation—of a party, ball game, dance, or dinner they attended recently. Tell students to be sure to apply each of the punctuation rules covered in this lesson, but tell them to leave out all end punctuation. Once students have finished writing, have them exchange papers.

2. Students should correct the papers by adding proper end punctuation.

661

1. Have students write a brief imaginative story. Tell students to include punctuation except for all end marks. Have students exchange papers.

2. Students should correct the papers by adding all proper end punctuation.

Optional Practice

Have students supply the necessary punctuation marks in the following sentences.

1. Help! These bookshelves are falling on me!
2. Did your watch stop? It is 1:00 A.M. now.
3. The Russian skaters earned a perfect score.
4. Carlos asked if Mr. Garcia was in his office
5. Where were you able to find shoes for $9.00?
6. What a shock!
7. The baby weighed 7 lbs. 3 oz. and was named Edward M. Miller, Jr.
8. Stop! Your time is up.
9. Do you like Italian food, Tina?
10. Summerdale Ave. isn't north of here, is it?

Extending the Lesson

Have students write the following kinds of sentences and insert appropriate punctuation.

1. two imperative sentences
2. two exclamatory sentences
3. two interrogative sentences
4. two declarative sentences
5. two sentences using initials or abbreviations
6. two sentences with indirect questions

662

Use a period after an abbreviation or an initial.

An **abbreviation** is a shortened form of a word. An **initial** is a first letter that stands for a word.

Dr. Orville N. Boynton   3 A.M. on Sept. 13

Maj. Jacob M. Levine   8 lb., 13 oz.

Certain abbreviations do not use periods. To check whether or not to use a period with an abbreviation, look up the abbreviation in your dictionary.

CIA (*Central Intelligence Agency*)
CB (*Citizens' Band*)
UN (*United Nations*)

Use a period after each number or letter for an item in an outline or a list.

(An Outline)   (A List)

I. Foods   1. beach towel

A. Fruits   2. suntan oil

1. Peaches   3. sunglasses

Use a period between dollars and cents and before a decimal.

$42.91   2.36

The Question Mark

Use a question mark at the end of an interrogative sentence.

An **interrogative sentence** is a sentence that asks a question.

Who was at the door?

The Exclamation Point

Use an exclamation point at the end of an exclamatory sentence.

An **exclamatory sentence** expresses excitement or other strong emotion.

662

That's wonderful! How lucky you were!

Use an exclamation point after an interjection.

An **interjection** is one or more words that show strong feeling. Sometimes the interjection is a sound.

Hurrah! Yuck! Oh, no! Great!

Exercise A Copy the following sentences, adding the necessary punctuation. Be prepared to tell what punctuation marks you used and why you used them.

1. Has anyone seen Col. Harms?
2. Mona said that she wants a watch for her birthday.
3. Incredible! That micrometer measures up to .0001 of an inch.
4. Does your plane leave at 6:00 A.M. or 6:00 P.M.?
5. Ouch! That plate is hot.
6. I. Types of fabric
   A. Natural products
      1. Cotton
7. The initials N.A.S. stand for the National Academy of Sciences.
8. Address the invitation to Dr. Jacob Morton, Jr., P.O. Box 1200, Nashville, Tennessee.
9. Did Rev. J.T. Smith give the sermon?
10. The U.S.S. *Arizona* was sunk at Pearl Harbor.

Exercise B Follow the directions for Exercise A.

1. Karen asked what UNICEF means.
2. The book was published by Random House, Inc. in 1968.
3. Have you heard the new FM station?
4. Is Sally an LPN or an RN.? *or L.P.N.*
5. Oh, no! He struck out!
6. Dr. O'Donnell's business card reads, "Mary O'Donnell, MD."

663

7. Does school end at 11 AM on Friday?
8. The IRS audited his financial records
   or I.R.S.
9. Dan handed the customer $237 change from the five-dollar bill
10. Stop! Did you bring the tickets for the concert?

The Comma

A comma is used to separate words that do not go together. When you are speaking, you can pause. When you are writing, you use commas for breaks in thought. In this way, commas help you to communicate clearly.

Using Commas in a Series

Use a comma after every item in a series except the last one.

A series is three or more items of the same kind. Your writing may contain a series of words, phrases, or clauses.

Words: Clair ordered soup, a salad, and milk.

Phrases: The cross-country team ran down the street, through the park, and into the forest preserve.

Clauses: The tour guide explained who founded Dallas, how it grew, and why it is an important city today.

Use commas after *first, second, third,* and so on, when these adverbs introduce a series.

There are four stages for writing a paper: first, pre-writing; second, writing a first draft; third, revising; and fourth, writing a final copy.

When there are two or more adjectives before a noun, use commas between them.

The weather reporter predicted another hot, humid day.

The Comma

Objective

To use commas correctly

Presenting the Lesson

1. Read page 664, going over rules and examples for the use of commas in a series.

2. Assign and discuss Exercises A and B on pages 665–666.

3. Read and discuss page 666, going over rules and examples of commas used with introductory words and with interruptions. Be certain that students understand and recognize prepositional phrases, verbal phrases, and adverb clauses. Study the list of interrupters on pages 666–667. Ask students to write original sentences using each interrupter.

4. Assign and discuss Exercises A and B on pages 667–668.

5. Read pages 668–670. Study rules and examples of comma usage, paying particular attention to explanations and examples of nouns of direct address and nouns in apposition. Again, be certain that students recognize direct quotations. Review the construction of compound sentences, pointing out the position of the comma before the conjunction.

664

Exercise A Number your paper from 1 to 10. Copy the following sentences and add commas where necessary.

1. Skiing, tobogganing, and ice skating are winter sports.
2. Julie goes to dance lessons on Monday, Wednesday, and Friday.
3. Mexican food is known for its hot, spicy flavors.
4. Craig started the car, put it in gear, and backed out of the driveway.
5. The soldier told his captors three things: first, his name; second, his rank; and third, his serial number.
6. The Christmas stocking was filled with fruit, nuts, and candy.
7. Jerry struck a match, turned on the gas, and lit the camp stove.
8. Cheryl learned three swimming strokes: first, the crawl; second, the backstroke; and third, the butterfly.
9. The baby waved his arms, kicked his legs, and talked to the stuffed animal.
10. Laura asked Barb where she bought the album, how much it cost, and whether she could borrow it.

Exercise B Follow the directions for Exercise A.

1. The mechanic listed the car's problems: first, faulty transmission; second, weak brakes; and third, bald tires.
2. Streamers, paper flowers, and balloons decorated the gym.
3. To make vanilla frosting, mix butter, powdered sugar, vanilla, and milk.
4. The radio announcer gave an accurate, informative report of the game.
5. Marti saddled the horse, mounted it, and rode off down the trail.

665

6. Read pages 671–672, going over rules and examples for the use of commas in dates, in place names, and in letters.
7. Read pages 672–673, discussing the use of commas in nonrestrictive clauses. Study the explanation and examples of restrictive and nonrestrictive clauses carefully, paying special attention to the ways to differentiate between the two kinds of clauses.
8. Read page 674, discussing the use of commas to avoid confusion.
9. Assign and discuss Exercises A and B on pages 674–675.

Individualizing the Lesson

Less-Advanced Students

Have students find one published example of each comma rule in the lesson. Students should copy the sentence and then write the rule that applies.

Advanced Students

Have students write two sentences applying each comma rule discussed in this lesson. After each sentence, students should write the comma rule that applies.

Optional Practice

Present the following sentences on the chalkboard or on a worksheet. Number the commas as indicated. Have students number their papers from 1 to 10 and write the rule that explains the use of each comma. Answers on page 666.

1. I was exposed to German measles,[1] but I didn't catch them.
2. On January 12,[2] 1980,[3] Andrea and her family moved to St. Paul,[4] Minnesota.

3. Dan Rather,[5] who reported the story,[6] seemed shaken by the bizarre,[7] frightening events.

4. The gardeners raked the grass,[8] pruned the hedges,[9] and turned the soil.

5. Howard,[10] come and eat your dinner.

1. compound sentence
2. dates
3. dates
4. place names
5. nonrestrictive clause
6. nonrestrictive clause
7. series (adjective before noun)
8. series
9. series
10. direct address

Extending the Lesson

Have students write the following kinds of senences as directed and insert commas where needed.

1. two sentences with direct quotations
2. two sentences with commas used to avoid confusion
3. two sentences with nonrestrictive clauses
4. two sentences with appositives
5. two sentences with nouns of direct address
6. two compound sentences

6. Lush, green, tropical foliage had overgrown the path through the hot, steamy jungle.

7. Seven-layer salad contains lettuce, peas, bacon, hard-boiled eggs, onions, mayonnaise, and cheese.

8. We visited cathedrals, art museums, and historical monuments on the tour.

9. First, I planned the menu; second, I went to the grocery store; third, I prepared the dinner; and fourth, I served it.

10. The waves roll in, crash on the beach, and roll out again.

Using Commas with Introductory Words

Use a comma to separate an introductory word, long phrase, or clause from the rest of the sentence.

Yes, I'd like a glass of water. (introductory word)

After three weeks without rain, the lawn became very dry and brown. (prepositional phrases)

Breathing hard, the runner kept walking after the race. (verbal phrase)

If it rains, the picnic will be postponed. (adverb clause)

As you can see, commas are used after introductory words like *yes* and *no*. They are also used after prepositional phrases, verbal phrases, and adverb clauses that begin sentences.

Sometimes the comma may be left out. When there would be little pause in speaking, no comma is used.

At midnight the band stopped playing.

Using Commas with Interrupters

Use commas to set off one or more words that interrupt the flow of thought in a sentence.

The defendant, I believe, is innocent.

Kevin, for example, plays two sports.

The price of gas, in fact, has gone down.

Mildred, of course, wants to be on the committee.

The following words are additional examples of interrupters. In a sentence, set them off with commas.

therefore	in any event	however
moreover	by the way	furthermore
I suppose	I think	nevertheless

Exercise A   Number your paper from 1 to 10. Copy the following sentences. Add commas where necessary.

1. No. *On Golden Pond* did not win the Oscar for best movie.
2. Before opening the door. Brad knocked.
3. Waxing the car. Tony found some rust spots.
4. Martin. however. refused to go.
5. Yes. Myrna accepted the job.
6. Exhausted from fighting the brush fire. the volunteers returned to town.
7. You know my brother. I believe.
8. To be honest with you. I really don't like that song.
9. After he had made the announcement. the President left the room.
10. If the Lakers win this game. they will win the championship.

Exercise B   Follow the directions for Exercise A.

1. The finale was. I think. the best part of the show.
2. George. on the other hand. prefers bluegrass music.
3. Yes. that is Lill's responsibility.
4. Miriam. however. walks to school.

5. After the last game of the season.the team has an awards dinner.
6. Although Cathy moved to Florida.we still call each other and write letters.
7. Worried about his final exams.Joe couldn't sleep.
8. When Bill cooks dinner.he always makes chili.
9. That book.by the way.is by Robert Peck.
10. Because Eddie had missed two practices.the coach wouldn't let him play in the game.

Using Commas with Nouns of Direct Address

Use commas to set off nouns of direct address.

Sometimes when you speak or write to someone, you use the person's name. The name of someone directly spoken to is a noun of **direct address.**

> Betsy, type this letter.
>
> On the table, Mom, is a note from Dad.
>
> Are there any messages, Lloyd?
>
> When you finish the test, class, turn your booklets over.

As in the last example, nouns of direct address may be common nouns.

Using Commas with Appositives

Use commas to set off most appositives.

An **appositive** is one or more words that explain or identify another word. The appositive directly follows the word it explains.

> Marcel Marceau, a mime, appeared in the movie *Silent Movie.*

Our dance teacher, Miss Eden, took us to a ballet.

Rugby, a form of football, is played with no time-outs or substitutions.

As in the final example, an appositive may contain a prepositional phrase.

A noun used as an appositive is called a **noun in apposition.** When the noun in apposition is a single name, it is not usually set off by commas.

My cousin Sally lives in Denver.

Using Commas with Quotations

Use commas to set off the explanatory words of a direct quotation.

The explanatory words are the statements like *he said, Greg replied,* or *Sheila asked.* They are not part of the quotation.

Explanatory words often come before the quotation. Use a comma after the explanatory words.

Carol said, "Meet me at the corner of State and Adams."

Now look at this quotation:

"Meet me at the corner of State and Adams," Carol said.

In the sentence above, the explanatory words come after the quotation. Notice that the comma belongs at the end of the quotation inside the quotation marks.

Sometimes a quotation is broken into two parts. The explanatory words separate the two parts. Here is an example of a *divided quotation.*

"Meet me," Carol said, "at the corner of State and Adams."

In a divided quotation, a comma is used within the quotation marks at the end of the first part of the sentence. A comma is also used after the explanatory words.

Indirect quotations do not tell the speaker's exact words. No commas are used.

> Carol said that we should meet her at the corner of State and Adams.

Using Commas in Compound Sentences

Use a comma before the conjunction between the two main clauses of a compound sentence.

> The temperature was ten degrees below zero, but the car started with no problem.

The comma is not necessary when the main clauses are very short and are joined by *and*.

> We danced and we sang.

Sometimes very short main clauses are joined by *but* or *or*. A comma is used since the words *but* and *or* mark a change in the flow of thought.

> Ann eats, but she doesn't gain weight.

Don't confuse compound sentences with compound subjects or compound predicates. There is no comma before the *and* that joins a compound subject or predicate.

> Tom parked the car and dropped some change into the parking meter.

Exercise A Copy these sentences. Add commas as needed.

1. Pac Man, a video game, has become very popular.
2. The doctor, a specialist in plastic surgery, examined the scar.
3. Mr. Wilson, I'd like to introduce my brother Fred.
4. Did you water the plants, Sylvia?
5. The dune buggy, a fiberglass shell with a Volkswagen engine, drove down the beach.

6. Mr. Schmidt, the building superintendent, will make minor repairs in the apartment.
7. Paul said, "The golf match is on TV at 1:00 P.M."
8. "I ordered four tickets for the concert," said Dad.
9. "That ball," said the angry tennis player, "was in bounds."
10. Amy was nervous before the play, but she remembered all her lines.

Exercise B   Follow the directions for Exercise A.

1. Is Sandy still attending the junior college, or did she transfer to the state university?
2. Jack cleaned out the leaves from the gutter, and then he painted it with rust-proof paint.
3. Milton Friedman, a well-known economist, won the Nobel Prize.
4. Nora reported on the Middle East, and Peter discussed the problems in South Africa.
5. Ralph asked, "Who is going to the banquet tomorrow night?"
6. "Sewing on a button is not that difficult, Marty," explained Debby.
7. "Your donations for the flood victims will be put to good use," said Father McDonald.
8. The sandwiches were made with pita, a Middle-Eastern flat bread.
9. "It is your turn," reminded Mom, "to do the dishes."
10. "Girls, let's meet by the south tennis courts before the match," said Ms. Snyder.

Using Commas in Dates

In dates, use a comma between the day of the month and the year.

September 4, 1982   July 20, 1947

671

When a date is part of a sentence, a comma follows the year.

The Tiffany Exhibit opened on June 10, 1982, in Chicago.

Using Commas in Place Names

Use a comma between the name of a city or town and the name of its state or country.

Seattle, Washington   Bonn, West Germany

Dublin, Ireland   Boise, Idaho

When an address is part of a sentence, use a comma after each item.

Simon addressed the letter to Mr. Edgar Evans, 1602 Fairview Road, Juneau, Alaska 99801.

Note that you do not put a comma between the state name and the ZIP code.

Using Commas in Letters

Use a comma after the salutation of a friendly letter. Use a comma after the closing of a friendly letter or a business letter.

Dear Margaret,   Yours truly,

Using Commas with Nonrestrictive Clauses

Use commas to set off nonrestrictive clauses.

A **nonrestrictive clause** is a clause that merely adds an idea to the sentence. The sentence would be complete without it. The meaning would be definite without it.

A **restrictive clause** is a clause that is essential to the meaning of

672

a sentence. The clause is needed for the sense of the sentence. If a restrictive clause is dropped from a sentence, the meaning of the sentence changes.

Nonrestrictive clause: Mr. Murphy, *who is the new coach of the team,* held a press conference.
Mr. Murphy held a press conference. (The clause could be dropped from the sentence.)

Restrictive clause: Mr. Murphy is the coach *who held the press conference.*
Mr. Murphy is the coach. (The clause cannot be dropped from the sentence.)

To see if a clause is nonrestrictive, read the sentence without the clause. If the meaning doesn't change, the clause is nonrestrictive. Use commas before and after it.

Restrictive clauses are often used to identify or to point out the person or thing they modify. Without this identification, the meaning of the sentence would not be clear. Nonrestrictive clauses, on the other hand, add no essential meaning to the sentence.

Restrictive clause: Mr. Greenberg is the instructor who taught me to drive. (The clause tells which instructor.)

Nonrestrictive clause: Mr. Greenberg, who is very patient, taught me to drive.
Mr. Greenberg taught me to drive. (The clause could be dropped.)

Restrictive clause: This is the theater that shows double features. (The clause tells which theater.)

Nonrestrictive clause: This theater, which has a balcony, holds 2,000 people.
This theater holds 2,000 people. (The clause could be dropped.)

Using Commas To Avoid Confusion

Use a comma whenever the reader might otherwise be confused.

Sometimes no rule applies, but a sentence might be misread if the commas weren't there.

Without commas, the following sentences could be misunderstood.

> Outside Mike barbecued chicken.
> Whoever knocked knocked loudly.

With commas, the sentences are clearer.

> Outside, Mike barbecued chicken.

> Whoever knocked, knocked loudly.

Exercise A Copy the following sentences. Add commas where necessary.

1. Dear Alice
   I will be moving soon. Please write to me at 102 Woodland Court, Nashville, Tennessee 37115.
   > Yours truly,
   > Margie
2. On March 4, 1933, President Roosevelt closed every bank in the country.
3. The letter was postmarked from Paris, France, on June 10, 1982.
4. Gary, Indiana, has many steel mills.
5. Johnny Morris, who used to play football for the Chicago Bears, is now a sports broadcaster.
6. On November 11, 1918, the Armistice ending World War I was signed.
7. The plane made intermediate stops in Huntsville, Alabama, and Memphis, Tennessee.
8. Ms. Bercher was stationed in Honolulu, Hawaii, from May 1, 1980, to September 1, 1982.

9. Send your application to Mr. Thomas Beale at the Beale Corporation, 200 South Michigan Avenue, Chicago, Illinois 60025.

10. Inside, Dad made a fire in the fireplace.

Exercise B   Follow the directions for Exercise A.

1. On August 3, 1923, Calvin Coolidge was sworn in as President of the United States.

2. Dear Mike,
   My sister's new address is P.O. Box 1978, Monterey, California 93940.

   Sincerely,
   Nick

3. On July 16, 1945, the first atomic bomb was exploded in the desert near Los Alamos, New Mexico.

4. The electrician you called, called back.

5. The South surrendered to the North on April 9, 1865, at Appomattox, Virginia.

6. The house is at 691 Gilmore Street, Long Beach, California.

7. Are you from Hollywood, Florida, or Hollywood, California?

8. Whoever screamed, screamed loudly.

9. My sister, who is sometimes called the family firecracker, was born on July 4, 1975.

10. This china, which my grandmother brought back from Vienna, Austria, is extremely fragile.

The Semicolon

Use a semicolon to join the parts of a compound sentence if no coordinating conjunction is used.

> We were bored with the programs on TV; we decided to write a play of our own.

1. Read pages 675–676. Go over rules and examples of the use of semicolons. Be sure that students can recognize and understand the meaning of *compound sentences, coordinating conjunctions,* and *conjunctive adverbs.*

2. Read pages 676–677. Go over rules and examples of the use of the colon.

3. Assign and discuss Exercises A and B on pages 677–678.

Individualizing the Lesson

Less-Advanced Students

1. Discuss with students the uses of a semicolon. Be sure they understand that a comma, semicolon, and colon cannot be used interchangeably.

2. Have students find five published examples of the uses of a semicolon. Tell them to copy the sentences; then have them write the rule that applies after each sentence.

Advanced Students

Have students write a letter using the following items.

Roland

a camping trip starting at eight a.m. Saturday, June 30 Larry will bring popcorn, peanuts, and peanut butter

Hector will drive

Kim has the tent, two sleeping bags, and a lantern

Martin will bring drinks such as water, milk, and juice

Tell students to be sure to use commas, semicolons, and colons properly.

When there are commas in the first part of a compound sentence, use a semicolon to separate the main clauses.

> The corner store sells bread, milk, and some canned goods; but it does not carry fresh fruit, vegetables, or meat.

When there are commas within parts of a series, use semicolons to separate the parts.

> The items we will make in woodshop this term are first, a chopping block; second, a tool box; and third, a footstool.

Use a semicolon before a conjunctive adverb that joins the clauses of a compound sentence.

You have learned that the parts of a compound sentence are sometimes joined by such words as *therefore, however, so, consequently, besides, nevertheless, then, yet,* and *moreover.* These words, called **conjunctive adverbs,** follow a semicolon.

> The food in that restaurant is good; however, the service is slow.

The Colon

Use a colon after the greeting in a business letter.

> Dear Mr. Blake: Dear Sir or Madam:

Use a colon between numerals indicating hours and minutes.

> 6:20 P.M.   7:10 A.M.

Use a colon to introduce a list of items. The colon indicates a pause before the items that follow.

> Our high school has girls' teams for most sports: track, basketball, swimming, volleyball, tennis, and softball.

Do not use a colon if the list immediately follows a verb or a preposition.

Scholarships are given for academic achievement, athletic ability, and financial need.

Exercise A   Copy the word before and after each missing semicolon or colon. Add the correct punctuation mark.

1. Dear Sir:
   The position that you inquired about has already been filled.
2. The customer gave her order to the waitress:French onion soup, spinach salad, and iced tea.
3. The villain appeared on the stage;the crowd booed.
4. Holiday traffic and road construction caused travel delays;it was not a good weekend for taking a trip.
5. On the hanger, the dress looked great;however, on me, it looked like a slipcover.
6. The play was supposed to start at 8:00;however, the curtain did not go up until 8:20.
7. Barb packed the following items:hiking boots, mosquito repellent, a poncho, and a change of clothes.
8. Snow fell all night;consequently, we had to dig our way out in the morning.
9. The tour stopped in these cities:Florence, Italy; Barcelona, Spain;and Lisbon, Portugal.
10. Karen does not enjoy chemistry;nevertheless, she does well in the course.

Exercise B   Follow the directions for Exercise A.

1. Kent broke his leg;therefore he had to learn to use crutches.
2. The junk shop was filled with old, broken-down chairs; rickety, wobbly tables;and dozens of useless items.
3. The fog is really bad;therefore, all flights to and from the airport have been canceled.
4. Tex made some hot, spicy chili and he served it with grated cheese, onions, and sour cream.

5. Her wallet contained the following items: ten dollars, two credit cards, a driver's license, a Social Security card, and several pictures.
6. Dear Reader:
   It's time to renew your subscription.
7. I enjoy watching the Academy Awards; however, I do not usually agree with the selection of winners.
8. The fireworks start at 9:00 PM on July 4.
9. The beaches are closed temporarily; the pollution level of the water is too high.
10. Indoor tennis has the following advantages over outdoor tennis: games are never canceled because of rain, there is no wind, and the sun doesn't get in the player's eyes.

The Dash

Using Dashes with Interrupters

You have learned about using commas with words or short phrases, such as *however* and *I think,* that interrupt a sentence. A **dash** is used with a long explanation that interrupts the thought.

The deluxe pizza—thin crust topped with double cheese, tomato sauce, pepperoni, sausage, green peppers, onions, and mushrooms—tasted delicious.

The microwave oven—it can cook a baked potato in minutes—has revolutionized cooking.

Using the Dash Before a Summary

Use a dash after a series to indicate that a summary statement will follow.

The Dash

Objective

To use the dash correctly

Presenting the Lesson

1. Read pages 678–679. Point out how the use of the dash differs from the use of the comma with interrupters.

2. Assign and discuss the exercise on page 679.

Individualizing the Lesson

Less-Advanced Students

1. Discuss with students the concepts of interrupters and summaries in sentences.

2. Have students write several sentences using dashes as interrupters and before summaries.

Spiders, termites, ants, and rodents—these are all household pests.

Fruits, vegetables, beans, nuts, and whole grains—this is the diet of many vegetarians.

Exercise   Copy these sentences. Insert dashes as needed.

1. School closings-one district closed four schools in the last ten years-are a result of the lower birth rate.
2. Bond paper, carbon paper, envelopes, and paper clips—these items were ordered from the stationery store.
3. Gila monsters, tarantulas, jellyfish, stingrays-all of them are venomous animals.
4. The state fair-it is usually held during the first two weeks in August-will feature live entertainment daily.
5. The James E. Sullivan Memorial Trophy-an award given to the amateur athlete who has done the most to promote sportsmanship-was given to Eric Heiden in 1980.
6. The young man wanted fame, wealth, and power-goals most successful business people have in common.
7. Azaleas, jasmine, camellias, and roses-all of these grew in the garden.
8. We can skip lunch-unless you are really hungry-and go shopping instead.
9. Golf, tennis, swimming, and sailing-this park has something for everyone.
10. The town newspaper-there were not enough ads to help pay printing costs-printed its last edition today.

The Hyphen

Use a hyphen if part of a word must be carried over from one line to the next.

Words are separated by hyphens only between syllables.

679

The Hyphen

Objective

To use the hyphen correctly in word division and in certain compound words

Presenting the Lesson

1. Read pages 679–680. Go over rules and examples of the use of the hyphen. Encourage students to check syllable division by consulting the dictionary. Be certain that students understand the meaning of compound numbers, compound nouns, and compound adjectives. Again, encourage students to verify the need for hyphens by consulting the dictionary.

2. Assign and discuss the Exercise on page 681.

Individualizing the Lesson

Less-Advanced Students

Work through the Exercise on page 681 with students.

Advanced Students

Have students do the Exercise on page 681 on their own.

Optional Practice

Have students insert hyphens in the following sentences. Students should consult the dictionary as necessary.

1. Mrs. Kramer, our next door neighbor, does not get along with her mother in law.
2. This encyclopedia is out of date; I need more up to the minute information.

The factory was patrolled by se-curity guards.

Only words having two or more syllables can be broken by a hyphen. Never divide one-syllable words, like *growl* or *weight*, at the end of a line. Check your dictionary if you are not sure of the syllables in a word.

A single letter should not be left at the end of a line. For instance, this division of *election* would be wrong: *e- lection*. A single letter should not begin a line either. This division of *ordinary* would be incorrect: *ordinar- y*.

Use a hyphen in compound numbers from twenty-one to ninety-nine.

fifty-two pencils   twenty-six cars

Use a hyphen in fractions.

a three-fifths share   one-sixth of the pie

Use a hyphen in certain compound nouns, such as *brother-in-law, drive-in,* and *commander-in-chief.*

My sister-in-law is a vice-president of the company.

Use a hyphen or hyphens between words that make up a compound adjective used before a noun.

The radio announcer gives a play-by-play account of the game.
but: The radio announcer describes the game play by play.

When compound adjectives are used after a noun, they are not usually hyphenated.

A dictionary will tell you if a word needs a hyphen. These are some examples of compound adjectives:

four-year-old girl	matter-of-fact approach
short-term loan	best-selling novel
well-used book	off-white paint
three-ring circus	half-baked idea

Exercise   Number your paper from 1 to 15. After the proper number, write the <u>word or words</u> that should be hyphenated. Add the necessary hyphens. Use your dictionary if necessary.

1. This is an <u>up-to-date</u> version of the *World Almanac*.
2. Brad made a <u>half-hearted</u> attempt to fix the lawnmower.
3. My <u>three-year-old</u> cousin got lost at the fair.
4. <u>Check-out</u> time at the hotel was noon.
5. Chuck Brown was on the city <u>all-star</u> football team.
6. The <u>well-to-do</u> executive donated large sums of money to her favorite charities.
7. My <u>great-grandmother</u> only made <u>forty-five</u> dollars a month at her first job.
8. <u>One-half</u> of the students have <u>part-time</u> jobs.
9. The newspaper reported the mayor's <u>off-the-cuff</u> remarks.
10. About <u>forty-nine</u> out of every 100 babies born each year are girls.
11. Fewer than <u>one-third</u> of the students ate a <u>well-bal-anced</u> diet.
12. The <u>two-for-one</u> sale was very successful.
13. Doug wrote a letter to his <u>brother-in-law</u>.
14. The executive wore a <u>three-piece</u> suit.
15. The quarterback asked for a <u>time-out</u>.

The Apostrophe

The apostrophe is frequently used to form the possessive of nouns. To use the apostrophe correctly, you should know whether a noun is singular or plural.

To form the possessive of a singular noun, add an apostrophe and an s.

athlete + 's = athlete's   Cas + 's = Cas's
lady + 's = lady's   Jessica + 's = Jessica's

681

to show omission of numbers in a date, and to form plurals of letters, figures, and words used as words.

2. Assign and discuss Exercises A and B on pages 682–683.

Individualizing the Lesson

Less-Advanced Students

Have students find published examples of words using apostrophes. Have students write the words on the chalkboard, and then go through the words orally. Students should define each word as singular possessive or plural possessive, and explain under which rule the apostrophe was added.

Advanced Students

1. Have students write ten sentences, making sure to use each rule about apostrophes at least once. Tell students not to insert apostrophes where they belong. Then have students exchange papers.

2. Students should rewrite the sentences, making sure to insert apostrophes properly.

Optional Practice

1. Have students form the possessive of the following words.

woman's	children's	nobody's
people's	fish's	Amy's
bus's	firefighter's	Ross's
Jones's	anyone's	horses's

2. Have students form contractions from the following words.

it is it's	could not couldn't	she had she'd
he will he'll	I will I'll	have not haven't
we have we've	will not won't	you are you're

To form the possessive of a plural noun that does not end in s, add an apostrophe and an s.

children + 's = children's   men + 's = men's

To form the possessive of a plural noun that ends in s, add only an apostrophe.

runners + ' = runners'   surfers + ' = surfers'
Masters + ' = Masters'   drivers + ' = drivers'

To form the possessive of indefinite pronouns, use an apostrophe and an s.

somebody + 's = somebody's   anyone + 's = anyone's

Do not use an apostrophe with a personal pronoun to show possession.

hers   ours   yours   its   theirs

The sailboat was blown off *its* course.

Use an apostrophe in a contraction.

In contractions, words are joined and letters are left out. An apostrophe replaces one or more letters that are left out.

we'll = we will   hadn't = had not
they've = they have   won't = will not
it's = it is   I'll = I will

Use an apostrophe to show the omission of numbers in a date.

the winter of '78 (the winter of 1978)
an '82 Mercury (a 1982 Mercury)

Use an apostrophe and s to form the plurals of letters, figures, and words used as words.

ABC's   two *3*'s   five *i*'s   *but*'s and *and*'s

Exercise A   Insert apostrophes where they are needed.

1. Where is the children's section of the library?
2. I'm going with Bess's cousin.

3. She's bringing the '72 yearbook to the reunion.
4. That's Tricia's favorite song.
5. There's a beautiful view of the Gilberts' apartment.
6. Someone's umbrella is in the closet.
7. I'm going to test drive that sports car.
8. They've realized that the problem is theirs.
9. Mimi's name has two *m*'s and two *i*'s.
10. Mr. Elliot couldn't attend the men's luncheon meeting.

Exercise B   Follow the directions for Exercise A.

1. Is that our neighbor's hammer you're borrowing?
2. The 1950's are sometimes called the Eisenhower years.
3. There were too many *well*'s and *you know*'s in your speech.
4. The children's puppy was a gift from their aunt.
5. The class of '83 planned its prom.
6. Doesn't the Barkers' car have a muffler?
7. Isn't Cathy's party from 8:00 until 11:00?
8. The two coaches' game plans were entirely different.
9. The toddler can't say *th*'s or *l*'s yet.
10. It is nobody's fault but yours.

Quotation Marks

Use quotation marks at the beginning and at the end of a direct quotation.

Quotation marks tell your reader that a speaker's exact words are being given. Here is an example:

Craig said, "Something is wrong with the radio."

Quotation marks are *not* used with indirect quotations. An indirect quotation does not tell the speaker's exact words.

Craig said that something was wrong with the radio.

683

Extending the Lesson

Have students form the possessives of the following words.

bird's   house's
apples'   his
cars'   class's

Quotation Marks

Objective

To use quotation marks correctly in direct quotations, and to use quotation marks and underlining correctly in titles

Presenting the Lesson

1. Read pages 683–684. Study the rule and examples of the use of quotation marks in direct quotations. Explain and illustrate the meaning of both direct and indirect

683

quotations. Point out the rules governing placement of quotation marks, commas, and end punctuation in relation to explanatory words.

2. Read page 684, explaining the placement of quotation marks, capital letters, commas, and end punctuation in divided quotations.

3. Assign the exercise on page 685. In discussing students' answers, have as many examples as possible written on the chalkboard.

4. Read page 685, discussing the use of question marks and exclamation points with quotation marks.

5. Assign and discuss Exercises A and B on pages 685–686.

6. Read pages 686–687. Study the examples of the use of quotation marks and paragraphing in dialogues.

7. Assign and discuss the Exercise on page 687.

8. Read pages 687–688, studying examples of the use of quotation marks and underlining for titles.

9. Assign and discuss Exercises A and B on pages 688–689.

Individualizing the Lesson

Less-Advanced Students

Have students write a dialogue of at least five lines between two observers at an outdoor concert. Students should punctuate the quotations correctly.

Advanced Students

Have students write ten sentences using quotations. Tell students to use direct quotations, divided quotations, question marks, exclamation points, and titles in their sentences.

At the beginning of a sentence there are often explanatory words. Use a comma directly after these words. Then begin the quotation with quotation marks. A period at the end of a sentence belongs *inside* the quotation marks.

The conductor said, "All aboard."

Sometimes explanatory words end the sentence. Then the quoted statement at the beginning of the sentence is followed by a comma. The comma belongs inside the quotation marks.

"All aboard," said the conductor.

Using Divided Quotations

Sometimes a quotation is divided into two parts by explanatory words. In that case, each part of the quotation is enclosed by quotation marks.

"A great city to visit," Roger said, "is Toronto."

In the example above, the divided quotation is a single sentence. The second part begins with a small letter. At times, however, the second part begins a new sentence. Then capitalize the first word of the second part.

"Let's go get some refreshments," Joy suggested. " The band is taking a break."

The first part of the divided quotation is followed by a comma. Commas always appear inside quotation marks.

"Your mail," Terry said, "is on the hall table."

The explanatory words in the middle of a divided quotation are followed by either a period or a comma. Use a period if the first part completes a sentence. Use a comma if the sentence continues after the explanatory words.

"In Florida," Don said, "we visited the Everglades."

"I want to go downtown today," Leslie explained. "I have to do some shopping."

Exercise Write each of the following sentences three ways as a direct quotation. Answers will vary.

> Example: I want a steady job.
> a. "I want a steady job," he said.
> b. He said, "I want a steady job."
> c. "I want," he said, "a steady job."

1. Try snorkeling if you go to the Bahamas.
2. No, Robert Redford was not in the movie *Ordinary People.*
3. I wish that I could go to the concert.
4. After all that planning, we still forgot a flashlight.
5. In the second period, the Blackhawks were leading.

Using Punctuation with Quotation Marks

Place question marks and exclamation points inside the quotation marks if they belong to the quotation itself.

> Katie asked, "Where can I find that information?"
> Larry screamed, "Watch out!"

Place question marks and exclamation points outside the quotation marks if they do not belong to the quotation.

> Did Kelly say, "Wait for me outside the cafeteria"?
> How happy I was when Ms. Piley said, "You got an A"!

Commas and periods, as you have seen, always appear within quotation marks.

Exercise A Copy the following sentences. Punctuate them correctly with quotation marks, end marks, and commas. (There are three indirect quotations that need only end punctuation.)

1. Stay back ordered the fire chief.
2. May I borrow your blue sweater asked Sue.
3. Oh no said Pat I think I did the wrong exercises

Have students punctuate the following sentences correctly.

1. "Wow! exclaimed Helen. That was the best game we've ever played."
2. Janis wondered if you were going to the museum exhibit.
3. "Can you help us? asked Bill. We'd really appreciate it."
4. Mr. Boone wondered what happened at the committee meeting last night.
5. Our English teacher said. Please review last week's notes before tomorrow's test."

Extending the Lesson

1. Divide students into pairs; then have them interview one another and take notes on the interview.
2. Have students write a newspaper story about the interview they conducted. Students should use a variety of quotations throughout the story.

4. Mr. Hardin explained how the clutch works in a car with standard transmission.
5. "My dog Grover is going to obedience school," said Mark.
6. The crowd shouted loudly, "We're number one!"
7. Eve said that she was going to summer school.
8. "The car started fine last night," said Fran. "Why won't it start now?"
9. Did Ellen say that she would be on the clean-up committee?
10. Did the doctor say, "I think we should X-ray your arm?"

Exercise B Write each of the following sentences as a direct quotation. In some examples, put the quotation first. In others, put the quotation last. Also, for variety, divide some quotations.

Answers will vary.

1. What language is spoken in Brazil?
2. Stop that!
3. I changed that flat tire on Denise's car.
4. There's a stream behind the cabin.
5. Can we join your book club?
6. After the Fourth of July, stores begin their summer clearance sales.
7. We hiked in the foothills.
8. Watch out!
9. Was that spider a black widow?
10. This afternoon I have to go to the orthodontist.

Using Long Quotations

You may wonder how to use quotation marks for quoting two or more sentences by the same speaker. Look at the following example.

"Once you have made a list of their birthdays, bring it to me," said the manager. "I want to ensure that everyone gets a card."

686

Using Quotation Marks for Dialogue

Dialogue is conversation between two or more people. It is punctuated in a special way. Begin a new paragraph each time the speaker changes.

> "I am trying to limit my TV watching," said Anne.
>
> "Well, I worked out a deal with my brother," replied Angela, "to try and cut down."
>
> "What did you do, Angela?" asked Tom.
>
> "I promised him that each week that I watched more TV than he did, I would do his chores."
>
> "Did it work?" asked Anne.
>
> "No!" exclaimed Angela. "Now we just watch TV together."

Exercise Rewrite the following conversation. Make correct paragraph divisions, and use the right punctuation.

> "What is the value of sports?"Mr. Munz asked."Well," answered Dick,"I think team sports,like football or basketball,help the players to learn cooperation."Jim added, "I think sports are valuable because they keep you fit."I agree with you,"said Frank."I also think that individual sports like golf or tennis are important."That's a good point,"agreed Tim. "I'll probably be playing tennis long after I've put away my football helmet."

Punctuating Titles

Use quotation marks to enclose the titles of magazine articles, chapters, short stories, essays, poems, songs, and short pieces of music.

Magazine article:	"Careers in Retailing"
Chapter title:	Chapter 5, "The Louisiana Purchase"
Short story:	"The Ransom of Red Chief"
Essay:	"Self-Reliance"
Poem:	"Fire and Ice"
Song:	"Hello, Dolly"

Underline the titles of books, newspapers, magazines, plays, movies, television programs, works of art, and long musical compositions.

In writing or typing, such titles are underlined, like this: <u>The Chocolate War</u>.

In print, these titles appear in italics instead.

Book title:	*Great Expectations*
Newspaper:	*Orlando Sentinel-Star*
Magazine:	*Sports Illustrated*
Play:	*The Wiz*
Movie:	*Rocky III*
Television program:	*Great Performances*
Work of art:	*American Gothic*
Long musical composition:	*Carmen*

Exercise A   Copy the following sentences, adding quotation marks or underlining titles where necessary.

1. The story "Blue Tea" appeared in the June issue of <u>Redbook</u> magazine.
2. The band played "Dixie."
3. Kathy read Jane Goodall's article about chimps, "Life and Death at Gombe."
4. <u>Custard and Company</u> is a book of poems by Ogden Nash.
5. The TV show <u>Hill Street Blues</u> is about a police precinct.
6. One of Barry's favorite movies was <u>Chariots of Fire</u>.
7. <u>The Washington Post</u> is the only newspaper that thoroughly investigated the Watergate break-in.
8. Ms. Avery played some of the music from the <u>Nutcracker Suite</u> during the Christmas holidays.
9. The play <u>The King and I</u> is based on a true story.
10. <u>The Spring House</u> and <u>Milk Cans</u> are two paintings by Andrew Wyeth.

Exercise B Follow the directions for Exercise A.

1. Marcy read us Robert Frost's poem "Birches."
2. Bill titled his research paper for economics class "Inflation: What Causes It. "
3. Dionne Warwick sang the song "Do You Know The Way to San Jose?"
4. The song "Raindrops Keep Falling on My Head" is from the movie Butch Cassidy and the Sundance Kid.
5. Did you read Chapter 1, "The New World?"
6. The community theater produced the play Annie Get Your Gun.
7. The Brethren is a book about the Supreme Court.
8. James Thurber, who wrote the story "The Secret Life of Walter Mitty," was a cartoonist for The New Yorker magazine.
9. The story was printed in The Detroit Free Press.
10. Brain, Coma, and Fever are all books by Robin Cook.

ADDITIONAL EXERCISES

Punctuation

A. Punctuation Copy these sentences, adding the necessary punctuation.

1. How thin you are!
2. How thin are you?
3. Mr. and Mrs. Antonelli are having a party at 8:00 P. M. on Saturday; R.S.V.P. was written on the invitation.
4. Dr. Tucker asked if her patient had been X-rayed yet.
5. Sal is 71.5 inches tall, just half an inch under six feet.
6. John W. Campbell, Jr. wrote the story on which the movie *The Thing* was based.
7. Oh, no! Didn't Spencer tell you to keep the cage closed?
8. The FBI trailed the suspect to St. Louis.
   or F.B.I.
9. The bus to Washington, D. C, is now boarding.
10. II. Relief programs of UNICEF
    A. African drought
    1. Food supplies

B. Commas Copy the following sentences. Add commas where necessary.

1. Carol asked if she should bring her own pliers, wrench, or hammer.
2. Georgia looked in her address book, rummaged through a stack of old mail, and finally found the address.
3. Friday, Saturday, and Sunday have been the warmest, most beautiful days this spring.
4. Gerrie put on her headphones, closed her eyes, and shut the world out.
5. Kip and Chad played chess, Mel and Al argued over a ping-pong score, and Esther leafed through an old magazine.

6. Playing Pac-Man, trying to solve the Rubik's cube, and watching cable TV were popular pastimes that year.
7. Bits of glass glittered like tiny, brilliant diamonds scattered in the alley.
8. Do the Rabbit, the Lynx, the Mustang, and the Cougar really move like the animals that they are named after?
9. First, most of the streetlights were broken; second, few houses had porch lights; third, it was a foggy night.
10. These are standard rules for cooking: first, read the entire recipe; second, gather all utensils and ingredients; third, clean up as you work.

C. Commas   Number your paper from 1 to 10. Copy the following sentences, adding commas where necessary.

1. After Robin bought the ticket, she put it in her pocket.
2. Well, the problem isn't really that simple.
3. Although the subway goes to Coney Island, many New Yorkers have never seen the ocean.
4. Really, I'm sure that I'm right.
5. Guinea pigs, to tell you the truth, are not much fun.
6. That plant, I'm sure, is poison ivy.
7. The wheelbarrow, however, was too heavy to be pushed up the ramp.
8. Almost everybody in town in fact, was at the game.
9. Left in the hot car, the dog began barking and whining.
10. Amazingly enough, Syl missed the free throw.

D. Commas   Copy the following sentences, adding commas where they are needed.

1. Skates became more popular, and skateboards were almost forgotten.
2. Joan of Arc, the French heroine, was declared a saint in 1920.
3. Yes, Mel, I remembered to buy Doritos and ginger ale.

c 4. My sister Carlene sang "Swing Low, Sweet Chariot."

5. He applied for a job at the post office, but he mailed his application to the wrong address.

6. Denny said, "I've started lifting weights."

7. "Whatever you do," said Nina, "don't look down."

8. James, have you seen my math book, the one with the red cover?

9. Ms. Willis, the career counselor, said that we should always be on time for job interviews.

10. "I tried and I succeeded," said Vince.

E. Commas Copy the following sentences. Use commas where necessary. Write *Correct* if no comma is necessary.

1. On March 13, 1852, the first newspaper cartoon of Uncle Sam appeared.

2. Dear Sandy,

   My vacation address is 215 Main Street, Carthage, Illinois 62321.

   Your friend,
   Luke

3. Mardi Gras, which is the day before Lent begins, is celebrated with a carnival in New Orleans, Louisiana.

4. What clubs are you in, in which you take an active part?

5. Otis, who really doesn't believe in horoscopes, said that he was born on May 3, 1967, around noon.

6. If Beth drives over, Vic will have a ride home.

c 7. The baseball player who broke Babe Ruth's record was Hank Aaron.

8. The pyramids near Cairo, Egypt, are all that are left of the Seven Wonders of the Ancient World.

9. The 1982 World's Fair, which was not officially recognized, was held in Knoxville, Tennessee.

10. Bronko Nagurski, who worked as a lumberjack to get in shape for football, was a legendary Bears fullback.

F. Semicolons and Colons Copy the <u>word</u> before and after each missing punctuation mark and add the correct punctuation mark. If necessary, replace a comma with a semicolon.

1. Donna can remember everything that she <u>hears</u>; <u>furthermore</u> she has a photographic memory.
2. Most of the students listed these <u>goals</u>: <u>more</u> education, an interesting job, and a happy family life.
3. Dear <u>Madam</u>:
   <u>We</u> have received your <u>letter</u>; it will be published in next week's column.
4. My grandmother likes songs by Hank Williams, Sr., who died in <u>1953</u>; I prefer Hank Williams, Jr.
5. Doctors now say that these activities cannot cause <u>colds</u>: sitting in a draft, getting one's feet wet, or swimming in chilly weather.
6. Please arrive promptly at 7:00 A.M. and bring the following <u>items</u>: <u>a</u> sleeping bag, a ground cover, a mess kit, and a canteen.
7. People from many parts of the world live in <u>Brazil</u>; <u>some</u> came to work in the rain forests.
8. Some of the amusement parks that Sheila visited were Old Country in Williamsburg, <u>Virginia</u>; <u>Kennywood</u> Park in Pittsburgh, <u>Pennsylvania</u>; <u>Kings</u> Island in Cincinnati, <u>Ohio</u>; <u>and</u> Astroworld in Houston, Texas.
9. Jackie had cut a lot of tape with the <u>scissors</u>; <u>therefore</u>, the blades were sticky.
10. The beach was <u>hot</u>; <u>however</u>, the lake was freezing.

G. The Dash and the Hyphen Copy these sentences. Insert dashes and hyphens where they are needed.

1. At eighty-six, my great-grandmother still has a happy-go-lucky view of life.
2. The commander-in-chief, the general, and the prime minister–these people will arrive at noon.

693

3. About two-thirds of the students will buy yearbooks.
4. Perhaps half of the student body-and that is just a rough guess-have long-term goals.
5. A green-eyed cat crouched on the railing.
6. Simms parked the car in an out-of-the-way spot.
7. The ten-year-old boy was half-asleep.
8. Kenwood, St. Mel's, Lane Technical-these schools have low drop-out rates.
9. Wild burros-the miners let them loose after the gold rush was over-still roam California.
10. Sue wore a nineteenth-century wedding gown, but her hairstyle was from the twenty-first century.

H. Apostrophes Copy the following sentences. Add apostrophes where they are needed.

1. Rachel likes the TR-7s made in the early 1970s.
2. The students theme for their dance hasnt been chosen.
3. Swing was dance music popular in the 30s.
4. Its somebodys problem, but not yours.
5. Chriss laces are flapping because he cant tie his shoes.
6. All three teachers classes discussed the womens movement.
7. The Hesses cat batted the bee with its paw.
8. Youre making your *r*s look almost like *v*s.
9. His *Im sorry*s didnt change the jurys verdict.
10. Thats true. The Celtics chances dont look good.

I. Quotation Marks Number your paper from 1 to 10. Copy the following sentences. Add the necessary quotation marks and other punctuation marks. Two sentences need only end punctuation.

1. I don't see that article in this magazine, said Beth. Maybe it's in last week's issue.
2. Have you included an outline with your term paper? asked Ms. Stranskey.

3. Heidi said, "The police photographer made a videotape of the scene of the crime."
4. Shawn said, "I think that I know why Pac-Man is popular. He looks like Charlie Brown."
5. Did Holly ask if Claire had called?
6. Max asked, "Does anybody have a pair of tweezers?"
7. Didn't the bus driver say, "There's no more room?"
8. "Help!" shouted George. "Where's the emergency brake?"
9. I said that I had cleared the calculator.
10. "Cheerful songs," Ms. Gaspar told us, "were popular during the Depression."

J. Quotation Marks and Underlining Copy the following sentences. Add quotation marks around titles or underline titles, where necessary.

1. The teacher assigned Tillie Olsen's story "I Stand Here Ironing."
2. David won the oratory contest by reciting Claude McKay's poem "If We Must Die."
3. Janine learned the words to the song "Sweet Home Chicago" from the movie <u>The Blues Brothers</u>.
4. The red hair of the child in Mary Cassatt's painting <u>Picking Flowers in a Field</u> blends with the flowers.
5. Karl shouts advice at the TV screen when <u>The Guiding Light</u> is on.
6. Juanita got some of the facts for her essay "Where Did the Family Car Go?" from a business newspaper, <u>The Wall Street Journal</u>.
7. <u>Grease</u> had a slightly longer run on Broadway than <u>Fiddler on the Roof</u> had.
8. <u>Mother Goose Suite</u> is a children's ballet.
9. Please read Chapter 15, "The Power of Ice," in <u>Physical Geography Today</u>.
10. Mimi got a subscription to <u>Sports Illustrated</u>.

MIXED REVIEW

Punctuation

A. Using punctuation correctly Copy these sentences, adding the correct punctuation.

1. Ouch! Did You have to use iodine?
2. The address of the Sports Car Club of America is 6750 S. Emporia, Englewood, Colorado 80112.
3. Yes, Mr. Barnes, Dr. Flores will see you right away.
4. Spartacus, who was a slave and a gladiator, led a revolt against the Romans in 71 B. C.; however, it failed.
5. "Has everyone here," Bill asked, "met Shondra?"
6. If you're using an out-of-date I D card, please get a new one before 8:30 A. M. tomorrow.
7. We've just received twenty-five pairs of men's boots.
8. The bandannas they're very popular cost $1.75 each.

B. Using punctuation in proofreading Proofread the following letter. Rewrite it, adding correct punctuation marks.

Dear Mr., Mrs., or Ms. Occupant:

Stop! You're probably asking yourself what you should stop. Well, stop worrying about what to get those hard-to-please people on your shopping list.

Everyone who appreciates natural beauty would be overjoyed to receive a gorgeous, healthy, orchid plant for the holidays. When they open these original gifts, how delighted your friends will be!

To make the holiday season of '85 one to remember, fill out the order form below.

If your order is mailed before December 5, 1985, you will receive a surprise too.

Very sincerely,

USING MECHANICS IN WRITING
Punctuation

A. You are a proofreader for a local newspaper. One day, the typesetting equipment goes haywire. The following article is an example of the results. Proofread the article. Make all necessary corrections in punctuation.

WHAT'S HAPPENING IN PORT CITY

there will be an exhibit of rare books at port City Public Library in steep street? The exhibit will be open daily from 9 am " 8 pm! [9:00 A.M.—8:00 P.M.]

at The Seaside Museum on River Street! there will be on exhibit of Whale photographs? Don't miss it; Admission will be #1.50 for Adults and $75 for children.

Port City art association, on Harbor Walk, will be exhibiting work by local artists. The Exhibition opens on Thurs? at 9;30. [A.M.]

B. Imagine this scene from a situation comedy program. On another planet, scientists have perfected a way to send beings over long distances. A visitor from that planet is sent to Earth. The alien visitor arrives in an average American apartment. It is empty except for a talking parrot. The visitor believes that the parrot is a typical inhabitant of Earth. Write a short conversation between the alien and the parrot. Include at least one divided quotation and at least one indirect quotation. Be sure to punctuate correctly.

697

These challenging and enjoyable activities allow the students to see how the concepts of grammar, usage, and mechanics may be applied in actual writing situations. Each exercise is designed to allow students practice in several of the skills they have acquired in this Section. The activities also provide opportunities for students to write creatively about a wide variety of interesting and unusual subjects.

697

Section Objectives

1. To develop a plan to improve spelling skills

2. To develop a plan to master the spelling of a particular word

3. To understand and apply common spelling rules

Preparing the Students

Ask students how a prospective employer assesses a job-seeker in an interview. No doubt students will mention appearance (neatness and clothing) and how the job-seeker expresses himself orally (vocabulary, grammar, and clear thinking).

What if there is no opportunity for a face-to-face interview, and a written application becomes the basis of the employer's assessment? Again, expression will be crucial, but this time spelling will be an important factor. Ask students if they think their spelling presents the best possible view of their intelligence and abilities.

Read the introduction on page 698.

Additional Resources

Diagnostic Test — page 10 in the test booklet

Mastery Test — pages 74–75 in the test booklet

Additional Exercises — pages 707–710 in the student text

Practice Book — pages 264–268

Duplicating Masters — pages 264–268

Special Populations — See special section at the front of this Teacher's Edition.

Spelling

Your written work may give people a first impression of you. One of the things that people will notice is whether or not you spell words correctly. Good spelling is a valuable skill that you will use all of your life.

Becoming a good speller, however, is not easy. Words in English often are not spelled the way they sound. Also, it seems that there are many exceptions to every spelling rule.

This section will help you become a better speller. First, it will present steps for improving your spelling and for learning to spell new words. Also, it will explain the spelling rules and the exceptions to them.

How To Improve Your Spelling

1. Locate and conquer your own specific spelling problems. What spelling errors do you make over and over? Study your past written assignments. Make a list of words you misspelled on them. Work on mastering those words.

2. Pronounce words carefully. Are you misspelling words because you aren't pronouncing them correctly? If you are writing *famly* for *family*, for instance, you are probably mispronouncing the word. Try to pronounce your words more precisely.

3. Try to remember the letters in unfamiliar words. Do you really look at the spelling of an unfamiliar or difficult word? That habit can help you to remember how to spell the word. Write the correct spelling of the word several times.

4. Always proofread your writing. Are some of your misspellings careless mistakes? By examining your writing, you may catch such errors. Read your work slowly, one word at a time.

5. Look up difficult words in a dictionary. Do you reach for the dictionary when you're unsure of a spelling? Get into the habit of letting the dictionary help you to spell well.

6. Learn the few important spelling rules explained in this section.

How To Spell a Particular Word Correctly

1. Look at the word and say it to yourself. Make sure to pronounce it correctly. Say it twice, looking at the syllables as you say them.

2. Look at the letters and say each one. Sound out the word from its spelling. Divide the word into syllables and pronounce each syllable.

699

How To Spell a Particular Word Correctly

Objective

To develop a plan to master the spelling of a particular word

Presenting the Lesson

Read the five steps on pages 699–700.

Individualizing the Lesson

Less-Advanced Students

Give students a spelling quiz of difficult words. Have students correct their own quiz by looking up the words in a dictionary. After several days have passed give the students the same spelling quiz.

Advanced Students

Have students divide into groups of two and give each other a spelling test. Have students check their answers in the dictionary.

Optional Practice

Have students practice using the five-step system with some difficult words. Words may be taken from misspellings in recent assignments or the lists on pages 705–706.

Spelling Rules

Objective

To understand and apply common spelling rules

---

3. Write the word without looking at your book or list.

4. Check to see if you spelled the word correctly. Look back at your book or list. If you spelled the word correctly, repeat the process.

5. If you made an error, note what it was. Then repeat steps 3 and 4 until you have written the word correctly three times.

Spelling Rules

Adding Prefixes

When a prefix is added to a word, the spelling of the word remains the same.

im- + patient = impatient   ir- + regular = irregular
re- + apply = reapply   mis- + lead = mislead
inter- + lock = interlock   de- + frost = defrost
dis- + respect = disrespect   il- + legible = illegible

Suffixes with Silent e

When a suffix beginning with a vowel is added to a word ending in a silent e, the e is usually dropped.

bake + -ing = baking   love + -able = lovable
style + -ish = stylish   like + -ing = liking
space + -ious = spacious   separate + -ion = separation

When a suffix beginning with a consonant is added to a word ending in a silent e, the e is usually retained.

face + -less = faceless   loose + -ly = loosely
love + -ly = lovely   place + -ment = placement
lame + -ness = lameness   care + -ful = careful

The following words are exceptions. Study them.

truly   argument   ninth   wholly

Exercise A Find the misspelled words. Spell them correctly.

1. John was ~~stareing~~ [staring] at the strangely dressed clown.
2. Jan is ~~eraseing~~ [erasing] that ~~mispelled~~ [misspelled] word.
3. Craig's handwriting is ~~definitly~~ [definitely] illegible.
4. The Dodgers were ~~loseing~~ [losing] in the ~~nineth~~ [ninth] inning.
5. Many people ~~dissagreed~~ [disagreed] with Darwin's theory of ~~createion~~ [creation].
6. The reporter ~~misquoted~~ [misquoted] the ~~fameous~~ [famous] writer.
7. These ~~arguements~~ [arguments] are wholly ~~unecessary~~ [unnecessary].
8. ~~Takeing~~ [Taking] the bus is ~~unrealiable~~ [unreliable] because the schedule is so ~~iregular~~ [irregular].
9. The detective ~~reexamined~~ [reexamined] all the likely suspects.
10. ~~Translateing~~ [Translating] that story from Spanish to English was ~~confuseing~~ [confusing].

Exercise B Add the prefixes and suffixes as shown and write the new word.

1. save + -ing [saving]
2. mis- + treat [mistreat]
3. im- + material [immaterial]
4. tote + -able [totable]
5. ir- + rational [irrational]
7. hope + -ing [hoping]
8. un- + necessary [unnecessary]
9. un- + waxed [unwaxed]
10. mis- + spell [misspell]
11. re- + arrange [rearrange]
12. race + -ing [racing]
13. re- + align [realign]
14. amaze + -ment [amazement]
15. pace + -ing [pacing]
17. retire + -ment [retirement]
18. value + -able [valuable]
19. dis- + agree [disagree]
20. dis- + appear [disappear]

Suffixes and Final *y*

When a suffix is added to a word ending in *y* preceded by a consonant, the *y* is usually changed to *i*.

heavy + -er = heavier study + -ous = studious
cry + -ed = cried twenty + -eth = twentieth
frilly + -est = frilliest tiny + -est = tiniest

701

Students should correct each mis-spelled word and then use the word in a sentence.

Advanced Students

Have students select twenty words from the list of commonly mis-spelled words on pages 705–706. Students should add suffixes to each word, use the new word in a sentence, and then write the rule that applies to the spelling of the new word.

A List of Commonly Misspelled Words

You may use the list of commonly misspelled words on pages 705–706 as a checklist for students to assess their spelling competence. The words may be used as spelling lists to practice the new skills and rules just studied. When presenting individual words, difficult spots should be pointed out and discussed. Root words, suffixes, and prefixes should be pointed out.

Optional Practice

Dictate the following words to the class. Have students write them, using the rules presented in this Section.

1. precede	11. praying
2. sipping	12. succeed
3. tasteful	13. usually
4. reenter	14. loveliest
5. niece	15. misshapen
6. either	16. unnatural
7. saving	17. rotting
8. thinness	18. displaying
9. hiking	19. ceiling
10. happiness	20. truly

Note the following exception: When *-ing* is added, the *y* does not change:

worry + -ing = worrying   curtsy + -ing = curtsying
carry + -ing = carrying   fly + -ing = flying

When a suffix is added to a word ending in *y* preceded by a vowel, the *y* usually does not change.

pray + -ing = praying   employ + -er = employer
relay + -ed = relayed   annoy + -ing = annoying

Exercise   Add the suffixes as shown and write the new word.

1. crazy + -ness *craziness*	8. sixty + -eth *sixtieth*	15. lazy + -er *lazier*
2. rally + -ing *rallying*	9. employ + -able *employable*	16. library + -an *librarian*
3. ready + -ness *readiness*	10. play + -ed *played*	17. play + -ful *playful*
4. carry + -er *carrier*	11. purify + -ing *purifying*	18. enjoy + -able *enjoyable*
5. tricky + -est *trickiest*	12. sleepy + -est *sleepiest*	19. holy + -ness *holiness*
6. hurry + -ing *hurrying*	13. decay + -ed *decayed*	20. try + -ed *tried*
7. marry + -age *marriage*	14. fury + -ous *furious*	

Adding the Suffixes *-ness* and *-ly*

When the suffix *-ly* is added to a word ending in *l*, both *l*'s are kept. When *-ness* is added to a word ending in *n*, both *n*'s are kept.

mental + -ly = mentally   open + -ness = openness
federal + -ly = federally   mean + -ness = meanness

Doubling the Final Consonant

In words of one syllable that end in one consonant preceded by one vowel, double the final consonant before adding *-ing*, *-ed*, or *-er*.

dig + -ing = digging   mar + -ed = marred
trap + -ed = trapped   grip + -ing = gripping
win + -er = winner   hop + -ed = hopped

In words of one syllable that end in one consonant preceded by two vowels, the final consonant is not doubled.

pour + -ing = pouring   read + -er = reader
thread + -ed = threaded   cool + -ing = cooling

Exercise A   Find the misspelled words. Spell them correctly.

1. The child ~~gleefuly~~ gleefully ~~riped~~ ripped open his birthday packages.
2. Joan ~~stoped~~ stopped writing and ~~taped~~ tapped her eraser on the desk.
3. The fox ~~cruely~~ cruelly attacked the ~~traped~~ trapped rabbit.
4. Dad's hair is ~~thining~~ thinning, and his waist is thickening.
5. The ~~federaly~~ federally funded program was ended last month.
6. The ~~sterness~~ sternness of their ~~leadder~~ leader strengthened the pioneers.
7. Waitresses know that students are ~~generaly~~ generally poor ~~tipers~~ tippers.
8. Is the water ~~runing~~ running?
9. The ~~leaness~~ leanness of veal makes it ~~especialy~~ especially good for dieters.
10. Are you bragging, or did you ~~realy~~ really do that?

Exercise B   Add the suffixes as shown and write the new word.

1. mean + -ness — meanness
2. rip + -ed — ripped
3. zoom + -ed — zoomed
4. tag + -ed — tagged
5. sip + -ed — sipped
6. careful + -ly — carefully
7. slim + -est — slimmest
8. fearful + -ly — fearfully
9. drag + -ing — dragging
10. even + -ness — evenness
11. look + -ed — looked
12. skip + -ed — skipped
13. get + -ing — getting
14. drip + -ed — dripped
15. open + -ness — openness
16. joyful + -ly — joyfully
17. moan + -ing — moaning
18. zip + -ed — zipped
19. drop + -ing — dropping
20. loop + -ing — looping

Words with the "Seed" Sound

There is only one English word ending in *sede: supersede.* Three words end in *ceed: exceed, proceed, succeed.* All other words ending with the sound of *seed* are spelled *cede:*

recede   precede   concede   secede

Words with *ie* and *ei*

There is a general rule for words with the long *e* (*ē*) sound. The word is spelled *ie* except after *c*.

I before E

field	grief	chief	piece	fierce
niece	reprieve	retrieve	believe	relief

Except after C

deceit	ceiling	receipt	perceive
conceit	receive	deceive	conceive

The following words are exceptions to the rule. Study them.

either	weird	leisure
species	seize	neither

Exercise Find the misspelled words in these sentences and spell them correctly.

1. I could not ~~beleive~~ [believe] the grief they experienced after the tragedy.
2. The ~~cheif~~ [chief] explained that federal law ~~superceeds~~ [supercedes] state law.
3. The reporter ~~conseded~~ [conceded] that she had ~~decieved~~ [deceived] her editors about the source of her story.
4. The proceeds from the fund-raising carnival ~~exceded~~ [exceeded] all expectations.
5. ~~Niether~~ [Neither] of them noticed the weird ~~speceis~~ [species] of bug crawling on the ~~cieling~~ [ceiling].
6. Jim, I believe, is the most ~~conceited~~ [conceited] person I know.
7. My ~~neice~~ [niece] offered me a piece of her three-~~teired~~ [tiered] wedding cake.
8. The store detective ~~siezed~~ [seized] the thief.
9. In her ~~liesure~~ [leisure] time Sandy rode her horse through the fields.
10. Good ~~greif~~ [grief]! I lost my ~~reciept~~ [receipt].

A List of Commonly Misspelled Words

abbreviate
accidentally
achievement
across
address
all right
altogether
always
amateur
analyze
anonymous
answer
apologize
appearance
appreciate
appropriate
argument
arrangement
associate
awkward
balance
bargain
beginning
believe
bicycle
bookkeeper
bulletin
bureau
business
cafeteria
calendar
campaign
candidate
certain
changeable
characteristic
column

committee
courageous
courteous
criticize
curiosity
cylinder
dealt
decision
definitely
despair
desperate
dictionary
dependent
description
desirable
different
disagree
disappear
disappoint
discipline
dissatisfied
efficient
eighth
eligible
eliminate
embarrass
emphasize
environment
enthusiastic
equipped
especially
exaggerate
excellent
exhaust
expense
experience
familiar

fascinating
February
financial
foreign
fourth
fragile
generally
government
grammar
guarantee
guard
gymnasium
handkerchief
height
humorous
imaginary
immediately
incredible
influence
intelligence
interesting
knowledge
laboratory
lightning
literature
loneliness
maintenance
marriage
mathematics
medicine
minimum
mischievous
missile
misspell
mortgage
municipal
necessary

nickel
ninety
noticeable
nuclear
nuisance
obstacle
occasionally
occur
opinion
opportunity
original
outrageous
parallel
particularly
permanent
permissible
persuade
picnicking
pleasant
pneumonia
politics
possess
possibility
practice
prejudice
preparation
privilege
probably
professor
pronunciation
propeller
psychology
quantity
realize
recognize
recommend
reference

referred
rehearse
repetition
representative
restaurant
rhythm
ridiculous
sandwich
schedule
scissors
secretary

separate
sergeant
similar
sincerely
sophomore
souvenir
specifically
strategy
strictly
success
surprise

syllable
sympathy
symptom
temperament
temperature
thorough
throughout
together
tomorrow
traffic
tragedy

transferred
truly
Tuesday
twelfth
undoubtedly
unnecessary
vacuum
vicinity
village
weird
writing

ADDITIONAL EXERCISES

Spelling

A. Prefixes Find the misspelled words. Spell them correctly.

1. The audience sounds ~~disatisfied~~ [dissatisfied] and disappointed.
2. The driver ~~missjudged~~ [misjudged] the distance and braked ~~uneccessarily~~ [unnecessarily].
3. The ~~unumbered~~ [unnumbered] pages contained many ~~mispelled~~ [misspelled] words.
4. You are ~~misstaken~~ [mistaken] about Tony's reaction to the unarmed robber.
5. That ~~interrsection~~ [intersection] is at an inconvenient location.

B. Suffixes Add the suffixes as shown. Write the new word.

1. zone + -ing — [zoning]
2. advertise + -ment — [advertisement]
3. pollute + -ion — [pollution]
4. argue + -ment — [argument]
5. believe + -able — [believable]
6. care + -less — [careless]
7. take + -ing — [taking]
8. waste + -ful — [wasteful]
9. space + -ious — [spacious]
10. complete + -ly — [completely]

C. Suffixes Add the suffixes as shown. Write the new word.

1. pity + -ful — [pitiful]
2. early + -er — [earlier]
3. dusty + -est — [dustiest]
4. study + -ing — [studying]
5. happy + -ly — [happily]
6. study + -ed — [studied]
7. vary + -ous — [various]
8. employ + -ment — [employment]
9. angry + -er — [angrier]
10. cry + -ed — [cried]

D. Suffixes Find the misspelled words. Spell them correctly.

1. She defended her boss ~~loyaly~~ [loyally], despite his ~~meaness~~ [meanness].
2. The water table was ~~continualy~~ [continually] dropping, ~~especialy~~ [especially] in the West.

707

Additional Exercises

These Additional Exercises may be used for additional practice of the concepts presented in this Section. Each exercise focuses on a single concept, and should be used after the page number indicated in parentheses.

Review

If you have not assigned these Additional Exercises before this time, you can also use them as an excellent Section Review.

c 3. The fire crew quickly chopped down the door.

4. The roaring ~~maching~~ ^{machine} ~~suddenlly~~ ^{suddenly} whimpered ~~pitifuly~~ ^{pitifully}.

c 5. The goalie had only the slimmest chance of stopping the puck.

6. Gus ~~usualy~~ ^{usually} arrived ~~punctualy~~ ^{punctually}; his ~~latness~~ ^{lateness} puzzled us.

7. Kevin looked around ~~fearfuly~~ ^{fearfully}, but Craig chatted cheerfully.

c 8. Claire was running to the bus stop when she nearly tripped over the curb.

9. Abby grinned ~~happilly~~ ^{happily} as the judges studied her painting.

10. Jeremy's height ~~realy~~ ^{really} made shopping for clothes a problem; ~~finaly~~ ^{finally}, he learned to sew.

E. Spelling   Find the misspelled words. Spell them correctly.

1. The ~~cheif~~ ^{chief} gave the brave a reprieve.

2. Some commercials are meant to ~~decieve~~ ^{deceive} us.

3. ~~Unbeleivable~~ ^{Unbelievable}! Judy has kicked the ball across the field.

4. The states that had seceded were ~~recieved~~ ^{received} back into the Union.

5. The dog was ~~niether~~ ^{neither} ~~feirce~~ ^{fierce} nor friendly.

6. This ~~reciept~~ ^{receipt} looks ~~wierd~~ ^{weird} to me.

7. Perhaps we have ~~succeded~~ ^{succeeded} in saving some endangered species.

8. Sam ~~conceeded~~ ^{conceded} that his niece had deceived him.

9. Pieces of plaster fell from the ~~cieling~~ ^{ceiling}.

10. Everyone was ~~releived~~ ^{relieved} when the flood waters ~~receeded~~ ^{receded}.

MIXED REVIEW

Spelling

A. Spelling words correctly Number your paper from 1 to 15. Correct the words that are spelled incorrectly.

1. He looked disappointed when the scores were ~~tallyed~~. [tallied]
2. The ~~libraryian~~ [librarian] made a ~~puzzleing~~ [puzzling] announcement.
3. The mules wearily plodded across the ~~feild~~. [field]
4. Cy traced the drawing onto a ~~thiner~~ [thinner] ~~peice~~ [piece] of paper.
5. Her puzzlement seemed ~~completly~~ [completely] unbelievable.
6. ~~Niether~~ [Neither] of the babies has a ~~carryage~~. [carriage]
7. Andrew cheerfully recopied his composition.
8. The puck ~~skided~~ [skidded] into the ~~defenseive~~ [defensive] zone.
9. The opposing team ~~recieved~~ [received] two ~~penaltys~~. [penalties]
10. Somebody is ~~pageing~~ [paging] the chief.
11. Betty is taller, but Joan is ~~heavyer~~. [heavier]
12. The puppies ~~cryed~~ [cried] ~~continueously~~. [continuously]
13. The workers are laying the foundation for the ~~pavment~~. [pavement]
14. Her statement ~~realy~~ [really] ~~endded~~ [ended] the ~~arguement~~. [argument]
15. I concede that, by ~~misstake~~, [mistake] I misspelled the word.

B. Using spelling in proofreading Proofread the following paragraph. Rewrite it, spelling all the words correctly.

I was ~~siting~~ [sitting] in a chair in the dining room with my foot propped up because of a skating ~~injurey~~. [injury] The phone in the ~~liveing~~ [living] room started ringing. I ~~waitted~~, [waited] hoping ~~ilogically~~ [illogically] that the phone could ~~percieve~~ [perceive] my feelings. However, it continued. I was becoming ~~nerveous~~. [nervous] ~~Surelly~~ [Surely] the caller must have something really important to say. Painfully I got up and ~~succeded~~ [succeeded] in hopping to the phone. I seized the ~~reciever~~. [receiver] My niece was calling. She ~~sayed~~ [said] that she was worrying about my foot. I impatiently reassured her and ~~slamed~~ [slammed] the phone down. Struggling back to my chair, I ~~steped~~ [stepped] onto a splinter of wood.

Mixed Review

These exercises provide review of the concepts presented in this Section. Each exercise challenges the students to apply several of the skills they have acquired during previous study. Because the "mixed" feature of these activities makes them more difficult, the teacher may wish to have less-advanced students do them orally or in small groups.

These challenging and enjoyable activities allow the students to see how the concepts of grammar, usage, and mechanics may be applied in actual writing situations. Each exercise is designed to allow students practice in several of the skills they have acquired in this Section. The activities also provide opportunities for students to write creatively about a wide variety of interesting and unusual subjects.

USING MECHANICS IN WRITING
Spelling

A. Write a review of a humorous movie. Choose any movie to review, but choose one that you found at least fairly funny. Use one of the following pairs of words in each sentence. At least one of the words in each pair is misspelled. Correct the misspelled words. Use all six pairs.

excellent
excelent performance

strongly   recommend
stronglly reccomend

amusing
amuseing scenes

unusual
unnusual situations

enthusiastic
enthuseiastic audience

writing
hilarious writeing

B. The following paragraph from an article for a magazine contains many misspelled words. Proofread the paragraph for spelling errors. List the misspelled words, spelled correctly.

Generally
Genrally, the high school years are years of opportunity

achievement   incredible
and acheivement. However, they are also years of incredable

schedules
ble stress. Most students have busy scedules at school.

important   decisions
They also have to make importent desisions about the future.

volunteers   leisure
ture. Many work after school, either for pay or as volonteers. For busy students, liesure time is important.

necessary
Students should be sure to get the necesary rest and relaxa-

occasionally
tion. Everyone needs a break ocassionally.

C. Write a story about an acrobat on a bicycle. Use as many of the following words as you can. Be sure to spell each word correctly.

accidentally, across, awkward, balance, bicycle, certain, courageous, definitely, desperate, humorous, immediately, incredible, mischievous, obstacle, outrageous

The Correct Form for Writing

Section Objectives

1. To use legible handwriting and to produce a neat, correct final copy

2. To use accepted form for headings, titles, margins, and spacing

3. To use the correct form in writing numbers

4. To use abbreviations correctly in writing

Preparing the Students

Read the introduction on page 711. Stress that good form enhances good content.

Additional Resources

Additional Exercises — pages 718–722 in the student text

Practice Book — pages 269–271

Duplicating Masters — pages 269–271

Special Populations — See special section at the front of this Teacher's Edition.

What you wear and how you speak give people an impression of you. Also, the way your papers look can give people a first impression. Content is the most important element of a paper. However, the form of your paper is important too. A paper that is carelessly written or difficult to read will probably affect your reader's attitude toward your work.

Care, neatness, and consistency are all part of good writing form. Your school may have specific rules for the correct form for written work. In this section you will learn about the kind of form that is accepted by many schools.

To use legible handwriting and to produce a neat, correct final copy

Presenting the Lesson

Read page 712. Go over suggestions for legible writing and why it is important to write a first draft. Stress the importance of proofreading.

Individualizing the Lesson

Less-Advanced Students

Explain to students that the neatness of a paper is important because it makes a paper easier to read. Explain that format, covered in the next part of the lesson, is also part of neatness.

Advanced Students

Have students look at newspapers and magazines for the layout of the pages. Discuss with students the differences layout—format and neatness—can make.

Optional Practice

Hold up a neatly-written paper alongside a sloppy or poorly-written paper. Ask students which paper is easier to read and why.

Extending the Lesson

Read students a paragraph from a first draft followed by the same paragraph from a revised final draft. Discuss the differences with students, pointing out the improvements after the revision.

Guidelines for Clear Writing

Neatness

A neat, legible paper can be read easily. Neatness also suggests that the writer cares about what he or she is writing. There are several ways to give your papers a neat appearance.

Legible Writing

Typewritten papers are usually more legible than handwritten ones. However, if you do not have a typewriter, make your handwriting clear and legible. Always use ink. Blue or black ink is easiest to read. Make sure that letters are distinct, since some letters look similar. For example, a's and o's can be confused unless they are formed carefully. So can e's and i's.

The First Draft and the Final Copy

You cannot expect the first draft of a paper to be in perfect form. You write a first draft from your pre-writing notes or an outline. You then correct or revise the first draft. You may have to change words and sentences or rearrange whole sections.

Afterward, make your final copy. Proofread this new copy. You may find errors or words left out. To insert a word, write it above the line. Use a caret ($\wedge$) to show where the word belongs. To change a word, draw a line through it and write the correction above it. If you have made more than about three corrections on a page, you should recopy the page.

Acceptable Form

The correct form for writing means more than a neat appearance. In a paper with acceptable form, the various parts are positioned correctly. Headings, titles, margins, and spacing should be in the correct form.

The Heading

A heading identifies your paper. It is usually placed in the upper right-hand corner of the first page. Place your name on the first line. Write the name of your class on the second line. Write the date on the third line. In a paper with a title page, place the heading in the upper right corner of that page.

Each page, except for page one, should be numbered. Beginning with page two, place the page number in the upper right-hand corner. To identify all pages, you might want to put your name under the page number.

Some teachers may require a different form for labeling your paper. Follow any special instructions you are given.

The Title

The title of a paper should appear near the top of the first page. In general, place the title two lines down from the last line of the heading. Begin the first line of your paper two lines below the title.

Correct form for a title also means proper capitalization. The first word and all important words in the title should be capitalized. Use capitals for only the first letters of words, not for every letter. Do not underline your title or place it in quotation marks.

When a paper is more than three pages long, sometimes a title page is used. This page precedes the paper.

Margins and Spacing

Use correct margins and spacing to achieve an attractive appearance. Margins of one inch at the top, bottom, and left side of the paper look pleasing.

713

Objective

To use accepted form for headings, titles, margins, and spacing

Presenting the Lesson

Read pages 712–715. Go over suggestions for correct placement of the heading and title, gauging margins, and the overall spacing of the paper. Be sure to modify or supplement suggestions with your own standards for format. Post or distribute samples of student papers illustrating proper form.

Individualizing the Lesson

Less-Advanced Students

Work with students on how to develop a good title for a paper. Use examples of good titles as well as examples of bad titles to help students understand how to write a title.

Advanced Students

Have students write a brief analysis of each of the following five titles

Jaws II
Gone with the Wind
In Cold Blood
Goodbye, Mr. Chips
A Tale of Two Cities

Students should explain why the title is good or bad, what they think the author was trying to indicate by the title, and what the title tells about the book or film.

Optional Practice

Explain to students the heading you want them to use on the papers in your class.

Have students write a one-page composition. Any topic may be used, or students may choose one of the following.

How My Hobby Became My Job
Life Has Changed for Me Because
History Should Have Taught Us This Lesson
Families Never Desert You
Music Is Essential

Students should write first drafts, which should be revised and proofread. They should apply all suggestions presented in this Section.

Writing Numbers

Objective

To use correct form in writing numbers

Presenting the Lesson

1. Read pages 714–715. Go over the guidelines and examples for the use of numbers in writing.
2. Assign and discuss the Exercise on page 715.

Individualizing the Lesson

Less-Advanced Students

Have students find five published examples of the use of numbers. Have them determine whether or not the published use follows the rules listed in this lesson. If not, have students speculate why not.

714

Try to keep the right-hand margin fairly even. Do not break too many words with hyphens, though, in order to keep the margin straight. A safe rule is to avoid hyphens in more than two lines in a row.

Double-spacing makes typed papers look neat. Paragraphs are usually indented five spaces. Skip two spaces after the punctuation mark at the end of a sentence.

Writing Numbers

The form for writing numbers should be consistent. Numbers under 100 are usually spelled out. Larger numbers are written in figures.

> The nursery charged *thirty-five* dollars to trim the tree.
> We need at least *eleven* more chairs.
> The sticker price on the car was *$8,175*.
> Over *350* invitations to the reception have been sent.

A number at the beginning of a sentence is always spelled out.

> *One million* people live in the New Orleans area.
> *Twenty-eight thousand* students attend the university.
> *Five hundred* dollars was the prize.

Figures rather than spelled-out words are used for these numbers: dates, street and room numbers, telephone numbers, temperatures, page numbers, decimals, and percentages.

> Humans first walked on the moon on July 20, 1969.
> The Marquette Building is at 140 South Dearborn.
> Dr. Blake is in Room 210.
> Jill's phone number is 555-5372.
> The high temperature today was 87 degrees.
> The map of China is on page 327.
> Scott ran the mile in 4.7 minutes.
> The current interest rate is 13½ percent.

In large sums of money or expressions of large quantities, commas are used to separate the figures. Commas are not used in dates, serial numbers, page numbers, addresses, or telephone numbers.

Correct: That mansion costs $350,000.
Correct: In 1980, the population of the United States was 226,504,825.
Incorrect: The stock market crash was in 1,929.
Correct: The stock market crash was in 1929.

Exercise Copy these sentences, correcting any errors in the writing of numbers.

1. Between 1970 and 1979, ~~one thousand one hundred and forty-three~~ [1,143] law enforcement officers were killed in the United States.
2. The Thompsons live in apartment ~~number six hundred and eighty-four~~ [684].
3. ~~2nd~~ [Second] prize is ~~five hundred dollars~~ [$500] and third prize is ~~two hundred dollars~~ [$200].
4. The interest rate for home loans hasn't been below ~~ten~~ [10] percent for over ~~4~~ [four] years.
5. The temperature on the lakefront was 76 degrees, but in the western suburbs it was ~~eighty-six~~ [86] degrees.
C 6. The author agreed to give 10 percent of the earnings to his agent.
7. ~~2~~ [Two] packages were delivered to ~~2,525~~ [2525] Harlem Avenue by mistake.
8. ~~1~~ [One] gallon weighs ~~eight and thirty-three hundredths~~ [8.33] pounds.
9. On December ~~fourteenth~~ [14], ~~1,911~~ [1911], Roald Amundsen reached the South Pole.
10. ~~400~~ [Four hundred] students attended the convention which was held at ~~three hundred and twenty-nine~~ [329] South Lakewood Avenue.

Using Abbreviations

Objective

To use abbreviations correctly in writing

Presenting the Lesson

1. Read pages 716–717. Go over rules and examples illustrating correct usage of abbreviations.

2. Assign and discuss the Exercise on page 717.

Individualizing the Lesson

Less-Advanced Students

Work through the Exercise, page 717, with students.

Advanced Students

Have students find examples of ten abbreviations in a newspaper or magazine. Have the class compile a list of abbreviations from this assignment.

Optional Practice

Have students write five sentences of their own using abbreviations.

Extending the Lesson

Explain to students that some abbreviations are called *acronyms* and actually are pronounced as a word, not as individual letters.

Use examples of *NATO, SEATO, scuba, radar, WAC,* and *WAVE.* Have the class do research to find what each acronym stands for.

Abbreviations are shortened forms of words. In formal writing, abbreviations are usually not acceptable.

Abbreviations, however, may be used for most titles before and after names. Abbreviations may also be used for government agencies and for time.

Titles before proper names:	Mrs., Mr., Ms., Gen., Dr., Rev., Sgt., Sen.
Titles after proper names:	Jr., M.D., D.D.S., Ph.D.
Government agencies:	FBI, VA, EPA, FTC
Dates and times:	A.M., P.M., B.C., A.D.

Notice that periods are not used in the abbreviations of government agencies.

A title is abbreviated only when it is used with a person's name, as in *Dr. Lauren Sherwood.* The following, for example, would not be acceptable: The dr. found a cure for the disease.

Abbreviations are not used for certain titles. *Honorable* and *Reverend* are not abbreviated when preceded by *the: the Reverend Lee Withers.* Abbreviations are not used for the titles of the President and Vice-President of the United States.

In most writing, abbreviations are not acceptable for the following: names of countries and states, months and days of the week, addresses, and firm names.

Incorrect:	Hebrew and Arabic are the official languages of Is.
Correct:	Hebrew and Arabic are the official languages of Israel.
Incorrect:	N.Y., N.Y., is called "The Big Apple."
Correct:	New York, New York, is called "The Big Apple."
Incorrect:	Sat., Sept. 25, is the homecoming dance.
Correct:	Saturday, September 25, is the homecoming dance.

Incorrect: The Baxter Co. headquarters are on Wacker Dr.
Correct: The Baxter Company headquarters are on Wacker Drive.

When you write paragraphs and compositions, abbreviations are not acceptable for the following: names of school courses, and the words *page*, *chapter*, and *Christmas*. Abbreviations for measurements, like *ft.*, *in.*, *hr.*, *oz.*, *qt.*, *mi.*, are also unacceptable.

Exercise   Correct the errors in abbreviations in these sentences.

1. The baby gained three lbs. in one mo. [pounds, month]
2. The Rev. Charles Potter is a chaplain with the U.S.A.F. [Reverend, United States Air Force]
3. Last Sat., Pres. Reagan attended a Xmas party for sr. citizens. [Saturday, President, Christmas, senior]
4. The Proctor & Gamble Co. is located on 6th St. in Cincin., OH. [Company, Sixth Street, Cincinnati, Ohio]
5. Dr. Greg Bradley, Ph.D., is teaching at the U. of Ill. [University of Illinois]
6. John R. Block is the Secy. of the Dept. of Agriculture. [Secretary, Department]
7. William H. Webster was appointed to a ten-yr. term as Dir. of the FBI on Feb. 23, 1978. [year, Director, February]
8. Homework for Hist. of World Civ. is to read p. 300–315 of Ch. 28. [History, Civilization, pages, Chapter]
9. Buddhism was founded in the first cent. B.C. in Ind. [century, India]
10. Many drs. work in govt. hospitals. [doctors, government]

Additional Exercises

These Additional Exercises may be used for additional practice of the concepts presented in this Section. Each exercise focuses on a single concept, and should be used after the page number indicated in parentheses.

Review

If you have not assigned these Additional Exercises before this time, you can also use them as an excellent Section Review.

ADDITIONAL EXERCISES

The Correct Form for Writing

A. Numbers in Sentences On your paper, correct any errors in the writing of numbers. Write *Correct* if a sentence has no errors.

1. The Cubs made ~~7~~ [seven] runs in the ~~4th~~ [fourth] inning.
2. The volcanic dust made the temperature ~~one~~ [1] degree lower for months and caused an early ~~1st~~ [first] frost.
3. The summer of ~~1,816~~ [1816] was cold; on July ~~Four~~ [4], the temperature in Savannah, Georgia, was 49° [degrees].
4. ~~116,000~~ [One hundred sixteen thousand] recreation workers had jobs in ~~nineteen-eighty~~ [1980].
5. I paid twenty-four dollars for that sweater.
6. About ~~forty-two~~ [42] percent of the land in Jamaica is used for agriculture.
  C 7. Square roots are listed on page 33.
8. In 1980, the resident population of the United States was ~~226504825~~ [226,504,825].
9. ~~$5~~ [Five dollars] is all that I paid for my ~~2nd~~ [second] bike.
10. That river is ~~eight hundred and sixty-nine~~ [869] miles long.

B. Abbreviations Correct the following errors in abbreviation.

1. American Samoa sent its first ~~rep.~~ [representative] to Congress in 1981.
2. Many ~~drs.~~ [doctors] in the Lee ~~Bldg.~~ [Building] do not have ~~Wed.~~ [Wednesday] office ~~hrs.~~ [hours]
3. Mr. Rios has worked for H.U.D. since last ~~Oct.~~ [October]
4. Has the ~~sgt.~~ [sergeant] asked the ~~Rev.~~ [Reverend] Yeaglin to speak?
5. The ~~Pres.~~ [President] signed the bill at 9:00 A.M.
6. The ~~phys. ed.~~ [physical education] class did exercises for twenty ~~mins.~~ [minutes]
7. The ~~prof.~~ [professor] told the class to read ~~p.~~ [page] 205.
8. The ~~labs.~~ [laboratories] and the ~~hosp.~~ [hospital] of NIH are located between Old Georgetown ~~Rd.~~ [Road] and Rockville Pike.
9. Cadets at West Point Military ~~Acad.~~ [Academy] are in the Army.
10. Nancy worked in a ~~dept.~~ [department] store during ~~Xmas.~~ [Christmas]

MIXED REVIEW

The Correct Form for Writing

Using the correct form for writing   The following composition contains errors in writing form and in the use of abbreviations and numbers. Copy the composition, correcting any errors.

Water: Heading for the Shallow End

Remember the lines "Water, water, everywhere,/Nor any drop to drink" from ~~lit.~~ [literature] class? Well, we might see that situation someday. Although almost ~~¾ th s~~ [three-fourths] of the earth is water, not even ~~three~~ [3] ~~%~~ [percent] of that water is fresh. Fresh water equals about one-thirtieth of our ~~aprox.~~ [approximately] ~~300000000~~ [300,000,000] cubic ~~mi.~~ [miles] of saltwater. Moreover, ~~⅔ s~~ [two-thirds] of the fresh water is frozen in glaciers and polar ice. The largest supply of fresh water, nearly ~~2%~~ [2 percent] of the world's total is in the Antarctic Icecap, which covers 6,000,000 ~~sq.~~ [square] miles. We can actually use less than ~~1%~~ [1 percent] of our water.

The ~~U.S.~~ [United States] spends more than $3,000,000,000 every ~~yr.~~ [year] to provide its population with water. ~~Drs.~~ [Doctors] suggest that we drink a ~~qt.~~ [quart] a day. Each person in the ~~U. S.~~ [United States] averages ~~90~~ [ninety] gallons daily to clean and garden~~,~~ [;] ~~2~~ [two] more are used for drinking and cooking.

More than ~~4 × s~~ [four times] as much water as we use directly is used for farming. ~~115~~ [One hundred fifteen] gallons are needed to grow wheat for ~~1~~ [one] loaf of bread. Producing one ~~lb.~~ [pound] of beef takes 4,000 gallons.

Industry uses ~~5~~ [five] times as much as people do. ~~Sixty-thous.~~ [60,000] gallons are needed to make one ton of steel. Industry not only uses a lot; it pollutes even more. Since the ~~govt.~~ [government] passed the Clean Water Act in ~~nineteen hundred and seventy-three~~ [1973], ~~corps.~~ [corporations] have kept surface water cleaner. The EPA, however, expresses concern about the growing pollution of ground water.

Our consumption of water is increasing faster than the ~~no.~~ [number] of humans. In ~~Ariz.~~ [Arizona], for instance, ground water is being used ~~8 × s~~ [eight times] faster than it can be replenished by the natural water cycle. In summary, unless we become more careful, we might find ourselves "sinking" for lack of water.

719

Mixed Review

These exercises provide review of the concepts presented in this Section. Each exercise challenges the students to apply several of the skills they have acquired during previous study. Because the "mixed" feature of these activities makes them more difficult, the teacher may wish to have less-advanced students do them orally or in small groups.

These challenging and enjoyable activities allow the students to see how the concepts of grammar, usage, and mechanics may be applied in actual writing situations. Each exercise is designed to allow students practice in several of the skills they have acquired in this Section. The activities also provide opportunities for students to write creatively about a wide variety of interesting and unusual subjects.

USING MECHANICS IN WRITING
The Correct Form for Writing

Following is the beginning of a report about the interesting origins of some American businesses. The passage needs editing to put it in the correct form. Rewrite the passage, making all the necessary corrections. Passages may vary.

Lisa Perkins
Social Studies
February 1

How It All Began

HOW IT ALL BEGAN

¶In November, 1902, President

in Nov., 1,902, Pres. Theodore Roosevelt went on a hunting trip. He refused to shoot a baby bear that he saw. Reporters heard the story, and soon a cartoon showing the incident appeared in newspapers. Morris Michtom, who owned a small shop in N.Y., saw the cartoons showing the cub. He made stuffed copies and called them "Teddy's Bear." He started a business that later became the Ideal Toy Corp., one of the largest toy businesses in this country.

CUMULATIVE REVIEW

Capitalization, Punctuation, and Spelling

A. Using capitalization, punctuation, and spelling correctly Copy the following sentences, correcting the errors in capitalization, punctuation, and spelling.

1. the editor. in. chief of the chicago sun. times, a well known newspaper, resigned.
2. "Is it illegal to make a U-turn on castro street?" asked gordon.
3. Clair, who will be leaveing soon, tryed out for the feild hockey team.
4. the beginning of standard time in the united states was at noon on november 18, 1883
5. "did your aunt visit the ship the *queen mary* when she was in long beach, california?" asked hank.
6. what truely amazeing architecture the city of chicago has!
7. there are three steps to makeing ice cream pie: first, mix chocolate cookie crumbs and melted butter to make the crust; second, pour in softened ice cream; and third, put the pie in the freezer until it hardens.
8. "didn't I leave a copy of that new book, blue highways, on your desk?" asked ms. castino.
9. there are twenty-two trophys on carls shelf.
10. robert frost, a new england poet, wrote the poem "mending fences."

721

B. Using proofreading skills Proofread the following paragraph. Copy it, correcting the errors in capitalization, punctuation, and spelling.

Have you ever ridden a train? Well, the Orient Express is no ordinary train. On october 4, 1883, the most fameous train in history made it's first trip from paris, france to giurgiu, romania. the idea for the orient express, known as "Train of Kings, the King of Trains," was concieved by Georges Nagelmakers, a belgian banker. he wanted his train to link the republics, kingdoms, and empires of europe in luxuryous fashion. what style the train had! The dineing car had cieling paintings, waiters in tailcoats, and french crystal. The train carryed all of the crowned heads of europe as well as other fameous people. the actress sarah bernhardt, the dancer anna pavlova, the magician harry houdini, and the spy mata hari all rode it. the orient express developed a legend of mystery and intrigue. this legend is carryed on in books and movies. agatha christies murder on the orient express and ian flemings from russia with love are two examples. as one passenger on the new orient express said, this is not just a train . . . it is a state of mind."

A

origin of word in, 28
part of speech listed in, 28
plurals in, 28
principal parts in, 485
pronunciation in, 28
slang in, 29
special forms or endings in, 28
syllables in entries, 28
synonyms in, 29
types of, 26
unabridged, 26
See also Words *and* Vocabulary.
Directions
following, 308–309
giving (in a speech), 372
for reading forms, 360–362
Direct objects, 398–400
compound, 407, 584
definition of, 398
diagraming, 401, 605
infinitive phrase as, 559
nouns as, 435–436
predicate words or, distinguishing, 404–405
pronouns as, 452
recognizing, 398–399
Direct quotations, 651
Discovery draft. *See* First draft.
Divided quotation, 651
Double negatives, 518–520
Drawing conclusions, 284–285

E

ei/ie, 704
Empty sentences, 52–53
Encyclopedia, 300–302
Ending compositions. *See*
Conclusions in compositions *and*
Compositions, conclusions.
Ending sentences in paragraphs, 100–101

English language
formal, 38–39
informal, 38–39
jargon, 42–43
nonstandard, 35–37
number of words in, 2
regional, 44–45
slang, 29, 40–41
standard, 35–37
English language words. *See*
English language *and* Words.
Entry words in dictionary, 28
Envelope, addressing, 331–332
Errors in reasoning, 280–283
Essay tests, 320–322
Examples
as context clues to word
meaning, 2
to develop a paragraph, 78–79,
94–95
Exclamation mark, or point
with exclamatory sentences, 409,
662–663
with interjections, 543–544
with quotation marks, 685–686
Exclamatory sentences
definition of, 409, 662–663
punctuation of, 662–663
Explanatory compositions, 211–239
explaining a process, 211–219
planning, 212–213
revising, 218–219
step-by-step order, 214–215
transitions in, 216–217
presenting an opinion, 221–229
developing an opinion,
222–223
first draft of, 226–227
organizing an opinion,
224–225
revising, 228–229
using transitions in, 226–227

F

G

Graphic aids, 316–317
Greek word roots, 14–15
Group discussions, 378–381
Guide cards, 298
Guidelines for writing
   compositions, 182–183
Guide words
   in dictionary, 26–27
   in encyclopedia, 300

H

have as helping verb, 479–480
Heading in letters, 328, 334
hear/here, 626
Hearing words, 20
Helping verbs, 392–393, 479–480
here/there, 517
Hyphen, 679–681

I

I
   capitalization of, 644
   with first-person point of view,
      118–119, 190–191, 253–255
ie/ei, 704
Imaginary narrative compositions
   (stories), 186–189
Imaginary subjects for paragraphs,
   114–115
Imperative sentences
   definition of, 409–410
   period with, 409, 661
   you as understood subject in,
      396–397
Importance of reasons as method
   of organization, 96–97, 150–151,
   224–225
in/into, 635
Indefinite pronouns, 460–461,
   574–575
Incidents in paragraphs, 78–79

Indenting first line of paragraphs
   in letters, 328–329
Indirect objects, 400–402, 452
Indirect question, 661
Inference, as context clue, 4–5
Infinitive, 557–561, 562–563
   phrase, 558–560
   split, 559
Informal English, 38–39
Initials,
   capitalization of, 643
   periods with, 661–662
Inside address of business letters,
   334–335
Interjections, 542–544, 662–663
Interrogative pronouns, 460
Interrogative sentences
   definition of, 409, 662
   period with, 661
   question mark with, 409, 662
Interviews and discussions,
   86–87
Interview, job, 354–359
Intransitive verbs, 399–400
Introductions
   in compositions, 168–169,
      192–193, 204–205, 214–215,
      226–227
   in speeches, 372
   in research papers, 253–255
Invitations. *See* Letters.
Irregular verbs, 484–490
   using a dictionary to find
      principal parts, 485
   and helping verbs, 485
   is, are, was, were, 479
   list of principal parts,
      485–486
   rules for, 485–490
   troublesome pairs of, 629–633
Italics, underlining for, 687–688
its/it's, 626

method of organization, 96–97
Multiple-choice tests, 320–321

N

Narrative compositions, 184–199
  choosing point of view in,
    190–191
  chronological order in, 196–197
  conflict in, 188–189
  dialogue in, 194–195
  first draft of, 192–193
  planning a story, 186–187
  plotting a story, 188–189
  point of view in, 190–191
  revising, 198–199
  transitions in, 196–197
Narrative paragraphs, 80–81,
  113–123
  choosing point of view in,
    118–119
  chronological order in, 116–117
  definition of, 80–81
  developing, 114–115
  first draft of, 120–121
  revising, 122–123
  transitions, 120–121
Nationalities, capitalization of, 649
Negatives
  double, 518–520
  n't not part of verb, 392–393
Nonfiction books, 294–295
Nonrestrictive clause, 672–673
Nonstandard English, 35–37, 625
Note cards, 245–247
Notes, social. *See* Letters.
Notetaking, 245–247, 312–313
Nouns, 431–446
  capitalization of, 432–433, 643
  clauses, 603–606
  as compound objects, 406–407
  as compound subjects, 406–407

common, 432–433
definition of, 432
as direct objects, 435–437
as indirect objects, 436–437
as objects of prepositions, 452,
  528–529, 605
plural forms of, 439–441
possessive forms of, 441–442
predicate, 403–404, 437–438
proper, 432–433, 643
in sentence patterns, 410–412
singular forms of, 439–441
as subjects, 390, 434–435
nowhere, 634
no words, *not* words. *See*
  Negatives.
Number of the verb, 571
Numbers in writing, 714–715
N LV Adj. sentence pattern, 411
N LV N sentence pattern, 411
N V sentence pattern, 410–411
N V N sentence pattern, 411
N V N N sentence pattern, 411

O

Objective tests, 318–321
Object of the preposition, 452,
  528–529, 605
Object of the verb, 605
Object pronouns, 449–450, 452
of, 636
Omniscient point of view, 190–191
Only-cause reasoning, 282–283
Opinion
  definition of, 274
  and facts, 274–275
  judgments, 276–277
  prediction, 276–277
  statement of obligation, 276–277
  supporting, 274–275
  in compositions, 222–225

as subjects, 449–451, 455
  with point of view, 118–119,
    190–191
them/those, 466–467
we/us, 465
who/whom, 464–465
Pronunciation of words as shown
  in dictionary, 28
Proofreading, 109, 178–179
Proper adjectives, 501, 643
Proper nouns, 432–433
Punctuation, 660–697
  accent mark, 28
  apostrophe, 681–683
  colon, 676–677
  comma, 664–675. *See also*
    Comma.
  in compound sentences, 60–61,
    586, 591–593, 670
  dash, 678–679
  at end of sentence, 661–663
  exclamation mark, or point,
    662–663
  hyphen, 679–681
  in letters, 327–339
  period, 661–662
  question mark, 662
  quotation mark, 683–689
  semicolon, 591–592,
    675–676
  and underlining, 687–688
Purpose of writing, 90–91,
  106–107
Purr words, 278–279

commas with, 675
definition of, 651
direct, 683–685
divided, 651
long, 686–687
punctuation with,
  685–686
Quotation marks, 683–689
  commas with, 685
  in dialogue, 687
  with divided quotations,
    684–685
  exclamation marks with,
    685–686
  question marks with,
    685–686
  for titles, 687–688

identifying audience of, 374
    organizing information in, 374
and gestures, 368
guidelines for content, 372–373
guidelines for presentation,
    376–377
informal, 372–373
    announcements, 372
    demonstrations, 372
    directions, 372–373
    introductions, 372
listening to, 370–371
and posture, 368
and practice, 376–377
Spelling, 698–720
and doubling final consonant,
    702–703
habits for improving, 699
ie/ei, 704
memory devices, 699–700
method of attack, 699–700
prefixes, 700–701
rules for, 700–704
suffixes, 700–703
words often misspelled, 705–706
words with "seed" sound, 703
SQ3R study method, 310–311
Standard English, 35–37, 625
Standardized tests, 322–325
State-of-being verbs, 389–390,
    403–404. *See also* Linking verbs.
stationary/stationery, 627
Statistics, 78–79
Step-by-step order
    in compositions, 214–215
    in paragraphs, 140–141
Stereotype, 280–281
Stories, writing, 114–115, 186–187
Study and research skills, 306–325
    assignments, understanding,
        308–309
    following directions, 308–309

graphic aids, 316–317
reading rate, 314–315
SQ3R study method, 310–311
standardized tests, 322–325
taking notes, 312–313
test-taking, 318–321
Style in paragraphs, 102–103, 109
Subject card, 297–298
Subject pronoun, 449–451
Subject of the sentence
    agreement with verb, 570–581
    complete, 389–390
    compound, 573–574, 584
    definition of, 388, 584
    diagraming, 390–391
    infinitive phrase as, 558–559
    nouns as, 434–435
    pronouns as, 449–451, 455
    simple, 389–390
    understood *(you)*, 396–397
    in unusual positions, 394
    of the verb, 390
Subordinate clause, 595–597
Suffixes, 6–7, 10–11, 700–703
Superlatives
    adjectives as, 505–506
    adverbs as, 512–513
Syllables
    as shown in dictionary, 28
    dividing words into, 679–681
Synonyms, 16–17, 29, 286–287

T

take/bring, 629
Talks. *See* Speech.
Tenses, verbs, 480–483
Taste words, 21
teach/learn, 629
Test-taking, 318–321
Thank-you notes. *See* Letters.
their/there/they're, 627
them/those, 466–467, 517

diagraming, 390–391
using dictionary to find principal
   parts of, 485
direct objects of, 398–400
future tense, 481
future perfect tense, 482
helping, 392–393, 479–480
indirect object of, 400–402
intransitive, 399–400,
   477–478
irregular, 484–490
linking, 402–405
main, 392–393, 479–480
in negative contractions,
   n't not part of, 392–393
number, definition of, 571
object of, 398–402
parts of, 392–393
passive, 491–492
past participle, 483–484
past tense, 481, 483–484
past perfect tense, 482
perfect tense, 482
plural forms of, 570–581
present tense, 480–481, 483
present perfect tense, 482
principal parts of, 483–484
regular, 483
in sentence patterns,
   410–412
separated parts of, 392–393
singular forms of, 570–581
state-of-being, 389–390,
   402–403, 476
subjects of, 390
tenses, 480–483
transitive, 399–400, 477–478
troublesome, 629–633
See also Irregular verbs.
Vertical file, 303
Vocabulary, 1–23. *See also* Words
  and Dictionary.

W

ways, 636
we/us, 465
weather/wether, 628
well/good, 517
whether/weather, 628
who/whom, 464–465
Word endings in dictionary, 28
Word parts, 8–15
Words, English language
  antonyms, 16–17
  base, 6–7
  combinations from Greek,
    14–15
  context clues to meanings of,
    1–5
  entry words in dictionary, 28
  as different parts of speech,
    544–545
  guide words, 26–27
  hearing, 20
  jargon, 42–43
  Latin roots of, 12–13
  purr, 278–279
  regional, 44–45
  sight, 20
  smell, 21
  snarl, 278–279
  for special fields, 22–23
  synonyms, 16–17
  slang, 29, 40–41
  taste, 21
  touch, 21
  transitional
    in compositions, 178–179,
      196–197, 216–217,
      224–227, 234–235
    in paragraphs, 120–121,
      132–133, 142–143
Writing
  choosing point of view, 118–119,
    190–191

Photographs

Jim Whitmer, ii, 24, 34, 156, 166, 184, 230, 306, 326, 366, 382; Tom McCarthy/Hillstrom Stock, xviii; James L. Ballard, 46, 58, 292; Jacqueline Durand, 70, 82, 136, 200, 240, 340; Brent Jones, 104; Ray F. Hillstrom, 112; Bob Adelman/Magnum, 124; Sylvia Johnson/Woodfin Camp, 146; Michael Hayman/Click Chicago, 210; A. Devaney/Gartman Agency, 220.

Cover

Sinjerli Variation II, 1977. Frank Stella. Petersburg Press, London and New York. © Vert Foncé, 1977.

Editorial Credits

Editor-in-Chief: Joseph F. Littell
Editorial Director: Joy Littell
Administrative Editor: Kathleen Laya
Managing Editor: Geraldine Macsai

Director of Secondary English: Bonnie Dobkin
Editors: James M. LiSacchi, Mary Schafer
Associate Editor: Robert D. Shepherd
Associate Designer: Mary E. MacDonald
Assistant Designer: Debbie Costello
Cover Design: Joy Littell, Mary E. MacDonald

Teaching Special Populations: Specific Suggestions

Section 1: The Sentences and Its Parts

LD   LD students will find it easier to distinguish sentences from fragments if you stress that a fragment contains only part of an idea.

You may want to limit your LD students to the simple subject-verb diagrams. Introduce other elements when and if your students are ready for them.

ESL   ESL students will have trouble distinguishing sentence fragments from sentences, as their command of syntax is likely to be poor. Provide extra practice using the diagrams on pages 387–388 and the questions *who*? and *what*? until the difference is clear. Use scrambled sentence exercises.

Stress word order in each of the four types of sentences. Demonstrate differences in intonation.

Practice with substitution drills. In the latter, the teacher provides a model sentence; students substitute cue words (from the teacher) to make new sentences.

> Model: I used the computer yesterday.
> Cues: played Ron piano
> Student responses: Ron played the piano yesterday.

ESL students will find the English verb system confusing. They will especially have difficulties with helping verbs. Demonstrate usage and correct form, and provide practice as needed. Give additional practice placing *who*? or *what*? before the verb in order to identify the subject. Stress the exercises in which the students must find the subject in unusual positions, and add to them if possible. The use of the sentence pattern charts will benefit ESL students; be sure, however, that they first recognize the parts of speech. ESL students will also find diagraming helpful because it provides visual representations of difficult syntactical patterns.

NSD   NSD students frequently have difficulty with the use of helping verbs and with the verb *be*.

The lessons on *The Parts of a Verb* and *Linking Verbs and Predicate Words* can be used as a diagnostic exercises, to determine where students' difficulties lie.

Section 2: Using Complete Sentences

LD and ESL   Because LD and ESL students will do a number of the exercises in this text orally, it will be helpful to spend some time on the lesson *What Is a Run-on Sentence*. Run-on errors, which are readily apparent in written work, are not easy to detect in oral work.

When teaching ESL students, see comments in the preceding Section. Identifying fragments and run-ons requires comprehension of examples. Check for understanding of vocabulary. Do many exercises orally. ESL students may not be able to generate their own sentences. Provide them with native English-speaking partners, or help them yourself.

Section 3: Using Nouns

LD   LD students may have difficulty using dictionaries to find the plurals of nouns. Frequent repetition and reinforcement will be necessary when teaching singular and plural nouns, particularly for irregular examples.

ESL   ESL students will understand proper and common nouns and possessives more readily through comparisons and contrasts with their own languages. They will need extra practice with forming plurals, the irregular ones in particular. Using a dictionary may be beyond their skill.

Word order will continue to be a problem. Be alert for negative transfer from the student's native language: for example, placing an adjective after a noun.

NSD   NSD students will need to spend some additional time working on *The Plurals of Nouns.* Encourage these students to use a dictionary.

Section 4: Using Pronouns

ESL   ESL students will find this Section difficult because pronouns are much more complicated in English than in many other languages. These students are likely to mistake case and gender and to omit pronouns. Review the rules, stressing that pronouns are not dropped in English. Provide extra practice: scrambled sentences, cloze exercises and substitution drills.

ESL students cannot usually judge what "sounds natural." Encourage reference to the charts on pages 448 and 450. Practice possessive pronouns, especially *its*, extensively.

Some ESL students will substitute a pronoun for the verb *be* forming a double subject (*Jenny, she pretty*). Be aware of this when teaching linking verbs.

Contractions may be entirely unfamiliar to ESL students. Review, practice, and encourage reference to the examples on page 463.

NSD   NSD students will have difficulty determining when to use the object form and when to use the subject form of pronouns. Pay particular attention to Parts 2 and 9 of this lesson.

Section 5: Using Verbs

LD   LD students may require additional explanation and drill in order to master linking verbs. Instructions for Exercises will have to be more explicit. They will also need more explanation and examples of irregular and active and passive forms of verbs in order to complete the Exercises.

ESL   ESL students frequently omit forms of *be*, drop *s* from third-person singular present tense, or drop *ed* from regular past tense. Go over rules very carefully and provide extra practice.

These students will have difficulty with helping verbs. Go over Part 2 carefully, using additional examples and exercises. Spend extra time on Part 5, pointing out the pattern of each group of irregular verbs.

NSD   Many NSD students, as already noted, have many difficulties with main verbs and helping verbs. If you have already used Section 1 as a diagnostic test, use Part 2 of this Section to concentrate on specific problems. Be especially aware of the faulty use of *be*.

Many NSD students will be more familiar with deviant than with standard usage of irregular verbs. They may not be able to distinguish aurally between standard and nonstandard usage. Repetition and patience will be essential when attempting to modify linguistic habits.

Section 6: Using Modifiers

ESL   ESL students may have difficulty using articles and placing adjectives in the sentences correctly. Practice with scrambled sentences and expansion drills. In an expansion drill, the teacher gives a base sentence (*The cat is gray.*), the student repeats it, the teacher gives a new word (*small*), and the student inserts it in the correct place in the sentence (*The small cat is gray*).

Make sure that these students know the vocabulary in this Section, and also concepts like *what kind, how many, to what extent,* etc.

Agreement in gender and number between an adjective and the noun it modifies is much simpler in English than in many languages. Point out that English does not require distinct forms for gender and number.

Give many examples of predicate adjectives, and use arrows, as in the examples on pages 501–502, to indicate the word modified.

ESL students may confuse adverbs and predicate adjectives, especially when they are used with linking verbs. Focus on the words modified. As you present the examples and the exercises on adverbs, ask the questions *how, when, where,* or *to what extent,* and encourage the students to do so. Give these students ample practice using adjectives and adverbs before moving on to comparative forms.

Double negatives are required in some languages. Compare the form in the ESL student's language and mark out the extra negative to show the difference.

NSD   NSD students often use *more* and *most* with adverbs as an emphatic statement (*most farthest, more better*). Provide extra examples of correct usage.

Many non-standard dialects use double negatives and incorrect modifiers. It will require repetition and patience to modify these linguistic habits.

Section 7: Using Prepositions and Conjunctions

LD   LD students may have trouble understanding relationships between sentence parts. Use extra examples to help recognition of correlative conjunctions.

ESL   For ESL students the functions of prepositions and conjunctions in English may be very confusing because their native languages use them quite differently. Contrast the usages whenever possible, and emphasize memorizing the list on page 529. Correct placement of prepositional phrases may require more sensitivity to English word order than these students have developed. Do many of the sentences orally, discussing the relationships among sentence parts and, when possible, the contrasts with the native language. You may also have to review *and, but,* and *or.*

Section 8: Review of Parts of Speech

LD   LD students will require some review of parts of speech before they can do the first Exercise. You can use the Exercises on pages 543–544 as the basis for an oral review.

ESL   ESL students will find this review very helpful. Stress the material on multiple functions of words, which is very important for non-native speakers.

Section 9: Using Verbals

LD   You may wish to limit your LD students to just finding verbals in a sentence rather than identifying the kind of verbal and its uses. You will have to modify Exercises to your students' abilities, and do most of the Exercises orally.

ESL   Review the concept of words used in more than one way before starting (Handbook Section 8). Call attention to spelling changes of verbs made into gerunds and participles. Give extra exercises and practice.

NSD   NSD students frequently drop the *ing* ending of verbals to an *in'* sound (*playin', jumpin',*). These students will need reinforcement of the spelling and pronunciation of participles and gerunds in order to recognize them aurally.

Section 10: Making Subjects and Verbs Agree

ESL   ESL students may need some review. The concepts *singular* and *plural* will be familiar, but the students may need to be reminded of their application to English words. Third-person singular present tense verbs end in *s* as do plural nouns, a fact which may cause confusion. Practice with substitution drills and fill-in sentences.

Compound subjects and indefinite pronouns may require extra practice; encourage their use in classroom conversation.

NSD   Stress the necessity of agreement between subject and verb. Use extra examples and practice for Part 4.

Section 11: Using Compound and Complex Sentences

LD   Work slowly through this Section with LD students. Do all Exercises orally with the class. Review the definition of a sentence before trying to teach main and subordinate clauses. Present two simple sentences and show different ways they can be put together.

ESL   ESL students may need careful explanation of the nuances in the uncombined sentences before they can combine them with the correct conjunction. Review uses of *and, but,* and *or.*

If students find combining sentences difficult, present an add-on sentence exercise: start with a noun or verb and have students place additional words where they belong in a sentence. After building two related sentences, have students add a conjunction to join them.

Encourage ESL students to practice writing complex sentences. Make sure students understand that a subordinate clause does not have only one position in a sentence, that it can appear first, last, or in the middle of a sentence.

It is important to make ESL students aware of which subordinating words are to be used when referring to people (*whom, whom,* etc.)

Section 12: The Right Word

LD Do not do this Section all at once; introduce *Words Often Confused* a few words as a time. Use extra examples of illustrative sentences and discuss mnemonic aids.

ESL Allow ESL students ample time for practice with confusing pairs of words. When discussing the introduction, stress that different types of English are appropriate at different times.

NSD This Section is of particular importance to NSD students. Emphasize that there is no "wrong" way of speaking, but that it is important to know how and when to use a form of English that is understood by most people. Go over Parts 2 and 3 carefully. Many NSD students will regularly substitute one verb for another similar verb. (Example: *set* for *sit*). If necessary, spend extra time on this lesson.

Section 13: Capitalization

LD LD students will have trouble copying all the sentences. Assign fewer sentences, or allow these students to complete them orally.

ESL ESL students will find some personal titles, proper nouns, outline/letter forms, and literary titles

unfamiliar. Have these students work with native speaking partners who can explain this material.

Section 14: Punctuation

LD LD students will have trouble copying all the sentences. Assign fewer sentences, or allow these students to complete them orally.

ESL ESL students will benefit from emphasis on the logic of punctuation. Point out any marks whose use may be unfamiliar, such as the hyphen or the apostrophe in possessives, and give extra practice in using them. A native English-speaking partner may be helpful.

Section 15: Spelling

ESL ESL students must learn English spelling through written use and practice. Discuss the rules at a leisurely pace, using a multisensory approach: see, hear, say, write.

NSD NSD students will usually need additional work in spelling. Encourage the use of the dictionary through dictionary drills.

Section 16: The Correct Form for Writing

LD You may have to modify the guidelines for correct writing form according to students' physical abilities.

ESL This is an important Section for ESL students. Not only does it give them an acceptable form model for their papers, but discusses writing conventions that are probably different than those of their native countries. Since most countries use the metric system, take time to go over the American numerical system. Also emphasize the acceptable form for dates, monetary amounts, and abbreviations, all of which vary from country to country.

Guidelines for Evaluating Composition

*Adapted from Teaching and Evaluating Student Writing,
copyright © 1985 by McDougal, Littell & Company*

Types of Evaluation

In order to give student writers the constant practice
and feedback they need, teachers must have a practical
method of evaluation. Obviously, if the student will be
writing constantly, a teacher cannot be expected to
evaluate each piece in a line-by-line, word-by-word
manner. Nor would such an evaluation necessarily be
useful to the developing writer. It is therefore suggested that a teacher learn to use two different evaluation methods—the holistic method and the more
detailed analytic method.

Holistic evaluation of writing is a quick, guided
method of rating pieces of writing. It can best be used
to evaluate daily writing samples or first drafts of more
complex pieces. With holistic evaluation, an evaluator
reads the written piece as a whole, considers certain
features, and immediately assigns a grade. The grade
may be a single rating for the entire piece of writing or
a set of ratings for the different features being
considered.

Analytic evaluation should occur only when the student has turned in the clean, final copy of a piece of
writing. In this detailed type of evaluation, the teacher
analyzes each aspect of a piece of writing, including
both content and mechanics.

Evaluators

The evaluation process can be utilized by three types
of evaluators: the writer of the piece, other students,
and the teacher. Each type of evaluation offers unique
benefits to the developing writer.

1. Self-Evaluation. In this type of evaluation, a
writer comments on his or her own work, noting which
parts were successful and which unsuccessful.

2. Peer Evaluation. Evaluating the writing of others
is often a strong learning experience. In peer evaluation, students work together in small groups to improve
a piece of writing. Student evaluators should always be
given a list of specific criteria that the writing is expected to meet, and should then comment on how well
each paper succeeds.

3. Teacher Evaluation. The teacher's comments and
suggestions may be incorporated at any point in the
writing process. Studies indicate that evaluation by the
teacher is most successful when it is done in combination with self- and peer evaluation. The evaluation that
follows provides for such a combination of evaluation
procedures.

Teacher evaluation should also involve direct communication with every student. Such help can be provided in student-teacher conferences.

Keeping a Record of Improvement

Both the teacher and students benefit when writing
folders are maintained throughout the school year. A
piece of writing from early in the year, along with its
evaluations, can be compared with later pieces. Progress from one piece to the next will be erratic, as the
writer takes risks using new techniques and appears to
move backwards until gaining mastery of each new
technique. However, over the course of the year, progress should be evident.

BIBLIOGRAPHY

Cooper, Charles R. and Lee Odell, eds. *Evaluating Writ-
ing: Describing, Measuring, Judging.* Urbana, Illinois:
National Council of Teachers of English, 1977.
Graves, Donald H. *Balance the Basics: Let Them Write.*
New York: The Ford Foundation, 1978.
Murray, Donald M. *A Writer Teaches Writing: A Practical
Method of Teaching Composition.* Boston: Houghton
Mifflin, 1968.
Payne, Lucile Vaughn, *The Lively Art of Writing.* Chicago:
Follett, 1965.

Using the Evaluation Form

The following form for composition evaluation may be used at any stage of the writing process, and may be re-used after each revision.

The form should be filled out by the student and turned in with the writing. There is also space on the form for peer evaluation, if desired. The teacher may ask students to turn in only final copies, or may ask to see work in progress. The student states whether the submitted writing is the final copy.

On the evaluation form, content may be rated at any point; mechanics should be graded only on a final copy.

Self-Evaluation: Besides the questions on the form, the student can ask himself or herself the questions concerning revising listed in the relevant composition chapter. The student may use 1, 3, and 5 subjectively.

Peer Evaluation: Members of the peer group should rate each feature as objectively as possible. In order to focus on ideas and organization, the group should evaluate content only.

Teacher Evaluation: The following standards for evaluating composition are provided to assist the teacher in rating papers with objectivity and consistency. In a conference, the teacher might discuss one or two of these areas in detail.

Standards for Evaluation

Content

	1—Low	3—Average	5—High
1	Unclear, unimaginative writing.	Understandable but unimaginative writing.	Imaginative, interesting writing.
2	Boring or poorly defined topic.	Topic adequately limited and defined.	Well-chosen, precisely developed topic.
3	Purpose unclear, or not achieved in the writing.	Purpose defined adequately. Not completely achieved.	Clear, well-defined purpose. Writing achieves purpose successfully.
4	Writing so lacking in detail that topic remains undeveloped.	Incomplete development. More information needed.	Topic thoroughly covered. Writing is rich in detail and supporting information.
5	Many irrelevant sentences or details.	Few irrelevant sentences or details.	Well-chosen, relevant sentences and details.
6	Disjointed ideas. No transitional words, phrases, or ideas.	Inconsistent flow. Some transitional devices.	Ideas flow well. Good use of transitional devices.
7	Lack of any logical organization of ideas.	Some organization of ideas evident.	Well-organized ideas. Type of organization suited to topic and purpose.
8	Dull, general words, poorly chosen. Inappropriate to audience.	Suitable but unimaginative language. Generally appropriate to audience.	Specific, vivid language. Appropriate to audience.

Mechanics

1	Many fragments and run-on sentences. Frequent mistakes in the use of nouns, verbs, pronouns, and subject-verb agreement.	Few fragments and run-ons. Some mistakes in the use of nouns, verbs, pronouns, and subject-verb agreement.	No fragments or run-ons. Few mistakes in the use of nouns, verbs, pronouns, and subject-verb agreement.
2	Frequent mistakes in capitalization.	Occasional mistakes in capitalization.	Infrequent mistakes in capitalization.
3	Punctuation marks frequently misused or missing.	Punctuation marks usually used correctly.	Infrequent mistakes in punctuation.
4	Frequent mistakes in spelling, without any indication of awareness of spelling patterns.	Occasional misspellings, usually indicating an approximation of the correct spelling and an awareness of spelling patterns.	Infrequent spelling mistakes.
5	Paragraphs not indented. Writing illegible. Incorrect headings or margins.	Some carelessness or inconsistency in form. Occasionally hard to read.	Correct form. Neat, legible handwriting.

Composition Evaluation Form

Writer _____   Date _____

Title _____   **Circle one:** Unfinished   Final Copy

Evaluation Symbols
1 Needs a great deal of work
3 Acceptable—could be improved
5 Very good. Needs no further revision.

Content

	Writer's Opinion	Peer Group Opinion	Teacher's Evaluation	Teacher's Comments
1. **Interest.** Is the writing interesting and understandable? Does it hold the reader's attention?				
2. **Topic.** Is the topic a good one? Has it been narrowed sufficiently?				
3. **Purpose.** Is the purpose of the writing clear? Has the writer accomplished this purpose?				
4. **Development.** Has the topic been developed well? Is there sufficient information?				
5. **Unity.** Are all ideas and details related to the topic? Do they all help to develop or strengthen the main idea?				
6. **Continuity.** Do ideas flow smoothly? Has the writer avoided any breaks in thought?				
7. **Organization.** Were ideas arranged in a logical order? Does this order suit the purpose of the writing?				
8. **Language.** Is the language appropriate to the writing? Does it suit the audience? Are the words vivid?				
Additional Guidelines				

Mechanics (to be graded by teacher on final copy only)

1. **Grammar and Usage.** Are there any fragments or run-ons? Is the correct form of every pronoun or verb used? Are adjectives and adverbs used correctly?				
2. **Capitalization.** Are all first words, initials, proper nouns, proper adjectives, and titles capitalized?				
3. **Punctuation.** Does each sentence have the proper end mark? Are all punctuation marks used correctly?				
4. **Spelling.** Are all words spelled correctly? Are plurals and possessive forms spelled correctly?				
5. **Form.** Is the writing legible? Is the heading correct? Are there sufficient margins?				